Algorithms

The JK Computer Science and Mathematics Series

Published by Pearson Education

R. Johnsonbaugh and M. Schaefer, **Algorithms**, 2004.

R. Johnsonbaugh and M. Kalin, **Applications Programming in ANSI C**, 3rd ed., 1996.

R. Johnsonbaugh and M. Kalin, **Applications Programming in C++**, 1999.

R. Johnsonbaugh and M. Kalin, **C for Scientists and Engineers**, 1997.

R. Johnsonbaugh, **Discrete Mathematics**, 5th ed., 2001.

R. Johnsonbaugh and M. Kalin, **Object-Oriented Programming in C++**, 2nd ed., 2000.

M. Kalin, **Object-Oriented Programming in JAVA™**, 2001.

Algorithms

Richard Johnsonbaugh
Marcus Schaefer

DePaul University

PEARSON
Prentice
Hall

Pearson Education
Upper Saddle River, New Jersey 07458

Library of Congress Cataloging-in-Publication Data

Johnsonbaugh, Richard,
   Algorithms / Richard Johnsonbaugh, Marcus Schaefer.
     p. cm.
   Includes bibliographical references and index.
   ISBN 0-02-360692-4
   1. Computer algorithms. I. Schaefer, Marcus, 1969- II. Title.

QA76.9.A43J67 2003
005.1--dc21

                                              2003054834

Vice President and Editorial Director, ECS: *Marcia J. Horton*
Senior Acquisitions Editor: *Kate Hargett*
Editorial Assistant: *Michael Giacobbe*
Vice President and Director of Production and Manufacturing, ESM: *David W. Riccardi*
Executive Managing Editor: *Vince O'Brien*
Managing Editor: *Camille Trentacoste*
Production Editor: *Kathryn Kasturas*
Director of Creative Services: *Paul Belfanti*
Creative Director: *Carole Anson*
Art Director and Cover Manager: *Jayne Conte*
Cover Designer: *Kiwi Design*
Managing Editor, AV Management and Production: *Patricia Burns*
Art Editor: *Gregory Dulles*
Manufacturing Manager: *Trudy Pisciotti*
Manufacturing Buyer: *Lisa McDowell*
Marketing Manager: *Pamela Shaffer*
Marketing Assistant: *Barrie Rheinhold*

Printed in the United States of America

10 9 8 7 6 5 4 3 2

ISBN: 0-02-360692-4

Pearson Education Ltd., *London*
Pearson Education Australia Pty. Ltd., *Sydney*
Pearson Education Singapore, Pte. Ltd.
Pearson Education North Asia Ltd., *Hong Kong*
Pearson Education Canada, Inc., *Toronto*
Pearson Educación de Mexico, S.A. de C.V.
Pearson Education—Japan, *Tokyo*
Pearson Education Malaysia, Pte. Ltd.
Pearson Education, Inc., *Upper Saddle River, New Jersey*

Contents

12 Parallel and Distributed Algorithms   559

Preface

Why We Wrote This Book

Intended for an upper-level undergraduate or graduate course in algorithms, this book is based on our combined 25 years of experience in teaching this course. Our major goals in writing this book were to

- Emphasize design techniques.
- Show that algorithms are fun and exciting.
- Include real-world applications.
- Provide numerous worked examples and exercises.

Faced with a new computational problem, a designer will often be able to solve it by using one of the algorithms in this book, perhaps after modifying or adapting it slightly. However, some problems cannot be solved by any of the algorithms in this book. For this reason, we present a repertoire of design techniques that can be used to solve the problem and help the reader to develop intuition about which techniques are likely to succeed. The chapters on **NP**-completeness and how to deal with it also tell how to recognize problems that are hard to solve and which techniques are available in that case.

Working with algorithms should be fun and exciting. The design of algorithms is a creative task requiring the solution of new problems and old problems in disguise. To be successful, we believe that it is important to enjoy the challenge that a new problem poses. To this end, we have included more examples and exercises of a combinatorial and recreational nature than is typical for a book of this type. All too often the challenge of an unsolved problem is experienced as a threat rather than as an opportunity, and we hope that these examples and exercises help to remove the threat.

Examples of real-word applications of algorithms in this book include data compression in Section 7.5, and the Boyer-Moore-Horspool algorithm in Section 9.4, which is used as part of the implementation of agrep. Most sections of the book introduce a motivating example in the first paragraph. The closest-pair problem (Section 5.3) begins with a pattern recognition example, and Section 8.4, which is concerned with the longest-common-subsequence problem, begins with a discussion of the analysis of proteins.

Algorithm design and analysis are best learned by experience. For this reason, we provide large numbers of worked examples and exercises. Worked examples show how to deal with algorithms, and exercises let the reader practice the techniques. There are over 300 worked examples throughout the book. These examples clarify and show how to develop algorithms, demonstrate applications of the theory, elucidate proofs, and help to motivate the material. The book contains over 1450 exercises, from routine to challenging, which were carefully developed through classroom testing. Close attention was paid to clarity and precision. Because some instant feedback is essential for students, we provide answers to about one-third of the end-of-section exercises (marked with "S" in the exercises) in the back of the book. Solutions to the remaining end-of-section exercises are reserved for instructors (see the Instructor Supplement section that follows).

Prerequisites

The principal computer science prerequisite is a data structures course that covers stacks, queues, linked lists, trees, and graphs. A course in discrete mathematics that covers logic, asymptotic notation (e.g., "big oh" notation), and recurrence relations and their solution by iteration is the main mathematics prerequisite. We do not use advanced methods such as generating functions. In one or two places, we use some basic concepts from calculus. The mathematics topics and data structures used in this book are summarized in Chapters 2 and 3. Some or all of these chapters can be used for reference or review or incorporated into an algorithms course as needed.

Content

Following the first three chapters (containing an introduction, mathematics topics, and data structures), the book presents five chapters that emphasize design techniques.

Chapter 4 features searching techniques, including novel applications such as region-finding in digital pictures.

The divide-and-conquer technique is introduced in Chapter 5. Among the problems considered are a tiling problem, finding the closest pair of points in the plane, and Strassen's matrix-product algorithm. Chapter 6 deals with sorting and selection. Divide-and-conquer is used to develop many of the algorithms in this chapter.

Chapter 7 shows how to use the greedy method to develop algorithms. After showing how to use the greedy method in a simple setting (coin changing), we present Kruskal's algorithm, Prim's algorithm, Dijkstra's algorithm, Huffman's algorithm, and a solution of the continuous-knapsack problem.

Chapter 8 covers the technique of dynamic programming. As in Chapter 7, we first show how dynamic programming operates in a simple setting (computing Fibonacci numbers). We next revisit the coin-changing problem (from Chapter 7 on the greedy method) and contrast dynamic programming with the greedy method. We then discuss optimal grouping of matrices, the longest-common-subsequence problem, and the algorithms of Floyd and Warshall.

Chapter 9 discusses text-searching techniques, including the Knuth-Morris-Pratt and Boyer-Moore-Horspool algorithms, and algorithms for non-exact searching.

In Chapter 10, we investigate **NP**-completeness—a theoretical approach to recognizing and understanding the limitations of algorithms. We include many examples from different areas such as cellular phone networks, games, and biological computing to illustrate the ubiquity and universality of **NP**-completeness.

It is widely believed that **NP**-complete problems cannot be solved efficiently by algorithms. Nevertheless, these problems arise in applications and have to be solved in practice. Chapter 11, Coping with **NP**-Completeness, presents a collection of techniques originating in practice and theory to deal with **NP**-complete problems. Among the approaches discussed are approximation, parameterization, and use of heuristics.

Chapter 12 presents fundamental algorithms for parallel architectures, including algorithms for the PRAM and sorting networks, and offers an introduction to computation in distributed environments.

Pedagogy

Each section (except Section 12.1, which is an introductory section) concludes with Section Exercises. The book contains over 1100 Section Exercises. Some of these exercises check for basic understanding of the material (e.g., some ask for a trace of an algorithm), while others check for a deeper understanding of the material (e.g., some investigate alternative algorithms). Exercises that are more challenging than average are indicated with a star, $\star$.

Each chapter ends with a Notes section, which is followed by Chapter Exercises. Notes sections contain suggestions for further reading and pointers to references. Chapter Exercises, some of which have hints, integrate the material of the chapter. The book contains over 350 Chapter Exercises. They are, on the whole, more challenging than the Section Exercises. We have included some very challenging Chapter Exercises marked with two stars. These will probably require instructor guidance, and some are appropriate for a small project.

Lower bounds for problems are integrated into the chapters that discuss those problems rather than being segregated into separate chapters. For example, after presenting several sorting algorithms, we discuss a lower bound for comparison-based sorting (Section 6.3).

We present and discuss many recent results, for example, parameterized complexity (Section 11.4), a recent area of research.

Algorithms are written in pseudocode that is close to the syntax of the familiar C, C++, and Java family of languages. Data types, semicolons, obscure features of the languages, and so on, are not used because we have found that specifying algorithms by writing actual code obscures the algorithm description and makes it difficult for someone not familiar with the language to understand the algorithm. The pseudocode used is completely described in Section 1.2.

Figures illustrate concepts, show how algorithms work, elucidate proofs, and motivate the material. Several figures illustrate proofs of theorems. The captions of these figures provide additional explanation and insight into the proofs.

Attention has been given to finding the most direct and comprehensible proofs of correctness [as examples, see Theorem 7.2.5 from which the correctness of both Kruskal's and Prim's algorithms are derived and the proof of the correctness of Dijkstra's algorithm (Theorem 7.4.5)].

We present several examples and arguments to show that our time bounds for algorithms are sharp. See, for example, the subsection in Section 7.3, Lower Bound Time Estimate, which shows that the upper bound for the worst-case time of Prim's algorithm using a binary heap is sharp, and the discussion just before Theorem 7.5.4, which shows that the upper bound for the worst-case time of Huffman's algorithm is sharp.

Instructor Supplement

An *Instructor's Guide*, which contains solutions to the end-of-section exercises not included in the book, is available at no cost from the publisher to instructors who adopt or sample this book. It should be requested from your local Prentice Hall representative.

World Wide Web Site

$\mathcal{WWW}$ The World Wide Web site

    http://condor.depaul.edu/~rjohnson

contains

- Expanded explanations of particular topics and additional information on algorithms. The logo shown indicates the availability of this information at this web site or via a link to another site.

- Algorithm animation software.

- PowerPoints.

- Late breaking news and references on the book's topics.

- Supplementary material.

- Computer programs.

- An errata list.

Acknowledgments

In writing this book, we have been assisted by many persons. Thanks go to the following reviewers who read all or some of the draft manuscript: Iyad A. Ajwa, Ashland University; Michael D. Frazier, Abilene Christian University; Norman Jacobson, University of California, Irvine; Joel Seiferas, University of Rochester; Amber Settle, DePaul University; and Jack Thompson, University of Tennessee at Chattanooga.

Ljubomir Perkovic, DePaul University, class-tested most of this material, meticulously read all of it, and provided detailed and very helpful comments.

We express our appreciation to Massimo DiPierro for furnishing the algorithm animation software available at this book's web site.

We are grateful to our friendly copy editor, Patricia Johnsonbaugh, for checking numerous details, catching text we intended not to write, and suggesting changes that improved the book.

We are indebted to Helmut Epp, Dean of the School of Computer Science, Telecommunications and Information Systems at DePaul University, for providing time and encouragement for the development of this book.

We have received consistent support from the people at Prentice Hall. Special thanks for their help go to Marcia Horton, vice president and editorial director, engineering and computer science; Petra Recter, executive acquisitions editor, computer science; Kate Hargett, senior acquisitions editor, computer science; Camille Trentacoste, managing editor, computer science; Kathy Kasturas, production editor; Sarah Parker, assistant editor, computer science; Pamela Shaffer, executive marketing manager, computer science; and Barrie Reinhold, marketing assistant, computer science.

R.J.
M.S.

CHAPTER 1
Introduction

Informally, an **algorithm** is a step-by-step method of solving some problem. Such an approach to problem-solving is not new; indeed, the word "algorithm" derives from the name of the ninth-century Persian mathematician al-Khowārizmī. Today, "algorithm" typically refers to a solution that can be executed by a computer. In this book, we will be concerned primarily with algorithms that can be executed by a "traditional" computer, that is, a computer, such as a personal computer, with a single processor that executes instructions step-by-step.

In Section 1.1, we discuss the concept of "algorithm" in more detail. Pseudocode, which is a precise way to specify algorithms, is explained in Section 1.2. Section 1.3 discusses the current state of algorithmic techniques. Section 1.4 provides a glimpse of alternative ways to perform computations that have been proposed, which may have a profound effect on algorithms and computation in the future.

1.1 Algorithms

Algorithms typically have the following properties:

- **Input.** The algorithm receives *input*.
- **Output.** The algorithm produces *output*.
- **Precision.** The steps are precisely stated.
- **Determinism.** The intermediate results of each step of execution are unique and are determined only by the inputs and results of the preceding steps.
- **Finiteness.** The algorithm *terminates*; that is, it stops after finitely many instructions have been executed.
- **Correctness.** The output produced by the algorithm is correct.
- **Generality.** The algorithm applies to a set of inputs.

Example 1.1.1 Finding the Maximum of Three Numbers. Consider the following algorithm that finds the maximum of three numbers a, b, and c:

1. $x = a$

2. If $b > x$, then $x = b$.

3. If $c > x$, then $x = c$.

The operator $=$ is the **assignment operator**; $y = z$ means to copy the value of z into y and leave z unchanged. The idea of the algorithm is to inspect the numbers one by one and copy the largest value seen into a variable x. At the conclusion of the algorithm, x will then be equal to the largest of the three numbers.

We verify that our algorithm has the properties listed previously. The algorithm receives the three values a, b, and c as input, and returns the value x as output.

The steps of the algorithm are stated sufficiently precisely so that the algorithm could be written in a programming language and executed by a computer.

Given values for the input, each intermediate step of the algorithm produces a unique result. For example, given the input

$$a = 1, \quad b = 5, \quad c = 3,$$

at line 2, x will be set to 5 regardless of who executes the algorithm.

The algorithm terminates after finitely many steps (three steps) correctly answering the given question (finding the largest of the three values input).

The algorithm is general; it can find the largest value of *any* three numbers.   □

There are two main tasks in the study of algorithms: designing an algorithm to solve a particular problem and analyzing a given algorithm. These two tasks are closely related. Analyzing algorithms provides insights into designing new algorithms.

Algorithm design is an art more than a science. The most famous and thorough text on the subject tellingly is called *The Art of Computer Programming* by Donald Knuth (see Knuth, 1997, 1998a, 1998b). As with any art (or science), however, there are basic techniques that can be identified. We will look at several important algorithmic design techniques: searching techniques (Chapter 4), divide-and-conquer methods (Chapter 5), greedy algorithms (Chapter 7), and dynamic programming (Chapter 8). Chapter 6 deals with sorting and selection and uses many of the divide-and-conquer techniques of Chapter 5.

In the **analysis of algorithms**, we ask the following questions:

- **Correctness.** Given an algorithm for a problem, does it solve the problem?

- **Termination.** Does the algorithm always stop after a finite number of steps?

- **Time analysis.** How many instructions does the algorithm execute?

- **Space analysis.** How much memory does the algorithm need to execute?

Throughout the book, we address the correctness issue. One typically constructs a mathematical proof that a given algorithm is correct. The fact that an algorithm terminates is often seen easily (as in Example 1.1.1) or follows from the time analysis of the algorithm.

However, correctness and termination are not enough. An algorithm that correctly solves a problem may not be practical for a computer because it takes too long to execute or requires too much space.

$\mathcal{WWW}$ **Example 1.1.2 Cryptography.** *Cryptography* refers to a method for persons to share information without any of the information being obtained by unauthorized users. From a correctness and termination point of view, it is not difficult to break most cryptographic systems that are in use right now. Suppose that we know the encryption function $e(s, k)$ that takes a plaintext s and a key k, and returns the encrypted text $e(s, k)$. The encryption algorithm is usually generally known and fast to compute (since it has to be executed for encryption). Here is an algorithm that, given an encrypted text c, returns the corresponding plaintext s, if there is one: For all possible keys k and all possible plaintexts s, compute $e(s, k)$ and compare it to c. If an s and k are found for which $e(s, k) = c$, return s and k. This brute-force attack breaks many available cryptosystems; however, the time it takes to do so makes it useless in practice.   □

It is important to know or be able to estimate the time and space required by algorithms. Knowing the time and space required by algorithms also allows us to compare algorithms that solve the same problem. For example, if one algorithm takes n steps to solve a problem and another algorithm takes n^2 steps to solve the same problem, we would surely prefer the first algorithm assuming that the space requirements are acceptable. In Chapter 2, we will give the technical definitions that allow us to make rigorous statements about the time and space required by algorithms.

Chapter 9 discusses some special algorithms for text searching; Chapter 10 introduces a class of problems for which time-efficient algorithms are not known. Many of these problems are quite practical (e.g., certain scheduling problems belong to this class of problems) and *must* be solved. Chapter 11 discusses techniques for dealing with these nasty problems.

Our concluding chapter (Chapter 12) discusses parallel and distributed algorithms. Parallel and distributed algorithms require *multiple* processors, rather than a *single* processor as in a personal computer, so that multiple instructions can be executed in parallel (i.e., simultaneously). The objective is to achieve faster solutions to problems by executing several instructions at the same time.

Exercises

[†]**1S.** Write an algorithm that finds the smallest element among a, b, and c.

[†]An exercise marked with "S" has a solution in the back of the book.

2. Write an algorithm that finds the second-smallest element among the distinct values a, b, and c.

3. Write the standard method of adding two positive decimal integers, taught in elementary schools, as an algorithm.

4S. Which properties of an algorithm—input, output, precision, determinism, finiteness, correctness, generality—if any, are lacking in the following? Explain. The input is a set S of integers and an integer m. The output is all subsets of S that sum to m.

    1. List all subsets of S and their sums.

    2. Proceed through the subsets listed in step 1 and output each whose sum is m.

5. Consult a manual for programming a video cassette recorder. Which properties of an algorithm—input, output, precision, determinism, finiteness, correctness, generality—are present? Which properties are lacking?

6. Goldbach's conjecture states that every even number greater than 2 is the sum of two prime numbers. Here is an algorithm that checks whether Goldbach's conjecture is true:

    1. Let $n = 4$.

    2. If n is not the sum of two primes, output "no" and stop.

    3. Else increase n by 2 and continue with step 2.

    4. Output "yes" and stop.

Which properties of an algorithm—input, output, precision, determinism, finiteness, correctness, generality—does this procedure have? Do any of them depend on the truth of Goldbach's conjecture (which mathematicians have not yet settled)?

1.2 Pseudocode for Algorithms

Although ordinary language is sometimes adequate to specify an algorithm, computer scientists prefer **pseudocode** because of its precision, structure, and universality. Pseudocode is so named because it resembles the actual code of computer languages such as C++ and Java. There are many versions of pseudocode. Unlike actual computer languages, which must be concerned about semicolons, uppercase and lowercase letters, special words, and so on, any version of pseudocode is acceptable as long as its instructions are unambiguous and it resembles in form, if not in exact syntax, the pseudocode described in this section.

    Our algorithms consist of a title, a brief description of the algorithm, the input and output parameters, and the functions containing the instructions of the algorithm. We could write the algorithm in Example 1.1.1 that finds the maximum of three numbers as follows.

Algorithm 1.2.1 Finding the Maximum of Three Numbers. This algorithm finds the largest of the numbers a, b, and c.

Input Parameters: a, b, c
Output Parameter: x

```
max(a, b, c, x) {
   x = a
   if (b > x) // if b is larger than x, update x
      x = b
   if (c > x) // if c is larger than x, update x
      x = c
}
```

The first line of a function consists of the name of the function followed, in parentheses, by the parameters of the function. The parameters describe the data, variables, arrays, and so on, that are available to the function. In Algorithm 1.2.1, the parameters are the three input values, a, b, and c, and the output parameter, x, that is assigned the maximum of the three input values. The statements to be executed by the function are enclosed in braces.

In the **if statement**

```
if (condition)
   action
```

if *condition* is true, *action* is executed and control passes to the statement following *action*. If *condition* is false, *action* is not executed and control passes immediately to the statement following *action*. As shown, we use indentation to identify the statements that make up *action*. In addition, if *action* consists of multiple statements, we enclose them in braces. An example of a multiple-statement *action* in an if statement is

```
if (x ≥ 0) {
   x = x + 1
   a = b + c
}
```

An alternative form of the if statement is the **if else statement**. In the if else statement

```
if (condition)
   action1
else
   action2
```

if *condition* is true, *action1* (but not *action2*) is executed and control passes to the statement following *action2*. If *condition* is false, *action2* (but not *action1*) is executed and control passes to the statement following *action2*.

If *action1* or *action2* consists of multiple statements, they are enclosed in braces.

Two slash marks // signal the beginning of a **comment**, which then extends to the end of the line. An example of a comment in Algorithm 1.2.1 is

// if b is larger than x, update x

Comments help the reader understand the algorithm but are not executed.

We show reserved words (e.g., if) in the regular typeface and user-chosen words (e.g., function names such as *max* and variables such as x) in italics.

The **return statement**

return x

terminates a function and returns the value of x to the invoker of the function. For example, rather than use an output parameter for the maximum of three numbers in Algorithm 1.2.1, we could have written the algorithm as

$max(a,b,c)$ {
   $x = a$
   if $(b > x)$ // if b is larger than x, update x
     $x = b$
   if $(c > x)$ // if c is larger than x, update x
     $x = c$
   return x
}

The statement

return

simply terminates a function. If there is no return statement, the function terminates just before the last brace.

We use the usual arithmetic operators $+$, $-$, $*$ (for multiplication), and $/$, as well as the relational operators $==$ (is equal to), $!=$ (is not equal to), $<$, $>$, $\le$ (is less than or equal to), and $\ge$ (is greater than or equal to), and the logical operators && (and), || (or), and ! (not). Notice that $=$ is the *assignment* operator and $==$ is the *equals* operator.

The **while loop** is written

while (*condition*)
   action

If *condition* is true, *action* is executed and this sequence is repeated; that is, if *condition* is true, *action* is executed again. This sequence is repeated until *condition* becomes false. Then, control passes immediately to the statement following *action*. If *action* consists of multiple statements, we enclose them in braces. Algorithm 1.2.2 uses a while loop to find the largest value in an array. If s is an array, $s.last$ is the last index in the array.

Algorithm 1.2.2 Finding the Maximum Value in an Array Using a While Loop. This algorithm finds the largest number in the array

$$s[1], s[2], \ldots, s[n].$$

```
    Input Parameter:    s
Output Parameters:    None

array_max_ver1(s) {
    large = s[1]
    i = 2
    while (i ≤ s.last) {
        if (s[i] > large) // larger value found
            large = s[i]
        i = i + 1
    }
    return large
}
```

The **do while loop** is like a while loop; the only difference is that the expression controlling the loop is tested at the bottom of loop. For this reason, the body of the loop is always executed at least once. The do while loop is written

```
do {
    action
} while (condition)
```

Example 1.2.3. After the segment

```
i = 2
do {
    i = i + 2
} while (i ≤ 0)
```

executes, the value of i is 4. ☐

The first form of the **for loop** is written

```
for var = init to limit
    action
```

When the for loop is executed, *init* and *limit* are expressions that have integer values. The variable *var* is first set to the value *init*. If *var* $\leq$ *limit*, *action* is executed and 1 is added to *var*. The process is repeated; that is, if *var* $\leq$ *limit*, *action* is executed again and 1 is added to *var*. Repetition continues until *var* $>$ *limit*. Then, control passes immediately to the statement following *action*. If *action* consists of multiple statements, we enclose them in braces. Algorithm 1.2.4 rewrites Algorithm 1.2.2 replacing the while loop with a for loop.

Algorithm 1.2.4 Finding the Maximum Value in an Array Using a For Loop.
This algorithm finds the largest value in the array $s[1], s[2], \ldots, s[n]$.

```
    Input Parameter:    s
Output Parameters:    None
```

```
array_max_ver2(s) {
    large = s[1]
    for i = 2 to s.last
        if (s[i] > large) // larger value found
            large = s[i]
    return large
}
```

The second form of the **for loop** is written

for *var* = *init* downto *limit*
    action

It operates similarly to the first form of the for loop, except that *action* is executed as long as *var* ≥ *limit*, and updating is performed by subtracting 1 from *var*.

We use the functions *print* and *println* for output. The function *println* adds a newline after printing its argument (which causes the next output to occur flush left on the next line); otherwise, the functions are the same. The operator + concatenates strings. If exactly one of +'s operands is a string, the other argument is converted to a string, after which the concatenation occurs. The concatenation operator is useful in the print functions.

Example 1.2.5. The segment

for *i* = 1 to *s.last*
    println(s[i])

prints the values in the array *s*, one per line. □

Example 1.2.6. The segment

for *i* = 1 to *s.last*
    print(s[i] + " ")
println()

prints the values in the array *s*, separated by space, on one line. The array values are followed by a newline. □

We assume that if *i* and *j* are integer variables, the quotient *i*/*j* is the value $\lfloor i/j \rfloor$.

Example 1.2.7. If *i* = 5 and *j* = 2, the value of *i*/*j* is 2. □

A structure containing data and functions is called a **class**. If *c* refers to a member, called an **object**, of a class containing a function *f*, *c.f*() invokes the function *f* on *c*.

Example 1.2.8. Suppose that *Card* is a class that models a playing card. Suppose further that class *Card* contains functions *set_suit* and *get_suit* to set and get the suit. If *c* refers to an object in the *Card* class, the segment

$c.set\_suit(\text{"diamonds"})$
$println(c.get\_suit())$

sets c's suit to diamonds and then prints *diamonds*.   □

Exercises

Write all algorithms in pseudocode as described in this section.

1S. Write an algorithm that returns the smallest value in the array

$$s[1], \ldots, s[n].$$

Use a while loop.

2. Write an algorithm that returns the smallest value in the array

$$s[1], \ldots, s[n].$$

Use a for loop.

3. Write an algorithm that outputs the largest and second largest values in the array $s[1], \ldots, s[n]$. Assume that $n > 1$ and the values in the array are distinct.

4S. Write an algorithm that outputs the smallest and second smallest values in the array $s[1], \ldots, s[n]$. Assume that $n > 1$ and the values in the array are distinct.

5. Write an algorithm that outputs the smallest and largest values in the array $s[1], \ldots, s[n]$.

6. Write an algorithm that returns the index of the first occurrence of the largest element in the array $s[1], \ldots, s[n]$.

7S. Write an algorithm that returns the index of the last occurrence of the largest element in the array $s[1], \ldots, s[n]$.

8. Write an algorithm that returns the index of the first occurrence of the value *key* in the array $s[1], \ldots, s[n]$. If *key* is not in the array, the algorithm returns the value 0.

9. Write an algorithm that returns the index of the last occurrence of the value *key* in the array $s[1], \ldots, s[n]$. If *key* is not in the array, the algorithm returns the value 0.

10S. Write an algorithm that returns the index of the first item that is less than its predecessor in the array $s[1], \ldots, s[n]$. (Assume that the $s[i]$ are real numbers.) If $n = 1$ or $s[i] \leq s[i + 1]$ for all i, the algorithm returns the value 0.

11. Write an algorithm that reverses the array $s[1], \ldots, s[n]$.

12. Write an algorithm whose input is an array $s[1], \ldots, s[n]$ and a value x. (Assume that all the values are real numbers.) If $n > 1$, the array satisfies $s[i] \le s[i+1]$ for all i. The algorithm inserts x into the array so that we have $s[i] \le s[i+1]$ for all i.

13S. Write an algorithm whose input is an array $s[1], \ldots, s[n]$ of bits. The algorithm rearranges the array so that all of the zeros precede all of the ones.

1.3 The Present

The pseudocode introduced in Section 1.2 allows us to write many traditional algorithms. However, it is occasionally necessary to relax the requirements of an algorithm stated in Section 1.1. Many algorithms currently in use are not general, deterministic, or even finite. An operating system, for example, is better thought of as a program that never terminates rather than as a finite program with input and output (such algorithms are called **online algorithms**). Algorithms written for more than one processor, whether for a multiprocessor machine or for a distributed environment (such as the Internet), are rarely deterministic. Also, many practical problems are too difficult to be solved efficiently, and compromises either in generality or correctness are necessary. We will see several variants of the narrow notion of an algorithm in this book, especially in Chapter 11, but also in other chapters.

As an illustration, we include an example that shows the usefulness of allowing an algorithm to make random decisions, thereby violating the requirement of determinism. In Section 1.4 we discuss what further changes in our notion of an algorithm the future might have in store.

Randomized Algorithms

A **randomized algorithm** does not require that the intermediate results of each step of execution be uniquely defined and depend only on the inputs and results of the preceding steps. By definition, when a randomized algorithm executes, at some points it makes *random* choices. These choices are made by a **random number generator**. When a random number generator is called, it computes a number and returns its value. When a sequence of calls is made to a random number generator, the sequence of numbers returned is random.[†]

In practice, a **pseudorandom number generator** is used. A pseudorandom number generator is an algorithm that produces numbers that ap-

---

[†]We are deliberately vague in using the notion of a random sequence, and we appeal to the reader's experience in playing games of chance. A correct mathematical definition of the notion of randomness was achieved only in the 20th century, 300 years after randomness had been introduced to mathematics by Blaise Pascal.

pear random. We shall assume the existence of a function

$$rand(i, j),$$

which returns a random integer between the integers i and j, inclusive. For example, for $i = 3$ and $j = 100$, when the pseudorandom number generator supplied by the Java programming language (scaled to produce random numbers in the desired range) was called 20 times, the following sequence was obtained:

46 11 57 91 10 42 69 48 98 84 100 52 48 37 58 41 45 15 60 39.

As an example, we describe a randomized algorithm that shuffles an array of numbers. More precisely, it inputs an array $a[1], \ldots, a[n]$ and moves the numbers to random positions.

The algorithm swaps $a[1]$ and $a[rand(1, n)]$. It then swaps $a[2]$ and $a[rand(2, n)]$. It continues in this manner until it swaps $a[n - 1]$ and $a[rand(n - 1, n)]$.

Algorithm 1.3.1 Array Shuffle. This algorithm shuffles the values in the array $a[1], a[2], \ldots, a[n]$.

Input Parameter: a
Output Parameter: a

```
shuffle(a) {
    for i = 1 to a.last − 1
        swap(a[i], a[rand(i, a.last)])
}
```

Example 1.3.2. Suppose that the array a

17	21	5	23	9

is input to *shuffle*. We first swap $a[i]$ and $a[j]$, where $i = 1$ and $j = rand(1, 5)$. If $j = 3$, after the swap we have

5	21	17	23	9

    ↑   ↑
    i j

Next, $i = 2$. If $j = rand(2, 5) = 5$, after the swap we have

5	9	17	23	21

      ↑   ↑
      i j

Next, $i = 3$. If $j = rand(3, 5) = 3$, the array does not change.
Finally, $i = 4$. If $j = rand(4, 5) = 5$, after the swap we have

5	9	17	21	23

.

$$\uparrow \qquad \uparrow$$
$$i \qquad j$$

Notice that the output (i.e., the rearranged array) depends on the random choices made by the random number generator.

Major bridge tournaments use computer programs to shuffle the cards. □

Randomized algorithms are normally run on traditional computers with the help of pseudorandom number generators (an active research area in computer science), although they could also be implemented by measuring unpredictable physical phenomena such as the radioactive decay of atomic particles. Some cryptographic software uses the random delay between user keystrokes as an input to generate a random key.

Exercises

1S. Write an algorithm to generate a random permutation of $1, 2, \ldots, n$.

2. Suppose that the only randomness to which your algorithm has access is the function $rand(1, 6)$. Can you use this function to implement a fair random coin toss (i.e., heads and tails occur with the same probability)?

1.4 The Future

We saw in Section 1.3 that there can be good reasons to extend the traditional notion of an algorithm and computation, and, indeed, many areas of computer science require such extended computational models. Computer games, cryptography, and computational geometry are unthinkable without randomness, and distributed computation is not deterministic. These are extensions of the algorithmic model that are already in place and used in practice. What can we expect in the future?

The fundamental unit of information in a traditional computer, such as a personal computer, is a **bit**, which has the value 0 or 1. The fundamental operations performed by the computer's processor, such as arithmetic and logical operations, are reduced to operations on bits, which are carried out by electronic circuits. The target machine for "traditional" algorithms is a traditional computer. Even randomized algorithms are usually run on traditional computers, as we mentioned earlier.

Recently, other ways have been proposed for performing operations necessary for computation, opening exciting possibilities for new kinds of algorithms.

Quantum Computing

$\mathcal{WWW}$ In a **quantum computer**, the fundamental unit of information is a **quantum bit** or **qubit**. Like a bit, a qubit has values 0 and 1, but it can also exist in an intermediate state, which is a superposition of the two classic states 0 and 1. This intermediate state collapses to 0 or 1 with certain probabilities when the qubit is observed. A quantum computer operates on qubits.

A quantum computer is no more powerful than a traditional computer; that is, any computation that a quantum computer can perform can also be performed on a traditional computer. What makes a quantum computer interesting and potentially useful is that it can perform some computations more efficiently than a traditional computer. For example, there is currently no efficient algorithm known for factoring an integer using a traditional computer. However, Peter Shor (see Shor, 1997) published an efficient factoring algorithm for a quantum computer. If a quantum computer could be built, Shor's algorithm would challenge popular public-key cryptosystems such as RSA whose security is based on the difficulty of factoring large integers.

Another example that illustrates the power of a quantum computer is an algorithm due to Lov Grover (see Grover, 1996) for searching for a given value in an unordered list. On a traditional computer, the best one can do is to check each item in the list, one-by-one, to see if it has the desired value. If there are n items in the list, in the worst case we would have to check them all, so the time is proportional to n. Grover's algorithm for a quantum computer searches the list in time proportional to $\sqrt{n}$ in the worst case.

Building a quantum computer is a challenge because qubits tend to be unstable, and the ones that have been built can process only a few qubits. Because of its potential usefulness, quantum computing is an active research area—both in developing algorithms for quantum computers and in constructing quantum computers.

A related area, which does not use quantum computers but still makes use of quantum physics principles, is **quantum cryptography**. The security of traditional cryptography methods rests on unproven mathematical assumptions. Quantum cryptography does not require these assumptions and has been shown to be successful in practical experiments.

DNA Computing

WWW DNA (deoxyribonucleic acid) encodes genetic information as a string of chemicals, called *bases*, typically denoted A, C, G, and T. In DNA computing, bits (0 and 1) are replaced by the bases A, C, G, and T. Strands of DNA represent data, just as strings of bits represent data in a traditional computer. A DNA computation begins by generating strands of DNA to represent possible solutions to a particular problem. The computation proceeds using biological processes that correspond to operations performed by a traditional computer. After the computation ends, any DNA strands that remain represent a solution to the problem.

Like the situation in which a quantum computer can efficiently solve a problem for which no efficient traditional algorithm is known, Len Adleman (see Adleman, 1994) showed how to use DNA computing to solve the Hamiltonian-cycle problem efficiently (see Section 2.5). No efficient traditional algorithm is known for the Hamiltonian-cycle problem. The size of Adleman's experimental problem was very small (seven vertices), and the solution took three weeks. Nevertheless, the experiment showed that DNA computing is possible.

After Adleman's experiment, other researchers began investigating DNA computing. Richard Lipton, Daniel Boneh, and Christopher Dunworth showed how a DNA computer might crack messages encoded using the United States Data Encryption Standard (DES), which was used for the secure exchange of information such as banking and national security matters.

DNA computing derives its power from *massive* parallelism. DES relies on one of 72 quadrillion "keys" to encode a message. The security results from the difficulty of discovering which key was used. Checking all possible keys is impossible using a traditional computer because it would take too long. However, a DNA computer could check all 72 quadrillion keys concurrently. Estimates indicate that the computation could take as little as two hours.

Exercises

1. Write a short article about the current status of quantum computing.

2. Write a short article about the current status of quantum cryptography.

3. What is the largest number of qubits currently implemented in a quantum computer? Cite a reference.

4. Write a short article about the current status of DNA computing.

Notes

The first half of Knuth, 1997, discusses the concept of algorithm. Knuth's expository article about algorithms (Knuth, 1977) and his article about the role of algorithms in the mathematical sciences (Knuth, 1985) are also recommended.

Stan Gudder (see Gudder, 2003) wrote an expository article about quantum computing that requires only linear algebra as a mathematics prerequisite, yet presents enough details to explain the basics of quantum computing.

Chapter Exercises

1.1. Choose a set, or subset, of instructions for running a particular computer application (e.g., a word processor). Which properties of an algorithm—input, output, precision, determinism, finiteness, correctness, generality—are present? Which properties are lacking?

1.2. [Requires basic probability theory.] Show that Algorithm 1.3.1 shuffles the array a filled with numbers 1 through n in a fair manner; that is, every possible permutation of 1 through n is obtained with the same probability.

1.3. [Requires basic probability theory.] Mister Wizard suggests the following modification of the shuffle algorithm (Algorithm 1.3.1):

> *new_shuffle*(a) {
>   for $i = 1$ to $a.last$
>   *swap*($a[i], a[rand(1, a.last)]$)
> }

Suppose that a initially contains the numbers 1 through n. Does *new_shuffle*(a) produce every possible permutation of 1 through n with the same probability?

1.4. One popular cryptographic method for encoding a message is substituting a letter for each letter of the alphabet. For example, the substitution

plaintext letter	abcdefghijklmnopqrstuvwxyz
ciphertext letter	HETJWOPSQYAZIVMBDUKNRGLCXF

turns the plaintext "omnia gallia est divisa in partes tres" into the ciphertext "MIVQH PHZZQH WKN QV BHUNWK NUWK". Note that the substitution is a permutation of the 26 letters of the alphabet, so we can uniquely decipher a ciphertext by reading the substitution backwards; that is, ciphertext "A" is plaintext "k", "B" is "p", and so on. Write a program that takes as an input a plaintext, generates a random substitution, and then encrypts the plaintext using that substitution. All substitutions should occur with the same probability.

1.5. [Requires basic probability theory.] Suppose that the only randomness to which your algorithm has access is $rand(1, 2)$, that is, a random fair coin toss. Can you use this function to write an algorithm that implements throwing a fair die (i.e., the outcomes should be $1, 2, 3, 4, 5, 6$ with equal probability)? *Hint:* It will make a difference whether you require your algorithm to terminate or not. Discuss both cases.

CHAPTER 2
Mathematics for Algorithms

In this chapter, we present the mathematics—notation, definitions, theorems—that we need in this book. Section 2.1 summarizes some basic results. Mathematical induction—*the* proof technique in discrete mathematics—is the subject of Section 2.2. Section 2.3 discusses the "big-oh" and related notations that are used to make precise statements about the time and space required by algorithms. Recurrence relations are presented in Section 2.4 together with techniques for solving them. The chapter concludes (Sections 2.5 and 2.6) with definitions and results about graphs and trees.

2.1 Definitions, Notation, and Basic Results

In this section, we summarize some definitions, notation, and basic results that will be used throughout the book.

Notation

We let $\mathbb{N}$ denote the set of natural numbers $\{1, 2, \ldots\}$, $\mathbb{R}$ denote the set of real numbers, and $\mathbb{R}_{\geq 0}$ denote the set of nonnegative real numbers.

If X is a finite set, we let $|X|$ denote the number of elements in X.

Polynomials

A **polynomial of degree** n is a function of the form

$$p(x) = c_n x^n + c_{n-1} x^{n-1} + \cdots + c_1 x + c_0,$$

with $c_n \neq 0$. The numbers c_i are called **coefficients**.

Example 2.1.1. The function

$$p(x) = 3x^5 - 12x^3 + 9x^2 - 200x + 4$$

is a polynomial of degree 5. The coefficients are

$$c_5 = 3, \quad c_4 = 0, \quad c_3 = -12, \quad c_2 = 9, \quad c_1 = -200, \quad c_0 = 4. \qquad \square$$

Intervals

If a and b are numbers, $[a, b]$ is called a **closed interval** and is defined to be the set

$$\{x \mid a \le x \le b\}.$$

If we are restricted to integers, a and b are integers and $[a, b]$ is understood to be the set

$$\{x \mid x \text{ is an integer and } a \le x \le b\}.$$

Similarly, if we are restricted to real numbers, a and b are real numbers and $[a, b]$ is understood to be the set

$$\{x \mid x \text{ is a real number and } a \le x \le b\}.$$

Example 2.1.2. If we are restricted to integers,

$$[2, 6] = \{2, 3, 4, 5, 6\}. \qquad \square$$

Example 2.1.3. If we are restricted to real numbers, $[2, 6]$ consists of all real numbers between 2 and 6, including 2 and 6. As examples, $2 \in [2, 6]$, $4.3019822 \in [2, 6]$, and $\pi \in [2, 6]$. $\qquad \square$

If a and b are numbers, (a, b) is called an **open interval** and is defined to be the set

$$\{x \mid a < x < b\}.$$

As for closed intervals, if we are restricted to integers, a and b are integers and (a, b) is understood to consist of integers; if we are restricted to real numbers, a and b are real numbers and (a, b) is understood to consist of real numbers.

If a and b are numbers, $[a, b)$ is defined to be the set

$$\{x \mid a \le x < b\},$$

and $(a, b]$ is defined to be the set

$$\{x \mid a < x \le b\}.$$

Either set $[a, b)$ or $(a, b]$ is called a **half-open interval**. As for closed and open intervals, if we are restricted to integers, a and b are integers and $[a, b)$ and $(a, b]$ are understood to consist of integers; if we are restricted to real numbers, a and b are real numbers and $[a, b)$ and $(a, b]$ are understood to consist of real numbers.

Sequences and Strings

A **finite sequence** a is a function from the set $\{0, 1, \ldots, n\}$ to a set X. The sequence is typically denoted $a_0, a_1, \ldots, a_n$ or $a[0], a[1], \ldots, a[n]$ or $a[0..n]$.

The subscript i in a_i is called the **index** of the sequence. It is frequently convenient to replace the set $\{0, 1, \ldots, n\}$ by some other finite set of consecutive integers. For example, if b is a function from the set $\{1, 2, \ldots, n\}$ to a set X, we would denote the sequence as $b_1, b_2, \ldots, b_n$ or $b[1], b[2], \ldots, b[n]$ or $b[1..n]$.

Example 2.1.4. If we let

$$a_0 = 4, \quad a_1 = 58, \quad a_2 = 0, \quad a_3 = 10, \quad a_4 = -54,$$

a is a finite sequence. The index of the term 10 is 3. The sequence is typically written

$$a_0, a_1, a_2, a_3, a_4$$

or

$$a[0], a[1], a[2], a[3], a[4]$$

or

$$a[0..4]$$

or

$$4, 58, 0, 10, -54. \qquad \square$$

An **infinite sequence** a is a function from the set $\{0, 1, \ldots\}$ to a set X. The sequence is typically denoted $a_0, a_1, \ldots$ or $a[0], a[1], \ldots$ or $\{a_i\}_{i=0}^{\infty}$ or simply $\{a_i\}$, if it is understood that the first index is zero. It is frequently convenient to allow the set $\{0, 1, \ldots\}$ to begin at some other integer. For example, if b is a function from the set $\{1, 2, \ldots\}$ to a set X, we would denote the sequence as $b_1, b_2, \ldots$ or $b[1], b[2], \ldots$ or $\{b_i\}_{i=1}^{\infty}$ or simply $\{b_i\}$, if it is understood that the first index is one.

Example 2.1.5. If we define

$$a_i = 3i + 1, \quad i \geq 0,$$

we obtain an infinite sequence a. The first four terms are

$$a_0 = 1, \quad a_1 = 4, \quad a_2 = 7, \quad a_3 = 10. \qquad \square$$

The term "sequence" refers to either a finite sequence or an infinite sequence.

A real-valued sequence (i.e., a sequence a for which a_i is a real number for all i) is **increasing** if $a_i < a_{i+1}$ for all i for which i and $i+1$ are indexes. A real-valued sequence is **decreasing** if $a_i > a_{i+1}$ for all i for which i and $i+1$ are indexes. A real-valued sequence is **nondecreasing** if $a_i \leq a_{i+1}$ for all i for which i and $i+1$ are indexes. A real-valued sequence is **nonincreasing** if $a_i \geq a_{i+1}$ for all i for which i and $i+1$ are indexes.

Example 2.1.6. The sequence

$$2, 5, 13, 104, 300$$

is increasing and nondecreasing.   □

Example 2.1.7. The sequence

$$2, 5, 13, 13, 104, 300, 300$$

is nondecreasing, but it is *not* increasing.   □

Example 2.1.8. The sequence a defined as

$$a_i = \frac{1}{i}, \quad i \geq 1$$

is decreasing and nonincreasing.   □

Example 2.1.9. The sequence

$$100, 90, 90, 74, 74, 74, 30$$

is nonincreasing, but it is *not* decreasing.   □

Example 2.1.10. The sequence

$$101$$

is increasing, decreasing, nonincreasing, and nondecreasing since there is *no* value of i for which both i and $i + 1$ are indexes.   □

A subsequence of a sequence is obtained by retaining only certain terms of the original sequence, while maintaining the order of terms in the given sequence. More formally, let $\{a_n\}$ be a sequence, and let $n_1, n_2, \ldots$ be an increasing sequence of integers whose values are indexes for a. The sequence $\{a_{n_k}\}$ is a **subsequence** of $\{a_n\}$. (The values $n_1, n_2, \ldots$ are the indexes of the terms retained in the original sequence a.)

Example 2.1.11. The sequence

$$3, -10, 7$$

is a subsequence of the sequence

$$b_1 = 2, \ b_2 = 3, \ b_3 = -14, \ b_4 = 2001, \ b_5 = -10, \ b_6 = 7, \ b_7 = 0, \ b_8 = 77.$$

The subsequence $3, -10, 7$ is obtained from the sequence b by retaining the second, fifth, and sixth terms. The expression n_k in the definition of "subsequence" is

$$n_1 = 2, \quad n_2 = 5, \quad n_3 = 6.$$

The subsequence is thus

$$b_2, b_5, b_6 \quad \text{or} \quad b_{n_1}, b_{n_2}, b_{n_3}.$$

Notice that the sequence

$$-10, 3, 7$$

is *not* a subsequence of b since the order of terms in b is *not* maintained. □

A **string** or **word over** X is a finite sequence $t[1], t[2], \ldots, t[n]$, where each $t[i] \in X$. The string is written $t[1]t[2] \cdots t[n]$. The **length** of the string t is n.

Example 2.1.12. Let $X = \{a, b, c\}$. If we let

$$t[1] = b, \quad t[2] = a, \quad t[3] = a, \quad t[4] = c,$$

we obtain a string over X. This string is written *baac*, and its length is 4. □

The **null string** or **empty word**, ε, is a string with no elements. Its length is zero.

If $t[1]t[2] \cdots t[n]$ is a string, we call $t[i..j]$, where $i, j \in \{1, \ldots, n\}$, a **substring** of t. If $i < j$, $t[i..j]$ is the substring $t[i] \cdots t[j]$. If $i = j$, $t[i..j] = t[i..i]$ is the substring $t[i]$. If $i > j$, by definition $t[i..j]$ is the null string.

Example 2.1.13. Let t be the string

$$t[1] = a, \quad t[2] = b, \quad t[3] = a, \quad t[4] = b, \quad t[5] = b.$$

Then, $t[2..4]$ is the substring *bab*, $t[5..5] = t[5]$ is the substring b, and $t[3..1]$ is the null string. □

Logic

We use $\vee$ to denote the Boolean operator *or*, $\wedge$ to denote the Boolean operator *and*, and $\bar{}$ to denote the Boolean operator *not*. We follow the usual precedence conventions: *not* has the highest precedence followed, in order, by *and* and *or*.

Example 2.1.14. The expression

$$p \vee q \wedge \bar{r}$$

is interpreted as

$$p \text{ or } q \text{ and not } r.$$

Because of the precedence conventions, the expression is equivalent to

$$p \text{ or } (q \text{ and } (not \ r)). \qquad \qquad \square$$

A **Boolean expression** is an expression containing variables, $\vee$'s, $\wedge$'s, $^-$'s, and grouping symbols (e.g., parentheses).

Example 2.1.15. The expression

$$(p_1 \vee \overline{p}_2 \wedge p_3) \vee \overline{(p_1 \vee p_4)}$$

is a Boolean expression. $\square$

A **literal** is a variable (e.g., p) or the negation of a variable (e.g., $\overline{p}$). A Boolean expression is in **conjunctive normal form** (CNF) if it is of the form

$$c_1 \wedge c_2 \wedge \cdots \wedge c_n,$$

where each c_i is of the form

$$p_1 \vee p_2 \vee \cdots \vee p_{n_i},$$

and each p_j is a literal. The c_i are called **clauses**.

Example 2.1.16. The Boolean expression in Example 2.1.15 is not in conjunctive normal form. $\square$

Example 2.1.17. The Boolean expression

$$(p \vee \overline{q} \vee r) \wedge (\overline{p} \vee s) \wedge (q \vee r) \wedge \overline{s}$$

is in conjunctive normal form. The clauses are

$$p \vee \overline{q} \vee r, \quad\quad \overline{p} \vee s, \quad\quad q \vee r, \quad\quad \overline{s}. \quad\quad\quad \square$$

A Boolean expression is in **disjunctive normal form** (DNF) if it is of the form

$$c_1 \vee c_2 \vee \cdots \vee c_n,$$

where each c_i is of the form

$$p_1 \wedge p_2 \wedge \cdots \wedge p_{n_i},$$

and each p_j is a literal.

We also find it convenient to use the Boolean connectives $\rightarrow$ (**implication**) and $\leftrightarrow$ (**equivalence**). The expression $p \rightarrow q$ is defined to be false when p is true and q is false; the expression is true for all other truth assignments to p and q. The expression $p \leftrightarrow q$ is defined to be true when p and q are both true or both false; the expression is false when one of p or q is true and the other is false.

Two Boolean formulas involving and, or, not, implication, and equivalence operators are said to be **equivalent** if the formulas have the same truth values regardless of the assignments to the variables. For example, the table

p	q	$p \to q$	$\overline{p} \vee q$
T	T	T	T
T	F	F	F
F	T	T	T
F	F	T	T

shows that the formulas $p \to q$ and $\overline{p} \vee q$ are equivalent. (T denotes true, and F denotes false.) Similarly, the formulas $p \leftrightarrow q$ and $(\overline{p} \vee q) \wedge (\overline{q} \vee p)$ are equivalent (see Exercise 34). Because of these equivalences, we sometimes extend the definition of "Boolean expression" to include the implication and equivalence operators as well as the and, or, and not operators.

Binomial Coefficients

The **binomial coefficient** $\binom{n}{k}$, $n \geq k \geq 0$, counts the number of k-element subsets of an n-element set. Its value is

$$\binom{n}{k} = \frac{n!}{(n-k)!k!}.$$

Useful bounds on the binomial coefficient are given in the next theorem.

Theorem 2.1.18.

$$\left(\frac{n}{k}\right)^k \leq \binom{n}{k} \leq \frac{n^k}{k!}$$

Proof. Note that

$$\frac{n-i}{k-i} \geq \frac{n}{k},$$

for $i = 0, 1, \ldots, k-1$. Therefore,

$$\binom{n}{k} = \frac{n!}{(n-k)!k!} = \frac{n(n-1)\cdots(n-k+1)}{k(k-1)\cdots 1}$$

$$= \frac{n}{k}\frac{n-1}{k-1}\cdots\frac{n-k+1}{1}$$

$$\geq \frac{n}{k}\frac{n}{k}\cdots\frac{n}{k}$$

$$= \left(\frac{n}{k}\right)^k.$$

Also,

$$\binom{n}{k} = \frac{n(n-1)\cdots(n-k+1)}{k!} \leq \frac{nn\cdots n}{k!} = \frac{n^k}{k!}. \qquad \blacksquare$$

The upper bound,

$$\binom{n}{k} \leq \left(\frac{en}{k}\right)^k,$$

of the same form as the lower bound in Theorem 2.1.18, can be proved using calculus techniques (see Exercise 38). ($e = 2.71828\ldots$ is the base of the natural logarithm function.)

Logarithms

In this subsection, we assume that b is a positive real number not equal to 1. If x is a positive real number, the **logarithm to the base b of x** is the exponent to which b must be raised to obtain x. We denote the logarithm to the base b of x as $\log_b x$, and the logarithm to the base 2 of x as $\lg x$.

Example 2.1.19. We have $\lg 8 = 3$ because $2^3 = 8$. □

Example 2.1.20. Given

$$2^{2^x} = n,$$

where n is a positive integer, solve for x.

From the definition of logarithm,

$$2^x = \lg n.$$

Again, from the definition of logarithm,

$$x = \lg(\lg n).$$ □

The following theorem lists important laws of logarithms.

Theorem 2.1.21 Laws of Logarithms. *Suppose that $b > 0$ and $b \neq 1$. Then*

(a) $b^{\log_b x} = x.$

(b) $\log_b(xy) = \log_b x + \log_b y.$

(c) $\log_b \left(\dfrac{x}{y} \right) = \log_b x - \log_b y.$

(d) $\log_b x^y = y \log_b x.$

(e) If $a > 0$ and $a \neq 1$, $\log_a x = \dfrac{\log_b x}{\log_b a}.$

(f) If $b > 1$ and $x > y > 0$, $\log_b x > \log_b y.$

Theorem 2.1.21(e) is known as the **change-of-base formula for logarithms**. If we know how to compute logarithms to the base b, we can perform the computation on the right side of the equation to obtain the logarithm to the base a. Theorem 2.1.21(f) says that if $b > 1$, $\log_b(x)$ is an increasing function.

Example 2.1.22. Let $b = 2$ and $x = 8$. Then $\log_b x = 3$. Now

$$b^{\log_b x} = 2^3 = 8 = x,$$

which illustrates Theorem 2.1.21(a). □

Example 2.1.23. Let $b = 2$, $x = 8$, and $y = 16$. Then $\log_b x = 3$, $\log_b y = 4$, and $\log_b(xy) = \log_2 128 = 7$. Now

$$\log_b(xy) = 7 = 3 + 4 = \log_b x + \log_b y,$$

which illustrates Theorem 2.1.21(b). □

Example 2.1.24. Let $b = 2$, $x = 8$, and $y = 16$. Then $\log_b x = 3$, $\log_b y = 4$, and

$$\log_b \left(\frac{x}{y} \right) = \log_2 \frac{1}{2} = -1.$$

Now

$$\log_b \left(\frac{x}{y} \right) = -1 = \log_b x - \log_b y,$$

which illustrates Theorem 2.1.21(c). □

Example 2.1.25. Let $b = 2$, $x = 4$, and $y = 3$. Then $\log_b x = 2$ and

$$\log_b x^y = \log_2 64 = 6.$$

Now

$$\log_b x^y = 6 = 3 \cdot 2 = y \log_b x,$$

which illustrates Theorem 2.1.21(d). □

Example 2.1.26. Suppose that we have a calculator that has a logarithm key that computes logarithms to the base 10 but does not have a key that computes logarithms to the base 2. We use Theorem 2.1.21(e) to compute $\log_2 40$.

Using our calculator, we compute

$$\log_{10} 40 = 1.602060, \qquad \log_{10} 2 = 0.301030.$$

Theorem 2.1.21(e) now gives

$$\log_2 40 = \frac{\log_{10} 40}{\log_{10} 2} = \frac{1.602060}{0.301030} = 5.321928. \qquad \square$$

Example 2.1.27. Show that if k and n are positive integers satisfying

$$2^{k-1} < n < 2^k,$$

then

$$k - 1 < \lg n < k.$$

By Theorem 2.1.21(f), the logarithm function is increasing. Therefore,

$$\lg 2^{k-1} < \lg n < \lg 2^k.$$

By Theorem 2.1.21(d),
$$\lg 2^{k-1} = (k-1)\lg 2.$$

Since
$$\lg 2 = \log_2 2 = 1,$$

we have
$$\lg 2^{k-1} = (k-1)\lg 2 = k-1.$$

Similarly,
$$\lg 2^k = k.$$

The given inequality now follows.   □

Inequalities

In this subsection, we derive some inequalities that will be useful later.

Theorem 2.1.28. *Let a and b be numbers such that* $0 \le a < b$. *Then*
$$\frac{b^{n+1} - a^{n+1}}{b - a} < (n+1)b^n.$$

Proof. If $0 \le a < b$, then
$$\frac{b^{n+1} - a^{n+1}}{b - a} = \sum_{i=0}^{n} a^i b^{n-i} < \sum_{i=0}^{n} b^i b^{n-i} = (n+1)b^n. \qquad \blacksquare$$

We may use Theorem 2.1.28 to show that the sequence $\{(1 + 1/n)^n\}$ is increasing and bounded above by 4. This fact will be used to derive another useful inequality.

Theorem 2.1.29. *The sequence* $\{(1+1/n)^n\}$ *is increasing and bounded above by* 4.

Proof. We first rewrite the inequality of Theorem 2.1.28 as
$$b^n[b - (n+1)(b-a)] < a^{n+1}.$$

If we set $a = 1 + 1/(n+1)$ and $b = 1 + 1/n$, the term in brackets reduces to 1 and we have
$$\left(1 + \frac{1}{n}\right)^n < \left(1 + \frac{1}{n+1}\right)^{n+1}.$$

Therefore, the sequence $\{(1 + 1/n)^n\}$ is increasing.

Next, we set $a = 1$ and $b = 1 + 1/(2n)$. This time the term in brackets reduces to $\frac{1}{2}$, and we have
$$\left(1 + \frac{1}{2n}\right)^n < 2.$$

Squaring both sides gives

$$\left(1 + \frac{1}{2n}\right)^{2n} < 4.$$

Since $\{(1 + 1/n)^n\}$ is increasing,

$$\left(1 + \frac{1}{n}\right)^n < \left(1 + \frac{1}{2n}\right)^{2n} < 4.$$

Therefore, the sequence $\{(1 + 1/n)^n\}$ is bounded above by 4. ∎

A calculus theorem states that an increasing sequence that is bounded above converges; thus, $\{(1 + 1/n)^n\}$ converges. The limit is $e = 2.71828\ldots$, the base of the natural logarithm function.

Since $\{(1 + 1/n)^n\}$ is increasing and $(1 + 1/n)^n = 2$ if $n = 1$, we have

$$2 \le \left(1 + \frac{1}{n}\right)^n < 4$$

for all n. Taking the logarithm to the base 2 gives our next inequality.

Theorem 2.1.30.

$$\frac{1}{n} \le \lg(n + 1) - \lg n < \frac{2}{n}$$

Proof. We have already noted that

$$2 \le \left(1 + \frac{1}{n}\right)^n < 4$$

for all n. Taking the logarithm to the base 2, we obtain

$$1 = \lg 2 \le \lg\left(1 + \frac{1}{n}\right)^n < \lg 4 = 2.$$

Since

$$\lg\left(1 + \frac{1}{n}\right)^n = \lg\left(\frac{n + 1}{n}\right)^n = n \lg\left(\frac{n + 1}{n}\right) = n[\lg(n + 1) - \lg n],$$

the preceding inequality becomes

$$1 \le n[\lg(n + 1) - \lg n] < 2.$$

Dividing by n yields the desired result. ∎

Upper Bounds, Lower Bounds, Supremum, Infimum

The maximum value in a nonempty finite set of real numbers is simply the largest element in the set. If the set is infinite, the set may fail to have a largest value. If the set is bounded above, the idea of "maximum" can be replaced by "least upper bound." We begin with precise definitions.

Definition 2.1.31. Let X be a nonempty set of real numbers.
  A number a is said to be an *upper bound* for X if $x \leq a$ for all $x \in X$.
  A number a is said to be a *lower bound* for X if $x \geq a$ for all $x \in X$.
  The number a is said to be the *least upper bound* of X if

(a) a is an upper bound for X.

(b) If b is an upper bound for X, then $a \leq b$.

  The number a is said to be the *greatest lower bound* of X if

(a) a is a lower bound for X.

(b) If b is a lower bound for X, then $a \geq b$.

  Part (b) of Definition 2.1.31 concerning least upper bounds may be equivalent stated as follows: If $b < a$, then b is not an upper bound for X. This last statement is equivalent to

(b′) If $b < a$, there exists $x \in X$ such that $b < x$.

In proving that a is the least upper bound of a set X, it is sometimes easier to use (b′) rather than (b). Part (b) of Definition 2.1.31 concerning greatest lower bounds may be rephrased in a similar way.

Example 2.1.32. We show that the least upper bound of the set

$$X = \{1 - 1/x \mid x > 0\}$$

is 1. Notice that X does not contain a largest value.
  First, we show that 1 is an upper bound for X. Since

$$1 \geq 1 - 1/x$$

for all $x > 0$, 1 is an upper bound for X.
  We now show that 1 is the least upper bound of X. We use the characterization (b′) to show that any value less than 1 is not an upper bound for X and, thus, that 1 is the least upper bound of X. If $b < 1$, then $1 - b$ is positive; so, there exists $x > 0$ satisfying $1/x < 1 - b$. Thus, $b < 1 - 1/x$. Therefore, b is not an upper bound for X, and 1 is the least upper bound of X. □

  It is a fundamental property of the real numbers that every nonempty set that is bounded above has a least upper bound, and every nonempty set that is bounded below has a greatest lower bound.
  We denote the least upper bound of a set X as $\mathrm{lub}\, X$. The least upper bound of a set X is also called the **supremum** of X; so, an alternative notation for the least upper bound of X is $\sup X$. Similarly, we denote the greatest lower bound of a set X as $\mathrm{glb}\, X$. The greatest lower bound of a set X is also called the **infimum** of X; so, an alternative notation for the greatest lower bound of X is $\inf X$. If a nonempty set X is not bounded above, we

set $\sup X = \infty$. Similarly, if a nonempty set X is not bounded below, we set $\inf X = -\infty$.

Exercises

In Exercises 1–3, give the degree of each polynomial and the values of the coefficients.

1S. $p(x) = 7x^3 + x^2 - 3$

2. $p(x) = -16x^8 + 14x^6 + 30x^5 - x^4 + x$

3. $p(x) = 100$

4S. Prove that if $p(x)$ and $q(x)$ are polynomials, then $p(x) + q(x)$, $p(x) - q(x)$, and $p(x)q(x)$ are also polynomials.

5. If $p(x)$ and $q(x)$ are polynomials, when is $p(x)/q(x)$ a polynomial?

6. If $p(x)$ is a polynomial of degree 5 and $q(x)$ is a polynomial of degree 3, what can you say about the degree of $p(x) + q(x)$?

7S. If $p(x)$ is a polynomial of degree 5 and $q(x)$ is a polynomial of degree 3, what can you say about the degree of $p(x) - q(x)$?

8. If $p(x)$ and $q(x)$ are polynomials, both of degree 5, what can you say about the degree of $p(x) - q(x)$?

9. If $p(x)$ is a polynomial of degree 5 and $q(x)$ is a polynomial of degree 3, what can you say about the degree of $p(x)q(x)$?

List the members of each set in Exercises 10–13. Assume that we are restricted to the set of integers.

10S. $[3,4]$ **11.** $(3,4)$ **12.** $[3,4)$ **13S.** $(3,4]$

14S. Suppose that two closed intervals have a nonempty intersection I. Can I be a closed interval? an open interval? a half-open interval?

15. Suppose that two open intervals have a nonempty intersection I. Can I be a closed interval? an open interval? a half-open interval?

16. Suppose that two half-open intervals have a nonempty intersection I. Can I be a closed interval? an open interval? a half-open interval?

17S. Suppose that a half-open interval and a closed interval have a nonempty intersection I. Can I be a closed interval? an open interval? a half-open interval?

Answer true or false for Exercises 18 and 19 and explain your answer.

18S. If a sequence is not increasing, then it is nonincreasing.

19. If a sequence is not increasing, then it is decreasing.

20S. Which sequences are both increasing and decreasing?

21. Which sequences are both nonincreasing and nondecreasing?

Determine whether each sequence in Exercises 22-28 is increasing, decreasing, nonincreasing, or nondecreasing.

22S. $5, 55, 555, 606, 1001, 2002, 2020, 3000, 4237$

23. $5, 55, 555, 555, 555, 606, 1001, 2002, 2020, 2020, 3000, 4237$

24. $5, -55, -555, -606, -1001, -2002, -2020, -3000, -4237$

25S. $5, -55, 555, -606, 1001, -2002, 2020, -3000, -4237$

26. $5, -55, -55, -606, -1001, -1001, -2020, -3000$

27. 5

28S. $5, 5$

Which Boolean expressions in Exercises 29-33 are in conjunctive normal form? Which are in disjunctive normal form?

29S. $(p \wedge \overline{(q \wedge r)}) \vee (\overline{p} \wedge s) \vee (q \wedge r) \vee \overline{s}$

30. $(p \vee q \vee r) \wedge (\overline{p} \vee s) \wedge (q \vee r) \wedge \overline{s}$

31. $p \vee (\overline{q} \wedge r) \vee \overline{q}$

32S. $\overline{p}$

33. $p \vee q$

34S. Show that $p \leftrightarrow q$ and $(\overline{p} \vee q) \wedge (\overline{q} \vee p)$ are equivalent.

35. Show that $\overline{p \wedge q}$ and $\overline{p} \vee \overline{q}$ are equivalent. This equivalence is one of *De Morgan's Laws.*

36. Show that $\overline{p \vee q}$ and $\overline{p} \wedge \overline{q}$ are equivalent. This equivalence is another of *De Morgan's Laws.*

37S. Write an expression equivalent to $p \to q$ involving only the $\wedge$ and $^-$ operators.

$\star$**38.** Prove that

$$\binom{n}{k} \le \left(\frac{en}{k}\right)^k.$$

Hint: Show that it is enough to prove that $k! \geq (k/e)^k$. Taking logarithms to the base e, this last inequality is equivalent to

$$\ln k + \ln(k-1) + \cdots + \ln 1 \geq k(\ln k - 1).$$

(ln denotes the logarithm to the base e.) To prove this last inequality, compare the sum on the left with $\int_1^k \ln x \, dx$.

Find the value of each expression in Exercises 39-43 without using a calculator.

39S. $\lg 64$ **40.** $\lg \frac{1}{128}$ **41.** $\lg 2$ **42S.** $2^{\lg 10}$ **43.** $\lg 2^{1000}$

Given that $\lg 3 = 1.584962501$ *and* $\lg 5 = 2.321928095$, *find the value of each expression in Exercises 44-48.*

44S. $\lg 6$ **45.** $\lg 30$ **46.** $\lg 59049$ **47S.** $\lg 0.6$ **48.** $\lg 0.0375$

Use a calculator with a logarithm key to find the value of each expression in Exercises 49-52.

49S. $\log_5 47$ **50.** $\log_7 0.30881$ **51.** $\log_9 8.888^{100}$ **52S.** $\log_{10}(\log_{10} 1054)$

In Exercises 53-55, use a calculator with a logarithm key to solve for x.

53S. $5^x = 11$ **54.** $5^{2x}6^x = 811$ **55.** $5^{11^x} = 10^{100}$

56S. Show that $x^{\log_b y} = y^{\log_b x}$.

57. Prove that the sequence $\{n^{1/n}\}_{n=3}^{\infty}$ is decreasing.

58. Prove that if $0 \leq a < b$, then

$$\frac{b^{n+1} - a^{n+1}}{b - a} > (n+1)a^n.$$

59S. Find appropriate values for a and b in the inequality in the preceding exercise to prove that the sequence $\{(1 - 1/n)^n\}_{n=1}^{\infty}$ is increasing and bounded above by $4/9$.

60. By using the result of the preceding exercise, or otherwise, prove that the sequence $\{(1 + 1/n)^{n+1}\}_{n=1}^{\infty}$ is decreasing.

61. Let X be a nonempty set of real numbers with least upper bound a. Prove that if $\varepsilon > 0$, there exists $x \in X$ such that $a - \varepsilon < x \leq a$.

62S. Prove that the least upper bound of a set is unique.

63. Assuming that every nonempty set bounded above has a least upper bound, prove that every nonempty set bounded below has a greatest lower bound.

2.2 Mathematical Induction

Mathematical induction can be used to prove a sequence of statements indexed by the positive integers. For example, it can be used to prove that

$$\sum_{i=1}^{n} i = \frac{n(n+1)}{2} \quad \text{for all } n \geq 1.$$

Here, the sequence of statements is

$$\text{Statement 1:} \quad \sum_{i=1}^{1} i = \frac{1(1+1)}{2}$$

$$\text{Statement 2:} \quad \sum_{i=1}^{2} i = \frac{2(2+1)}{2}$$

$$\text{Statement 3:} \quad \sum_{i=1}^{3} i = \frac{3(3+1)}{2}$$

$$\vdots \qquad\qquad \vdots$$

$$\text{Statement } n: \quad \sum_{i=1}^{n} i = \frac{n(n+1)}{2}$$

$$\vdots \qquad\qquad \vdots$$

(Statements 1–3 are obtained by everywhere replacing n by 1 in the original equation, then n by 2, and then n by 3.)

Suppose that we wish to use mathematical induction to prove a sequence of statements $S(1), S(2), \ldots$. We must

(Basis Step.) Prove that $S(1)$ is true.

(Inductive Step.) *Assume* that $S(n)$ is true, and prove that $S(n+1)$ is true, for all $n \geq 1$.

The assumption in the Inductive Step is often called the *inductive assumption*.

Example 2.2.1. Prove that

$$\sum_{i=1}^{n} i = \frac{n(n+1)}{2} \quad \text{for all } n \geq 1.$$

Basis Step. We must show that the equation is true for $n = 1$; that is, we must show that

$$\sum_{i=1}^{1} i = \frac{1(1+1)}{2}.$$

The truth is immediate since both sides are equal to 1.

Inductive Step. We must assume that the equation is true for n and prove that it is true for $n + 1$. Thus, we are assuming that

$$\sum_{i=1}^{n} i = \frac{n(n+1)}{2}.$$

We must prove that

$$\sum_{i=1}^{n+1} i = \frac{(n+1)(n+2)}{2}.$$

(In constructing a proof using mathematical induction, it is a good idea to write out explicitly the cases for n and $n + 1$ as we have done so that it is clear what is assumed and what is to be proved.)

The key to mathematical induction is to find case n "within" case $n + 1$. Here, the sum for $n+1$ is obtained from the sum for n by adding the $(n+1)$st term. In mathematical notation,

$$\sum_{i=1}^{n+1} i = \left(\sum_{i=1}^{n} i \right) + (n+1).$$

Since we are assuming that

$$\sum_{i=1}^{n} i = \frac{n(n+1)}{2},$$

we obtain

$$\sum_{i=1}^{n+1} i = \left(\sum_{i=1}^{n} i \right) + (n+1) = \frac{n(n+1)}{2} + (n+1).$$

A little algebra shows that

$$\frac{n(n+1)}{2} + (n+1) = \frac{(n+1)(n+2)}{2}.$$

Therefore,

$$\sum_{i=1}^{n+1} i = \frac{(n+1)(n+2)}{2},$$

and the proof is complete. □

If we want to prove that the statements

$$S(n_0), S(n_0 + 1), \ldots,$$

where $n_0 \neq 1$, are true, we must change the Basis Step and the Inductive Step to

(Modified Basis Step.) Prove that $S(n_0)$ is true.

(Modified Inductive Step.) Assume that $S(n)$ is true, and prove that $S(n + 1)$ is true, for all $n \geq n_0$.

Example 2.2.2 Geometric Sum. Prove that if a and $r \neq 1$ are real numbers,

$$\sum_{i=0}^{n} ar^i = \frac{a(r^{n+1} - 1)}{r - 1} \quad \text{for all } n \geq 0.$$

The sum on the left is called a **geometric sum**.

Basis Step. Since $n = 0$ is the first statement, the Basis Step becomes

$$\sum_{i=0}^{0} ar^i = \frac{a(r^{0+1} - 1)}{r - 1}.$$

Since both expressions are equal to a, the equation is true for $n = 0$.

Inductive Step. We must assume that the inequality is true for n and prove that it is true for $n + 1$. Thus, we are assuming that

$$\sum_{i=0}^{n} ar^i = \frac{a(r^{n+1} - 1)}{r - 1}.$$

We must prove that

$$\sum_{i=0}^{n+1} ar^i = \frac{a(r^{n+2} - 1)}{r - 1}.$$

Here, case n is "within" case $n + 1$ in the sense that

$$\sum_{i=0}^{n+1} ar^i = \sum_{i=0}^{n} ar^i + ar^{n+1}.$$

By the inductive assumption,

$$\sum_{i=0}^{n+1} ar^i = \sum_{i=0}^{n} ar^i + ar^{n+1} = \frac{a(r^{n+1} - 1)}{r - 1} + ar^{n+1}.$$

A little algebra shows that

$$\frac{a(r^{n+1} - 1)}{r - 1} + ar^{n+1} = \frac{a(r^{n+2} - 1)}{r - 1}.$$

We have completed the Inductive Step.   □

We may use the formula for the geometric sum to prove an inequality that we will need in Section 3.6. (See Exercise 9 for another way to prove Theorem 2.2.3.)

Theorem 2.2.3.

$$\sum_{i=1}^{n} i r^i < \frac{r}{(1-r)^2} \quad \text{for all } n \geq 1 \text{ and } 0 < r < 1.$$

Proof. Using the geometric sum, we obtain the inequality

$$\sum_{i=0}^{n} r^i = \frac{1 - r^{n+1}}{1 - r} < \frac{1}{1 - r} \quad \text{for all } n \geq 0. \tag{2.2.1}$$

If we sum the terms in

$$
\begin{array}{cccccc}
r & r^2 & r^3 & r^4 & \cdots & r^n \\
r^2 & r^3 & r^4 & \cdots & & r^n \\
r^3 & r^4 & \cdots & & r^n & \\
r^4 & \cdots & & & & \\
\vdots & \vdots & & & & \\
& r^n & & & & \\
r^n & & & & &
\end{array}
$$

in the diagonal direction ($\nearrow$), we obtain one r, two r^2's, three r^3's, and so on; that is, we obtain the sum

$$\sum_{i=1}^{n} i r^i.$$

Multiplying inequality (2.2.1) by r yields

$$\sum_{i=1}^{n+1} r^i < \frac{r}{1 - r} \quad \text{for all } n \geq 0. \tag{2.2.2}$$

Thus, the sum of the entries in the first column is less than $r/(1-r)$. Similarly, the sum of the entries in the second column is less than $r^2/(1-r)$, and so on. It follows from the preceding discussion that

$$\sum_{i=1}^{n} i r^i < \frac{1}{1 - r} \sum_{i=1}^{n} r^i.$$

Again using inequality (2.2.2), we obtain the desired result

$$\sum_{i=1}^{n} i r^i < \frac{1}{1 - r} \sum_{i=1}^{n} r^i < \left(\frac{1}{1 - r} \right) \left(\frac{r}{1 - r} \right) = \frac{r}{(1 - r)^2}. \qquad \blacksquare$$

Example 2.2.4. Prove that

$$2n + 1 \leq 2^n \quad \text{for all } n \geq 3.$$

Basis Step. Since $n = 3$ is the first statement, the Basis Step becomes

$$2 \cdot 3 + 1 \leq 2^3.$$

Since $2 \cdot 3 + 1 = 7$ and $2^3 = 8$, the inequality is true for $n = 3$.

Inductive Step. We must assume that the inequality is true for n and prove that it is true for $n + 1$. Thus, we are assuming that

$$2n + 1 \leq 2^n.$$

We must prove that
$$2(n + 1) + 1 \leq 2^{n+1}.$$

Here, case n is "within" case $n + 1$ in the sense that

$$2(n + 1) + 1 = (2n + 1) + 2.$$

Noting that $2 \leq 2^n$, for $n \geq 1$, we obtain

$$2(n + 1) + 1 = (2n + 1) + 2 \leq 2^n + 2 \leq 2^n + 2^n = 2^{n+1}.$$

We have completed the Inductive Step.   □

In the form of mathematical induction that we have been using, in order to prove case $n + 1$, we assume the truth of case n. In other words, to prove case $n+1$, we assume the truth of the *immediately preceding case* (case n). In the **strong form of mathematical induction**, we assume the truth of *all* of the preceding cases. When the strong form of mathematical induction is used, the proof typically is written so that in the Inductive Step, the statement for n (rather than for $n + 1$) is proved, assuming the truth of the statements for all $k < n$. Thus, the strong form of mathematical induction may be stated as follows:

(**Basis Step.**) Prove that $S(1)$ is true.

(**Inductive Step.**) Assume that $S(k)$ is true for all $k < n$, and prove that $S(n)$ is true, for all $n > 1$.

Example 2.2.5. Use mathematical induction to show that postage of four cents or more can be achieved by using only 2-cent and 5-cent stamps.

Before giving a formal proof, we discuss the idea of the proof. Consider the Inductive Step, where we want to prove that n-cents postage can be achieved using only 2-cent and 5-cent stamps. It would be particularly easy to prove this statement if we could assume that we can make postage of $n - 2$ cents. We could then simply add a 2-cent stamp to make n-cents postage. How simple! Using the strong form of mathematical induction, we can assume the truth of the statement for all $k < n$. In particular, we *can* assume the truth of the statement for $k = n - 2$. Thus the strong form of mathematical induction allows us to give a correct proof based on our informal reasoning.

There is one subtle point to which we must attend. We are only considering postage of four cents or more. Thus when $n = 5$, $n - 2$ is not a valid value; that is, because $n - 2 < 4$, we cannot assume that we can make postage for $n - 2$ cents. Therefore, besides the case $n = 4$, we must explicitly verify the case $n = 5$. Only when $n \geq 6$, is $n - 2$ a valid value. Thus we must explicitly verify the cases $n = 4$ and $n = 5$, which thus become the Basis Steps.

Basis Steps. We can make four-cents postage by using two 2-cent stamps. We can make five-cents postage by using one 5-cent stamp. The Basis Steps are verified.

Inductive Step. We assume that $n \geq 6$ and that postage of k cents or more can be achieved by using only 2-cent and 5-cent stamps for $4 \leq k < n$.

By the inductive assumption, we can make postage of $n - 2$ cents. We add a 2-cent stamp to make n-cents postage. The Inductive Step is complete. □

Loop Invariants

A **loop invariant** is a statement about program variables that is true just before a loop begins executing, and is also true after each iteration of the loop. In particular, a loop invariant is true after the loop finishes, at which point the invariant tells us something about the state of the variables. Ideally, this statement tells us that the loop produces the expected result, that is, that the loop is correct. For example, a loop invariant for a while loop

while (*condition*)
    // loop body

is true just before *condition* is evaluated the first time, and it is also true each time the loop body is executed.

We can use mathematical induction to prove that an invariant has the desired behavior. The Basis Step proves that the invariant is true before the condition that controls looping is tested for the first time. The Inductive Step assumes that the invariant is true and then proves that if the condition that controls looping is true (so that the loop body is executed again), the invariant is true after the loop body executes. Since a loop iterates a finite number of times, the form of mathematical induction used here proves that a *finite* sequence of statements is true, rather than an infinite sequence of statements as in our previous examples. Whether the sequence of statements is finite or infinite, the steps needed for the proof by mathematical induction are the same. We illustrate a loop invariant with an example.

Example 2.2.6. We use a loop invariant to prove that the following algorithm computes $n!$:

```
factorial(n) {
    i = 1
    fact = 1
```

```
while (i < n) {
    i = i + 1
    fact = fact * i
}
return fact
}
```

We prove that $fact = i!$ is an invariant for the while loop. Just before the while loop begins executing, $i = 1$ and $fact = 1$, so $fact = 1!$. We have proved the Basis Step.

Assume that $fact = i!$. If $i < n$ is true (so that the loop body executes again), i becomes $i + 1$ and $fact$ becomes

$$fact * (i + 1) = i! * (i + 1) = (i + 1)!.$$

We have proved the Inductive Step. Therefore, $fact = i!$ is an invariant for the while loop.

The while loop terminates when $i = n$. Because $fact = i!$ is an invariant, at this point, $fact = n!$, which is the value the algorithm returns. Therefore, the algorithm correctly computes $n!$.   □

Exercises

In Exercises 1-7, use induction to prove that each equation is true for every positive integer n.

1S. $\displaystyle\sum_{i=1}^{n} (2i - 1) = n^2$

2. $\displaystyle\sum_{i=1}^{n} i(i + 1) = \frac{n(n + 1)(n + 2)}{3}$

3. $\displaystyle\sum_{i=1}^{n} i(i!) = (n + 1)! - 1$

4S. $\displaystyle\sum_{i=1}^{n} i^2 = \frac{n(n + 1)(2n + 1)}{6}$

5. $\displaystyle\sum_{i=1}^{n} (-1)^{i+1} i^2 = \frac{(-1)^{n+1} n(n + 1)}{2}$

6. $\displaystyle\sum_{i=1}^{n} i^3 = \left[\frac{n(n + 1)}{2}\right]^2$

7S. $\displaystyle\sum_{i=1}^{n} \frac{1}{(2i-1)(2i+1)} = \frac{n}{2n+1}$

8S. Prove that $\displaystyle\sum_{i=1}^{n} \frac{i}{2^i} < 2$ for all $n \geq 1$.

9. [Requires calculus.] This exercise offers an alternative proof of Theorem 2.2.3.

Assume that r is a real number satisfying $0 < r < 1$.

(a) Differentiate both sides of the geometric sum

$$\sum_{i=0}^{n} r^i = \frac{1 - r^{n+1}}{1-r}$$

with respect to r to show that

$$\sum_{i=1}^{n} i r^{i-1} = \frac{1 - r^{n+1} - (n+1)(1-r)r^n}{(1-r)^2} \quad \text{for all } n \geq 1.$$

(b) Use part (a) to show that

$$\sum_{i=1}^{n} i r^i < \frac{r}{(1-r)^2} \quad \text{for all } n \geq 1.$$

10. Prove that

$$\sum_{i=1}^{n} \left[\frac{i(i+1)}{2} \right] r^i < \frac{1}{(1-r)^3} \quad \text{for all } n \geq 1.$$

In Exercises 11–13, use induction to prove the inequality.

11S. $n! \geq 2^{n-1}$ for all $n \geq 1$

12. $\displaystyle\frac{1}{2n} \leq \frac{1 \cdot 3 \cdot 5 \cdots (2n-1)}{2 \cdot 4 \cdot 6 \cdots (2n)}$ for all $n \geq 1$

13. $(1+x)^n \geq 1 + nx$ for all real numbers $x \geq -1$ and integers $n \geq 1$

14S. Show that postage of six cents or more can be achieved by using only 2-cent and 7-cent stamps.

15. Show that postage of 24 cents or more can be achieved by using only 5-cent and 7-cent stamps.

16. Use the

$$\text{If } S(n) \text{ is true, then } S(n+1) \text{ is true.}$$

form of the Inductive Step to prove the statement in Example 2.2.5.

17S. Use the

$$\text{If } S(n) \text{ is true, then } S(n+1) \text{ is true.}$$

form of the Inductive Step to prove the statement in Exercise 14.

18. Use the

$$\text{If } S(n) \text{ is true, then } S(n+1) \text{ is true.}$$

form of the Inductive Step to prove the statement in Exercise 15.

19S. Use a loop invariant to prove that the following algorithm computes a^n:

```
exp(a, n) {
    i = 1
    pow = 1
    while (i ≤ n) {
        pow = pow * a
        i = i + 1
    }
    return pow
}
```

20. Use a loop invariant to prove that the following algorithm converts the positive binary integer, which is stored in the array b, to decimal. For example, the binary integer 10011, which is 19 in decimal, is stored as $b[1] = b[2] = 1$, $b[3] = b[4] = 0$, $b[5] = 1$.

```
to_decimal(b) {
    i = 0
    n = 0
    while (i < b.last) {
        n = n * 2 + b[b.last - i]
        i = i + 1
    }
    return n
}
```

21. Use a loop invariant to prove that the following algorithm converts the positive integer n to binary. The binary representation is stored in the array b. The preceding exercise shows how the binary integer is stored in b.

```
to_binary(n, b) {
    i = 0
    while (n > 0) {
        i = i + 1
```

$$b[i] = n \bmod 2$$
$$n = n/2$$
$$\}$$
$$\}$$

2.3 Analysis of Algorithms

A computer program, even though derived from a correct algorithm, might be useless for certain types of input because the time needed to run the program or the space needed to hold the data, program variables, and so on, is too great. **Analysis of an algorithm** refers to the process of deriving estimates for the time and space needed to execute the algorithm. In this section, we focus on the problem of estimating the time to execute an algorithm.

The time needed to execute an algorithm is a function of the input. Usually, it is difficult to obtain an explicit formula for this function, and we settle for less. Instead of dealing directly with the input, we use parameters that characterize the *size* of the input. For example, if the input is an array of size n, we would say that the size of the input is n. Sometimes two or more parameters characterize the size of the input. For example, if the input is an $m \times n$ array, we would characterize the size of the input using the two parameters m and n.

Among all inputs of size n, we can ask for the maximum time needed to execute an algorithm. This time is called the **worst-case time** for the algorithm for inputs of size n. Another important case is **average-case time**—the average time needed to execute the algorithm over some finite set of inputs all of size n.

Since we are primarily concerned with *estimating* the time of an algorithm rather than computing its exact time, as long as we count some fundamental, dominating steps of the algorithm, we will obtain a useful measure of the time. For example, if the principal activity of an algorithm is making comparisons, as might happen in a sorting algorithm, we might count the number of comparisons. As another example, if an algorithm consists of a single loop whose body executes in at most C steps, for some constant C, we might count the number of iterations of the loop.

Example 2.3.1. Consider Algorithm 1.2.2, which finds the maximum value in an array:

```
array_max_ver1(s) {
    large = s[1]
    i = 2
    while (i ≤ s.last) {
        if (s[i] > large) // larger value found
            large = s[i]
```

$$i = i + 1$$
    }
  return *large*
}

The input is an array of size n, and a reasonable definition of the execution time is the number of iterations of the while loop. Thus, the worst-case and average-case times for the algorithm are each $n - 1$ since the loop is always executed $n - 1$ times.   □

Usually, we are less interested in the exact time required by an algorithm than we are in how the time grows as the size of the input increases. For example, suppose that the worst-case time of an algorithm is

$$t(n) = 60n^2 + 5n + 1$$

for input of size n. For large n, the term $60n^2$ is approximately equal to $t(n)$ (see Figure 2.3.1). In this sense, $t(n)$ grows like $60n^2$.

n	$t(n) = 60n^2 + 5n + 1$	$60n^2$
10	6051	6000
100	600,501	600,000
1000	60,005,001	60,000,000
10,000	6,000,050,001	6,000,000,000

Figure 2.3.1 Comparing the growth of $t(n)$ with $60n^2$.

If $t(n)$ measures the time for input of size n in seconds, then

$$T(n) = n^2 + \frac{5}{60}n + \frac{1}{60}$$

measures the time for input of size n in minutes. Now this change of units does not affect how the time grows as the size of the input increases but only the units in which we measure the time for input of size n. Thus, when we describe how the time grows as the size of the input increases, we not only seek the dominant term [e.g., $60n^2$ for $t(n)$], but we also may ignore constant coefficients. Under these assumptions, $t(n)$ grows like n^2 as n increases. We say that $t(n)$ is of **order** n^2 and write

$$t(n) = \Theta(n^2),$$

which is read "$t(n)$ is theta of n^2." The basic idea is to replace an expression, such as $t(n) = 60n^2 + 5n + 1$, with a simpler expression, such as n^2, that grows at the same rate as $t(n)$. The formal definitions follow.

Definition 2.3.2. Let f and g be nonnegative functions on the positive integers.
    We write

$$f(n) = O(g(n))$$

and say that $f(n)$ *is of order at most* $g(n)$ or $f(n)$ *is big oh of* $g(n)$ if there exist constants $C_1 > 0$ and N_1 such that

$$f(n) \le C_1 g(n) \quad \text{for all } n \ge N_1.$$

We write

$$f(n) = \Omega(g(n))$$

and say that $f(n)$ *is of order at least* $g(n)$ or $f(n)$ *is omega of* $g(n)$ if there exist constants $C_2 > 0$ and N_2 such that

$$f(n) \ge C_2 g(n) \quad \text{for all } n \ge N_2.$$

We write

$$f(n) = \Theta(g(n))$$

and say that $f(n)$ *is of order* $g(n)$ or $f(n)$ *is theta of* $g(n)$ if $f(n) = O(g(n))$ and $f(n) = \Omega(g(n))$.

Definition 2.3.2 can be loosely paraphrased as follows: $f(n) = O(g(n))$ if, except for a constant factor and a finite number of exceptions, f is bounded above by g. We also say that g is an **asymptotic upper bound** for f. Similarly, $f(n) = \Omega(g(n))$ if, except for a constant factor and a finite number of exceptions, f is bounded below by g. We also say that g is an **asymptotic lower bound** for f. Also, $f(n) = \Theta(g(n))$ if, except for a constant factor and a finite number of exceptions, f is bounded above and below by g. We also say that g is an **asymptotic tight bound** for f.

According to Definition 2.3.2, if $f(n) = O(g(n))$, all that we can conclude is that, except for a constant factor and a finite number of exceptions, f is bounded *above* by g, so g grows at least as fast as f. For example, if $f(n) = n$ and $g(n) = 2^n$, then $f(n) = O(g(n))$, but g grows considerably faster than f. On the other hand, if $f(n) = \Theta(g(n))$, we can draw the conclusion that, except for a constant factor and a finite number of exceptions, f is bounded *above* and *below* by g, so f and g grow at the same rate. Notice that $n = O(2^n)$, but $n \ne \Theta(2^n)$.

Example 2.3.3. Since

$$60n^2 + 5n + 1 \le 60n^2 + 5n^2 + n^2 = 66n^2 \quad \text{for all } n \ge 1,$$

we may take $C_1 = 66$ and $N_1 = 1$ in Definition 2.3.2 and conclude that

$$60n^2 + 5n + 1 = O(n^2).$$

Since

$$60n^2 + 5n + 1 \ge= 60n^2 \quad \text{for all } n \ge 1,$$

we may take $C_2 = 60$ and $N_2 = 1$ in Definition 2.3.2 and conclude that

$$60n^2 + 5n + 1 = \Omega(n^2).$$

Since $60n^2 + 5n + 1 = O(n^2)$ and $60n^2 + 5n + 1 = \Omega(n^2)$,

$$60n^2 + 5n + 1 = \Theta(n^2). \qquad \square$$

We show, more generally, that a nonnegative polynomial in n of degree k is $\Theta(n^k)$.

Theorem 2.3.4. *Let*

$$p(n) = a_k n^k + a_{k-1} n^{k-1} + \cdots + a_1 n + a_0$$

be a nonnegative polynomial (i.e., $p(n) \geq 0$ for all n) in n of degree k. Then

$$p(n) = \Theta(n^k).$$

Proof. We first show that $p(n) = O(n^k)$. Let

$$C_1 = |a_k| + |a_{k-1}| + \cdots + |a_1| + |a_0|.$$

Then, for all n,

$$
\begin{aligned}
p(n) &= a_k n^k + a_{k-1} n^{k-1} + \cdots + a_1 n + a_0 \\
&= |a_k n^k + a_{k-1} n^{k-1} + \cdots + a_1 n + a_0| \qquad \text{since } p(n) \geq 0 \\
&\leq |a_k| n^k + |a_{k-1}| n^{k-1} + \cdots + |a_1| n + |a_0| \\
&\leq |a_k| n^k + |a_{k-1}| n^k + \cdots + |a_1| n^k + |a_0| n^k \\
&= (|a_k| + |a_{k-1}| + \cdots + |a_1| + |a_0|) n^k \\
&= C_1 n^k.
\end{aligned}
$$

Therefore, $p(n) = O(n^k)$.

To show that $p(n) = \Omega(n^k)$, we write

$$p(n) = n^k \left(a_k + \frac{a_{k-1}}{n} + \frac{a_{k-2}}{n^2} + \cdots + \frac{a_1}{n^{k-1}} + \frac{a_0}{n^k} \right),$$

and use the fact that

$$\frac{a_{k-1}}{n} + \frac{a_{k-2}}{n^2} + \cdots + \frac{a_1}{n^{k-1}} + \frac{a_0}{n^k}$$

gets arbitrarily close to zero for large n. Stated more precisely in calculus terms,

$$\lim_{n \to \infty} \left(\frac{a_{k-1}}{n} + \frac{a_{k-2}}{n^2} + \cdots + \frac{a_1}{n^{k-1}} + \frac{a_0}{n^k} \right) = 0.$$

We first show that $a_k > 0$. Since the degree of $p(n)$ is k, $a_k \neq 0$. Assume by way of contradiction that $a_k < 0$. Choose $\varepsilon > 0$ so that $a_k + \varepsilon < 0$. Then for all sufficiently large n

$$\left| \frac{a_{k-1}}{n} + \frac{a_{k-2}}{n^2} + \cdots + \frac{a_1}{n^{k-1}} + \frac{a_0}{n^k} \right| < \varepsilon.$$

Thus, for some n,

$$
\begin{aligned}
p(n) &= n^k \left(a_k + \frac{a_{k-1}}{n} + \frac{a_{k-2}}{n^2} + \cdots + \frac{a_1}{n^{k-1}} + \frac{a_0}{n^k} \right) \\
&\leq n^k \left(a_k + \left| \frac{a_{k-1}}{n} + \frac{a_{k-2}}{n^2} + \cdots + \frac{a_1}{n^{k-1}} + \frac{a_0}{n^k} \right| \right) \\
&< n^k (a_k + \varepsilon) < 0,
\end{aligned}
$$

which contradicts the fact that $p(n)$ is nonnegative.

Since $a_k > 0$, there exists N such that for $n \geq N$,

$$
\left| \frac{a_{k-1}}{n} + \frac{a_{k-2}}{n^2} + \cdots + \frac{a_1}{n^{k-1}} + \frac{a_0}{n^k} \right| < \frac{a_k}{2}.
$$

In particular, for $n \geq N$,

$$
\frac{a_{k-1}}{n} + \frac{a_{k-2}}{n^2} + \cdots + \frac{a_1}{n^{k-1}} + \frac{a_0}{n^k} > -\frac{a_k}{2}.
$$

Taking $C_2 = a_k / 2$, we have

$$
\begin{aligned}
p(n) &= n^k \left(a_k + \frac{a_{k-1}}{n} + \frac{a_{k-2}}{n^2} + \cdots + \frac{a_1}{n^{k-1}} + \frac{a_0}{n^k} \right) \\
&> n^k \left(a_k - \frac{a_k}{2} \right) = C_2 n^k,
\end{aligned}
$$

for $n \geq N$. Therefore $p(n) = \Omega(n^k)$.

Since $p(n) = O(n^k)$ and $p(n) = \Omega(n^k)$, $p(n) = \Theta(n^k)$.	∎

Example 2.3.5. Since $\lg n < n$ for all $n \geq 1$,

$$
2n + 3 \lg n < 2n + 3n = 5n \quad \text{for all } n \geq 1.
$$

Thus,

$$
2n + 3 \lg n = O(n).
$$

Also,

$$
2n + 3 \lg n \geq 2n \quad \text{for all } n \geq 1.
$$

Thus,

$$
2n + 3 \lg n = \Omega(n).
$$

Therefore,

$$
2n + 3 \lg n = \Theta(n).
$$	□

Example 2.3.6. If $a > 1$ and $b > 1$ (to ensure that $\log_b a > 0$), by the change-of-base formula for logarithms [Theorem 2.1.21(e)],

$$
\log_b n = \Theta(\log_a n).
$$

Thus, when using big-oh, omega, or theta notations, we need not worry about which number is used as the base for the logarithm function (as long as the base is greater than 1). For this reason, we sometimes simply write log without specifying the base.   □

Example 2.3.7. If we replace each integer $1, 2, \ldots, n$ by n in the sum $1 + 2 + \cdots + n$, the sum does not decrease and we have

$$1 + 2 + \cdots + n \leq n + n + \cdots + n = n \cdot n = n^2 \quad \text{for all } n \geq 1.$$

Thus,

$$1 + 2 + \cdots + n = O(n^2).$$

To obtain a lower bound, we might imitate the preceding argument and replace each integer $1, 2, \ldots, n$ by 1 in the sum $1 + 2 + \cdots + n$ to obtain

$$1 + 2 + \cdots + n \geq 1 + 1 + \cdots + 1 = n \cdot 1 = n \quad \text{for all } n \geq 1.$$

In this case, we conclude that

$$1 + 2 + \cdots + n = \Omega(n),$$

and while the preceding expression is true, we cannot deduce a Θ-estimate for $1 + 2 + \cdots + n$, since the upper bound n^2 and lower bound n are not equal. We must be craftier in deriving a lower bound.

One way to get a sharper lower bound is to argue as in the previous paragraph, but first throw away the first half of the terms to obtain

$$
\begin{aligned}
1 + 2 + \cdots + n \quad &\geq \quad \lceil n/2 \rceil + \cdots + (n - 1) + n \\
&\geq \quad \lceil n/2 \rceil + \cdots + \lceil n/2 \rceil + \lceil n/2 \rceil \\
&= \quad \lceil (n + 1)/2 \rceil \lceil n/2 \rceil \geq (n/2)(n/2) = \frac{n^2}{4}.
\end{aligned}
$$

We can now conclude that

$$1 + 2 + \cdots + n = \Omega(n^2).$$

Therefore,

$$1 + 2 + \cdots + n = \Theta(n^2).$$ □

We can use the method of Example 2.3.7 to show more generally that

$$1^k + 2^k + \cdots + n^k = \Theta(n^{k+1})$$

(see Exercise 46).

Example 2.3.8. We use an argument similar to that in Example 2.3.7 to show that

$$\lg n! = \Theta(n \lg n).$$

By properties of logarithms, we have

$$\lg n! = \lg n + \lg(n-1) + \cdots + \lg 2 + \lg 1.$$

Since lg is an increasing function,

$$\begin{aligned}
\lg n! &= \lg n + \lg(n-1) + \cdots + \lg 2 + \lg 1 \\
&\leq \lg n + \lg n + \cdots + \lg n + \lg n = n \lg n.
\end{aligned}$$

We conclude that

$$\lg n! = O(n \lg n).$$

For $n \geq 4$, we have

$$\begin{aligned}
\lg n + \lg(n-1) &+ \cdots + \lg 2 + \lg 1 \\
&\geq \lg n + \lg(n-1) + \cdots + \lg\lceil n/2 \rceil \\
&\geq \lg\lceil n/2 \rceil + \lg\lceil n/2 \rceil + \cdots + \lg\lceil n/2 \rceil \\
&= \lceil (n+1)/2 \rceil \lg\lceil n/2 \rceil \\
&\geq (n/2) \lg(n/2) \\
&= (n/2) \lg n - n/2 \\
&\geq n \lg n/4
\end{aligned}$$

(since $\lg n \geq 2$ for $n \geq 4$). Therefore,

$$\lg n! = \Omega(n \lg n).$$

It follows that

$$\lg n! = \Theta(n \lg n). \qquad \square$$

The number H_n, defined by

$$H_n = \sum_{i=1}^{n} \frac{1}{i},$$

is called the nth **harmonic number**. It occurs frequently in the analysis of algorithms. Our next theorem gives a theta notation for the nth harmonic number.

Theorem 2.3.9.

$$\sum_{i=1}^{n} \frac{1}{i} = \Theta(\lg n)$$

Proof. By Theorem 2.1.30,

$$\frac{1}{n} \leq \lg(n+1) - \lg n < \frac{2}{n}.$$

Therefore,

$$\sum_{i=1}^{n} \frac{1}{i} \le \sum_{i=1}^{n} [\lg(i+1) - \lg i] = \lg(n+1) \le \lg 2n = 1 + \lg n \le 2 \lg n,$$

if $n \ge 2$. Thus,

$$\sum_{i=1}^{n} \frac{1}{i} = O(\lg n).$$

Also,

$$\sum_{i=1}^{n} \frac{1}{i} > \frac{1}{2} \sum_{i=1}^{n} [\lg(i+1) - \lg i] = \frac{1}{2} \lg(n+1) \ge \frac{1}{2} \lg n.$$

Thus,

$$\sum_{i=1}^{n} \frac{1}{i} = \Omega(\lg n).$$

We conclude that

$$\sum_{i=1}^{n} \frac{1}{i} = \Theta(\lg n). \qquad\blacksquare$$

The asymptotic notation can be extended to functions of two or more variables as follows. If f and g are nonnegative functions of two variables on the positive integers, we write

$$f(m, n) = O(g(m, n))$$

if there exist constants C and N such that

$$f(m, n) \le C g(m, n) \quad \text{for all } m \ge N \text{ and } n \ge N.$$

For example,

$$(1 + 2 + \cdots + m)(1 + 2 + \cdots + n) = O(m^2 n^2).$$

We may also extend the definition of the omega and theta notations to functions of two or more variables in a similar way.

We next define what it means for the worst-case or average-case time of an algorithm to be of order at most $g(n)$.

Definition 2.3.10. If an algorithm requires $t(n)$ units of time to terminate in the worst case for an input of size n and

$$t(n) = O(g(n)),$$

we say that the *worst-case time required by the algorithm is of order at most $g(n)$* or that the *worst-case time required by the algorithm is $O(g(n))$*.

If an algorithm requires $t(n)$ units of time to terminate in the average case for an input of size n and

$$t(n) = O(g(n)),$$

we say that the *average-case time required by the algorithm is of order at most* $g(n)$ or that the *average-case time required by the algorithm is $O(g(n))$*.

By replacing O by Ω and "at most" by "at least" in Definition 2.3.10, we obtain the definition of what it means for the worst-case or average-case time of an algorithm to be of order at least $g(n)$. If the worst-case time required by an algorithm is $O(g(n))$ and $\Omega(g(n))$, we say that the worst-case time required by the algorithm is $\Theta(g(n))$. An analogous definition applies to the average-case time of an algorithm. If the worst-case time of an algorithm is $O(g(n))$, we also say that the *time* of the algorithm is $O(g(n))$ [since *any* time (e.g., average-case time) must also be $O(g(n))$].

Example 2.3.11. Suppose that an algorithm is known to take

$$60n^2 + 5n + 1$$

units of time to terminate in the worst case for inputs of size n. We showed in Example 2.3.3 that

$$60n^2 + 5n + 1 = \Theta(n^2).$$

Thus the worst-case time required by this algorithm is $\Theta(n^2)$.   □

Example 2.3.12. Find a theta notation in terms of n for the number of times the statement $x = x + 1$ is executed in the segment

```
for i = 1 to n
   for j = 1 to i
      x = x + 1
```

First, i is set to 1 and, as j runs from 1 to 1, $x = x + 1$ is executed one time. Next, i is set to 2 and, as j runs from 1 to 2, $x = x + 1$ is executed two times, and so on. Thus the total number of times that $x = x + 1$ is executed is (see Example 2.3.7)

$$1 + 2 + \cdots + n = \Theta(n^2).$$

Thus a theta notation for the number of times that the statement $x = x + 1$ is executed is $\Theta(n^2)$.   □

Example 2.3.13. Find a theta notation in terms of n for the number of times the statement $x = x + 1$ is executed in the segment

```
j = n
while (j ≥ 1) {
   for i = 1 to j
      x = x + 1
   j = j/2
}
```

Let $t(n)$ denote the number of times the statement $x = x + 1$ is executed. The first time we arrive at the body of the while loop, the statement $x = x + 1$ is executed n times. Therefore $t(n) \geq n$ and $t(n) = \Omega(n)$.

Next we derive a big-oh notation for $t(n)$. After j is set to n, we arrive at the while loop for the first time. The statement $x = x + 1$ is executed n times. Then j is reset to $\lfloor n/2 \rfloor$; hence $j \leq n/2$. If $j \geq 1$, we will execute $x = x + 1$ at most $n/2$ additional times in the next iteration of the while loop, and so on. If we let k denote the number of times we execute the body of the while loop, the number of times we execute $x = x + 1$ is at most

$$n + \frac{n}{2} + \frac{n}{4} + \cdots + \frac{n}{2^{k-1}}.$$

This geometric sum (see Example 2.2.2) is equal to

$$\frac{n\left(1 - \frac{1}{2^k}\right)}{1 - \frac{1}{2}}.$$

Now

$$t(n) \leq \frac{n\left(1 - \frac{1}{2^k}\right)}{1 - \frac{1}{2}} = 2n\left(1 - \frac{1}{2^k}\right) \leq 2n,$$

so $t(n) = O(n)$. Thus a theta notation for the number of times $x = x + 1$ is executed is $\Theta(n)$. $\square$

Certain growth functions occur so often that they are given special names, as shown in Figure 2.3.2. The functions in Figure 2.3.2, with the exception of $\Theta(n^k)$, are arranged so that if $\Theta(f(n))$ is above $\Theta(g(n))$, then for some N, $f(n) \leq g(n)$ for all $n \geq N$. Thus, if algorithms A and B have run times that are $\Theta(f(n))$ and $\Theta(g(n))$, respectively, and $\Theta(f(n))$ is above $\Theta(g(n))$ in Figure 2.3.2, then algorithm A is more time-efficient than algorithm B for sufficiently large inputs.

Theta Form	Name
$\Theta(1)$	Constant
$\Theta(\lg \lg n)$	Log log
$\Theta(\lg n)$	Log
$\Theta(n^c)$, $0 < c < 1$	Sublinear
$\Theta(n)$	Linear
$\Theta(n \lg n)$	$n \log n$
$\Theta(n^2)$	Quadratic
$\Theta(n^3)$	Cubic
$\Theta(n^k)$, $k \geq 1$	Polynomial
$\Theta(c^n)$, $c > 1$	Exponential
$\Theta(n!)$	Factorial

Figure 2.3.2 Common growth functions.

A problem that has a worst-case polynomial-time algorithm is considered to have a "good" algorithm; the interpretation is that such a problem has an efficient solution. Such problems are called **feasible** or **tractable**.

A problem that does not have a worst-case polynomial-time algorithm is said to be **intractable**. Any algorithm, if there is one, that solves an intractable problem is guaranteed to take a long time to execute in the worst case, even for modest sizes of the input.

Certain problems are so hard that they have no algorithms at all. A problem for which there is no algorithm is said to be **unsolvable**. A large number of problems are known to be unsolvable, some of considerable practical importance. One of the earliest problems to be proved unsolvable is the **halting problem**: Given an arbitrary program and a set of inputs, will the program eventually halt?

A large number of solvable problems have an as yet undetermined status; they are thought to be intractable, but none of them has been proved to be intractable. Most of these problems belong to the class of **NP-complete problems** (see Chapter 10). *Many* practical problems are known to be NP-complete. It is known that if any **NP**-complete problem has a polynomial-time algorithm, *all* **NP**-complete problems have polynomial-time algorithms. Since no polynomial-time algorithm has been discovered for any **NP**-complete problem, this is taken as strong evidence that the **NP**-complete problems are intractable.

An example of an **NP**-complete problem is as follows:

> Given a collection C of finite sets and a positive integer $k \leq |C|$, does C contain at least k mutually disjoint sets?

Another example of an **NP**-complete problem is the Hamiltonian-cycle problem (see Definition 2.5.34).

Exercises

Select a theta notation from Figure 2.3.2 for each expression in Exercises 1–12.

1S. $6n + 1$ **2.** $2n^2 + 1$

3. $6n^3 + 12n^2 + 1$ **4S.** $3n^2 + 2n \lg n$

5. $2 \lg n + 4n + 3n \lg n$ **6.** $6n^6 + n + 4$

7S. $2 + 4 + 6 + \cdots + 2n$ **8.** $(6n + 1)^2$

9. $(6n + 4)(1 + \lg n)$ **10S.** $\dfrac{(n + 1)(n + 3)}{n + 2}$

11. $\dfrac{(n^2 + \lg n)(n + 1)}{n + n^2}$ **12.** $2 + 4 + 8 + 16 + \cdots + 2^n$

In Exercises 13–19, select a theta notation from among $\Theta(1)$, $\Theta(\lg n)$, $\Theta(n)$, $\Theta(n \lg n)$, $\Theta(n^2)$, $\Theta(n^3)$, $\Theta(2^n)$, or $\Theta(n!)$ for the number of times the statement $x = x + 1$ is executed.

13S. for $i = 1$ to $2n$
    $x = x + 1$

14. for $i = 1$ to $2n$
    for $j = 1$ to n
        $x = x + 1$

15. for $i = 1$ to n
    for $j = 1$ to i
        for $k = 1$ to j
            $x = x + 1$

16S. for $i = 1$ to n
    for $j = 1$ to i
        for $k = 1$ to i
            $x = x + 1$

17. $i = n$
while $(i \geq 1)$ {
    $x = x + 1$
    $i = i/2$
}

18. $j = n$
while $(j \geq 1)$ {
    for $i = 1$ to j
        $x = x + 1$
    $j = j/3$
}

19S. $i = n$
while $(i \geq 1)$ {
    for $j = 1$ to n
        $x = x + 1$
    $i = i/2$
}

20S. Find a theta notation for the number of times the statement $x = x + 1$ is executed.

$i = 2$
while $(i < n)$ {
    $i = i * i$
    $x = x + 1$
}

21. Prove that $n! = O(n^n)$.

22. Prove that $2^n = O(n!)$.

23S. Prove that $\sum_{i=1}^{n} i \lg i = \Theta(n^2 \lg n)$.

★24. Prove that $n^{n+1} = 2^{(n+1)\lg n} \le 2^{n^2}$ for all $n \ge 1$.

25. Prove that $\lg(n^k + c) = \Theta(\lg n)$ for every fixed $k > 0$ and $c > 0$.

26S. Prove that if n is a power of 2, say $n = 2^k$, then

$$\sum_{i=0}^{k} \lg(n/2^i) = \Theta(\lg^2 n).$$

27. Suppose that $f(n) = O(g(n))$, and $g(n) > 0$ for all $n \ge 1$. Prove that for some constant C, $f(n) \le Cg(n)$ for *all* $n \ge 1$.

Determine whether each statement in Exercises 28–37 is true or false. Justify your response.

28S. $n^n = O(2^n)$

29. If $f(n) = \Theta(h(n))$ and $g(n) = \Theta(h(n))$, then $f(n) + g(n) = \Theta(h(n))$.

30. If $f(n) = \Theta(g(n))$, then $cf(n) = \Theta(cg(n))$ for any $c > 0$.

31S. If $f(n) = \Theta(g(n))$, then $2^{f(n)} = \Theta(2^{g(n)})$.

32. If $f(n) = \Theta(g(n))$, then $\lg f(n) = \Theta(\lg g(n))$. Assume that $f(n) \ge 1$ and $g(n) \ge 1$ for all $n = 1, 2, \ldots$.

33. If $f(n) = O(g(n))$, then $g(n) = O(f(n))$.

34S. If $f(n) = O(g(n))$, then $g(n) = \Omega(f(n))$.

35. If $f(n) = \Theta(g(n))$, then $g(n) = \Theta(f(n))$.

36. $f(n) + g(n) = \Theta(h(n))$, where $h(n) = \max\{f(n), g(n)\}$.

37S. $f(n) + g(n) = \Theta(h(n))$, where $h(n) = \min\{f(n), g(n)\}$.

38S. Suppose that the worst-case time of an algorithm is $\Theta(n)$. What is the error in the following reasoning? Since $2n = \Theta(n)$, the worst-case time to run the algorithm with input of size $2n$ is approximately the same as the worst-case time to run the algorithm with input of size n.

39. What is wrong with the following "proof" that any algorithm has a run time that is $O(n)$?

We must show that the time required for an input of size n is at most a constant times n.

Basis Step. Suppose that $n = 1$. If the algorithm takes C units of time for an input of size 1, the algorithm takes at most $C \cdot 1$ units of time. Thus, the assertion is true for $n = 1$.

Inductive Step. Assume that the time required for an input of size n is at most $C'n$ and that the time for processing an additional item is C''. Let C be the maximum of C' and C''. Then the total time required for an input of size $n + 1$ is at most

$$C'n + C'' \leq Cn + C = C(n + 1).$$

The inductive step has been verified.

By induction, for input of size n, the time required is at most a constant times n. Therefore, the run time is $O(n)$.

In Exercises 40–45, determine whether the statement is true or false. If the statement is true, prove it. If the statement is false, give a counterexample. Assume that $f(n) \geq 0$ and $g(n) > 0$ for all n. These exercises require calculus.

40S. If

$$\lim_{n \to \infty} \frac{f(n)}{g(n)} = 0,$$

then $f(n) = O(g(n))$.

41. If

$$\lim_{n \to \infty} \frac{f(n)}{g(n)} = 0,$$

then $f(n) = \Theta(g(n))$.

42. If

$$\lim_{n \to \infty} \frac{f(n)}{g(n)} = c > 0,$$

then $f(n) = O(g(n))$.

43S. If

$$\lim_{n \to \infty} \frac{f(n)}{g(n)} = c > 0,$$

then $f(n) = \Theta(g(n))$.

44. If $f(n) = O(g(n))$, then

$$\lim_{n \to \infty} \frac{f(n)}{g(n)}$$

exists and is equal to some real number.

45. If $f(n) = \Theta(g(n))$, then

$$\lim_{n \to \infty} \frac{f(n)}{g(n)}$$

exists and is equal to some real number.

46S. Prove that

$$1^k + 2^k + \cdots + n^k = \Theta(n^{k+1}).$$

2.4 Recurrence Relations

A **recurrence relation** relates the nth element of a sequence to certain of its predecessors. We often use a recurrence relation to describe the time required by an algorithm, especially a *recursive algorithm*. Thus, recurrence relations arise naturally in the analysis of algorithms.

Definition 2.4.1. A *recurrence relation* for the sequence $a_0, a_1, \ldots$ is an equation that relates a_n to certain of its predecessors $a_0, a_1, \ldots, a_{n-1}$.

Initial conditions for the sequence $a_0, a_1, \ldots$ are explicitly given values for a finite number of the terms of the sequence.

A recurrence relation and initial conditions can be used to define a sequence.

$\mathcal{WWW}$ **Example 2.4.2 Fibonacci Sequence.** The **Fibonacci sequence**, $f_1, f_2, \ldots$, is defined by the recurrence relation

$$f_n = f_{n-1} + f_{n-2}, \quad n \geq 3,$$

and initial conditions

$$f_1 = f_2 = 1.$$

As examples,

$$f_3 = f_2 + f_1 = 1 + 1 = 2,$$
$$f_4 = f_3 + f_2 = 2 + 1 = 3,$$
$$f_5 = f_4 + f_3 = 3 + 2 = 5. \qquad \square$$

The Fibonacci sequence originally arose in a puzzle about rabbits (see Exercises 1 and 2). After returning from the Orient in 1202, Fibonacci wrote his most famous work, *Liber Abaci*, which, in addition to containing what we now call the Fibonacci sequence, advocated the use of Hindu-Arabic numerals. This book was one of the main influences in bringing the decimal number system to Western Europe. Fibonacci signed much of his work "Leonardo Bigollo." *Bigollo* translates as "traveler" or "blockhead." There is some evidence that Fibonacci enjoyed having his contemporaries consider him a blockhead for advocating the new number system.

The following example shows how we can use a recurrence relation and initial condition to represent the time required to execute an algorithm.

Example 2.4.3. Let c_n denote the number of times the statement $x = x + 1$ is executed in the algorithm

example(n) {
  if ($n == 1$)
    return

```
    for i = 1 to n
        x = x + 1
    example(n/2)
}
```

We have the initial condition

$$c_1 = 0,$$

since, when $n = 1$, *example* simply returns.

When $n > 1$, the statement $x = x + 1$ is executed n times. Then, *example* is called with input $\lfloor n/2 \rfloor$, which causes $x = x + 1$ to be executed $c_{\lfloor n/2 \rfloor}$ additional times. (By *definition*, $c_{\lfloor n/2 \rfloor}$ is the number of times that $x = x + 1$ is executed with input $\lfloor n/2 \rfloor$.) Thus, we obtain the recurrence relation

$$c_n = n + c_{\lfloor n/2 \rfloor}. \qquad \qquad \square$$

Solving Recurrence Relations

To *solve* a recurrence relation for a sequence $\{c_n\}$ is to give a formula for c_n that does not involve c_i for any i. The situation is similar to solving an algebraic equation (e.g., the quadratic equation). The difference is that in an algebraic equation, the unknown is a number; in a recurrence relation, the unknown is a sequence.

In this subsection, we discuss one technique for solving a recurrence relation in which the nth term is given in terms of the immediately preceding term [the $(n-1)$st term] *only*. The solution technique is called **iteration** or **substitution**. We illustrate the technique with an example.

Example 2.4.4. Solve the recurrence relation

$$c_n = c_{n-1} + n, \quad n \ge 1,$$

with initial condition
$$c_0 = 0.$$

We use the iteration technique, which begins by writing the recurrence relation:
$$c_n = c_{n-1} + n.$$

We then substitute for c_{n-1}. Replacing n in the recurrence relation by $n - 1$, we obtain a formula for c_{n-1}:

$$c_{n-1} = c_{n-2} + (n-1).$$

We then substitute for c_{n-1} in the original recurrence relation to obtain

$$
\begin{aligned}
c_n &= c_{n-1} + n \\
&= [c_{n-2} + (n-1)] + n.
\end{aligned}
$$

Since

$$c_{n-2} = c_{n-3} + (n-2),$$

we repeat by substituting for c_{n-2}:

$$
\begin{aligned}
c_n &= c_{n-2} + (n-1) + n \\
&= [c_{n-3} + (n-2)] + (n-1) + n.
\end{aligned}
$$

Notice that after each substitution, the subscript on the right side of the equation is reduced by 1. We continue until the subscript is reduced to 0, at which point we may substitute using the initial condition:

$$
\begin{aligned}
c_n &= c_{n-1} + n \\
&= c_{n-2} + (n-1) + n \\
&= c_{n-3} + (n-2) + (n-1) + n \\
&\ \ \vdots \\
&= c_1 + 2 + 3 + \cdots + (n-2) + (n-1) + n \\
&= c_0 + 1 + 2 + 3 + \cdots + (n-2) + (n-1) + n \\
&= 0 + 1 + 2 + 3 + \cdots + (n-2) + (n-1) + n \\
&= \frac{n(n+1)}{2}.
\end{aligned}
$$

We have obtained an explicit solution for c_n. $\square$

A recurrence relation such as

$$c_n = n + c_{\lfloor n/2 \rfloor} \tag{2.4.1}$$

(see Example 2.4.3), which is typical of recurrence relations that describe the time required by divide-and-conquer algorithms (see Chapter 5), is not immediately solved by the iteration technique. However, the preceding recurrence relation *can* be solved by the iteration technique when n is a power of 2.

Example 2.4.5. Solve the recurrence relation (2.4.1) when n is a power of 2. The initial condition is $c_1 = 0$.

Since we assume that n is a power of 2, $n = 2^k$, for some k. Then (2.4.1) becomes

$$c_n = c_{2^k} = 2^k + c_{2^k/2} = 2^k + c_{2^{k-1}}.$$

We can solve this recurrence relation using the iteration technique. We write

$$
\begin{aligned}
c_{2^k} &= 2^k + c_{2^{k-1}} \\
&= 2^k + 2^{k-1} + c_{2^{k-2}} \\
&\ \ \vdots \\
&= 2^k + 2^{k-1} + \cdots + 2^1 + c_{2^0}.
\end{aligned}
$$

Since $c_{2^0} = c_1 = 0$,

$$
\begin{aligned}
c_{2^k} &= 2^k + 2^{k-1} + \cdots + 2^1 + c_{2^0} \\
&= 2^k + 2^{k-1} + \cdots + 2^1 + c_1 \\
&= 2^k + 2^{k-1} + \cdots + 2^1 + 0 \\
&= \frac{2^{k+1} - 2}{2 - 1} = 2^{k+1} - 2.
\end{aligned}
$$

Since $n = 2^k$, we have

$$
c_n = c_{2^k} = 2^{k+1} - 2 = 2 \cdot 2^k - 2 = 2n - 2. \qquad \square
$$

The following example shows how to estimate c_n, defined by (2.4.1), when n is an arbitrary integer.

Example 2.4.6. Show that $c_n = \Theta(n)$, where c_n is defined by (2.4.1).

Let n be an arbitrary integer. Then n lies between two powers of 2; that is, there exists k such that

$$
2^{k-1} \le n < 2^k.
$$

We can use induction to show that c_n is an increasing sequence (see Exercise 30). Thus,

$$
c_{2^{k-1}} \le c_n < c_{2^k}.
$$

By Example 2.4.5,

$$
c_{2^k} = 2^{k+1} - 2.
$$

Now

$$
c_n < c_{2^k} = 2^{k+1} - 2 < 4n.
$$

Therefore, $c_n = O(n)$.

Again by Example 2.4.5,

$$
c_{2^{k-1}} = 2^k - 2.
$$

Now

$$
c_n \ge c_{2^{k-1}} = 2^k - 2 > n - 2 \ge \frac{n}{2},
$$

for $n \ge 4$. Therefore, $c_n = \Omega(n)$. We conclude that $c_n = \Theta(n)$. $\qquad \square$

Our next theorem, whose proof is given in the following subsection, gives asymptotic bounds for the solution of many divide-and-conquer recurrence relations.

Theorem 2.4.7 Main Recurrence Theorem. *Let a, b, and k be integers satisfying $a \ge 1$, $b \ge 2$, and $k \ge 0$.[†] In the following, n/b denotes either $\lfloor n/b \rfloor$ or $\lceil n/b \rceil$. In the case of the floor function, the initial condition $T(0) = u$ is given; and in the case of the ceiling function, the initial condition $T(1) = u$ is given.*

[†]More general versions of this theorem are known. For example, the theorem is correct if a and b are any real numbers satisfying $a \ge 1$ and $b > 1$.

Upper Bound: *If*
$$T(n) \leq aT(n/b) + f(n)$$

and
$$f(n) = O(n^k),$$

then
$$T(n) = \begin{cases} O(n^k) & \text{if } a < b^k \\ O(n^k \log n) & \text{if } a = b^k \\ O(n^{\log_b a}) & \text{if } a > b^k. \end{cases}$$

Lower Bound: *If*
$$T(n) \geq aT(n/b) + f(n)$$

and
$$f(n) = \Omega(n^k),$$

then
$$T(n) = \begin{cases} \Omega(n^k) & \text{if } a < b^k \\ \Omega(n^k \log n) & \text{if } a = b^k \\ \Omega(n^{\log_b a}) & \text{if } a > b^k. \end{cases}$$

Exact: *If*
$$T(n) = aT(n/b) + f(n)$$

and
$$f(n) = \Theta(n^k),$$

then
$$T(n) = \begin{cases} \Theta(n^k) & \text{if } a < b^k \\ \Theta(n^k \log n) & \text{if } a = b^k \\ \Theta(n^{\log_b a}) & \text{if } a > b^k. \end{cases}$$

Proof. This theorem is proved in the following subsection. ∎

Example 2.4.8. Use Theorem 2.4.7 to find a Θ-notation for c_n as defined by (2.4.1).

Recurrence relation (2.4.1) has the form
$$T(n) = aT(n/b) + f(n)$$

with $a = 1$, $b = 2$, $f(n) = n$, and $k = 1$. Since $a < b^k$, Theorem 2.4.7 states that $c_n = \Theta(n)$. □

Example 2.4.9. Use Theorem 2.4.7 to find a Θ-notation for $T(n)$ given by the recurrence relation
$$T(n) = 2T(\lceil n/2 \rceil) + n.$$

The recurrence relation has the form

$$T(n) = aT(n/b) + f(n)$$

with $a = 2$, $b = 2$, $f(n) = n$, and $k = 1$. Since $a = b^k$, Theorem 2.4.7 states that $T(n) = \Theta(n \log n)$. $\qquad\square$

Example 2.4.10. Use Theorem 2.4.7 to find a Θ-notation for $T(n)$ given by the recurrence relation

$$T(n) = 7T(\lfloor n/4 \rfloor) + n.$$

The recurrence relation has the form

$$T(n) = aT(n/b) + f(n)$$

with $a = 7$, $b = 4$, $f(n) = n$, and $k = 1$. Since $a > b^k$, Theorem 2.4.7 states that $T(n) = \Theta(n^{\log_4 7})$. Since $\log_4 7$ is approximately 1.4037, we have $T(n) = \Theta(n^{1.4037})$ (approximately). $\qquad\square$

Example 2.4.11. Use Theorem 2.4.7 to find a big-oh notation for $T(n)$, where $T(n)$ satisfies
$$T(n) \leq T(\lfloor n/2 \rfloor) + T(\lceil n/2 \rceil) + n^2.$$

Assume that $T(n)$ is nondecreasing.

Since $T(n)$ is nondecreasing,

$$T(\lfloor n/2 \rfloor) \leq T(\lceil n/2 \rceil).$$

Therefore,
$$T(n) \leq 2T(\lceil n/2 \rceil) + n^2.$$

We may now apply Theorem 2.4.7 with $a = b = k = 2$ and $f(n) = n^2$. Since $a < b^k$, we conclude that

$$T(n) = O(n^2). \qquad\square$$

†Proof of Main Recurrence Theorem

Our proof of the Main Recurrence Theorem was inspired by the methods presented in Brassard, 1996.

Throughout this section, we assume that a, b, and k are integers satisfying $a \geq 1$, $b \geq 2$, and $k \geq 0$. We further assume that c is a positive real number. We consider the recurrence relations

$$T(n) = aT(\lfloor n/b \rfloor) + cn^k, \quad n \geq 1,$$

---

†This subsection can be omitted without loss of continuity.

with initial condition $T(0) = u > 0$; and

$$T(n) = aT(\lceil n/b \rceil) + cn^k, \quad n \geq 2,$$

with initial condition $T(1) = u > 0$. We can use induction to prove that for either recurrence relation, $T(n)$ is well-defined for all n (see Exercises 38 and 39). We use the notation n/b to denote either $\lfloor n/b \rfloor$ or $\lceil n/b \rceil$. Thus,

$$T(n) = aT(n/b) + cn^k, \tag{2.4.2}$$

stands for either recurrence relation. We begin by using iteration to solve recurrence relation (2.4.2) when n is a power of b. The solution uses the formula

$$\sum_{i=0}^{m} x^{m-i}y^i = \frac{x^{m+1} - y^{m+1}}{x - y}, \quad x \neq y.$$

Lemma 2.4.12. *If $n > 1$ is a power of b and $a \neq b^k$, the solution of recurrence relation (2.4.2) is*

$$T(n) = C_1 n^{\log_b a} + C_2 n^k, \tag{2.4.3}$$

for some constants C_1 and C_2. If $a < b^k$, $C_2 > 0$. If $a > b^k$, $C_2 < 0$.

If $n > 1$ is a power of b and $a = b^k$, the solution of recurrence relation (2.4.2) is

$$T(n) = C_3 n^k + C_4 n^k \log_b n, \tag{2.4.4}$$

for some constants C_3 and C_4, $C_4 > 0$.

Proof. Suppose that $n = b^m$ for some positive integer m. Notice that $m = \log_b n$, $n^k = (b^k)^m$, and $a^m = n^{\log_b a}$. Now

$$
\begin{aligned}
T(n) = T(b^m) &= aT(b^{m-1}) + c(b^k)^m \\
&= a[aT(b^{m-2}) + c(b^k)^{m-1}] + c(b^k)^m \\
&= a^2 T(b^{m-2}) + c[a(b^k)^{m-1} + (b^k)^m] \\
&= a^2[aT(b^{m-3}) + c(b^k)^{m-2}] + c[a(b^k)^{m-1} + (b^k)^m] \\
&= a^3 T(b^{m-3}) + c[a^2(b^k)^{m-2} + a(b^k)^{m-1} + (b^k)^m] \\
&\;\;\vdots \\
&= a^m T(b^0) + c \sum_{i=1}^{m} a^{m-i}(b^k)^i.
\end{aligned}
$$

If $a \neq b^k$, we have

$$
\begin{aligned}
T(n) &= a^m T(1) + c\left[\frac{(b^k)^{m+1} - a^{m+1}}{b^k - a} - a^m\right] \\
&= a^m T(1) + \frac{c(b^k)^{m+1}}{b^k - a} + c\left[\frac{-a^{m+1}}{b^k - a} - a^m\right]
\end{aligned}
$$

$$
\begin{aligned}
&= a^m T(1) + \frac{c(b^k)^{m+1}}{b^k - a} - \left[\frac{cb^k}{b^k - a} \right] a^m \\
&= C_1 a^m + C_2 (b^k)^m \\
&= C_1 n^{\log_b a} + C_2 n^k,
\end{aligned}
$$

where

$$
C_1 = T(1) - \left[\frac{cb^k}{b^k - a} \right] \quad \text{and} \quad C_2 = \frac{cb^k}{b^k - a}.
$$

We note that if $a < b^k$, $C_2 > 0$; and if $a > b^k$, $C_2 < 0$.

If $a = b^k$, we have

$$
\begin{aligned}
T(n) &= a^m T(1) + c \sum_{i=1}^{m} a^m \\
&= a^m T(1) + c(m-1) a^m \\
&= a^m [T(1) - c] + c a^m m \\
&= C_3 n^k + C_4 n^k \log_b n,
\end{aligned}
$$

where

$$
C_3 = T(1) - c \quad \text{and} \quad C_4 = c > 0. \qquad \blacksquare
$$

Lemma 2.4.12 solves recurrence relation (2.4.2) when n is a power of b. We next use the technique demonstrated in Example 2.4.6 to estimate the solution of recurrence relation (2.4.2) for all n. The technique is given in Lemma 2.4.14, and the estimate is given in Lemma 2.4.15.

We call a function f defined on the positive integers **smooth** if for any positive integer $m \geq 2$, there are positive constants C and N, depending on m, such that

$$
f(mn) \leq Cf(n) \quad \text{and} \quad f(n) \leq f(n+1)
$$

for all $n \geq N$.

Example 2.4.13. The function $f(n) = n^k$ is smooth because for any positive integer $m \geq 2$,

$$
f(mn) = (mn)^k = m^k n^k = Cf(n) \quad \text{for all } n \geq 1,
$$

where $C = m^k$, and

$$
f(n) \leq f(n+1) \quad \text{for all } n \geq 1. \qquad \square
$$

If X is a subset of the set of positive integers, we define

$$
f(n) = \Theta(g(n)) \quad \text{for all } n \in X,
$$

to mean that there exist positive constants N, C_1, and C_2 such that

$$
C_1 g(n) \leq f(n) \leq C_2 g(n) \quad \text{for all } n \in X \text{ and } n \geq N.
$$

An important property of a smooth function f is that if t is a nondecreasing function and $t(n) = \Theta(f(n))$ for n a power of b, then $t(n) = \Theta(f(n))$ (without any restriction on n).

Lemma 2.4.14. *If t is a nondecreasing function, f is a smooth function, and $t(n) = \Theta(f(n))$ for n a power of b, then $t(n) = \Theta(f(n))$.*

Proof. Since $t(n) = \Theta(f(n))$ for n a power of b, there are positive constants N_1, C_1, and C_2 such that

$$C_1 f(n) \le t(n) \le C_2 f(n)$$

for n a power of b and $n \ge N_1$. Since f is smooth, there are positive constants C_3 and N_2 such that

$$f(bn) \le C_3 f(n) \quad \text{and} \quad f(n) \le f(n+1)$$

for all $n \ge N_2$. Let k_0 be the smallest integer such that $b^{k_0} \ge N_2$. Let $N = \max\{N_1, N_2, b^{k_0}\}$. Let n be any integer, $n \ge N$. Choose k such that

$$b^k \le n < b^{k+1}.$$

Then,

$$t(n) \le t(b^{k+1}) \le C_2 f(b^{k+1}) \le C_2 C_3 f(b^k) \le C_2 C_3 f(n)$$

and

$$t(n) \ge t(b^k) \ge C_1 f(b^k) \ge \frac{C_1}{C_3} f(b^{k+1}) \ge \frac{C_1}{C_3} f(n).$$

Therefore, $t(n) = \Theta(f(n))$. ∎

We can now estimate the solution of recurrence relation (2.4.2).

Lemma 2.4.15. *Let $T(n)$ denote the function defined by recurrence relation (2.4.2). Then*

$$T(n) = \begin{cases} \Theta(n^k) & \text{if } a < b^k \\ \Theta(n^k \log n) & \text{if } a = b^k \\ \Theta(n^{\log_b a}) & \text{if } a > b^k. \end{cases}$$

Proof. We use Lemma 2.4.14, and we begin by using induction to prove that T is nondecreasing. For the basis step, we have for the floor function

$$T(1) = aT(\lfloor 1/b \rfloor) + c = aT(0) + c \ge T(0).$$

For the ceiling function, we have

$$T(2) = aT(\lceil 2/b \rceil) + c2^k = aT(1) + c2^k \ge T(1).$$

Now assume that T is nondecreasing on $\{i \mid i \le n\}$. We show that T is nondecreasing on $\{i \mid i \le n + 1\}$. We have

$$T(n+1) = aT((n+1)/b) + c(n+1)^k \ge aT(n/b) + cn^k = T(n).$$

Therefore, T is nondecreasing.

If n is a power of b and $a \neq b^k$, by Lemma 2.4.12,

$$T(n) = C_1 n^{\log_b a} + C_2 n^k.$$

If $a < b^k$, $C_2 > 0$ and $\log_b a < k$; therefore, the dominant term is n^k. Thus, $T(n) = \Theta(n^k)$ for n a power of b. Since T is nondecreasing and n^k is a smooth function (see Example 2.4.13), by Lemma 2.4.14 $T(n) = \Theta(n^k)$.

If $a > b^k$, $C_2 < 0$. Since $T(n)$ takes on nonnegative values, we must have $C_1 > 0$. Because $\log_b a > k$, the dominant term is $n^{\log_b a}$. Thus, $T(n) = \Theta(n^{\log_b a})$ for n a power of b. Since T is nondecreasing and $n^{\log_b a}$ is a smooth function (see Exercise 40), by Lemma 2.4.14 $T(n) = \Theta(n^{\log_b a})$.

If n is a power of b and $a = b^k$, by Lemma 2.4.12,

$$T(n) = C_3 n^k + C_4 n^k \log_b n,$$

$C_4 > 0$. Since $C_4 > 0$, the dominant term is $n^k \log_b n$. Therefore, $T(n) = \Theta(n^k \log_b n)$ for n a power of b. Since T is nondecreasing and $n^k \log_b n$ is a smooth function (see Exercise 41), by Lemma 2.4.14 $T(n) = \Theta(n^k \log_b n)$. ∎

We are now ready to prove the Main Recurrence Theorem (Theorem 2.4.7).

Proof of Main Recurrence Theorem. Assume that $T(n) \leq aT(n/b) + f(n)$ and $f(n) = O(n^k)$. In case a/b denotes the floor, define

$$T_{u,v}(n) = \begin{cases} u & \text{if } n = 0 \\ aT_{u,v}(n/b) + vn^k & \text{if } n > 0. \end{cases}$$

In case a/b denotes the ceiling, define

$$T_{u,v}(n) = \begin{cases} u & \text{if } n = 1 \\ aT_{u,v}(n/b) + vn^k & \text{if } n > 1. \end{cases}$$

By Lemma 2.4.15,

$$T_{u,v}(n) = \begin{cases} \Theta(n^k) & \text{if } a < b^k \\ \Theta(n^k \log n) & \text{if } a = b^k \\ \Theta(n^{\log_b a}) & \text{if } a > b^k. \end{cases}$$

Since $f(n) = O(n^k)$, there exist N and C_1 such that

$$f(n) \leq C_1 n^k, \quad \text{for } n \geq N.$$

Let

$$\begin{aligned} x &= \max\{T(n)/T_{1,1}(n) \mid 1 \leq n \leq N\}, \\ y &= \max\{x, C_1\}. \end{aligned}$$

For $n \leq N$,

$$T(n) \leq xT_{1,1}(n) = T_{x,x}(n) \leq T_{x,y}(n),$$

(see Exercises 42 and 43).

We now use induction to show that

$$T(n) \leq T_{x,y}(n)$$

for all n. The basis steps are $n = 1, \ldots, N$.

Assume that $n > N$. Now

$$
\begin{aligned}
T(n) &\leq aT(n/b) + f(n) \\
&\leq aT(n/b) + C_1 n^k \\
&\leq aT_{x,y}(n/b) + C_1 n^k \quad \text{inductive assumption} \\
&\leq aT_{x,y}(n/b) + y n^k \\
&= T_{x,y}(n).
\end{aligned}
$$

If $a < b^k$, by Lemma 2.4.15, $T_{x,y}(n) = \Theta(n^k)$. Since $T(n) \leq T_{x,y}(n)$, it follows that $T(n) = O(n^k)$. The cases $a = b^k$ and $a > b^k$ are handled similarly.

The lower-bound case $[T(n) \geq aT(n/b) + f(n)$ and $f(n) = \Omega(n^k)]$ is similar and left as an exercise (see Exercise 44).

The exact case $[T(n) = aT(n/b) + f(n)$ and $f(n) = \Theta(n^k)]$ follows from the upper-bound and lower-bound cases. ∎

Exercises

Exercises 1–12 concern the Fibonacci sequence $\{f_n\}$.

1S. Suppose that at the beginning of the year, there is one pair of rabbits, and that every month each pair produces a new pair that becomes productive after one month. Suppose further that no deaths occur. Let a_n denote the number of rabbits at the end of the nth month. Show that $a_1 = 1$, $a_2 = 2$, and $a_n - a_{n-1} = a_{n-2}$. Explain why $a_n = f_{n+1}$, $n \geq 1$.

2. Fibonacci's original question was: Under the conditions of Exercise 1, how many rabbits are there after one year? Answer Fibonacci's question.

3. Use mathematical induction to show that

$$\sum_{k=1}^{n} f_k = f_{n+2} - 1, \quad n \geq 1.$$

4S. Use mathematical induction to show that

$$f_n^2 = f_{n-1} f_{n+1} + (-1)^{n+1}, \quad n \geq 2.$$

5. Show that

$$f_{n+2}^2 - f_{n+1}^2 = f_n f_{n+3}, \quad n \geq 1.$$

6. Use mathematical induction to show that

$$\sum_{k=1}^{n} f_k^2 = f_n f_{n+1}, \quad n \geq 1.$$

7S. Use mathematical induction to show that f_n is even if and only if n is divisible by 3, $n \geq 1$.

8. Use mathematical induction to show that for $n \geq 6$,

$$f_n > \left(\frac{3}{2}\right)^{n-1}.$$

9. Use mathematical induction to show that for $n \geq 1$, $f_n \leq 2^{n-1}$.

10S. Use mathematical induction to show that for $n \geq 1$,

$$\sum_{k=1}^{n} f_{2k} = f_{2n+1} - 1, \qquad \sum_{k=1}^{n} f_{2k-1} = f_{2n}.$$

$\star$**11.** Use mathematical induction to show that every integer $n \geq 1$ can be expressed as the sum of distinct Fibonacci numbers, no two of which are consecutive.

12. Show that the representation in Exercise 11 is unique if we do not allow f_1 as a summand.

Use iteration to solve each recurrence relation in Exercises 13–18.

13S. $a_n = a_{n-1} + 3, \; n > 1; a_1 = 2$

14. $a_n = 2a_{n-1}, \; n > 0; a_0 = 1$

15. $a_n = 2a_{n-1} + 1, \; n > 1; a_1 = 1$

16S. $a_n = 2na_{n-1}, \; n > 0; a_0 = 1$

17. $a_n = 2^n a_{n-1}, \; n > 0; a_0 = 1$

$\star$**18.** $a_n = 2 + \sum_{i=1}^{n-1} a_i, \; n > 1; a_1 = 1$

Exercises 19–23 refer to the following algorithm, which computes a^n. The number of multiplications required to compute a^n is denoted c_n.

```
exp1(a, n) {
   if (n == 1)
      return a
   m = n/2
   return exp1(a, m) * exp1(a, n − m)
}
```

19S. Explain how the preceding algorithm computes a^n.

20. Find a recurrence relation and initial conditions for the sequence $\{c_n\}$.

21. Compute c_2, c_3, and c_4.

22S. Solve the recurrence relation of Exercise 20 in case n is a power of 2.

23. Prove that $c_n = n - 1$ for every positive integer n.

Exercises 24–29 refer to the following algorithm, which also computes a^n. The number of multiplications required to compute a^n is denoted c_n.

```
exp2(a, n) {
   if (n == 1)
      return a
   m = n/2
   power = exp2(a, m)
   power = power * power
   if (n is even)
      return power
   else
      return power * a
}
```

24S. Explain how the preceding algorithm computes a^n.

25. Show that
$$c_n = \begin{cases} c_{(n-1)/2} + 2 & \text{if } n \text{ is odd} \\ c_{n/2} + 1 & \text{if } n \text{ is even}. \end{cases}$$

26. Compute c_1, c_2, c_3, and c_4.

27S. Solve the recurrence relation of Exercise 25 in case n is a power of 2.

28. Show, by an example, that c is not nondecreasing.

29. Prove that $c_n = \Theta(\lg n)$.

30S. Show that the sequence $\{c_n\}$ defined by (2.4.1) is an increasing sequence.

Find a theta notation for each sequence in Exercises 31–37.

31S. $T(n) = 2T(n/2) + f(n); \ f(n) = n^2$

32. $T(n) = 2T(n/2) + f(n); \ f(n) = 5$

33. $T(n) = 4T(n/2) + f(n); \ f(n) = n$

34S. $T(n) = 4T(n/2) + f(n); \ f(n) = n^2$

35. $T(n) = 4T(n/2) + f(n);\ f(n) = n^3$

36. $T(n) = 4T(n/3) + f(n);\ f(n) = n$

37S. $T(n) = 4T(n/3) + f(n);\ f(n) = n^2$

38S. Prove that $T(n)$ is well-defined for all n by recurrence relation (2.4.2) when n/b denotes $\lfloor n/b \rfloor$.

39. Prove that $T(n)$ is well-defined for all n by recurrence relation (2.4.2) when n/b denotes $\lceil n/b \rceil$.

40. Prove that $f(n) = n^{\log_b a}$ is a smooth function.

41S. Prove that $f(n) = n^k \log_b n$ is a smooth function.

42. Define $T_{u,v}$ as in the proof of Theorem 2.4.7. Prove that $xT_{1,1}(n) = T_{x,x}(n)$ for all n and x.

43. Define $T_{u,v}$ as in the proof of Theorem 2.4.7. Prove that if $u_1 \le u_2$ and $v_1 \le v_2$, then $T_{u_1,v_1}(n) \le T_{u_2,v_2}(n)$ for all n.

44S. Prove Theorem 2.4.7 for the case $T(n) \ge aT(n/b) + f(n)$ and $f(n) = \Omega(n^k)$.

2.5 Graphs

When a **graph** is drawn (see Figure 2.5.1), it typically resembles a map with cities connected by streets. In graph terminology, the cities are **vertices**, and the streets are **edges**. The formal definition follows.

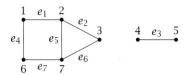

Figure 2.5.1 A graph.

Definition 2.5.1. A *graph* (or *undirected graph*) G consists of a set V of *vertices* (or *nodes*) and a set E of *edges* (or *arcs*) such that each edge $e \in E$ is associated with an unordered pair of vertices. We write $G = (V, E)$. If there is a unique edge e associated with the vertices v and w, we write $e = (v, w)$ or $e = (w, v)$. In this context, (v, w) denotes an edge between v and w and *not* an ordered pair.

Example 2.5.2. Figure 2.5.1 shows a graph $G = (V, E)$ where

$$V = \{1, 2, 3, 4, 5, 6, 7\},$$

and
$$E = \{e_1, e_2, e_3, e_4, e_5, e_6, e_7\}.$$
We write $e_1 = (1, 2)$ or $e_1 = (2, 1)$, $e_2 = (2, 3)$ or $e_2 = (3, 2)$, and so on. □

An undirected graph models a street system in which each street is a two-way street; that is, each street can be traversed in either direction A **directed graph** models a street system in which each street is a one-way street.

Definition 2.5.3. A *directed graph* (or *digraph*) G consists of a set V of *vertices* (or *nodes*) and a set E of *edges* (or *arcs*) such that each edge $e \in E$ is associated with an ordered pair of vertices. We write $G = (V, E)$. If there is a unique edge e associated with the ordered pair (v, w) of vertices, we write $e = (v, w)$. In this context, (v, w) denotes an edge from v, called the *tail*, to w, called the *head*.

Example 2.5.4. Figure 2.5.2 shows a directed graph $G = (V, E)$ where
$$V = \{1, 2, 3, 4, 5, 6, 7\}$$
and
$$E = \{(2, 1), (3, 2), (4, 5), (6, 1), (6, 7), (7, 2), (7, 3)\}.$$
As shown, an edge (v, w) is drawn as an arrow from v to w.

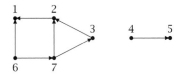

Figure 2.5.2 A directed graph. □

Definition 2.5.5. An edge e in an undirected graph that is associated with the pair of vertices v and w is said to be *incident on v and w*, and v and w are said to be *incident on e*, *endpoints of e*, and *adjacent vertices*.

Example 2.5.6. In Figure 2.5.1, edge e_1 is incident on vertices 1 and 2, vertices 1 and 2 are incident on edge e_1, and vertices 1 and 2 are adjacent. □

Definition 2.5.7. If v is a vertex in an undirected graph, the *neighborhood of v*, $N(v)$, is the set of vertices adjacent to v. The *degree of v* is the number of edges incident on v, except that each edge of the form (v, v) contributes 2 to the degree of v.

If v is a vertex in a directed graph, the *outdegree of v* is the number of edges of the form (v, w), and the *indegree of v* is the number of edges of the form (w, v).

Example 2.5.8. In the graph in Figure 2.5.1, the neighborhood of vertex 2, $N(2)$, is the set $\{1, 3, 7\}$, and the neighborhood of vertex 4, $N(4)$, is the set

{5}. The degree of vertex 2 is 3, and the degree of vertex 4 is 1. In the graph in Figure 2.5.2, the outdegree of vertex 7 is 2, and the indegree of vertex 7 is 1.   □

Definitions 2.5.1 and 2.5.3 allow distinct edges to be associated with the same pair of vertices. For example, in Figure 2.5.3, edges e_1 and e_2 are both associated with the vertex pair $\{1, 2\}$. Edges incident on vertices v_i and v_j, with $v_i \neq v_j$, are called **parallel edges**. An edge incident on a single vertex is called a **loop**. For example, in Figure 2.5.3, edge $e_3 = (2, 2)$ is a loop. A vertex, such as 3 in Figure 2.5.3, that is not incident on any edge is called an **isolated vertex**. A graph with neither loops nor parallel edges is called a **simple graph**. The graph in Figure 2.5.1 is a simple graph, but the graph in Figure 2.5.3 is *not* a simple graph. Notice that in a simple graph, the degree of a vertex v is equal to $|N(v)|$, the number of vertices in the neighborhood of v.

Figure 2.5.3 A graph with parallel edges (e_1 and e_2), a loop (e_3), and an isolated vertex (3). This graph is not a simple graph.

A **weighted graph** (undirected or directed) models a street system in which distances are indicated on the streets.

Definition 2.5.9. A *weighted graph* (undirected or directed) G consists of a set V of vertices, a set E of edges, and a function w from E to the real numbers. The sets V and E are as described in the definitions of graph and digraph. We call $w(e)$ the *weight* or *cost of e*. We write $G = (V, E, w)$.

Example 2.5.10. The graph in Figure 2.5.4 is a weighted graph. The weight of each edge is shown on the edge. For example, the weight of edge $(1, 2)$ is 9, and the weight of edge $(2, 7)$ is 2.

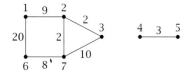

Figure 2.5.4 A weighted graph.   □

Graph Representations

One way to represent an undirected simple graph is to use an **adjacency matrix**. For example, to represent the graph in Figure 2.5.1, we first choose an ordering of the vertices, say $1, 2, 3, 4, 5, 6, 7$. Next, we label the rows and columns of a matrix with the ordered vertices. The entry in this matrix in row i, column j, is 1 if (i, j) is an edge, or 0 if (i, j) is not an edge. The adjacency matrix for the graph in Figure 2.5.1 is

$$
\begin{array}{c c}
& \begin{array}{c c c c c c c}
1 & 2 & 3 & 4 & 5 & 6 & 7
\end{array} \\
\begin{array}{c}
1 \\
2 \\
3 \\
4 \\
5 \\
6 \\
7
\end{array} &
\left(
\begin{array}{c c c c c c c}
0 & 1 & 0 & 0 & 0 & 1 & 0 \\
1 & 0 & 1 & 0 & 0 & 0 & 1 \\
0 & 1 & 0 & 0 & 0 & 0 & 1 \\
0 & 0 & 0 & 0 & 1 & 0 & 0 \\
0 & 0 & 0 & 1 & 0 & 0 & 0 \\
1 & 0 & 0 & 0 & 0 & 0 & 1 \\
0 & 1 & 1 & 0 & 0 & 1 & 0
\end{array}
\right)
\end{array}.
$$

The definition of "adjacency matrix" can be extended to accommodate other types of graphs (e.g., directed graphs, nonsimple graphs). For example, in the adjacency matrix of a directed graph, the entry in row i, column j, is 1 if there is an edge from vertex i to vertex j, and 0 otherwise.

The adjacency matrix of a graph with many edges missing has many zeros in its adjacency matrix. An algorithm that must inspect every entry in the adjacency matrix—whether zero or one—may be inefficient. To overcome this difficulty, it is more common to represent a graph using adjacency lists. Adjacency lists, in effect, omit the zeros. We discuss this representation after discussing linked lists (see Section 3.3).

Some Special Graphs

We define some special graphs that appear frequently in computer science and graph theory.

Definition 2.5.11. The *complete graph on n vertices*, denoted K_n, is the simple graph with n vertices in which there is an edge between every pair of distinct vertices.

Example 2.5.12. Two ways to draw the complete graph on four vertices, K_4, are shown in Figure 2.5.5.

Figure 2.5.5 Two ways to draw the complete graph K_4. ☐

Definition 2.5.13. A graph $G = (V, E)$ is *bipartite* if there exist subsets V_1 and V_2 (either possibly empty) of V such that $V_1 \cap V_2 = \varnothing$, $V_1 \cup V_2 = V$, and each edge in E is incident on one vertex in V_1 and one vertex in V_2.

Example 2.5.14. The graph in Figure 2.5.6 is bipartite since, if we let

$$V_1 = \{1, 2, 3\} \quad \text{and} \quad V_2 = \{4, 5\},$$

Figure 2.5.6 A bipartite graph.

each edge is incident on one vertex in V_1 and one vertex in V_2.   □

Definition 2.5.15. The *complete bipartite graph on m and n vertices*, denoted $K_{m,n}$, is the simple graph whose vertex set is partitioned into disjoint sets V_1 with m vertices and V_2 with n vertices in which there is an edge between each pair of vertices v_1 and v_2, where v_1 is in V_1 and v_2 is in V_2.

Example 2.5.16. The complete bipartite graph on two and four vertices, $K_{2,4}$, is shown in Figure 2.5.7.

Figure 2.5.7 The complete bipartite graph $K_{2,4}$.   □

Paths and Cycles

If we think of a graph as modeling streets and cities, a path corresponds to a trip beginning at some city, passing through several cities, and terminating at some city. We begin by giving a formal definition of path.

Definition 2.5.17. Let v_0 and v_n be vertices in a graph. A *path from v_0 to v_n of length n* is an alternating sequence of $n + 1$ vertices and n edges beginning with vertex v_0 and ending with vertex v_n,

$$(v_0, e_1, v_1, e_2, v_2, \ldots, v_{n-1}, e_n, v_n),$$

in which edge e_i is incident on vertices v_{i-1} and v_i for $i = 1, \ldots, n$.

The formalism in Definition 2.5.17 means: Start at some vertex v_0; go along edge e_1 to v_1; go along edge e_2 to v_2; and so on.

Example 2.5.18. In the graph in Figure 2.5.8,

$$(2, e_1, 1, e_4, 4, e_3, 1, e_1, 2, e_2, 3)$$

is a path of length 5 from 2 to 3.

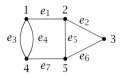

Figure 2.5.8 A graph with a path $(2, e_1, 1, e_4, 4, e_3, 1, e_1, 2, e_2, 3)$ of length 5.□

Example 2.5.19. In the graph in Figure 2.5.8, the path (4) consisting solely of vertex 4 is a path of length 0 from vertex 4 to vertex 4. □

In the absence of parallel edges, in denoting a path we may suppress the edges. For example, the path

$$(1, e_1, 2, e_2, 3, e_6, 5, e_5, 2)$$

in Figure 2.5.8 may also be written

$$(1, 2, 3, 5, 2).$$

In a *weighted* graph, the length of a path is defined to be the sum of the weights of the edges in the path.

Example 2.5.20. The length of the path $(1, 2, 3, 7)$ in the weighted graph in Figure 2.5.4 is

$$9 + 2 + 10 = 21.$$ □

A **connected graph** is a graph in which we can get from any vertex to any other vertex on a path. The formal definition follows.

Definition 2.5.21. A graph G is *connected* if given any vertices v and w in G, there is a path from v to w.

Example 2.5.22. The graph in Figure 2.5.8 is connected because, given any vertices v and w in G, there is a path from v to w. The graph in Figure 2.5.4 is *not* connected because, for example, there is no path from vertex 3 to vertex 4. □

As we can see from Figures 2.5.4 and 2.5.8, a connected graph consists of one "piece," whereas a graph that is not connected consists of two or more "pieces." These "pieces" are **subgraphs** of the original graph and are called **components**. We give the formal definitions beginning with "subgraph."

Definition 2.5.23. Let $G = (V, E)$ be a graph. We call (V', E') a *subgraph* of G if

(a) $V' \subseteq V$ and $E' \subseteq E$.

(b) For every edge $e' \in E'$, if e' is incident on v' and w', then $v', w' \in V'$.

Example 2.5.24. The graph in Figure 2.5.9 is a subgraph of the graph in Figure 2.5.8 since properties (a) and (b) of Definition 2.5.23 are satisfied.

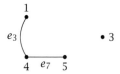

Figure 2.5.9 A subgraph of the graph in Figure 2.5.8.   □

We can now define "component."

Definition 2.5.25. Let G be a graph and let v be a vertex in G. The subgraph G' of G consisting of all edges and vertices in G that are contained in some path beginning at v is called the *component* of G containing v.

Example 2.5.26. The graph in Figure 2.5.8 has one component, namely itself. Indeed, a graph is connected if and only if it has exactly one component.   □

Example 2.5.27. The graph in Figure 2.5.1 has the two components shown in Figure 2.5.10.

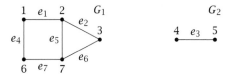

Figure 2.5.10 Two components, G_1 and G_2, of the graph in Figure 2.5.1. □

In geometry, the diameter of an object is the maximum distance between two elements of the object. We can define the diameter of a graph analogously, where the distance between two vertices is defined as the length of a shortest path between them.

Definition 2.5.28. Let G be a graph. If there is no path from vertex v to vertex w, we define $dist(v, w) = \infty$. If there is a path from vertex v to vertex w, we define $dist(v, w)$ to be the length of a shortest path from v to w. The *diameter of G* is

$$\max\{dist(v, w) \mid v \text{ and } w \text{ are vertices in } G\}.$$

Example 2.5.29. The diameter of the graph in Figure 2.5.8 is 2 since $dist(3, 4) = 2$, and $dist(v, w) \leq 2$ for all vertices v and w.   □

Example 2.5.30. The diameter of a graph that is not connected is ∞ since there are vertices v and w with $dist(v, w) = \infty$.   □

The definition of "path" (Definition 2.5.17) allows repetition of vertices or edges or both. Subclasses of paths are obtained by prohibiting duplicate vertices or edges or by making the vertices v_0 and v_n of Definition 2.5.17 identical.

Definition 2.5.31. Let v and w be vertices in a graph G.

A *simple path* from v to w is a path from v to w with no repeated vertices.

A *cycle* is a path of nonzero length from v to v with no repeated edges. A graph with no cycles is an *acyclic graph*.

A *simple cycle* is a cycle from v to v in which, except for the beginning and ending vertices that are both equal to v, there are no repeated vertices.

Example 2.5.32. Examples of paths, simple paths, cycles, and simple cycles in the graph in Figure 2.5.11 are shown in the following table:

Path	Simple Path?	Cycle?	Simple Cycle?
$(1, 4, 5, 7, 4, 3)$	No	No	No
$(1, 2, 1)$	No	No	No
$(2, 5, 7, 4, 3)$	Yes	No	No
$(4, 5, 7, 4, 1, 3, 4)$	No	Yes	No
$(1, 2, 5, 7, 4, 1)$	No	Yes	Yes
(6)	Yes	No	No

Figure 2.5.11 A graph to demonstrate paths, simple paths, cycles, and simple cycles. □

Example 2.5.33. The graph in Figure 2.5.6 is an acyclic graph. □

We conclude this subsection by defining two special kinds of cycles: **Hamiltonian cycles** and **Euler cycles**.

Definition 2.5.34. A *Hamiltonian cycle* in a graph G is a cycle that contains each vertex in G exactly once, except for the starting and ending vertex that appears twice.

Example 2.5.35. The cycle $(1, 2, 5, 4, 7, 6, 3, 1)$ is a Hamiltonian cycle for the graph in Figure 2.5.11. □

Example 2.5.36. We argue by contradiction to show that the graph in Figure 2.5.12 does not contain a Hamiltonian cycle. Suppose that the graph has a

Hamiltonian cycle C. Since each vertex in a Hamiltonian cycle has degree 2, the edges incident on vertex 1 must be in C. Also, the edges incident on vertices 3 and 5 must be in C. But now vertex 4 has degree 3. Therefore, the graph in Figure 2.5.12 does not contain a Hamiltonian cycle.

Figure 2.5.12 A graph that does not contain a Hamiltonian cycle.   □

The **Hamiltonian-cycle problem** is: Given a graph G, find a Hamiltonian cycle in G. In Sections 4.5, 10.2 and 11.2, we will discuss algorithms for solving the Hamiltonian-cycle problem. No efficient algorithms are known for the Hamiltonian-cycle problem; indeed, this problem is known to be **NP**-complete.

Hamiltonian cycles are named after Sir William Rowan Hamilton (1805–1865), who was one of Ireland's greatest scholars. Hamilton marketed a puzzle, called "A Voyage Around the World," in the form of a solid dodecahedron, which is a regular polyhedron whose 12 sides are pentagons (see Figure 2.5.13). The vertices were labeled from Brussels to Zanzibar. The problem was to start at some city, travel along the edges, visit each city exactly one time, and return to the initial city, that is, find a Hamiltonian cycle on the dodecahedron. We leave the solution of this puzzle as an exercise (see Exercise 63).

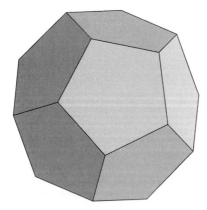

Figure 2.5.13 A dodecahedron.

Hamilton was professor of astronomy at the University of Dublin, where he published articles on astronomy, physics, and mathematics. In mathematics, Hamilton is most famous for inventing the quaternions, a generalization of the complex number system. The quaternions provided inspiration for the development of modern abstract algebra. In this connection, Hamilton introduced the term *vector*.

A close relative of the Hamiltonian-cycle problem is the **traveling-salesperson problem**: Given a weighted graph G, find a minimum-length Hamiltonian cycle in G. If we think of the vertices of G as cities and the edge weights as distances, the traveling-salesperson problem is to find a shortest route in which the salesperson can visit each city one time, starting and ending at the same city. Like the Hamiltonian-cycle problem, the traveling-salesperson problem is known to be **NP**-complete.

Example 2.5.37. The cycle $C = (1, 2, 3, 4, 1)$ is a Hamiltonian cycle for the graph G in Figure 2.5.14. Replacing any of the edges in C by either of the edges labeled 11 would increase the length of C; thus, C is a minimum-length Hamiltonian cycle for G. Therefore, C solves the traveling-salesperson problem for G.

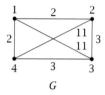

Figure 2.5.14 A graph for the traveling-salesperson problem. □

Definition 2.5.38. An *Euler cycle* in a graph G is a path from v to v with no repeated edges that contains all of the edges and all of the vertices of G.

Example 2.5.39. The cycle $(1, 3, 2, 4, 1, 5, 2, 6, 1)$ is an Euler cycle for the graph in Figure 2.5.15. Notice, however, that the graph does not have a Hamiltonian cycle.

Figure 2.5.15 A graph that contains an Euler cycle. □

It can be shown that a graph G has an Euler cycle if and only if G is connected and the degree of every vertex is even (see Exercise 74). Using the techniques of Chapter 3, it is possible to give an efficient algorithm for finding an Euler cycle in a connected graph in which the degree of every vertex is even (see Exercise 4.8).

Example 2.5.40. The graph in Figure 2.5.11 does not have an Euler cycle because there are vertices (e.g., vertex 3) of odd degree. We observed previously that it does have a Hamiltonian cycle, however. □

Euler cycles are named after Leonard Euler (1707–1783), who solved the Königsberg problem in 1736 in a paper that is regarded as the first paper in graph theory. Two islands lying in the Pregel River in Königsberg (now Kaliningrad in Russia) were connected to each other and the river banks by seven bridges (see Figure 2.5.16). The problem is to begin at some point, traverse every bridge exactly one time, and return to the starting point. The bridge configuration can be modeled as a graph after which the problem becomes that of finding an Euler cycle in the graph (see Exercise 75).

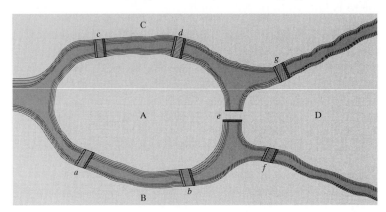

Figure 2.5.16 The Königsberg-bridge problem. Two islands, A and D, are connected to each other and the river banks, B and C, by seven bridges, a, b, c, d, e, f, and g. The problem is to begin at some point, traverse every bridge exactly one time, and return to the starting point.

Graph Complement

The **complement** of a simple graph G is the simple graph $\overline{G}$ with the same vertices as G. An edge exists in $\overline{G}$ if and only if it does not exist in G.

Example 2.5.41. A graph and its complement are shown in Figure 2.5.17.

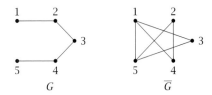

Figure 2.5.17 A graph G and its complement $\overline{G}$. G and $\overline{G}$ have the same vertices, but $\overline{G}$ has an edge precisely where G does not have an edge.   □

Graph Isomorphism

Suppose that G_1 and G_2 are simple, undirected graphs. If A_1 is an adjacency matrix for G_1 corresponding to some ordering of G_1's vertices and A_2 is an adjacency matrix for G_2 corresponding to some ordering of G_2's vertices, we would not, in general, expect that $A_1 = A_2$. (Even if $G_1 = G_2$, we would not, in general, have $A_1 = A_2$ since different orderings of the vertices for A_1 and A_2 could result in $A_1 \neq A_2$.) However, if $A_1 = A_2$ for *some* orderings of the vertices of the two graphs, we would consider G_1 and G_2 to be essentially the same graphs. The formal terminology is that G_1 and G_2 are **isomorphic graphs**. In this subsection, all graphs are simple and undirected.

Definition 2.5.42. Simple, undirected graphs G_1 and G_2 are *isomorphic* if for some orderings of the vertices, their adjacency matrices are equal.

Example 2.5.43. The adjacency matrix of the graph G_1 in Figure 2.5.18 relative to the ordering $1, 2, 3, 4, 5, 6, 7, 8, 9, 10$ of the vertices is

$$
\begin{pmatrix}
0 & 1 & 0 & 0 & 1 & 1 & 0 & 0 & 0 & 0 \\
1 & 0 & 1 & 0 & 0 & 0 & 1 & 0 & 0 & 0 \\
0 & 1 & 0 & 1 & 0 & 0 & 0 & 1 & 0 & 0 \\
0 & 0 & 1 & 0 & 1 & 0 & 0 & 0 & 1 & 0 \\
1 & 0 & 0 & 1 & 0 & 0 & 0 & 0 & 0 & 1 \\
1 & 0 & 0 & 0 & 0 & 0 & 0 & 1 & 1 & 0 \\
0 & 1 & 0 & 0 & 0 & 0 & 0 & 0 & 1 & 1 \\
0 & 0 & 1 & 0 & 0 & 1 & 0 & 0 & 0 & 1 \\
0 & 0 & 0 & 1 & 0 & 1 & 1 & 0 & 0 & 0 \\
0 & 0 & 0 & 0 & 1 & 0 & 1 & 1 & 0 & 0
\end{pmatrix}.
$$

The adjacency matrix of the graph G_2 in Figure 2.5.18 relative to the ordering $5, 6, 1, 2, 7, 4, 10, 8, 3, 9$ of the vertices is

$$
\begin{pmatrix}
0 & 1 & 0 & 0 & 1 & 1 & 0 & 0 & 0 & 0 \\
1 & 0 & 1 & 0 & 0 & 0 & 1 & 0 & 0 & 0 \\
0 & 1 & 0 & 1 & 0 & 0 & 0 & 1 & 0 & 0 \\
0 & 0 & 1 & 0 & 1 & 0 & 0 & 0 & 1 & 0 \\
1 & 0 & 0 & 1 & 0 & 0 & 0 & 0 & 0 & 1 \\
1 & 0 & 0 & 0 & 0 & 0 & 0 & 1 & 1 & 0 \\
0 & 1 & 0 & 0 & 0 & 0 & 0 & 0 & 1 & 1 \\
0 & 0 & 1 & 0 & 0 & 1 & 0 & 0 & 0 & 1 \\
0 & 0 & 0 & 1 & 0 & 1 & 1 & 0 & 0 & 0 \\
0 & 0 & 0 & 0 & 1 & 0 & 1 & 1 & 0 & 0
\end{pmatrix}.
$$

Since the matrices are equal, G_1 and G_2 are isomorphic.

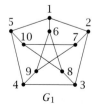 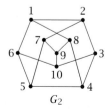

Figure 2.5.18 Isomorphic graphs. Either is called the Petersen graph.

Any graph isomorphic to the graphs in Figure 2.5.18 is called the **Petersen graph**. The Petersen graph is much used as an example; in fact, D. A. Holton and J. Sheehan wrote an entire book about it (see Holton, 1993).   □

Graphs G_1 and G_2 are isomorphic when orderings of their vertices, say $v_1, \ldots, v_n$ for G_1 and $w_1, \ldots, w_n$ for G_2, produce equal adjacency matrices. The existence of such orderings implies that there is a one-to-one, onto function f, defined by $f(v_i) = w_i$ from the vertex set of G_1 to the vertex set of G_2. Producing equal adjacency matrices requires that v_i and v_j are adjacent in G_1 if and only if $f(v_i)$ and $f(v_j)$ are adjacent in G_2. These observations lead to the following theorem whose proof is left as an exercise (see Exercise 86).

Theorem 2.5.44. *Let G_1 and G_2 be simple, undirected graphs. The following are equivalent.*

(a) *G_1 and G_2 are isomorphic.*

(b) *There is a one-to-one, onto function f from the vertex set of G_1 to the vertex set of G_2 satisfying: Vertices v_i and v_j are adjacent in G_1 if and only if the vertices $f(v_i)$ and $f(v_j)$ are adjacent in G_2.*

Proof. Exercise 86.   ∎

If G_1 and G_2 are isomorphic graphs, we call the function f of Theorem 2.5.44(b) an **isomorphism** of G_1 and G_2.

Example 2.5.45. The graphs in Figure 2.5.19 are not isomorphic. Notice that G_1 has a vertex, 1, of degree 3, but G_2 does not have a vertex of degree 3. If G_1 and G_2 were isomorphic and f was the isomorphism, vertex $f(1)$ in G_2 would have degree 3. Therefore, G_1 and G_2 are not isomorphic. Even though G_1 and G_2 are not isomorphic, they nevertheless have the same number of edges and vertices.

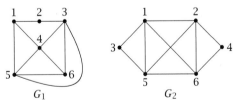

Figure 2.5.19 Nonisomorphic graphs.   □

Although the graph-isomorphism problem is not known to be **NP**-complete and is also not expected to be **NP**-complete, no polynomial-time algorithm is known for it.

Graph Coloring

Graph coloring refers to coloring the *vertices* so that adjacent vertices have different colors. The details are given in the following definition.

Definition 2.5.46. Let G be a graph. An *m-coloring* of G is an assignment of at most m distinct colors to the vertices of G so that adjacent vertices are assigned different colors. The *chromatic number of* G, $\chi(G)$, is the smallest m for which G has an *m*-coloring.

Example 2.5.47. A 3-coloring is shown in Figure 2.5.20. Since the graph G contains K_3 as a subgraph and K_3 requires three colors, there is no 2-coloring of G. Therefore, the chromatic number of G is 3.

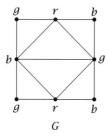

Figure 2.5.20 A graph colored with three colors: r, b, and g. □

Exercises

For each graph $G = (V, E)$ in Exercises 1–3, find V, E, all parallel edges, all loops, all isolated vertices, and tell whether G is a simple graph. Also, tell on which vertices edge e_1, if present, is incident.

1S.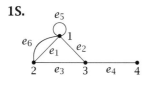

2.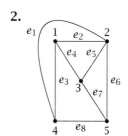

3.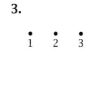

4S. Find the neighborhood of each vertex in Exercise 1.

5. Find the degree of each vertex in Exercise 1.

6. Find the neighborhood of each vertex in Exercise 2.

7S. Find the degree of each vertex in Exercise 2.

8. Find the neighborhood of each vertex in Exercise 3.

9. Find the degree of each vertex in Exercise 3.

10S. Find the indegree and outdegree of each vertex in Figure 2.5.2.

11. Draw K_3 and K_5.

12. How many edges does K_n have?

13S. Draw $K_{2,3}$ and $K_{3,3}$.

14. How many edges does $K_{m,n}$ have?

15S. Write the adjacency matrix of the graph in Figure 2.5.6 relative to the ordering $1, 2, 3, 4, 5$.

16. Write the adjacency matrix of the graph in Figure 2.5.6 relative to the ordering $2, 4, 1, 3, 5$.

17. Write the adjacency matrix of the graph in Figure 2.5.11 relative to the ordering $1, 2, 3, 4, 5, 6, 7$.

18S. Write the adjacency matrix of the graph in Figure 2.5.12 relative to the ordering $1, 2, 3, 4, 5$.

State which graphs in Exercises 19–33 are bipartite. If the graph is bipartite, specify disjoint vertex sets V_1 and V_2 satisfying the conditions in Definition 2.5.13.

19S.
    20.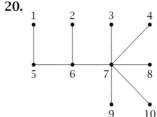

21. Figure 2.5.1   **22S.** Figure 2.5.3   **23.** K_4

24. Figure 2.5.8   **25S.** Figure 2.5.11   **26.** Figure 2.5.12

27. Figure 2.5.14   **28S.** The graph G_1 in Figure 2.5.18

29. The graph G_1 in Figure 2.5.19

30. The graph G_2 in Figure 2.5.19

31S. The graph in Exercise 1

32. The graph in Exercise 2

33. The graph in Exercise 3

Find the diameter of each graph in Exercises 34–36.

34S. The graph in Exercise 19

35. The graph in Figure 2.5.20

36. K_n

In Exercises 37–46, tell whether the given path in the graph is

(a) A simple path   (b) A cycle   (c) A simple cycle

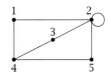

37S. $(2, 2)$ **38.** $(5, 4, 3, 2)$

39. $(1, 4, 3, 4, 5)$ **40S.** $(4, 3, 2, 5, 4)$

41. $(2, 3, 4, 1, 2, 5, 4, 3, 2)$ **42.** $(2, 3, 4, 5, 2, 2)$

43S. $(1, 4, 3, 2, 5)$ **44.** (4)

45. $(4, 3, 4)$ **46S.** $(2, 2, 3, 4, 5, 2)$

47S. Find all simple cycles in the following graph.

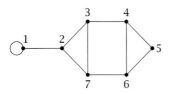

48. Find all simple paths from 1 to 5 in the graph of Exercise 47.

In Exercises 49–51, find the length of the given path in Figure 2.5.4.

49S. $(6, 7, 2, 3)$ **50.** $(1, 2, 7, 6, 1)$ **51.** $(2, 3, 7, 2, 1, 6)$

52S. Find all connected subgraphs of the following graph containing all of the vertices of the original graph and having as few edges as possible. Which of these subgraphs is a simple path (with a suitable ordering of the vertices)? Which of these subgraphs is a cycle (with a suitable ordering of the vertices)? Which of these subgraphs is a simple cycle (with a suitable ordering of the vertices)?

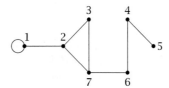

In Exercises 53–60, determine whether the graph has a Hamiltonian cycle. If the graph has a Hamiltonian cycle, exhibit one. If the graph does not have a Hamiltonian cycle, prove that it does not.

53S. The graph in Figure 2.5.1

54. The graph in Figure 2.5.8

55. The graph G_1 in Figure 2.5.19

56S. The graph G_2 in Figure 2.5.19

57. K_4 **58.** K_5 **59S.** $K_{3,4}$ **60.** $K_{4,4}$

61S. When does K_n contain a Hamiltonian cycle?

62. When does $K_{m,n}$ contain a Hamiltonian cycle?

63. Model a dodecahedron (see Figure 2.5.13) as a graph and find a Hamiltonian cycle in it.

64S. If we model a cube as a graph, similar to modeling the dodecahedron as a graph, does the resulting graph contain a Hamiltonian cycle?

65. Show that the cycle $(5, 2, 1, 3, 4, 5)$ solves the traveling-salesperson problem for the following graph.

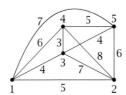

In Exercises 66–71, determine whether the graph has an Euler cycle. If the graph has an Euler cycle, exhibit one. If the graph does not have an Euler cycle, prove that it does not.

66S. The graph in Figure 2.5.1

67. The graph in Figure 2.5.12

68. K_4 **69S.** K_5 **70.** $K_{3,4}$ **71.** $K_{4,4}$

72S. When does K_n contain an Euler cycle?

73. When does $K_{m,n}$ contain an Euler cycle?

★**74.** Prove that graph G has an Euler cycle if and only if G is connected and the degree of every vertex is even.

75S. Model the Königsberg-bridge problem (see Figure 2.5.16) as a graph so that the bridge problem has a solution if and only if the graph has an Euler cycle. Does the bridge problem have a solution?

76S. Draw the complement of the graph in Figure 2.5.6.

77. Draw the complement of the graph in Figure 2.5.11.

78. Draw the complement of the graph in Figure 2.5.12.

⋆**79S.** Show that if G is a simple graph, either G or $\overline{G}$ is connected.

80. A simple graph G is *self-complementary* if G and $\overline{G}$ are isomorphic.

   (a) Find a self-complementary graph having five vertices.

   (b) Find another self-complementary graph.

In Exercises 81–83, determine whether the graphs G_1 and G_2 are isomorphic. If the graphs are isomorphic, give orderings of the vertices that produce equal adjacency matrices; otherwise, give a proof that the graphs are not isomorphic.

81S.

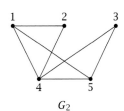

G_1 G_2

82.

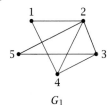
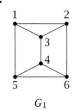
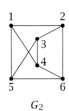

G_1 G_2

83.

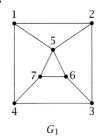
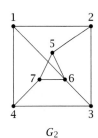

G_1 G_2

84S. Prove that the following graph is the Petersen graph; that is, prove that it is isomorphic to the graphs in Figure 2.5.18.

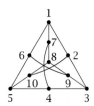

85. Draw a graph with 10 vertices. Label each vertex with one of the 10 distinct two-element subsets of $\{1, 2, 3, 4, 5\}$. Put an edge between two vertices if their labels (i.e., subsets) have no elements in common. Prove that your graph is the Petersen graph; that is, prove that it is isomorphic to the graphs in Figure 2.5.18.

86. Prove Theorem 2.5.44.

In Exercises 87–91, find the chromatic number of the graph, and prove that your value is correct.

87S. The graph in Figure 2.5.1   88. K_n 89. $K_{m,n}$

90S. The graph $G = (V, E)$, with $V = \{1, 2, \ldots, n\}$, $n > 1$, and

$$E = \{(i, i + 1) \mid 1 \le i \le n - 1\}$$

91. The graph consisting of the simple cycle $(1, 2, \ldots, n - 1, 1)$, $n > 3$, and a vertex n adjacent to each of $1, 2, \ldots, n - 1$. This graph is called a *wheel graph*.

92. Why is $\chi(G)$ called the *chromatic* number of G?

2.6 Trees

Trees form one of the most widely used subclasses of graphs. We begin by giving the formal definition.

Definition 2.6.1. A *(free) tree* T is a simple graph satisfying the following: If v and w are vertices in T, there is a unique simple path from v to w.

Example 2.6.2. Figure 2.6.1 shows a tree. We can directly verify that if v and w are any vertices, there is a unique simple path from v to w.   □

A **rooted tree** is a tree in which a particular vertex is designated the root. Figure 2.6.2 shows the way the tree in Figure 2.6.1 could be drawn with 5 as the root. First, we place the root, 5, at the top. Under the root and on the same level, we place the vertices 2, 4, 6, and 7, which can be reached from the root on a simple path of length 1. Under each of these vertices and on the same level, we place the vertices 1, 3, 8, and 9, which can be reached from the root on a simple path of length 2. We conclude by placing vertex

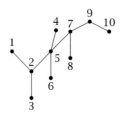

Figure 2.6.1 A (free) tree.

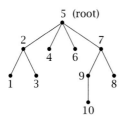

Figure 2.6.2 The tree in Figure 2.6.1 as a rooted tree with 5 as the root.

10 under vertex 9 since vertex 10 can be reached from the root on a simple path of length 3. Since the simple path from the root to any given vertex is unique, each vertex is on a uniquely determined level. We call the level of the root level 0. The vertices under the root are said to be on level 1, and so on. Thus, the **level of a vertex** v is the length of the simple path from the root to v. In the tree in Figure 2.6.2, vertex 5 is on level 0; vertices 2, 4, 6, and 7 are on level 1; vertices 1, 3, 8, and 9 are on level 2; and vertex 10 is on level 3. The **height** of a rooted tree is the maximum level number that occurs. The height of the tree in Figure 2.6.2 is 3.

We next define some useful terminology.

Definition 2.6.3. Let T be a tree with root v_0. Suppose that x, y, and z are vertices in T and that $(v_0, v_1, \ldots, v_n)$ is a simple path in T. Then

(a) v_{n-1} is the *parent* of v_n.

(b) $v_0, \ldots, v_{n-1}$ are *ancestors* of v_n.

(c) v_n is a *child* of v_{n-1}.

(d) If x is an ancestor of y, y is a *descendant* of x.

(e) If x and y are children of z, x and y are *siblings*.

(f) If x has no children, x is a *terminal* or a *leaf vertex*.

(g) If x is not a terminal vertex, x is an *internal* or *inner vertex*.

(h) The *subtree of T rooted at x* is the rooted tree $T' = (V, E)$, where V is x together with the descendants of x, and

$$E = \{e \mid e \text{ is an edge on a simple path from } x \text{ to some vertex in } V\}.$$

In T', x is designated the root.

Example 2.6.4. In the rooted tree in Figure 2.6.2,

(a) The parent of 3 is 2.

(b) The ancestors of 10 are 5, 7, and 9.

(c) The children of 7 are 8 and 9.

(d) The descendants of 7 are 8, 9, and 10.

(e) Vertices 2 and 7 are siblings.

(f) The terminal vertices are 1, 3, 4, 6, 8, and 10.

(g) The internal vertices are 2, 5, 7, and 9.

(h) The subtree rooted at 7 is shown in Figure 2.6.3.

Figure 2.6.3 The subtree rooted at 7 of the tree in Figure 2.6.2.   □

Our next theorem gives several equivalent characterizations of trees.

Theorem 2.6.5. *Let T be a graph with n vertices. The following are equivalent.*

(a) T is a tree.

(b) T is connected and acyclic.

(c) T is connected and has n − 1 edges.

(d) T is acyclic and has n − 1 edges.

Proof. To show that (a)-(d) are equivalent, we prove four results: (a) implies (b); (b) implies (c); (c) implies (d); and (d) implies (a).

[(a) implies (b).] Let T be a tree. Then, T is connected because there is a simple path from any vertex to any other vertex. Assume, by way of contradiction, that T contains a cycle C'. We can show (see Exercise 27) that C' contains a simple cycle

$$C = (v_0, \ldots, v_n),$$

$v_0 = v_n$, (see Figure 2.6.4). Since T is a simple graph, C cannot be a loop; so C contains at least two distinct vertices v_i and v_j, $i < j$. Now

$$(v_i, v_{i+1}, \ldots, v_j) \quad \text{and} \quad (v_i, v_{i-1}, \ldots, v_0, v_{n-1}, \ldots, v_j)$$

are distinct simple paths from v_i to v_j, which contradicts the definition of tree. Therefore, a tree cannot contain a cycle. This portion of the proof is complete.

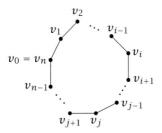

Figure 2.6.4 A simple cycle.

[(b) implies (c).] Suppose that T is connected and acyclic. We prove that T has $n - 1$ edges by induction on n.

If $n = 1$, T consists of one vertex and zero edges, so the result is true if $n = 1$.

Now suppose that the result holds for a connected, acyclic graph with n vertices. Let T be a connected, acyclic graph with $n + 1$ vertices. Choose a simple path P of maximum length. If P ends at vertex v, v has degree 1 because T is acyclic (see Figure 2.6.5). Let T^* be T with v and the edge incident on v removed. Then T^* is connected and acyclic; and because T^* contains n vertices, by the inductive hypothesis T^* contains $n - 1$ edges. Therefore, T contains n edges. The inductive argument is complete and this portion of the proof is complete.

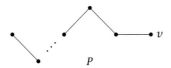

Figure 2.6.5 The proof of Theorem 2.6.5 [(b) implies (c)]. P is a simple path. v and the edge incident on v are removed so that the inductive hypothesis can be invoked.

[(c) implies (d).] Suppose that T is connected and has $n - 1$ edges. We must show that T is acyclic.

Suppose that T contains at least one cycle. Since removing an edge from a cycle does not disconnect a graph, we may remove edges, but no vertices, from cycle(s) in T until the resulting graph T^* is connected and acyclic. Now T^* is an acyclic, connected graph with n vertices. We may use our just proven result, (b) implies (c), to conclude that T^* has $n - 1$ edges. But now T has more than $n - 1$ edges. This is a contradiction. Therefore, T is acyclic. This portion of the proof is complete.

[(d) implies (a).] Suppose that T is acyclic and has $n - 1$ edges. We must show that T is a tree, that is, that T is a simple graph and that T has a unique simple path from any vertex to any other vertex.

The graph T cannot contain any loops because loops are cycles and T is acyclic. Similarly, T cannot contain distinct edges e_1 and e_2 incident on v

and w because we would then have the cycle (v, e_1, w, e_2, v). Therefore, T is a simple graph.

Suppose, by way of contradiction, that T is not connected. Let $T_1, T_2, \ldots, T_k$ be the components of T. Since T is not connected, $k > 1$. Suppose that T_i has n_i vertices. Each T_i is connected and acyclic, so we may use our previously proven result, (b) implies (c), to conclude that T_i has $n_i - 1$ edges. Now

$$
\begin{aligned}
n - 1 \quad &= \quad (n_1 - 1) + (n_2 - 1) + \cdots + (n_k - 1) \quad &\text{(counting edges)} \\
&< \quad (n_1 + n_2 + \cdots + n_k) - 1 \quad &\text{(since } k > 1) \\
&= \quad n - 1, \quad &\text{(counting vertices)}
\end{aligned}
$$

which is false. Therefore, T is connected.

Suppose that there are distinct simple paths P_1 and P_2 from a to b in T (see Figure 2.6.6). Let c be the first vertex after a on P_1 that is not on P_2; let d be the vertex preceding c on P_1; and let e be the first vertex after d on P_1 that is also on P_2. Let

$$(v_0, v_1, \ldots, v_{n-1}, v_n)$$

be the portion of P_1 from $d = v_0$ to $e = v_n$. Let

$$(w_0, w_1, \ldots, w_{m-1}, w_m)$$

be the portion of P_2 from $d = w_0$ to $e = w_m$. Now

$$(v_0, \ldots, v_n = w_m, w_{m-1}, \ldots, w_1, w_0)$$

is a cycle (in fact, a simple cycle) in T, which is a contradiction. Thus there is a unique simple path from any vertex to any other vertex in T. Therefore, T is a tree. This completes the proof.

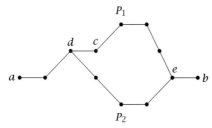

Figure 2.6.6 The proof of Theorem 2.6.5 [(d) implies (a)]. P_1 and P_2 are simple paths from a to b. c is the first vertex after a on P_1 not on P_2. d is the vertex preceding c on P_1. e is the first vertex after d on P_1 that is also on P_2. Thus, P_1 is the path that goes from a to d, then follows along the top, and terminates by going from e to b. Similarly, P_2 is the path that goes from a to d, then follows along the bottom, and terminates by going from e to b. As shown, a cycle results, which gives a contradiction. ■

Binary Trees

Binary trees are among the most important special types of rooted trees. Every vertex in a binary tree has at most two children (see Figure 2.6.7). Moreover, each child is designated a **left child** or **right child**. When a binary tree is drawn, a left child is drawn to the left and a right child is drawn to the right.

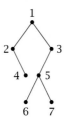

Figure 2.6.7 A binary tree.

Definition 2.6.6. A *binary tree* is a rooted tree in which each vertex has either no children, one child, or two children. If a vertex has one child, that child is designated as either a left child or a right child (but not both). If a vertex has two children, one child is designated a left child and the other a right child.

Example 2.6.7. In the binary tree in Figure 2.6.7, vertex 2 is the left child of vertex 1, and vertex 3 is the right child of vertex 1. Vertex 4 is the right child of vertex 2; vertex 2 has no left child. Vertex 5 is the left child of vertex 3; vertex 3 has no right child.   □

   The following theorem establishes an important connection between the height of a binary tree and the number of terminal vertices in it.

Theorem 2.6.8. *If a binary tree of height h has t terminal vertices, then*

$$\lg t \le h.$$

Proof. We prove the equivalent inequality

$$t \le 2^h$$

by induction on h.
   If $h = 0$, the binary tree consists of a single vertex. In this case, $t = 1$ and thus $t \le 2^h$.
   Assume that the result holds for a binary tree whose height is less than h. Let T be a binary tree of height $h > 0$ with t terminal vertices. Suppose first that the root of T has only one child. If we eliminate the root and the edge incident on the root, the resulting tree has height $h - 1$ and the same number of terminal vertices as T. By the inductive assumption, $t \le 2^{h-1}$. Since $2^{h-1} < 2^h$, in this case $t \le 2^h$.

Now suppose that the root of T has children v_1 and v_2. Let T_i be the sub-tree rooted at v_i and suppose that T_i has height h_i and t_i terminal vertices, $i = 1, 2$. By the inductive assumption,

$$t_i \le 2^{h_i}, \quad i = 1, 2.$$

The terminal vertices of T consist of the terminal vertices of T_1 and T_2. Hence

$$t = t_1 + t_2.$$

Combining the preceding inequality and equation, we obtain

$$t = t_1 + t_2 \le 2^{h_1} + 2^{h_2} \le 2^{h-1} + 2^{h-1} = 2^h.$$

The inductive step has been verified and the proof is complete. ∎

Exercises

Which of the graphs in Exercises 1–4 are trees? Explain.

1S.

2.

3.

4S.

5S. For which values of m and n is $K_{m,n}$ a tree?

6. For which values of n is K_n a tree?

7. Find the level of each vertex in the tree shown.

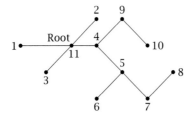

8S. Find the height of the tree in Exercise 7.

9. Draw the tree in Exercise 7 as a rooted tree with vertex 1 as the root. What is the height of the resulting tree?

10. Draw the tree in Exercise 7 as a rooted tree with vertex 4 as the root. What is the height of the resulting tree?

11S. Show that if T is a rooted tree, the diameter of T is less than or equal to twice the height of T.

12. Show that a tree is a bipartite graph.

13. Show that any tree can be 2-colored.

   Answer the questions in Exercises 14–19 for the tree in Figure 2.6.2.

14S. Find the parent of 6.

15. Find the ancestors of 8.

16. Find the children of 5.

17S. Find the descendants of 5.

18. Find the siblings of 2.

19. Draw the subtree rooted at 2.

20S. What can you say about two vertices in a rooted tree that have the same parent?

21. What can you say about two vertices in a rooted tree that have the same ancestors?

22. What can you say about a vertex in a rooted tree that has no ancestors?

23S. What can you say about two vertices in a rooted tree that have a descendant in common?

24. What can you say about a vertex in a rooted tree that has no descendants?

25. If $P_1 = (v_0, \ldots, v_n)$ and $P_2 = (w_0, \ldots, w_m)$ are distinct simple paths from a to b in a simple graph G, is

$$(v_0, \ldots, v_n = w_m, w_{m-1}, \ldots, w_1, w_0)$$

necessarily a cycle? Explain. (This exercise is relevant to the last paragraph of the proof of Theorem 2.6.5.)

26S. Show that a graph with n vertices and fewer than $n - 1$ edges is not connected.

27. Show that any cycle contains a simple cycle.

28. Prove that a rooted tree with at least n terminal vertices in which each vertex has at most three children has height at least $\log_3 n$.

Notes

The topics in this chapter are covered in more detail in discrete mathematics books (see, e.g., Johnsonbaugh, 2001; and Graham, 1989). The first half of Knuth, 1997, introduces the concept of algorithm and various mathematical topics, including mathematical induction. Recurrence relations are treated more fully in Graham, 1989; Liu, 1985; Roberts, 1984; and Tucker, 1995. Books specifically on graph theory are West, 2000, and Wilson, 1996.

The clever proof of Theorem 2.1.29 is apparently due to Fort in 1862 [see Chrystal (1964), vol. II, page 77].

Euler's original paper on the Königsberg bridges, edited by J. R. Newman, was reprinted as Newman, 1953.

Chapter Exercises

2.1. Use induction to prove that

$$\frac{1 \cdot 3 \cdot 5 \cdots (2n - 1)}{2 \cdot 4 \cdot 6 \cdots (2n)} \le \frac{1}{\sqrt{n + 1}}, \quad n \ge 1.$$

2.2. Use induction to prove that

$$(a_1 a_2 \cdots a_{2^n})^{1/2^n} \le \frac{a_1 + a_2 + \cdots + a_{2^n}}{2^n}$$

for all $n \ge 1$. The a_i are positive real numbers.

2.3. Given n 0's and n 1's distributed in any manner whatsoever around a circle (see the following figure), show, using induction on n, that it is possible to start at some number and proceed clockwise around the circle to the original starting position so that, at any point during the cycle, we have seen at least as many 0's as 1's. In the following figure, a possible starting point is marked with an arrow.

In Exercises 2.4-2.8, suppose that $n > 1$ people are positioned in a field (Euclidean plane) so that each has a unique nearest neighbor. Suppose further that each person has a pie that is hurled at the nearest neighbor. A survivor is a person that is not hit by a pie.

2.4. Give an example to show that if n is even, there may be no survivor.

2.5. Give an example to show that there may be more than one survivor.

2.6. Use induction on n to show that if n is odd, there is always at least one survivor. This result is due to Carmony, 1979.

2.7. Prove or disprove: If n is odd, one of a pair of persons farthest apart is a survivor.

2.8. Prove or disprove: If n is odd, a person who throws a pie the greatest distance is a survivor.

2.9. Explain precisely what $f(n) \neq O(g(n))$ means.

2.10. Give examples of functions $f(n)$ and $g(n)$ satisfying

$$f(n) \neq O(g(n)) \quad \text{and} \quad g(n) \neq O(f(n)).$$

2.11. Give examples of increasing functions $f(n)$ and $g(n)$ satisfying

$$f(n) \neq O(g(n)) \quad \text{and} \quad g(n) \neq O(f(n)).$$

2.12. Prove that for $k \in \{1, 2, \ldots\}$ and $c > 1$, $n^k = O(c^n)$.

2.13. Find a theta notation for the solution of the recurrence relation $T(n) = 2T(n/2) + \lg n$.

2.14. Find a theta notation for the solution of the recurrence relation $T(n) = 2T(n/2) + n \lg n$.

Exercises 2.15–2.21 explore an inductive proof of the Main Recurrence Theorem (Theorem 2.4.7).

⋆**2.15.** Assume that T satisfies $T(n) \leq aT(\lfloor n/b \rfloor) + f(n)$, $f(n) = O(n^k)$, and $a < b^k$. Choose a suitable constant C, and then use induction to prove that $T(n) \leq Cn^k + T(0)$ for all $n \geq 0$. Notice that this proves that $T(n) = O(n^k)$.

⋆**2.16.** Assume that T satisfies $T(n) \leq aT(\lceil n/b \rceil) + f(n)$, $f(n) = O(n^k)$, and $a < b^k$. Use induction to prove an inequality from which we can deduce $T(n) = O(n^k)$.

⋆**2.17.** Assume that T satisfies $T(n) \leq aT(\lfloor n/b \rfloor) + f(n)$, $f(n) = O(n^k)$, and $a = b^k$. Choose a suitable constant C, and then use induction to prove that $T(n) \leq Cn^k \log n + T(1) + T(2) + \cdots + T(\lceil b \rceil)$ for all $n \geq 1$. Notice that this proves that $T(n) = O(n^k \log n)$.

⋆**2.18.** Assume that T satisfies $T(n) \leq aT(\lceil n/b \rceil) + f(n)$, $f(n) = O(n^k)$, and $a = b^k$. Use induction to prove an inequality from which we can deduce $T(n) = O(n^k \log n)$.

⋆**2.19.** Assume that T satisfies $T(n) \le aT(\lfloor n/b \rfloor) + f(n)$, $f(n) = O(n^k)$, and $a > b^k$. Use induction to prove an inequality from which we can deduce $T(n) = O(n^{\log_b a})$.

⋆**2.20.** Assume that T satisfies $T(n) \le aT(\lceil n/b \rceil) + f(n)$, $f(n) = O(n^k)$, and $a > b^k$. Use induction to prove an inequality from which we can deduce $T(n) = O(n^{\log_b a})$.

⋆**2.21.** Use induction to prove inequalities from which we can deduce the lower-bound case of Theorem 2.4.7.

A directed Euler cycle *in a directed graph G is a sequence of edges of the form*

$$(v_0, v_1), (v_1, v_2), \ldots, (v_{n-1}, v_n),$$

where $v_0 = v_n$, every edge in G occurs exactly one time, and all vertices appear.

2.22. Show that a directed graph G contains a directed Euler cycle if and only if the undirected graph obtained by ignoring the directions of the edges of G is connected and the indegree of v = outdegree of v, for every vertex v in G.

A de Bruijn sequence for n *(in 0's and 1's) is a sequence*

$$a_1, \ldots, a_{2^n}$$

of 2^n bits having the property that if s is a bit string of length n, for some m,

$$s = a_m a_{m+1} \cdots a_{m+n-1}.$$

In the preceding equation, we define $a_{2^n+i} = a_i$ for $i = 1, \ldots, 2^n - 1$.

2.23. Verify that 00011101 is de Bruijn sequence for $n = 3$.

2.24. Let G be a directed graph with vertices corresponding to all bit strings of length $n - 1$. A directed edge exists from vertex $x_1 \cdots x_{n-1}$ to $x_2 \cdots x_n$. Show that a directed Euler cycle in G corresponds to a de Bruijn sequence.

2.25. Prove that there is a de Bruijn sequence for every $n = 1, 2, \ldots$.

2.26. A *closed path* is a path from v to v. Show that a graph G is bipartite if and only if every closed path in G has even length. *Hint:* First prove the result for connected graphs.

2.27. Show that a graph is bipartite if and only if it does not contain a simple cycle of odd length.

⋆**2.28.** Show that there are $\lfloor n!e - 1 \rfloor$ simple paths in K_n. ($e = 2.71828\ldots$ is the base of the natural logarithm.)

2.29. For which values of m and n does the following graph contain a Hamiltonian cycle?

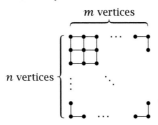

2.30. For which values of m and n does the graph in Exercise 2.29 contain an Euler cycle?

The eccentricity *of a vertex v in a tree T is the maximum length of a simple path that begins at v. A vertex v in a tree T is a* center *for T if the eccentricity of v is a minimum.*

2.31. Find the eccentricity of each vertex in the tree in Figure 2.6.1.

2.32. Find the center(s) in the tree in Figure 2.6.1.

2.33. Show that a tree has either one or two centers.

2.34. Show that if a tree has two centers they are adjacent.

2.35. Prove that T is a tree if and only if T is connected and when an edge is added between any two vertices, exactly one cycle is created.

CHAPTER 3
Data Structures

A **data structure** is data together with structural relations on the data to promote efficient processing of the data. For example, an array structures data sequentially and provides random (i.e., constant-time) access to the data. Some data structures can be described abstractly in terms of the operations on the data (see Section 3.1).

In this chapter, we discuss several basic data structures that are useful in building algorithms. Stacks and queues are presented in Section 3.2. Section 3.3 discusses linked lists with applications to graph representation. In Section 3.4, we discuss binary trees and operations on them. Priority queues, binary heaps, and heapsort are introduced in Section 3.5. The chapter concludes with algorithms to manage disjoint sets (Section 3.6). Any of these topics can be skipped or reviewed if the reader is already familiar with them. The sections can also be covered at the time they are needed. For example, algorithms for managing disjoint sets (Section 3.6) are used in Kruskal's algorithm (Section 7.2).

3.1 Abstract Data Types

An **abstract data type** (**ADT**) consists of data together with functions that operate on the data. An abstract data type is "abstract" in the sense that how the data are represented and how the functions are implemented are not specified. Only the *behavior* of the functions is specified.

For example, a **stack**, which we discuss in detail in Section 3.2, is an abstract data type with functions

- *stack_init*(): Make the stack empty.
- *empty*(): Return true if the stack is empty. Return false if the stack is not empty.
- *push*(*val*): Add the item *val* to the stack.
- *pop*(): Remove the item most recently added to the stack.

- *top*(): Return the item most recently added to the stack, but do not remove it.

Notice that the preceding function specifications define a stack but do not tell how to implement the stack. In a specific implementation, *as long as the functions have the properties specified*, the ADT is a stack. Of course, in practice, we would want an efficient implementation.

If *a* is an instance of an abstract data type and *f* is one of its functions, in pseudocode we denote the application of *f* to *a* as

$a.f(arg\_list)$

where *arg_list* is a list of arguments to *f*, separated by commas.

Example 3.1.1. Suppose that *s* is a stack. Then

$s.stack\_init()$

makes *s* an empty stack; *s* contains no data. The value of *s.empty*() is true. Executing

$s.push(16)$

adds 16 to the stack. The stack now contains 16. The value of *s.empty*() is false. Executing

$s.push(5)$
$s.push(33)$

adds 5 and 33 to the stack. The stack now contains 16, 5, and 33. Executing

$i = s.top()$

copies 33, the most recently added item, to *i*. The operation does *not* remove 33. The stack still contains 16, 5, and 33. Executing

$s.pop()$

removes 33, the most recently added item. The stack now contains 16 and 5. Executing

$s.pop()$

removes 5, the most recently added item. The stack now contains only 16.

□

Throughout the remainder of this chapter, we will define and implement several abstract data types.

Exercises

1S. Suppose that *s* is a stack. List the contents of the stack after each *push* or *pop*. Give the value of *i* after each statement $i = s.top()$ executes. Give the value of *b* after each statement $b = s.empty()$ executes.

$s.stack\_init()$
$b = s.empty()$
$s.push(-3)$
$b = s.empty()$
$i = s.top()$
$s.pop()$
$b = s.empty()$
$s.push(38)$
$s.push(88)$
$s.push(70)$
$b = s.empty()$
$i = s.top()$
$s.pop()$
$i = s.top()$

2. How do abstract data types relate to classes, which are a major component of object-oriented programming languages?

3.2 Stacks and Queues

Stacks

In Section 3.1, we defined a **stack** as an abstract data type with the functions

- $stack\_init()$: Make the stack empty.
- $empty()$: Return true if the stack is empty. Return false if the stack is not empty.
- $push(val)$: Add the item *val* to the stack.
- $pop()$: Remove the item most recently added to the stack.
- $top()$: Return the item most recently added to the stack, but do not remove it.

A stack may be implemented in many different ways. One of the simplest ways is to use an array. (In Section 3.3, we use a linked list to implement a stack.) We use a variable t to index the top of the stack. When an item is pushed onto the stack, we increment t and put the item in the cell at index t. When an item is popped off the stack, we decrement t.

Example 3.2.1. Suppose that we use an array, whose first index is 0, to store items in a stack s, and a variable t to index the last item pushed onto the stack.

After

$s.stack\_init()$

s is an empty stack, so $t = -1$ [see Figure 3.2.1(a)].

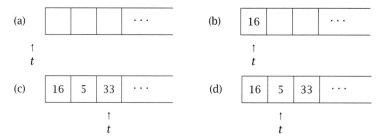

Figure 3.2.1 Implementing a stack s using an array, whose first index is 0. The top of the stack is at index t. An empty stack, shown in (a), has $t = -1$. After $s.push(16)$, we have the situation shown in (b). After $s.push(5)$ and $s.push(33)$, we have the situation shown in (c). After $s.pop()$, we have the situation shown in (d).

After

$s.push(16)$

t is incremented to 0, and 16 is copied to the cell at index 0 [see Figure 3.2.1(b)]. The stack contains 16.

After

$s.push(5)$

t is incremented to 1, and 5 is copied to the cell at index 1. After

$s.push(33)$

t is incremented to 2, and 33 is copied to the cell at index 2 [see Figure 3.2.1(c)]. The stack contains 16, 5, and 33.

After

$s.pop()$

t is decremented to 1 [see Figure 3.2.1(d)]. The stack contains 16 and 5.   □

If we represent a stack using an array, the functions $stack\_init$, $empty$, $push$, pop, and top are reasonably straightforward to write.

Algorithm 3.2.2 Initializing a Stack. This algorithm initializes a stack to empty. An empty stack has $t = -1$.

  Input Parameters: None
Output Parameters: None

```
stack_init() {
    t = -1
}
```

Algorithm 3.2.3 Testing for an Empty Stack. This algorithm returns true if the stack is empty or false if the stack is not empty. An empty stack has $t = -1$.

Input Parameters: None
Output Parameters: None

```
empty() {
   return t == -1
}
```

Algorithm 3.2.4 Adding an Element to a Stack. This algorithm adds the value *val* to a stack. The stack is represented using an array *data*. The algorithm assumes that the array is not full. The most recently added item is at index t unless the stack is empty, in which case, $t = -1$.

Input Parameter: *val*
Output Parameters: None

```
push(val) {
   t = t + 1
   data[t] = val
}
```

Algorithm 3.2.5 Removing an Element From a Stack. This algorithm removes the most recently added item from a stack. The algorithm assumes that the stack is not empty. The most recently added item is at index t.

Input Parameters: None
Output Parameters: None

```
pop() {
   t = t - 1
}
```

Algorithm 3.2.6 Returning the Top Element in a Stack. This algorithm returns, but does not remove, the most recently added item in a stack. The algorithm assumes that the stack is not empty. The stack is represented using an array *data*. The most recently added item is at index t.

Input Parameters: None
Output Parameters: None

```
top() {
   return data[t]
}
```

Each of Algorithms 3.2.2–3.2.6 runs in constant time.

None of the stack algorithms does any error checking. For example, Algorithm 3.2.4 (*push*) does not check for a full array, that is, whether the index t

is at the end of the array. In practice, such a situation must be dealt with. The algorithm could be modified to return values that signal whether the push succeeded or not. Another approach is to throw an exception if the array capacity would be exceeded. This exception could be caught and handled by the function that called *push*. Yet another way to deal with the situation is to allocate a new, larger array, copy the data from the old array to the new array, and then continue.

Similarly, Algorithms 3.2.5 (*pop*) and 3.2.6 (*top*) are incorrect if the array is empty, that is, if $t = -1$. The *pop* algorithm could be modified similarly to *push* to return values that signal whether the function succeeded or not, or it could throw an exception if the array is empty. Since *top* returns a value, it could not also return a value to signal success or failure; an exception could be thrown, however. (See Exercises 4–6.)

Example 3.2.7. The function *one*

    Input Parameter: *s* (the stack)
Output Parameters: None

```
one(s) {
   if (s.empty())
      return false
   val = s.top()
   s.pop()
   flag = s.empty()
   s.push(val)
   return flag
}
```

returns true if there is exactly one element in the stack and false otherwise. The stack contents before and after *one* executes are identical. The code uses the *abstract data type* stack (i.e., it does not refer to *data* or *t*). □

Queues

A **queue** is similar to a stack. The difference is that when an item is deleted from a queue, the *least recently* item is deleted. In some applications, the add and delete functions for a queue are called push and pop just as for a stack. We prefer the common alternative names, enqueue (for add) and dequeue (for delete) to avoid confusion with stacks. We also refer to adding an element at the **rear** of a queue and deleting an element from the **front** of a queue. (The terminology is consistent with a queue of people waiting in line, for example, for tickets to a rock concert.) Thus, a queue is an abstract data type with the functions

- *queue_init*(): Make the queue empty.

- *empty*(): Return true if the queue is empty. Return false if the queue is not empty.

- *enqueue(val)*: Add the item *val* to the queue.
- *dequeue()*: Remove the item least recently added to the queue.
- *front()*: Return the item least recently added to the queue, but do not remove it.

Example 3.2.8. Suppose that q is a queue. Then

> $q.queue\_init()$

makes q an empty queue; q contains no data. The value of $q.empty()$ is true. Executing

> $q.enqueue(16)$

adds 16 to the queue. The queue now contains 16. The value of $q.empty()$ is false.
Executing

> $q.enqueue(5)$
> $q.enqueue(33)$

adds 5 and 33 to the queue. The queue now contains 16, 5, and 33.
Executing

> $i = q.front()$

copies 16, the least recently added item, to i. The operation does *not* remove 16. The queue still contains 16, 5, and 33.
Executing

> $q.dequeue()$

removes 16, the least recently added item. The queue now contains 5 and 33.
Executing

> $s.dequeue()$

removes 5, the least recently added item. The queue now contains only 33.

□

Like a stack, a queue may be implemented in many different ways, and one of the simplest ways is to use an array. In a queue, items are added at the rear and deleted from the front; thus, we use two variables, r and f, to track the indexes of the rear and front of the queue. An empty queue has both r and f equal to -1.

When an item is added (at the rear) to an empty queue, we set r and f to 0 and put the item in the cell at index 0. When an item is added to a nonempty queue, we increment r and put the item in the cell at index r. If r is the index of the last cell in the array, we "wrap around" by setting r to 0. In either case, f does not change.

When an item is deleted (at the front) from a queue, we increment f. If f is the index of the last cell in the array, we "wrap around" by setting f to 0. In either case, r does not change. When an item is deleted from the queue and the queue becomes empty, we set r and f to -1.

Example 3.2.9. Suppose that we use an array of size 4, whose first index is 0, to store items in a queue q.

After

$q.queue\_init()$

q is an empty queue so $r = f = -1$ [see Figure 3.2.2(a)].

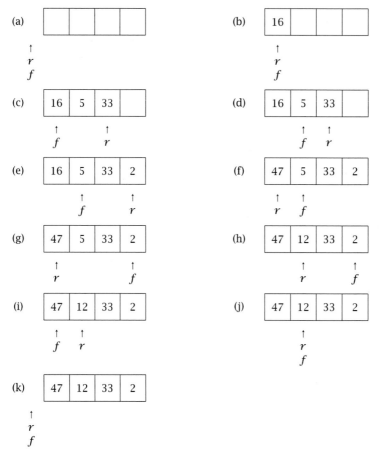

Figure 3.2.2 Implementing a queue q using an array of size 4, whose first index is 0. The rear of the queue is at index r, and the front of the queue is at index f. An empty queue, shown in (a), has $r = f = -1$. After $q.enqueue(16)$, we have the situation shown in (b). After $q.enqueue(5)$ and $q.enqueue(33)$, we have the situation shown in (c). After $q.dequeue()$, we have the situation shown in (d). After $q.enqueue(2)$, we have the situation shown in (e). After $q.enqueue(47)$, we have the situation shown in (f). After $q.dequeue()$ and $q.dequeue()$, we have the situation shown in (g). After $q.enqueue(12)$, we have the situation shown in (h). After $q.dequeue()$, we have the situation shown in (i). After $q.dequeue()$, we have the situation shown in (j). After $q.dequeue()$, we have the situation shown in (k).

After

q.enqueue(16)

r and *f* are set to 0, and 16 is copied to the cell at index 0 [see Figure 3.2.2(b)]. The queue contains 16.

After

q.enqueue(5)

r is incremented to 1, and 5 is copied to the cell at index 1. After

q.enqueue(33)

r is incremented to 2, and 33 is copied to the cell at index 2 [see Figure 3.2.2(c)]. The queue contains 16, 5, and 33.

After

q.dequeue()

f is incremented to 1 [see Figure 3.2.2(d)]. The queue contains 5 and 33.

After

q.enqueue(2)

r is incremented to 3, and 2 is copied to the cell at index 3 [see Figure 3.2.2(e)]. The queue contains 5, 33, and 2.

After

q.enqueue(47)

r wraps around to 0, and 47 is copied to the cell at index 0 [see Figure 3.2.2(f)]. The queue contains 5, 33, 2, and 47.

After

q.dequeue()
q.dequeue()

f is incremented to 3 [see Figure 3.2.2(g)]. The queue contains 2 and 47.

After

q.enqueue(12)

r is incremented to 1, and 12 is copied to the cell at index 1 [see Figure 3.2.2(h)]. The queue contains 2, 47, and 12.

After

q.dequeue()

f wraps around to 0 [see Figure 3.2.2(i)]. The queue contains 47 and 12.

After

q.dequeue()

f is incremented to 1 [see Figure 3.2.2(j)]. The queue contains 12.

After

q.dequeue()

the queue becomes empty, so *r* and *f* are reset to −1 [see Figure 3.2.2(k)]. □

We next write the queue functions *queue_init*, *empty*, *enqueue*, *dequeue*, and *front*.

Algorithm 3.2.10 Initializing a Queue. This algorithm initializes a queue to empty. An empty queue has $r = f = -1$.

Input Parameters: None
Output Parameters: None

queue_init() {
  $r = f = -1$
}

Algorithm 3.2.11 Testing for an Empty Queue. This algorithm returns true if the queue is empty or false if the queue is not empty. An empty queue has $r = f = -1$.

Input Parameters: None
Output Parameters: None

empty() {
  return $r == -1$
}

Recall (see Figure 3.2.2) that r (rear) is the index of the most recently added item in a queue, and that r wraps around the end of the array [i.e., if r is the index of the last cell in the array, r "increments" to zero; see Figure 3.2.2(e) and (f)].

Algorithm 3.2.12 Adding an Element to a Queue. This algorithm adds the value *val* to a queue. The queue is represented using an array *data* of size *SIZE*. The algorithm assumes that the queue is not full. The most recently added item is at index r (rear), and the least recently added item is at index f (front). If the queue is empty, $r = f = -1$.

Input Parameter: *val*
Output Parameters: None

enqueue(*val*) {
  if (*empty*())
    $r = f = 0$
  else {
    $r = r + 1$
    if ($r == SIZE$)
      $r = 0$
  }
  $data[r] = val$
}

Recall (see Figure 3.2.2) that f (front) is the index of the least recently added item in a queue, and that f wraps around the end of the array [i.e., if f is the index of the last cell in the array, f "increments" to zero; see Figure 3.2.2(h) and (i)].

Algorithm 3.2.13 Removing an Element From a Queue. This algorithm removes the least recently added item from a queue. The queue is represented using an array of size *SIZE*. The algorithm assumes that the queue is not empty. The most recently added item is at index r (rear), and the least recently added item is at index f (front). If the queue is empty, $r = f = -1$.

Input Parameters: None
Output Parameters: None

```
dequeue() {
    // does queue contain one item?
    if (r == f)
        r = f = -1
    else {
        f = f + 1
        if (f == SIZE)
            f = 0
    }
}
```

Algorithm 3.2.14 Returning the Front Element in a Queue. This algorithm returns, but does not remove, the least recently added item in a queue. The algorithm assumes that the queue is not empty. The queue is represented using an array *data*. The least recently added item is at index f (front).

Input Parameters: None
Output Parameters: None

```
front() {
    return data[f]
}
```

Each of Algorithms 3.2.10–3.2.14 runs in constant time.

None of the queue algorithms does any error checking. For example, Algorithm 3.2.12 (*enqueue*) does not check for a full queue. The suggested ways to implement error checking for a stack (see the discussion following Algorithm 3.2.6) can also be used for a queue (see Exercises 8–10).

Exercises

1S. What is the output? s is a stack.

```
s.stack_init()
s.push(100)
s.push(54)
println(s.top())
s.pop()
println(s.top())
s.push(60)
s.push(630)
println(s.top())
s.pop()
println(s.top())
s.pop()
println(s.top())
```

2. What is the output? *q* is a queue.

```
q.queue_init()
q.enqueue(100)
q.enqueue(54)
println(q.front())
q.dequeue()
println(q.front())
q.enqueue(60)
q.enqueue(630)
println(q.front())
q.dequeue()
println(q.front())
q.dequeue()
println(q.front())
```

3. Write a function *is_full* that returns true or false to indicate whether the array that implements a stack is full. Assume that *SIZE* specifies the size of the array.

4S. Write a version of *push* that checks for a full array. If the array is full, the function simply returns false. If the array is not full, the behavior is the same as the original *push*, except that the function also returns true. Assume that *SIZE* specifies the size of the array.

5. Write a version of *push* that checks for a full array. If the array is full, the function allocates a new array that is twice as large as the original array. The function then copies the data from the old array to the new array and then proceeds as in the original function. Assume that *SIZE* specifies the size of the array currently being used.

6. Write a version of *pop* that checks for an empty stack. If the stack is empty, the function simply returns false. If the stack is not empty, the

behavior is the same as the original *pop*, except that the function also returns true.

7S. Write a function *is_full* that returns true or false to indicate whether the array that implements a queue is full.

8. Write a version of *enqueue* that checks for a full array. If the array is full, the function simply returns false. If the array is not full, the behavior is the same as the original *enqueue* except that the function also returns true.

9. Write a version of *enqueue* that checks for a full array. If the array is full, the function allocates a new array that is twice as large as the original array. The function then copies the data from the old array to the new array and then proceeds as in the original function. Assume that *SIZE* specifies the size of the array currently being used.

10S. Write a version of *dequeue* that checks for an empty queue. If the queue is empty, the function simply returns false. If the queue is not empty, the behavior is the same as the original *dequeue* except that the function also returns true.

11. Write a function *rear* that returns, but does not remove, the most recently added item in a queue. Assume that the queue is not empty.

12. Write a function *invert* to invert the contents of a stack. *Example:* If *s* is a stack containing $3, 6, -1$, where 3 is the most recently added item, 6 is the second most recently added item, and -1 is the least recently added item, after *invert*(*s*), *s* contains the same elements, but -1 is the most recently added item, 6 is the second most recently added item, and 3 is the least recently added item. Use the *abstract data type* stack (i.e., do not refer to *data* or *t*). You may use additional stacks (i.e., you are not restricted to using just the input stack).

13S. Write a function *one* that returns true if there is exactly one element in a queue and false otherwise. Use the *abstract data type* queue (i.e., do not refer to *data*, *r*, *f*, etc.). Assume that the abstract data type queue has a function *insert_front*(*val*) that adds the item *val* to the front of the queue.

3.3 Linked Lists

An array provides constant-time access to a cell by specifying its index; that is, evaluating the expression $a[i]$, where a is an array and i is an index, takes constant time. However, inserting at the beginning of an array of n elements takes time $\Theta(n)$ because all n items must move over one cell to make room for the added element. Deleting the first element from an array of n elements also takes time $\Theta(n)$. A **linked list** provides constant time insertions and deletions anywhere in the list, but accessing an element takes time $\Theta(n)$ in the worst case.

To implement a linked list, we can use a *node* structure with a data field *data* and a field *next* that references the next node in the list (see Figure 3.3.1). When this structure is implemented in a computer, the reference field is typically the address of the next node. A linked list consists of several nodes (see Figure 3.3.2), together with a variable (*start* in Figure 3.3.2) that references the first node in the list. The *next* field of the last node has the special value null (shown as a diagonal line in Figure 3.3.2). Such a linked list is called a **singly-linked list**. Unless specified otherwise, by "linked list" we mean a singly-linked list.

Figure 3.3.1 A node structure with a data field *data* and a field *next* that references the next node in the list.

Figure 3.3.2 A singly-linked list of nodes. For the purposes of illustration, the data are shown as integers. As shown, *start* is a reference to the first node in the list. The *next* field in each node, except the last, references the next node in the list. The *next* field of the last node is null, shown as a diagonal line.

The key algorithms for manipulating a linked list are inserting and deleting an element. Figure 3.3.3 shows how the insertion algorithm works.

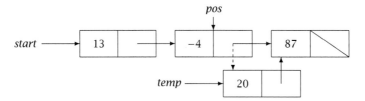

Figure 3.3.3 Inserting in a linked list. The original list is $13, -4, 87$, and the value 20 is to be inserted after -4. As shown, *pos* references the node that will precede the node containing the inserted value. A new node, *temp*, is obtained. Then 20 in inserted at *temp.data*, and *temp.next* is set to *pos.next*. Finally, *pos.next* is set to *temp*. The updated reference is shown as a dashed line.

Algorithm 3.3.1 Inserting in a Linked List. This algorithm inserts the value *val* after the node referenced by *pos*. The operator, new, is used to obtain a new *node*.

Input Parameters: *val, pos*
Output Parameters: None

insert(*val, pos*) {
 temp = new *node*
 temp.data = *val*
 temp.next = *pos.next*
 pos.next = *temp*
}

  Notice that *insert* (Algorithm 3.3.1) runs in constant time.
  Deleting in a linked list involves adjusting one reference (see Figure 3.3.4).

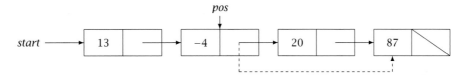

Figure 3.3.4 Deleting in a linked list. The original list is $13, -4, 20, 87$, and *pos* references the node preceding the node to be deleted. The node is deleted by resetting *pos.next* to *pos.next.next*. The updated reference is shown as a dashed line.

Algorithm 3.3.2 Deleting in a Linked List. This algorithm deletes the node after the node referenced by *pos*.

Input Parameter: *pos*
Output Parameters: None

delete(*pos*) {
 pos.next = *pos.next.next*
}

  Notice that *delete* (Algorithm 3.3.2) runs in constant time.
  Algorithms 3.3.1 and 3.3.2 show that we can insert and delete in a linked list in constant time. However, accessing a node in a linked list containing n nodes takes time $\Theta(n)$ in the worst case. For example, to access the last node we must begin at the first node and step through the list, node by node, until arriving at the last node. We frequently do step through the nodes in a linked list, node by node, to perform some action on each node. As an example, Algorithm 3.3.3 prints the data in each node in a linked list.

Algorithm 3.3.3 Printing the Data in a Linked List. This algorithm prints the data in each node in a linked list. The first node is referenced by *start*.

Input Parameter: *start*
Output Parameters: None

```
print(start) {
  while (start != null) {
    println(start.data)
    start = start.next
  }
}
```

Algorithm 3.3.3 runs in time $\Theta(n)$ when the linked list contains n nodes.

Algorithm 3.3.2 for deleting in a linked list requires a reference to the node preceding the node to be deleted. If we use nodes with references to the preceding and next nodes (see Figure 3.3.5), we can delete a node in constant time by specifying a reference to it (see Exercise 11). A list using such nodes (see Figure 3.3.6) is called a **doubly-linked list**. Exercises 9–11 ask for algorithms to manipulate a doubly-linked list.

prev   data   next

Figure 3.3.5 A node structure with a data field *data*, a field *prev* that references the previous node in the list, and a field *next* that references the next node in the list.

start →   13   −4   87

Figure 3.3.6 A doubly-linked list of nodes. The data are shown as integers. As shown, *start* is a reference to the first node in the list. The *prev* field in each node, except the first, references the previous node in the list. The *prev* field of the first node is null, shown as a diagonal line. The *next* field in each node, except the last, references the next node in the list. The *next* field of the last node is null.

A linked list can be used to implement a stack. We simply push and pop at the start of the list. Algorithms 3.3.4–3.3.8 provide the details.

Algorithm 3.3.4 Initializing a Stack. This algorithm initializes a stack to empty. The stack is implemented as a linked list. The start of the linked list, referenced by t, is the top of the stack. An empty stack has t = null.

Input Parameters: None
Output Parameters: None

```
stack_init() {
  t = null
}
```

Algorithm 3.3.5 Testing for an Empty Stack. This algorithm returns true if the stack is empty or false if the stack is not empty. An empty stack has $t = $ null.

Input Parameters: None
Output Parameters: None

```
empty() {
    return t == null
}
```

Algorithm 3.3.6 Adding an Element to a Stack. This algorithm adds the value *val* to a stack. The stack is implemented using a linked list. The start of the linked list, referenced by t, is the top of the stack.

Input Parameter: *val*
Output Parameters: None

```
push(val) {
    temp = new node
    temp.data = val
    temp.next = t
    t = temp
}
```

Algorithm 3.3.7 Removing an Element From a Stack. This algorithm removes the most recently added item from a stack. The stack is implemented using a linked list. The start of the linked list, referenced by t, is the top of the stack. The algorithm assumes that the stack is not empty.

Input Parameters: None
Output Parameters: None

```
pop() {
    t = t.next
}
```

Algorithm 3.3.8 Returning the Top Element in a Stack. This algorithm returns, but does not remove, the most recently added item in a stack. The stack is implemented using a linked list. The start of the linked list, referenced by t, is the top of the stack. The algorithm assumes that the stack is not empty.

Input Parameters: None
Output Parameters: None

top() {
   return *t.data*
}

    Each of Algorithms 3.3.4–3.3.8, like their counterparts using an array (Algorithms 3.2.2–3.2.6), runs in constant time. The linked list versions require somewhat more overhead; they use additional storage (for the references) and require additional time for memory management (getting and returning nodes).

    A queue can also be implemented using a linked list (see Exercise 12).

Adjacency Lists for Graphs

The most common way to represent a graph is to use linked lists, called **adjacency lists**. An array, *adj*, is used to access the various linked lists; *adj*[*i*] is a reference to the first node in a linked list of nodes representing the vertices adjacent to vertex *i*. Many algorithms execute more efficiently if a graph is represented using adjacency lists rather than an adjacency matrix (see the discussion following Algorithm 3.3.11).

Example 3.3.9. The graph in Figure 3.3.7(a) can be represented using adjacency lists as shown in Figure 3.3.7(b).

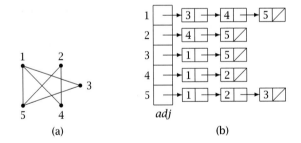

        (a)   (b)

Figure 3.3.7 (a) A graph. (b) A representation of the graph in (a) using adjacency lists. For *i* = 1 to 5, *adj*[*i*] is a reference to the first node in a linked list of nodes representing the vertices adjacent to vertex *i*. □

    Algorithm 3.3.10 computes the degree of each vertex in a graph. The graph is represented using adjacency lists. A glance at Figure 3.3.7 shows that it suffices to count the nodes in each linked list.

Algorithm 3.3.10 Computing Vertex Degrees Using Adjacency Lists. This algorithm computes the degree of each vertex in a graph. The graph is represented using adjacency lists; *adj*[*i*] is a reference to the first node in a linked list of nodes representing the vertices adjacent to vertex *i*. The *next* field in each node, except the last, references the next node in the list. The *next* field of the last node is null. The vertices are 1, 2, ...

Input Parameter: *adj*
Output Parameters: None

```
degrees1(adj) {
  for i = 1 to adj.last {
    count = 0
    ref = adj[i]
    while (ref != null) {
      count = count + 1
      ref = ref.next
    }
    println("vertex " + i + " has degree " + count)
  }
}
```

If a graph has m edges and n vertices, the for loop in Algorithm 3.3.10 executes n times. Notice that an edge (i, j) is represented twice in the adjacency lists: j appears once on i's list, and i appears once on j's list. Therefore, there are $2m$ total nodes in the adjacency lists. Thus, the *total* time required by the while loop in Algorithm 3.3.10 is $\Theta(m)$. Therefore, the time for Algorithm 3.3.10 is $\Theta(m + n)$.

We now contrast Algorithm 3.3.10 with a version in which the graph is represented using an adjacency matrix.

Algorithm 3.3.11 Computing Vertex Degrees Using an Adjacency Matrix.
This algorithm computes the degree of each vertex in a graph. The graph is represented using an adjacency matrix *am*, where $am[i][j]$ is 1 if there is an edge between i and j, and 0 if not. The vertices are $1, 2, \ldots$.

Input Parameter: *am*
Output Parameters: None

```
degrees2(am) {
  for i = 1 to am.last {
    count = 0
    for j = 1 to am.last
      if (am[i][j] == 1)
        count = count + 1
    println("vertex " + i + " has degree " + count)
  }
}
```

If a graph has n vertices, because of the nested for loops, Algorithm 3.3.11 runs in time $\Theta(n^2)$. This time is independent of the number of edges in the graph. If a graph has m edges, where m is considerably less than the maximum possible number of edges, $n(n-1)/2 = \Theta(n^2)$, (a not uncommon situation), Algorithm 3.3.10 is more efficient than Algorithm 3.3.11. For example, if $m = \Theta(n \lg n)$, Algorithm 3.3.10 runs in time $\Theta(n \lg n)$, whereas Algorithm 3.3.11 runs in time $\Theta(n^2)$.

Exercises

In Exercises 1–8, "linked list" means "singly-linked list." The node structure is that shown in Figure 3.3.1.

1S. Suppose that *start* is a reference to the first node in a linked list. What is the value of *start* after

      while (*start* != null)
        start = *start.next*

2. Suppose that *start* is a reference to the first node in a linked list or, if the linked list is empty, *start* = null. Write an algorithm that is passed *start* and a value *val*. The algorithm adds a node at the beginning of the linked list whose data field is *val* and returns *start*. What is the worst-case time of your algorithm?

3. Write an algorithm that receives a reference to the first node in a linked list and returns a reference to the last node in the list. What is the worst-case time of your algorithm?

4S. Write an algorithm that receives a reference to the first node in a linked list and returns the number of elements in the list. What is the worst-case time of your algorithm?

5. Write an algorithm to append one linked list to another. For example, if the lists are $78, 80, 0, -3$ and $10, 20, -10$, after the algorithm executes, one list, $78, 80, 0, -3, 10, 20, -10$, results. You may modify only the *next* fields of the nodes. What is the worst-case time of your algorithm?

6. Write an algorithm to reverse a linked list. You may modify only the *next* fields of the nodes. What is the worst-case time of your algorithm?

7S. Write an algorithm to *merge* two linked lists. Assume that the data in each list are in nondecreasing order. The result is one linked list, containing all of the data, in nondecreasing order. You may modify only the *next* fields of the nodes. What is the worst-case time of your algorithm? For example, if the lists are $3, 6, 6, 10, 45, 45, 50$ and $2, 3, 55, 60$, after the merge, the result is $2, 3, 3, 6, 6, 10, 45, 45, 50, 55, 60$.

8. Write an algorithm to "intertwine" two linked lists containing equal numbers of elements. The result is a linked list whose first element is the first element of the first list, whose second element is the first element of the second list, whose third element is the second element of the first list, whose fourth element is the second element of the second list, and so on. You may modify only the *next* fields of the nodes. What is the worst-case time of your algorithm? For example, if the lists are $6, 3, 8, 1, 44$ and $9, -3, 10, 100, 54$, after intertwining, the result is

$$6, 9, 3, -3, 8, 10, 1, 100, 44, 54.$$

Exercises 9–11 ask for algorithms that manipulate a doubly-linked list. These algorithms should run in constant time. The node structure is that shown in Figure 3.3.5.

9S. Write an algorithm *init* that sets up an empty list. An empty list consists of two nodes, *head* and *tail*, for internal use; *head.next* references *tail*, and *tail.prev* references *head*.

10. Write an algorithm *insert* that inserts a node with a specified value before the node referenced by *pos*. (In particular, if *pos* references *tail*, *insert* inserts an item at the end of a possibly empty list.)

11. Write an algorithm *delete* that deletes the node referenced by *pos*.

12S. Implement a queue using a singly-linked list. Write *queue_init*, *empty*, *enqueue*, *dequeue*, and *front*.

13. Draw adjacency lists for the graph

14. Write an algorithm that constructs adjacency lists for a graph. The algorithm first uses the function *read(n)* to read a value for n, which signifies that the vertices are $1, 2, \ldots, n$. Assume that adj = new $node[n]$ constructs an array of *node* references (initialized to null) named *adj* of size n, indexed from 1 to n. Then, the algorithm repeatedly uses the function *read(i, j)* to read edges (i, j). The end of the list of edges is detected when *read* returns false.

A digraph can be represented using adjacency lists. In the array adj, adj[i] is a reference to the first node in a linked list of nodes representing edges of the form (i, j) (i.e., from i to j).

15S. Draw adjacency lists for the digraph

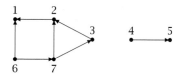

16. Write a $\Theta(m + n)$ algorithm that prints the indegree and outdegree of every vertex in an m-edge, n-vertex digraph, where the digraph is represented using adjacency lists.

3.4 Binary Trees

Binary Tree Traversals

In this subsection, we discuss basic algorithms for traversing binary trees: **preorder**, **inorder**, and **postorder**. In the following subsection, as an application we introduce **binary search trees**.

Recall (see Section 2.6) that a binary tree is a rooted tree in which each node has either no children, one child, or two children. If a node has one child, that child is designated as either a left child or a right child (but not both). If a node has two children, one child is designated a left child and the other a right child. When a binary tree is drawn (see Figure 3.4.1), a left child is drawn to the left and a right child is drawn to the right.

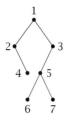

Figure 3.4.1 A binary tree.

To **traverse** a binary tree is to visit each node in the tree in some prescribed order. Depending on the application, "visit" may be interpreted in various ways. For example, if we want to print the data in each node in a binary tree, we would interpret "visit" as "print the data." The three most common traversal orders are preorder, inorder, and postorder. Each is most easily defined recursively. We begin with preorder.

Definition 3.4.1. *Preorder traversal* of a binary tree rooted at *root* is defined by the rules:

1. If *root* is empty, stop.

2. Visit *root*.

3. Execute preorder on the binary tree rooted at the left child of the root.

4. Execute preorder on the binary tree rooted at the right child of the root.

Example 3.4.2. Consider executing preorder on the binary tree in Figure 3.4.1.

Beginning with *root* = 1, we visit 1. We then execute preorder on the subtree rooted at 2 (i.e., the subtree rooted at 1's left child):

The order of visitation of this subtree is 2 (root), (no left subtree), 4 (right subtree). The overall order of visitation so far is $1, 2, 4$.

Since we have finished executing preorder on 1's left subtree, we next execute preorder on 1's right subtree:

You should verify that the order of visitation for this subtree is $3, 5, 6, 7$.

Therefore, the order of visitation for the tree in Figure 3.4.1 is

$$1, 2, 4, 3, 5, 6, 7. \qquad \square$$

The preorder algorithm is a direct translation of the definition of preorder (Definition 3.4.1). In specifying the algorithm, we assume that if v refers to an empty node, the value of v is the special value null. Also, if v refers to a nonempty node, $v.left$ refers to the left child of v, if v has a left child; otherwise, $v.left$ is equal to null. Similarly, if v refers to a nonempty node, $v.right$ refers to the right child of v, if v has a right child; otherwise, $v.right$ is equal to null.

Algorithm 3.4.3 Preorder. This algorithm performs a preorder traversal of the binary tree with root $root$.

Input Parameter: *root*
Output Parameters: None

```
preorder(root) {
   if (root != null) {
      // visit root
      preorder(root.left)
      preorder(root.right)
   }
}
```

We take as a measure of the time required to execute the preorder algorithm (Algorithm 3.4.3) the total number of times the line

```
if (root != null) {
```

is executed throughout all of the recursive calls. We can use induction to show that if a binary tree has n nodes, the preorder algorithm runs in time $\Theta(n)$.

Theorem 3.4.4. *If a binary tree has n nodes, the preorder algorithm (Algorithm 3.4.3) runs in time $\Theta(n)$.*

Proof. We use induction to prove that if a binary tree has n nodes, the line, which we subsequently call the *conditional line,*

```
if (root != null) {
```

is executed $2n + 1$ times, thus proving the theorem.

The proof is by induction on n. The basis step is $n = 0$. In this case, the conditional line is executed $1 = 2 \cdot 0 + 1$ time. This verifies the basis step.

Now assume that $n > 0$ and if a binary tree has $m < n$ nodes, the conditional line is executed $2m + 1$ times.

Let T be an n-node binary tree with root *root*. Suppose that T's left subtree contains n_l nodes and T's right subtree contains n_r nodes. When *preorder* is called with input *root*, first the line

> if (*root* != null) {

is executed, which accounts for one execution of the conditional line.

Next, *preorder* is called with input *root.left*. The tree rooted at *root.left* has $n_l < n$ nodes; so, by the inductive assumption, the conditional line is executed a total of $2n_l + 1$ times while processing T's left subtree. Similarly, the tree rooted at *root.right* has $n_r < n$ nodes; so, by the inductive assumption, the conditional line is executed a total of $2n_r + 1$ times while processing T's right subtree. The total number of times the conditional line is executed is, therefore,

$$1 + (2n_l + 1) + (2n_r + 1) = 2(n_l + n_r + 1) + 1 = 2n + 1.$$

The inductive step is complete.   ∎

As an application of the preorder algorithm, we adapt it to obtain an algorithm that counts the nodes in a binary tree. "Visit node" is interpreted as "count node."

Algorithm 3.4.5 Counting Nodes in a Binary Tree. This algorithm returns the number of nodes in the binary tree with root *root*.

Input Parameter: *root*
Output Parameters: None

```
count_nodes(root)
   if (root == null)
      return 0
   count = 1 // count root
   count = count + count_nodes(root.left) // add in nodes in left subtree
   count = count + count_nodes(root.right) // add in nodes in right subtree
   return count
}
```

By Theorem 3.4.4, Algorithm 3.4.5 runs in time $\Theta(n)$ when the input is an n-node binary tree.

Algorithm 3.4.5 could be more concisely written as

```
count_nodes(root)
   if (root == null)
      return 0
```

$$\text{return } 1 + count\_nodes(root.left) + count\_nodes(root.right)$$
}

We first wrote the algorithm in detail to illustrate a version derived from preorder.

Inorder and postorder traversal are like preorder traversal except for the position of the "visit" statement.

Definition 3.4.6. *Inorder traversal* of a binary tree rooted at *root* is defined by the rules:

1. If *root* is empty, stop.
2. Execute inorder on the binary tree rooted at the left child of the root.
3. Visit *root.*
4. Execute inorder on the binary tree rooted at the right child of the root.

Postorder traversal of a binary tree rooted at *root* is defined by the rules:

1. If *root* is empty, stop.
2. Execute postorder on the binary tree rooted at the left child of the root.
3. Execute postorder on the binary tree rooted at the right child of the root.
4. Visit *root.*

Example 3.4.7. Inorder visits the nodes of the binary tree in Figure 3.4.1 in the order

$$2, 4, 1, 6, 5, 7, 3. \qquad \square$$

Example 3.4.8. Postorder visits the nodes of the binary tree in Figure 3.4.1 in the order

$$4, 2, 6, 7, 5, 3, 1. \qquad \square$$

The inorder and postorder algorithms are modest perturbations of the preorder algorithm (Algorithm 3.4.3).

Algorithm 3.4.9 Inorder. This algorithm performs an inorder traversal of the binary tree with root *root.*

Input Parameter: *root*
Output Parameters: None

```
inorder(root) {
   if (root != null) {
      inorder(root.left)
      // visit root
      inorder(root.right)
   }
}
```

Algorithm 3.4.10 Postorder. This algorithm performs a postorder traversal of the binary tree with root *root*.

    Input Parameter: *root*
Output Parameters: None

```
postorder(root) {
    if (root != null) {
        postorder(root.left)
        postorder(root.right)
        // visit root
    }
}
```

The proof of Theorem 3.4.4 can be adapted to prove that both inorder and postorder run in time $\Theta(n)$ when the input is an n-node binary tree (see Exercises 1 and 2).

Binary Search Trees

In a **binary search tree**, data are stored in the nodes. Data items can be compared; that is, $<$, $\leq$, and so on, are defined on the data. The data are placed in a binary search tree so that, for every node v, each data item in v's left subtree, if any, is less than or equal to the data item in v, and each data item in v's right subtree, if any, is greater than or equal to the data item in v.

Example 3.4.11. Figure 3.4.2 shows a binary search tree containing the data

OLD PROGRAMMERS NEVER DIE THEY JUST LOSE THEIR MEMORIES

Data item x is less than data item y if $x < y$ in lexicographic (i.e., dictionary) order. By inspection, we see that for every node v, each data item in v's left subtree is less than or equal to the data item in v, and each data item in v's right subtree is greater than or equal to the data item in v. For example, the left subtree of PROGRAMMERS contains OLD, and OLD < PROGRAMMERS. The right subtree of PROGRAMMERS contains THEIR and THEY, and THEIR > PROGRAMMERS and THEY > PROGRAMMERS. □

The same data can be placed in many different ways in a binary search tree (except in an empty or one-node tree). For example, Figure 3.4.3 shows the same data as in Figure 3.4.2 arranged in a different way in a binary search tree.

If we run the inorder algorithm on a binary search tree and interpret "visit node" as "print the contents of the node," the data are printed in nondecreasing order. We leave the formal specification of the algorithm as an exercise (see Exercise 15). Since the inorder algorithm runs in linear time, printing the data in nondecreasing order also runs in linear time.

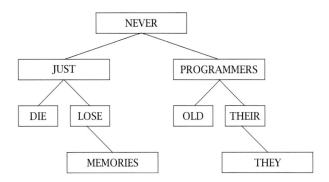

Figure 3.4.2 A binary search tree.

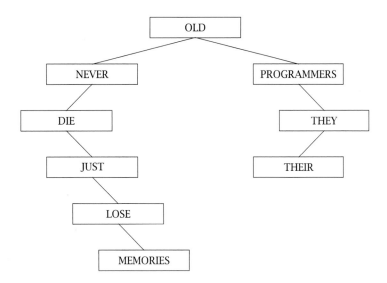

Figure 3.4.3 The data of Figure 3.4.2 arranged in a different way in a binary search tree.

Theorem 3.4.12. *When the inorder algorithm (Algorithm 3.4.9) is run on a binary search tree and "visit node" means to print the contents of the node, the data are printed in nondecreasing order.*

Proof. The proof is by induction on the number n of nodes in the binary search tree. The basis step is $n = 0$, and its truth is self-evident.

Now suppose when *inorder* is run on a binary search tree that contains less than $n > 0$ nodes, the data are printed in nondecreasing order. Let T be an n-node binary search tree, $n > 0$. Let T_1 and T_2 be the left and right subtrees, respectively, of T. When *inorder* executes with input T, it is first called recursively on T_1. Since T_1 has fewer nodes than T, by the inductive assumption the data in T_1 are printed in nondecreasing order. Next, *inorder* prints the contents of T's root. Since T is a binary search tree, each data item in T_1 is less than or equal to the contents of T's root; thus, the items printed to this point are in nondecreasing order. Finally, *inorder* is called recursively on T_2. Since T_2 has fewer nodes than T, by the inductive assumption the data in T_2 are printed in nondecreasing order. Since T is a binary search tree, each data item in T_2 is greater than or equal to the contents of T's root; thus, the data items in T are printed in nondecreasing order. The inductive step is complete.   ■

Example 3.4.13. When *inorder* is run on either of the binary search trees in Figures 3.4.2 or 3.4.3, the output is

DIE JUST LOSE MEMORIES NEVER OLD PROGRAMMERS THEIR THEY   □

We can construct a binary search tree by repeatedly inserting data items into an initially empty tree. To insert an item, say *val*, we begin at the root. If the tree is empty, we construct a node, which becomes the root, and store *val* in the node. If the tree is not empty, we compare *val* with the data item in the root, say *root_val*. If *val* ≤ *root_val*, *val* should be placed in the root's left subtree. Therefore, if the root has no left child, we create one and insert *val* into it. If the root has a left child, we recursively insert *val* in the root's left subtree. If *val* > *root_val*, we proceed similarly. If the root has no right child, we create one and insert *val* into it. If the root has a right child, we recursively insert *val* in the root's right subtree.

Algorithm 3.4.14 Inserting Into a Binary Search Tree. This algorithm inserts the value *val* into a binary search tree with root *root*. If the tree is empty, *root* = null. The algorithm returns the root of the tree containing the added item. We assume that

new *node*

creates a new node with data field *data* and reference fields *left* and *right*.

Input Parameters: *root*, *val*
Output Parameters: None

```
BSTinsert(root, val) {
    // set up node to be added to tree
    temp = new node
    temp.data = val
    temp.left = temp.right = null
    if (root == null) // special case: empty tree
        return temp
    BSTinsert_recurs(root, temp)
    return root
}
```

```
BSTinsert_recurs(root, temp) {
  if (temp.data ≤ root.data)
    if (root.left == null)
      root.left == temp
    else
      BSTinsert_recurs(root.left, temp)
  else
    if (root.right == null)
      root.right == temp
    else
      BSTinsert_recurs(root.right, temp)
}
```

In the worst case, the insert algorithm (Algorithm 3.4.14) traces a path from the root to a node at the lowest level of the tree; therefore, the worst-case time is $\Theta(h)$, where h is the height of the tree.

An algorithm to search for a particular data item in a binary search tree can be constructed similarly to the insert algorithm (Algorithm 3.4.14) and is left as an exercise (see Exercise 17).

We conclude this section by discussing an algorithm to delete a node N from a binary search tree. If N has no children, deletion is straightforward; we simply delete N (see Figure 3.4.4). If N has exactly one child, we replace N by N's child (see Figure 3.4.5). The case in which N has two children is more

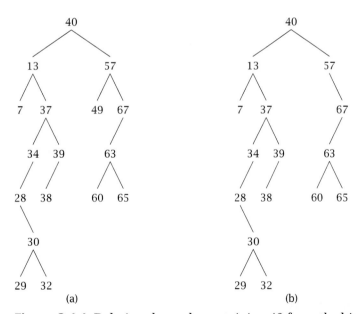

Figure 3.4.4 Deleting the node containing 49 from the binary search tree in (a). Since the node containing 49 has no children, we simply remove it. The result is the tree shown in (b).

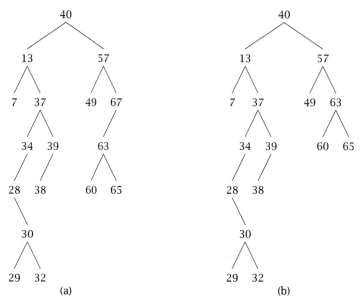

Figure 3.4.5 Deleting the node containing 67 from the binary search tree in (a). Since 67 has exactly one child, we replace the node containing 67 by 67's child. The result is the tree shown in (b).

complicated. In this case, we first locate a node M containing a minimum data item in N's right subtree (see Figure 3.4.6). We will show that we can ensure that M has no left child. We then replace N's data item with M's data item. Since M's data item is a smallest value, this transformation yields a binary search tree. Finally, we replace M by M's right child.

We first write an algorithm, which handles the first two cases—deleting a node with no children or exactly one child (Figures 3.4.4 and 3.4.5). We call the algorithm *replace* since it replaces the deleted node with its child (interpreted as null when there is no child).

Algorithm 3.4.15 Deleting from a Binary Search Tree, Special Case. This algorithm deletes the node referenced by *ref* from a binary search tree with root *root*. The node referenced by *ref* has zero children or exactly one child. We assume that each node N in the tree has a parent field, N.*parent*. If N is the root, N.*parent* is null. The algorithm returns the root of the tree that results from deleting the node.

    Input Parameters: *root, ref*
    Output Parameters: None

```
BSTreplace(root, ref) {
    // set child to ref's child, or null, if no child
    if (ref.left == null)
        child = ref.right
```

```
    else
        child = ref.left
    if (ref == root) {
        if (child != null)
            child.parent = null
        return child
    }
    if (ref.parent.left == ref) // is ref left child?
        ref.parent.left = child
    else
        ref.parent.right = child
    if (child != null)
        child.parent = ref.parent
    return root
}
```

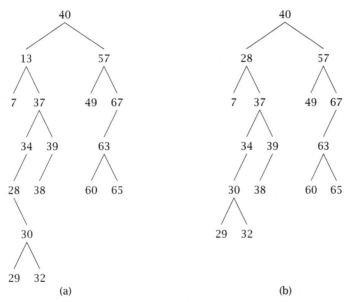

(a)   (b)

Figure 3.4.6 Deleting 13 from the binary search tree in (a). We first locate the node containing the minimum data item, 28, in 13's right subtree. Notice that 28 has no left child. We then replace 13 by 28. Finally, we replace the node containing 28 by its child (30). The result is the tree shown in (b).

Algorithm 3.4.15 runs in constant time.

We now write the general algorithm to delete from a binary search tree. Algorithm 3.4.15 takes care of the case in which the node to delete has zero or one children. The remaining case is that in which the node *N* to delete has two children (Figure 3.4.6). In this case, we first locate a node *M* containing a minimum data item in *N*'s right subtree. We can find such a node by moving to N's right child and then repeatedly moving to a left child until we reach a node M without a left child. We then replace N's data with M's data and delete node M using Algorithm 3.4.15.

Algorithm 3.4.16 Deleting from a Binary Search Tree. This algorithm deletes the node referenced by *ref* from a binary search tree with root *root*. We assume that each node N in the tree has a parent field, $N.parent$. If N is the root, $N.parent$ is null. The algorithm returns the root of the tree that results from deleting the node.

>   Input Parameters: *root, ref*
>   Output Parameters: None

BSTdelete(*root, ref*) {
    // if zero or one children, use Algorithm 3.4.15
    if (*ref.left* == null || *ref.right* == null)
       return *BSTreplace*(*root, ref*)
    // find node *succ* containing a minimum data item in *ref*'s right subtree
    succ = *ref.right*
    while (*succ.left* != null)
       succ = *succ.left*
    // "move" *succ* to *ref*, thus deleting *ref*
    ref.data = *succ.data*
    // delete *succ*
    return *BSTreplace*(*root, succ*)
}

All statements in Algorithm 3.4.16, except for the while loop, execute in constant time. In the worst case, the while loop traces a path from the root to a node at the lowest level of the tree; therefore, the worst-case time of Algorithm 3.4.16 is $\Theta(h)$, where h is the height of the tree.

Exercises

1S. Prove that inorder runs in time $\Theta(n)$ when the input is an n-node binary tree.

2. Prove that postorder runs in time $\Theta(n)$ when the input is an n-node binary tree.

3. Write a linear-time algorithm that swaps the left and right children of each node in a binary tree. For example, if the original tree is

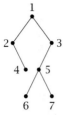

after the algorithm executes, the tree becomes

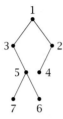

4S. Write an algorithm that returns the number of terminal nodes in a binary tree.

5. Prove that the algorithm

```
funnyorder(root) {
    if (root != null) {
        // visit root
        funnyorder(root.right)
        funnyorder(root.left)
    }
}
```

visits the nodes in the reverse order of postorder.

6. A *binary expression tree* is a binary tree in which the internal nodes represent binary operators and the terminal nodes represent values (or variables that contain values). An operator operates on its left and right subtrees. For example, the binary expression tree

represents the expression $(3 + 1) * (4 - 5)$. Write a postorder algorithm that prints the data in a binary expression tree.

WWW The postorder output of a binary expression tree is said to be in *reverse Polish notation* (*RPN*). Reverse Polish notation does not require parentheses or rules about operator precedence; it is unambiguous as written. The

Polish logician, Jan Łukasiwicz (1878–1956), introduced parenthesis-free notation. Some calculators (e.g., Hewlett Packard calculators) use RPN; so, for example, to compute $3 * 4$, you enter 3, then enter 4, and then push the $*$ key. The PostScript language, which is used to print text and graphics (this book is an example), also uses RPN.

7S. Write an algorithm, based on inorder traversal, whose input is a binary expression tree (see the preceding exercise) and whose output is a fully-parenthesized version of the expression in which the operators appear between the operands. ("Fully-parenthesized" means that there is one pair of parentheses for each operator.) For example, if the input is the expression tree of the preceding exercise, the output is $((3 + 1) * (4 - 5))$.

8. Trace *BSTinsert*, Algorithm 3.4.14, when 20 is inserted in the binary search tree in Figure 3.4.4(a).

9. Trace *BSTinsert*, Algorithm 3.4.14, when 95 is inserted in the binary search tree in Figure 3.4.4(a).

10S. Trace *BSTinsert*, Algorithm 3.4.14, when 10 is inserted in the binary search tree in Figure 3.4.4(a).

11. Trace *BSTdelete*, Algorithm 3.4.16, when 7 is deleted from the binary search tree in Figure 3.4.4(a).

12. Trace *BSTdelete*, Algorithm 3.4.16, when 28 is deleted from the binary search tree in Figure 3.4.4(a).

13S. Trace *BSTdelete*, Algorithm 3.4.16, when 57 is deleted from the binary search tree in Figure 3.4.4(a).

14. Trace *BSTdelete*, Algorithm 3.4.16, when 40 is deleted from the binary search tree in Figure 3.4.4(a).

15. Write an inorder algorithm that prints the data in a binary search tree.

16S. Write a nonrecursive version of Algorithm 3.4.14 (inserting in a binary search tree).

17. Write an algorithm to search for a particular item in a binary search tree. The worst-case time must be $\Theta(h)$, where h is the height of the tree. If the item is found, the algorithm returns a reference to the location where it was found. If the item is not found, the algorithm returns null.

18. True or false? Explain. If T is a binary tree in which, for every node v, the data item in v's left child is less than or equal to the data item in v, and the data item in v's right child is greater than or equal to the data item in v, then T is a binary search tree.

19S. Write a linear-time algorithm that determines whether a binary tree is a binary search tree.

3.5 Priority Queues, Binary Heaps, and Heapsort

Priority Queues

The abstract data type known as a **priority queue** allows us to insert an item with a specified priority (given by a number) and to delete an item having the *highest* priority. For example, if we are processing jobs with specified priorities and there is a single processor available, as the jobs arrive we can insert them into a priority queue. When the processor becomes available, we can delete a job from the priority queue—which, by definition, has the highest priority—and process it.

In the discussion that follows, we list only the priority of an item. In practice, a data item has other attributes besides its priority (e.g., an identification number, time started, time stopped).

Example 3.5.1. Suppose that items with the priorities

$$57, 32, 100, 56, 44$$

are inserted into an initially empty priority queue. If we delete an item from the priority queue, 100 will be removed, regardless of the order in which the items were inserted, because the highest priority is 100. The priority queue contains

$$57, 32, 56, 44.$$

If we delete another item from the priority queue, 57 will be removed since it now has the highest priority. The priority queue contains

$$32, 56, 44.$$

If we now insert 37, the priority queue contains

$$32, 56, 44, 37.$$

If we delete another item from the priority queue, 56 will be removed since it now has the highest priority. The priority queue contains

$$32, 44, 37. \qquad \square$$

Consider implementing a priority queue using an array. If an item is inserted by putting it at the end of the array, insertion takes time $\Theta(1)$. To delete an item, we must first locate the item having the greatest priority. Since the items are in no particular order, we would have to scan all the items to find one having the largest priority. Scanning an n-element array takes time $\Theta(n)$. After finding an item having the largest priority, we then have to remove it. This entails shifting all items to its right one cell to the left, which takes time $O(n)$. Thus, deletion always takes time $\Theta(n)$.

When using a priority queue, we typically perform many insertions and deletions. Suppose, for example, that we perform n insertions and n deletions in an initially empty priority queue. Since each insertion takes constant time, the total time for the insertions is $\Theta(n)$. The time for a deletion is $O(n)$ and, since we perform n deletions, the total time for the deletions is $O(n^2)$. The time for deletions dominates. Thus, the total time to perform n insertions and n deletions in an initially empty priority queue is $O(n^2)$. This estimate is sharp. In the worst case, performing n insertions and n deletions takes time $\Theta(n^2)$ (see Exercise 3).

Suppose that we still implement a priority queue using an array, but we maintain nondecreasing order. Now, when we insert an item, we first have to determine where it should be inserted to maintain nondecreasing order. If the item is to be inserted in the cell at index i, for each $j \geq i$ we will have to shift the item in the cell at index j to the cell at index $j + 1$ to make room for the inserted item. In the worst case (when the item to be inserted is smaller than all the others), all items have to move. Moving all items in an n-element array takes time $\Theta(n)$. We can determine where to insert the item by scanning all the items, which takes time $\Theta(n)$. Thus, in the worst case, insertion takes time $\Theta(n)$. [Using binary search (see Section 4.1), we can determine where to insert the item in time $O(\lg n)$. However, in the worst case, moving the items still takes time $\Theta(n)$; so, binary search does not improve the asymptotic worst-case time of the insertion algorithm.] Deleting an item takes time $\Theta(1)$, since the item with largest priority is at the end of the array.

Again, suppose that we perform n insertions and n deletions in an initially empty priority queue. Since each deletion takes constant time, the total time for the deletions is $\Theta(n)$. The time for an insertion is $O(n)$ and, since we perform n insertions, the total time for the insertions is $O(n^2)$. The time for insertions dominates. Thus, the total time to perform n insertions and n deletions in an initially empty priority queue is $O(n^2)$. This estimate is sharp. In the worst case, performing n insertions and n deletions takes time $\Theta(n^2)$ (see Exercise 4).

The two proposed ways to implement a priority queue represent the extremes of data organization and times for inserting and deleting. In the first implementation, the array is not sorted, insertion takes time $\Theta(1)$, and deletion takes time $O(n)$. In the second implementation, the array is sorted, insertion takes time $O(n)$, and deletion takes time $\Theta(1)$. For both implementations, in the worst case performing n insertions and n deletions takes time $\Theta(n^2)$. We can use a **heap** to maintain a "weak order," an organization that is not completely sorted but is not random either. By doing so, we can perform both insertions and deletions in time $O(\lg n)$. Thus, performing n insertions and n deletions takes time $O(n \lg n)$, which, in the worst case, is better than either of the other implementations.

Heaps

We begin by defining a *heap structure*.

Definition 3.5.2. A *heap structure* is a binary tree in which all levels, except possibly the last (bottom) level, have as many nodes as possible. On the last level, all of the nodes are at the left.

Example 3.5.3. Figure 3.5.1 shows a heap structure. Levels 0 (the root), 1, and 2 (the next-to-last level) have as many nodes as possible. On level 3 (the last level), all of the nodes are at the left.

Level

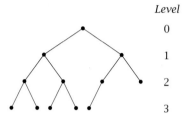

0

1

2

3

Figure 3.5.1 A heap structure. All levels, except the last level, 3, have as many nodes as possible. On the last level, all of the nodes are at the left. □

Definition 3.5.4. A *binary minheap* is a heap structure in which values are assigned to the nodes so that the value of each node is less than or equal to the values of its children (if any). A *binary maxheap* is a heap structure in which values are assigned to the nodes so that the value of each node is greater than or equal to the values of its children (if any).

Throughout the remainder of this section, we will discuss binary maxheaps and abbreviate "binary maxheap" to "heap." (The algorithms for manipulating minheaps are similar to those for manipulating maxheaps.)

Example 3.5.5. Figure 3.5.2 shows a heap. The value of each node is greater than or equal to the values of its children (if any).

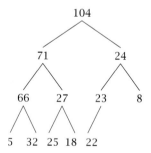

Figure 3.5.2 A heap. The value of each node is greater than or equal to the values of its children (if any). For example, the value 24 is greater than or equal to the values of the children, 23 and 8. □

A heap is "weakly sorted" in the sense that the values along a path from the root to a terminal node are in nonincreasing order. For example, in Figure 3.5.2 the values 104, 71, 66, 5, along the path from the root to the terminal node with value 5, are in nonincreasing order. At the same time, the values along a *level* are, in general, in no particular order. For example, in Figure 3.5.2 the values 5, 32, 25, 18, 22 on level 3 are in neither nonincreasing nor nondecreasing order. (See also Exercise 21.)

In a heap, the maximum value is at the root. Thus, if we implement a priority queue using a heap, the item with highest priority is at the root. In order to use a heap to implement a priority queue, we must represent the heap. We do so using an array! We number the nodes level by level, left to right, starting at the root. In Figure 3.5.3, we have numbered the nodes in the heap structure of Figure 3.5.1.

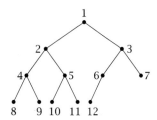

Figure 3.5.3 A heap structure with the nodes numbered level by level, left to right, starting at the root.

To represent a heap, we store the value in node number i in cell i of an array. In Figure 3.5.4, we represent the heap of Figure 3.5.2 as an array.

104	71	24	66	27	23	8	5	32	25	18	22
1	2	3	4	5	6	7	8	9	10	11	12

Figure 3.5.4 The heap of Figure 3.5.2 as an array. The value in node number i is stored in cell i of the array.

It is apparent from Figure 3.5.3 that the parent of node i, assuming that the node is not the root, is $\lfloor i/2 \rfloor$. Also, the left child of node i, assuming that the node has a left child, is $2 * i$, and the right child of node i, assuming that the node has a right child, is $2 * i + 1$. We will use these formulas in our subsequent heap algorithms.

In order to implement a priority queue as a heap, we must write algorithms to return the largest value in the heap, to delete the largest value from a heap, and to insert an arbitrary value into a heap. Returning the largest value in the heap is straightforward since the largest value is at the root.

Algorithm 3.5.6 Largest. This algorithm returns the largest value in a heap. The array v represents the heap.

    Input Parameter: v
Output Parameters: None

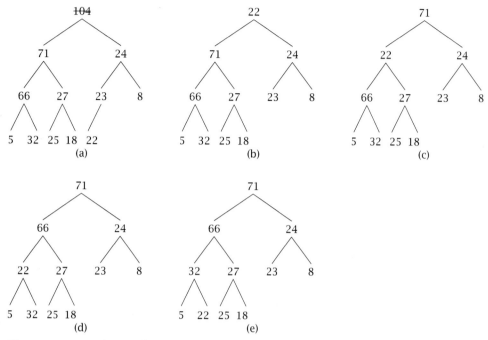

Figure 3.5.5 Deleting from a heap. The root, which contains the largest value, 104, is to be deleted [see (a)]. To maintain a heap structure, we move the value at the bottom level, farthest right, 22, to the root [see (b)]. The root is not greater than or equal to its children; so, we swap the root's value, 22, with the largest child, 71, [see (c)]. The node with value 22 is not greater than or equal to its children; so, we again swap 22 with the largest child, 66, [see (d)]. Again, the node with value 22 is not greater than or equal to its children; so, we again swap 22 with the largest child, 32, [see (e)]. Since 22 now has no children, the algorithm terminates. The structure shown in (e) is a heap.

```
heap_largest(v) {
    return v[1]
}
```

Algorithm 3.5.6 runs in constant time.

We next discuss the delete algorithm, whose implementation is shown in Figure 3.5.5. Before writing the delete algorithm, we write a separate algorithm to repeatedly swap a value with the larger child. We allow the operation to begin at an arbitrary node rather than at the root as in Figure 3.5.5, since we will need this more general version later. Thus, we assume that v is an array representing a heap structure indexed from 1 to n. We further assume that the left subtree of node i is a heap and the right subtree of node i is also a heap [see Figure 3.5.6(a)]. After $siftdown(v, i, n)$ is called, the subtree rooted at i is a heap [see Figure 3.5.6(b)]. To make the algorithm more efficient, we do not actually swap values; rather, we copy the value $v[i]$ to a temporary variable and repeatedly move the larger child up, if necessary.

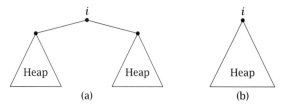

Figure 3.5.6 The siftdown algorithm. Initially, the left and right subtrees of node i are heaps [see (a)]. After *siftdown* is called, the subtree rooted at i is a heap [see (b)].

After locating the cell where $v[i]$ goes, we copy it to that cell.

Algorithm 3.5.7 Siftdown. The array v represents a heap structure indexed from 1 to n. The left and right subtrees of node i are heaps. After

$$siftdown(v, i, n)$$

is called, the subtree rooted at i is a heap.

  Input Parameters: v, i, n
Output Parameter: v

```
siftdown(v, i, n) {
    temp = v[i]
    // 2 * i ≤ n tests for a left child
    while (2 * i ≤ n) {
        child = 2 * i
        // if there is a right child and it is bigger than the left child, move child
        if (child < n && v[child + 1] > v[child])
            child = child + 1
        // move child up?
        if (v[child] > temp)
            v[i] = v[child]
        else
            break // exit while loop
        i = child
    }
    // insert original v[i] in correct spot
    v[i] = temp
}
```

In the worst case, the variable i in Algorithm 3.5.7 travels all the way from the root to the last level; thus, in the worst-case, the while loop in Algorithm 3.5.7 executes $\Theta(h)$ times, where h is the height of the subtree rooted at i. We show that if the subtree rooted at i has m nodes, $h = \lfloor \lg m \rfloor$; thus, the worst-case time of Algorithm 3.5.7 is $\Theta(\lg m)$.

Theorem 3.5.8. *The height of a heap structure containing m nodes is $\lfloor \lg m \rfloor$.*

Proof. Suppose that a heap structure containing m nodes has height $h > 0$. Then, level i, $i < h$, contains the maximum number of nodes 2^i (see Figure 3.5.1). Thus, levels 0 through $h - 1$ contain

$$2^0 + 2^1 + \cdots + 2^{h-1} = 2^h - 1$$

nodes. (We have used the formula for the geometric sum; see Example 2.2.2.) Level h contains 1 to 2^h nodes. Thus, m satisfies

$$(2^h - 1) + 1 \le m \le (2^h - 1) + 2^h = 2^{h+1} - 1$$

or

$$2^h \le m < 2^{h+1}.$$

Notice that the last inequality is also true if $h = 0$. Taking the logarithm to the base 2 of each expression in the last inequality yields

$$h \le \lg m < h + 1.$$

Therefore,

$$h = \lfloor \lg m \rfloor. \qquad \blacksquare$$

We now write the delete algorithm.

Algorithm 3.5.9 Delete. This algorithm deletes the root (the item with largest value) from a heap containing n elements. The array v represents the heap.

Input Parameters: v, n
Output Parameters: v, n

```
heap_delete(v, n) {
    v[1] = v[n]
    n = n - 1
    siftdown(v, 1, n)
}
```

When the input is a heap structure of size n, *siftdown* runs in time $\Theta(\lg n)$ in the worst case; therefore, the worst-case time of *heap_delete* is $\Theta(\lg n)$.

We turn next to the insert algorithm, whose implementation is shown in Figure 3.5.7. As in the delete algorithm, we do not actually swap values in the insert algorithm; rather we repeatedly move the parent down, if necessary. After locating the cell where the added value goes, we copy it to that cell.

Algorithm 3.5.10 Insert. This algorithm inserts the value *val* into a heap containing n elements. The array v represents the heap.

Input Parameters: val, v, n
Output Parameters: v, n

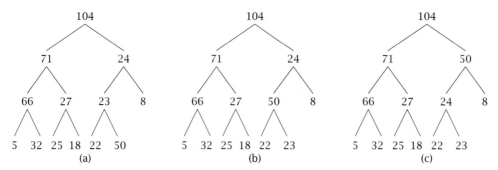

Figure 3.5.7 Inserting the value 50 into the heap in Figure 3.5.2. To maintain a heap structure, the value added, 50, is inserted in the bottom level, farthest left [see (a)]. (If the bottom level were full, we would begin another level at the left.) Since 50 is larger than its parent, we swap 50 with its parent [see (b)]. Again 50 is larger than its parent; so, we again swap 50 with its parent [see (c)]. This time 50 is not larger than its parent, so the insert algorithm terminates.

$heap\_insert(val, v, n)$ {
    $i = n = n + 1$
    // i is the child and $i/2$ is the parent.
    // If $i > 1$, i is not the root.
    while ($i > 1$ && $val > v[i/2]$) {
        $v[i] = v[i/2]$
        $i = i/2$
    }
    $v[i] = val$
}

Suppose that we use Algorithm 3.5.10 to insert into a heap containing n elements. In the worst case, the value added travels all the way from last level to the root; thus, the worst-case time of Algorithm 3.5.10 is $\Theta(h)$, where h is the height of the tree, which now contains $n + 1$ elements. By Theorem 3.5.8, the height of the tree is $\lfloor \lg(n + 1) \rfloor$. Therefore, the worst-case time of Algorithm 3.5.10 is $\Theta(\lg n)$.

Suppose that we have an array of n elements that we want to organize into a heap. We could use Algorithm 3.5.10 to insert the elements one at a time into an initially empty heap. Since each insertion takes time $O(\lg n)$, the total time is $O(n \lg n)$. This estimate is sharp; that is, the worst-case time to construct a heap in this way is $\Theta(n \lg n)$ (see Exercise 25). We can do better by repeatedly using *siftdown* (Algorithm 3.5.7).

Example 3.5.11. Consider the problem of organizing the data shown in Figure 3.5.8(a) into a heap. Notice that the left and right subtrees of the parent having the largest index 4 are trivially heaps. Thus we may call *siftdown* on node 4. The result is shown in Figure 3.5.8(b).

The left and right subtrees of the node having the next largest index, 3, are heaps. Thus we may call *siftdown* on node 3. The result is shown in Figure 3.5.8(c).

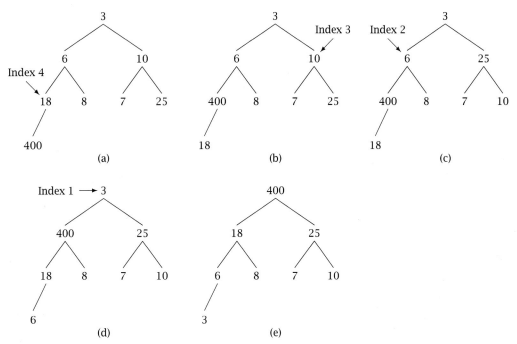

Figure 3.5.8 Making a heap. The input is shown in (a). *siftdown* is first called on the parent having the largest index, 4. The result is shown in (b). *siftdown* is next called on the node having the next largest index, 3. The result is shown in (c). *siftdown* is next called on the node having the next largest index, 2. The result is shown in (d). Finally, *siftdown* is called on the root. The result, shown in (e), is a heap.

Now the left and right subtrees of the node having the next largest index, 2, are heaps. Thus we may call *siftdown* on node 2. The result is shown in Figure 3.5.8(d).

Finally, the left and right subtrees of the root are heaps. Thus we may call *siftdown* on node 1. The result, shown in Figure 3.5.8(e), is a heap. □

We state the algorithm to make a heap as Algorithm 3.5.12.

Algorithm 3.5.12 Heapify. This algorithm rearranges the data in the array v, indexed from 1 to n, so that it represents a heap.

Input Parameters: v, n
Output Parameters: v

heapify(v, n) {
    // $n/2$ is the index of the parent of the last node
    for $i = n/2$ downto 1
       siftdown(v, i, n)
}

We show that Algorithm 3.5.12 runs in linear time.

Theorem 3.5.13. *The time for Algorithm 3.5.12 is* $\Theta(n)$.

Proof. The time for Algorithm 3.5.12 is bounded by the worst-case time of all of the calls to *siftdown*.

There is one node on level 0, namely the root. The worst-case time for this call to *siftdown* (counting iterations of *siftdown*'s while loop) is h, where $h = \lfloor \lg n \rfloor$ is the height of the tree.

There are two nodes on level 1; so, the worst-case time for these two calls is $2(h-1)$.

In general, on level i, $i < h$, there are 2^i nodes; so, the worst-case time for these 2^i calls is bounded by $2^i(h-i)$. [*siftdown* may not be called on all nodes on level $h-1$ (see Figure 3.5.8); however, its worst-case time is bounded by $2^{h-1} \cdot 1$.] It follows that the time of Algorithm 3.5.12 is bounded by

$$\sum_{i=0}^{h-1} 2^i(h-i).$$

Now

$$\sum_{i=0}^{h-1} 2^i(h-i) = \sum_{i=1}^{h} 2^{h-i}i = 2^h \sum_{i=1}^{h} \frac{i}{2^i}.$$

Taking $r = 1/2$ in Theorem 2.2.3, we obtain

$$\sum_{i=1}^{h} \frac{i}{2^i} < 2.$$

Therefore,

$$2^h \sum_{i=1}^{h} \frac{i}{2^i} < 2^h \cdot 2 = 2^{\lfloor \lg n \rfloor} \cdot 2 \le 2^{\lg n} \cdot 2 = 2n,$$

and the time for Algorithm 3.5.12 is $O(n)$.

On the other hand, the for loop in Algorithm 3.5.12 executes $\Theta(n)$ times; so, the time for Algorithm 3.5.12 is $\Omega(n)$. Therefore, the time for Algorithm 3.5.12 is $\Theta(n)$. ∎

Indirect Heaps

In some applications (see, e.g., Sections 7.3 and 7.4), we need to modify a value in a heap. To specify which element to modify, we provide its index. The problem is that in the current implementation, the indexes of the various values change. In order to modify a value in a heap efficiently, we maintain an array of values, *key*, which does not change unless a *value* (as opposed to the *index* of a value) in the heap is modified. For example, the siftdown algorithm would not modify *key*. We then maintain two additional arrays: *into*[i], whose value is the index in the heap structure where *key*[i] is found; and *outof*[j], whose value is the index in *key* where the value of node j in

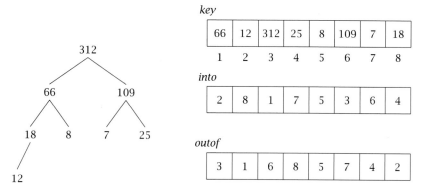

Figure 3.5.9 An indirect heap. The heap structure is shown at the left. The *key* array stores the values contained in the heap structure. The value $key[i]$ is stored at index $into[i]$ in the heap structure. For example, the value $25 = key[4]$ is stored at index $into[4] = 7$ in the heap structure. The value at index j in the heap structure is at index $outof[j]$ in the *key* array. For example, the value, 18, at index 4 in the heap structure is at index $outof[4] = 8$ in the *key* array. Notice that *into* and *outof* are inverses of each other in the sense that $into[outof[j]] = j$ for all j, and $outof[into[i]] = i$ for all i.

the heap structure is found (see Figure 3.5.9). Such a structure is sometimes called an **indirect heap**.

Example 3.5.14. As an example of manipulating an indirect heap, we show how to swap the value 66 at index 2 and the value 18 at index 4 in the indirect heap in Figure 3.5.9.

In Figure 3.5.9, $outof[2] = 1$ gives the index of 66 in the *key* array, and $outof[4] = 8$ gives the index of 18 in the *key* array. These values in *outof* must be swapped:

$temp = outof[2]$
$outof[2] = outof[4]$
$outof[4] = temp$

The changes are shown in Figure 3.5.10 (next page).

Similarly, the *into* values must also be swapped:

$temp = into[outof[2]]$
$into[outof[2]] = into[outof[4]]$
$into[outof[4]] = temp$

(see Figure 3.5.10). □

Consider writing an *increase* algorithm. The input is an index into the *key* array, which specifies the value to be increased, and the replacement value. The algorithm is illustrated in Figure 3.5.11.

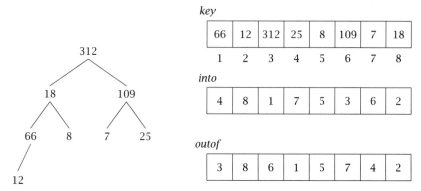

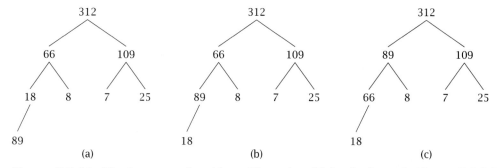

Figure 3.5.10 The heap structure of Figure 3.5.9 after swapping the value 66 at index 2 and the value 18 at index 4. The values *outof* [2] and *outof* [4] are swapped as are the corresponding *into* values, *into*[*outof* [2]] and *into*[*outof* [4]].

(a)　　　　　　　(b)　　　　　　　(c)

Figure 3.5.11 The increase algorithm. The value 12 in the heap in Figure 3.5.9 is to be increased to 89 [see (a)]. Since 89 is larger than its parent (18), 18 must move down [see (b)]. Again, 89 is larger than its parent (66), so 66 must move down [see (c)]. This time 89 is not larger than its parent (312); thus, the heap is restored and the increase algorithm terminates.

Algorithm 3.5.15 Increase. This algorithm increases a value in an indirect heap and then restores the heap. The input is an index i into the *key* array, which specifies the value to be increased, and the replacement value *newval*.

Input Parameters:　*i, newval*
Output Parameters:　None

```
increase(i, newval) {
    key[i] = newval
    // p is the parent index in the heap structure
    // c is the child index in the heap structure
    c = into[i]
```

```
    p = c/2
    while (p ≥ 1) {
        if (key[outof[p]] ≥ newval)
            break // exit while loop
        // move value at p down to c
        outof[c] = outof[p]
        into[outof[c]] = c
        // move p and c up
        c = p
        p = c/2
    }
    // "put" newval in heap structure at index c
    outof[c] = i
    into[i] = c
}
```

The worst-case time of Algorithm 3.5.15 occurs when the value to be increased is at the bottom of the heap and migrates to the root. In this case, the while loop iterates h times, where h is the height of the heap. By Theorem 3.5.8, $h = \lfloor \lg n \rfloor$; thus, the worst-case time of Algorithm 3.5.15 is $\Theta(\lg n)$, where n is the number of items in the heap.

We leave the details of implementing other heap algorithms, when the heap is implemented as an indirect heap, to the exercises (see Exercises 27–32).

Heapsort

Figure 3.5.12 shows how a heap can be used to sort an array. The algorithm that results is called **heapsort**. We write it as Algorithm 3.5.16.

Algorithm 3.5.16 Heapsort. This algorithm sorts the array $v[1], \ldots, v[n]$ in nondecreasing order. It uses the siftdown and heapify algorithms (Algorithms 3.5.7 and 3.5.12).

```
Input Parameters:   v, n
Output Parameter:   v

heapsort(v, n) {
    // make v into a heap
    heapify(v, n)
    for i = n downto 2 {
        // v[1] is the largest among v[1], ..., v[i].
        // Put it in the correct cell.
        swap(v[1], v[i])
        // Heap is now at indexes 1 through i − 1.
        // Restore heap.
        siftdown(v, 1, i − 1)
    }
}
```

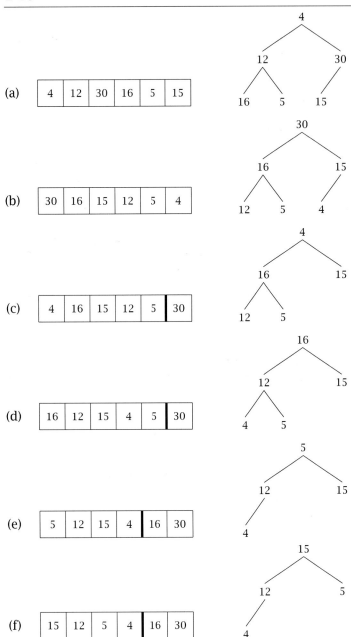

Figure 3.5.12 The first steps in the heapsort algorithm. The input array is considered a heap structure [see (a)]. First, *heapify* is called [see (b)]. The largest element, at index 1, is swapped with the last element; and the elements, except the last, are considered a heap structure [see (c)]. Next, *siftdown* is called [see (d)]. The second-largest element, at index 1, is swapped with the next-to-last element; and the elements, except the last two, are considered a heap structure [see (e)]. Again, *siftdown* is called [see (f)]. The process is repeated until the array is sorted.

In the heapsort algorithm, the call to *heapify* takes time $\Theta(n)$. Each call to *siftdown* takes time $O(\lg n)$. Since the calls to *siftdown* are in a for loop that runs in time $\Theta(n)$, the total time for the calls to *siftdown* is $O(n \lg n)$. Therefore, heapsort runs in time $O(n \lg n)$. Corollary 6.3.3 shows that any comparison-based sorting algorithm, of which heapsort is an example, has worst-case time $\Omega(n \lg n)$. Therefore, the worst-case time of heapsort is $\Theta(n \lg n)$. It is also possible to show directly that the worst-case time of heapsort is $\Theta(n \lg n)$ by constructing input that requires time $\Theta(n \lg n)$ (see Exercise 3.12).

Notice that except for the input array, heapsort uses a constant amount of storage. In practice, heapsort is the fastest general sorting algorithm that, except for the input array, uses a constant amount of storage and guarantees worst-case time $\Theta(n \lg n)$. [In practice, quicksort (see Section 6.2) is faster on average than heapsort. However, in addition to the input array, quicksort, if properly implemented, uses $O(\lg n)$ storage and has worst-case time $\Theta(n^2)$.]

Exercises

1S. A priority queue is implemented using an array. An item is inserted by putting it at the end of the array. Write algorithms to initialize a priority queue to empty, to delete an item with the highest priority, to return an item with the highest priority, and to insert an item with a specified priority.

2. A priority queue is implemented using an array. An item is inserted by putting it in a cell that maintains nondecreasing order. Write algorithms to initialize a priority queue to empty, to delete an item with the highest priority, to return an item with the highest priority, and to insert an item with a specified priority.

3. A priority queue is implemented using an array. An item is inserted by putting it at the end of the array. Show that, in the worst case, performing n insertions and n deletions in an initially empty priority queue takes time $\Theta(n^2)$.

4S. A priority queue is implemented using an array. An item is inserted by putting it in a cell that maintains nondecreasing order. Show that, in the worst case, performing n insertions and n deletions in an initially empty priority queue takes time $\Theta(n^2)$.

5. Show how to implement a stack using a priority queue.

6. Show how to implement a queue using a priority queue.

Unless specified otherwise, all heaps are maxheaps.

7S. Trace siftdown (Algorithm 3.5.7) on the following heap structure when $i = 1$.

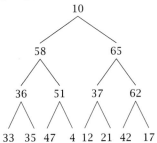

8. Trace delete (Algorithm 3.5.9) on the heap in Figure 3.5.5(e).

9. Trace delete (Algorithm 3.5.9) on the heap in Figure 3.5.7(c).

10S. Trace insert (Algorithm 3.5.10) when 61 is inserted into the heap in Figure 3.5.5(e).

11. Trace insert (Algorithm 3.5.10) when 210 is inserted into the heap in Figure 3.5.7(c).

12. Trace heapify (Algorithm 3.5.12) for the input

2	5	9	15	27	35	38	99

13. Trace heapify (Algorithm 3.5.12) for the input

75	6	24	102	27	15	8	99	72	25	8	84

14S. Given the *key* array

18	24	71	5	22	23	66	32	8	25	27

show the *into* and *outof* arrays when the heap in Figure 3.5.5(e) is implemented as an indirect heap.

15. Given the *key* array

104	50	8	24	23	22	71	27	18	25	66	32	5

show the *into* and *outof* arrays when the heap in Figure 3.5.7(c) is implemented as an indirect heap.

16. Trace the increase algorithm (Algorithm 3.5.15) for the indirect heap in Figure 3.5.9 when 18 is increased to 380. (Show the changes to the *into* and *outof* arrays.)

17. Trace the increase algorithm (Algorithm 3.5.15) for the indirect heap in Figure 3.5.9 when 12 is increased to 471. (Show the changes to the *into* and *outof* arrays.)

18S. Continue Figure 3.5.12 until heapsort terminates to show how it sorts the array.

19. Trace heapsort (Algorithm 3.5.16) for the input

94	88	82	64	63	22	21	7

20. Trace heapsort (Algorithm 3.5.16) for the input

4	18	23	64	63	22	21	7	67	3	102	55

21S. Let $x_1, \ldots, x_n$ be numbers. Construct a heap in which the values in the bottom level are, left to right, $x_1, \ldots, x_n$.

22. Assuming the data in a heap are distinct, what are the possible locations of the smallest element?

23. Assuming the data in a heap are distinct, what are the possible locations of the second-smallest element?

24S. Assuming the data in a heap are distinct, what are the possible locations of the second-largest element?

25. Show that inserting n elements into an initially empty heap takes time $\Theta(n \lg n)$ in the worst case.

26. Write an $O(\lg n)$ *siftup* algorithm for a heap. The input to *siftup* is an index i and a heap structure in which the value of each node is greater than or equal to the values of its children (if any), except for the node at index i, which may have a value greater than its parent. *siftup* restores the heap. Show that your algorithm does run in time $O(\lg n)$.

27S. Write a constant-time algorithm that returns the largest value in an indirect heap. Show that your algorithm does run in constant time.

28. Write a version of siftdown for an indirect heap. Show that your algorithm runs in time $O(\lg n)$.

29. Write an algorithm that deletes the root from an indirect heap. Show that your algorithm runs in time $O(\lg n)$.

30S. Write an algorithm that inserts a value into an indirect heap. Show that your algorithm runs in time $O(\lg n)$.

31. Write a version of heapify for an indirect heap. Show that your algorithm runs in time $O(n)$.

32. Write a version of siftup (see Exercise 26) for an indirect heap. Show that your algorithm runs in time $O(\lg n)$.

33S. Suppose that in heapsort, we replace the call to heapify with repeated calls to the insert algorithm (Algorithm 3.5.10) to create the initial heap. What is the worst-case time of this version of heapsort?

3.6 Disjoint Sets

In this section, we discuss an abstract data type that contains nonempty pairwise disjoint sets (i.e., for all sets X and Y in the container, $X \neq \emptyset$, $Y \neq \emptyset$, and either $X = Y$ or $X \cap Y = \emptyset$). Furthermore, each set X in the container has one of its members *marked* as a representative of that set. The operations supported are:

- *makeset*(i): Construct the set $\{i\}$.

- *findset*(i): Return the marked member of the set to which i belongs.

- *union*(i, j): Replace the sets containing i and j with their union. (It is assumed that i and j do not belong to the same set.)

We assume that the elements of the sets are positive integers.

Example 3.6.1. After

> *makeset*(1)
> *makeset*(2)
> *makeset*(3)
> *makeset*(4)
> *makeset*(5)

we have

$$\{1\}, \quad \{2\}, \quad \{3\}, \quad \{4\}, \quad \{5\}.$$

Each element is marked; so, the value of

> *findset*(i)

is i, for all i.

After

> *union*$(1, 4)$
> *union*$(3, 5)$

we have

$$\{1, 4\}, \quad \{2\}, \quad \{3, 5\}.$$

If we assume that 4 is marked, the value of

> *findset*(1)

or

> *findset*(4)

is 4.

Notice that *findset* can be used to check whether elements i and j belong to the same set. For example,

> *findset*$(1) == $ *findset*(4)

is true; but

> *findset*$(2) == $ *findset*(3)

is false. (The value of *findset*(2) is 2, and the value of *findset*(3) is either 3 or 5, whichever is marked.)

After

   union(4, 2)

we have

$$\{1, 2, 4\}, \quad \{3, 5\};$$

and after

   union(1, 5)

we have

$$\{1, 2, 3, 4, 5\}.$$

Now the value of *findset*(*i*) is the same for all *i*. (The common value is whichever element is marked in the set $\{1, 2, 3, 4, 5\}$.) □

To implement the disjoint-set abstract data type, we represent a set as a tree with the marked element as the root. The elements in a set are not arranged in any special way, and the tree is not necessarily a binary tree.

Example 3.6.2. Three of the many ways to represent the set $\{2, 4, 5, 8\}$, with 5 as the marked element, are shown in Figure 3.6.1.

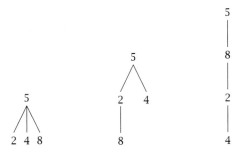

Figure 3.6.1   Representations of the set $\{2, 4, 5, 8\}$, with 5 as the marked element. □

We represent disjoint sets using an array, *parent*, in which the value, *parent*[*i*], is the parent of *i*, unless *i* is the root. In the latter case, the value of *parent*[*i*] is *i*.

Example 3.6.3. If the disjoint sets

$$\{2, 4, 5, 8\}, \quad \{1\}, \quad \{3, 6, 7\}$$

are represented by the trees shown in Figure 3.6.2, the *parent* array is

1	5	7	5	5	7	7	2
1	2	3	4	5	6	7	8

Figure 3.6.2 Disjoint sets represented as trees.   □

We turn now to algorithms to manipulate disjoint sets represented as trees. We begin with the first version of *makeset*, which is straightforward.

Algorithm 3.6.4 Makeset, Version 1. This algorithm represents the set $\{i\}$ as a one-node tree.

> Input Parameter: i
> Output Parameters: None

```
makeset1(i) {
    parent[i] = i
}
```

The first version of *findset* simply follows a path from the input element to the root.

Algorithm 3.6.5 Findset, Version 1. This algorithm returns the root of the tree to which i belongs.

> Input Parameter: i
> Output Parameters: None

```
findset1(i) {
    while (i != parent[i])
        i = parent[i]
    return i
}
```

Algorithm 3.6.5 returns the root since, by convention, i is equal to the root precisely when i and $parent[i]$ are equal.

To compute the union of two sets, we must merge the trees that represent them. To merge the trees, we make one root a child of the other root. The following algorithm gives the details. The algorithm assumes that the input is the two roots.

Algorithm 3.6.6 Mergetrees, Version 1. This algorithm receives as input the roots of two distinct trees and combines them by making one root a child of the other root.

Input Parameters: i, j
Output Parameters: None

$mergetrees1(i, j)$ {
  $parent[i] = j$
}

Example 3.6.7. Given the disjoint sets as represented in Figure 3.6.2, after

$mergetrees1(5, 1)$

we obtain

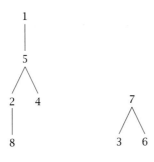

After

$mergetrees1(7, 1)$

we obtain

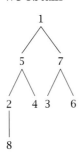

□

The union algorithm receives as input two *arbitrary* values (i.e., the values are not necessarily roots). It first invokes *findset1* (Algorithm 3.6.5) to find the roots of the trees and then invokes *mergetrees1* (Algorithm 3.6.6).

Algorithm 3.6.8 Union, Version 1. This algorithm receives as input two arbitrary values i and j and constructs the tree that represents the union of the sets to which i and j belong. The algorithm assumes that i and j belong to different sets.

Input Parameters: i, j
Output Parameters: None

```
union1(i, j) {
    mergetrees1(findset1(i), findset1(j))
}
```

We next consider the time required by our disjoint-set algorithms. When these algorithms are used, there are typically *many* calls to the various algorithms; thus, we are interested in the total time required when these algorithms are called repeatedly. Therefore, we assume throughout the remainder of this section that there are n makeset operations and a total of m union and findset operations. We also assume that the makeset operations are performed first.

Since the makeset algorithm (Algorithm 3.6.4) runs in constant time, the n makeset operations take time $\Theta(n)$. The worst-case time of findset (Algorithm 3.6.5) for any tree occurs when the argument is a node at the lowest level. In this case, the time is proportional to the height of the tree. The maximum height of a tree with n nodes is $n - 1$ (which occurs when each parent has exactly one child). Thus, the time of findset is $O(n)$. The union algorithm (Algorithm 3.6.8) calls the findset algorithm twice and the mergetrees algorithm (Algorithm 3.6.6) once. Since the mergetrees algorithm runs in time $\Theta(1)$ and the findset algorithm runs in time $O(n)$, the union algorithm runs in time $O(n)$. The findset and union algorithms are called a total of m times. Therefore, the time required by the findset and union algorithms is $O(mn)$, and the time required by all of the algorithms is $O(n + mn)$, where there are n makeset operations and a total of m union and findset operations.

If $m < n$, we can derive a sharper estimate. In this case, the height of any tree is at most m (see Exercise 7); so, the time required by the findset and union algorithms is $O(m^2)$. Thus, the time required by all of the algorithms is $O(n + m^2)$. It follows that for any value of m, the time required by all of the algorithms is $O(n + m \cdot \min\{m, n\})$. We leave as an exercise (see Exercise 8) to show that this estimate is sharp, that is, that the worst-case time required by all of the algorithms is $\Omega(n + m \cdot \min\{m, n\})$. It follows that the worst-case time required by all of the algorithms is $\Theta(n + m \cdot \min\{m, n\})$, where there are n makeset operations and a total of m union and findset operations.

The time of the findset algorithm, and by extension the time of the union algorithm, is bounded by the height of the tree. It follows that we can improve the performance of our algorithms if we can constrain the tree heights.

Notice that when we execute $union1(5, 1)$ for the trees in Figure 3.6.2, we obtain

We have increased the maximum height among the trees to 3 because we made the tree with the greater height a subtree of the tree with the smaller height. Had we made the tree with the smaller height a subtree of the tree with the greater height

we would not have increased the maximum height among all trees. In order to make the tree with the smaller height a subtree of the tree with the greater height, we maintain an array *height*, in which *height*[*i*] is the height of the tree rooted at *i*. The revised algorithms follow.

Algorithm 3.6.9 Makeset, Version 2. This algorithm represents the set {*i*} as a one-node tree and initializes its height to 0.

Input Parameter: *i*
Output Parameters: None

```
makeset2(i) {
    parent[i] = i
    height[i] = 0
}
```

The findset algorithm is unchanged.

Algorithm 3.6.10 Findset, Version 2. This algorithm returns the root of the tree to which *i* belongs.

Input Parameter: *i*
Output Parameters: None

```
findset2(i) {
    while (i != parent[i])
        i = parent[i]
    return i
}
```

Algorithm 3.6.11 Mergetrees, Version 2. This algorithm receives as input the roots of two distinct trees and combines them by making the root of the tree of smaller height a child of the other root. If the trees have the same height, we arbitrarily make the root of the first tree a child of the other root.

Input Parameters: *i*, *j*
Output Parameters: None

```
mergetrees2(i, j) {
  if (height[i] < height[j])
    parent[i] = j
  else if (height[i] > height[j])
    parent[j] = i
  else {
    parent[i] = j
    height[j] = height[j] + 1
  }
}
```

The union algorithm now calls *mergetrees2* and *findset2*.

Algorithm 3.6.12 Union, Version 2. This algorithm receives as input two arbitrary values i and j and constructs the tree that represents the union of the sets to which i and j belong. The algorithm assumes that i and j belong to different sets.

  Input Parameters: i, j
Output Parameters: None

```
union2(i, j) {
  mergetrees2(findset2(i), findset2(j))
}
```

Example 3.6.13. Suppose that we begin by calling *makeset2*[i] for $i = 1$ to 8. The resulting trees are the singleton nodes and the arrays are

parent

1	2	3	4	5	6	7	8
1	2	3	4	5	6	7	8

height

0	0	0	0	0	0	0	0
1	2	3	4	5	6	7	8

When *union2*$(8, 2)$ is called, *mergetrees2* is called as *mergetrees2*$(8, 2)$. Since *height*[8] and *height*[2] are equal, *mergetrees2* executes

    $parent[8] = 2$
    $height[2] = height[2] + 1$

The trees become

and the arrays become

parent

1	2	3	4	5	6	7	2
1	2	3	4	5	6	7	8

height

0	1	0	0	0	0	0	0
1	2	3	4	5	6	7	8

Similarly, after

union2(4, 5)
union2(3, 7)

the trees become

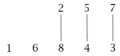

and the arrays become

parent

1	2	7	5	5	6	7	2
1	2	3	4	5	6	7	8

height

0	1	0	0	1	0	1	0
1	2	3	4	5	6	7	8

When *union2*(3, 6) is called, *mergetrees2* is called as *mergetrees2*(7, 6). Since *height*[7] > *height*[6], *mergetrees2* executes

parent[6] = 7

The trees become

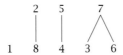

and the arrays become

parent

1	2	7	5	5	7	7	2
1	2	3	4	5	6	7	8

height

0	1	0	0	1	0	1	0
1	2	3	4	5	6	7	8

□

In version 1 of our disjoint-set algorithms, the height of a k-node tree was at most $k - 1$. We show that, in version 2, the height of a k-node tree is at most $\lfloor \lg k \rfloor$.

Theorem 3.6.14. *Using version 2 of the disjoint-set algorithms (Algorithms 3.6.9–3.6.12), the height of a k-node tree is at most $\lfloor \lg k \rfloor$.*

Proof. The proof is by induction on k, and the basis step is $k = 1$. Since a one-node tree has height zero, the statement is true in this case.

Now suppose that $k > 1$, and for all $p < k$, the height of a p-node tree is at most $\lfloor \lg p \rfloor$. Let T be a k-node tree. Since $k > 1$, T is the union of two trees: T_1, of height h_1 with $k_1 < k$ nodes; and T_2, of height h_2 with $k_2 < k$ nodes. By the inductive assumption, $h_1 \le \lfloor \lg k_1 \rfloor$ and $h_2 \le \lfloor \lg k_2 \rfloor$. If $h_1 \neq h_2$, the height of T is

$$\max\{h_1, h_2\} \le \max\{\lfloor \lg k_1 \rfloor, \lfloor \lg k_2 \rfloor\} \le \lfloor \lg k \rfloor.$$

Now suppose that $h_1 = h_2$. We may assume that $k_1 \geq k_2$. Notice that $k_2 \leq k/2$. (If this last inequality is false, we have $k_2 > k/2$ and $k_1 \geq k_2 > k/2$, which implies that $k = k_1 + k_2 > k$.) The height of T is

$$1 + h_2 \leq 1 + \lfloor \lg k_2 \rfloor \leq 1 + \lfloor \lg k/2 \rfloor = 1 + \lfloor (\lg k) - 1 \rfloor = \lfloor \lg k \rfloor.$$

The inductive step is complete. ∎

Consider the time required by version 2 of the disjoint-set algorithms. The makeset algorithm (Algorithm 3.6.9) still runs in constant time, and the n makeset operations take time $\Theta(n)$. By Theorem 3.6.14, the height of any tree is bounded by $\lg n$. Thus, the time of findset (Algorithm 3.6.10) is $O(\lg n)$. The union algorithm (Algorithm 3.6.12) calls the findset algorithm twice and the mergetrees algorithm (Algorithm 3.6.11) once. Since the mergetrees algorithm runs in time $\Theta(1)$ and the findset algorithm runs in time $O(\lg n)$, the union algorithm runs in time $O(\lg n)$. The findset and union algorithms are called a total of m times. Therefore, the time required by the findset and union algorithms is $O(m \lg n)$, and the time required by all of the algorithms is $O(n + m \lg n)$, where there are n makeset operations and a total of m union and findset operations.

As for version 1 of our disjoint-set algorithms, if $m < n$ we can derive a sharper estimate. We first note that after makeset initializes the parent array, each cell in the parent array is modified at most one time—by a call to union. In a tree containing k nodes, each node, except the root, has had its cell in the parent array modified (since it is no longer a root). Therefore, a tree with p nodes was constructed by exactly $p - 1$ calls of the union algorithm. Let k be the number of times the union algorithm was called. From our preceding comments, each tree has at most $k + 1 \leq m + 1$ nodes. By Theorem 3.6.14, the height of any tree is bounded by $\lg(m + 1)$. Thus, the time required by the findset and union algorithms is $O(m \lg m)$, and the time required by all of the algorithms is $O(n + m \lg m)$. It follows that for any value of m, the time required by all of the algorithms is $O(n + m \cdot \min\{\lg m, \lg n\})$. We leave as an exercise (see Exercise 9) to show that this estimate is sharp, that is, that the worst-case time required by all of the algorithms is $\Omega(n + m \cdot \min\{\lg m, \lg n\})$. It follows that the worst-case time required by all of the algorithms is $\Theta(n + m \cdot \min\{\lg m, \lg n\})$, where there are n makeset operations and a total of m union and findset operations.

The final enhancement to the disjoint-set algorithms involves the findset algorithm. Again, our goal is to decrease the heights of the trees. In the call *findset(i)*, after locating the root, we make every node on the path from i to the root, except the root itself, a child of the root, thereby potentially decreasing the height of the tree. This process is called **path compression**.

Example 3.6.15. After the call

findset(11)

the tree in Figure 3.6.3(a) becomes the tree shown in Figure 3.6.3(b).

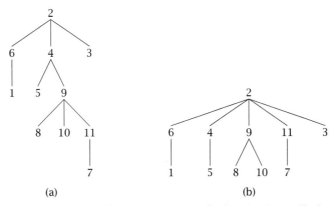

Figure 3.6.3 Path compression. *findset*(11) is called on tree (a). Every node on the path from 11 to the root, except the root itself, becomes a child of the root, yielding tree (b). □

The fastest known implementation of the disjoint-set algorithms combines path compression and an analog of the *height* array. The *height* array no longer gives the *exact* heights of the trees because path compression can reduce the height of the tree. For this reason, we rename the *height* array the *rank* array; $rank[i]$ is an *upper bound* on the height of the tree rooted at i. The version of the union algorithm that uses the *rank* array is called **union by rank**. The algorithms follow.

Algorithm 3.6.16 Makeset, Version 3. This algorithm represents the set $\{i\}$ as a one-node tree and initializes its rank to 0.

    Input Parameter: i
Output Parameters: None

makeset3(i) {
   parent[i] = i
   rank[i] = 0
}

Algorithm 3.6.17 Findset, Version 3. This algorithm returns the root of the tree to which i belongs and makes every node on the path from i to the root, except the root itself, a child of the root.

    Input Parameter: i
Output Parameters: None

findset3(i) {
   root = i
   while (*root* != *parent*[*root*])
     root = *parent*[*root*]

```
    j = parent[i]
    while (j != root) {
        parent[i] = root
        i = j
        j = parent[i]
    }
    return root
}
```

Algorithm 3.6.18 Mergetrees, Version 3. This algorithm receives as input the roots of two distinct trees and combines them by making the root of the tree of smaller rank a child of the other root. If the trees have the same rank, we arbitrarily make the root of the first tree a child of the other root.

Input Parameters: i, j
Output Parameters: None

```
mergetrees3(i, j) {
    if (rank[i] < rank[j])
        parent[i] = j
    else if (rank[i] > rank[j])
        parent[j] = i
    else {
        parent[i] = j
        rank[j] = rank[j] + 1
    }
}
```

Algorithm 3.6.19 Union, Version 3. This algorithm receives as input two arbitrary values i and j and constructs the tree that represents the union of the sets to which i and j belong. The algorithm assumes that i and j belong to different sets.

Input Parameters: i, j
Output Parameters: None

```
union3(i, j) {
    mergetrees3(findset3(i), findset3(j))
}
```

The analysis of the time required by the disjoint-set algorithms using both path compression and union by rank (Algorithms 3.6.16–3.6.19) is complicated and, through the years, increasingly sharper upper bounds on the time were obtained. Finally, in 1975, R. E. Tarjan (see Tarjan, 1975) proved that the worst-case running time is

$$\Theta(t\alpha(t, n)),$$

where n is the number of makeset operations, $t = m + n$ is the total number of operations, and α is a function with an *extremely* slow rate of growth. For the α defined by Tarjan, $\alpha(t, n) \leq 4$, for all $n \leq 10^{19728}$. (Other definitions of α in the literature differ from Tarjan's definition by an additive constant.) Whichever essentially equivalent way α is defined, for all practical values of n, $\alpha(t, n)$ is bounded by a constant. So, from a practical standpoint (but *not* from a theoretical standpoint!), the worst-case time of the disjoint-set algorithms using both path compression and union by rank is linear in t.

Exercises

In Exercises 1–3, show the trees that result after the following statements are executed:

for $i = 1$ to 8
   makeset(i)
union$(1, 2)$
union$(3, 4)$
union$(5, 6)$
union$(5, 7)$
union$(5, 8)$
union$(4, 8)$
union$(3, 2)$

1S. Substitute *makeset1* for *makeset* and *union1* for *union*.

2. Substitute *makeset2* for *makeset* and *union2* for *union*.

3. Substitute *makeset3* for *makeset* and *union3* for *union*.

4S. What happens if union, version 1, (Algorithm 3.6.8) is erroneously called with i and j in the same tree?

5. What happens if union, version 2, (Algorithm 3.6.12) is erroneously called with i and j in the same tree?

6. What happens if union, version 3, (Algorithm 3.6.19) is erroneously called with i and j in the same tree?

7S. Show that if $m < n$, after executing Algorithms 3.6.4, 3.6.5, and 3.6.8, the maximum height of a tree is m.

8. Show that the worst-case time required by Algorithms 3.6.4, 3.6.5, and 3.6.8 is
$$\Omega(n + m \cdot \min\{m, n\}).$$

9. Show that the worst-case time required by Algorithms 3.6.9, 3.6.10, and 3.6.12 is
$$\Omega(n + m \cdot \min\{\lg m, \lg n\}).$$

10S. Write a recursive version of the findset algorithm without path compression (Algorithm 3.6.5).

11. Write a recursive version of the findset algorithm with path compression (Algorithm 3.6.17).

12. An alternative to path compression is *path halving*. In path halving, when the path is traversed from the node to the root, we make the grandparent of every other node i on the path the new parent of i. Write the path-halving algorithm. Path compression requires two passes from the node to the root (one to find the root and one to reset the parents), but path halving requires only one pass. Tarjan and van Leeuwen (see Tarjan, 1984) showed that path halving, together with union by rank, also gives worst-case time $\Theta(t\alpha(t,n))$.

Notes

Classic books on data structures are Aho, 1983; Knuth, 1997; and Tarjan, 1983. Recent books on data structures and their implementation in programming languages are Standish, 1998, and Weiss, 2001.

The heapsort algorithm and the term "heap" were invented by J. W. J. Williams (see Williams, 1964). Fibonacci heaps (see Fredman, 1987) and relaxed heaps (see Driscoll, 1988) improve the asymptotic times of binary heaps.

Chapter Exercises

3.1. Write a version of *push* for a stack that throws an exception if the array is full. If the array is not full, the behavior is the same as the original *push*. Assume that *SIZE* specifies the size of the array.

3.2. Write a version of *pop* for a stack that throws an exception if the stack is empty. If the stack is not empty, the behavior is the same as the original *pop*.

3.3. Write a version of *top* for a stack that throws an exception if the stack is empty. If the stack is not empty, the behavior is the same as the original *top*.

3.4. Write a version of *enqueue* for a queue that throws an exception if the array is full. If the array is not full, the behavior is the same as the original *enqueue*.

3.5. Write a version of *dequeue* for a queue that throws an exception if the queue is empty. If the queue is not empty, the behavior is the same as the original *dequeue*.

3.6. Write a version of *front* for a queue that throws an exception if the queue is empty. If the queue is not empty, the behavior is the same as the original *front*.

A deque *(pronounced "deck") is like a queue, except that items may be added and deleted at the rear or the front.*

3.7. Implement a deque using an array. Do not incorporate error checking into your functions.

3.8. Implement a deque using an array. Incorporate error checking into your functions.

3.9. Implement a deque using a linked list. Do not incorporate error checking into your functions.

3.10. Implement a deque using a linked list. Incorporate error checking into your functions.

3.11. Let T_1 be a binary tree with root r_1 and let T_2 be a binary tree with root r_2. The binary trees are *isomorphic* if there is a one-to-one, onto function f from the vertex set of T_1 to the vertex set of T_2 satisfying

- Vertices v_i and v_j are adjacent in T_1 if and only if the vertices $f(v_i)$ and $f(v_j)$ are adjacent in T_2.
- $f(r_1) = r_2$.
- v is a left child of w in T_1 if and only if $f(v)$ is a left child of $f(w)$ in T_2.
- v is a right child of w in T_1 if and only if $f(v)$ is a right child of $f(w)$ in T_2.

Write an algorithm, which runs in linear time in the worst case, to determine whether two binary trees are isomorphic. Prove that your algorithm does run in linear time.

3.12. Find input that produces worst-case time for heapsort (Algorithm 3.5.16).

3.13. A *d-heap* is like a binary heap except that the nodes have d children or less rather than two children or less. Write d-heap versions of siftdown, delete, insert, and heapify. Also write an algorithm that returns the largest value in a d-heap. The asymptotic times should be the same as the binary heap algorithms. Show that your algorithms do have the same asymptotic times as those for a binary heap. In practice, the 3- or 4-heap algorithms tend to run faster than the binary heap algorithms.

3.14. Implement a d-heap (see Exercise 3.13) as an indirect heap. Write versions of siftdown, delete, insert, and heapify. Also write an algorithm that returns the largest value in an indirect d-heap. The asymptotic times should be the same as the binary heap algorithms. Show that your algorithms do have the same asymptotic times as those for a binary heap.

3.15. Implement the disjoint-set abstract data type by using linked lists to represent the sets. Make your algorithms as efficient as you can, and provide sharp asymptotic time bounds.

3.16. Prove a version of Theorem 3.6.14 in which *height*[i] is replaced by *count*[i], where *count*[i] is the number of nodes in the tree rooted at i.

CHAPTER 4
Searching

In this chapter, we discuss **searching algorithms**. Our first algorithm, the binary-search algorithm (see Section 4.1), efficiently solves the problem of searching for a given value in a sorted array. In Sections 4.2 and 4.3, we discuss depth-first and breadth-first search in graphs. Besides being useful in their own right, these searching techniques are the basis of many other algorithms. For example, topological sorting (see Section 4.4) is based on depth-first search. A topological sort of a directed acyclic graph is an ordering of the vertices $v_1, \ldots, v_n$ such that, if (v_i, v_j) is a directed edge, then v_i precedes v_j in the ordering.

A special instance of depth-first search is called *backtracking*. In the worst-case, backtracking typically degenerates to exhaustive search; but, in many applications, it is quite useful. We show how backtracking can be used to solve the n-queens problem and the Hamiltonian-cycle problem.

4.1 Binary Search

Searching an *unsorted* list can take a long time. Imagine trying to find a phone number in a directory in which the names are not sorted. The best that we can do is to start at the beginning and go through the names one-by-one until the desired one is found. Fortunately, we can search a *sorted* list quickly.

WWW   Suppose that we are given an array L, which is sorted in *nondecreasing* order; that is,

$$L[i] \le L[i+1] \le \cdots \le L[j],$$

and that we are searching for the value *key*. The **binary-search algorithm** begins by computing the midpoint $k = \lfloor (i+j)/2 \rfloor$ of the array. If $L[k]$ is equal to *key*, the problem is solved. Otherwise, the array is divided into two parts of nearly equal size

$$L[i], \ldots, L[k-1], \qquad L[k+1], \ldots, L[j].$$

If $j - i$ is odd, the second part has one more element than the first part; but if $j - i$ is even, the parts are the same size. We then compare $L[k]$ with *key*. If $key < L[k]$, because the array is sorted in nondecreasing order, if *key* is present, it must be in

$$L[i], \ldots, L[k-1].$$

Thus we ignore the second part and search for *key* in $L[i], \ldots, L[k-1]$. On the other hand, if $key > L[k]$ and *key* is present, it must be in

$$L[k+1], \ldots, L[j].$$

In this case, we ignore the first part and search for *key* in $L[k+1], \ldots, L[j]$. We formally state the binary-search algorithm as Algorithm 4.1.1.

Algorithm 4.1.1 Binary Search. This algorithm searches for the value *key* in the nondecreasing array $L[i], \ldots, L[j]$. If *key* is found, the algorithm returns an index k such that $L[k]$ equals *key*. If *key* is not found, the algorithm returns -1, which is assumed not to be a valid index.

   Input Parameters: L, i, j, key
Output Parameters: None

```
bsearch(L, i, j, key) {
    while (i ≤ j) {
        k = (i + j)/2
        if (key == L[k]) // found
            return k
        if (key < L[k]) // search first part
            j = k - 1
        else // search second part
            i = k + 1
    }
    return -1 // not found
}
```

Algorithm *bsearch* is an iterative algorithm, and each iteration evaluates the expression $i \le j$. Since the body of the loop executes in constant time, we define the time of *bsearch* to be the number of times the expression $i \le j$ is evaluated. If the input array has n elements, we let c_n denote the worst-case time of *bsearch*.

Example 4.1.2. We compute c_4, the worst-case time of *bsearch* when the input is $L[0], \ldots, L[3]$. When the body of the while loop executes the first time, since $i = 0$ and $j = 3$ the line

   $k = (i + j)/2$

sets k to 1. Since we are computing the *worst-case* time, we assume that $key \ne L[1]$. If $key < L[1]$, j is set to 0; but if $key > L[1]$, i is set to 2. Since we are computing the worst-case time, we assume that $key > L[1]$, which results in a larger subarray in which to search during the next iteration of the while loop.

When the body of the while loop executes the second time with $i = 2$ and $j = 3$, the line

$$k = (i + j)/2$$

sets k to 2. We assume that $key \neq L[2]$. If $key < L[2]$, j is set to 1; but if $key > L[2]$, i is set to 3. Since we are computing the worst-case time, we assume that $key > L[2]$, which results in another iteration of the while loop.

When the body of the while loop executes the third time with $i = 3$ and $j = 3$, the line

$$k = (i + j)/2$$

sets k to 3. We assume that $key \neq L[3]$. If $key < L[3]$, j is set to 2; but if $key > L[3]$, i is set to 4. In either case, the while loop terminates. Since the expression $i \leq j$ was evaluated four times, $c_4 = 4$. □

We next derive a recurrence relation for the sequence $\{c_n\}$, which gives the worst-case time of *bsearch*. Assume that $L[0], \ldots, L[n-1]$ is input to *bsearch* and that *key* is not found. When the body of the while loop executes the first time, the line

$$k = (i + j)/2$$

sets k to $(n-1)/2$. Since *key* is not in the array L, either i is set to $k + 1$, which results in a subarray of size $\lfloor n/2 \rfloor$ for the next iteration of the while loop; or j is set to $k - 1$, which results in a subarray of size $\lfloor (n-1)/2 \rfloor$ for the next iteration of the while loop. Since we are computing the worst-case time of *bsearch*, we assume that i is set to $k + 1$. By definition, the resulting subarray has worst-case time $c_{\lfloor n/2 \rfloor}$. Therefore,

$$c_n = 1 + c_{\lfloor n/2 \rfloor}.$$

For this recurrence relation,

$$c_n = \Theta(\lg n)$$

(see Theorem 2.4.7). Thus, for input of size n, the worst-case time of *bsearch* is $\Theta(\lg n)$.

A Lower Bound for the Searching Problem

We show that *any* comparison-based algorithm that searches a sorted array of size n requires $\Omega(\lg n)$ time in the worst case. It then will follow that binary search (Algorithm 4.1.1) is asymptotically optimal. By "comparison-based," we mean that the only way that the algorithm can obtain information about where in the array *key*, the value that is sought, might occur is to compare *key* with an element in the array. Notice that Algorithm 4.1.1 is a comparison-based searching algorithm. For example, a comparison-based searching algorithm is *not* allowed to glean information from the value of *key* or the value of a data item (e.g., a comparison-based searching algorithm is *not* allowed to interpret the value of *key* as a number to help locate *key*).

Throughout the remainder of this subsection, we abbreviate "comparison-based searching algorithm that searches a sorted array" to "searching algorithm." We use *three-way comparisons*, which we subsequently abbreviate to "comparisons," in which the result of the comparison is either less than, equals, or greater than. We also use a *decision tree* to depict a searching algorithm (see Figure 4.1.1). In such a decision tree, each internal vertex denotes a three-way comparison of *key* with an item in the array. If the result of the comparison is "less than," the algorithm follows the left edge. If the result of the comparison is "equals," the algorithm follows the middle edge. If the result of the comparison is "greater than," the algorithm follows the right edge. The state of the data after the comparison is shown on the edge. The process is repeated (i.e., if an internal vertex is reached, another comparison is performed, the algorithm follows an edge, and the state of the data changes) until a terminal vertex is reached, at which point, *key* is found or it is determined that *key* is not present.

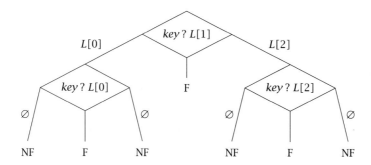

Figure 4.1.1 Binary search in an array of size three as a decision tree. F designates found, and NF designates not found. The input is the array $L[0], L[1], L[2]$. Each internal vertex denotes the comparison of *key* with an item in the array. If the result of the comparison is "less than," the algorithm follows the left edge. If the result of the comparison is "equals," the algorithm follows the middle edge. If the result of the comparison is "greater than," the algorithm follows the right edge. The state of the data after the comparison is shown on the edge. For example, *key* and $L[1]$ are compared first. If $key < L[1]$, the algorithm follows the left edge, the array to search becomes $L[0]$, and the algorithm next compares *key* and $L[0]$. If *key* equals $L[1]$, the algorithm follows the middle edge where it terminates, having found *key*. If $key > L[1]$, the algorithm follows the right edge, the array to search becomes $L[2]$, and the algorithm next compares *key* and $L[2]$.

Example 4.1.3. Figure 4.1.1 depicts binary search (Algorithm 4.1.1) for input of size three as a decision tree.   □

The worst-case time for a searching algorithm is at least as large as the number of comparisons performed in the worst case since it does additional work (e.g., updating variables) beyond making comparisons. In a decision-tree depiction of the algorithm, the maximum number of comparisons occurs on a path of maximum length from the root to a terminal vertex, which is equal to the height of the tree. For example in Figure 4.1.1, the height of the tree is two; thus, the maximum number of comparisons for this algorithm for input of size three is equal to two.

Suppose that an array of n distinct elements and *key* are input to a searching algorithm. In the decision tree depiction of the algorithm, there must be at least n terminal vertices to account for the n possible distinct elements in the array that might be equal to *key*. By Exercise 28, Section 2.6, a tree with at least n terminal vertices in which each vertex has at most three children has height at least $\log_3 n$. Thus, in the worst case, the algorithm performs at least $\log_3 n$ comparisons, and the worst-case time of the algorithm is $\Omega(\log_3 n)$. The change-of-base formula for logarithms (see Example 2.3.6) shows that $\Theta(\log_3 n) = \Theta(\lg n)$; therefore, any comparison-based algorithm that searches for *key* in a sorted array has worst-case time $\Omega(\lg n)$. In particular, binary search (Algorithm 4.1.1) is asymptotically optimal.

Exercises

Exercises 1–4 refer to the array

$$L[1] = 3, \quad L[2] = 6, \quad L[3] = 8, \quad L[4] = 11,$$

which is input to Algorithm 4.1.1.

1S. Trace Algorithm 4.1.1 for *key* = 6.

2. Trace Algorithm 4.1.1 for *key* = 10.

3. Trace Algorithm 4.1.1 for *key* = 3.

4S. Trace Algorithm 4.1.1 for *key* = 24.

5S. Write a recursive version of Algorithm 4.1.1.

6. Prove that in the worst case, the expression $i \le j$ in Algorithm 4.1.1 is evaluated $2 + \lfloor \lg n \rfloor$ times when the size of the input array is n.

7. Give an example to show that if the input to Algorithm 4.1.1 is *not* in nondecreasing order, Algorithm 4.1.1 may not find *key* even if it is present.

8S. Suppose that the input to Algorithm 4.1.1 is *not* in nondecreasing order. Could Algorithm 4.1.1 erroneously find *key* even though it is not present?

9. Professor Larry proposes the following version of binary search:

```
bsearch(L, i, j, key) {
    while (i ≤ j) {
        k = (i + j)/2
        if (key == L[k])
            return k
        if (key < L[k])
            j = k
        else
            i = k
    }
    return −1
}
```

Is the Professor's version correct (i.e., does it find *key* if it is present and return −1 if it is not present)? If the Professor's version is correct, what is the worst-case time?

10. Professor Curly proposes the following version of binary search:

```
bsearch(L, i, j, key) {
    if (i > j)
        return −1
    k = (i + j)/2
    if (key == L[k])
        return k
    flag = bsearch(L, i, k − 1, key)
    if (flag == −1)
        return bsearch(L, k + 1, j, key)
    else
        return flag
}
```

Is the Professor's version correct (i.e., does it find *key* if it is present and return −1 if it is not present)? If the Professor's version is correct, what is the worst-case time?

11S. Professor Moe proposes the following version of binary search:

```
bsearch(L, i, j, key) {
    if (i > j)
        return −1
    k = (i + j)/2
    if (key == L[k])
        return k
    if (key < L[k])
        return bsearch(L, i, k, key)
    else
        return bsearch(L, k + 1, j, key)
}
```

Is the Professor's version correct (i.e., does it find *key* if it is present and return -1 if it is not present)? If the Professor's version is correct, what is the worst-case time?

12. Suppose that we replace the line

    $$k = (i + j)/2$$

    with

    $$k = i + (j - i)/3$$

    in Algorithm 4.1.1. Is the resulting algorithm still correct (i.e., does it find *key* if it is present and return -1 if it is not present)? If it is correct, what is the worst-case time?

13. Suppose that we replace the line

    $$k = (i + j)/2$$

    with

    $$k = j - 2$$

    in Algorithm 4.1.1. Is the resulting algorithm still correct (i.e., does it find *key* if it is present and return -1 if it is not present)? If it is correct, what is the worst-case time?

    In Exercises 14–16, trace the decision tree of Figure 4.1.1 for the array 3, 6, 12 and the given value of key.

14S. *key* = 3   15. *key* = 5   16. *key* = 13

17S. Draw the decision tree for binary search in an array of size four.

18. What is the worst-case lower bound given by the decision tree for a three-way-comparison searching algorithm when the input is an array of size four?

19. What is the worst-case lower bound given by the decision tree for a three-way-comparison searching algorithm when the input is an array of size five?

20S. What is the worst-case lower bound given by the decision tree for a three-way-comparison searching algorithm when the input is an array of size 100?

    Exercises 21–29 refer to the following problem. There are n coins identical in appearance, but one is either heavier or lighter than the others, which all weigh the same. Identify the bad coin and determine whether it is heavier or lighter than the others using only a pan balance, which compares the weights of two sets of coins.

21S. Write an algorithm to solve the coin-weighing problem for $n = 5$ using three weighings in the worst case.

22. Prove that the coin-weighing problem for $n = 5$ cannot be solved using two weighings in the worst case.

23. Write an algorithm to solve the coin-weighing problem for $n = 4$ using three weighings in the worst case.

24S. Prove that the coin-weighing problem for $n = 4$ cannot be solved using two weighings in the worst case.

25. Write an algorithm to solve the coin-weighing problem for $n = 4$ using two weighings in the worst case. This algorithm must find the bad coin, but it need not determine whether it is heavier or lighter than the other coins.

26. Write an algorithm to solve the coin-weighing problem for $n = 12$ using three weighings in the worst case.

27S. Prove that the coin-weighing problem for $n = 12$ cannot be solved using two weighings in the worst case.

28. What is wrong with the following argument, which supposedly shows that the 12-coins problem requires at least four weighings in the worst case if we begin by weighing four coins against four coins?

If we weigh four coins against four coins and they balance, we must then determine the bad coin from the remaining four coins. But Exercise 24 shows that determining the bad coin from among four coins requires at least three weighings in the worst case. Therefore, in the worst case, if we begin by weighing four coins against four coins, the 12-coins problem requires at least four weighings.

29. Write an optimal algorithm to solve the coin-weighing problem for $n = 13$. Prove that your algorithm is optimal.

4.2 Depth-First Search

A *binary (digital) image* is a two-dimensional array, each of whose entries, called *pixels*, is 0 or 1 (see Figure 4.2.1). The image is interpreted as black (1) on a white (0) background. One of the important steps in analyzing an image is to identify its regions—groups of contiguous pixels having the same value. For example, in Figure 4.2.1 there are two regions formed by the pixels of value 1 (two balls). One technique to identify the regions begins at a pixel of value 1, goes to an unvisited neighbor pixel N (defined as any of the four touching pixels; see Figure 4.2.2[†]) of value 1, and repeats; that is, we next

---

[†]An alternative definition of "neighbor" includes as neighbors of P the four pixels above and left of P, above and right of P, below and left of P, and below and right of P.

$$
\begin{array}{cccccccccc}
0 & 0 & 0 & 0 & 0 & 0 & 0 & 0 & 0 & 0 \\
0 & 0 & 1 & 0 & 0 & 0 & 0 & 0 & 0 & 0 \\
0 & 1 & 1 & 1 & 0 & 0 & 0 & 1 & 0 & 0 \\
1 & 1 & 1 & 1 & 1 & 0 & 1 & 1 & 1 & 0 \\
0 & 1 & 1 & 1 & 0 & 0 & 0 & 1 & 0 & 0 \\
0 & 0 & 1 & 0 & 0 & 0 & 0 & 0 & 0 & 0 \\
0 & 0 & 0 & 0 & 0 & 0 & 0 & 0 & 0 & 0
\end{array}
$$

Figure 4.2.1 A binary (digital) image of two balls. Each entry (pixel) is 0 or 1. The image is interpreted as black (1) on a white (0) background.

$$
\begin{array}{ccc}
 & N & \\
N & P & N \\
 & N &
\end{array}
$$

Figure 4.2.2 The four neighbors (N) of pixel (P).

go to an unvisited neighbor of N of value 1. If a pixel c, which was visited from pixel p, has no unvisited neighbors of value 1, we go to another of p's unvisited neighbors of value 1. By definition, the region containing the initial pixel consists of all the visited pixels. If all of the pixels of value 1 have been visited, we stop. Otherwise, we identify a new region by repeating this procedure starting at an unvisited pixel of value 1. We continue until all regions have been found. This technique is known as **depth-first search** and is the basis of many searching algorithms.

Example 4.2.1. We show how depth-first search operates on the image in Figure 4.2.1. The order of visitation of the pixels depends on the start pixel and which neighbor is visited when a pixel has more than one unvisited neighbor.

In Figure 4.2.3, we show the leftmost pixels of value 1 as a graph. The vertices correspond to the pixels, and an edge indicates that the corresponding pixels are neighbors. Suppose that we begin at pixel 1.

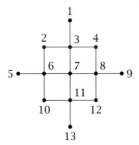

Figure 4.2.3 The leftmost pixels of value 1 in Figure 4.2.1 as a graph. The vertices correspond to the pixels, and an edge indicates that the corresponding pixels are neighbors.

We first visit 3—the unvisited neighbor of 1 (see Figure 4.2.4). We next visit an unvisited neighbor of 3—any of 2, 7, or 4. Suppose that we visit 7. We next visit an unvisited neighbor of 7—any of 6, 11, or 8. Suppose that we visit 11. We next visit an unvisited neighbor of 11—any of 10, 13, or 12. Suppose that we visit 13. We should next visit an unvisited neighbor of 13, but the sole neighbor of 13 has already been visited. Since 13 was visited from 11, we next visit an unvisited neighbor of 11—either 10 or 12. Suppose that we visit 10. Continuing in this way, we find an order of visitation

$$1 \quad 3 \quad 7 \quad 11 \quad 13 \quad 10 \quad 6 \quad 2 \quad 5 \quad 12 \quad 8 \quad 9 \quad 4.$$

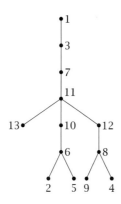

Figure 4.2.4 Depth-first search of the graph of Figure 4.2.3 as a tree. If c was visited from p, we draw p as the parent of c.

At this point we have identified the pixels in the leftmost ball in Figure 4.2.1. We would next find an unvisited pixel of value 1 (i.e., a pixel in the rightmost ball) and execute another depth-first search, which would identify the pixels in the rightmost ball. □

Depth-first search of a graph is inherently recursive: We first visit the initial vertex *start*, find an unvisited vertex v adjacent to *start*, and perform another depth-first search beginning at v. If there are no unvisited vertices adjacent to *start*, we simply return.

In order to implement depth-first search efficiently, we represent the graph using adjacency lists (see Section 3.3). In this way, we can quickly access the vertices adjacent to a given vertex. We also use an array *visit* to track which vertices have been visited. We set *visit*[i] to true if vertex i has been visited or to false if vertex i has not been visited. We begin by initializing all of the entries in *visit* to false. We then perform a depth-first search beginning at the start vertex. Algorithm 4.2.2 implements depth-first search.

Algorithm 4.2.2 Depth-First Search. This algorithm executes a depth-first search beginning at vertex *start* in a graph with vertices $1, \ldots, n$ and outputs the vertices in the order in which they are visited.

The graph is represented using adjacency lists; $adj[i]$ is a reference to the first node in a linked list of nodes representing the vertices adjacent to vertex i. Each node has members *ver*, the vertex adjacent to i, and *next*, the next node in the linked list or null, for the last node in the linked list.

To track visited vertices, the algorithm uses an array *visit*; $visit[i]$ is set to true if vertex i has been visited or to false if vertex i has not been visited.

Input Parameters: *adj, start*
Output Parameters: None

```
dfs(adj, start) {
    n = adj.last
    for i = 1 to n
        visit[i] = false
    dfs_recurs(adj, start)
}

dfs_recurs(adj, start) {
    println(start)
    visit[start] = true
    trav = adj[start]
    while (trav != null) {
        v = trav.ver
        if (!visit[v])
            dfs_recurs(adj, v)
        trav = trav.next
    }
}
```

Example 4.2.3. We trace Algorithm 4.2.2 when the input is the graph with adjacency lists (see Figure 4.2.5)

$$adj[1] \rightarrow 2 \rightarrow 3$$
$$adj[2] \rightarrow 1 \rightarrow 4$$
$$adj[3] \rightarrow 1 \rightarrow 4$$
$$adj[4] \rightarrow 2 \rightarrow 3 \rightarrow 5$$
$$adj[5] \rightarrow 4$$

and the start vertex is 1.

Figure 4.2.5 A graph to illustrate depth-first search (Algorithm 4.2.2) and breadth-first search (Algorithm 4.3.2).

When *dfs* is called, the cells of the array *visit* are initialized to false; then, *dfs* calls *dfs_recurs* with *start* = 1.

In this call of *dfs_recurs*, *start* = 1 so *visit*[1] is set to true and *trav* is set to *adj*[1] [see Figure 4.2.6(a)]. Since *trav* is not equal to null, the body of the while loop executes, and *v* is set to 2. Because vertex 2 is not visited, *dfs_recurs* is called with *v* = 2. In Figure 4.2.6(a), we indicate the next call of *dfs_recurs* by writing "1 calls 2."

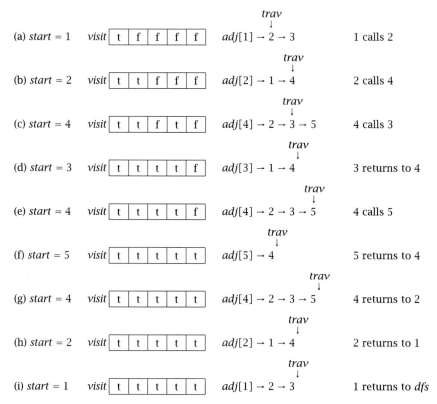

Figure 4.2.6 A trace of depth-first search (Algorithm 4.2.2) for the graph of Figure 4.2.5. In the array *visit*, true is abbreviated to t, and false is abbreviated to f.

In the next call of *dfs_recurs*, *start* = 2 so *visit*[2] is set to true and *trav* is set to *adj*[2]. Since *trav* is not equal to null, the body of the while loop executes, and *v* is set to 1. Because vertex 1 is visited, *trav* moves to the next node, which contains vertex 4 [see Figure 4.2.6(b)]. Again, *trav* is not equal to null, and the body of the while loop executes again; *v* is set to 4. Because vertex 4 is not visited, *dfs_recurs* is called with *v* = 4.

In the next call of *dfs_recurs*, *start* = 4 so *visit*[4] is set to true and *trav* is set to *adj*[4]. Since *trav* is not equal to null, the body of the while loop executes, and *v* is set to 2. Because vertex 2 is visited, *trav* moves to the next node, which contains vertex 3 [see Figure 4.2.6(c)]. Again, *trav* is not equal to null, and the body of the while loop executes again; v is set to 3. Because vertex 3 is not visited, *dfs_recurs* is called with $v = 3$.

In the next call of *dfs_recurs*, *start* = 3 so *visit*[3] is set to true and *trav* is set to *adj*[3]. Since *trav* is not equal to null, the body of the while loop executes, and v is set to 1. Because vertex 1 is visited, *trav* moves to the next node, which contains vertex 4. Again, *trav* is not equal to null, and the body of the while loop executes again; v is set to 4. Because vertex 4 is also visited and this is the last node in this list, *trav* becomes null [see Figure 4.2.6(d)], and *dfs_recurs* with *start* = 3 returns to its caller, *dfs_recurs* with *start* = 4. In Figure 4.2.6(d), we indicate this return by writing "3 returns to 4."

Execution of *dfs_recurs* with *start* = 4 resumes with *trav* set to the node containing vertex 3 [see Figure 4.2.6(c)]. The next statement to execute is

$$trav = trav.next$$

which moves *trav* to the node containing 5 [see Figure 4.2.6(e)]. Since *trav* is not equal to null, the body of the while loop executes, and v is set to 5. Because vertex 5 is not visited, *dfs_recurs* is called with $v = 5$.

In the next call of *dfs_recurs*, *start* = 5 so *visit*[5] is set to true and *trav* is set to *adj*[5]. Since *trav* is not equal to null, the body of the while loop executes, and v is set to 4. Because vertex 4 is visited and this is the last node in this list, *trav* becomes null [see Figure 4.2.6(f)], and *dfs_recurs* with *start* = 5 returns to its caller, *dfs_recurs* with *start* = 4.

Execution of *dfs_recurs* with *start* = 4 resumes with *trav* set to the node containing vertex 5 [see Figure 4.2.6(e)]. The next statement to execute is

$$trav = trav.next$$

Because the node containing vertex 5 is the last node in this list, *trav* becomes null [see Figure 4.2.6(g)], and *dfs_recurs* with *start* = 4 returns to its caller, *dfs_recurs* with *start* = 2.

Execution of *dfs_recurs* with *start* = 2 resumes with *trav* set to the node containing vertex 4 [see Figure 4.2.6(b)]. The next statement to execute is

$$trav = trav.next$$

Because the node containing vertex 4 is the last node in this list, *trav* becomes null [see Figure 4.2.6(h)], and *dfs_recurs* with *start* = 2 returns to its caller, *dfs_recurs* with *start* = 1.

Execution of *dfs_recurs* with *start* = 1 resumes with *trav* set to the node containing vertex 2 [see Figure 4.2.6(a)]. The next statement to execute is

$$trav = trav.next$$

which moves *trav* to the node containing 3. Because vertex 3 is visited and this is the last node in this list, *trav* becomes null [see Figure 4.2.6(i)]. Now *dfs_recurs* with *start* = 1 returns to its caller, *dfs*, and the algorithm terminates. □

Suppose that a graph with m edges and n vertices is input to the depth-first-search algorithm (Algorithm 4.2.2). The for loop in *dfs* runs in time $\Theta(n)$. After *dfs* calls *dfs_recurs*, in the worst case each node in each adjacency list is visited one time, as happens in Example 4.2.3. Since there are $2m$ nodes altogether in the adjacency lists, the total time for all of the calls of *dfs_recurs* is $\Theta(m)$ in the worst case. Therefore, in the worst case depth-first search runs in time $\Theta(m + n)$. In particular, depth-first search is linear in the size of the graph.

Depth-first search (Algorithm 4.2.2) can be applied without change to a directed graph. The adjacency list for vertex i represents vertices j, where (i, j) is an edge from i to j.

We can use depth-first search to test whether a graph is connected. We simply run depth-first search using any vertex as a start vertex and then check whether all nodes were visited. The graph is connected if and only if all nodes were visited, that is, if and only if all nodes are reachable from the start vertex.

Algorithm 4.2.4 Testing Whether a Graph is Connected. This algorithm tests whether a graph is connected; it returns true if the graph is connected or false if the graph is not connected. The input is a graph with vertices $1, \ldots, n$.

The graph is represented using adjacency lists; $adj[i]$ is a reference to the first node in a linked list of nodes representing the vertices adjacent to vertex i. Each node has members *ver*, the vertex adjacent to i, and *next*, the next node in the linked list or null, for the last node in the linked list.

In the array *visit*, $visit[i]$ is set to true if vertex i has been visited or to false if vertex i has not been visited.

```
Input Parameter:    adj
Output Parameters:  None
is_connected(adj) {
   n = adj.last
   for i = 1 to n
      visit[i] = false
   dfs_recurs(adj, 1)
   for i = 1 to n
      if (!visit[i])
         return false
   return true
}
dfs_recurs(adj, start) {
   visit[start] = true
   trav = adj[start]
   while (trav != null) {
      v = trav.ver
      if (!visit[v])
         dfs_recurs(adj, v)
      trav = trav.next
   }
}
```

Suppose that a graph with m edges and n vertices is input to Algorithm 4.2.4. We already observed that, in the worst-case, depth-first search runs in time $\Theta(m + n)$. Except for constant-time statements, Algorithm 4.2.4 differs from Algorithm 4.2.2 only in that a $\Theta(n)$ for loop was added to check whether all of the vertices were visited; thus, in the worst case, Algorithm 4.2.4 also runs in time $\Theta(m + n)$.

Exercises

In Exercises 1–6, list the order in which the vertices are visited when the depth-first-search algorithm (Algorithm 4.2.2) is executed with the given input. Assume that the vertices are listed in increasing order in each adjacency list.

1S.   Start vertex = 1

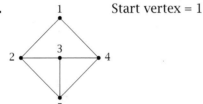

2.   Start vertex = 3

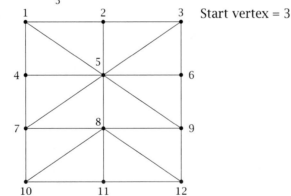

3.   Start vertex = 4

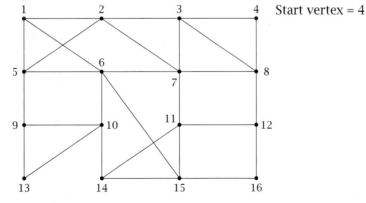

4S. Graph of Exercise 1, start vertex = 3

5. Graph of Exercise 2, start vertex = 8

6. Graph of Exercise 3, start vertex = 6

In Exercises 7–12, list the order in which the vertices are visited when the depth-first-search algorithm (Algorithm 4.2.2) is executed with the given input. Assume that the vertices are listed in decreasing order in each adjacency list.

7S. The graph of Exercise 1, start vertex = 1

8. The graph of Exercise 1, start vertex = 2

9. The graph of Exercise 2, start vertex = 3

10S. The graph of Exercise 2, start vertex = 4

11. The graph of Exercise 3, start vertex = 5

12. The graph of Exercise 3, start vertex = 6

13S. Give a trace of the depth-first-search algorithm (Algorithm 4.2.2) similar to that in Example 4.2.3 when the input is the graph of Figure 4.2.5 and the start vertex is 5. Assume that the vertices are listed in increasing order in each adjacency list.

14. Give a trace of the depth-first-search algorithm (Algorithm 4.2.2) similar to that in Example 4.2.3 when the input is the graph of Figure 4.2.5 and the start vertex is 1. Assume that the vertices are listed in decreasing order in each adjacency list.

15. Give a trace of the depth-first-search algorithm (Algorithm 4.2.2) similar to that in Example 4.2.3 when the input is the graph of Exercise 1 and the start vertex is 1. Assume that the vertices are listed in increasing order in each adjacency list.

16S. Give a trace of the depth-first-search algorithm (Algorithm 4.2.2) similar to that in Example 4.2.3 when the input is the graph of Exercise 1 and the start vertex is 3. Assume that the vertices are listed in decreasing order in each adjacency list.

17. What is the best-case time of the depth-first-search algorithm (Algorithm 4.2.2)?

18. Modify Algorithm 4.2.2 so that it tracks the parent p of a vertex c (p is the *parent* of c if c was visited from p).

19. Write an algorithm that uses the output of your algorithm in Exercise 18 to print each vertex and its parent.

20S. Write a nonrecursive version of depth-first search.

21. Write a version of depth-first search in which the input graph is represented using an adjacency matrix. What is the worst-case time of your algorithm?

4.3 Breadth-First Search

In depth-first search, after we visit a vertex—the *current* vertex—we immediately go to an unvisited adjacent vertex (if there is one), which becomes the current vertex. The procedure is then repeated. In **breadth-first search**, after we visit the current vertex, before going to an unvisited adjacent vertex, we visit *all* unvisited vertices adjacent to the current vertex. The current vertex then becomes the least recently visited vertex that has not yet served as the current vertex, and the procedure is repeated. Breadth-first search concludes when every vertex has served as the current vertex.

Example 4.3.1. We show how breadth-first search visits the vertices in the graph of Figure 4.3.1 when the start vertex is 1. We begin by visiting vertex 1. The list of vertices visited so far, in order, is 1.

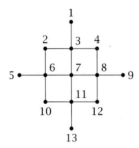

Figure 4.3.1 A graph for breadth-first search.

Since the current vertex is 1, we visit all unvisited vertices adjacent to 1: vertex 3 (see Figure 4.3.2). The current vertex becomes 3. The list of vertices visited so far, in order, is 1, 3.

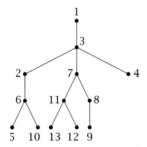

Figure 4.3.2 Breadth-first search of the graph of Figure 4.3.1 as a tree. If c was visited from p, we draw p as the parent of c.

We next visit all unvisited vertices adjacent to 3: vertices 2, 7, and 4. Suppose that the vertices 2, 7, and 4 are visited in this order. The current vertex becomes 2—the least recently visited vertex that has not yet served as the current vertex. The list of vertices visited so far, in order, is $1, 3, 2, 7, 4$.

We next visit all unvisited vertices adjacent to 2: vertex 6. The current vertex becomes 7. The list of vertices visited so far, in order, is $1, 3, 2, 7, 4, 6$.

We next visit all unvisited vertices adjacent to 7: vertices 11 and 8 in this order. The current vertex becomes 4. The list of vertices visited so far, in order, is $1, 3, 2, 7, 4, 6, 11, 8$.

Since all vertices adjacent to 4 have been visited, the current vertex becomes 6.

We next visit all unvisited vertices adjacent to 6: vertices 5 and 10 in this order. The current vertex becomes 11. The list of vertices visited so far, in order, is $1, 3, 2, 7, 4, 6, 11, 8, 5, 10$.

We next visit all unvisited vertices adjacent to 11: vertices 13 and 12 in this order. The current vertex becomes 8. The list of vertices visited so far, in order, is $1, 3, 2, 7, 4, 6, 11, 8, 5, 10, 13, 12$.

We next visit all unvisited vertices adjacent to 8: vertex 9. The current vertex becomes 5. The list of vertices visited so far, in order, is

$$1, 3, 2, 7, 4, 6, 11, 8, 5, 10, 13, 12, 9.$$

Since all vertices have been visited, the current vertex becomes 10, then 13, then 12, then 9, after which the algorithm concludes. The vertices were visited in the order $1, 3, 2, 7, 4, 6, 11, 8, 5, 10, 13, 12, 9$.   □

Just as in depth-first search, in order to implement breadth-first search efficiently we represent the graph using adjacency lists (see Section 3.3). We also use an array *visit* to track which vertices have been visited. We set *visit*[i] to true if vertex i has been visited or to false if vertex i has not been visited. We begin by initializing all of the entries in *visit* to false. Since the current vertex is the *least recently* visited vertex that has not yet served as the current vertex, we use a queue (see Section 3.2) to store pending current vertices. Algorithm 4.3.2 implements breadth-first search.

Algorithm 4.3.2 Breadth-First Search. This algorithm executes a breadth-first search beginning at vertex *start* in a graph with vertices $1, \ldots, n$ and outputs the vertices in the order in which they are visited.

The graph is represented using adjacency lists; *adj*[i] is a reference to the first node in a linked list of nodes representing the vertices adjacent to vertex i. Each node has members *ver*, the vertex adjacent to i, and *next*, a reference to the next node in the linked list or null, for the last node in the linked list.

To track visited vertices, the algorithm uses an array *visit*; *visit*[i] is set to true if vertex i has been visited or to false if vertex i has not been visited.

The algorithm uses an initially empty queue q to store pending current vertices. The expression

q.enqueue(*val*)

adds *val* to *q*. The expression

  q.front()

returns the value at the front of *q* but does not remove it. The expression

  q.dequeue()

removes the item at the front of *q*. The expression

  q.empty()

returns true if *q* is empty or false if *q* is not empty.

  Input Parameters: *adj, start*
  Output Parameters: None

```
bfs(adj, start) {
  n = adj.last
  for i = 1 to n
    visit[i] = false
  visit[start] = true
  println(start)
  // q is an initially empty queue
  q.enqueue(start)
  while (!q.empty()) {
    current = q.front()
    q.dequeue()
    trav = adj[current]
    while (trav != null) {
      v = trav.ver
      if (!visit[v]) {
        visit[v] = true
        println(v)
        q.enqueue(v)
      }
      trav = trav.next
    }
  }
}
```

Example 4.3.3. We trace Algorithm 4.3.2 when the input is the graph with adjacency lists (see Figure 4.2.5)

$$adj[1] \rightarrow 2 \rightarrow 3$$
$$adj[2] \rightarrow 1 \rightarrow 4$$
$$adj[3] \rightarrow 1 \rightarrow 4$$
$$adj[4] \rightarrow 2 \rightarrow 3 \rightarrow 5$$
$$adj[5] \rightarrow 4$$

and the start vertex is 1.

When *bfs* is called, the cells of the array *visit* are initialized to false; and the start vertex, 1, is marked as visited and pushed on the queue [see Figure 4.3.3(a)].

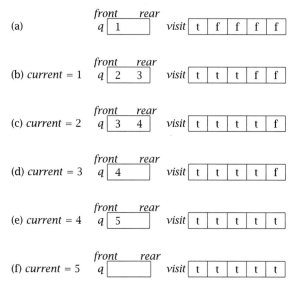

Figure 4.3.3 A trace of breadth-first search (Algorithm 4.3.2) for the graph of Figure 4.2.5. In the array *visit*, true is abbreviated to t, and false is abbreviated to f.

We then execute the first while loop. Since the queue is not empty, the body of the while loop executes. Since 1 is at the front of the queue, *current* is set to 1, 1 is removed from the queue, and *trav* is set to the first node in 1's adjacency list, which contains vertex 2. Since *trav* is not null, the body of the second while loop executes, where *v* is set to 2. Because 2 is not visited, it is marked as visited and added to the queue. The variable *trav* is then advanced to the next node, which contains vertex 3. Since *trav* is again not null, the body of the second while loop executes again, where *v* is set to 3. Because 3 is not visited, it is marked as visited and added to the queue. The variable *trav* then becomes null, and the second while loop terminates [see Figure 4.3.3(b)].

We again execute the first while loop. Since the queue is not empty, the body of the while loop executes. Since 2 is at the front of the queue, *current* is set to 2, 2 is removed from the queue, and *trav* is set to the first node in 2's adjacency list, which contains vertex 1. Since *trav* is not null, the body of the second while loop executes, where *v* is set to 1. Because 1 is visited, *trav* is advanced to the next node, which contains vertex 4. Since *trav* is not null, the body of the second while loop executes again, where *v* is set to 4. Because 4 is not visited, it is marked as visited and added to the queue. The variable *trav* then becomes null, and the second while loop terminates [see Figure 4.3.3(c)].

We again execute the first while loop. Since the queue is not empty, the body of the while loop executes. Since 3 is at the front of the queue, *current* is set to 3, 3 is removed from the queue, and *trav* is set to the first node in 3's adjacency list, which contains vertex 1. Since *trav* is not null, the body of the second while loop executes, where v is set to 1. Because 1 is visited, *trav* is advanced to the next node, which contains vertex 4. Since *trav* is not null, the body of the second while loop executes again, where v is set to 4. Because 4 is also visited, *trav* then becomes null, and the second while loop terminates [see Figure 4.3.3(d)].

We again execute the first while loop. Since the queue is not empty, the body of the while loop executes. Since 4 is at the front of the queue, *current* is set to 4, 4 is removed from the queue, and *trav* is set to the first node in 4's adjacency list, which contains vertex 2. Since *trav* is not null, the body of the second while loop executes, where v is set to 2. Because 2 is visited, *trav* is advanced to the next node, which contains vertex 3. Since *trav* is not null, the body of the second while loop executes again, where v is set to 3. Because 3 is also visited, *trav* is advanced to the next node, which contains vertex 5. Since *trav* is not null, the body of the second while loop executes again, where v is set to 5. Because 5 is not visited, it is marked as visited and added to the queue. The variable *trav* then becomes null, and the second while loop terminates [see Figure 4.3.3(e)].

We again execute the first while loop. Since the queue is not empty, the body of the while loop executes. Since 5 is at the front of the queue, *current* is set to 5, 5 is removed from the queue, and *trav* is set to the only node in 5's adjacency list, which contains vertex 4. Since *trav* is not null, the body of the second while loop executes, where v is set to 4. Because 4 is visited, *trav* then becomes null, and the second while loop terminates [see Figure 4.3.3(f)]. Since the queue is now empty, the algorithm terminates.   □

Suppose that a graph with m edges and n vertices is input to the breadth-first-search algorithm (Algorithm 4.3.2). The for loop in *bfs* runs in time $\Theta(n)$. In the nested while loops, in the worst case each node in each adjacency list is visited one time, as happens in Example 4.3.3. Since there are $2m$ nodes altogether in the adjacency lists, the total time for the nested while loops is $\Theta(m)$ in the worst case. Therefore, in the worst case, breadth-first search runs in time $\Theta(m + n)$.

Breadth-first search (Algorithm 4.3.2) can be applied without change to a directed graph. The adjacency list for vertex i represents vertices j, where (i, j) is an edge from i to j.

Notice that in breadth-first search, after the start vertex is visited, *all* vertices V_1 adjacent to the start vertex are visited before any other vertices are visited; that is, V_1 is the set of vertices reachable from the start vertex on a path of minimum length 1. Next, all vertices V_2 not yet visited that are adjacent to some vertex in V_1 are visited before any other vertices are visited; that is, V_2 is the set of vertices reachable from the start vertex on a path of minimum length 2. (A vertex in V_2 cannot be reachable from the start vertex on a path of length 1 because, if it could, it would be in V_1 and thus already visited.) These observations lead to the following shortest-path algorithm. In Algorithm 4.3.4, the array *length* plays a role similar to the array *visit* in Algorithm 4.3.2.

Algorithm 4.3.4 Finding Shortest Path Lengths Using Breadth-First Search.
This algorithm finds the length of a shortest path from the start vertex *start* to every other vertex in a graph with vertices $1, \ldots, n$.

The graph is represented using adjacency lists; *adj*[*i*] is a reference to the first node in a linked list of nodes representing the vertices adjacent to vertex *i*. Each node has members *ver*, the vertex adjacent to *i*, and *next*, a reference to the next node in the linked list or null, for the last node in the linked list.

In the array *length*, *length*[*i*] is set to the length of a shortest path from *start* to vertex *i* if this length has been computed or to ∞ if the length has not been computed. If there is no path from *start* to *i*, when the algorithm terminates, *length*[*i*] is ∞.

```
 Input Parameters:    adj, start
 Output Parameter:    length

shortest_paths(adj, start, length) {
   n = adj.last
   for i = 1 to n
      length[i] = ∞
   length[start] = 0
   // q is an initially empty queue
   q.enqueue(start)
   while (!q.empty()) {
      current = q.front()
      q.dequeue()
      trav = adj[current]
      while (trav != null) {
         v = trav.ver
         if (length[v] == ∞) {
            length[v] = 1 + length[current]
            q.enqueue(v)
         }
         trav = trav.next
      }
   }
}
```

Although Algorithm 4.3.4 computes only the lengths of shortest paths and not the shortest paths themselves, by tracking the vertex *current* from which vertex *v* is visited, an auxiliary algorithm can be written that outputs the shortest paths (see Exercises 21 and 22).

Since Algorithm 4.3.4 is essentially identical to Algorithm 4.3.2, which runs in time $\Theta(m + n)$ in the worst case when the input is a graph with m edges and n vertices, Algorithm 4.3.4 also runs in time $\Theta(m + n)$ in the worst case. In particular, this shortest-path problem can be solved in linear time. In Section 7.4, we will discuss Dijkstra's algorithm—an enhancement of Algorithm 4.3.4—that finds shortest paths in a *weighted* graph.

Exercises

In Exercises 1–6, list the order in which the vertices are visited when the breadth-first-search algorithm (Algorithm 4.3.2) is executed with the given input. Assume that the vertices are listed in increasing order in each adjacency list.

1S. The graph of Exercise 1, Section 4.2; start vertex = 1

2. The graph of Exercise 1, Section 4.2; start vertex = 3

3. The graph of Exercise 2, Section 4.2; start vertex = 3

4S. The graph of Exercise 2, Section 4.2; start vertex = 8

5. The graph of Exercise 3, Section 4.2; start vertex = 4

6. The graph of Exercise 3, Section 4.2; start vertex = 6

In Exercises 7–12, list the order in which the vertices are visited when the breadth-first-search algorithm (Algorithm 4.3.2) is executed with the given input. Assume that the vertices are listed in decreasing order in each adjacency list.

7S. The graph of Exercise 1, Section 4.2; start vertex = 1

8. The graph of Exercise 1, Section 4.2; start vertex = 2

9. The graph of Exercise 2, Section 4.2; start vertex = 3

10S. The graph of Exercise 2, Section 4.2; start vertex = 4

11. The graph of Exercise 3, Section 4.2; start vertex = 5

12. The graph of Exercise 3, Section 4.2; start vertex = 6

13S. Give a trace of the breadth-first-search algorithm (Algorithm 4.3.2) similar to that in Example 4.3.3 when the input is the graph of Figure 4.2.5 and the start vertex is 5. Assume that the vertices are listed in increasing order in each adjacency list.

14. Give a trace of the breadth-first-search algorithm (Algorithm 4.3.2) similar to that in Example 4.3.3 when the input is the graph of Figure 4.2.5 and the start vertex is 1. Assume that the vertices are listed in decreasing order in each adjacency list.

15. Give a trace of the breadth-first-search algorithm (Algorithm 4.3.2) similar to that in Example 4.3.3 when the input is the graph of Exercise 1, Section 4.2, and the start vertex is 1. Assume that the vertices are listed in increasing order in each adjacency list.

16S. Give a trace of the breadth-first-search algorithm (Algorithm 4.3.2) similar to that in Example 4.3.3 when the input is the graph of Exercise 1, Section 4.2, and the start vertex is 3. Assume that the vertices are listed in decreasing order in each adjacency list.

17. What is the best-case time of the breadth-first-search algorithm (Algorithm 4.3.2)?

18. Modify Algorithm 4.3.2 so that it tracks the parent p of a vertex c (p is the *parent* of c if c was visited from p).

19. Write an algorithm that uses the output of your algorithm in Exercise 18 to print each vertex and its parent.

20S. Write a version of breadth-first search in which the input graph is represented using an adjacency matrix. What is the worst-case time of your algorithm?

21. Modify Algorithm 4.3.4 so that it tracks the vertex *current* from which vertex v is visited.

22. Use the output of your modified algorithm of Exercise 21 to write an algorithm that prints a shortest path from *start* to all other vertices in the graph.

4.4 Topological Sort

Figure 4.4.1 shows a list of courses and prerequisites. (Course A is a *prerequisite* for course B if A must be taken before B.) A **topological sort** of the courses is a list of courses in the order in which they could be taken to satisfy the prerequisite requirements. In other words, if course c_i is a prerequisite for course c_j, then c_i precedes c_j in the topological sort. By inspection, we see that

> MATH 120, MATH 130, COMPSCI 100, MATH 140, COMPSCI 150, ENG 110, COMPSCI 200, PHY 130, MATH 200, COMPSCI 240

is a topological sort of the courses in Figure 4.4.1. In this example, other topological sorts are also possible.

Course	Prerequisites
COMPSCI 100	MATH 120
COMPSCI 150	MATH 140
COMPSCI 200	COMPSCI 100, COMPSCI 150, ENG 110
COMPSCI 240	COMPSCI 200, PHYS 130
ENG 110	*None*
MATH 120	*None*
MATH 130	MATH 120
MATH 140	MATH 130
MATH 200	MATH 140, PHYS 130
PHYS 130	*None*

Figure 4.4.1 Courses and prerequisites.

In order for a topological sort to exist, there must not be any cyclical prerequisite structure, that is, a situation in which c_1 is a prerequisite for c_2, c_2 is a prerequisite for $c_3, \ldots, c_{n-1}$ is a prerequisite for c_n, *and c_n* is a prerequisite for c_1. If such a situation existed, no topological sort would be possible, and no student would be able to take any of the classes $c_1, \ldots, c_n$!

A list of courses and prerequisites such as that in Figure 4.4.1 can be modeled as a directed graph (see Figure 4.4.2). The vertices represent the courses, and there is an edge from the vertex representing course c_i to the vertex representing course c_j if c_i is a prerequisite to c_j. The requirement that there must not be any cyclical prerequisite structure means that in the graph there must not be any directed cycles. A directed graph with no directed cycles is called a *directed acyclic graph* or a *dag*. A *topological sort of a dag G* is, then, an ordering $v_1, \ldots, v_n$ of all of the vertices of G such that, if (v_i, v_j) is a directed edge, then v_i precedes v_j in the ordering.

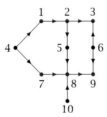

Figure 4.4.2 The prerequisite structure of Figure 4.4.1 as a directed graph. The vertices represent the courses: 1-MATH 130, 2-MATH 140, 3-MATH 200, 4-MATH 120, 5-COMPSCI 150, 6-PHYS 130, 7-COMPSCI 100, 8-COMPSCI 200, 9-COMPSCI 240, and 10-ENG 110. If course c_i is a prerequisite to course c_j, then there is an edge from the vertex representing c_i to the vertex representing c_j.

We can use depth-first search to construct a topological sort of a dag G. Suppose that we run a depth-first search from an arbitrary start vertex v_1 in

G. The depth-first search visits v_1, then visits an unvisited vertex v_2 from v_1, then visits an unvisited vertex v_3 from v_2, and so on. Eventually the depth-first search reaches a vertex v_k with no edges of the form (v_k, v'), where v' is unvisited [see Figure 4.4.3(a)]. We suppose that v_k is the first such vertex. In fact, there are *no* edges at all of the form (v_k, v') (i.e., the outdegree of v_k is 0), for if there was such an edge, v' would be visited, and the graph would contain a directed cycle [see Figure 4.4.3(b)]. (This observation can be used to determine whether an arbitrary directed graph is a dag; see Exercise 4.11.) It follows that v_k can be placed last in the topological sort.

(a)   (b)

Figure 4.4.3 (a) Depth-first search beginning at vertex v_1 and continuing until reaching the first vertex v_k with no edges of the form (v_k, v'), where v' is unvisited. (b) If there is an edge of the form (v_k, v'), v' would be visited and therefore one of the already visited vertices v_i. In this case, the graph would contain a directed cycle.

Let v_k be the first vertex in the depth-first search that is identified as having outdegree 0. Notice that when *dfs_recurs* (in Algorithm 4.2.2) is called with *start* = v_k, this is the first instance of *dfs_recurs* to return. Thus, in Algorithm 4.2.2, we can identify the last vertex in a topological sort at the point shown in Figure 4.4.4.

```
dfs_recurs(adj, start) {
    println(start)
    visit[start] = true
    trav = adj[start]
    while (trav != null) {
        v = trav.ver
        if (!visit[v])
            dfs_recurs(adj, v)
        trav = trav.next
    }
    // vertex identified here
}
```

Figure 4.4.4 The first time any call of *dfs_recurs* reaches the line marked "vertex identified here," the current *start* can be placed last in the topological sort; the next time a call of *dfs_recurs* reaches the line marked "vertex identified here," the current *start* can be placed next to last in the topological sort; and so on.

Consider how the depth-first search continues. Since v_k was marked as visited, any time later when *start* = v' and v' is adjacent to $v = v_k$, v_k is ignored in *dfs_recurs* because of the line

if (!*visit*[v])

In effect, the algorithm continues as though all edges into v_k were deleted. Thus, when *dfs_recurs* next reaches the point marked

// vertex identified here

with *start* = w, w can be placed next to last in the topological sort. If depth-first search concludes and there are still unvisited vertices, another depth-first search is begun at an unvisited vertex. This discussion leads to the following algorithm that computes a topological sort of a dag.

Algorithm 4.4.1 Topological Sort. This algorithm computes a topological sort of a directed acyclic graph with vertices $1, \ldots, n$. The vertices in the topological sort are stored in the array *ts*.

The graph is represented using adjacency lists; *adj*[i] is a reference to the first node in a linked list of nodes representing the vertices adjacent to vertex i. Each node has members *ver*, the vertex adjacent to i, and *next*, a reference to the next node in the linked list or null, for the last node in the linked list.

To track visited vertices, the algorithm uses an array *visit*; *visit*[i] is set to true if vertex i has been visited or to false if vertex i has not been visited.

Input Parameter: *adj*
Output Parameter: *ts*

```
top_sort(adj, ts) {
    n = adj.last
    // k is the index in ts where the next vertex is to be stored in the
    // topological sort. k is assumed visible in top_sort_recurs.
    k = n
    for i = 1 to n
        visit[i] = false
    for i = 1 to n
        if (!visit[i])
            top_sort_recurs(adj, i, ts)
}

top_sort_recurs(adj, start, ts) {
    visit[start] = true
    trav = adj[start]
    while (trav != null) {
        v = trav.ver
        if (!visit[v])
            top_sort_recurs(adj, v, ts)
```

$$trav = trav.next$$
$$\}$$
$$ts[k] = start$$
$$k = k - 1$$
$$\}$$

Example 4.4.2. We show how Algorithm 4.4.1 constructs a topological sort of the graph of Figure 4.4.2. We assume that the vertices are listed in increasing order on each adjacency list.

First, *top_sort* calls *top_sort_recurs* with $i = 1$. Vertex 1 is marked as visited, and we begin traversing 1's adjacency list. The only vertex on the list is 2. Since 2 is not visited, *top_sort_recurs* is called with $v = 2$.

Vertex 2 is marked as visited, and we begin traversing 2's adjacency list. The first vertex on the list is 3. Since 3 is not visited, *top_sort_recurs* is called with $v = 3$.

Vertex 3 is marked as visited. Since 3's adjacency list is empty, 3 is placed last in the topological sort, and *top_sort_recurs* with $start = 3$ returns to its caller *top_sort_recurs* with $start = 2$.

Execution of *top_sort_recurs* with $start = 2$ resumes by moving to the next node on 2's adjacency list, which contains vertex 5. Since 5 is not visited, *top_sort_recurs* is called with $v = 5$.

Vertex 5 is marked as visited, and we begin traversing 5's adjacency list. The only vertex on the list is 8. Since 8 is not visited, *top_sort_recurs* is called with $v = 8$.

Vertex 8 is marked as visited, and we begin traversing 8's adjacency list. The only vertex on the list is 9. Since 9 is not visited, *top_sort_recurs* is called with $v = 9$.

Vertex 9 is marked as visited. Since 9's adjacency list is empty, 9 is placed before 3 in the topological sort, and *top_sort_recurs* with $start = 9$ returns to its caller *top_sort_recurs* with $start = 8$.

Execution of *top_sort_recurs* with $start = 8$ resumes by attempting to move to the next node on 8's adjacency list. Since there are no more nodes on 8's list, 8 is placed before 9 in the topological sort, and *top_sort_recurs* with $start = 8$ returns to its caller *top_sort_recurs* with $start = 5$.

Execution of *top_sort_recurs* with $start = 5$ resumes by attempting to move to the next node on 5's adjacency list. Since there are no more nodes on 5's list, 5 is placed before 8 in the topological sort, and *top_sort_recurs* with $start = 5$ returns to its caller *top_sort_recurs* with $start = 2$.

Execution of *top_sort_recurs* with $start = 2$ resumes by attempting to move to the next node on 2's adjacency list. Since there are no more nodes on 2's list, 2 is placed before 5 in the topological sort, and *top_sort_recurs* with $start = 2$ returns to its caller *top_sort_recurs* with $start = 1$.

Execution of *top_sort_recurs* with $start = 1$ resumes by attempting to move to the next node on 1's adjacency list. Since there are no more nodes on 1's list, 1 is placed before 2 in the topological sort, and *top_sort_recurs* with $start = 1$ returns to its caller *top_sort*. At this point, the array *ts* is

				1	2	5	8	9	3

.

Since 2 and 3 are visited, but 4 is not visited, *top_sort* next calls *top_sort_recurs* with $i = 4$. The reader should check that, after this call, the array *ts* becomes

		4	7	1	2	5	8	9	3

.

Since 5 is visited, but 6 is not visited, *top_sort* next calls *top_sort_recurs* with $i = 6$. The reader should check that, after this call, the array *ts* becomes

	6	4	7	1	2	5	8	9	3

.

Since 7, 8, and 9 are visited, but 10 is not visited, *top_sort* next calls *top_sort_recurs* with $i = 10$. The reader should check that, after this call, the array *ts* becomes

10	6	4	7	1	2	5	8	9	3

.

The algorithm then terminates.   □

Suppose that a graph with m edges and n vertices is input to topological sort (Algorithm 4.4.1). The for loops in *top_sort* each run in time $\Theta(n)$. After *top_sort* finishes calling *top_sort_recurs*, each node in each adjacency list is visited one time. Since there are m nodes altogether in the adjacency lists, the total time for all of the calls of *top_sort_recurs* is $\Theta(m)$. Therefore, topological sort runs in time $\Theta(m + n)$.

Exercises

In Exercises 1–3, find the topological sort produced by Algorithm 4.4.1. Assume that the vertices are listed in increasing order in each adjacency list.

1S.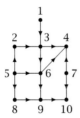

2.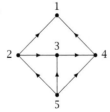

3.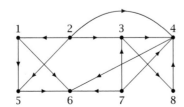

In Exercises 4–7, find the topological sort produced by Algorithm 4.4.1. Assume that the vertices are listed in decreasing order in each adjacency list.

4S. The graph of Figure 4.4.2

5. The graph of Exercise 1

6. The graph of Exercise 2

7S. The graph of Exercise 3

8S. Give a trace of the topological-sort algorithm (Algorithm 4.4.1) similar to that in Example 4.4.2 when the input is the graph of Figure 4.4.2. Assume that the vertices are listed in decreasing order in each adjacency list.

9. Give a trace of the topological-sort algorithm (Algorithm 4.4.1) similar to that in Example 4.4.2 when the input is the graph of Exercise 1. Assume that the vertices are listed in increasing order in each adjacency list.

10. Give a trace of the topological-sort algorithm (Algorithm 4.4.1) similar to that in Example 4.4.2 when the input is the graph of Exercise 2. Assume that the vertices are listed in increasing order in each adjacency list.

11S. Give a trace of the topological-sort algorithm (Algorithm 4.4.1) similar to that in Example 4.4.2 when the input is the graph of Exercise 1. Assume that the vertices are listed in decreasing order in each adjacency list.

12. Give a trace of the topological-sort algorithm (Algorithm 4.4.1) similar to that in Example 4.4.2 when the input is the graph of Exercise 2. Assume that the vertices are listed in decreasing order in each adjacency list.

13. Give a topological sort of the graph in Figure 4.4.2 different from that obtained in Example 4.4.2.

14S. Give an example of a dag with at least four vertices that has a unique topological sort.

15. Give an example of a dag G with at least four vertices in which every permutation of the vertices of G is a topological sort of G.

16. Prove that a directed graph in which every vertex v has at least one outgoing edge [i.e., an edge of the form (v, v')] and at least one incoming edge [i.e., an edge of the form (v'', v)] is *not* a dag.

17S. What is the best-case time of the topological-sort algorithm (Algorithm 4.4.1)?

18. Is Algorithm 4.4.1 still correct if the line

    if ($!visit[i]$)

in *top_sort* is omitted? Explain.

19. Determine whether the following is true or false. If it is true, prove it. If it is false, give a counterexample.

Let G be a dag with $n > 1$ vertices, and let G' be the undirected graph obtained from G by ignoring the direction of the edges. Suppose that G' is connected. In any topological sort $v_1, \ldots, v_n$ of G, (v_i, v_{i+1}) is an edge for some $i \in \{1, \ldots, n-1\}$.

20S. Write a version of topological sort in which the input graph is represented using an adjacency matrix. What is the worst-case time of your algorithm?

21. Write an algorithm that inputs a dag G and an ordering a of the vertices of G. The algorithm returns true if a is a topological sort of G or false if a is not a topological sort of G. What is the worst-case time of your algorithm?

4.5 Backtracking

$\mathcal{WWW}$ The n-**queens problem** is to place n queens on an $n \times n$ board so that no two queens are in the same row, column, or diagonal (see Figure 4.5.1). In chess terminology, this is the problem of placing n queens on an $n \times n$ board so that no queen attacks another queen.

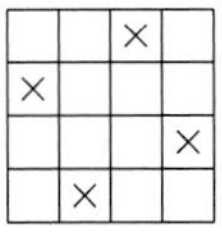

Figure 4.5.1 The 4-queens problem. Queens, shown as $\times$, are placed so that no two queens are in the same row, column, or diagonal.

The n-queens problem can be solved using depth-first search. The graph to which depth-first search is applied is a tree, called the **search tree**, with vertices that represent boards containing n or fewer queens. The root is the board with no queens. The tree is generated dynamically; that is, we place queens successively in the columns beginning in the left column and working from top to bottom. The next queen placed in a column is shown as a child. When it is impossible to place a queen in a column, we return to the parent and adjust the queen in the preceding column. Depth-first search applied to a dynamically generated tree is called **backtracking**. The name derives from the situation in which we cannot place the next queen and return to the parent.

Example 4.5.1. Figure 4.5.2 shows part of the search tree for the four-queens problem that is generated using backtracking.

We begin at the root with an empty board [board (0)]. We use the notation "board (*i*)" to indicate the board that is generated after *i* attempts to place

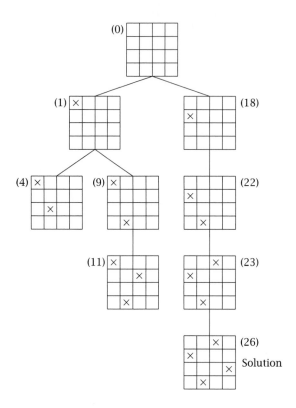

Figure 4.5.2 Part of the search tree for the four-queens problem generated by backtracking. We place queens successively in the columns beginning in the left column and working from top to bottom. The children of the root, which represents an empty board, show various possibilities for placing a queen in column 1. At the next level are various possibilities for placing a queen in column 2, given the position of the queen in column 1. The next two levels are generated similarly. The notation (i) by a board B indicates that B was generated after i attempts to place a queen.

a queen. We then place queens successively in the columns beginning in the left column and working from top to bottom. We first place a queen in the upper-left corner [board (1)].

Since a queen in column 2, row 1, or column 2, row 2, conflicts with the queen in column 1, we next place a queen in column 2, row 3 [board (4)].

It is now impossible to place a queen in column 3 because every position conflicts with one of the queens already present. We therefore backtrack to board (1) and generate another child of (1) by moving the queen down in column 2 in board (4); the result is board (9).

Since a queen in column 3, row 1, conflicts with the queen in column 1, we next place a queen in column 3, row 2 [board (11)].

It is now impossible to place a queen in column 4 because every position conflicts with one of the queens already present. We therefore backtrack to board (9) and attempt to generate another child of (9) by moving the queen down in column 3 in board (11); however, both potential positions conflict. We therefore backtrack to board (1) and attempt to generate another child of (1) by moving the queen down in column 2 in board (9). Since the queen in column 2 is in the last row, this is impossible. We therefore backtrack to board (0), where we generate another child of (0) by moving the queen down in column 1 in board (1) [board (18)].

We are then able to generate successive children starting at board (18) until we find a solution [board (26)].   □

We implement the backtracking solution of the n-queens problem recursively. The key function is rn_queens. When $rn\_queens(k, n)$ is called, queens have been properly placed in columns 1 through $k - 1$, and rn_queens tries to place a queen in column k. If it is successful and k equals n, it prints a solution. The algorithm can be terminated at this point if only one solution is desired. Our version, which outputs *all* solutions, continues. If $rn\_queens(k, n)$ succeeds in placing a queen in column k, and k does not equal n, it calls

$$rn\_queens(k + 1, n),$$

which tries to place a queen in the next column. If $rn\_queens(k, n)$ does not succeed in placing a queen in column k, it backtracks by returning to its caller

$$rn\_queens(k - 1, n),$$

which tries to adjust the queen in column $k - 1$. The backtracking solution is obtained by calling

$$rn\_queens(1, n).$$

We track the positions of the queens by using an array *row*. The value of $row[k]$ is the row in which the queen in column k is placed.

To test for a valid position for a queen in column k, we write a function $position\_ok(k, n)$, which returns true if the queen in column k does not conflict with the queens in columns 1 through $k - 1$ or false if it does conflict. The queens in columns i and k conflict if either they are in the same row

$$row[k] == row[i]$$

or in the same diagonal

$$|row[k] - row[i]| == k - i$$

(see Figure 4.5.3).

The first version of the algorithm is

```
n_queens(n) {
   rn_queens(1, n)
}
```

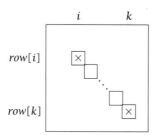

Figure 4.5.3 Two queens in column i, row $row[i]$, and in column k, row $row[k]$, $i < k$, are in the same diagonal if the absolute difference $|row[k] - row[i]|$, which measures the row gap between them, equals $k - i$, the column gap between them.

```
rn_queens(k, n) {
    for row[k] = 1 to n
        if (position_ok(k, n))
            if (k == n) {
                for i = 1 to n
                    print(row[i] + " ")
                println()
            }
            else
                rn_queens(k + 1, n)
}

position_ok(k, n)
    for i = 1 to k - 1
        // abs is absolute value
        if (row[k] == row[i] || abs(row[k] - row[i]) == k - i)
            return false
    return true
}
```

We can reduce the time of *position_ok* from $O(k)$ to constant time by tracking which rows and diagonals cannot be used by a queen because they are occupied by previous queens. We maintain an array *row_used*, where *row_used*$[r]$ is true if a queen occupies row r. To track the diagonals, we arbitrarily number the diagonals in the direction ↘ as shown in Figure 4.5.4(a). We call these the *ddiag*s (downward *diag*onals). We maintain a second array *ddiag_used*, where *ddiag_used*$[d]$ is true if a queen occupies *ddiag* d. Notice that the queen in column k, row r, is in *ddiag* $n - k + r$. Similarly, we arbitrarily number the diagonals in the direction ↗ [see Figure 4.5.4(b)]. We call these the *udiag*s (upward *diag*onals). We maintain a third array *udiag_used*, where *udiag_used*$[d]$ is true if a queen occupies *udiag* d. Notice that the queen in column k, row r, is in *udiag* $k + r - 1$.

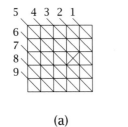
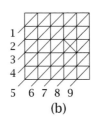

(a)   (b)

Figure 4.5.4 Board (a) shows the numbering of the diagonals in the direction ↘ in a 5×5 board. These diagonals are called the *ddiag*s. The queen in column k, row r, is in *ddiag* $n - k + r$. For example, the queen in column 4, row 3, (shown as ×) is in *ddiag* $n - k + r = 5 - 4 + 3 = 4$. Board (b) shows the numbering of the diagonals in the direction ↗ in a 5×5 board. These diagonals are called the *udiag*s. The queen in column k, row r, is in *udiag* $k + r - 1$. For example, the queen in column 4, row 3, (shown as ×) is in *udiag* $k + r - 1 = 4 + 3 - 1 = 6$.

The final version of our n-queens algorithm is given as Algorithm 4.5.2.

Algorithm 4.5.2 Solving the n-Queens Problem Using Backtracking. The n-queens problem is to place n queens on an $n \times n$ board so that no two queens are in the same row, column, or diagonal. Using backtracking, this algorithm outputs all solutions to this problem. We place queens successively in the columns beginning in the left column and working from top to bottom. When it is impossible to place a queen in a column, we return to the previous column and move its queen down.

The value of *row*[k] is the row where the queen in column k is placed.

The algorithm begins when *n_queens* calls *rn_queens*$(1, n)$. When

$$rn\_queens(k, n)$$

is called, queens have been properly placed in columns 1 through $k - 1$, and *rn_queens*(k, n) tries to place a queen in column k. If it is successful and k equals n, it prints a solution. If it is successful and k does not equal n, it calls

$$rn\_queens(k + 1, n).$$

If it is not successful, it backtracks by returning to its caller

$$rn\_queens(k - 1, n).$$

The value of *row_used*[r] is true if a queen occupies row r and false otherwise. The value of *ddiag_used*[d] is true if a queen occupies *ddiag* diagonal d and false otherwise [see Figure 4.5.4(a)]. According to the numbering system used, the queen in column k, row r, is in *ddiag* diagonal $n - k + r$. The value of *udiag_used*[d] is true if a queen occupies *udiag* diagonal d and false otherwise [see Figure 4.5.4(b)]. According to the numbering system used, the queen in column k, row r, is in *udiag* $k + r - 1$.

The function *position_ok*(*k*, *n*) assumes that queens have been placed in columns 1 through *k* − 1. It returns true if the queen in column *k* does not conflict with the queens in columns 1 through *k* − 1 or false if it does conflict.

Input Parameter: *n*
Output Parameters: None

```
n_queens(n) {
   for i = 1 to n
      row_used[i] = false
   for i = 1 to 2 * n − 1
      ddiag_used[i] = udiag_used[i] = false
   rn_queens(1, n)
}

// When rn_queens(k, n) is called, queens have been
// properly placed in columns 1 through k − 1.
rn_queens(k, n) {
   for row[k] = 1 to n
      if (position_ok(k, n)) {
         row_used[row[k]] = true
         ddiag_used[n − k + row[k]] = true
         udiag_used[k + row[k] − 1] = true
         if (k == n) {
            // Output a solution. Stop if only one solution is desired.
            for i = 1 to n
               print(row[i] + " ")
            println()
         }
         else
            rn_queens(k + 1, n)
         row_used[row[k]] = false
         ddiag_used[n − k + row[k]] = false
         udiag_used[k + row[k] − 1] = false
      }
}

// position_ok(k, n) returns true if the queen in column k
// does not conflict with the queens in columns 1
// through k − 1 or false if it does conflict.
position_ok(k, n) {
   return !(row_used[row[k]]
            || ddiag_used[n − k + row[k]]
            || udiag_used[k + row[k] − 1])
}
```

Time for n-Queens

To obtain an upper bound for the worst-case time of Algorithm 4.5.2, we bound the number of times that $rn\_queens(k,n)$ is called for each value of k.

For $k = 1$, $rn\_queens(k,n)$ is called one time (by n_queens). For $k > 1$, there are $n(n-1)\cdots(n-k+2)$ ways to place $k-1$ queens in the first $k-1$ columns in distinct rows; thus, $rn\_queens(k,n)$ is called at most

$$n(n-1)\cdots(n-k+2)$$

times. Ignoring recursive calls, $rn\_queens(k,n)$ executes in time $\Theta(n)$ for $k < n$. Therefore, the worst-case time for $rn\_queens(k,n)$ is at most

$$n, \text{ for } k = 1, \quad \text{and} \quad n[n(n-1)\cdots(n-k+2)], \text{ for } 1 < k < n. \quad (4.5.1)$$

When $k = n$, all rows except one are occupied; thus, $position\_ok(k,n)$ is true for at most one value of k. The inner for loop in rn_queens executes in time $\Theta(n)$. Therefore, the time for rn_queens for $k = n$ is $O(n)$. There are $n(n-1)\cdots 2$ ways to place $n-1$ queens in the first $n-1$ columns in distinct rows; thus, the worst-case time of $rn\_queens(n,n)$ is at most

$$n[n(n-1)\cdots 2]. \quad (4.5.2)$$

Combining equations (4.5.1) and (4.5.2), we find that the worst-case time of rn_queens is at most

$$n[1 + n + n(n-1) + \cdots + n(n-1)\cdots 2]$$
$$= n \cdot n! \left[\frac{1}{n!} + \frac{1}{(n-1)!} + \frac{1}{(n-2)!} + \cdots + \frac{1}{1!} \right].$$

A result from calculus tells us that

$$e = \sum_{i=0}^{\infty} \frac{1}{i!},$$

where e is the base of the natural logarithm. Therefore, the worst-case time of rn_queens is at most

$$n \cdot n! \left[\frac{1}{n!} + \frac{1}{(n-1)!} + \frac{1}{(n-2)!} + \cdots + \frac{1}{1!} \right] \leq n \cdot n! \sum_{i=1}^{\infty} \frac{1}{i!} = n \cdot n!(e-1).$$

It follows that the worst-case time of rn_queens is $O(n \cdot n!)$. The for loops in n_queens run in time $\Theta(n)$; thus, the worst-case time for Algorithm 4.5.2 is $O(n \cdot n!)$.

Existence of Solutions to the n-Queens Problem

In this subsection, we show that the n-queens problem has a solution for each $n \geq 4$. The proof explicitly constructs a solution for each $n \geq 4$. However, if *all* solutions or the *number* of solutions are desired, it appears that an algorithm such as Algorithm 4.5.2 is required.

Theorem 4.5.3. *The n-queens problem has a solution for every $n \geq 4$.*

We use the notation introduced previously in this section in which row[k] designates the row in which the queen in column k is placed. Then, if $n \geq 4$ is even and n mod 3 = 0 or 1, one solution is obtained by setting

$$row[k] = 2k \qquad\qquad for\ 1 \leq k \leq n/2,$$
$$row[k] = 2k - n - 1 \quad for\ n/2 + 1 \leq k \leq n.$$

If $n \geq 8$ is even and n mod 3 = 2, one solution is obtained by setting

$$row[1] = 4,$$
$$row[k] = n - 2(k - 1) \quad for\ 2 \leq k \leq n/2 - 2,$$
$$row[n/2 - 1] = n,$$
$$row[n/2] = 2,$$
$$row[n/2 + 1] = n - 1,$$
$$row[n/2 + 2] = 1,$$
$$row[k] = 2(n - k) + 1 \quad for\ n/2 + 3 \leq k \leq n - 1,$$
$$row[n] = n - 3.$$

If $n > 4$ is odd, one solution is obtained by first solving the $(n - 1)$-queens problem as described previously and then setting row[n] = n.

Proof. Suppose that n is even and n mod 3 = 0 or 1. We first show that no two queens are in the same row.

Since distinct values of k, $1 \leq k \leq n/2$, yield distinct values of $2k$, no two queens in columns 1 through $n/2$ are in the same row. Similarly, no two queens in columns $n/2 + 1$ through n are in the same row.

Notice that a queen in column k_1, $1 \leq k_1 \leq n/2$, is in an even-numbered row, and a queen in column k_2, $n/2 + 1 \leq k_2 \leq n$, is in an odd-numbered row. It follows that no two queens, one from column k_1, $1 \leq k_1 \leq n/2$, and one from column k_2, $n/2 + 1 \leq k_2 \leq n$, are in the same row. Therefore, no two queens are in the same row.

If two queens in columns k_1 and k_2, $1 \leq k_1 < k_2 \leq n/2$, are in the same diagonal, we must have (see Figure 4.5.3)

$$k_2 - k_1 = 2(k_2 - k_1),$$

which is impossible. Therefore, no two queens in columns 1 through $n/2$ are in the same diagonal. Similarly, no two queens in columns $n/2 + 1$ through n are in the same diagonal.

If two queens in column k_1, $1 \leq k_1 \leq n/2$, and column k_2,

$$n/2 + 1 \leq k_2 \leq n,$$

are in the same diagonal, we must have

$$k_2 - k_1 = |2k_2 - n - 1 - 2k_1|.$$

Thus, either

$$k_2 - k_1 = 2k_2 - n - 1 - 2k_1, \tag{4.5.3}$$

or

$$k_2 - k_1 = -2k_2 + n + 1 + 2k_1. \tag{4.5.4}$$

Equation (4.5.3) may be rewritten as

$$k_2 - k_1 = n + 1.$$

However, this is impossible since $k_2 - k_1 \leq n - 1$.
  Equation (4.5.4) may be rewritten as

$$3(k_2 - k_1 - 1) + 2 = n.$$

Thus, $n \bmod 3 = 2$, which contradicts the fact that $n \bmod 3 = 0$ or 1. There-fore, no two queens are in the same diagonal.
  The case when $n \geq 8$ is even and $n \bmod 3 = 2$ is similar and left as an exercise (see Exercise 8).
  If n is even, it may be verified (see Exercise 9) that no queen is on the main diagonal; that is, for every column k, we have $row[k] \neq k$. Thus, if $n > 4$ is odd and we first solve the $(n - 1)$-queens problem, we can add a queen in column n, row n. Since the added queen does not conflict with the other queens, we obtain a solution to the n-queens problem when n is odd and greater than 4. ∎

Form of a Backtracking Algorithm

Suppose that we solve a problem using backtracking as in Algorithm 4.5.2 in which the solution is of the form

$$x[1], \ldots, x[n].$$

Suppose also that the values of $x[i]$ are in the set S (e.g., in Algorithm 4.5.2, $S = \{1, \ldots, n\}$). The general form of a backtracking algorithm becomes

```
backtrack(n) {
   rbacktrack(1, n)
}

rbacktrack(k, n) {
   for each x[k] ∈ S
      if (bound(k))
         if (k == n) {
            // Output a solution. Stop if only one solution is desired.
```

```
    for i = 1 to n
        print(x[i] + " ")
    println()
}
else
    rbacktrack(k + 1, n)
}
```

The function *bound*(k) assumes that

$$x[1], \ldots, x[k-1]$$

is a partial solution and that $x[k]$ has been assigned a value. It then returns true if

$$x[1], \ldots, x[k]$$

is a partial solution and false otherwise. The key to writing a useful backtracking algorithm is to write an efficient bound function that eliminates many potential nodes from the search tree.

The Hamiltonian-Cycle Problem

Recall (see Section 2.5) that a Hamiltonian cycle in a graph G is a cycle in which every vertex, except the beginning and ending vertices which coincide, occurs exactly one time. For example,

$$(1, 3, 5, 2, 4, 1)$$

is a Hamiltonian cycle for the graph of Figure 4.5.5.

Figure 4.5.5 A graph with a Hamiltonian cycle: $(1, 3, 5, 2, 4, 1)$.

Determining whether a graph has a Hamiltonian cycle is known to be **NP**-complete (see Section 10.2), so there is likely no polynomial-time algorithm for this problem. However, we can write a backtracking algorithm to solve the Hamiltonian-cycle problem; the time is often acceptable for graphs of modest size.

Suppose that a graph with vertices $1, \ldots, n$ has a Hamiltonian cycle

$$(x[1], x[2], \ldots, x[n], x[1]).$$

We represent this cycle as the array

$$x[1], \ldots, x[n].$$

Since a Hamiltonian cycle contains all of the vertices and can begin at any vertex, we assume that $x[1] = 1$. In our algorithm, if the graph has a Hamiltonian cycle, we return true and terminate the algorithm as soon as we find one Hamiltonian cycle. If the graph has no Hamiltonian cycle, we return false. We represent the graph using the adjacency matrix adj so that, given vertices i and j, we can quickly determine whether (i, j) is an edge. Translating the general form of the backtracking algorithm into the solution of the Hamiltonian-cycle problem, we obtain

```
hamilton(adj, x) {
   x[1] = 1
   rhamilton(adj, 2, x)
}

rhamilton(adj, k, x) {
   n = adj.last
   for x[k] = 2 to n
      if (path_ok(adj, k, x))
         if (k == n)
            return true
         else if (rhamilton(adj, k + 1, x))
            return true
   return false
}
```

Notice that the lines

```
if (k == n)
   return true
else if (rhamilton(adj, k + 1, x))
   return true
```

can be combined as

```
if (k == n || rhamilton(adj, k + 1, x))
   return true
```

The bound function, which we rename as *path_ok*, assumes that

$$(x[1], \ldots, x[k-1])$$

is a path from $x[1]$ to $x[k-1]$ and that the vertices $x[1], \ldots, x[k-1]$ are distinct. It must then check whether $(x[k-1], x[k])$ is an edge and whether $x[k]$ is different from each of $x[1], \ldots, x[k-1]$. If these conditions are satisfied, then $(x[1], \ldots, x[k])$ is a path from $x[1]$ to $x[k]$ and $x[1], \ldots, x[k]$ are distinct. If $k = n$, *path_ok* must also check whether $(x[n], x[1])$ is an edge.

As in the solution to the n-queens problem, we maintain an array *used* in which $used[i]$ is true if vertex i is one of $x[1], \ldots, x[k-1]$, or false otherwise. We obtain

```
path_ok(adj, k, x) {
  n = adj.last
  if (used[x[k]])
    return false
  if (k < n)
    return adj[x[k − 1]][x[k]]
  else
    return adj[x[n − 1]][x[n]] && adj[x[1]][x[n]]
}
```

With appropriate modifications of *hamilton* and *rhamilton*, we obtain the following backtracking algorithm that searches for Hamiltonian cycles.

Algorithm 4.5.4 Searching for a Hamiltonian Cycle. This algorithm inputs a graph with vertices $1, \ldots, n$. The graph is represented as an adjacency matrix adj; $adj[i][j]$ is true if (i, j) is an edge or false if it is not an edge. If the graph has a Hamiltonian cycle, the algorithm computes one such cycle

$$(x[1], \ldots, x[n], x[1]).$$

If the graph has no Hamiltonian cycle, the algorithm returns false and the contents of the array x are not specified.

In the array *used*, $used[i]$ is true if i has been selected as one of the vertices in a potential Hamiltonian cycle or false if i has not been selected.

The function $path\_ok(adj, k, x)$ assumes that $(x[1], \ldots, x[k-1])$ is a path from $x[1]$ to $x[k − 1]$ and that the vertices $x[1], \ldots, x[k − 1]$ are distinct. It then checks whether $x[k]$ is different from each of $x[1], \ldots, x[k − 1]$ and whether $(x[k − 1], x[k])$ is an edge. If $k = n$, $path\_ok$ also checks whether $(x[n], x[1])$ is an edge.

```
  Input Parameter:    adj
  Output Parameter:   x

hamilton(adj, x) {
  n = adj.last
  x[1] = 1
  used[1] = true
  for i = 2 to n
    used[i] = false
  rhamilton(adj, 2, x)
}

rhamilton(adj, k, x) {
  n = adj.last
  for x[k] = 2 to n
    if (path_ok(adj, k, x)) {
      used[x[k]] = true
```

$$if \ (k == n \ || \ rhamilton(adj, k + 1, x))$$
$$return \ true$$
$$used[x[k]] = false$$
$$\}$$
$$return \ false$$
$$\}$$

$$path\_ok(adj, k, x) \ \{$$
$$n = adj.last$$
$$if \ (used[x[k]])$$
$$return \ false$$
$$if \ (k < n)$$
$$return \ adj[x[k-1]][x[k]]$$
$$else$$
$$return \ adj[x[n-1]][x[n]] \ \&\& \ adj[x[1]][x[n]]$$
$$\}$$

The same technique we used to obtain an upper bound on the running time of the n-queens algorithm can be used to show that the worst-case time of Algorithm 4.5.4 is $O(n!)$ (see Exercise 23).

If G is the graph consisting of K_{n-1} (the complete graph on $n-1$ vertices), with vertices labeled $1, \ldots, n-1$, and one additional, isolated vertex labeled n, the running time of Algorithm 4.5.4 is $\Omega((n-1)!)$ (see Exercise 24). Thus, the worst-case time of Algorithm 4.5.4 is $\Omega((n-1)!)$.

Exercises

1S. Show that there is no solution to the 2-queens problem.

2. Show that there is no solution to the 3-queens problem.

3. Show all solutions to the 4-queens problem.

4S. Show all solutions to the 5-queens problem in which one queen is in the first column, second row.

5. How many solutions are there to the 5-queens problem?

6. Show all solutions to the 6-queens problem in which one queen is in row 2, column 1, and a second queen is in row 4, column 2.

7S. Show that if *rn_queens* is written as

$$rn\_queens(k, n) \ \{$$
$$if \ (k == 1)$$
$$m = (n + 1)/2$$
$$else$$
$$m = n$$

```
        for row[k] = 1 to m
           if (position_ok(k, n))
              if (k == n) {
                 for i = 1 to n
                    print(row[i] + " ")
                 println()
              }
              else
                 rn_queens(k + 1, n)
     }
```

the algorithm still finds a solution if there is one (although it does not find *all* solutions).

8. Prove Theorem 4.5.3 for the case n even, $n \geq 8$, and $n \bmod 3 = 2$.

9. Prove that if n is even, Theorem 4.5.3 places no queen on the main diagonal; that is, for every column k, we have $row[k] \neq k$.

10S. Give an example to show that if we use the solution for $n \bmod 3 = 0$ or 1 given in Theorem 4.5.3 for a board satisfying $n \bmod 3 = 2$, we may not obtain a solution.

11. Give an example to show that if we use the solution for $n \bmod 3 = 2$ given in Theorem 4.5.3 for a board satisfying $n \bmod 3 = 0$, we may not obtain a solution.

12. Give an example to show that if we use the solution for $n \bmod 3 = 2$ given in Theorem 4.5.3 for a board satisfying $n \bmod 3 = 1$, we may not obtain a solution.

The minimum-queens problem *asks for the minimum number of queens that can attack all of the squares of an $n \times n$ board (i.e., the minimum number of queens such that each row, column, and diagonal contains at least one queen). In Exercises 13–17, solve the minimum-queens problem for the given values of n.*

13S. $n = 3$ 14. $n = 4$ 15. $n = 5$ 16S. $n = 6$ 17. $n = 7$

18. Write a backtracking algorithm that determines whether k queens can attack all squares of an $n \times n$ board.

In Exercises 19–22, use your solution to Exercise 18 to solve the minimum-queens problem for the given values of n.

19S. $n = 7$ 20. $n = 8$ 21. $n = 9$ 22S. $n = 10$

23S. Show that the worst-case time of Algorithm 4.5.4 is $O(n!)$.

24. Let G be the graph consisting of K_{n-1} (the complete graph on $n-1$ vertices), with vertices labeled $1, \ldots, n-1$, and one additional, isolated vertex labeled n. Show that if G is input to Algorithm 4.5.4, the running time is $\Omega((n-1)!)$.

25. Trace Algorithm 4.5.4 for the graph of Figure 4.5.5.

26S. How many times is *path_ok* called when the input to Algorithm 4.5.4 is K_n, the complete graph on n vertices?

27. How many times is *path_ok* called when the input to Algorithm 4.5.4 is a graph with n vertices and no edges?

28. Write a backtracking algorithm that outputs all permutations of $1, 2, \ldots, n$.

29S. Write a backtracking algorithm that outputs all subsets of $\{1, 2, \ldots, n\}$.

Notes

Depth-first search was first used to find paths in mazes (see Exercises 4.21–4.23); Lucas, 1882, described results due to Trémaux, and Tarry, 1895, gave an algorithm to traverse a maze. Tarjan demonstrated the importance of depth-first search by using it as the basis of several graph algorithms including algorithms to construct a topological sort (see Tarjan, 1974) and, with Hopcroft, to determine whether a graph is planar (see Hopcroft, 1974).

One of the earliest applications of breadth-first search was to find a shortest path in a maze (see Moore, 1959).

The first linear-time algorithm for topological sorting was given by Knuth in 1968 (see Knuth, 1997). The algorithm in Section 4.3 based on depth-first search is due to Tarjan, 1974.

The term "backtracking" seems to have been introduced by Walker (see Walker, 1960). Early descriptions of backtracking with many examples are Golomb, 1965; and Wells, 1971. Articles dealing with techniques for estimating the efficiency of backtracking are Chen, 1992, 1994; and Knuth, 1975.

Exercise 4.10 is due to Itai and Rodeh (see Itai, 1978).

Chapter Exercises

4.1. Write an $O(n \lg n)$ algorithm that receives as input an array a of n real numbers sorted in nondecreasing order and a value *val*. The algorithm returns true if there are distinct indexes i and j such that $a[i] + a[j] = val$ and false otherwise.

4.2. Write an $O(n)$ algorithm that receives as input an array a of n real numbers sorted in nondecreasing order and a value *val*. The algorithm returns true if there are distinct indexes i and j such that $a[i] + a[j] = val$ and false otherwise.

Exercises 4.3–4.5 concern the following variant of the coin-weighing problem (see Exercises 21–29, Section 4.1). We are given n coins, some of which are bad, but are otherwise identical in appearance. All of the good coins have the same weight. All of the bad coins also have the same weight, but they are lighter than the good coins. We assume that there is at least one bad coin among the n coins. The task is to determine the number of bad coins.

4.3. Show that at least $\log_3 n$ weighings are necessary to determine the number of bad coins.

4.4. Show how to determine the number of bad coins in at most $n - 1$ weighings.

$\star$**4.5.** Show how to determine the number of bad coins in at most $O(\lg^2 n)$ weighings.

4.6. Write a region-finding algorithm based on depth-first search in which the input is a matrix of 1's and 0's. The output is the input matrix where all of the 1's in one region are replaced by 2's, all of the 1's in another region are replaced by 3's, and so on. What is the worst-case time of your algorithm?

4.7. Write an algorithm that determines whether an undirected graph is bipartite. If the graph is bipartite, in addition to determining that it is bipartite, the algorithm divides the vertices into disjoint sets V_1 and V_2 so that every edge is incident on one vertex in V_1 and one vertex in V_2. What is the worst-case time of your algorithm?

4.8. Write an algorithm that finds an Euler cycle in a connected graph if there is one. What is the worst-case time of your algorithm?

4.9. Show that there are graphs that contain exponentially many different cycles. More precisely, show that for every n there is a graph with n vertices that contains $\Omega(2^n)$ different cycles.

4.10. The *girth* of a graph G is the length of a shortest cycle in G. Write an algorithm to determine the girth of a graph G in time $\Theta(mn)$, where m is the number of edges and n is the number of vertices in G. *Hint:* Breadth-first search takes time $\Theta(m + n)$. [Exercise 11.23 asks for an algorithm that computes the girth of a graph G to within an additive error of 1 in time $O(n^2)$, where n is the number of vertices in G.]

4.11. Write an algorithm that inputs a directed graph G and, if G is a dag, outputs a topological sort of G and returns true. If G is not a dag, the algorithm returns false. What is the worst-case time of your algorithm?

4.12. Write a backtracking algorithm to determine whether two undirected simple graphs are isomorphic. Represent the graphs by using adjacency matrices. If the graphs are not isomorphic, the algorithm simply outputs a statement to that effect. If the graphs are isomorphic, the algorithm outputs a statement to that effect and orderings of their vertices for which their adjacency matrices are equal. What is the worst-case time of your algorithm?

4.13. The *subset-sum problem* is: Given a set $\{c_1, \ldots, c_n\}$ of positive integers and a positive integer M, find all subsets $\{c_{k_1}, \ldots, c_{k_j}\}$ of $\{c_1, \ldots, c_n\}$ with

$$\sum_{i=1}^{j} c_{k_i} = M.$$

Write a backtracking algorithm to solve the subset-sum problem. What is the worst-case time of your algorithm?

4.14. Write a backtracking algorithm that finds all m-colorings of a graph. What is the worst-case time of your algorithm?

4.15. Suppose that c is a coloring of a graph G with vertices $1, \ldots, n$ in which vertex i is colored c_i. Suppose c' is another coloring of G. We say that c and c' are *equivalent colorings* of G if there is a permutation p of the colors such that

$$p(c_i) = c'_i \quad \text{for all } i = 1, \ldots, n.$$

Write a backtracking algorithm that finds colorings of a graph G using colors chosen from $1, \ldots, m$, where

- No two distinct colorings generated by the algorithm are equivalent.
- Any coloring of G using colors chosen from $1, \ldots, m$ is equivalent to some coloring generated by the algorithm.

What is the worst-case time of your algorithm?

In chess, the knight's move consists of moving two squares horizontally or vertically and then moving one square in the perpendicular direction (assuming that the position obtained is on the board). For example, legal moves for the knight K are shown on the following board as ×'s:

WWW *The* knight's tour *of an $n \times n$ board begins at some square, visits every square exactly one time making legal moves, and returns to the initial square. Exercises 4.16–4.19 are concerned with the knight's tour.*

4.16. Show that there is no knight's tour for a 4×4 board.

4.17. Show a knight's tour for a 6×6 board.

4.18. Show that there is no knight's tour on an $n \times n$ board if n is odd.

4.19. Write a backtracking algorithm that searches an $n \times n$ board for a knight's tour. If there is a knight's tour, the algorithm outputs one such tour; if there is none, the algorithm outputs a statement to that effect. What is the worst-case time of your algorithm?

4.20. Suppose that a 3×3 board contains two black knights in squares labeled B and two white knights in squares labeled W as shown:

B		B
W		W

Solve the problem of swapping the positions of the black and white knights by making legal moves for the knights.

Exercises 4.21–4.23 refer to mazes. A maze consists of passageways with various connections among the passageways. The goal is to begin at the position marked Start *and end at the position marked* Finish. *As an example, the following diagram shows the famous maze at Hampton Court in England.*

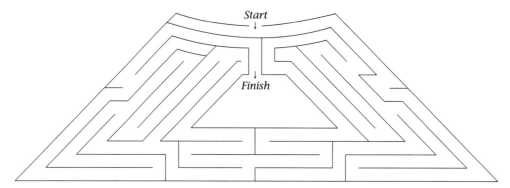

4.21. Write a backtracking algorithm that finds a path from the start to the finish in a maze. What is the worst-case time of your algorithm? Finding a path in a maze using backtracking is one of the earliest applications of backtracking, although the term "backtracking" was introduced later.

4.22. Use your algorithm of Exercise 4.21 to find a path from the start to the finish in the Hampton Court maze.

4.23. Use breadth-first search to find a shortest path from the start to the finish in a maze. What is the worst-case time of your algorithm? Finding a shortest path in a maze using breadth-first search is one of the earliest applications of breadth-first search.

CHAPTER 5
Divide and Conquer

A **divide-and-conquer algorithm** proceeds as follows. If the problem is small, it is solved directly. If the problem is large, the problem is divided into two or more parts called *subproblems*. Each subproblem is then solved after which solutions to the subproblems are combined into a solution to the original problem. The divide-and-conquer technique is also used to solve the subproblems; that is, the subproblems are further divided into subproblems, which are divided into subproblems, and so on. Eventually, small problems result that can be solved directly. The solutions to the various subproblems are then combined into a solution to the original problem. *Recursion* is often used to solve a subproblem. As an example, an array of two or more elements can be sorted by using a divide-and-conquer algorithm in which the original array is divided into two parts. If either part consists of one element, that part is already sorted. Parts containing two or more elements are sorted recursively. Finally, the two sorted arrays are merged into a single sorted array. The sorting algorithm is called *mergesort* and is discussed in Section 5.2.

We begin in Section 5.1 by introducing the divide-and-conquer technique with a tiling problem. After discussing mergesort (Section 5.2), we turn to a geometry problem that has an elegant divide-and-conquer solution (Section 5.3). The chapter concludes with a divide-and-conquer algorithm for multiplying matrices (Section 5.4), which is asymptotically faster than the algorithm derived directly from the definition of matrix multiplication.

In succeeding chapters, we will again have occasion to use the divide-and-conquer technique (see, e.g., Section 6.2, Quicksort, and Section 6.5, Selection).

5.1 A Tiling Problem

A *right tromino*, hereafter called simply a *tromino*, is an object made up of three 1×1 squares, as shown in Figure 5.1.1. We call an $n \times n$ board, with one 1×1 square (on the unit grid lines) removed, a *deficient board*

Figure 5.1.1 A tromino.

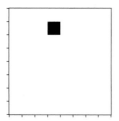

Figure 5.1.2 A deficient 8×8 board. The missing square is shown in black. The gap between successive marks along the sides is one unit.

(see Figure 5.1.2). Our tiling problem can then be stated as follows: Given a deficient $n \times n$ board, where n is a power of 2, tile the board with trominoes. By a *tiling* of the board with trominoes, we mean an exact covering of the board by trominoes without having any of the trominoes overlap each other or extend outside the board.

Example 5.1.1. Figure 5.1.3 shows a tiling of a deficient 8×8 board with trominoes.

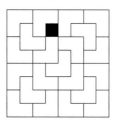

Figure 5.1.3 A tiling of a deficient 8×8 board with trominoes.   □

Suppose that we are given a deficient $n \times n$ board, where n is a power of 2. If $n = 2$, we can tile the board because the board *is* a tromino (see Figure 5.1.1). Suppose that $n > 2$. A divide-and-conquer approach to solving the tiling problem begins by dividing the original problem (tile the $n \times n$ board) into subproblems (tile smaller boards). We divide the original board into four $n/2 \times n/2$ subboards [see Figure 5.1.4(a)]. Since n is a power of 2, $n/2$ is also a power of 2. The subboard that contains the missing square [in Figure 5.1.4(a), the upper-left subboard] is a deficient $n/2 \times n/2$ subboard, so we can recursively tile it. The other three $n/2 \times n/2$ subboards are not deficient, so we cannot directly recursively tile these subboards. However, if we place a tromino as shown in Figure 5.1.4(b) so that each of its 1×1 squares lies in

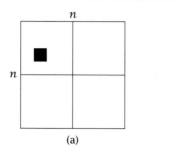   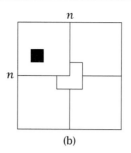

(a)   (b)

Figure 5.1.4 Using divide and conquer to tile a deficient $n \times n$ board with trominoes. In (a), the original $n \times n$ board is divided into four $n/2 \times n/2$ subboards. The subboard containing the missing square is then tiled recursively. A tromino is placed as shown in (b) so that each of its 1×1 squares lies in one of the three remaining subboards. These 1×1 squares are then considered as missing. The remaining subboards are then tiled recursively.

one of the three remaining subboards, we can consider each of these 1×1 squares as missing in the remaining subboards. We can then recursively tile these deficient subboards. Our tiling problem is solved.

Example 5.1.2. Figure 5.1.5 shows how our algorithm tiles a deficient 4×4 board.

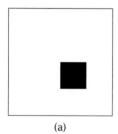   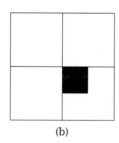   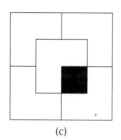

(a)   (b)   (c)

Figure 5.1.5 Tiling the deficient 4×4 board shown in (a). First, the board is divided into four 2×2 subboards as shown in (b). The subboard that contains the missing square is recursively tiled; in this case, the deficient 2×2 board is a tromino. Next, we place a tromino as shown in (c) so that each of its 1×1 squares lies in one of the three remaining subboards. Each of these 1×1 squares is considered as missing in the remaining subboards. We can then recursively tile these deficient subboards. Again, each of the deficient 2×2 boards is a tromino, so the problem is solved.   □

Example 5.1.3. Figure 5.1.6 (next page) shows how our algorithm tiles a deficient 8×8 board.   □

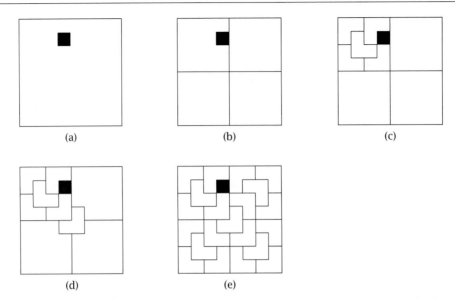

Figure 5.1.6 Tiling the deficient 8×8 board shown in (a). First, the board is divided into four 4×4 subboards as shown in (b). The subboard that contains the missing square is recursively tiled as shown in (c). Next, we place a tromino as shown in (d) so that each of its 1×1 squares lies in one of the three remaining subboards. Each of these 1×1 squares is considered as missing in the remaining subboards. We can then recursively tile each of these deficient 4×4 subboards as shown in (e). The problem is solved.

$\mathcal{WWW}$ We formally state our tiling algorithm as Algorithm 5.1.4.

Algorithm 5.1.4 Tiling a Deficient Board with Trominoes. This algorithm constructs a tiling by trominoes of a deficient $n \times n$ board where n is a power of 2.

Input Parameters: n, a power of 2 (the board size);
                                 the location L of the missing square
Output Parameters: None

```
tile(n, L) {
   if (n == 2) {
      // the board is a right tromino T
      tile with T
      return
   }
   divide the board into four n/2 × n/2 subboards
   place one tromino as in Figure 5.1.4(b)
   // each of the 1 × 1 squares in this tromino is considered as missing
   let m₁, m₂, m₃, m₄ denote the locations of the missing squares
```

$$tile(n/2, m_1)$$
$$tile(n/2, m_2)$$
$$tile(n/2, m_3)$$
$$tile(n/2, m_4)$$
}

In Algorithm 5.1.4, "tile with T" can be interpreted in many ways. It could mean printing the location and orientation of T, or it could mean drawing T using a graphics system (see Exercises 5.1 and 5.2). In any case, we assume that "tile with T" takes constant time. We also assume that dividing the board, placing the tromino as in Figure 5.1.4(b), and computing m_1, m_2, m_3, m_4 each takes constant time. It follows that the time required by Algorithm 5.1.4 is proportional to the number of trominoes placed on the board. Since the number of 1×1 squares on a deficient $n \times n$ board is $n^2 - 1$ and each tromino occupies three squares, Algorithm 5.1.4 places

$$\frac{n^2 - 1}{3} = \Theta(n^2)$$

trominoes on the board. Therefore, the time required by Algorithm 5.1.4 is $\Theta(n^2)$.

If we can tile a deficient $n \times n$ board, where n is not necessarily a power of 2, then the number of squares, $n^2 - 1$, must be divisible by 3. Chu and Johnsonbaugh (see Chu, 1986) showed that the converse is true, except when n is 5. More precisely, if $n \neq 5$, any deficient $n \times n$ board can be tiled with trominoes if and only if 3 divides $n^2 - 1$ (see Exercises 11 and 12). Some deficient 5×5 boards can be tiled and some cannot (see Exercises 6 and 7).

Some real-world problems can be modeled as tiling problems. One example is the *VLSI layout problem*—the problem of packing many components on a computer chip (see Wong, 1986). (VLSI is short for Very Large Scale Integration.) The problem is to tile a rectangle of minimum area with the desired components. The components are sometimes modeled as rectangles and L-shaped figures similar to trominoes. In practice, other constraints are imposed such as the proximity of various components that must be interconnected and restrictions on the ratios of width to height of the resulting rectangle.

Exercises

In Exercises 1–4, show how Algorithm 5.1.4 tiles the given deficient board.

1S.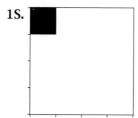

2.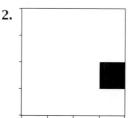

3. 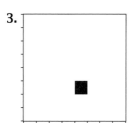   **4S.**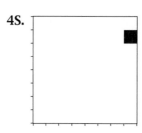

5S. Let c_n denote the time required by Algorithm 5.1.4. Write a recurrence relation and an initial condition for c_n. Show that $c_n = \Theta(n^2)$.

6. Give a tiling of a 5×5 board with trominoes in which the upper-left square is missing.

7. Show a deficient 5×5 board that is impossible to tile with trominoes. Prove that your board cannot be tiled with trominoes.

8S. Show how to tile with trominoes any $2i \times 3j$ board with no squares missing, where i and j are positive integers.

9. Show how to tile any deficient 7×7 board with trominoes.

10. Show how to tile any deficient 11×11 board with trominoes. *Hint:* Subdivide the board into overlapping 7×7 and 5×5 boards and two 6×4 boards. Then, use Exercises 6, 8, and 9.

11S. Write an algorithm that tiles any deficient $n \times n$ board with trominoes if n is odd, $n > 5$, and 3 divides $n^2 - 1$. *Hint:* Use the hint for Exercise 10.

12. Write an algorithm that tiles any deficient $n \times n$ board with trominoes if n is even, $n > 8$, and 3 divides $n^2 - 1$. *Hint:* Use Algorithm 5.1.4 with $n = 4$ and Exercises 8 and 11.

13. A *3D-septomino* is a three-dimensional $2 \times 2 \times 2$ cube with one $1 \times 1 \times 1$ corner cube removed. A *deficient cube* is an $n \times n \times n$ cube with one $1 \times 1 \times 1$ cube removed. Give an algorithm to tile a deficient $n \times n \times n$ cube with 3D-septominoes when n is a power of 2. (An unsolved problem is to determine which deficient cubes can be tiled with 3D-septominoes.)

A straight tromino is an object made up of three squares in a row. Exercises 14–16 deal with straight trominoes.

14S. Which deficient 4×4 boards can be tiled with straight trominoes?

15. Which deficient 5×5 boards can be tiled with straight trominoes?

16. Which deficient 8×8 boards can be tiled with straight trominoes?

17S. This exercise and the one that follows are due to Anthony Quas.

A $2^n \times 2^n$ *L-shape*, $n \geq 0$, is a figure of the form

$2^n \times 2^n$	
$2^n \times 2^n$	$2^n \times 2^n$

with no missing squares. Write an algorithm to tile any $2^n \times 2^n$ L-shape with trominoes.

18. Use the preceding exercise to give a different algorithm to tile any $2^n \times 2^n$ deficient board with trominoes.

5.2 Mergesort

$\mathcal{WWW}$ **Mergesort** divides the array to be sorted into two nearly equal parts. Each part is then sorted. The two sorted halves are then *merged* into one sorted array. We begin by discussing the merge algorithm.

Example 5.2.1 Merging Two Sorted Arrays. Suppose that the goal is to merge the sorted arrays

14	20	36

10	12	30	40	44

.

We begin by examining the first element in each array:

14	20	36

10	12	30	40	44

.

Since $10 < 14$ and the arrays are *sorted*, 10 is the smallest element. It is copied into the output array

10	$\cdots$

,

and we move to the next item in the second array

14	20	36

10	12	30	40	44

.

Since $12 < 14$, 12 is copied into the output array

10	12	$\cdots$

,

and we move to the next item in the second array

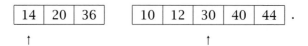

This time $30 > 14$, so 14 is copied into the output array

| 10 | 12 | 14 | $\cdots$ |

and we move to the next item in the first array

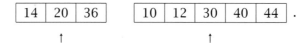

After the next values, 20, 30, and 36, are copied to the output array, we have

| 14 | 20 | 36 | | 10 | 12 | 30 | 40 | 44 | .

Since all of the data from the first array have been copied to the output array, we conclude by copying the remainder of the second array to the output array to obtain

| 10 | 12 | 14 | 20 | 30 | 36 | 40 | 44 | .

The merge is complete.   □

We state the merge algorithm as Algorithm 5.2.2.

Algorithm 5.2.2 Merge. This algorithm receives as input indexes i, m, and j, and an array a, where $a[i], \ldots, a[m]$ and $a[m+1], \ldots, a[j]$ are each sorted in nondecreasing order. These two nondecreasing subarrays are merged into a single nondecreasing array.

Input Parameters: a, i, m, j
Output Parameter: a

```
merge(a, i, m, j) {
    p = i // index in a[i], ..., a[m]
    q = m + 1 // index in a[m + 1], ..., a[j]
    r = i // index in a local array c
    while (p ≤ m && q ≤ j) {
        // copy smaller value to c
        if (a[p] ≤ a[q]) {
            c[r] = a[p]
            p = p + 1
        }
        else {
            c[r] = a[q]
```

$$q = q + 1$$
}
$$r = r + 1$$
}
// copy remainder, if any, of first subarray to c
while ($p \leq m$) {
$$c[r] = a[p]$$
$$p = p + 1$$
$$r = r + 1$$
}
// copy remainder, if any, of second subarray to c
while ($q \leq j$) {
$$c[r] = a[q]$$
$$q = q + 1$$
$$r = r + 1$$
}
// copy c back to a
for $r = i$ to j
$$a[r] = c[r]$$
}

In Algorithm 5.2.2, at every iteration of every while loop, an element of a is copied into c; thus, each element in the array a is accessed once. Thus, if a has n elements, the total time to execute the while loops is $\Theta(n)$. Also, the for loop executes in time $\Theta(n)$. Thus, the time to execute merge is $\Theta(n)$.

Having written the merge algorithm, mergesort is straightforward.

Algorithm 5.2.3 Mergesort. This algorithm sorts the array $a[i], \ldots, a[j]$ in nondecreasing order. It uses the merge algorithm (Algorithm 5.2.2).

Input Parameters: a, i, j
Output Parameter: a

$mergesort(a, i, j)$ {
  // if only one element, just return
  if ($i == j$)
    return
  // divide a into two nearly equal parts
  $m = (i + j)/2$
  // sort each half
  $mergesort(a, i, m)$
  $mergesort(a, m + 1, j)$
  // merge the two sorted halves
  $merge(a, i, m, j)$
}

We next consider the worst-case time of mergesort (Algorithm 5.2.3). We let t_n denote the worst-case time for mergesort to sort an array of n elements.

Suppose that an array of size $n > 1$ is input to mergesort. After the array is divided into two nearly equal parts, the sizes of the two parts are $\lceil n/2 \rceil$ and $\lfloor n/2 \rfloor$. By definition, the worst-case times to sort these two halves are $t_{\lceil n/2 \rceil}$ and $t_{\lfloor n/2 \rfloor}$. Since the time to merge the two halves is $2n$ (counting the number of times an array element is copied in the merge algorithm), we obtain the recurrence relation

$$t_n = t_{\lceil n/2 \rceil} + t_{\lfloor n/2 \rfloor} + 2n.$$

An induction proof (see Exercise 12) shows that t_n is nondecreasing. Therefore,

$$
\begin{aligned}
t_n &= t_{\lceil n/2 \rceil} + t_{\lfloor n/2 \rfloor} + 2n \\
&\leq t_{\lceil n/2 \rceil} + t_{\lceil n/2 \rceil} + 2n \\
&= 2t_{\lceil n/2 \rceil} + 2n.
\end{aligned}
$$

By the Main Recurrence Theorem (Theorem 2.4.7), $t_n = O(n \lg n)$. Similarly,

$$t_n \geq 2t_{\lfloor n/2 \rfloor} + 2n.$$

Again, by the Main Recurrence Theorem, $t_n = \Omega(n \lg n)$. Therefore, $t_n = \Theta(n \lg n)$, and the worst-case time of mergesort is $\Theta(n \lg n)$.

Example 5.2.4. We show how mergesort sorts the array

12	30	21	8	6	9	1	7

.

The array is first divided into two equal parts

12	30	21	8		6	9	1	7

.

Each part is then sorted by mergesort. The process begins by dividing each part into equal parts

12	30		21	8		6	9		1	7

and then each of these parts into equal parts

12		30		21		8		6		9		1		7

.

This subdividing process now ends because each part contains only one item. Each pair is then merged

12	30		8	21		6	9		1	7

.

Each of these pairs is then merged

8	12	21	30		1	6	7	9

.

Finally these pairs are merged

| 1 | 6 | 7 | 8 | 9 | 12 | 21 | 30 |

to obtain the sorted array. □

Stable Sorts

Suppose that duplicates occur in the input to a sorting algorithm; specifically, suppose that in the input array a we have $a[i] = a[j]$ with $i < j$. Let i' be the index in the (sorted) output where $a[i]$ is located, and let j' be the index in the (sorted) output where $a[j]$ is located. The sorting algorithm is **stable** if for all such i and j, we have $i' < j'$. In words, a sorting algorithm is stable if the relative positions of items with duplicate keys are unchanged by the algorithm. Mergesort is stable because, when merge (Algorithm 5.2.2) encounters equal keys, it copies the one with the smaller index to the output array.

Stability may be important if the items to sort comprise several fields, but the key involves only some subset of the fields.

Example 5.2.5. Suppose that weather data are entered daily and that a record comprises the date and the maximum temperature for that date. Example data might be:

Mar 1; 51
Mar 2; 49
Mar 3; 52
Mar 4; 58
Mar 5; 52
Mar 6; 56
Mar 7; 52
Mar 8; 51

If the data are sorted in nondecreasing order of maximum temperature using a stable sort, the output would be

Mar 2; 49
Mar 1; 51
Mar 8; 51
Mar 3; 52
Mar 5; 52
Mar 7; 52
Mar 6; 56
Mar 4; 58

Because the sort is stable, dates with equal temperatures are listed in chronological order, which might be helpful in analyzing the data. □

In-Place Merge and Mergesort

Merge (Algorithm 5.2.2) receives an array that contains two sorted subarrays and merges them into a second array, which is then sorted. The reader may wonder whether a second array is necessary. The answer is "No." Several versions of merge have been designed so that the merging is done in place. By "in place," we mean that only one extra cell (in addition to the input array) is allowed, together with $O(1)$ storage for handling array indexing. One of the most efficient in-place merge algorithms is due to Huang and Langston (see Huang, 1988). In practice, in-place merging is much slower than merging using an extra array.

In-place merging gives rise to an in-place version of mergesort. However, since the merging is slower than merging using an extra array, in practice, the resulting version of mergesort runs much slower than Algorithm 5.2.3.

An alternative to using an in-place version of merge in mergesort is to obtain an in-place version of mergesort directly (see, e.g., Katajainen, 1996). The key observation that makes a direct in-place version of mergesort possible is that if we have an array a consisting of a sorted subarray of size m followed by a sorted subarray of size n, then the subarrays can be merged into a using extra storage, say an array b, of size $\min\{m, n\}$. For example, if $m \le n$, we copy the first m elements of a into b and then merge b and the last n elements of a into a using the standard merge algorithm (see Exercise 13).

Now suppose that we have an array of size n. The idea of in-place mergesort is to sort the first $n/2$ elements using the last part of the array as the extra storage. (When we do so, we have to be careful to *swap* data rather than overwrite data; for details, see Katajainen, 1996.) Next, we sort the $n/4$ elements following the first $n/2$ elements, using the last fourth of the array as the extra storage. We then merge the two sorted subarrays using the last fourth of the array as the extra storage. We then repeatedly sort half of the unsorted end of the array and merge it with the already sorted first part of the array, using the end of the array as the extra storage until the entire array is sorted. In practice, an optimized version of this algorithm runs much faster than in-place mergesort using in-place merging; however, experiments by Katajainen, et al., show that the optimized version is about 50 percent slower than mergesort implemented with a version of merge that uses a second array (as in Algorithm 5.2.3).

Exercises

Show how merge *merges the arrays in Exercises 1–4.*

1S. 14   24   27
     17   26   54

2. 14   24   27   28   31   45   47   51
    7   10   11   29   31

3. 7   10   11   29   31
    47   50   71   79   101

4S. 7   10   11   29   31

    9   28   71   79   101

Show how mergesort *sorts each array in Exercises 5–8.*

5S. 14   40   31   28   3   15   17   51

6. 3   14   15   17   28   31   40   51

7. 51   40   31   28   17   15   14   3

8S. 23   23   23   23   23   23   23   23

9S. Write a nonrecursive version of mergesort. Make your algorithm as efficient as you can.

10. Give a formal proof using mathematical induction that mergesort is stable.

11. Suppose we merge two sorted *linked* lists of sizes m and n by changing reference fields in the list. Show that the best-case time is $\Theta(\min\{m, n\})$ and the worst-case time is $\Theta(m+n)$. Give examples of input that produce the best-case time and the worst-case time.

12S. Let t_n be the worst-case time of mergesort. Show that t_n is nondecreasing.

13. Write an algorithm that, given an array a consisting of a sorted subarray of size m followed by a sorted subarray of size n, merges them into a using an extra array b of size $\min\{m, n\}$.

5.3 Finding a Closest Pair of Points

A lumber store stocks several different kinds of plywood. Each is classified according to several features (e.g., number of knotholes per square foot, smoothness). In Figure 5.3.1, the different kinds of plywood are plotted as points in the plane, where the x-coordinate measures the number of knotholes per square foot, and the y-coordinate measures the smoothness. Notice that the distance between two points gives a dissimilarity measure: If the distance is small, the types of plywood represented by the points are similar; if the distance is large, the types of plywood represented by the points are dissimilar. The store decides to reduce the number of different kinds of plywood in stock by identifying two types of plywood that are most similar and eliminating one of them. The problem then is to identify a closest pair of points and eliminate a type of plywood that corresponds to one of the points. (We say *a* closest pair since it is possible that several pairs achieve the same minimum distance.) Our distance measure is ordinary Euclidean distance.

WWW   The **closest-pair problem** furnishes an example of a problem from computational geometry. **Computational geometry** is concerned with the design

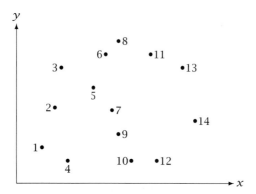

Figure 5.3.1 Types of plywood. Each type of plywood is plotted as a point in the plane; the x-coordinate measures the number of knotholes per square foot, and the y-coordinate measures the smoothness. The closest pair of points (6 and 8) represents the most similar types of plywood.

and analysis of algorithms to solve geometry problems. Efficient geometric algorithms are useful in fields such as pattern recognition, computer graphics, statistics, image processing, and very-large-scale-integration (VLSI) design.

One way to solve the closest-pair problem is to list the distance between each pair and choose the minimum in this list of distances. Since there are $n(n - 1)/2 = \Theta(n^2)$ pairs, this "list-all" algorithm's time is $\Theta(n^2)$. We can do better; we will give a divide-and-conquer closest-pair algorithm whose worst-case time is $\Theta(n \lg n)$.

We begin by finding a vertical line l that divides the points into two nearly equal parts (see Figure 5.3.2). [If n is even, we divide the points into parts each having $n/2$ points. If n is odd, we divide the points into parts, one having $(n + 1)/2$ points and the other having $(n - 1)/2$ points.]

We then recursively solve the problem for each of the parts. We let δ_L be the distance between a closest pair in the left part; we let δ_R be the distance between a closest pair in the right part; and we let

$$\delta = \min\{\delta_L, \delta_R\}.$$

Unfortunately, δ may not be the distance between a closest pair from the original set of points because a pair of points, one from the left part and the other from the right part, might be closer (see Figure 5.3.2). Thus we must consider distances between points on opposite sides of the line l.

We first note that if the distance between a pair of points is less than δ, the points must lie in the vertical strip of width 2δ centered at l (see Figure 5.3.2). (Any point not in this strip is at least δ away from every point on the other side of l.) Thus, we can restrict our search for a pair closer than δ to points in this strip.

If there are n points in the strip and we check *all* pairs in the strip, the worst-case time to process the points in the strip is $\Theta(n^2)$. In this case the

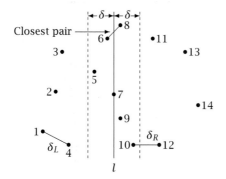

Figure 5.3.2 n points in the plane. The problem is to find a closest pair. For this set, the closest pair is 6 and 8. Line l divides the points into two approximately equal parts. The closest pair in the left half is 1 and 4, which is δ_L apart. The closest pair in the right half is 10 and 12, which is δ_R apart. Any pair (e.g., 6 and 8) closer together than $\delta = \min\{\delta_L, \delta_R\}$ must lie in the vertical strip of width 2δ centered at l.

worst-case time of our algorithm will be $\Omega(n^2)$, which is at least as bad as exhaustive search; thus we must avoid checking all pairs in the strip.

We order the points in the strip in nondecreasing order of the y-coordinates. We then examine the points in this order. When we examine a point p in the strip, any point following p whose distance to p is less than δ must lie strictly within or on the base of the rectangle of height δ whose base contains p and whose vertical sides are at a distance δ from l (see Figure 5.3.3). We need not compute the distance between p and points below p. These distances would already have been considered since we are examining the points in nondecreasing order of their y-coordinates. (We are only interested in distances from p to other points within the rectangle that are on the other side of l; however, our algorithm checks the distance from p to *all* other points within the rectangle.) We will show that this rectangle contains at most eight points, including p itself; so if we compute the distances between p and the next seven points in the strip, we can be sure that we will compute the distance between p and all points in the rectangle. Of course, if fewer than seven points follow p in the list, we compute the distances

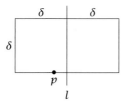

Figure 5.3.3 Any point whose y-coordinate is greater than or equal to p's y-coordinate and whose distance to p is less than δ must lie within the rectangle.

between p and all of the remaining points. By restricting the search in the strip in this way, the time spent processing the points in the strip is $O(n)$. (Since there are at most n points in the strip, the time spent processing the points in the strip is at most $7n$.)

We show that the rectangle of Figure 5.3.3 contains at most eight points. Figure 5.3.4 shows the rectangle of Figure 5.3.3 divided into eight equal squares. Notice that the length of a diagonal of a square is

$$\left[\left(\frac{\delta}{2}\right)^2 + \left(\frac{\delta}{2}\right)^2\right]^{1/2} = \frac{\delta}{\sqrt{2}} < \delta;$$

thus each square contains at most one point. (A point on l is assigned to the square on the side of l to which the point belongs. Other points on edges of squares are arbitrarily assigned to adjoining squares.) Therefore the $2\delta \times \delta$ rectangle contains at most eight points.

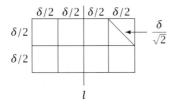

Figure 5.3.4 The large rectangle contains at most eight points because each square contains at most one point.

Example 5.3.1. We show how the closest-pair algorithm finds a closest pair for the input of Figure 5.3.2.

The algorithm begins by finding a vertical line l that divides the points into two equal parts

$$S_1 = \{1, 2, 3, 4, 5, 6, 7\}, \qquad S_2 = \{8, 9, 10, 11, 12, 13, 14\}.$$

For this input there are many possible choices for the dividing line. The particular line chosen here happens to go through point 7.

Next we recursively solve the closest-pair problem for S_1 and S_2. The closest pair of points in S_1 is 1 and 4. We let δ_L denote the distance between points 1 and 4. The closest pair of points in S_2 is 10 and 12. We let δ_R denote the distance between points 10 and 12. We let

$$\delta = \min\{\delta_L, \delta_R\} = \delta_R.$$

We next order the points in the vertical strip of width 2δ centered at l in nondecreasing order of their y-coordinates:

$$10, \quad 9, \quad 7, \quad 5, \quad 6, \quad 8.$$

We then examine the points in this order. We compute the distances between each point and the remaining points.

We first compute the distances from 10 to each of 9, 7, 5, 6, and 8. Since each of these distances exceeds δ, at this point we have not found a closer pair.

We next compute the distances from 9 to each of 7, 5, 6, and 8. Since the distance between points 9 and 7 is less than δ, we have discovered a closer pair. We update δ to the distance between points 9 and 7.

We next compute the distances from 7 to each of 5, 6, and 8. Since each of these distances exceeds δ, at this point we have not found a closer pair.

We next compute the distances from 5 to each of 6 and 8. Since each of these distances exceeds δ, at this point we have not found a closer pair.

We next compute the distance from 6 to 8. Since the distance between 6 and 8 is less that δ, we have discovered a closer pair. We update δ to the distance between points 6 and 8. Since there are no more points in the strip to consider, the algorithm terminates. The closest pair is 6 and 8, and the distance between them is δ.   □

Before we give a formal statement of the closest-pair algorithm, there are several technical points to resolve.

In order to terminate the recursion, we check the number of points in the input and if there are three or fewer points, we find a closest pair directly. Dividing the input and using recursion only if there are four or more points ensures that each of the two parts contains at least one pair of points and, therefore, that there is a closest pair in each part.

Before invoking the recursive procedure, we sort the entire set of points by x-coordinate. This makes it easy to divide the points into two nearly equal parts.

We use mergesort (see Section 5.2) to sort by y-coordinate. However, instead of sorting each time we examine points in the vertical strip, we assume, as in mergesort, that each half is sorted by y-coordinate.

We can now formally state the closest-pair algorithm. To simplify the description, our version outputs only the distance between a closest pair of points, but not the points themselves. We leave this enhancement as an exercise (see Exercise 10).

Algorithm 5.3.2 Finding the Distance Between a Closest Pair of Points.
This algorithm finds the distance between a closest pair of points. The input is an array $p[1], \ldots, p[n]$ of $n \geq 2$ points. If p is a point, $p.x$ is the x-coordinate of p, and $p.y$ is the y-coordinate of p. The function *merge* is Algorithm 5.2.2 and *mergesort* is Algorithm 5.2.3. The function *merge* uses as the key the y-coordinate of the point. The function *mergesort* uses as the key either the x- or y-coordinate of the point; the comments indicate which. The function $dist(p, q)$ returns the Euclidean distance between points p and q.

    Input Parameter: p
Output Parameters: None

```
closest_pair(p) {
   n = p.last
   mergesort(p, 1, n) // sort by x-coordinate
   return rec_cl_pair(p, 1, n)
}
```

// *rec_cl_pair* assumes that the input is sorted by *x*-coordinate.
// At termination, the input is sorted by *y*-coordinate.

```
rec_cl_pair(p, i, j) {
   if (j − i < 3) {
      mergesort(p, i, j) // sort by y-coordinate
      // find the distance delta between a closest pair
      delta = dist(p[i], p[i + 1])
      if (j − i == 1) // two points
         return delta
      // three points
      if (dist(p[i + 1], p[i + 2]) < delta)
         delta = dist(p[i + 1], p[i + 2])
      if (dist(p[i], p[i + 2]) < delta)
         delta = dist(p[i], p[i + 2])
      return delta
   }
   k = (i + j)/2
   l = p[k].x
   deltaL = rec_cl_pair(p, i, k)
   deltaR = rec_cl_pair(p, k + 1, j)
   delta = min(deltaL, deltaR)
   // p[i], ..., p[k] is now sorted by y-coordinate, and
   // p[k + 1], ..., p[j] is now sorted by y-coordinate.
   merge(p, i, k, j)
   // p[i], ..., p[j] is now sorted by y-coordinate.

   // store points in the vertical strip in v.
   t = 0
   for k = i to j
      if (p[k].x > l − delta && p[k].x < l + delta) {
         t = t + 1
         v[t] = p[k]
      }
   // look for closer pairs in the strip by comparing
   // each point in the strip to the next 7 points.
   for k = 1 to t − 1
      for s = k + 1 to min(t, k + 7)
         delta = min(delta, dist(v[k], v[s]))
   return delta
}
```

We show that the worst-case time of the closest-pair algorithm (Algorithm 5.3.2) is $\Theta(n \lg n)$.

Theorem 5.3.3. *The worst-case time of Algorithm 5.3.2 is $\Theta(n \lg n)$.*

Proof. The function *closest_pair* begins by sorting the points by x-coordinate, which takes time $\Theta(n \lg n)$ in the worst case. Next, *closest_pair* calls *rec_cl_pair*. We let a_n denote the worst-case time of *rec_cl_pair* for input of size n. If $n > 3$, *rec_cl_pair* first calls itself with input sizes $\lfloor n/2 \rfloor$ and $\lfloor (n+1)/2 \rfloor$. Merging the points, extracting the points in the strip, and checking the distances in the strip each takes time $O(n)$. Thus, we obtain the recurrence relation

$$a_n \leq a_{\lfloor n/2 \rfloor} + a_{\lfloor (n+1)/2 \rfloor} + cn, \quad n > 3,$$

whose solution satisfies (see the Main Recurrence Theorem, Theorem 2.4.7)

$$a_n = O(n \lg n).$$

Sorting the points by x-coordinate takes time $\Theta(n \lg n)$, and the worst-case time of *rec_cl_pair* is $O(n \lg n)$; thus, the worst-case time of *closest_pair* is $\Theta(n \lg n)$. ∎

It can be shown (see Exercise 15) that there are at most six points in the rectangle of Figure 5.3.3 when the base is included and the other sides are excluded. This result is the best possible since it is possible to place six points in the rectangle (see Exercise 13). By considering the possible locations of the points in the rectangle, D. Lerner and R. Johnsonbaugh have shown that it suffices to compare each point in the strip with the next three points (rather than the next seven). This result is the best possible since checking the next two points does not lead to a correct algorithm (see Exercise 12).

Making reasonable assumptions about what kinds of computations are allowed and using a decision tree model together with advanced methods, Preparata (see Preparata, 1985: Theorem 5.2, page 188) shows that Algorithm 5.3.2 is asymptotically optimal.

Exercises

In Exercises 1 and 2, describe how the closest-pair algorithm finds a closest pair of points for the given input.

1S. $(8, 4), (3, 11), (12, 10), (5, 4), (1, 2), (17, 10), (8, 7), (8, 9), (11, 3), (1, 5), (11, 7), (5, 9), (1, 9), (7, 6), (3, 7), (14, 7)$

2. $(10, 1), (7, 7), (3, 13), (6, 10), (16, 4), (10, 5), (7, 13), (13, 8), (4, 4), (2, 2), (1, 8), (10, 13), (7, 1), (4, 8), (12, 3), (16, 10), (14, 5), (10, 9)$

3S. In order to terminate the recursion in the closest-pair algorithm, if there are three or fewer points in the input, we find a closest pair directly. Why can't we replace "three" by "two"?

4. Show that the worst-case time of *rec_cl_pair* for input of size n is $\Theta(n \lg n)$.

5. What can you conclude about input to the closest-pair algorithm when the output is zero for the distance between a closest pair?

6S. Give an example of input for which the closest-pair algorithm puts some points on the dividing line l into the left half and other points on l into the right half.

7. Explain why, in some cases, when dividing a set of points by a vertical line into two nearly equal parts, it is necessary for the line to contain some of the points.

8. Show that there are at most four points in the lower half of the rectangle of Figure 5.3.4.

9S. What would the worst-case time of the closest-pair algorithm be if instead of merging $p[i], \ldots, p[k]$ and $p[k+1], \ldots, p[j]$, we used mergesort to sort $p[i], \ldots, p[j]$?

10. Write a closest-pair algorithm that finds one closest pair as well as the distance between the pair of points.

11. Write an algorithm that finds the distance between a closest pair of points on a (straight) line.

12S. Give an example of input for which comparing each point in the strip with the next two points gives incorrect output.

13. Give an example to show that it is possible to place six points in the rectangle of Figure 5.3.3 when the base is included and the other sides are excluded.

14. When we compute the distances between a point p in the strip and points following it, can we stop computing distances from p if we find a point q such that the distance between p and q exceeds δ? Explain.

$\star$**15S.** Show that there are at most six points in the rectangle of Figure 5.3.3 when the base is included and the other sides are excluded.

5.4 Strassen's Matrix Product Algorithm

If A is a matrix, we let A_{ij} denote the entry in row i, column j. Recall that the **matrix product** of A and B, where A is an $m \times p$ matrix (i.e., A has m

rows and p columns) and B is a $p \times n$ matrix, is defined as the $m \times n$ matrix C, where

$$C_{ij} = \sum_{k=1}^{p} A_{ik}B_{kj}, \qquad 1 \le i \le m,\ 1 \le j \le n.$$

Matrix multiplication is a fundamental operation on matrices and is used in many different contexts. For example, if A is the adjacency matrix of a simple graph G with vertices $1, \ldots, n$, entry ij in

$$A^k = \underbrace{A \cdot A \cdots A}_{k\ A\text{'s}}$$

is equal to the number of paths of length k from vertex i to vertex j (see Exercise 7). An adjacency matrix is an example of a *square matrix*—a matrix in which the number of rows is equal to the number of columns. In the remainder of this section, we deal only with square matrices. Algorithm 5.4.1 computes the product of two square matrices directly from the definition.

Algorithm 5.4.1 Matrix Product. This algorithm computes the product C of the $n \times n$ matrices A and B directly from the definition of the matrix product.

Input Parameters: A, B
Output Parameter: C

```
matrix_product(A, B, C) {
    n = A.last
    for i = 1 to n
        for j = 1 to n {
            C[i][j] = 0
            for k = 1 to n
                C[i][j] = C[i][j] + A[i][k] * B[k][j]
        }
}
```

Since Algorithm 5.4.1 performs n^3 multiplications and n^3 additions, it requires $\Theta(n^3)$ arithmetic operations. For many years, $\Theta(n^3)$ was considered to be the minimum number of arithmetic operations, and it was quite a surprise when a more efficient algorithm was discovered.

Consider a divide-and-conquer approach to computing the matrix product. The input is A and B—two $n \times n$ matrices, where n is a power of 2. If $n > 1$, we divide each of A and B into four $n/2 \times n/2$ matrices

$$A = \begin{pmatrix} \mathbf{a}_{11} & \mathbf{a}_{12} \\ \mathbf{a}_{21} & \mathbf{a}_{22} \end{pmatrix}, \qquad B = \begin{pmatrix} \mathbf{b}_{11} & \mathbf{b}_{12} \\ \mathbf{b}_{21} & \mathbf{b}_{22} \end{pmatrix},$$

and then compute the matrix product as

$$AB = \begin{pmatrix} \mathbf{a}_{11}\mathbf{b}_{11} + \mathbf{a}_{12}\mathbf{b}_{21} & \mathbf{a}_{11}\mathbf{b}_{12} + \mathbf{a}_{12}\mathbf{b}_{22} \\ \mathbf{a}_{21}\mathbf{b}_{11} + \mathbf{a}_{22}\mathbf{b}_{21} & \mathbf{a}_{21}\mathbf{b}_{12} + \mathbf{a}_{22}\mathbf{b}_{22} \end{pmatrix}. \qquad (5.4.1)$$

[Exercise 1 is to verify that equation (5.4.1) correctly computes AB.] Each of the terms $\mathbf{a}_{ik}\mathbf{b}_{kj}$ is itself a *matrix* product and is computed recursively, unless $\mathbf{a}_{ik}$ and $\mathbf{b}_{kj}$ are 1×1.

Let c_n denote the number of multiplications and additions required by an algorithm based on equation (5.4.1) to compute the product of two $n \times n$ matrices. Computing the products of the eight $n/2 \times n/2$ submatrices requires $8c_{n/2}$ additions and multiplications, and combining them requires $4(n/2)^2 = n^2$ additions. Thus, we obtain the recurrence relation

$$c_n = 8c_{n/2} + n^2.$$

Unfortunately, the solution of this recurrence relation is $c_n = \Theta(n^3)$ (see the Main Recurrence Theorem, Theorem 2.4.7), which is no better asymptotically than Algorithm 5.4.1. Strassen (see Strassen, 1969) showed how to compute the expressions in equation (5.4.1) using only *seven* matrix products and $\Theta(n^2)$ additions and subtractions to combine them. The recurrence relation for this technique is

$$c_n = 7c_{n/2} + f(n),$$

where $f(n) = \Theta(n^2)$. The solution satisfies $c_n = \Theta(n^{\lg 7}) = \Theta(n^{2.807})$ (see the Main Recurrence Theorem, Theorem 2.4.7). Strassen's algorithm is, then, asymptotically faster than Algorithm 5.4.1.

Strassen's algorithm computes the quantities

$$
\begin{aligned}
\mathbf{q}_1 &= (\mathbf{a}_{11} + \mathbf{a}_{22}) * (\mathbf{b}_{11} + \mathbf{b}_{22}) \\
\mathbf{q}_2 &= (\mathbf{a}_{21} + \mathbf{a}_{22}) * \mathbf{b}_{11} \\
\mathbf{q}_3 &= \mathbf{a}_{11} * (\mathbf{b}_{12} - \mathbf{b}_{22}) \\
\mathbf{q}_4 &= \mathbf{a}_{22} * (\mathbf{b}_{21} - \mathbf{b}_{11}) \\
\mathbf{q}_5 &= (\mathbf{a}_{11} + \mathbf{a}_{12}) * \mathbf{b}_{22} \\
\mathbf{q}_6 &= (\mathbf{a}_{21} - \mathbf{a}_{11}) * (\mathbf{b}_{11} + \mathbf{b}_{12}) \\
\mathbf{q}_7 &= (\mathbf{a}_{12} - \mathbf{a}_{22}) * (\mathbf{b}_{21} + \mathbf{b}_{22}).
\end{aligned}
$$

We can verify (see Exercise 6) that

$$AB = \begin{pmatrix} \mathbf{q}_1 + \mathbf{q}_4 - \mathbf{q}_5 + \mathbf{q}_7 & \mathbf{q}_3 + \mathbf{q}_5 \\ \mathbf{q}_2 + \mathbf{q}_4 & \mathbf{q}_1 + \mathbf{q}_3 - \mathbf{q}_2 + \mathbf{q}_6 \end{pmatrix}. \tag{5.4.2}$$

Computing the $\mathbf{q}$'s and combining them to obtain AB requires only seven matrix products and $\Theta(n^2)$ additions and subtractions. Therefore, Strassen's algorithm requires only $\Theta(n^{\lg 7}) = \Theta(n^{2.807})$ arithmetic operations.

Various schemes have been proposed to extend Strassen's algorithm so that it can compute the product of $n \times n$ matrices where n is not a power of 2. One technique is to expand the size of the matrices by adding extra rows and columns of zeros—for example, adding rows and columns of zeros to make the size a power of 2. A more complicated scheme along the same lines was suggested by Strassen himself (see Strassen, 1969).

Strassen's algorithm requires considerable overhead and is practical only for large values of n (e.g., $n \geq 50$). For modest values of n, Algorithm 5.4.1 typically runs faster than Strassen's algorithm.

An algorithm by Coppersmith and Winograd (see Coppersmith, 1987) runs in time $\Theta(n^{2.376})$ and, so, is asymptotically faster than Strassen's algorithm. Since the product of two $n \times n$ matrices contains n^2 terms, *any* algorithm that multiplies two $n \times n$ matrices requires at least $\Omega(n^2)$ arithmetic operations. At the present time, no sharper lower bound is known for the matrix-product problem.

Exercises

1S. Prove that equation (5.4.1) correctly computes the matrix product.

2. Show how the $\Theta(n^3)$ recursive matrix-product algorithm based on equation (5.4.1) computes

$$\begin{pmatrix} 3 & 1 & 0 & 2 \\ 4 & -1 & 1 & 1 \\ 1 & 1 & -2 & 0 \\ -1 & -1 & 1 & 4 \end{pmatrix} \begin{pmatrix} 2 & -5 & 1 & 2 \\ 0 & -3 & -1 & 3 \\ 1 & 2 & 3 & 5 \\ 3 & 1 & -2 & 3 \end{pmatrix}.$$

3. Estimate the number of additions and multiplications the $\Theta(n^3)$ recursive matrix-product algorithm based on equation (5.4.1) performs. How does this compare with Algorithm 5.4.1?

4S. Show how Strassen's algorithm computes

$$\begin{pmatrix} 3 & 1 \\ 4 & -1 \end{pmatrix} \begin{pmatrix} 2 & -5 \\ 6 & -3 \end{pmatrix}.$$

5. Show how the extension of Strassen's algorithm that adds an extra column and row of zeros computes

$$\begin{pmatrix} 1 & 3 & -2 \\ 4 & -1 & 6 \\ 1 & 3 & -3 \end{pmatrix} \begin{pmatrix} -2 & 5 & 1 \\ 6 & -3 & 3 \\ -3 & 1 & 2 \end{pmatrix}.$$

6. Verify equation (5.4.2).

7S. Suppose that A is the adjacency matrix of a simple graph G with vertices $1, \ldots, n$. Show that entry ij in A^k is equal to the number of paths of length k from vertex i to vertex j.

Notes

Algorithm 5.1.4 is due to Solomon W. Golomb (Golomb, 1954). Golomb introduced *polyominoes*, of which trominoes are a special case. A *polyomino of order s* consists of s squares joined at the edges. A tromino is a polyomino of order 3. Three squares in a row form the only other type of polyomino of order 3. No one has yet found a simple formula for the number of polyominoes of order s. Numerous problems using polyominoes have been devised (see Martin, 1991).

Preparata, 1985, and Edelsbrunner, 1987, are good references on the closest-pair problem and computational geometry, in general. These references also give algorithms to solve the closest-pair problem in an arbitrary number of dimensions. A more recent computational geometry reference is de Berg, 1997.

Chapter Exercises

5.1. Implement Algorithm 5.1.4 in the following way. Assume that the board to be tiled is in the usual xy-coordinate system. Assume further that the board to be tiled is designated by the coordinates of its lower-left corner, and that the missing square is also designated by the coordinates of its lower-left corner. The following figure shows a 4×4 board located at $(0, 0)$ whose missing square is located at $(3, 2)$:

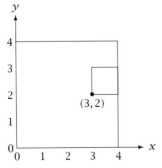

Assume also that the location of a tromino is given by the coordinates of its inner corner. For example, the tromino in the figure

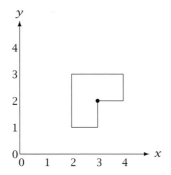

is located at $(3, 2)$. Finally, assume that the orientations of the trominoes are designated as follows:

UL   UR   LL   LR

(The terminology arises from the orientation of the trominoes if they are placed in the corners of a square: LL is lower left, UL is upper left, etc.) The output from a board of size 4 at $(0, 0)$, with the missing square at $(3, 2)$, might be

```
2 2 LL
1 3 UL
3 3 UL
3 1 LR
1 1 LL
```

5.2. Implement Algorithm 5.1.4 so that it draws the tiling.

5.3. Which rectangles can be tiled with trominoes?

5.4. Which deficient rectangles can be tiled with trominoes?

5.5. Write an $O(n \lg n)$ algorithm that receives as input an array a of n real numbers and a value *val*. (The array is not necessarily sorted.) The algorithm returns true if there are distinct indexes i and j such that $a[i] + a[j] = val$ and false otherwise.

5.6. Write an $O(n \lg n)$ algorithm that receives as input two n-element arrays a and b of real numbers and a value *val*. (The arrays are not necessarily sorted.) The algorithm returns true if there are indexes i and j such that $a[i] + b[j] = val$ and false otherwise.

5.7. Write an $O(n)$ algorithm that computes the union $A \cup B$ of two n-element sets A and B of real numbers. The sets are represented as arrays sorted in nondecreasing order. (There are no duplicates in either array.) The output is an array sorted in nondecreasing order that represents the union. (There are no duplicates in the output array either.)

5.8. Repeat Exercise 5.7 with "union" replaced by "intersection."

5.9. Write an $O(n \lg m)$ algorithm that computes the union $A \cup B$ of an m-element set A and an n-element set B, where $m \le n$. The sets A and B contain real numbers and are represented as arrays. (The arrays are not necessarily sorted, and there are no duplicates in either array.) The output is an array that represents the union. (The output array is not necessarily sorted, and it contains no duplicates.)

5.10. Repeat Exercise 5.9 with "union" replaced by "intersection."

5.11. Explain how to tweak the input so that *any* sorting algorithm becomes a stable sorting algorithm.

5.12. Implement merge (Algorithm 5.2.2) and an in-place merge (see Section 5.2 for a reference) and compare the times for various array sizes.

5.13. Implement mergesort (Algorithm 5.2.3), mergesort using an in-place merge, and an in-place mergesort (see Section 5.2 for references for in-place merge and in-place mergesort). Compare the times for arrays of various sizes containing sorted and unsorted data.

5.14. Write an $O(n \lg n)$ algorithm that finds the distance δ between a closest pair of points in the plane and, if $\delta > 0$, also finds *all* pairs δ apart.

5.15. Write an $O(n \lg n)$ algorithm that finds the distance δ between a closest pair of points in the plane and *all* pairs less than 2δ apart.

5.16. Write an $O(n \lg n)$ algorithm that finds a closest pair of points in the plane in which Euclidean distance is replaced by

$$\text{dist}(p, q) = |p_x - q_x| + |p_y - q_y|,$$

where $p = (p_x, p_y)$ and $q = (q_x, q_y)$. This distance is known as the *taxicab* or *Manhattan distance* because $\text{dist}(p, q)$ is equal to the number of blocks between points p and q if we are moving within a street system comprising square blocks and p and q are at the corners of blocks.

5.17. Write a version of Strassen's algorithm (see Section 5.4) that multiplies $n \times n$ matrices, where n is any positive integer. What is the time of your algorithm?

CHAPTER 6

Sorting and Selection

In Section 6.1, we begin with insertion sort, a straightforward sort that is useful for sorting small arrays. We then turn in Section 6.2 to a more sophisticated sort, quicksort, that is efficient for sorting large arrays. In Section 6.3, we address the question: How fast can we sort? Two special sorts (counting sort and radix sort) are discussed in Section 6.4. The selection problem (finding the kth smallest element in an array) is closely related to sorting and is the topic of Section 6.5.

6.1 Insertion Sort

In this section, we discuss insertion sort, one of the simplest $\Theta(n^2)$ sorting algorithms, but which can sort small arrays very fast. In the following section, we turn to a more sophisticated $\Theta(n \lg n)$ sorting algorithm that is used to sort large arrays efficiently.

$\mathcal{WWW}$ **Insertion sort** divides the array to be sorted into two parts: The first part consists of everything but the last element, and the second part is the last element. After sorting the first part, insertion sort *inserts* the last element in the correct position into the now sorted first part.

Suppose that we want to sort $a[1], \ldots, a[n]$. To implement insertion sort, we begin by solving the smallest problem: Sort $a[1], a[2]$. Since $a[1]$ is already sorted, we insert $a[2]$ into $a[1]$ (i.e., if $a[2] \geq a[1]$, we do nothing; if $a[2] < a[1]$, we swap $a[1]$ and $a[2]$). We next insert $a[3]$ into the now sorted array $a[1], a[2]$; then we insert $a[4]$ into the now sorted array $a[1], a[2], a[3]$; and so on.

At the ith iteration, we insert $val = a[i]$ into the sorted array

$$a[1], \ldots, a[i-1].$$

We first compare val with $a[i-1]$. If $val \geq a[i-1]$, we stop since

$$a[1], \ldots, a[i]$$

is already sorted. If $val < a[i-1]$, we move $a[i-1]$ one cell to the right (i.e., we copy $a[i-1]$ to $a[i]$), and we then compare val with $a[i-2]$. If $val \geq a[i-2]$, we copy val to $a[i-1]$ and stop since now

$$a[1], \ldots, a[i]$$

is sorted. If $val < a[i-2]$, we move $a[i-2]$ one cell to the right. We continue shifting data to the right until we obtain the correct position for val after which we insert val. The algorithm terminates when $a[n]$ is inserted into the proper position in the array

$$a[1], \ldots, a[n-1].$$

Example 6.1.1. Suppose that the array to sort is

| 36 | 14 | 27 | 40 | 31 | .

Insertion sort first inserts 14 into the one-element array 36. Since $14 < 36$, 36 moves one cell to the right

| | 36 | ,

after which 14 is inserted into the first cell

| 14 | 36 | .

Insertion sort next inserts 27 into the array $14, 36$. Since $27 < 36$, 36 moves one cell to the right

| 14 | | 36 | .

Since $27 > 14$, 14 does not move, and 27 is inserted into the second cell

| 14 | 27 | 36 | .

Insertion sort next inserts 40 into the array $14, 27, 36$. Since $40 > 36$, 36 does not move; the array is already sorted

| 14 | 27 | 36 | 40 | .

Finally, insertion sort inserts 31 into the array $14, 27, 36, 40$. Since $31 < 40$, 40 moves one cell to the right

| 14 | 27 | 36 | | 40 | .

Since $31 < 36$, 36 moves one cell to the right

| 14 | 27 | | 36 | 40 |

.

Since $31 > 27$, 27 does not move, and 31 is inserted into the third cell

| 14 | 27 | 31 | 36 | 40 |

.

The array is sorted. □

We state insertion sort as Algorithm 6.1.2.

Algorithm 6.1.2 Insertion Sort. This algorithm sorts the array a by first inserting $a[2]$ into the sorted array $a[1]$; next inserting $a[3]$ into the sorted array $a[1], a[2]$; and so on; and finally inserting $a[n]$ into the sorted array $a[1], \dots, a[n-1]$.

Input Parameter: a
Output Parameter: a

```
insertion_sort(a) {
    n = a.last
    for i = 2 to n {
        val = a[i] // save a[i] so it can be inserted into the correct place
        j = i − 1
        // if val < a[j], move a[j] right to make room for a[i]
        while (j ≥ 1 && val < a[j]) {
            a[j + 1] = a[j]
            j = j − 1
        }
        a[j + 1] = val // insert val
    }
}
```

In the worst case in Algorithm 6.1.2, the while loop executes the maximum number of times, which occurs when *val* is always inserted at index one. Such a situation occurs when the input is sorted in *decreasing* order. In this case, when $i = 2$ the while loop body executes once. When $i = 3$, the while loop body executes twice, and so on. Thus, in the worst case, the total number of times that the while loop body executes is

$$1 + 2 + \cdots + (n-1) = \frac{(n-1)n}{2} = \Theta(n^2).$$

Thus, the worst-case time of Algorithm 6.1.2 is $\Theta(n^2)$.

Exercises

Show how insertion sort sorts each array in Exercises 1–4.

1S. 14   40   31   28   3   15   17   51

2. 3   14   15   17   28   31   40   51

3. 51   40   31   28   17   15   14   3

4S. 23   23   23   23   23   23   23   23

5S. Give an example of input of size 5 that produces the best-case time for insertion sort.

6. What is the best-case time of insertion sort?

An inversion *in an array a is a pair of indexes* (i, j), $i < j$, *with* $a[i] > a[j]$ *(i.e., a pair of indexes that references values that are out of order).*

7S. List all inversions for the array of Exercise 1. Assume that the first index is one.

8. List all inversions for the array of Exercise 2. Assume that the first index is one.

9. List all inversions for the array of Exercise 3. Assume that the first index is one.

10S. List all inversions for the array of Exercise 4. Assume that the first index is one.

11. Show an array of size 5 having the maximum number of inversions.

12. What is the maximum number of inversions in an array of size n?

⋆**13S.** What is the average number of inversions in an array of size n? Assume that the data are distinct and that all permutations are equally likely.

14. Show that, in effect, each iteration of the while loop in insertion sort (Algorithm 6.1.2) removes one inversion.

15. Give a reasonable definition of "nearly sorted." Argue that insertion sort can sort a nearly-sorted array quickly.

16S. Show that any sorting algorithm that moves data only by swapping adjacent elements has worst-case time $\Omega(n^2)$.

17. *Binary insertion sort* sorts the array $a[1], \ldots, a[n]$ by first using binary search (see Section 4.1) to determine where to insert $a[2]$ in $a[1]$. It then inserts $a[2]$ in the proper position in $a[1]$. Next, it uses binary search to determine where to insert $a[3]$ in $a[1], a[2]$ and inserts it; next, it uses binary search to determine where to insert $a[4]$ in $a[1], a[2], a[3]$ and inserts it; and so on. What is wrong with the following statement? Since binary search is $\Theta(\lg n)$ in the worst case and there are $n - 1$ elements to insert, the worst-case time of binary insertion sort is $\Theta(n \lg n)$.

18. Answer Exercise 17 with "array" replaced by "linked list."

19. If the size of an array is small, say less than some number s, whose exact value depends on the implementation, system, and so on, insertion sort can run faster than mergesort (see Section 5.2). Modify mergesort to take this fact into account, and, thereby, make mergesort run faster.

6.2 Quicksort

$\mathcal{WWW}$ Like mergesort (see Section 5.2), **quicksort** first divides the array to be sorted into two parts and then sorts each part. In quicksort, this division process is called **partition**. Unlike mergesort, which divides the array into two nearly equal parts, the sizes of the two parts into which partition divides the array can range from nearly equal to highly unequal. The division depends on a particular element, called the *partition element*, that is chosen. Partition rearranges the data so that the partition element is in the correct position (i.e., the partition element is in the cell where it would be *if* the entire array was sorted). In addition, the particular version of partition that we discuss places all data less than the partition element to the left of the partition element (but not necessarily in sorted order) and all data greater than or equal to the partition element to the right of the partition element (again not necessarily in sorted order). Because the data are on the correct sides of the partition element, once quicksort sorts each side, the entire array is sorted.

Example 6.2.1. Quicksort begins by partitioning the array to be sorted. If the array

12	30	21	8	6	9	1	7

is partitioned using 12 as the partition element, the result could be

7	8	6	9	1	12	21	30

(The arrangement of the data to the left and right of the partition element is determined by the particular version of partition that is used.) The partition element, 12, is in the cell where it would be if the entire array was sorted. The data to the left of 12 are less than 12, and the data to the right of 12 are greater than or equal to 12. The quicksort algorithm concludes by sorting the part to the left of 12 and the part to the right of 12

1	6	7	8	9	12	21	30

after which the array is sorted. □

Jon Bentley (see Bentley, 2000, page 117) attributes our first version of partition to Nico Lomuto. We use the first element *val* as the partition element. At the kth iteration of partition, there is a section of the array a following *val* containing data less than *val* and an index h marking the end of this

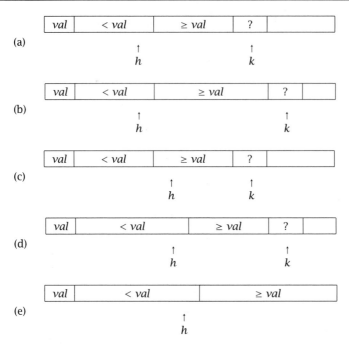

Figure 6.2.1 Partitioning an array a. The situation just before another iteration of the algorithm is shown in (a). If $a[k] \geq val$, we may extend the second section of the array to include $a[k]$ by simply incrementing k [see (b)]. If $a[k] < val$, we may increment h and then swap $a[h]$ and $a[k]$ [see (c)], thereby extending the first section and shifting the second section's collection of values one to the right. We then increment k [see (d)]. We are now ready for another iteration of the algorithm. After iterating through the array, we have the situation shown in (e), so if we then swap val and $a[h]$, the partitioning is complete.

section of the array. This section of the array is followed by another section containing data greater than or equal to val. The cell following this section has index k [see Figure 6.2.1(a)]. Either or both of these sections might be empty. If $a[k] \geq val$, we may extend the second section of the array to include $a[k]$ by simply incrementing k [see Figure 6.2.1(b)]. If $a[k] < val$, we may increment h and then swap $a[h]$ and $a[k]$ [see Figure 6.2.1(c)], thereby extending the first section and shifting the second section's collection of values one to the right. We then increment k [see Figure 6.2.1(d)]. We are now ready for another iteration of partition. After iterating through the array, we have the situation shown in Figure 6.2.1(e), so if we then swap val and $a[h]$, the partitioning is complete. We conclude with val at index h, all data less than val to the left of val's cell, and all data greater than or equal to val to the right of val's cell.

We state the partition algorithm as Algorithm 6.2.2.

Algorithm 6.2.2 Partition. This algorithm partitions the array

$$a[i], \ldots, a[j]$$

by inserting $val = a[i]$ at the index h where it would be if the array was sorted. When the algorithm concludes, values at indexes less than h are less than val, and values at indexes greater than h are greater than or equal to val. The algorithm returns the index h.

```
Input Parameters:   a, i, j
Output Parameter:   a

partition(a, i, j) {
    val = a[i]
    h = i
    for k = i + 1 to j
        if (a[k] < val) {
            h = h + 1
            swap(a[h], a[k])
        }
    swap(a[i], a[h])
    return h
}
```

Example 6.2.3. We show how Algorithm 6.2.2 partitions the array

| 12 | 30 | 21 | 8 | 6 | 9 | 1 | 7 | .

Since 30 and 21 are greater than 12, k simply increments giving

| 12 | 30 | 21 | 8 | 6 | 9 | 1 | 7 | .

$\uparrow$ h $\uparrow$ k

Since $8 < 12$, h increments and we swap $a[h]$ and $a[k]$ giving

| 12 | 8 | 21 | 30 | 6 | 9 | 1 | 7 | .

$\uparrow$ h $\uparrow$ k

Next k increments giving

| 12 | 8 | 21 | 30 | 6 | 9 | 1 | 7 | .

$\uparrow$ h $\uparrow$ k

Since $6 < 12$, h increments and we swap $a[h]$ and $a[k]$ giving

| 12 | 8 | 6 | 30 | 21 | 9 | 1 | 7 |

$$\begin{array}{cc} \uparrow & \uparrow \\ h & k \end{array}$$

Next k increments giving

| 12 | 8 | 6 | 30 | 21 | 9 | 1 | 7 |

$$\begin{array}{cc} \uparrow & \uparrow \\ h & k \end{array}$$

Each of 9, 1, and 7 is less than 12, so for each of these values, h increments and $a[h]$ and $a[k]$ are swapped, giving

| 12 | 8 | 6 | 9 | 1 | 7 | 21 | 30 |

$$\begin{array}{c} \uparrow \\ h \end{array}$$

After swapping $a[h]$ and the partition element, 12,

| 7 | 8 | 6 | 9 | 1 | 12 | 21 | 30 |

$$\begin{array}{c} \uparrow \\ h \end{array}$$

all values to the left of 12 are less than 12, and all values to the right of 12 are greater than or equal to 12. The partitioning is complete.   □

The proof that Algorithm 6.2.2 is correct is given in Figure 6.2.1.

If we define the time of Algorithm 6.2.2 to be the number of comparisons of array elements, the time for an array of size n is $n - 1$.

Having written partition, it is straightforward to write quicksort.

Algorithm 6.2.4 Quicksort. This algorithm sorts the array

$$a[i], \ldots, a[j]$$

by using the partition algorithm (Algorithm 6.2.2).

 Input Parameters: a, i, j
Output Parameter: a

```
quicksort(a, i, j) {
    if (i < j) {
        p = partition(a, i, j)
        quicksort(a, i, p - 1)
        quicksort(a, p + 1, j)
    }
}
```

Because of all of the swapping in partition, it is not surprising that quick-sort is *not* stable. We leave as an exercise (Exercise 12) the problem of constructing a concrete example.

In the following subsection, we discuss the worst-case time of quicksort.

Worst-Case Time for Quicksort

As we remarked earlier, in general a divide-and-conquer algorithm is most efficient when the division is as even as possible. Thus, we suspect that worst-case time for quicksort occurs when the division is as *uneven* as possible. We show that this is indeed the case.

Suppose we input an n-element array a to quicksort that has the property that every time partition is called, the partition element is placed at either the beginning or the end of the array (resulting in the worst possible division). Such a situation can occur. If a is sorted in increasing order, the partition element is always placed at the beginning of the array (see Exercise 9). When quicksort is first called, partition takes time $n - 1$. Quicksort is then called twice, once with an empty array and again with an array of size $n - 1$. The next call to partition takes time $n - 2$. Quicksort is again called twice, once with an empty array and again with an array of size $n - 2$. The next call to partition takes time $n - 3$. The process continues. The total time for all of the calls to partition is

$$(n - 1) + (n - 2) + (n - 3) + \cdots + 1 = \frac{(n - 1)n}{2} = \Theta(n^2).$$

Therefore, the worst-case time to execute quicksort is $\Omega(n^2)$. We show that the time for quicksort is always $O(n^2)$, so that the worst-case time to execute quicksort is $\Theta(n^2)$.

Theorem 6.2.5. *The worst-case time for quicksort for an array of size n is $\Theta(n^2)$.*

Proof. We have already noted that if an n-element input array is sorted in increasing order, the time for quicksort is $\Theta(n^2)$. Thus, the worst-case time of quicksort is $\Omega(n^2)$. We show that the worst-case time of quicksort is $O(n^2)$, thus proving the theorem.

Let c_n be the worst-case time for quicksort for an array of size n. Then $c_1 \geq 1$. We use mathematical induction to show that $c_n \leq c_1 n^2$, thus proving that the worst-case time of quicksort is $O(n^2)$. The basis step is immediate.

Suppose that $n > 1$ and $c_p \leq c_1 p^2$ for all $p < n$. We show that $c_n \leq c_1 n^2$. Suppose that the input is the array $a[1], \ldots, a[n]$. Quicksort first partitions a, which takes time (i.e., the number of comparisons) at most n. If the partition element is at index p, the recursive call to sort the left side takes time at most c_{p-1}, and the recursive call to sort the right side takes time at most c_{n-p}. Thus, if the partition element is at index p, the worst-case time is at most

$$n + c_{p-1} + c_{n-p}.$$

Since the partition element could be at any index between 1 and n,

$$c_n \le n + \max_{1 \le p \le n} c_{p-1} + c_{n-p}.$$

By the inductive assumption, $c_{p-1} \le c_1(p-1)^2$ and $c_{n-p} \le c_1(n-p)^2$. Therefore,

$$c_n \le n + \max_{1 \le p \le n} c_{p-1} + c_{n-p} \le n + c_1 \max_{1 \le p \le n} (p-1)^2 + (n-p)^2.$$

The function $y = (p-1)^2 + (n-p)^2$ on $[1, n]$ is a parabola symmetric about the line $p = (n+1)/2$ that opens up (see Figure 6.2.2). Thus, the maximum occurs at the points $p = 1$ and $p = n$; and the value of this maximum is $(n-1)^2$. It follows that

$$c_n \le n + c_1 \max_{1 \le p \le n} (p-1)^2 + (n-p)^2 \le n + c_1(n-1)^2.$$

Now

$$n + c_1(n-1)^2 = c_1 n^2 + (1 - 2c_1)n + c_1.$$

Since $n > 1$ and $c_1 \ge 1$, the expression $(1 - 2c_1)n + c_1$ is negative. Therefore,

$$n + c_1(n-1)^2 = c_1 n^2 + (1 - 2c_1)n + c_1 \le c_1 n^2,$$

and

$$c_n \le c_1 n^2.$$

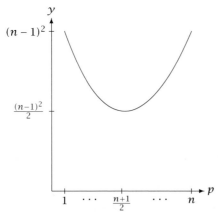

Figure 6.2.2 The graph of $y = (p-1)^2 + (n-p)^2$ on $[1, n]$. The maximum occurs at the points $p = 1$ and $p = n$, and the value of this maximum is $(n-1)^2$. ∎

Randomized Quicksort

Although the worst-case time of quicksort is $\Theta(n^2)$, it often performs much better. In fact, as a practical sorting algorithm, quicksort is often the choice, and many system sorting procedures use a version of quicksort. If partition divides the array to be sorted into two equal parts, quicksort is very fast. For example, if partition always divides the array to be sorted into two equal parts and c_n is the time required to sort an n-item array, the recurrence relation is

$$c_n = n - 1 + 2c_{n/2}.$$

By the Main Recurrence Theorem, Theorem 2.4.7, $c_n = \Theta(n \lg n)$. This discussion shows that the choice of the partition element is very important.

One way to help avoid a bad partition element is to choose it randomly (rather than to always choose the first element as in Algorithm 6.2.2). The resulting algorithm (Algorithm 6.2.6) is called *random_partition*. When *random_partition* replaces *partition* in quicksort, we call the resulting algorithm (Algorithm 6.2.7) *random_quicksort*.

Algorithm 6.2.6 Random Partition. This algorithm partitions the array

$$a[i], \ldots, a[j]$$

by inserting *val* = $a[k]$ at the index h where it would be if the array was sorted. The index k is chosen randomly. We assume that the function

$$rand(i, j)$$

executes in constant time and returns a random integer between i and j, inclusive. After inserting *val* at index h, values at indexes less than h are less than *val*, and values at indexes greater than h are greater than or equal to *val*. The algorithm returns the index h.

```
 Input Parameters:    a, i, j
 Output Parameter:    a

random_partition(a, i, j) {
    k = rand(i, j)
    swap(a[i], a[k])
    return partition(i, j) // Algorithm 6.2.2
}
```

Since *rand* runs in constant time, the time of Algorithm 6.2.6 for an n-element array, like partition (Algorithm 6.2.2), is $n - 1$ (again counting comparisons of array elements).

Random quicksort is obtained by replacing *partition* in the original quicksort algorithm (Algorithm 6.2.4) by *random_partition*.

Algorithm 6.2.7 Random Quicksort. This algorithm sorts the array

$$a[i], \ldots, a[j]$$

by using the random-partition algorithm (Algorithm 6.2.6).

Input Parameters: a, i, j
Output Parameter: a

```
random_quicksort(a, i, j) {
   if (i < j) {
      p = random_partition(a, i, j)
      random_quicksort(a, i, p - 1)
      random_quicksort(a, p + 1, j)
   }
}
```

Although the worst-case time of random quicksort, $\Theta(n^2)$, is the same as quicksort, its *expected* run time is $\Theta(n \lg n)$.

Theorem 6.2.8. *The expected run time of random quicksort (Algorithm 6.2.7) is* $\Theta(n \lg n)$.

Proof. Let c_n be the expected run time of random quicksort when

$$a[1], \ldots, a[n]$$

is input to quicksort.

If $n > 1$, random quicksort first calls random partition, which takes time $n-1$. After random partition is called, random quicksort is called recursively on each part of the array. Thus, if the partition element is placed at index p, the total time is

$$n - 1 + c_{p-1} + c_{n-p}, \quad n > 1.$$

Since all indexes p are equally likely, we have

$$c_n = n - 1 + \frac{1}{n} \sum_{p=1}^{n} (c_{p-1} + c_{n-p}), \quad n > 1.$$

Noting that each term $c_0, \ldots, c_{n-1}$ appears twice in the preceding equation, we may rewrite the equation as

$$c_n = n - 1 + \frac{2}{n} \sum_{p=0}^{n-1} c_p, \quad n > 1.$$

This recurrence relation is not readily solved by the methods discussed in Section 2.4; however, it can be transformed into a recurrence relation that we can solve by iteration.

We rewrite the preceding recurrence relation as

$$nc_n = n(n - 1) + 2 \sum_{p=0}^{n-1} c_p, \quad n > 1,$$

by multiplying by n. If we write the recurrence relation for c_{n-1}

$$(n-1)c_{n-1} = (n-1)(n-2) + 2\sum_{p=0}^{n-2} c_p, \quad n > 2,$$

and subtract this equation from that for nc_n, most terms cancel and we obtain

$$nc_n - (n-1)c_{n-1} = n(n-1) - (n-1)(n-2) + 2c_{n-1}, \quad n > 2.$$

The preceding equation simplifies to

$$nc_n = 2(n-1) + (n+1)c_{n-1}, \quad n > 2.$$

Dividing by $n(n+1)$, we obtain

$$\frac{c_n}{n+1} = \frac{2(n-1)}{n(n+1)} + \frac{c_{n-1}}{n}, \quad n > 2.$$

Replacing $2(n-1)$ by $2n$, we obtain

$$\frac{c_n}{n+1} \le \frac{2}{n+1} + \frac{c_{n-1}}{n}, \quad n > 2.$$

Since we now have an inequality involving only c_n and c_{n-1}, we can estimate c_n using iteration. We obtain

$$\frac{c_n}{n+1} \le \frac{2}{n+1} + \frac{c_{n-1}}{n}$$

$$\le \frac{2}{n+1} + \frac{2}{n} + \frac{c_{n-2}}{n-1} \le \cdots$$

$$\le 2\left(\frac{1}{n+1} + \frac{1}{n} + \cdots + \frac{1}{4}\right) + \frac{c_2}{3}.$$

By Theorem 2.3.9,

$$\frac{1}{n+1} + \frac{1}{n} + \cdots + \frac{1}{4} = O(\lg n).$$

Therefore,

$$c_n = O(n \lg n).$$

Similarly, since $n > 2$, we may replace $2(n-1)$ by n to obtain

$$\frac{c_n}{n+1} \ge \frac{1}{n+1} + \frac{c_{n-1}}{n}, \quad n > 2.$$

We now obtain

$$\frac{c_n}{n+1} \ge \frac{1}{n+1} + \frac{1}{n} + \cdots + \frac{1}{4} + \frac{c_2}{3}.$$

Again by Theorem 2.3.9,

$$\frac{1}{n+1} + \frac{1}{n} + \cdots + \frac{1}{4} = \Omega(\lg n).$$

Therefore,

$$c_n = \Omega(n \lg n).$$

Since $c_n = O(n \lg n)$ and $c_n = \Omega(n \lg n)$, $c_n = \Theta(n \lg n)$ and the proof is complete. ∎

Exercises

1S. Show how partition (Algorithm 6.2.2) partitions the array in Exercise 1, Section 6.1.

2. Show how partition (Algorithm 6.2.2) partitions the array in Exercise 2, Section 6.1.

3. Show how partition (Algorithm 6.2.2) partitions the array in Exercise 3, Section 6.1.

4S. Show how partition (Algorithm 6.2.2) partitions the array in Exercise 4, Section 6.1.

5S. Show how quicksort (Algorithm 6.2.4) sorts the array in Exercise 1, Section 6.1.

6. Show how quicksort (Algorithm 6.2.4) sorts the array in Exercise 2, Section 6.1.

7. Show how quicksort (Algorithm 6.2.4) sorts the array in Exercise 3, Section 6.1.

8S. Show how quicksort (Algorithm 6.2.4) sorts the array in Exercise 4, Section 6.1.

9S. Show that if an array is sorted in increasing order, when quicksort is called, partition (Algorithm 6.2.2) always places the partition element at the beginning of the array.

10. Show that if an array is sorted in decreasing order, when quicksort is called, partition (Algorithm 6.2.2) always places the partition element at the beginning or end of the array.

11. Give an example of an array of size 5 that is not sorted in increasing or decreasing order and produces worst-case time for quicksort.

12S. Give an example to show that quicksort is *not* stable.

13. What is the time of quicksort when the values of all of the data are equal?

14. Show possible values returned by *rand* that produce worst-case time when *random_quicksort* sorts $12, 6, 20, 5, 10$.

15S. Professor Groucho suggests changing the partition algorithm (Algorithm 6.2.2) to

```
partition(a, i, j) {
    val = a[i]
    h = i
    for k = i + 1 to j
        if (a[k] ≤ val) {
            h = h + 1
            swap(a[h], a[k])
        }
    swap(a[i], a[h])
    return h
}
```

When this version of partition is used with quicksort, does quicksort correctly sort *a*?

16. Professor Larry suggests changing the quicksort algorithm (Algorithm 6.2.4) to

```
quicksort(a, i, j) {
    if (i < j) {
        p = partition(a, i, j)
        quicksort(a, i, p)
        quicksort(a, p, j)
    }
}
```

Does this algorithm correctly sort *a*? If so, what is its worst-case time?

Given an array $a[i], \ldots, a[j]$, with $j - i \geq 2$, let $k = \lfloor (i+j)/2 \rfloor$, and choose as the partition element the median among $a[i], a[k], a[j]$ (i.e., the value that would be in the middle if $a[i], a[k], a[j]$ was sorted). Median-of-three partitioning uses as the partition element the median among $a[i], a[k], a[j]$.

17S. Show how median-of-three partitioning partitions the array in Exercise 1, Section 6.1.

18. Show how median-of-three partitioning partitions the array in Exercise 2, Section 6.1.

19. Show how median-of-three partitioning partitions the array in Exercise 3, Section 6.1.

20S. Show how median-of-three partitioning partitions the array in Exercise 4, Section 6.1.

21. Write pseudocode for median-of-three partitioning.

22. What is the running time for median-of-three partitioning?

23S. What is the running time for a version of quicksort that uses median-of-three partitioning if the input is a sorted array?

24. Solve the recurrence relation

$$c_n = 2 + \sum_{i=1}^{n-1} c_i, \quad n \geq 2,$$

with initial condition $c_1 = 1$.

6.3 A Lower Bound for the Sorting Problem

In Section 4.1, we used decision trees to give a lower bound on a searching problem. In a similar way, decision trees can be used to give a lower bound on the number of comparisons required in the worst case to sort an array. We show that to sort n items, *any* comparison-based sorting algorithm has worst-case time $\Omega(n \lg n)$. By "comparison-based," we mean that the only way that the algorithm can obtain information about where an element in the array should be placed is to compare one element in the array with another. A comparison-based sorting algorithm may not take action based on the *value* of a data item (e.g., a comparison-based sorting algorithm is *not* allowed to conclude that an item whose value is "small" should be placed early in the array). Notice that heapsort, insertion sort, mergesort, and quicksort are all comparison-based sorting algorithms. In Section 6.4, we will see that if an algorithm can obtain information about where an element in the array should be placed by means other than simply comparing array elements, it is possible to sort faster than $\Theta(n \lg n)$ (but only for inputs satisfying certain conditions).

Throughout the remainder of this section, we abbreviate "comparison-based sorting algorithm" to "sorting algorithm." We use a *decision tree* to depict a sorting algorithm (see Figure 6.3.1). In such a decision tree, each internal vertex denotes a comparison. If the result of the comparison is true, the algorithm follows the left edge; otherwise, it follows the right edge. The state of the data after the comparison is shown on the edge. The process is repeated (i.e., if an internal vertex is reached, another comparison is performed, the algorithm follows the left or right edge, and the state of the data changes) until a terminal vertex is reached, at which point the data are sorted.

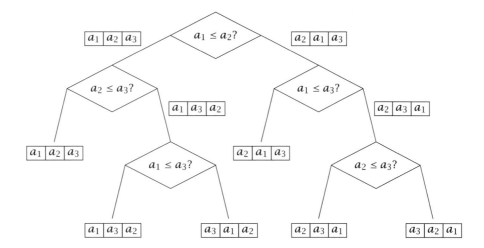

Figure 6.3.1 Insertion sort for three items as a decision tree. The input is an array containing the values a_1, a_2, a_3. Each internal vertex denotes a comparison. If the result of the comparison is true, insertion sort follows the left edge; otherwise, it follows the right edge. The values in the array after a comparison are shown on the edge. For example, a_1 and a_2 are compared first. If $a_1 \leq a_2$, the algorithm follows the left edge, the array is unchanged, and the algorithm next compares a_2 and a_3. If $a_1 > a_2$, the algorithm follows the right edge, the values in the array become a_2, a_1, a_3, and the algorithm next compares a_1 and a_3. The terminal vertices show the array after it is sorted.

Example 6.3.1. Figure 6.3.1 depicts insertion sort (see Section 6.1) for input of size three as a decision tree.   □

The worst-case time for a sorting algorithm is at least as large as the number of comparisons performed in the worst-case since it does additional work (e.g., moving data) beyond making comparisons. In a decision-tree depiction of the algorithm, the maximum number of comparisons occurs on a path of maximum length from the root to a terminal vertex, which is equal to the height of the tree. For example in Figure 6.3.1, the height of the tree is three; thus, the maximum number of comparisons for this algorithm is equal to three.

We now use decision trees to give a lower bound on the number of comparisons required in the worst case to sort n items.

Theorem 6.3.2. *If $f(n)$ is the number of comparisons needed to sort n items in the worst case by a comparison-based sorting algorithm, then $f(n) = \Omega(n \lg n)$.*

Proof. Let T be the decision tree that represents the algorithm for input of size n, and let h denote the height of T. Then the algorithm requires h

comparisons in the worst case, so

$$h = f(n).$$

Since n distinct items can be arranged in $n!$ ways, T has at least $n!$ terminal vertices. By Theorem 2.6.8,

$$\lg n! \leq h.$$

Now $\lg n! = \Theta(n \lg n)$ (see Example 2.3.8); thus, for some positive constant C,

$$Cn \lg n \leq \lg n!$$

for all but finitely many integers n. Combining the previous equation and inequalities, we obtain

$$Cn \lg n \leq f(n)$$

for all but finitely many integers n. Therefore,

$$f(n) = \Omega(n \lg n). \qquad \blacksquare$$

Corollary 6.3.3. *The worst-case time of a comparison-based sorting algorithm is $\Omega(n \lg n)$.*

Proof. By Theorem 6.3.2, the number of comparisons required by a comparison-based sorting algorithm in the worst case is $\Omega(n \lg n)$. Thus the *total* time required by the algorithm in the worst case is also $\Omega(n \lg n)$. $\qquad \blacksquare$

Exercises

1S. Trace the decision tree of Figure 6.3.1 for input $6, 3, 12$.

2. Trace the decision tree of Figure 6.3.1 for input $12, 6, 3$.

3. Trace the decision tree of Figure 6.3.1 for input $6, 12, 3$.

4S. Give an algorithm that sorts four items using five comparisons in the worst case.

5. Use a decision tree to find a lower bound on the number of comparisons required to sort five items in the worst case. Give an algorithm that uses this number of comparisons to sort five items in the worst case.

6. Use a decision tree to find a lower bound on the number of comparisons required to sort six items in the worst case. Give an algorithm that uses this number of comparisons to sort six items in the worst case.

7S. Consider an algorithm that sorts an array of size n as follows. If $n = 1, 2, 3$, it uses a sort that minimizes the number of comparisons. If $n > 3$, the algorithm first recursively sorts the first $n - 1$ items. Then binary search is used to determine the correct position for the nth item, after which it is inserted in its correct position. Determine the number of comparisons used in the worst case for $n = 4, 5, 6$. Does any algorithm use fewer comparisons for $n = 4, 5, 6$?

6.4 Counting Sort and Radix Sort

In this section, we consider two sorting algorithms, **counting sort** and **radix sort**, that require specific knowledge about the input. Because of this requirement, these algorithms are able to use the input in a particular way, and, as a result, neither is comparison based. Each runs in *linear time* and, thus, faster than any comparison-based sorting algorithm [the lower bound for which is $\Theta(n \lg n)$; see Section 6.3].

Counting Sort

WWW   **Counting sort** sorts an array $a[1], \ldots, a[n]$ of integers, each in the range 0 to m, inclusive. To sort the array, counting sort counts the number of integers of each value. It then uses this information to sort the original array.

Example 6.4.1. Suppose that the input is

$$a[1] = 5, \quad a[2] = 8, \quad a[3] = 3, \quad a[4] = 8, \quad a[5] = 10, \quad a[6] = 7.$$

If $c[k]$ is the number of occurrences of value k in the array a,

$$c[3] = 1, \quad c[5] = 1, \quad c[7] = 1, \quad c[8] = 2, \quad c[10] = 1.$$

In order to sort a, we modify c so that $c[k]$ is equal to the number of elements in a less than or equal to k:

$$c[3] = 1, \quad c[5] = 2, \quad c[7] = 3, \quad c[8] = 5, \quad c[10] = 6.$$

We then copy the items from a into another array b, which will be sorted. Copying begins with the last element in a.

The last element in a is 7. Since $c[7] = 3$, there are three elements in a less than or equal to 7. Therefore, 7 should be in the third cell once a is sorted. Thus, 7 is copied to the third cell of b:

| | | 7 | | | | .

We also decrement $c[7]$ to 2 so that if there is another occurrence of 7, it will be placed in the second cell.

The predecessor of 7 in a is 10 and $c[10] = 6$, so 10 is copied to the sixth cell of b:

| | | 7 | | | 10 | .

We also decrement $c[10]$ to 5.

The predecessor of 10 in a is 8 and $c[8] = 5$, so the last 8 is copied to the fifth cell of b:

| | | 7 | | 8 | 10 | .

We also decrement $c[8]$ to 4.

The predecessor of the last 8 in a is 3 and $c[3] = 1$, so 3 is copied to the first cell of b:

| 3 | | 7 | | 8 | 10 | .

We also decrement $c[3]$ to 0 even though there cannot be another occurrence of 3.

The predecessor of 3 in a is 8 and $c[8] = 4$, so the first 8 is copied to the fourth cell of b:

| 3 | | 7 | 8 | 8 | 10 | .

We also decrement $c[8]$ to 3. Notice that the sort is stable.

The predecessor of the first 8 in a is 5 and $c[5] = 2$, so 5 is copied to the second cell of b:

| 3 | 5 | 7 | 8 | 8 | 10 | .

The sort is completed by copying b back to a.   □

Algorithm 6.4.2 Counting Sort. This algorithm sorts the array

$$a[1], \ldots, a[n]$$

of integers, each in the range 0 to m, inclusive.

Input Parameters: a, m
Output Parameter: a

counting_sort(a, m) {
    // set $c[k]$ = the number of occurrences of value k in the array a.
    // begin by initializing c to zero.
    for $k = 0$ to m
       $c[k] = 0$
    $n = a.last$
    for $i = 1$ to n
       $c[a[i]] = c[a[i]] + 1$
    // modify c so that $c[k]$ = number of elements $\leq k$
    for $k = 1$ to m
       $c[k] = c[k] + c[k-1]$

```
// sort a with the result in b
for i = n downto 1 {
    b[c[a[i]]] = a[i]
    c[a[i]] = c[a[i]] - 1
}
// copy b back to a
for i = 1 to n
    a[i] = b[i]
}
```

The time of each for loop in Algorithm 6.4.2 is either $\Theta(m)$ or $\Theta(n)$. Thus Algorithm 6.4.2 runs in time $\Theta(m + n)$. Notice that if $m \leq n$ or, more generally, if m is a function of n satisfying $m = O(n)$, Algorithm 6.4.2 runs in linear time, $\Theta(n)$.

Notice that counting sort is stable (see Exercise 5).

Radix Sort

$\mathcal{WWW}$ Suppose that, like the situation for counting sort, we again need to sort integers; but, unlike the situation for counting sort, the integers are large. For discussion purposes, we assume that the integers are positive and have up to five digits. **Radix sort** sorts these integers (see Example 6.4.3) by first using a stable sort (e.g., counting sort) to sort these integers on the least significant digit (the one's digit), then sorting on the second least significant digit (the 10's digit), and so on, until finally sorting on the most significant digit (the 10,000's digit). We will show that after these five sorts, the integers are indeed sorted (see Theorem 6.4.5).

Example 6.4.3. We show how radix sort sorts the array

33101	26440	16341	20101	801

.

We assume that it uses counting sort to sort on a particular digit.

Since the least significant digits are, in order,

$$1 \quad 0 \quad 1 \quad 1 \quad 1,$$

after using counting sort to sort on the least significant digit, the array becomes

26440	33101	16341	20101	801

.

Notice that the integers that end with 1 are in the same order as in the original array because counting sort is *stable*.

The array becomes

33101	20101	801	26440	16341

after sorting on the 10's digit.

The array becomes

| 33101 | 20101 | 16341 | 26440 | 801 |

after sorting on the 100's digit.
   The array becomes

| 20101 | 801 | 33101 | 16341 | 26440 |

after sorting on the 1000's digit.
   The array becomes

| 801 | 16341 | 20101 | 26440 | 33101 |

after sorting on the 10,000's digit and is now sorted. Notice that if counting sort was not stable, we could not guarantee that 20101 would precede
26440.   □

   We state radix sort as Algorithm 6.4.4.

Algorithm 6.4.4 Radix Sort. This algorithm sorts the array

$$a[1], \ldots, a[n]$$

of integers. Each integer has at most k digits.

   Input Parameters a, k
Output Parameter: a

```
radix_sort(a, k) {
   for i = 0 to k − 1
      counting_sort(a, 10) // key is digit in 10^i's place
}
```

   In Algorithm 6.4.4, the time for each call of counting sort is $\Theta(n + 10) = \Theta(n)$. Since counting sort is called k times, the time for radix sort is $\Theta(kn)$. If we consider k to be bounded by a constant, radix sort runs in linear time, $\Theta(n)$.
   We next prove that radix sort (Algorithm 6.4.4) is correct.

Theorem 6.4.5. *Radix sort (Algorithm 6.4.4) is correct.*

Proof. Let x be an element in the array input to radix sort. We show that when the algorithm terminates, every element whose value is greater than x follows x, thus proving that radix sort is correct.
   Let

$$y = b_i 10^i + b_{i-1} 10^{i-1} + \cdots + b_0, \quad b_i \neq 0,$$

be the decimal expansion of an element in the array greater than x. Suppose that the decimal expansion of x is

$$x = a_i 10^i + a_{i-1} 10^{i-1} + \cdots + a_0.$$

Let k be the largest index with $b_k \neq a_k$. Since $y > x$, $b_k > a_k$. When counting sort sorts on the 10^k's place, y is placed after x. On subsequent calls of counting sort, both x and y have the same key and, since counting sort is stable, y still follows x. ∎

Example 6.4.6 Sorting Punch Cards. Radix sort was originally used to sort punch cards. Each card had 80 columns, and the value of a column was indicated by punches. A card sorting machine was first programmed to examine the last column after which the machine distributed the cards into bins so that all of the cards in a particular bin had the same value in the last column. The operator then gathered the cards, being careful to put the stack with the lowest value first, the stack with the second lowest value second, and so on. After gathering the cards, they were then sorted by the machine on the second to last column. This process was repeated until the cards were sorted. □

Exercises

Show how counting sort sorts each array in Exercises 1–4.

1S. 15 3 17 2 9 10 8   **2.** 15 8 17 2 9 8 15 8

3. 4 4 4 4 4 4   **4S.** 2 3 4 5

5S. Give a formal proof that counting sort is stable.

6. Write a version of counting sort that sorts an array of integers in *nonincreasing* order.

7. Professor Larry proposes modifying counting sort as follows:

```
counting_sort(a, m) {
    for k = 0 to m − 1
        c[k] = 0
    for i = 1 to n
        c[a[i]] = c[a[i]] + 1
    for k = 1 to m
        c[k] = c[k] + c[k − 1]
    for i = 1 to n {
        b[c[a[i]]] = a[i]
        c[a[i]] = c[a[i]] − 1
    }
    for i = 1 to n
        a[i] = b[i]
}
```

Does the Professor's version sort a? If so, is it stable?

8S. Write a stable version of counting sort that sorts the array a by copying the elements in a to their proper positions from the *beginning* of a rather than from the end of a as in Algorithm 6.4.2.

Show how radix sort sorts each array in Exercises 9–12.

9S. 34   9134   20134   29134   4   134

10. 4   34   134   9134   20134   29134

11. 29134   20134   9134   134   34   4

12S. 10000   1000   10   1   100

13S. How much space does radix sort (Algorithm 6.4.4) require?

14. What is the worst-case time of radix sort if we replace counting sort by insertion sort?

15. What is the worst-case time of radix sort if we replace counting sort by mergesort?

6.5 Selection

Consider the incomes listed in Figure 6.5.1. The **median** income is the income that would be in the middle if the incomes were sorted. Since the sorted order is

25,160   30,570   55,300   72,815   77,800   137,230   260,750,

the median income is $72,815.

Name	Income
Hewitt	$30,570
Chu	260,750
Zemanski	55,300
Royer	72,815
Brown	137,230
Moy	77,800
Johnson	25,160

Figure 6.5.1 Incomes. The median income is $72,815, the income that would be in the middle if the incomes were sorted.

The selection problem generalizes the problem of finding the median. The **selection problem** is: Given an array a and an integer k, find the kth smallest element. The selection problem, thus, includes the problem of finding the median: We simply set $k = n/2$.

Any sorting algorithm can be used to solve the selection problem. After sorting the array in nondecreasing order, the element in the kth cell is the kth smallest element. However, since the selection problem does *not* require that the array be sorted, the goal is to solve the problem faster by doing less work than sorting the entire array.

Most fast practical algorithms that solve the selection problem use a version of the partition algorithm (see Algorithms 6.2.2 and 6.2.6). Suppose that we execute the partition algorithm and the partition element *val* happens to be placed in the kth cell. Since the partition algorithm places all of the elements less than *val* to the left of *val* and all of the elements greater than or equal to *val* to the right of *val*, it follows that *val* is the kth smallest element. Of course, in general, the partition algorithm does *not* place the partition element in the kth cell. If the partition element is placed in the ith cell, $i < k$, the kth smallest element must be among the elements that are to the right of the ith cell. In this case, we ignore the left side of the array and call partition again using as input the right side of the array. Similarly, if the partition element is placed in the ith cell, $i > k$, the kth smallest element must be among the elements that are to the left of the ith cell; and we ignore the right side of the array and call partition again using as input the left side of the array. We continue until partition places the partition element in the kth cell.

Example 6.5.1. Suppose that we want to find the 10th smallest element in the array

17	21	5	23	9	37	15	3	11	25	31	13	29	7	19

  ↑   ↑   ↑
  1   10   15

We seek the element that would be at index 10 if the array was sorted.

After partition (Algorithm 6.2.2) is called, we obtain

7	5	9	15	3	11	13	17	37	25	31	23	29	21	19

  ↑   ↑   ↑   ↑
  1   8   10   15

The partition element 17 is placed at index 8.

Since $8 < 10$, we next call partition on the part of the array to the right of 17; the result is

19	25	31	23	29	21	37

  ↑   ↑   ↑
  9   10   15

The partition element 37 is placed at index 15.

Since $10 < 15$, we next call partition on the part of the array to the left of 37; the result is

$$\boxed{19 \mid 25 \mid 31 \mid 23 \mid 29 \mid 21} \;.$$

$$\begin{array}{ccccc} \uparrow & \uparrow & & & \uparrow \\ 9 & 10 & & & 14 \end{array}$$

The partition element 19 is placed at index 9.

Since $9 < 10$, we next call partition on the part of the array to the right of 19; the result is

$$\boxed{21 \mid 23 \mid 25 \mid 29 \mid 31} \;.$$

$$\begin{array}{ccccc} \uparrow & & \uparrow & & \uparrow \\ 10 & & 12 & & 14 \end{array}$$

The partition element 25 is placed at index 12.

Since $10 < 12$, we next call partition on the part of the array to the left of 25; the result is

$$\boxed{21 \mid 23} \;.$$

$$\begin{array}{cc} \uparrow & \uparrow \\ 10 & 11 \end{array}$$

The partition element 21 is placed at index 10. The algorithm thus terminates, having found 21 as the 10th smallest element in the array. $\qquad \square$

Just as for quicksort (see Section 6.2), the worst-case time of the selection algorithm is $\Theta(n^2)$ (see Exercise 7). To help avoid this problem, we use the randomized version of partition (Algorithm 6.2.6).

Algorithm 6.5.2 Random Select. Let *val* be the value in the array

$$a[i], \ldots, a[j]$$

that would be at index k ($i \leq k \leq j$) if the entire array was sorted. This algorithm rearranges the array so that *val* is at index k, all values at indexes less than k are less than *val*, and all values at indexes greater than k are greater than or equal to *val*. The algorithm uses the random-partition algorithm (Algorithm 6.2.6).

Input Parameters: a, i, j, k
Output Parameter: a

```
random_select(a, i, j, k) {
    if (i < j) {
        p = random_partition(a, i, j)
        if (k == p)
            return
        if (k < p)
            random_select(a, i, p - 1, k)
```

```
        else
            random_select(a, p + 1, j, k)
    }
}
```

Although the worst-case time of random select is still $\Theta(n^2)$, its *expected* run time is much better.

Suppose, for example, that partition always divides the array to be sorted into two nearly equal parts, the value p returned by partition is not equal to k unless the array size is 1, and c_n is the time required by random select when the input is an n-item array. The recurrence relation is

$$c_n = n - 1 + c_{n/2},$$

since partition takes time $n - 1$, and the size of the array input to the recursive call of random select is $n/2$. By the Main Recurrence Theorem, Theorem 2.4.7, $c_n = \Theta(n)$. This example suggests that the expected time of random select is $\Theta(n)$. We prove that this is indeed so.

Theorem 6.5.3. *The expected time of random select (Algorithm 6.5.2) is* $\Theta(n)$.

Proof. Let c_n be the expected time of random select for the input

$$a[1], \ldots, a[n].$$

If $n > 1$, random select first calls random partition,

$$p = random\_partition(a, i, j),$$

which takes time $n - 1$. Thus, $c_n = \Omega(n)$. If $p \neq k$, random partition is called recursively on an array of size $p - 1$ or $n - p$. The expected time for the call on the array of size $p - 1$ is c_{p-1}, and the expected time for the call on the array of size $n - p$ is c_{n-p}. Thus, the expected time for the recursive call is at most

$$\max\{c_{p-1}, c_{n-p}\}.$$

If $p = k$, the algorithm simply returns; so even in this case, $\max\{c_{p-1}, c_{n-p}\}$ serves as an *upper bound* for the additional time required by random select after random partition is called.

Since all indexes p are equally likely, we have

$$c_n \leq n + \frac{1}{n} \sum_{p=1}^{n} \max\{c_{p-1}, c_{n-p}\}, \quad n > 1.$$

Now $\max\{c_{p-1}, c_{n-p}\} = c_{n-p}$, if $p \leq n - p$, and $\max\{c_{p-1}, c_{n-p}\} = c_{p-1}$, if $p > n - p$; thus, we may rewrite the previous estimate for c_n as

$$c_n \leq n + \frac{2}{n} \sum_{p=\lfloor n/2 \rfloor}^{n-1} c_p.$$

We assume that $c_1 \geq 1$, and we use mathematical induction to prove that

$$c_n \leq 4c_1 n, \quad n \geq 1.$$

It will then follow that $c_n = \Theta(n)$.

The basis step ($n = 1$) is clearly true. For the inductive step, assume that $c_p \leq 4c_1 p$ for $p < n$. Then

$$
\begin{aligned}
c_n \quad &\leq \quad n + \frac{2}{n} \sum_{p=\lfloor n/2 \rfloor}^{n-1} c_p \\
&\leq \quad c_1 n + \frac{2}{n} \sum_{p=\lfloor n/2 \rfloor}^{n-1} 4c_1 p \\
&= \quad c_1 n + \frac{8c_1}{n} \left[\left(n - 1 + \left\lfloor \frac{n}{2} \right\rfloor \right) \left(n - \left\lfloor \frac{n}{2} \right\rfloor \right) \cdot \frac{1}{2} \right],
\end{aligned}
\tag{6.5.1}
$$

where we have used the formula

$$\sum_{i=u}^{v} i = \frac{(v+u)(v+1-u)}{2}$$

for an arithmetic sum. If n is even, the last expression in (6.5.1) equal to $c_1(4n - 2)$ (see Exercise 8), which is less than $4c_1 n$. If n is odd, the last expression in (6.5.1) is equal to

$$c_1 \left(4n - \frac{3}{n} \right)$$

(see Exercise 9), which is also less than $4c_1 n$. In either case,

$$c_n \leq 4c_1 n,$$

and the proof is complete. ∎

Any algorithm that solves the selection problem when the input consists of n distinct values runs in time $\Omega(n)$ because the algorithm must access each element in the array at least one time, which takes time $\Omega(n)$. We can argue by contradiction to show that the algorithm must access each element in the array at least once. If the algorithm did not access a particular element, say $a[i]$, we could change the value of $a[i]$ so that the kth smallest element would also change. Since the algorithm does not access $a[i]$, when the altered array is input to the algorithm, the algorithm still chooses the same value as the kth smallest element that it chose before $a[i]$ was changed. That this is not the correct kth smallest element yields the desired contradiction. In particular, the expected time of Algorithm 6.5.2 is optimal.

Algorithm 6.5.2 was invented by Hoare (see Hoare, 1961). Although its worst-case time is $\Theta(n^2)$, if the partitioning algorithm is changed to guarantee a good partition, worst-case time $\Theta(n)$ can be obtained. This version is due to Blum, Floyd, Pratt, Rivest, and Tarjan (see Blum, 1973). Because the overhead is substantial, it is mainly of theoretical interest.

The time of Algorithm 6.5.2 can be improved (i.e., the constants can be lowered) for large arrays by recursively choosing the partition element from a subset of the array that is likely (on average) to yield a good partition. This version of Algorithm 6.5.2 is due to Floyd and Rivest (see Floyd, 1975) and is the most practical selection algorithm known for large arrays.

Exercises

In Exercises 1–5, trace a version of Algorithm 6.5.2 for the input given where random partition is replaced by partition (Algorithm 6.2.2).

1S. The array in Exercise 1, Section 6.1, and $k = 4$

2. The array in Exercise 1, Section 6.1, and $k = 7$

3. The array in Exercise 1, Section 6.1, and $k = 1$

4S. The array in Exercise 2, Section 6.1, and $k = 4$

5. The array in Exercise 4, Section 6.1, and $k = 4$

6S. Give an example where the time of Algorithm 6.5.2 is $\Theta(n^2)$.

7. Prove that the worst-case time of Algorithm 6.5.2 is $\Theta(n^2)$.

8. Show that if n is even, the last expression in (6.5.1) is equal to $c_1(4n - 2)$.

9S. Show that if n is odd, the last expression in (6.5.1) is equal to

$$c_1 \left(4n - \frac{3}{n} \right).$$

10. In Algorithm 6.5.2, we assume that $i \leq k \leq j$. Show, by giving examples, what happens if $i > k$ or $k > j$.

11. Consider an algorithm that finds the kth smallest element in an array of size n that works as follows. If $k < n - k$, the algorithm builds a binary minheap (see Section 3.5) and performs k deletions. If $k \geq n - k$, it builds a binary maxheap and performs $n - k + 1$ deletions. In either case, the last item deleted is the kth smallest. What is the worst-case time of this algorithm (in terms of n and k)? What is the worst-case time for this algorithm to find the median?

Notes

Knuth, 1998, is the standard reference on sorting and searching algorithms. See Sedgewick, 1978, for a detailed discussion of the quicksort algorithm.

Chapter Exercises

Exercises 6.1–6.6 refer to selection sort. *Selection sort first finds the maximum value in the array. After swapping the maximum value with the last element in the array, selection sort then sorts the remaining elements.*

6.1. Write pseudocode for selection sort.

6.2. Trace selection sort for the arrays of Exercises 1–4, Section 6.1.

6.3. What is the worst-case time of selection sort?

6.4. Give an example of input of size 5 that produces the worst-case time for selection sort.

6.5. What is the best-case time of selection sort?

6.6. Give an example of input of size 5 that produces the best-case time for selection sort.

6.7. Implement insertion sort, selection sort (selection sort is described before Exercise 6.1), heapsort (see Section 3.5), mergesort (see Section 5.2), mergesort that uses insertion sort for small arrays (see Exercise 19, Section 6.1), quicksort, quicksort using median-of-three partitioning (median-of-three partitioning is described before Exercise 17, Section 6.2), random quicksort, quicksort that uses insertion sort for small arrays, quicksort that uses median-of-three partitioning and insertion sort for small arrays, and random quicksort that uses insertion sort for small arrays, and compare the times of each for several inputs of different sizes. Include arrays sorted in nondecreasing order, arrays sorted in nonincreasing order, arrays with many duplicates, and arrays with data in random order.

6.8. Implement insertion sort and counting sort, and compare the times for several arrays containing small integers. Include arrays sorted in nondecreasing order, arrays sorted in nonincreasing order, arrays with many duplicates, and arrays with data in random order.

6.9. Implement insertion sort, heapsort (see Section 3.5), mergesort (see Section 5.2), quicksort, random quicksort, and radix sort and compare the times of each for several integer inputs of different sizes. Include arrays sorted in nondecreasing order, arrays sorted in nonincreasing order, arrays with many duplicates, and arrays with data in random order.

Exercises 6.10 and 6.11 explore an alternative partitioning algorithm:

```
partition(a, i, j) {
    m = i
    n = j
    j = j + 1
    while (true) {
        do {
            i = i + 1
        } while (i ≤ n && a[i] < a[m])
        do {
            j = j - 1
        } while (a[j] > a[m])
        if (i < j)
            swap(a[i], a[j])
        else
            break // exit while loop
    }
    swap(a[m], a[j])
    return j
}
```

6.10. Show that the alternative algorithm properly partitions the array.

6.11. Compare the times required by the alternative algorithm and Lomuto's partition algorithm (Algorithm 6.2.2).

6.12. An n-element array contains only the numbers $0, 1, 2$. Write an $O(n)$ algorithm to sort the numbers. Legal operations on the data are swapping two elements in the array and testing whether an element in the array is 0, 1, or 2.

6.13. Write an $O(n \lg n)$ algorithm to compute the union of two sets of real numbers. The input consists of two arrays, each representing one of the sets. In each of these arrays, each value appears only one time. The output is an array representing the union of the two sets in which each value appears only one time. If n is the sum of the sizes of the input arrays, the algorithm must run in time $O(n \lg n)$.

WWW *Exercises 6.14–6.16 refer to* Shell sort. *Shell sort sorts the array a by first calling insertion sort g_1 times to sort the g_1 subarrays*

$$a[0 + i], a[g_1 + i], a[2g_1 + i], a[3g_1 + i], \ldots,$$

for $i = 1$ to g_1. It next calls insertion sort g_2 times to sort the g_2 subarrays

$$a[0 + i], a[g_2 + i], a[2g_2 + i], a[3g_2 + i], \ldots,$$

for $i = 1$ to g_2, and so on. The sequence $\{g_i\}_{i=1}^{k}$ satisfies

$$g_1 > g_2 > \cdots g_k = 1.$$

Shell sort is named after its inventor Donald Shell. Its performance depends on the choice of the sequence $\{g_i\}_{i=1}^{k}$. Although the analysis of its run time is incomplete, for many choices of g_i, its worst-case performance is somewhat smaller than $O(n^2)$ and somewhat larger than $\Omega(n \lg n)$.

6.14. Show how Shell sort sorts the array of Exercise 1, Section 6.1, where $g_1 = 3$, $g_2 = 2$, and $g_3 = 1$.

6.15. Show how Shell sort sorts the array of Exercise 1, Section 6.1, where $g_1 = 3$ and $g_2 = 1$.

6.16. Write pseudocode for Shell sort.

6.17. **Bucket sort** assumes that keys are randomly distributed over some interval, say $[a, b]$. The interval $[a, b]$ is divided into k equal subintervals, called *buckets*. (For example, if we are sorting names, the buckets might correspond to the first letter of the last name.) Bucket sort begins by putting each element in the array to sort in the appropriate bucket. It then sorts each bucket using an appropriate sorting algorithm. Show that at this point, if we enumerate the items in the first bucket (in sorted order) followed by the items in the second bucket (again, in sorted order) and so on, the entire array is sorted. Making appropriate assumptions, what is the expected time of your algorithm?

6.18. Write an $O(n \lg n)$ algorithm that returns the number of inversions ("inversion" is defined before Exercise 7, Section 6.1) in an array.

6.19. Implement random select, random select where random partition is replaced by partition (Algorithm 6.2.2), random select where for small arrays we use insertion sort, random select where for small arrays we use insertion sort and where random partition is replaced by partition (Algorithm 6.2.2), and the algorithm described in Exercise 11, Section 6.5. Compare the times of each for several inputs of different sizes and different values of k. Include arrays sorted in nondecreasing order, arrays sorted in nonincreasing order, arrays with many duplicates, and arrays with data in random order.

CHAPTER 7
Greedy Algorithms

A **greedy algorithm** builds a solution to a problem in steps. At each iteration, it adds a part of the solution. For example, a greedy coin-changing algorithm might choose a coin at each step. Which part of the solution to add next is determined by a **greedy rule**. The rule is "greedy" in the sense that among all of the parts of a solution that might be chosen, the best available is selected. For example, a greedy coin-changing algorithm that seeks to minimize the number of coins chosen might choose a coin of largest denomination. A greedy algorithm may or may not be optimal. If it is not optimal, it is sometimes close to optimal and so yields a solution that in many applications is good enough. Algorithms that produce near-optimal solutions are called *approximation algorithms*; we discuss them in Chapter 11.

After formally discussing the greedy coin-changing algorithm in Section 7.1, we turn to two greedy algorithms to solve the problem of finding a minimal spanning tree in a graph (Kruskal's and Prim's algorithms, Sections 7.2 and 7.3). Dijkstra's greedy algorithm for finding shortest paths in a graph is the subject of Section 7.4. In Section 7.5, we discuss data compression—specifically, Huffman's greedy algorithm. The continuous-knapsack problem of Section 7.6 concerns optimally packing objects, which can be subdivided, into a knapsack of a specified capacity. We discuss a greedy algorithm to solve this problem.

7.1 Coin Changing

Suppose that we want to make change for an amount A using the fewest number of coins. Suppose further that the available denominations are 1, 5, and 10. A greedy algorithm might use the rule: Select the largest denomination available. The rationale behind this rule is that using large denominations tends to advance toward the goal A faster than using small denominations. As an example, using our rule to make change for $A = 18$, we would first choose a coin of denomination 10. We would then need to make change for $A = 8$. Thus we would next choose a coin of denomination 5. Since we would then need to make change for $A = 3$, we would conclude by choosing three coins of denomination 1. Our greedy algorithm would thus use five coins to make change for $A = 18$. By considering the various possibilities, we can verify that five coins are optimal for $A = 18$; that is, one cannot use four or fewer coins to make change for $A = 18$. Greedy coin changing is given as Algorithm 7.1.1.

Algorithm 7.1.1 Greedy Coin Changing. This algorithm makes change for an amount A using coins of denominations

$$denom[1] > denom[2] > \cdots > denom[n] = 1.$$

  Input Parameters: *denom*, A
  Output Parameters: None

```
greedy_coin_change(denom, A) {
    i = 1
    while (A > 0) {
        c = A/denom[i]
        println("use " + c + " coins of denomination " + denom[i])
        A = A − c * denom[i]
        i = i + 1
    }
}
```

Since the while loop in Algorithm 7.1.1 executes n times in the worst case, the worst-case time of Algorithm 7.1.1 is $\Theta(n)$.

A greedy algorithm *always* uses the same greedy rule to select the next part of the solution. The algorithm begins by applying the greedy rule to the original input, and the first part of the solution is obtained. In Algorithm 7.1.1, to make change for an amount A, the algorithm begins by determining how many coins of the largest denomination to include. After a greedy algorithm applies its greedy rule to the original input, a new problem results from having a partial solution. The *same* greedy rule is applied to the modified problem. In Algorithm 7.1.1, after selecting c coins of the largest denomination d, a new problem results: Make change for $A − c * d$. Algorithm 7.1.1 then determines how many coins of the second largest denomination to include, and so on. The greedy rule is repeatedly applied until a solution to the original problem is obtained.

A greedy rule may *seem* reasonable, yet it may or may not lead to an optimal solution. It turns out that for the denominations 1, 5, and 10, Algorithm 7.1.1 *is* optimal; that is, for any value A, it always uses the minimum number of coins to make change (see Theorem 7.1.2). If we change the denominations to 1, 6, and 10, Algorithm 7.1.1 is no longer optimal. For example, we can make change for $A = 12$ by using two coins of denomination 6. Algorithm 7.1.1, however, selects one coin of denomination 10 and two of denomination 1 and, so, is not optimal. To prove that a greedy algorithm is not optimal, a *counterexample* is required—input for which the greedy algorithm delivers a solution that is *not* optimal. Our counterexample for denominations 1, 6, and 10 is $A = 12$.

One technique for showing that a greedy algorithm is optimal is to compare the solution given by the greedy algorithm with an optimal solution. If the solutions are the same size, the greedy algorithm is optimal. We illustrate this technique by proving that Algorithm 7.1.1 is optimal for denominations 1, 5, and 10.

Theorem 7.1.2. *Algorithm 7.1.1 is optimal for denominations 1, 5, and 10.*

Proof. We use induction on A to prove that to make change for an amount A, the output of Algorithm 7.1.1 and the optimal solution are identical. The cases $A = 1, 2, 3, 4, 5, 10$ are readily verified.

The inductive assumption is that to make change for an amount k, where $k < A$, the output of Algorithm 7.1.1 and the optimal solution are identical. Suppose first that $5 < A < 10$. Let *Opt* be an optimal solution. Now *Opt* must use a coin of denomination 5. (If *Opt* does not use a coin of denomination 5, it is restricted to coins of denomination 1. Because $A > 5$, *Opt* must use at least five 1's. But now *Opt* is not optimal because it could trade in five coins of denomination 1 for one of denomination 5.) Now *Opt* with one coin of denomination 5 removed is optimal for $A - 5$. (If *Opt* with one coin of denomination 5 removed is not optimal for $A - 5$, there is another solution for $A - 5$ that uses fewer coins. Adding a coin of denomination 5 to the solution to the $A - 5$ problem produces a solution for A using fewer coins than *Opt*, which is impossible.) By the inductive assumption, the output of Algorithm 7.1.1 for $A - 5$ and *Opt* with one coin of denomination 5 removed are identical. Adding a coin of denomination 5 to the output of Algorithm 7.1.1 for $A - 5$ yields the output of Algorithm 7.1.1 for A. Thus, the output of Algorithm 7.1.1 and the optimal solution are identical for $5 < A < 10$.

The argument is similar for the case $A > 10$, so we omit some details. Suppose that $A > 10$. Let *Opt* be an optimal solution. Now *Opt* must use a coin of denomination 10. Then *Opt* with one coin of denomination 10 removed is optimal for $A - 10$. By the inductive assumption, the output of Algorithm 7.1.1 for $A - 10$ and *Opt* with one coin of denomination 10 removed are identical. Adding a coin of denomination 10 to the output of Algorithm 7.1.1 for $A - 10$ yields the output of Algorithm 7.1.1 for A. Thus, the output of Algorithm 7.1.1 and the optimal solution are identical for $A > 10$. The inductive step is complete. ∎

Recall that Algorithm 7.1.1 is *not* optimal for denominations 1, 6, and 10. It is instructive to replace 5 by 6 in the proof of Theorem 7.1.2 and find the error in the resulting argument (see Exercise 6).

In Section 8.2, we will show how the greedy coin-changing algorithm can be improved using dynamic programming to yield an algorithm that *is* optimal for any denominations.

Exercises

1S. Trace Algorithm 7.1.1 for $n = 37$ and denominations 1, 5, and 25.

2. Trace Algorithm 7.1.1 for $n = 37$ and denominations 1, 5, 10, and 25.

3. What is the best-case time of Algorithm 7.1.1?

4S. Give a proof along the lines of the proof of Theorem 7.1.2 that Algorithm 7.1.1 is optimal for denominations 1, 13, and 25.

5. Give a counterexample to show that Algorithm 7.1.1 is not optimal for denominations 1, 10, and 11.

6. Replace 5 by 6 in the proof of Theorem 7.1.2 and find the error in the resulting argument.

Tell whether Algorithm 7.1.1 is optimal for each set of coins in Exercises 7–12. If Algorithm 7.1.1 is optimal, give an argument to support your answer. If Algorithm 7.1.1 is not optimal, give a counterexample.

7S. 1, 4, 10   **8.** 1, 8, 12

9. 1, 5, 10, 25, 50   **10S.** 1, 5, 11

11. 1, 5, 14, 18   **12.** 1, 5, 10, 20, 25, 40

13S. Prior to 1971, the British system of coins consisted of denominations $\frac{1}{2}$, 1, 3, 6, 12, 24, 30, 60, and 240. Tell whether Algorithm 7.1.1 is optimal for this system of coins. If Algorithm 7.1.1 is optimal, give an argument to support your answer. If Algorithm 7.1.1 is not optimal, give a counterexample.

14. Euro coin denominations are 1, 2, 5, 10, 20, 50, 100, and 200. Tell whether Algorithm 7.1.1 is optimal for this system. If Algorithm 7.1.1 is optimal, give an argument to support your answer. If Algorithm 7.1.1 is not optimal, give a counterexample.

15. Show that Algorithm 7.1.1 is optimal for denominations $d_1 > d_2 > \cdots > d_n = 1$ if d_i divides d_{i-1} for $i = 2, \ldots, n$.

★16S. Notice that Algorithm 7.1.1 is optimal for the denominations

$$d_1 = 50, \quad d_2 = 10, \quad d_3 = 5, \quad d_4 = 1,$$

and that

$$d_i \geq 2d_{i+1} - d_{i+2}, \quad 1 \leq i \leq n - 2.$$

Show, by giving counterexamples that, nevertheless, the preceding condition is neither necessary nor sufficient for Algorithm 7.1.1 to be optimal.

⋆**17.** Notice that Algorithm 7.1.1 is optimal for the denominations

$$d_1 = 50, \quad d_2 = 10, \quad d_3 = 5, \quad d_4 = 1,$$

and that

$$d_i \text{ divides } d_{i-2} - d_{i-1}, \quad 3 \le i \le n.$$

Show, by giving counterexamples that, nevertheless, the preceding condition is neither necessary nor sufficient for Algorithm 7.1.1 to be optimal.

18. Given coins of denominations

$$1 = d[1] < d[2] < \cdots < d[n],$$

prove or disprove whether the following sets $c[i][j]$ equal to the minimum number of coins needed to make change for an amount j, $1 \le j \le m$, using only the denominations

$$d[1], \ldots, d[i].$$

```
for i = 0 to n
  c[i][0] = 0
for j = 1 to m
  c[0][j] = 0
for i = 1 to n
  for j = 1 to m
    if (d[i] divides j)
      c[i][j] = j/d[i]
    else
      c[i][j] = min(c[i][j − 1] + 1, c[i − 1][j])
```

7.2 Kruskal's Algorithm

Figure 7.2.1 shows six cities and the costs (in hundreds of thousands of dollars) of rebuilding roads between them. The road commission has decided

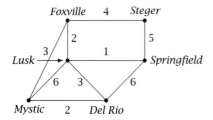

Figure 7.2.1 Cities and the costs (in hundreds of thousands of dollars) of rebuilding roads between them.

to rebuild enough roads so that each pair of cities will be connected, either directly or by going through other cities, by rebuilt roads. Figure 7.2.2 shows one possibility that costs

$$2 + 6 + 1 + 5 + 4 = 18.$$

The road commission needs an algorithm to find a minimum-cost set of roads meeting its criterion.

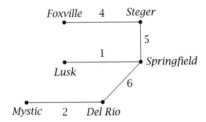

Figure 7.2.2 A subset of the roads of Figure 7.2.1. If these roads are rebuilt, each pair of cities will be connected, either directly or by going through other cities, by rebuilt roads. The cost of rebuilding these roads is 18.

Roads, cities, and costs can be modeled as a weighted graph where the vertices represent the cities, the edges represent the roads, and the weights represent the costs (see Figure 7.2.3). A **spanning tree** for a graph G is a subgraph of G that is a tree containing all of G's vertices. A **minimal spanning tree** is a spanning tree of minimum weight. Every connected graph has a spanning tree and, therefore, a minimal spanning tree. Thus, the problem of finding a minimum-cost set of roads directly or indirectly connecting all of the cities is the problem of finding a minimal spanning tree.

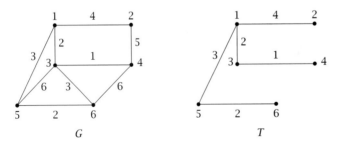

Figure 7.2.3 The graph G of Figure 7.2.1 with integers replacing the city names and a spanning tree T. No other spanning tree has a smaller weight, so T is a *minimal* spanning tree.

Example 7.2.1. In Figure 7.2.3, the weight of the spanning tree T for the graph G is 12. No other spanning tree for G has weight less than 12. [The only set of five edges whose weights sum to less than 12 is

$$\{(3,4), (5,6), (1,3), (3,6), (1,5)\},$$

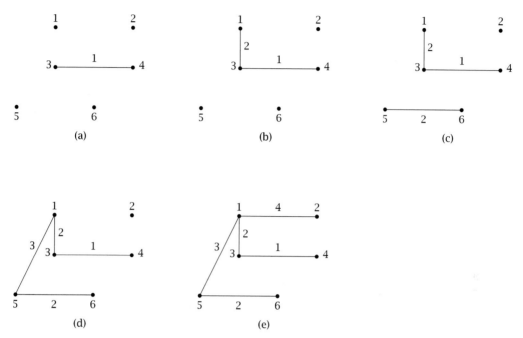

Figure 7.2.4 Kruskal's algorithm with input the graph G of Figure 7.2.3. The algorithm begins with all of the vertices and no edges. It then repeatedly adds an edge of minimum weight that does not make a cycle. In this case, it first selects edge (3,4) since it has minimum weight [graph (a)]. It next selects an edge of minimum weight 2; we assume that it selects edge (1,3) [graph (b)]. It next selects edge (5,6) since it has minimum weight [graph (c)]. It next selects an edge of minimum weight 3; we assume that it selects edge (1,5) [graph (d)]. Finally, it selects edge (1,2) since it has minimum weight [graph(e)] to complete the minimal spanning tree.

but these edges do not form a tree.] Thus, T is a minimal spanning tree.

Since G models the road system of Figure 7.2.1, the minimal spanning tree T is a solution to the problem of finding a minimum-cost subset of roads directly or indirectly connecting all of the cities. □

$\mathcal{WWW}$ In this section and the next, we discuss the problem of finding a minimal spanning tree in a connected, weighted graph. Unless specified otherwise, all of the weights are assumed to be positive. **Kruskal's algorithm** is a greedy algorithm for finding a minimal spanning tree in a graph G. The algorithm begins with all of the vertices of G and no edges. It then applies the greedy rule: Add an edge of minimum weight that does not make a cycle.

Example 7.2.2. We show how Kruskal's algorithm finds a minimal spanning tree for the graph G in Figure 7.2.3. Kruskal's algorithm first selects edge (3,4) since it has minimum weight [see Figure 7.2.4(a)].

Kruskal's algorithm next selects edge (1,3) or (5,6); either edge has minimum weight 2 and neither makes a cycle when added to {(3,4)}. When more than one edge has the same minimum weight, any can be selected. Different spanning trees may result, but all will be minimal. Suppose that we arbitrarily select edge $(1, 3)$ [see Figure 7.2.4(b)].

Kruskal's algorithm next selects edge $(5, 6)$ since it has minimum weight 2 and does not make a cycle when added to $\{(3, 4), (1, 3)\}$ [see Figure 7.2.4(c)].

Kruskal's algorithm next selects edge $(1, 5)$ or $(3, 6)$; both have minimum weight 3 and neither makes a cycle when added to

$$\{(3, 4), (1, 3), (5, 6)\}.$$

Suppose that we arbitrarily select edge $(1, 5)$ [see Figure 7.2.4(d)].

Kruskal's algorithm next considers selecting edge $(3, 6)$, which has minimum weight 3. Since $(3, 6)$ makes a cycle when added to

$$\{(3, 4), (1, 3), (5, 6), (1, 5)\},$$

it does *not* select $(3, 6)$.

Finally, Kruskal's algorithm selects edge $(1, 2)$ because it has minimum weight 4 and does not make a cycle when added to

$$\{(3, 4), (1, 3), (5, 6), (1, 5)\}$$

[see Figure 7.2.4(e)].

Since we now have a spanning tree, Kruskal's algorithm terminates with the minimal spanning tree shown in Figure 7.2.4(e).   □

To implement Kruskal's algorithm, several issues need to be addressed. First, we must represent the graph. Since we are selecting edges by weight, we represent the graph as a list of edges and their weights. Second, we must select the edges in nondecreasing order of weight. We can sort the edges in nondecreasing order by weight and then examine them in sorted order. Third, we must be able to determine whether adding an edge would create a cycle. We observe that adding edge (v, w) creates a cycle when there is a path between v and w formed by edges already selected, that is, when v and w are in the same *component* (see Definition 2.5.25) of the graph of edges already selected. We keep track of components by recording the set of vertices belonging to each component.

Example 7.2.3. Consider the graph G of Figure 7.2.3. Its representation is

$$(1, 2, 4)\ (1, 3, 2)\ (1, 5, 3)\ (2, 4, 5)\ (3, 4, 1)\ (3, 5, 6)\ (3, 6, 3)\ (4, 6, 6)\ (5, 6, 2),$$

where (v_1, v_2, w) is interpreted as edge (v_1, v_2) of weight w.

We first sort the edges in nondecreasing order by weight:

$$(3, 4, 1)\ (1, 3, 2)\ (5, 6, 2)\ (1, 5, 3)\ (3, 6, 3)\ (1, 2, 4)\ (2, 4, 5)\ (3, 5, 6)\ (4, 6, 6).$$

When Kruskal's algorithm starts, no edges have been selected, so each vertex belongs to a component consisting of itself:

$$\{1\}\quad \{2\}\quad \{3\}\quad \{4\}\quad \{5\}\quad \{6\}.$$

The first edge $(3, 4)$ is selected, and the components to which vertices 3 and 4 belong are merged; the components become

$$\{1\} \quad \{2\} \quad \{3,4\} \quad \{5\} \quad \{6\}.$$

Next edge $(1, 3)$ is selected, and the components to which vertices 1 and 3 belong are merged; the components become

$$\{1,3,4\} \quad \{2\} \quad \{5\} \quad \{6\}.$$

Next edge $(5, 6)$ is selected, and the components to which vertices 5 and 6 belong are merged; the components become

$$\{1,3,4\} \quad \{2\} \quad \{5,6\}.$$

Next edge $(1, 5)$ is selected, and the components to which vertices 1 and 5 belong are merged; the components become

$$\{1,3,4,5,6\} \quad \{2\}.$$

Next edge $(3, 6)$ is examined but rejected because its vertices belong to the same component $\{1, 3, 4, 5, 6\}$. Finally, edge $(1, 2)$ is selected, and the components to which vertices 1 and 2 belong are merged; the components become

$$\{1,2,3,4,5,6\},$$

and Kruskal's algorithm terminates. □

The algorithms to manage disjoint sets (see Section 3.6) can be used to handle the components. Algorithm *makeset* can be used to initialize each vertex to its own component;

$$findset(v) == findset(w)$$

can be used to test whether vertices v and w belong to the same component; and $union(v, w)$ can be used to merge the components to which vertices v and w belong. Algorithm 7.2.4 formally states Kruskal's algorithm.

Algorithm 7.2.4 Kruskal's Algorithm. Kruskal's algorithm finds a minimal spanning tree in a connected, weighted graph with vertex set $\{1, \dots, n\}$. The input to the algorithm is *edgelist*, an array of *edge*, and n. The members of *edge* are

- v and w, the vertices on which the edge is incident.
- *weight*, the weight of the edge.

The output lists the edges in a minimal spanning tree. The function *sort* sorts the array *edgelist* in nondecreasing order of *weight*.

Input Parameters: *edgelist*, n
Output Parameters: None

```
kruskal(edgelist, n) {
  sort(edgelist)
  for i = 1 to n
    makeset(i)
  count = 0
  i = 1
  while (count < n − 1) {
    if (findset(edgelist[i].v) != findset(edgelist[i].w)) {
      println(edgelist[i].v + " " + edgelist[i].w)
      count = count + 1
      union(edgelist[i].v, edgelist[i].w)
    }
    i = i + 1
  }
}
```

After Kruskal's algorithm adds $n − 1$ edges, an acyclic, $(n − 1)$-edge subgraph of the original n-vertex graph is obtained. By Theorem 2.6.5, the subgraph is a tree and, therefore, a spanning tree.

There are n *makeset* operations, at most $2m$ *findset* operations, and $n − 1$ *union* operations. Because the graph input to Kruskal's algorithm is connected, $m \geq n − 1$. Thus the number of union and findset operations is $O(m)$. Using union by rank alone, or union by rank and path compression, these operations take time $O(m \lg m)$ (see Section 3.6). In the worst case, comparison-based sorting takes time $\Theta(m \lg m)$. Thus the worst-case time of Algorithm 7.2.4 is $\Theta(m \lg m)$.

In Section 7.1, we noted that greedy algorithms may or may not be optimal. Fortunately, Kruskal's algorithm is optimal. We deduce this from a slightly stronger result.

Theorem 7.2.5. *Let G be a connected, weighted graph, and let G′ be a subgraph of a minimal spanning tree of G. Let C be a component of G′, and let S be the set of all edges with one vertex in C and the other not in C. If we add a minimum weight edge in S to G′, the resulting graph is also contained in a minimal spanning tree of G.*

Before proving Theorem 7.2.5, we show how it implies the correctness of Kruskal's algorithm (Algorithm 7.2.4).

Theorem 7.2.6 Correctness of Kruskal's Algorithm. *Kruskal's algorithm (Algorithm 7.2.4) is correct; that is, it finds a minimal spanning tree.*

Proof. We use induction to show that at each iteration of Kruskal's algorithm, the subgraph constructed is contained in a minimal spanning tree. It then follows that, at the termination of Kruskal's algorithm, the subgraph constructed *is* a minimal spanning tree.

When we begin, the subgraph, which consists of no edges, is contained in every minimal spanning tree. Thus the basis step is true.

Turning to the inductive step, let G' denote the subgraph constructed by Kruskal's algorithm prior to another iteration of the algorithm. The inductive assumption is that G' is contained in a minimal spanning tree. Let (v, w) be the next edge selected by Kruskal's algorithm, and let C be the component of G' to which v belongs. Edge (v, w) is a minimum weight edge with one vertex in C and one not in C because it is a minimum weight edge from *any* component to any other. Therefore, by Theorem 7.2.5, when (v, w) is added to G', the resulting graph is also contained in a minimal spanning tree. The inductive step is complete and the theorem is proved.   ■

We conclude by proving Theorem 7.2.5.

Proof of Theorem 7.2.5. Let G be a connected, weighted graph, and let G' be a subgraph of G that is contained in a minimal spanning tree T of G. Let C be a component of G', and let (v, w) be a minimum weight edge with v in C and w not in C. We must show that the graph obtained by adding (v, w) to G' is contained in a minimal spanning tree of G.

If T also contains (v, w), the proof is complete; so, suppose that T does not contain (v, w). If we add the edge (v, w) to T and remove an edge from the cycle S created by adding (v, w), the resulting subgraph T' is also a spanning tree. We choose the edge to remove as follows.

Let w' be the first vertex on S, going from v to w, that is not in C, and let v' be the vertex on S just before w' (v' is in C) (see Figure 7.2.5). Add (v, w) to T and remove (v', w') from T to obtain T'. Since (v, w) is a minimum weight edge with one vertex in C and the other not in C,

$$\text{weight}(v', w') \geq \text{weight}(v, w).$$

Therefore

$$\text{weight}(T) \geq \text{weight}(T').$$

Since T is a *minimal* spanning tree, we must have

$$\text{weight}(T) = \text{weight}(T').$$

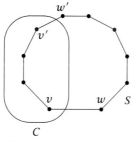

Figure 7.2.5 The proof of Theorem 7.2.5. Vertex w' is the first vertex on cycle S, going from v to w, that is not in C. Vertex v' is the vertex on S just before w'. The spanning tree T is modified by adding edge (v, w) and removing edge (v', w'). The tree T' obtained is also a minimal spanning tree.

Therefore T' is a minimal spanning tree. Since T' contains all of the edges of G' as well as (v, w), the proof is complete. ∎

Exercises

Trace Kruskal's algorithm for each graph in Exercises 1–3.

1S.

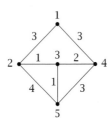

2.

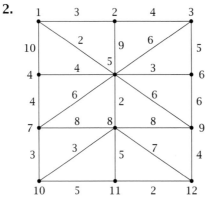

3.

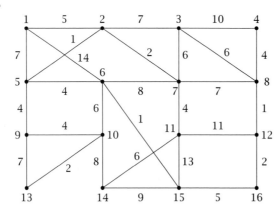

4S. What is the worst-case time (in terms of n) of Kruskal's algorithm when the input is the complete graph on n vertices?

5. In Kruskal's algorithm, sorting all of the edges will be more work than necessary if not all of the edges are examined for possible inclusion in the minimal spanning tree; so, suppose that instead of sorting the edges, we place them in a binary minheap and remove them from the minheap as needed. Analyze the worst-case time of this implementation of Kruskal's algorithm in terms of the number of edges, the number of vertices, and the number of edges examined for possible inclusion in a minimal spanning tree.

6. Consider a possible divide-and-conquer approach to finding a minimal spanning tree in a connected, weighted graph G. Suppose that we divide the vertices of G into two disjoint subsets V_1 and V_2. We then find a minimal spanning tree T_1 for V_1 and a minimal spanning tree T_2 for V_2. Finally, we find a minimum weight edge e connecting T_1 and T_2. We then let T be the graph obtained by combining T_1, T_2, and e.

   (a) Is T always a spanning tree?

   (b) If T is a spanning tree, is it always a minimal spanning tree?

7S. Let T be a minimal spanning tree for a graph G, let e be an edge in T, and let T' be T with e removed. Show that e is a minimum weight edge between components of T'.

8. Let G be a connected, weighted graph, let v be a vertex in G, and let e be an edge of minimum weight incident on v. Show that e is contained in some minimal spanning tree.

9. Let G be a connected, weighted graph, and let v be a vertex in G. Suppose that the weights of the edges incident on v are distinct. Let e be the edge of minimum weight incident on v. Show that e is contained in every minimal spanning tree.

10S. Let T and T' be two spanning trees of a connected graph G. Suppose that an edge e is in T but not in T'. Show that there is an edge e' in T', but not in T, such that $(T - \{e\}) \cup \{e'\}$ and $(T' - \{e'\}) \cup \{e\}$ are spanning trees of G.

In Exercises 11–13, tell whether the statement is true or false. If the statement is true, prove it; otherwise, give a counterexample. In each exercise, G is a connected, weighted graph.

11S. If all of the weights in G are distinct, distinct spanning trees of G have distinct weights.

12. If all of the weights in G are distinct, G has a unique minimal spanning tree.

13. If e is an edge in G whose weight is less than the weight of every other edge, e is in every minimal spanning tree of G.

7.3 Prim's Algorithm

$\mathcal{WWW}$ **Prim's algorithm** is another greedy algorithm that finds a minimal spanning tree in a connected, weighted graph. Unless specified otherwise, all of the weights are assumed to be positive. Unlike Kruskal's algorithm, whose partial solutions are not necessarily connected, a partial solution in Prim's algorithm is a tree.

Prim's algorithm begins with a start vertex and no edges and then applies the greedy rule: Add an edge of minimum weight that has one vertex in the current tree and the other not in the current tree.

Example 7.3.1. We show how Prim's algorithm finds a minimal spanning tree for the graph G in Figure 7.2.3 assuming that the start vertex is 5.

Prim's algorithm first selects edge $(5, 6)$ since, among all of the edges incident on the start vertex 5, it has minimum weight. Edge $(5, 6)$ has one vertex in the current tree and the other not in the current tree.

At the next iteration, possible edges to add are

$$(5, 1), (5, 3), (6, 3), (6, 4)$$

since each has one vertex in the current tree and the other not in the current tree [see Figure 7.3.1(a)]. Edges $(5, 1)$ and $(6, 3)$ each have minimum weight 3 and either can be selected; different spanning trees will result, but each will have minimum weight. We arbitrarily assume that $(5, 1)$ is selected.

At the next iteration, possible edges to add are

$$(1, 2), (1, 3), (5, 3), (6, 3), (6, 4)$$

[see Figure 7.3.1(b)]. Edge $(1, 3)$, which has minimum weight 2, is selected.

At the next iteration, possible edges to add are

$$(1, 2), (3, 4), (6, 4)$$

[see Figure 7.3.1(c)]. Notice that $(5, 3)$ and $(6, 3)$ are no longer candidates for selection because vertices 3, 5, and 6 are all in the tree. Edge $(3, 4)$, which has minimum weight 1, is selected.

At the final iteration, possible edges to add are

$$(1, 2), (2, 4)$$

[see Figure 7.3.1(d)]. Edge $(1, 2)$, which has minimum weight 4, is selected. We obtain the minimal spanning shown in Figure 7.3.1(e).   □

To implement Prim's algorithm, we must keep track of candidate edges to add to the current tree. We can simplify this task if we retain only *one* minimum weight edge from each vertex not in the current tree to the current tree. For example, Figure 7.3.1(b) shows three edges from vertex 3, which is not in the current tree, to the tree: $(3, 1)$ of weight 2, $(3, 5)$ of weight 6, and $(3, 6)$ of weight 3. We would not select $(3, 5)$ or $(3, 6)$ because the

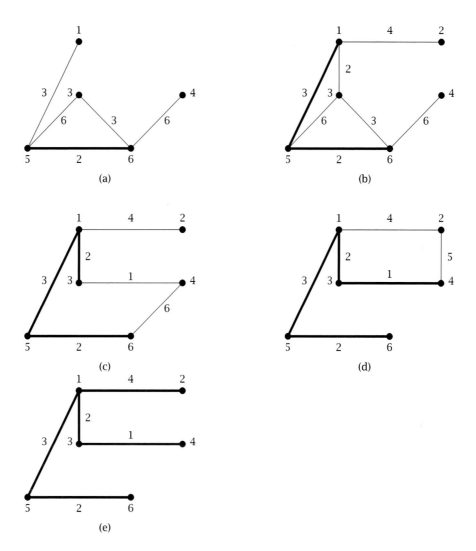

Figure 7.3.1 Prim's algorithm. The start vertex is 5. Edges chosen are shown as thick lines. Candidate edges for selection at the next iteration are shown as thin lines. Edge $(5, 6)$ is selected first because, among the edges incident on the start vertex 5, $(5, 6)$ has minimum weight. Next [see (a)], among the candidate edges, $(5, 1)$, which has minimum weight, is selected. Next [see (b)], among the candidate edges, $(1, 3)$, which has minimum weight, is selected. Next [see (c)], among the candidate edges, $(3, 4)$, which has minimum weight, is selected. Finally [see (d)], among the candidate edges, $(1, 2)$, which has minimum weight, is selected yielding the minimal spanning tree (e).

weight of each exceeds the weight of $(3, 1)$. Therefore, we retain only $(3, 1)$ as a candidate edge from vertex 3 to the current tree. If we retain only one minimum weight edge from each vertex not in the current tree to the current tree, Figure 7.3.1(b) becomes Figure 7.3.2.

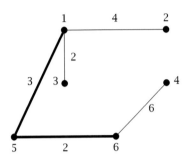

Figure 7.3.2 Modifying Figure 7.3.1(b) to implement Prim's algorithm. Instead of considering *all* edges from vertices not in the current tree to the tree, we consider only a *least weight* edge from each vertex not in the current tree to the tree.

We keep a list h of vertices v not in the tree and the minimum weight of an edge from v to a vertex in the tree. We also maintain an array *parent* that tells us which edges give minimum weights. If (v, w) is an edge of minimum weight where v is not in the tree and w is in the tree, then $parent[v] = w$.

Example 7.3.2. For Figure 7.3.2, the following table shows the list h and the parent of each vertex in h

h		$parent[v]$
Vertex (v)	Minimum Weight from v to Tree	
2	4	1
3	2	1
4	6	6

The *parent* array is

$$parent[2] = 1, \quad parent[3] = 1, \quad parent[4] = 6. \qquad \square$$

After the vertex v with a minimum weight edge to the tree is deleted from the h list, the vertices still in the h list may need their weights adjusted. For example, if, in the original h list, the weight corresponding to vertex w was 10 but there is an edge from w to v of weight less than 10, say 5, the adjusted weight corresponding to w becomes 5 (see Figure 7.3.3). Thus, after selecting vertex v, we examine each vertex w not in the tree adjacent to v. If the weight of edge (v, w) is less than the weight in the h list corresponding to w, we update the weight corresponding to w to the weight of edge (v, w). We also update $parent[w]$ to v. In order to perform this updating efficiently, we represent the graph using adjacency lists.

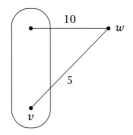

Current Tree

Figure 7.3.3 Updating a vertex's weight entry in the h list. Before vertex v was added to the tree, the least weight edge from w to the tree was 10. Since edge (v, w) has weight 5, after v is added to the tree, the weight corresponding to w becomes 5. Also, $parent[w]$ becomes v.

Example 7.3.3. We show a trace of Prim's algorithm for the graph G of Figure 7.2.3. We assume that the start vertex is 5.

Initially, the h list and parents of vertices in h are

h		$parent[v]$
Vertex (v)	Minimum Weight from v to Tree	
1	3	5
2	∞	–
3	6	5
4	∞	–
6	2	5

As shown, if there is no edge from a vertex not in the tree to the tree, we set its weight to ∞. The $parent$ array is

$$parent[1] = 5, \quad parent[3] = 5, \quad parent[5] = 0, \quad parent[6] = 5.$$

As shown, to indicate the start vertex, we set its parent to zero.

We then select the minimum weight 2 in the h list and delete this entry from the h list, which corresponds to selecting edge $(5, 6)$. We then examine all of the vertices adjacent to 6 not in the tree to determine whether any entries in the h list need updating. In this case, vertices 3 and 4 in the h list have their weights adjusted. Since the edge $(3, 6)$ has weight 3, but 3's old weight in the h list was 6, vertex 3's weight entry is updated to 3. Similarly, since there is an edge from 4 to 6 of weight 6, 4's weight entry is updated to 6. The h list and parents of vertices in h become

h		$parent[v]$
Vertex (v)	Minimum Weight from v to Tree	
1	3	5
2	∞	–
3	3	6
4	6	6

The *parent* array becomes

$$parent[1] = 5, \quad parent[3] = 6, \quad parent[4] = 6,$$
$$parent[5] = 0, \quad parent[6] = 5.$$

Next, we select the minimum weight 3 in the h list and delete this entry from the h list. Since there is a tie, we could select the entry corresponding to either vertex 1 or 3. We arbitrarily choose vertex 1, which corresponds to selecting edge $(1, 5)$. We then examine all of the vertices adjacent to 1 not in the tree to determine whether any entries in the h list need updating. In this case, vertices 2 and 3 in the h list have their weights adjusted. The h list and parents of vertices in h become

	h	$parent[v]$
Vertex (v)	Minimum Weight from v to Tree	
2	4	1
3	2	1
4	6	6

and the *parent* array becomes

$$parent[1] = 5, \quad parent[2] = 1, \quad parent[3] = 1,$$
$$parent[4] = 6, \quad parent[5] = 0, \quad parent[6] = 5.$$

Next, we select the minimum weight 2 in the h list and delete this entry from the h list, which corresponds to selecting edge $(1, 3)$. We then examine all of the vertices adjacent to 3 not in the tree to determine whether any entries in the h list need updating. In this case, vertex 4 in the h list has its weight adjusted. The h list and parents of vertices in h become

	h	$parent[v]$
Vertex (v)	Minimum Weight from v to Tree	
2	4	1
4	1	3

and the *parent* array becomes

$$parent[1] = 5, \quad parent[2] = 1, \quad parent[3] = 1,$$
$$parent[4] = 3, \quad parent[5] = 0, \quad parent[6] = 5.$$

Next, we select the minimum weight 1 in the h list and delete this entry from the h list, which corresponds to selecting edge $(3, 4)$. We then examine all of the vertices adjacent to 4 not in the tree to determine whether any entries in the h list need updating. In this case, no vertex has its weight adjusted. The h list and parent of the vertex in h become

	h	$parent[v]$
Vertex (v)	Minimum Weight from v to Tree	
2	4	1

and the *parent* array becomes

$$parent[1] = 5, \quad parent[2] = 1, \quad parent[3] = 1,$$
$$parent[4] = 3, \quad parent[5] = 0, \quad parent[6] = 5.$$

We select the remaining weight 4 in the *h* list and delete this entry from the *h* list, which corresponds to selecting edge $(1, 2)$. The *h* list becomes empty and the *parent* array is unchanged. Prim's algorithm terminates with the minimal spanning tree *T* shown in Figure 7.2.3. □

In Prim's algorithm, we assume that *h* is an abstract data type that supports the following operations: If *key* is an array of size *n*, the expression

$h.init(key, n)$

initializes *h* to the values in *key*. The expression

$h.del()$

deletes the item in *h* with the smallest weight and returns the corresponding vertex. The expression

$h.isin(w)$

returns true if vertex *w* is in *h* and false otherwise. The expression

$h.keyval(w)$

returns the weight corresponding to vertex *w*. Finally, the expression

$h.decrease(w, wgt)$

changes the weight corresponding to vertex *w* to *wgt* (a smaller value).

Algorithm 7.3.4 Prim's Algorithm. This algorithm finds a minimal spanning tree in a connected, weighted, *n*-vertex graph. The graph is represented using adjacency lists; $adj[i]$ is a reference to the first node in a linked list of nodes representing the vertices adjacent to vertex *i*. Each node has members *ver*, the vertex adjacent to *i*; *weight*, representing the weight of edge (i, ver); and *next*, a reference to the next node in the linked list or null, for the last node in the linked list. The start vertex is *start*. In the minimal spanning tree, the parent of vertex $i \neq start$ is $parent[i]$, and $parent[start] = 0$. The value ∞ is the largest available integer value.

Input Parameters: *adj, start*
Output Parameter: *parent*

```
prim(adj, start, parent) {
    n = adj.last
    // key is a local array
    for i = 1 to n
        key[i] = ∞
    key[start] = 0
    parent[start] = 0
    // the following statement initializes the
    // container h to the values in the array key
```

```
h.init(key, n)
for i = 1 to n {
    v = h.del()
    ref = adj[v]
    while (ref != null) {
        w = ref.ver
        if (h.isin(w) && ref.weight < h.keyval(w)) {
            parent[w] = v
            h.decrease(w, ref.weight)
        }
        ref = ref.next
    }
}
}
```

There are several ways to implement the abstract data type h in Prim's algorithm (Algorithm 7.3.4). One efficient way is to use a binary minheap (see Section 3.5). We analyze the worst-case time of Prim's algorithm assuming that h is implemented using a binary minheap and that the graph has n vertices and m edges. The worst-case time of the various heap operations involved are summarized in Figure 7.3.4 (see Section 3.5 for details).

Operation	Worst-Case Time
$init(key, n)$	$\Theta(n)$
$del()$	$\Theta(\lg n)$
$isin(w)$	$\Theta(1)$
$keyval(w)$	$\Theta(1)$
$decrease(w, ref.weight)$	$\Theta(\lg n)$

Figure 7.3.4 The worst-case time for binary minheap operations.

Each for loop takes time $\Theta(n)$. The *init* operation takes time $\Theta(n)$. The delete operation *del*, which takes time $O(\lg n)$, is in a for loop whose time is $\Theta(n)$; thus, the total worst-case time for the delete operations is $O(n \lg n)$. The *total* time for the while loop is $\Theta(m)$ since each iteration of the while loop inspects another node on some adjacency list and there are $2m$ nodes altogether. Each *isin* and *keyval* operation takes constant time to evaluate. The decrease operation *decrease*, which takes time $O(\lg n)$, is in the while loop whose total time is $\Theta(m)$; thus, the total worst-case time for the decrease operations is $O(m \lg n)$. Since $m \geq n - 1$, the dominant term is $m \lg n$ and the worst-case time is $O(m \lg n)$. [In the following subsection, we show that this estimate is sharp; that is, the worst-case time is $\Theta(m \lg n)$.]

If, instead of using a binary heap to implement Prim's algorithm, we use a Fibonacci heap (see Fredman, 1987), we can improve the worst-case time of Prim's algorithm to $\Theta(m + n \lg n)$.

The proof of correctness of Prim's algorithm is similar to the proof of correctness of Kruskal's algorithm.

Theorem 7.3.5 Correctness of Prim's Algorithm. *Prim's algorithm (Algorithm 7.3.4) is correct; that is, it finds a minimal spanning tree.*

Proof. We use induction to show that, at each iteration of Prim's algorithm, the tree constructed is contained in a minimal spanning tree. It then follows that at the termination of Prim's algorithm, the tree constructed *is* a minimal spanning tree.

When we begin, the tree consists of no edges and is contained in every minimal spanning tree. Thus the basis step is true.

Turning to the inductive step, let T denote the tree constructed by Prim's algorithm prior to another iteration of the algorithm. The inductive assumption is that T is contained in a minimal spanning tree. Let (v, w) be the next edge selected by Prim's algorithm, where v is in T and w is not in T. Let G' be T together with all of the vertices not in T. Then T is a component of G' and (v, w) is a minimum weight edge with one vertex in T and one not in T. By Theorem 7.2.5, when (v, w) is added to G', the resulting graph is also contained in a minimal spanning tree. The inductive step is complete and the theorem is proved. ∎

[†]Lower Bound Time Estimate

In this subsection, we show that the worst-case time for Prim's algorithm using a binary heap is $\Theta(m \lg n)$, where m denotes the number of edges and n denotes the number of vertices.

The bottleneck is the decrease operation

$$h.decrease(w, ref.weight)$$

To obtain worst-case time, we must construct a graph in which the decrease operation takes time $\Theta(\lg i)$ sufficiently often when the heap contains i vertices. We can guarantee such behavior if the next vertex's key to decrease has the maximum key in the heap which is then decreased so that it becomes the smallest key in the heap (in which case the vertex moves from a terminal node in the heap to the root). We construct such a graph with $n \geq 4$ vertices and $m \geq 4n$ edges as follows. [If $m < 4n$, for any graph the worst-case time T satisfies

$$T \geq Cn \lg n \geq \frac{C}{4} m \lg n = \Omega(m \lg n).$$

The first inequality results from the fact that any implementation of Prim's algorithm that uses comparisons of weights can sort an array of size $\Theta(n)$, and, so, has worst-case time $\Omega(n \lg n)$ (see Exercise 15).]

Our graph G has vertices $1, 2, \ldots, n$. For $i = 1, \ldots, n - 1$, we construct edges $(i, i + 1)$ of weight 1 (see Figure 7.3.5). We next construct edges

$$(1, n), (1, n - 1), \ldots, (1, 4), (1, 3)$$

of decreasing weight. We next construct edges

$$(2, n), (2, n - 1), \ldots, (2, 5), (2, 4)$$

[†]This subsection can be omitted without loss of continuity.

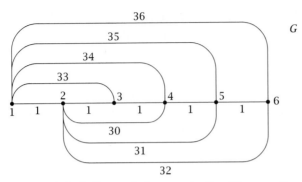

Figure 7.3.5 Part of the graph G with $n = 6$ vertices for input to Prim's algorithm. The edges shown as curves are given the weights $n^2, n^2 - 1,$ $n^2 - 2, \ldots,$ which here become $36, 35, \ldots$. This graph produces worst-case time $\Theta(m \lg n)$. After vertices 1 and 2 are deleted from the heap, the heap contains keys $33, 34, 35, 36$ (the original minimum weights of edges from vertices $3, 4, 5, 6$ to vertex 1). We then examine the edges $(2, 6), (2, 5), (2, 4),$ $(2, 3)$ in this order. Since the weight of $(2, 6)$ is 32, 6's key is decreased from 36 to 32. Since 36 was the largest key and 32 will become the smallest key, vertex 6 moves from a terminal vertex in the heap to the root, which takes time at least $C \lg(n - 2)$. Similarly, when keys $35, 34, 33$ are decreased, they too each take time at least $C \lg(n - 2)$. The total time to decrease these keys is at least $C(n - 2) \lg(n - 2)$.

of decreasing weight, where the weight of $(2, n)$ is less than the weight of $(1, 3)$. We continue in this way, stopping when m edges have been constructed. We assume that the weights assigned in this part of the construction are, in order, $n^2, n^2 - 1, n^2 - 2, \ldots$.

Suppose that G is input to Prim's algorithm and that the start vertex is 1. After 1 is deleted from the heap and the keys are decreased, we have

Vertex	Minimum Weight to Tree
2	1
3	$n^2 - (n - 3)$
4	$n^2 - (n - 4)$
$\vdots$	$\vdots$
$n - 2$	$n^2 - 2$
$n - 1$	$n^2 - 1$
n	n^2

Vertex 2 is deleted next. Assume that when the keys are decreased, the edges are examined in the order

$$(2, n), (2, n - 1), \ldots, (2, 4), (2, 3).$$

After vertex 2 is deleted from the heap, n's key is largest. Therefore, it is a terminal vertex in the heap. Since its new value is less than any of the current keys, the time to decrease n's key is at least $C \lg(n - 2)$ for some constant C. Now $(n - 1)$'s key is largest. Therefore, it is a terminal vertex in the heap. Since its new value is less than any of the current keys, the time to decrease $(n - 1)$'s key is also at least $C \lg(n - 2)$. Similarly, the time to decrease each of the other keys is also at least $C \lg(n - 2)$. The total time to decrease the keys (if all of these edges are present) is at least $C(n - 2) \lg(n - 2)$.

Vertex 3 is deleted next. Assume that when the keys are decreased, the edges are examined in the order

$$(3, n), (3, n - 1), \ldots, (3, 5), (3, 4).$$

Arguing as in the preceding paragraph, we see that the time to decrease each of the keys is at least $C \lg(n - 3)$, and the total time to decrease the keys (if all of these edges are present) is at least $C(n - 3) \lg(n - 3)$.

Let T be the time for all of the decrease operations for our graph G. Then

$$T \geq C[(n - 2) \lg(n - 2) + (n - 3) \lg(n - 3) + \cdots + (k + 1) \lg(n - p)],$$

where the last edges constructed were k edges of the form (p, i). (The inequality could be strict since the right side may not account for all of the keys that eventually decrease to 1.) We show that

$$T \geq \frac{C}{2} m \lg\left(\frac{n - 2}{2}\right).$$

First, suppose that $n - p \geq \lceil (n - 2)/2 \rceil$. Then

$$
\begin{aligned}
T &\geq C[(n - 2) \lg(n - 2) + (n - 3) \lg(n - 3) + \cdots + (k + 1) \lg(n - p)] \\
&\geq C\left[(n - 2) \lg\left\lceil\frac{n - 2}{2}\right\rceil + \cdots + (k + 1) \lg\left\lceil\frac{n - 2}{2}\right\rceil\right] \\
&\geq C[(n - 2) + \cdots + (k + 1)] \lg\left\lceil\frac{n - 2}{2}\right\rceil \\
&\geq C[(n - 3) + \cdots + k] \lg\left(\frac{n - 2}{2}\right).
\end{aligned}
$$

Since the sum

$$(n - 3) + \cdots + k$$

counts all of the edges except those of weight 1 and those incident on vertex 1,

$$(n - 3) + \cdots + k = m - (n - 1) - (n - 2).$$

Because $m \geq 4n$,

$$m - (n - 1) - (n - 2) \geq \frac{m}{2}$$

(see Exercise 12). It follows that

$$T \geq \frac{C}{2} m \lg\left(\frac{n - 2}{2}\right).$$

Now suppose that $n - p < \lceil (n - 2)/2 \rceil$. In this case,

$$
\begin{aligned}
T &\geq C[(n-2)\lg(n-2) + (n-3)\lg(n-3) + \cdots + (k+1)\lg(n-p)] \\
&\geq C\left[(n-2)\lg(n-2) + \cdots + \left\lceil \frac{n-2}{2} \right\rceil \lg\left\lceil \frac{n-2}{2} \right\rceil\right] \\
&\geq C\left[(n-2)\lg\left\lceil \frac{n-2}{2} \right\rceil + \cdots + \left\lceil \frac{n-2}{2} \right\rceil \lg\left\lceil \frac{n-2}{2} \right\rceil\right] \\
&\geq C\left[(n-2) + \cdots + \left\lceil \frac{n-2}{2} \right\rceil\right] \lg\left(\frac{n-2}{2}\right) \\
&\geq \frac{C}{2} m \lg\left(\frac{n-2}{2}\right).
\end{aligned}
$$

The last inequality follows from the inequality

$$
(n-2) + \cdots + \left\lceil \frac{n-2}{2} \right\rceil \geq \frac{n(n-1)}{4},
$$

which holds for $n \geq 4$ (see Exercise 13), and the fact that the maximum number of edges in the graph is $n(n-1)/2$.

In either case, we have

$$
T \geq \frac{C}{2} m \lg\left(\frac{n-2}{2}\right) = \Omega(m \lg n).
$$

We showed earlier that the worst-case time of Prim's algorithm using a binary heap is $O(m \lg n)$. It follows that the worst-case time of Prim's algorithm using a binary heap is $\Theta(m \lg n)$.

Exercises

1S. Trace Prim's algorithm for the graph of Exercise 1, Section 7.2. Assume that the start vertex is 1.

2. Trace Prim's algorithm for the graph of Exercise 2, Section 7.2. Assume that the start vertex is 8.

3. Trace Prim's algorithm for the graph of Exercise 3, Section 7.2. Assume that the start vertex is 11.

4S. Write an algorithm whose input is the *parent* array constructed by Prim's algorithm and whose output is a list of the edges in the minimal spanning tree constructed by Prim's algorithm.

5. Explain why we can't eliminate the *parent* array in Algorithm 7.3.4 and replace the statement

   $parent[w] = v$

with

$$println(v + \text{“ ”} + w)$$

6. What is the worst-case time (in terms of n) of Prim's algorithm when the input is the complete graph on n vertices? Assume that h is implemented using a binary minheap.

7S. What is the worst-case time of Prim's algorithm if h is implemented using an array that is always sorted from largest to smallest weight?

8. What is the worst-case time of Prim's algorithm if h is implemented using an unsorted array?

9. Are there graphs for which Prim's algorithm is faster than Kruskal's algorithm?

10S. Are there graphs for which Prim's algorithm is slower than Kruskal's algorithm?

11. Provide an implementation of Prim's algorithm that uses an adjacency matrix instead of adjacency lists. What is the worst-case time of your algorithm? Assume that h is implemented using a binary minheap.

12. Show that if $m \geq 4n$,

$$m - (n - 1) - (n - 2) \geq \frac{m}{2}.$$

13S. Show that if $n \geq 4$,

$$(n - 2) + (n - 3) + \cdots + \left\lceil \frac{n - 2}{2} \right\rceil \geq \frac{n(n - 1)}{4}.$$

14. Show that any implementation of Prim's algorithm must examine each edge's weight at least once, and thus has time $\Omega(m)$.

15. Show that any implementation of Prim's algorithm that uses comparisons of weights can sort an array of size $\Theta(n)$ and, so, has worst-case time $\Omega(n \lg n)$.

7.4 Dijkstra's Algorithm

The map in Figure 7.4.1(a) shows six cities and the time in minutes to drive between cities that are directly connected by a road. A computer technician based in Riverview, who is desperately needed in Wolf, must find the quickest route from Riverview to Wolf.

WWW   The map in Figure 7.4.1(a) can be considered a graph [see Figure 7.4.1(b)] in which the cities become vertices, the roads become edges, and the times

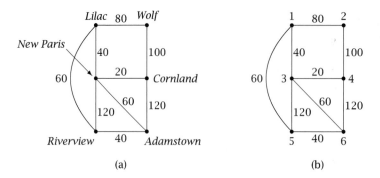

Figure 7.4.1 The map (a) shows six cities and the time in minutes to drive between cities that are directly connected by a road. The map is shown in (b) as a graph in which the cities become vertices, the roads become edges, and the times become the weights of edges.

become the weights of edges. Now the computer-technician's problem becomes the problem of finding a shortest path from vertex 5 to vertex 2. **Dijkstra's algorithm** is a greedy algorithm that finds shortest paths from a designated vertex to all other vertices in a connected, weighted graph; in particular, Dijkstra's algorithm solves the computer-technician's problem. In this section, unless specified otherwise, all of the weights are positive.

The following example shows that not just any greedy approach correctly finds shortest paths from a designated vertex to all of the other vertices.

Example 7.4.1. Consider the following greedy rule for the graph of Figure 7.4.2: Add a minimum-weight edge to an existing path if the addition does not create a cycle. Suppose that we want to find the length of a shortest path from vertex 1 to vertex 4. The designated vertex is 1; we would first choose edge $(1, 2)$, then edge $(2, 3)$, and finally edge $(3, 4)$, which gives a path of length 14 from 1 to 4. This is not a shortest path because $1, 2, 4$ has length 11.

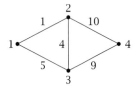

Figure 7.4.2 A graph for finding shortest paths.   □

Dijkstra's algorithm correctly finds shortest paths from a designated vertex s to all of the other vertices in nondecreasing order of length; the first path found is from s to s of length zero. It then applies the greedy rule: Among all of the vertices that can extend a shortest path already found by one edge, choose the one that results in the shortest path.

Example 7.4.2. We show how Dijkstra's algorithm correctly finds shortest paths in the graph of Figure 7.4.2 with designated vertex 1. It first adds vertex 2 to produce the path $1, 2$ of minimum length 1. It next extends this path by vertex 3 to produce the path $1, 2, 3$ of minimum length 5. (It could have added vertex 3 to vertex 1 to produce the path $1, 3$ also of minimum length 5.) Finally, it adds vertex 4 to extend path $1, 2$ to produce the path $1, 2, 4$ of minimum length 11.   □

Example 7.4.3. We show how Dijkstra's algorithm finds shortest paths in the graph in Figure 7.4.1(b) beginning at vertex 5. The first path is from 5 to 5 of length 0.

Vertices 1, 3, and 6 can extend the shortest path from 5 to 5 as follows:

Vertex Added	To Path	Path Length
1	5	60
3	5	120
6	5	40

Since length 40 is the minimum, we add vertex 6 and edge $(5, 6)$ to the path from 5 to 5 to obtain the path $5, 6$ of length 40. We now have the following shortest paths:

Shortest Path	Length
5	0
5, 6	40

Vertices 1, 3, and 4 can extend the shortest paths found as follows:

Vertex Added	To Path	Path Length
1	5	60
3	5, 6	100
4	5, 6	160

Notice that we do not consider adding vertex 3 to path 5 because that would give a path of length 120. Adding 3 to path $5, 6$ is better since that results in a path of length 100. Since length 60 is the minimum, we add vertex 1 and edge $(5, 1)$ to the path from 5 to 5 to obtain the path $5, 1$ of length 60. We now have the following shortest paths:

Shortest Path	Length
5	0
5, 6	40
5, 1	60

Vertices 2, 3, and 4 can extend the shortest paths found as follows:

Vertex Added	To Path	Path Length
2	5, 1	140
3	5, 6	100
4	5, 6	160

Since length 100 is the minimum, we add vertex 3 and edge $(6, 3)$ to the path $5, 6$ to obtain the path $5, 6, 3$ of length 100. We now have the following shortest paths:

Shortest Path	Length
5	0
5, 6	40
5, 1	60
5, 6, 3	100

Vertices 2 and 4 can extend the shortest paths found as follows:

Vertex Added	To Path	Path Length
2	5, 1	140
4	5, 6, 3	120

Since length 120 is the minimum, we add vertex 4 and edge $(3, 4)$ to the path $5, 6, 3$ to obtain the path $5, 6, 3, 4$ of length 120. We now have the following shortest paths:

Shortest Path	Length
5	0
5, 6	40
5, 1	60
5, 6, 3	100
5, 6, 3, 4	120

Vertex 2 can extend the shortest paths found in one way

Vertex Added	To Path	Path Length
2	5, 1	140

so we add vertex 2 and edge $(1, 2)$ to the path $5, 1$ to obtain the path $5, 1, 2$ of length 140. We have now found all of the shortest paths

Shortest Path	Length
5	0
5, 6	40
5, 1	60
5, 6, 3	100
5, 6, 3, 4	120
5, 1, 2	140

and Dijkstra's algorithm terminates.

Referring to Figure 7.4.1, we see that the shortest path from Riverview to Wolf goes through Lilac and takes 140 minutes. □

Examples 7.4.2 and 7.4.3 show that Dijkstra's algorithm operates just like Prim's algorithm; the only difference is the value associated with a vertex. In Prim's algorithm, the value associated with vertex v is the minimum weight of an edge from v to the current tree. In Dijkstra's algorithm, the value associated with vertex v is the minimum of all of the sums of the form

$$length(w) + \text{weight}(v, w),$$

where w marks the end of a shortest path already found. [In this case, $length(w)$ *is* the length of a shortest path from the designated vertex to w.] Thus, Dijkstra's algorithm may be implemented similarly to Prim's algorithm.

Algorithm 7.4.4 Dijkstra's Algorithm. This algorithm finds shortest paths from the designated vertex *start* to all of the other vertices in a connected, weighted, n-vertex graph. The graph is represented using adjacency lists; $adj[i]$ is a reference to the first node in a linked list of nodes representing the vertices adjacent to vertex i. Each node has members *ver*, the vertex adjacent to i; *weight*, representing the weight of edge (i, ver); and *next*, a reference to the next node in the linked list or null, for the last node in the linked list. In a shortest path, the predecessor of vertex $i \neq start$ is $predecessor[i]$, and $predecessor[start] = 0$. The value ∞ is the largest available integer value. The abstract data type h supports the same operations as in Prim's algorithm.

Input Parameters: *adj, start*
Output Parameter: *predecessor*

```
dijkstra(adj, start, predecessor) {
    // key is a local array
    n = adj.last
    for i = 1 to n
        key[i] = ∞
    key[start] = 0
    predecessor[start] = 0
    // the following statement initializes the
    // container h to the values in the array key
    h.init(key, n)
    for i = 1 to n {
        v = h.min_weight_index()
        min_cost = h.keyval(v)
        v = h.del()
        ref = adj[v]
```

```
        while (ref != null) {
          w = ref.ver
          if (h.isin(w) && min_cost + ref.weight < h.keyval(w)) {
            predecessor[w] = v
            h.decrease(w, min_cost + ref.weight)
          } // end if
          ref = ref.next
        } // end while
     } // end for
}
```

Since the implementations of Dijkstra's and Prim's algorithms (see Section 7.3 for a detailed analysis of Prim's algorithm) are essentially the same, their worst-case times are also the same. Using a binary minheap to implement h, the worst-case time of Dijkstra's algorithm is $O(m \lg n)$ for a graph with m edges and n vertices. A graph similar to that in Figure 7.3.5 can be used to show that the estimate for the time using a binary heap is sharp; that is, the worst-case time of Dijkstra's algorithm using a binary heap is $\Theta(m \lg n)$ (see Exercise 11). If we use a Fibonacci heap instead, we can improve the worst-case time of Dijkstra's algorithm to $\Theta(m + n \lg n)$.

We conclude by proving the correctness of Dijkstra's algorithm. The main observation that drives the proof is that Dijkstra's algorithm finds shortest paths in nondecreasing order of length.

Theorem 7.4.5 Correctness of Dijkstra's Algorithm. *Dijkstra's algorithm (Algorithm 7.4.4) is correct; that is, it finds shortest paths from a designated vertex to all of the other vertices.*

Proof. We use induction to show that at each iteration of Dijkstra's algorithm, when v is deleted from h, $key(v)$ is the length of a shortest path from *start* to v.

When we begin, $v = start$, $key(v) = 0$, and the length of a shortest path from *start* to *start* is zero, so the basis step is true.

Turning to the inductive step, assume that v has just been deleted from h and that for all vertices i previously deleted from h, $key(i)$ is the length of a shortest path from *start* to i.

First we show that if there is a path from *start* to a vertex w whose length is less than $key(v)$, then w was previously deleted from h. Suppose by way of contradiction that w is still in h. Let P be a shortest path from *start* to w, let w' be the vertex nearest *start* on P that is in h, and let w'' be the predecessor of w' on P (see Figure 7.4.3). Then w'' is not in h, so by the inductive assumption, $key(w'')$ is the length of a shortest path from *start* to w''. Now

$$key(w') \leq key(w'') + \text{weight}(w'', w') \leq \text{length of } P < key(v).$$

But this inequality shows that v is not the vertex in h with minimum key [$key(w')$ is smaller]. This contradiction completes the proof that, if there is

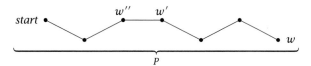

Figure 7.4.3 The proof of Theorem 7.4.5. P is a shortest path from *start* to w, w' is the vertex nearest *start* on P that is in h, and w'' is the predecessor of w' on P.

a path from *start* to a vertex w whose length is less than $key(v)$, then w was previously deleted from h.

The preceding result shows, in particular, that if there were a path from *start* to v whose length is less than $key(v)$, v would already have been deleted from h. Therefore, every path from *start* to v has length at least $key(v)$. By construction, there is a path from *start* to v of length $key(v)$, so this is a shortest path from *start* to v. The proof is complete. ∎

Exercises

1S. Trace Dijkstra's algorithm for the graph of Exercise 1, Section 7.2. Assume that the start vertex is 1.

2. Trace Dijkstra's algorithm for the graph of Exercise 2, Section 7.2. Assume that the start vertex is 8.

3. Trace Dijkstra's algorithm for the graph of Exercise 3, Section 7.2. Assume that the start vertex is 11.

4S. Write an algorithm whose input is the *predecessor* array constructed by Dijkstra's algorithm and whose output is a list of shortest paths from the start vertex to all of the other vertices in the graph.

5. What is the worst-case time (in terms of n) of Dijkstra's algorithm when the input is the complete graph on n vertices? Assume that h is implemented using a binary minheap.

6. What is the worst-case time of Dijkstra's algorithm if h is implemented using an array that is always sorted from largest to smallest weight?

7S. What is the worst-case time of Dijkstra's algorithm if h is implemented using an unsorted array?

8. Provide an implementation of Dijkstra's algorithm that uses an adjacency matrix instead of adjacency lists. What is the worst-case time of your algorithm? Assume that h is implemented using a binary minheap.

9. Modify Dijkstra's algorithm so that it accepts a weighted graph that is not necessarily connected. At termination, what is $key(v)$ if there is no path from the start vertex to v?

10S. True or false? Dijkstra's algorithm finds the length of a shortest path in a connected, weighted graph even if some weights are negative. If true, prove it; otherwise, provide a counterexample.

11. Show that the worst-case time of Dijkstra's algorithm using a binary heap is $\Theta(m \lg n)$.

7.5 Huffman Codes

Text containing the characters shown in Figure 7.5.1 is to be encoded by representing each character by a bit string. How often each character appears in the text, called the *frequency* of the character, is also shown in Figure 7.5.1. The goal is to represent the data using the minimum number of bits.

Character	Frequency
space	60
A	22
O	16
R	13
S	6
T	4

Figure 7.5.1 Characters and their frequencies.

Data compression refers to minimizing the number of bits used to represent data. It is important to compress data when large amounts of data are to be stored or transmitted. Data compression is a key component of digital television technology in which huge amounts of data must be transmitted quickly. Data compression is also used in digital video disks (DVDs).

The most common way to represent characters is by using fixed-length bit strings. For example, ASCII (American Standard Code for Information Interchange) represents each character by a string of seven bits.

Example 7.5.1. The ASCII codes for the characters in Figure 7.5.1 are given in Figure 7.5.2. For example,

STAR OR RATS

would be encoded as

1010011 1010100 1000001 1010010 0100000 1001111
1010010 0100000 1010010 1000001 1010100 1010011.

Character	ASCII Code
space	0100000
A	1000001
O	1001111
R	1010010
S	1010011
T	1010100

Figure 7.5.2 Characters and their ASCII codes.

Space separates the codes for readability, but there would not be any space between the codes in the actual encoding.

The text in Figure 7.5.1 contains

$$60 + 22 + 16 + 13 + 6 + 4 = 121$$

characters; thus, $121 \cdot 7 = 847$ bits are required to encode the text. □

$\mathcal{WWW}$ **Huffman codes** provide alternatives to ASCII and other fixed-length codes by using variable-length bit strings to represent characters. The idea is to use short bit strings to represent the most frequently used characters and to use longer bit strings to represent less frequently used characters. In this way, it is generally possible to represent text in less space than if ASCII were used. VCR Plus+, a device that automatically programs a videocassette recorder, uses a Huffman code to generate numbers that the user then enters to choose which programs to record. The numbers are published in many television listings.

Example 7.5.2. Figure 7.5.3 shows a Huffman code for the characters in Figure 7.5.1. Notice that the characters are represented by variable-length bit strings. For example, the space character is represented by a bit string of length 1, *A* is represented by a bit string of length 3, and *T* is represented by a bit string of length 4. Notice also that the most frequently used character (the space character) uses a short bit string, whereas the least frequently used characters (*S* and *T*) use longer bit strings.

Character	Huffman Code
space	0
A	111
O	110
R	101
S	1001
T	1000

Figure 7.5.3 Characters and their Huffman codes.

As an example,

STAR OR RATS

would be encoded as

1001 1000 111 101 0 110 101 0 101 111 1000 1001.

Space separates the codes for readability, but there would not be any space between the codes in the actual encoding.

The text in Figure 7.5.1 would require $22 \cdot 3 = 66$ bits to encode the A's since there are 22 A's and each is A is represented by 3 bits. The total number of bits required to encode the text is

$$60 \cdot 1 + 22 \cdot 3 + 16 \cdot 3 + 13 \cdot 3 + 6 \cdot 4 + 4 \cdot 4 = 253.$$

Example 7.5.1 showed that if ASCII is used, 847 bits are required to encode the text.   □

If we use a code in which some character is represented by a bit string that is the initial segment of a bit string that represents another character, text might not be unambiguously decoded. For example, if A is represented by 100, B by 101, and T by 100101, the encoding 100101 would be ambiguous; 100101 could represent AB or T. A code in which no character is represented by a bit string that is the initial segment of a bit string that represents another character is called a **prefix code**.

Notice that the code in Figure 7.5.3 is a prefix code. Example 7.5.2 showed that the Huffman code in Figure 7.5.3 stores the text in Figure 7.5.1 in 253 bits. We will show later that no other prefix code stores the text in Figure 7.5.1 in fewer than 253 bits; that is, the Huffman code in Figure 7.5.3 is optimal for the text in Figure 7.5.1.

A Huffman code may be defined by a binary tree (see Figure 7.5.4) called a **Huffman coding tree**. The code for a particular character is obtained by following the path from the root to the character and noting the bits on the edges of the path. For example, for the Huffman coding tree of Figure 7.5.4, the code for character T is 1000. The Huffman coding tree of Figure 7.5.4 is an alternate description of the code given in tabular form in Figure 7.5.3.

Our problem is to construct an *optimal* Huffman code. More precisely, the problem is: Given a table of characters and their frequencies, construct a Huffman code that represents the text using as few bits as possible.

Example 7.5.2 shows that the problem of constructing an optimal Huffman coding tree given a table of n characters and their frequencies

$$f_1, f_2, \ldots, f_n$$

is equivalent to minimizing the sum

$$\sum_{i=1}^{n} f_i p_i,$$

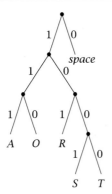

Figure 7.5.4 A Huffman coding tree.

where p_i is the number of bits for character i, or, equivalently, the length of the path from the root to the character with frequency f_i. This sum is called the **weighted path length** of the Huffman coding tree T and is denoted WPL(T).

An alternative way to view the weighted path length is to assign the frequency of each character to the terminal vertex that represents that character and then assign each internal vertex the sum of its children. Figure 7.5.5 shows the Huffman coding tree of Figure 7.5.4 rewritten in this way for the frequencies in Figure 7.5.1. Since each terminal vertex's value appears as a summand in each vertex on a path to the root (see Figure 7.5.6), when the values of all the internal vertices are summed, the value of each terminal

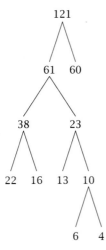

Figure 7.5.5 The Huffman coding tree of Figure 7.5.4 and its weighted path length. The value of each terminal vertex is the frequency of the character it represents, and the value of each internal vertex is the sum of the values of its children. The sum of the values of all of the internal vertices is equal to the weighted path length (253).

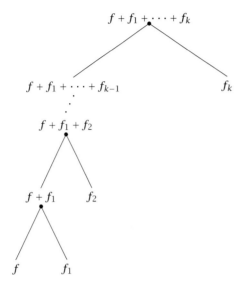

Figure 7.5.6 A Huffman coding tree. A frequency (e.g., f) appears as a summand in each vertex on the path to the root.

vertex is counted p times, where p is the length of the path from the vertex to the root. It follows that the weighted path length is equal to the sum of the values of the internal vertices. For example, the sum of the values of the internal vertices of the Huffman coding tree of Figure 7.5.5 is

$$121 + 61 + 38 + 23 + 10 = 253,$$

the same value obtained by a different computation in Example 7.5.2.

A greedy algorithm to construct an optimal Huffman coding tree might begin by finding the two smallest frequencies and putting them at the bottom of the tree. The idea is that the least frequently used characters should have the longest bit codes. For the frequencies in Figure 7.5.1, the smallest frequencies are 4 and 6. In a representation such as that of Figure 7.5.5, the parent of 4 and 6 has value $10 = 4 + 6$. The tree that we eventually construct, with 4 and 6 removed, has all of the original frequencies except that 4 and 6 are replaced by 10. This suggests that after placing 4 and 6 at the bottom of the tree, we consider a new problem: Construct an optimal Huffman coding tree for the frequencies 10, 13, 16, 22, and 60 (and ultimately give vertex 10 children corresponding to 4 and 6; see Figure 7.5.7).

For the 10, 13, 16, 22, 60 problem, we find the two smallest frequencies, 10 and 13, and put them at the bottom of the tree. We then consider the problem of constructing an optimal Huffman coding tree for the frequencies 16, 22, 23, and 60 (and ultimately giving vertex 23 children corresponding to 10 and 13).

For the 16, 22, 23, 60 problem, we find the two smallest frequencies, 16 and 22, and put them at the bottom of the tree. We then consider the

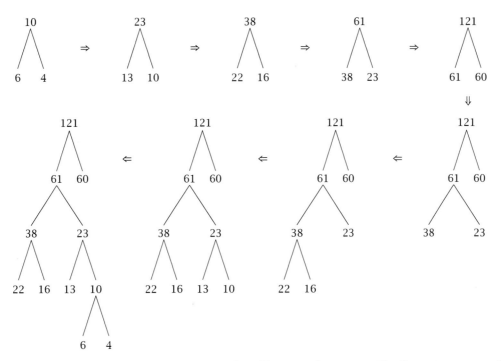

Figure 7.5.7 Constructing an optimal Huffman coding tree. The frequencies are 4, 6, 13, 16, 22, and 60. The smallest frequencies (4 and 6) are the children of 4 + 6. The new problem has frequencies 10, 13, 16, 22, and 60. The smallest frequencies (10 and 13) are the children of 10 + 13. The new problem has frequencies 16, 22, 23, and 60. The smallest frequencies (16 and 22) are the children of 16 + 22. The new problem has frequencies 23, 38, and 60. The smallest frequencies (23 and 38) are the children of 23 + 38. The new problem has frequencies 60 and 61. These frequencies are the children of 60 + 61. When the trees are combined, an optimal Huffman coding tree results.

problem of constructing an optimal Huffman coding tree for the frequencies 23, 38, and 60 (and ultimately giving vertex 38 children corresponding to 16 and 22).

For the 23, 38, 60 problem, we find the two smallest frequencies, 23 and 38, and put them at the bottom of the tree. We then consider the problem of constructing an optimal Huffman coding tree for the frequencies 60 and 61 (and ultimately giving vertex 61 children corresponding to 23 and 38). There is only one way to construct such a tree (see Figure 7.5.7). After giving vertex 61 children 23 and 38, giving vertex 38 children 16 and 22, giving vertex 23 children 10 and 13, and giving vertex 10 children 4 and 6, we obtain the Huffman coding tree shown in Figure 7.5.7. The Huffman-coding-tree algorithm is stated formally as Algorithm 7.5.3.

Algorithm 7.5.3 Huffman's Algorithm. This algorithm constructs an optimal Huffman coding tree. The input is an array a of $n \geq 2$ nodes. Each *node* has an integer member *character* to identify a particular character, another integer member *key* to identify that character's frequency, and *left* and *right* members. After the Huffman coding tree is constructed, a *left* member of a *node* references its left child, and a *right* member of a *node* references its right child or, if the *node* is a terminal vertex, its *left* and *right* members are null. The algorithm returns a reference to the root of the Huffman coding tree. The operator, new, is used to obtain a new node.

If *a* is an array, the expression

$$h.init(a)$$

initializes the container *h* to the data in *a*. The expression

$$h.del()$$

deletes the *node* in *h* with the smallest key and returns the *node*. The expression

$$h.insert(ref)$$

inserts the *node* referenced by *ref* into *h*.

Input Parameter:	*a*
Output Parameters:	None

```
huffman(a) {
   h.init(a)
   for i = 1 to a.last − 1 {
      ref = new node
      ref.left = h.del()
      ref.right = h.del()
      ref.key = ref.left.key + ref.right.key
      h.insert(ref)
   }
   return h.del()
}
```

If we use a binary minheap (see Section 3.5) to implement the container *h* in Algorithm 7.5.3, initialization of the heap takes time $\Theta(n)$. The for loop executes $n - 1$ times. Within the for loop, deletion from the heap and insertion into the heap each take time $O(\lg n)$. Thus the total time for deletions and insertions is $O(n \lg n)$. The final deletion also takes time $O(\lg n)$. Thus the overall time for Algorithm 7.5.3 is $O(n \lg n)$.

The preceding estimate for the time for Algorithm 7.5.3 is sharp; that is, the worst-case time is $\Theta(n \lg n)$. When Algorithm 7.5.3 receives the input

$$1 \quad 1 \quad 3 \quad 6 \quad 12 \quad 24 \quad 48 \ldots,$$

the time is $\Theta(n \lg n)$. First, the two smallest frequencies $(1, 1)$ are removed from the heap. When the key $2 = 1 + 1$ is inserted into the heap, 2 becomes the smallest key; thus, this insertion requires time at least $C \lg(n-1)$ (see Section 3.5). The keys in the heap are now

$$2 \quad 3 \quad 6 \quad 12 \quad 24 \quad 48 \ldots .$$

Next, the key $5 = 2 + 3$ is inserted into the heap. Now 5 becomes the smallest key; thus, this insertion requires time at least $C \lg(n-2)$. The keys in the heap are now

$$5 \quad 6 \quad 12 \quad 24 \quad 48 \ldots .$$

Next, the key $11 = 5 + 6$ is inserted into the heap. This insertion requires time at least $C \lg(n-3)$. The process continues. Therefore, the time for this input is at least

$$C[\lg(n-1) + \lg(n-2) + \lg(n-3) + \cdots] = \Omega(n \lg n)$$

(see Example 2.3.8). Since the time is always $O(n \lg n)$, the worst-case time is $\Theta(n \lg n)$.

As the first step in proving the correctness of Algorithm 7.5.3, we show that there is always an optimal Huffman coding tree in which the two smallest frequencies have the same parent.

Theorem 7.5.4. *Given a table of characters and their frequencies, there is an optimal Huffman coding tree in which the two smallest frequencies have the same parent.*

Proof. Let T be an optimal Huffman coding tree, and let f_1 and f_2 be the smallest frequencies. If f_1 is not at the lowest level of T, choose a frequency f that is at the lowest level of T. Then $f \geq f_1$. Let T' be the tree that results from swapping f and f_1. We show that T' is also an optimal Huffman coding tree.

Let p be length of the path in T from the root to f, and let p_1 be length of the path in T from the root to f_1 (see Figure 7.5.8). Then $p \geq p_1$. The weighted path lengths of T and T' are related as follows:

$$
\begin{aligned}
\text{WPL}(T') &= \text{WPL}(T) - pf + pf_1 - p_1 f_1 + p_1 f \\
&= \text{WPL}(T) - (p - p_1)(f - f_1).
\end{aligned}
$$

Since $(p - p_1)(f - f_1) \geq 0$, it follows that

$$\text{WPL}(T') \leq \text{WPL}(T).$$

Since T is optimal, we must have

$$\text{WPL}(T') = \text{WPL}(T).$$

Therefore T' is an optimal Huffman coding tree.

If f_2 is not a sibling of f_1 in T', we swap f_2 with f_1's sibling to obtain a tree T''. An argument like that in the preceding paragraph shows that T'' is

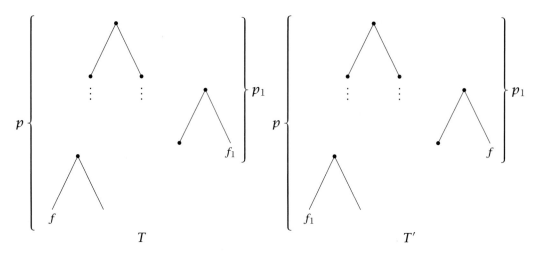

Figure 7.5.8 The proof of Theorem 7.5.4. T is an optimal Huffman coding tree, f_1 is one of the smallest two frequencies, and f is at the lowest level of T. f and f_1 are swapped to obtain T'. Let p be the length of the path in T from the root to f, and let p_1 be the length of the path in T from the root to f_1. The weighted path length of T' is the same as that of T except that pf is replaced by pf_1, and p_1f_1 is replaced by p_1f. Comparing the weighted path lengths of T and T' shows that T' is also an optimal Huffman coding tree.

also an optimal Huffman coding tree. Thus, we obtain an optimal Huffman coding tree in which f_1 and f_2 have the same parent. ∎

After one more result, we can prove the correctness of Algorithm 7.5.3.

Theorem 7.5.5. *Let T be a Huffman coding tree for the frequencies*

$$f_1, f_2, f_3, \ldots, f_n,$$

and suppose that f_1 and f_2 have the same parent. Let T' be T with nodes f_1 and f_2 deleted and the parent of f_1 and f_2 labeled $f_1 + f_2$. Then

$$\mathrm{WPL}(T) = \mathrm{WPL}(T') + f_1 + f_2.$$

Furthermore, if T is optimal for the frequencies $f_1, f_2, f_3, \ldots, f_n$, then T' is optimal for the frequencies $f_1 + f_2, f_3, \ldots, f_n$.

Proof. The weighted path length is the sum of all of the values of the internal nodes. Since T has one more internal node than T', whose value is $f_1 + f_2$, the equation follows.

Suppose, by way of contradiction, that T is optimal for the frequencies $f_1, f_2, f_3, \ldots, f_n$ but T' is not optimal for the frequencies $f_1 + f_2, f_3, \ldots, f_n$. Let T'' be an optimal Huffman coding tree for the frequencies $f_1 + f_2$, $f_3, \ldots, f_n$. Then

$$\mathrm{WPL}(T'') < \mathrm{WPL}(T').$$

Now T'' has a node whose value is $f_1 + f_2$. Attach two children to this node with values f_1 and f_2 to obtain a Huffman coding tree T'''. The equation already established shows that

$$\text{WPL}(T''') = \text{WPL}(T'') + f_1 + f_2.$$

Now

$$\text{WPL}(T''') = \text{WPL}(T'') + f_1 + f_2 < \text{WPL}(T') + f_1 + f_2 = \text{WPL}(T).$$

But this is a contradiction because T is an optimal Huffman coding tree for the frequencies $f_1, f_2, f_3, \ldots, f_n$. Therefore T' is optimal for the frequencies $f_1 + f_2, f_3, \ldots, f_n$. ∎

We can now prove the correctness of Huffman's algorithm (Algorithm 7.5.3).

Theorem 7.5.6 Correctness of Huffman's Algorithm. *Huffman's algorithm (Algorithm 7.5.3) is correct; that is, the Huffman coding tree constructed is optimal.*

Proof. We use induction on the number n of frequencies. The basis step is $n = 2$. In this case, there is a unique Huffman coding tree that must therefore be optimal.

Assume that $n > 2$ and that the theorem is true for $n - 1$ frequencies. Suppose that we have input $f_1, f_2, \ldots, f_n$, where f_1 and f_2 are the smallest frequencies. By Theorem 7.5.4, there is an optimal Huffman coding tree T in which f_1 and f_2 have the same parent. Let TA be the Huffman coding tree constructed by Algorithm 7.5.3. We must show that

$$\text{WPL}(TA) = \text{WPL}(T).$$

By the inductive assumption, the Huffman coding tree TA_1 constructed by Algorithm 7.5.3 for $f_1 + f_2, f_3, \ldots, f_n$ is optimal. Let T_1 denote T with f_1 and f_2 deleted. By Theorem 7.5.5, T_1 is also optimal for $f_1 + f_2, f_3, \ldots, f_n$. Thus

$$\text{WPL}(T_1) = \text{WPL}(TA_1).$$

Again using Theorem 7.5.5, we have

$$\text{WPL}(T) = \text{WPL}(T_1) + f_1 + f_2$$

and

$$\text{WPL}(TA) = \text{WPL}(TA_1) + f_1 + f_2.$$

Now

$$\begin{aligned}
\text{WPL}(T) &= \text{WPL}(T_1) + f_1 + f_2 \\
&= \text{WPL}(TA_1) + f_1 + f_2 \\
&= \text{WPL}(TA).
\end{aligned}$$

Therefore TA is optimal and the proof is complete. ∎

Exercises

In Exercises 1–4, decode each bit string using the following Huffman coding tree.

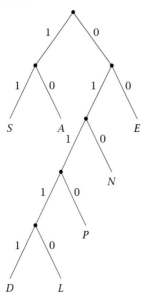

1S. 011000010

3. 01111001001110

2. 01110100110

4S. 1110011101001111

In Exercises 5–8, encode each string using the Huffman coding tree for Exercises 1–4.

5S. DEN

7. LEADEN

6. NEED

8S. PENNED

9S. Construct an optimal Huffman coding tree for the characters α with frequency 5, β with frequency 6, γ with frequency 6, δ with frequency 11, and ϵ with frequency 20.

10. How many bits are required to store the characters in Exercise 9?

11. Construct an optimal Huffman coding tree for the characters I with frequency 75, U with frequency 200, B with frequency 25, S with frequency 275, C with frequency 50, H with frequency 100, M with frequency 25, and P with frequency 250.

12S. How many bits are required to store the characters in Exercise 11?

13. Construct two optimal Huffman coding trees of different heights for the text of Exercise 11.

14. Professor Gig A. Byte needs to store text made up of the characters *A* with frequency 6, *B* with frequency 2, *C* with frequency 3, *D* with frequency 2, and *E* with frequency 8. Professor Byte suggests using the variable-length codes

Character	Code
A	1
B	00
C	01
D	10
E	0

which, he argues, store the text in less space than that used by an optimal Huffman code. Is the professor correct? Explain.

15S. Write an algorithm whose input is the Huffman coding tree constructed by Algorithm 7.5.3 and whose output is a list of characters and their codes.

16. Show that the converse of the last statement in Theorem 7.5.5 is false; that is, give an example of a nonoptimal Huffman coding tree *T* with frequencies f and f' having the same parent in which *T* with f and f' deleted is optimal.

17. What factors in addition to saving space should be considered when choosing a code, such as ASCII or a Huffman code, to encode strings?

7.6 The Continuous-Knapsack Problem

A draft report has five chapters. Figure 7.6.1 shows the lengths of the chapters and their importance, where the scale is 1 (low) to 10 (high). The report must be at most 600 pages long. The problem is to edit the report (e.g., by deleting pages or rewriting) so that the overall importance is maximized.

Chapter	Pages	Importance
1	120	5
2	150	5
3	200	4
4	150	8
5	140	3

Figure 7.6.1 A draft report, the number of pages in each chapter, and the importance of each chapter, where the scale is 1 (low) to 10 (high).

For example, we could delete chapter 5 and 20 pages of chapter 3 to obtain a 600-page report. The overall importance of this draft is

$$5 + 5 + \left(\frac{180}{200}\right)4 + 8 = 21.6.$$

[Chapter 3's importance is 4, but since we deleted 20 of its pages, it contributes only $(180/200)4$ to the sum. Since we deleted chapter 5, it contributes zero to the sum.] In general, if x_i is the amount of chapter i used (e.g., $x_3 = 180/200$) and p_i is the importance of chapter i (e.g., $p_1 = 5$), we define the *importance* of the resulting draft to be

$$\sum_{i=1}^{n} x_i p_i.$$

The problem, then, is to maximize the preceding sum subject to the condition that the report must consist of at most 600 pages. (Before continuing, the reader is invited to find a draft whose importance is greater than 21.6.)

The report-revision problem is an example of a **knapsack problem**: Given n objects and a knapsack of capacity C, where object i has *weight* w_i and earns *profit* p_i, find values of x_i that maximize the total profit

$$\sum_{i=1}^{n} x_i p_i$$

subject to the constraints

$$\sum_{i=1}^{n} x_i w_i \le C, \qquad 0 \le x_i \le 1.$$

The constraint $\sum_{i=1}^{n} x_i w_i \le C$ guarantees that the capacity of the knapsack is not exceeded.

In the report-revision problem, the capacity of the knapsack is $C = 600$; the weights are

$$w_1 = 120, \quad w_2 = 150, \quad w_3 = 200, \quad w_4 = 150, \quad w_5 = 140;$$

and the profits are

$$p_1 = 5, \quad p_2 = 5, \quad p_3 = 4, \quad p_4 = 8, \quad p_5 = 3.$$

If we delete chapter 5 and 20 pages of chapter 3, the knapsack will be filled to capacity:

$$120 + 150 + 180 + 150 + 0 = 600.$$

For these selections, the values of x_i are

$$x_1 = 1, \quad x_2 = 1, \quad x_3 = \frac{180}{200} = 0.9, \quad x_4 = 1, \quad x_5 = 0,$$

and the total profit is

$$\sum_{i=1}^{n} x_i p_i = 1 \cdot 5 + 1 \cdot 5 + 0.9 \cdot 4 + 1 \cdot 8 + 0 \cdot 3 = 21.6.$$

Two versions of the knapsack problem result from placing conditions on the x_i. In the **0/1-knapsack problem**, each x_i must be 0 or 1; that is, each selection must take none (0) or all (1) of an object. In this version, the objects are considered to be indivisible. In the **continuous-knapsack problem**, which we discuss in this section, each x_i is allowed to take *any* value between 0 and 1, including 0 or 1; that is, each selection may take none, all, or any portion of an object. In this version, the objects are considered to be divisible into any portion. The report-revision problem is an example of the *continuous*-knapsack problem, since we are allowed to take none, all, or any portion of a chapter.

A greedy algorithm to solve the continuous-knapsack problem would examine the objects in some order and use a greedy rule to decide how much of each object to select. A greedy rule could not look only at the weights and ignore the profits. Even if an object had a small weight and so, apparently, should be selected for inclusion in the knapsack, it might yield so little profit that it would be better to omit it. Exercise 5 requests an example to show that looking only at the weights and ignoring the profits does not necessarily give an optimal solution. Similarly, looking only at the profits and ignoring the weights also does not necessarily give an optimal solution (see Exercise 6). Since we want to maximize the profit and minimize the weight, we should maximize the *ratio* of profit to weight. Thus, the greedy rule is to select the objects in nonincreasing order of the ratio of profit to weight. We take *all* of the object if the capacity of the knapsack is not exceeded. If the capacity of the knapsack would be exceeded, we take whatever portion of the object fills the knapsack and stop.

Example 7.6.1. We show how the greedy algorithm chooses objects for the weights (pages) and profits (importance) given in Figure 7.6.1. The capacity of the knapsack is 600.

The ratios of profit to weight are:

$$\frac{p_1}{w_1} = \frac{5}{120} = .0417$$

$$\frac{p_2}{w_2} = \frac{5}{150} = .0333$$

$$\frac{p_3}{w_3} = \frac{4}{200} = .0200$$

$$\frac{p_4}{w_4} = \frac{8}{150} = .0533$$

$$\frac{p_5}{w_5} = \frac{3}{140} = .0214.$$

Thus, we examine the objects in the order: 4, 1, 2, 5, 3. We therefore take all of the objects 4, 1, 2, and 5. At this point, the weight of the objects selected is $150 + 120 + 150 + 140 = 560$. Since the knapsack's capacity is 600, we select $40/200$ of object 3 to fill the knapsack. We obtain a profit of

$$5 + 5 + 0.2 \cdot 4 + 8 + 3 = 21.8. \hspace{2cm} \Box$$

A formal statement of the greedy algorithm to solve the continuous-knapsack problem follows.

Algorithm 7.6.2 Greedy Algorithm for the Continuous-Knapsack Problem.
The input to the algorithm is the knapsack capacity C, and an array a of size n, each of whose entries specifies an *id* (e.g., the first item might have *id* 1, the second item might have *id* 2, etc.), a profit p, and a weight w. The output tells how much of each object to select to maximize the profit. Objects not selected do not appear in the output. The function *sort* sorts the array a in nonincreasing order of the ratio of profit to weight.

Input Parameters: a, C
Output Parameters: None

```
continuous_knapsack(a, C) {
    n = a.last
    for i = 1 to n
        ratio[i] = a[i].p/a[i].w
    sort(a, ratio)
    weight = 0
    i = 1
    while (i ≤ n && weight < C) {
        if (weight + a[i].w ≤ C) {
            println("select all of object " + a[i].id)
            weight = weight + a[i].w
        }
        else {
            r = (C − weight)/a[i].w
            println("select " + r + " of object " + a[i].id)
            weight = C
        }
        i = i + 1
    }
}
```

In the worst case, the for loop and while loop each take time $\Theta(n)$, and optimal comparison-based sorting (e.g., mergesort or heapsort) takes time $\Theta(n \lg n)$. Thus Algorithm 7.6.2 runs in time $\Theta(n \lg n)$ in the worst case.

We show that Algorithm 7.6.2 is correct.

Theorem 7.6.3 Correctness of the Greedy Algorithm for the Continuous-Knapsack Problem. *Algorithm 7.6.2 yields a maximum profit for the continuous-knapsack problem.*

Proof. We assume that the sum of the weights of the objects exceeds the capacity of the knapsack; otherwise, Algorithm 7.6.2 selects all of the objects and surely gives a maximum profit.

Algorithm 7.6.2 first sorts the objects in nonincreasing order of ratio of profit to weight. Let x_i denote the portion of object i selected by Algorithm 7.6.2, and let P be the total profit obtained. Consider an arbitrary solution in which x_i' is the portion of object i chosen and P' is the total profit obtained. We show that $P' \leq P$ thus proving the theorem.

Since

$$\sum_{i=1}^{n} x_i' w_i \leq C = \sum_{i=1}^{n} x_i w_i,$$

we have

$$0 \leq \sum_{i=1}^{n} (x_i - x_i') w_i. \tag{7.6.1}$$

Let k be the smallest index with $x_k < 1$. First, consider $i < k$. Because Algorithm 7.6.2 picks all of object i, $x_i = 1$. Therefore

$$x_i - x_i' \geq 0.$$

The objects are sorted in nonincreasing order of ratio of profit to weight, so

$$\frac{p_i}{w_i} \geq \frac{p_k}{w_k}.$$

Therefore

$$(x_i - x_i') \left(\frac{p_i}{w_i} \right) \geq (x_i - x_i') \left(\frac{p_k}{w_k} \right)$$

for all $i < k$.

If $i = k$, then

$$(x_i - x_i') \left(\frac{p_i}{w_i} \right) \geq (x_i - x_i') \left(\frac{p_k}{w_k} \right).$$

Finally, suppose that $i > k$. Because Algorithm 7.6.2 picks none of these objects, $x_i = 0$. Therefore

$$x_i - x_i' \leq 0.$$

The objects are sorted in nonincreasing order of ratio of profit to weight, so

$$\frac{p_i}{w_i} \leq \frac{p_k}{w_k}.$$

Therefore

$$(x_i - x_i') \left(\frac{p_i}{w_i} \right) \geq (x_i - x_i') \left(\frac{p_k}{w_k} \right)$$

for all $i > k$.

It follows that for all i, we have

$$(x_i - x_i') \left(\frac{p_i}{w_i} \right) \geq (x_i - x_i') \left(\frac{p_k}{w_k} \right). \tag{7.6.2}$$

Therefore

$$P - P' = \sum_{i=1}^{n} (x_i - x_i')p_i$$

$$= \sum_{i=1}^{n} (x_i - x_i')w_i \left(\frac{p_i}{w_i}\right)$$

$$\geq \sum_{i=1}^{n} (x_i - x_i')w_i \left(\frac{p_k}{w_k}\right) \quad \text{by (7.6.2)}$$

$$= \left(\frac{p_k}{w_k}\right) \sum_{i=1}^{n} (x_i - x_i')w_i$$

$$\geq 0 \quad \text{by (7.6.1)}$$

and the theorem is proved.   ■

Exercises

In Exercises 1–3, solve the continuous-knapsack problem for the given weights, profits, and knapsack capacity. Tell which objects are chosen and give the maximum profit.

1S. $w_1 = 120$, $w_2 = 150$, $w_3 = 200$; $p_1 = 5$, $p_2 = 5$, $p_3 = 4$; $C = 300$

2. $w_1 = 12$, $w_2 = 15$, $w_3 = 20$, $w_4 = 15$; $p_1 = 4$, $p_2 = 3$, $p_3 = 6$, $p_4 = 8$; $C = 50$

3. $w_1 = 20$, $w_2 = 50$, $w_3 = 60$, $w_4 = 15$, $w_5 = 20$, $w_6 = 30$; $p_1 = 2$, $p_2 = 3$, $p_3 = 4$, $p_4 = 4$, $p_5 = 1$, $p_6 = 6$; $C = 140$

4S. What is maximized for the continuous-knapsack problem if $p_i = 1$ for all i?

5. Consider a greedy rule for the continuous-knapsack problem that selects the objects in nondecreasing order of weight. We take all of the object if the capacity of the knapsack is not exceeded. If the capacity of the knapsack would be exceeded, we take whatever portion of the object fills the knapsack and stop. Give an example to show that this greedy algorithm does not necessarily maximize the profit.

6. Consider a greedy rule for the continuous-knapsack problem that selects the objects in nonincreasing order of profit. We take all of the object if the capacity of the knapsack is not exceeded. If the capacity of the knapsack would be exceeded, we take whatever portion of the object fills the knapsack and stop. Give an example to show that this greedy algorithm does not necessarily maximize the profit.

7S. Give an example to show that the greedy algorithm of this section, suitably modified for the 0/1-knapsack problem, does *not* necessarily maximize the profit. (Exercise 8.13 is to give a *dynamic-programming* algorithm that *does* solve the 0/1-knapsack problem optimally.)

8. Suppose that one attempts, by imitating the proof of Theorem 7.6.3, to *prove* that the greedy algorithm of this section, suitably modified for the 0/1-knapsack problem, maximizes the profit. Where does the argument fail?

Notes

Standard references on greedy algorithms are Lawler, 1976, and Papadimitriou, 1982.

Tarjan, 1983, presents minimal-spanning-tree algorithms and their implementations. Kruskal discovered his algorithm (Kruskal, 1956) while in graduate school. Prim's algorithm was published as Prim, 1957, but it was previously discovered by V. Jarnik in 1930.

Dijkstra's shortest-path algorithm is in Dijkstra, 1959. In this paper, Dijkstra also discusses Prim's algorithm.

Huffman's algorithm (Huffman, 1952) was the subject of his master's thesis at MIT.

Chapter Exercises

7.1. Show that Algorithm 7.1.1 is optimal for all A for the denominations

$$d_1 > d_2 > \cdots > d_n = 1$$

if and only if it is optimal for all A satisfying $1 \le A < d_1 + d_2$.

7.2. Show that the value $d_1 + d_2$ in Exercise 7.1 is the best possible; that is, give a counterexample to show that if $d_1 + d_2$ is replaced by $d_1 + d_2 - 1$, the result is false.

7.3. Given the denominations

$$d_1 > d_2 > \cdots > d_n = 1,$$

where $n > 1$, suppose that Algorithm 7.1.1 is optimal for the denominations $d_2, \ldots, d_n$. Let q be the quotient when d_1 is divided by d_2. Let $p = q + 1$, and let $\delta = p d_2 - d_1$. Let g denote the number of coins used by Algorithm 7.1.1 to make change for $A = \delta$. Show that Algorithm 7.1.1 is optimal for the denominations $d_1, \ldots, d_n$ if and only if

$$1 + g \le p.$$

This result is due to Magazine, Nemhauser, and Trotter.

7.4. A private plane flying from Los Angeles to St. Louis must stop periodically to refuel. Develop a greedy algorithm to minimize the number of stops, and prove that your algorithm is optimal.

7.5. The *activity-selection problem* is: Given n activities and their starting and finishing times, find a subset of k nonconflicting activities with k as large as possible. Two activities *conflict* if there is a point in time when both are active. More precisely, if one activity starts at time s_1 and finishes at time f_1, and a second activity starts at time s_2 and finishes at time f_2, they conflict if either $s_1 < s_2 < f_1$ or $s_2 < s_1 < f_2$. Develop a greedy algorithm to solve the activity-selection problem, and prove that your algorithm is optimal. What is the worst-case time of your algorithm?

7.6. Suppose that we are given n tasks each of which takes the same amount of time to complete. Suppose further that each task has a deadline by which it is supposed to finish and a penalty that is accessed if the task does not finish by the deadline. The problem is to find a schedule of all of the tasks that minimizes the total penalty. Develop a greedy algorithm to solve this problem, and prove that your algorithm is optimal. What is the worst-case time of your algorithm?

7.7. Suppose that n programs having lengths $L_1, \ldots, L_n$ are stored on a tape. If the programs are stored in the order $i_1, \ldots, i_n$, the time to retrieve program i_k is

$$T_k = \sum_{j=1}^{k} L_{i_j}.$$

(We assume that retrieval starts at the beginning of the tape. The formula results from the fact that in order to retrieve program i_k, we must pass all of the programs stored before program i_k.) The *average retrieval time* (i.e., the average time to retrieve each program one time) is defined as

$$\frac{1}{n} \sum_{k=1}^{n} T_k.$$

Develop a greedy algorithm to minimize the average retrieval time, and prove that your algorithm is optimal. What is the worst-case time of your algorithm?

In Exercises 7.8–7.11, a problem is given for which no polynomial-time algorithm is known. Develop a greedy algorithm for each problem, which may or may not always give an optimal solution. Analyze the worst-case time of your algorithm. Does your algorithm always yield an optimal solution? If so, prove it; it not, give example input for which your algorithm is not optimal. If your algorithm is optimal and runs in polynomial time, you are immediately famous.

7.8. Vertex-Cover Problem. A *vertex cover* of a graph $G = (V, E)$ is a subset W of V such that for each edge $(v, w) \in E$, either $v \in W$ or $w \in W$. The *size* of a vertex cover W is the number of vertices in W. Given a graph, find a vertex cover of minimum size.

7.9. Bin-Packing Problem. Given n objects of sizes $s_1, \ldots, s_n$, where $0 < s_i \leq 1$, find the smallest number of bins, each of capacity one, into which the objects can be packed.

7.10. Subset-Sum Problem. Given n positive integers $s_1, \ldots, s_n$ and a positive integer C, what is the largest sum $S \leq C$ of a subsequence of $s_1, \ldots, s_n$?

7.11. Traveling-Salesperson Problem. Given a weighted graph G, find a minimum-weight Hamiltonian cycle in G (see Section 2.5).

CHAPTER 8
Dynamic Programming

Dynamic programming is an algorithm design technique that resembles divide-and-conquer. The difference between the techniques is that dynamic programming typically provides many ways to divide the original problem into subproblems, but it is not evident which division will lead to a solution of the original problem. Therefore, dynamic programming solves all subproblems that might potentially be needed. To avoid solving the same subproblems over and over, once the solution to a subproblem is computed, it is stored in a table. When a solution to a subproblem is needed, instead of recomputing the solution, the algorithm obtains it from the table. A dynamic-programming algorithm computes the simplest subproblems first and then works its way up to the original problem.

To illustrate the design of a dynamic-programming algorithm, in Section 8.1 we derive an algorithm to compute the Fibonacci numbers. In Section 8.2, we revisit the coin-changing problem from Section 7.1. The greedy algorithm of Section 7.1 did not always produce an optimal solution. We show how dynamic programming can be used to construct an algorithm that always produces an optimal solution. How matrices to be multiplied are grouped can greatly affect the number of scalar multiplications (i.e., the number of multiplications of the elements that make up the matrices). A dynamic-programming algorithm can efficiently find a grouping of the matrices that minimizes the number of scalar multiplications (see Section 8.3). The longest-common-subsequence problem, which is used to compare proteins, is discussed in Section 8.4. In Section 8.5, we discuss a dynamic-programming algorithm to solve the problem of finding a shortest path between each pair of vertices in a graph. A related problem, the transitive-closure problem, is also discussed in Section 8.5.

8.1 Computing Fibonacci Numbers

Recall (see Example 2.4.2) that the Fibonacci sequence, $f_1, f_2, \ldots$, is defined by the recurrence relation

$$f_n = f_{n-1} + f_{n-2}, \quad n \geq 3, \tag{8.1.1}$$

and initial conditions

$$f_1 = f_2 = 1.$$

A dynamic-programming algorithm to compute f_n begins by computing the simplest problems first, namely, f_1 and f_2. It then uses equation (8.1.1) to compute $f_3, \ldots, f_n$ in this order. After each f_i is computed, it is stored in an array, and, when a value is needed later, it is obtained from the array.

Algorithm 8.1.1 Computing the Fibonacci Numbers, Version 1. This dynamic-programming algorithm computes the Fibonacci number $f[n]$. It uses the formulas

$$f[1] = 1; \quad f[2] = 1; \quad f[n] = f[n-1] + f[n-2], \ n \geq 3.$$

At the conclusion of the algorithm, the array f holds the first n Fibonacci numbers.

Input Parameter: n
Output Parameters: None

```
fibonacci1(n) {
    // f is a local array
    f[1] = 1
    f[2] = 1
    for i = 3 to n
        f[i] = f[i − 1] + f[i − 2]
    return f[n]
}
```

Example 8.1.2. Figure 8.1.1 shows the array f computed by Algorithm 8.1.1 for $n = 5$. The algorithm first computes $f[1]$ and $f[2]$. It next computes $f[3]$ using the formula

$$f[3] = f[2] + f[1]$$

to obtain the value $f[3] = 2$. Notice that the values $f[2]$ and $f[1]$ have already been computed and stored in the array f.

1	1	2	3	5

Figure 8.1.1 The array f computed by Algorithm 8.1.1 for $n = 5$.

It next computes $f[4]$ using the formula

$$f[4] = f[3] + f[2]$$

to obtain the value $f[4] = 3$. Again, the values needed, $f[3]$ and $f[2]$, have already been computed and stored in the array f.

Finally, it computes $f[5]$ using the formula

$$f[5] = f[4] + f[3]$$

to obtain the value $f[5] = 5$. Again, the values needed, $f[4]$ and $f[3]$, have already been computed and stored in the array f. □

Because of the for loop, Algorithm 8.1.1 runs in time $\Theta(n)$. See Exercise 8.3 for an algorithm that computes the nth Fibonacci number using at most $O(\lg n)$ arithmetic operations.

Notice that, to compute the next Fibonacci number, Algorithm 8.1.1 uses only the *two* preceding Fibonacci numbers. Space can be saved by replacing the array f by two variables to hold the two preceding Fibonacci numbers (see Algorithm 8.1.3). It is frequently the case in a dynamic-programming algorithm that solutions to only certain subproblems are needed to solve the current problem.

Algorithm 8.1.3 Computing the Fibonacci Numbers, Version 2. This dynamic-programming algorithm computes the nth Fibonacci number. It uses the formulas $f_1 = 1$, $f_2 = 1$, and equation (8.1.1). It saves the two preceding Fibonacci numbers in the variables *f_twoback* and *f_oneback* in order to compute the next Fibonacci number.

Input Parameter: n
Output Parameters: None

```
fibonacci2(n) {
  if (n == 1)
    return 1
  if (n == 2)
    return 1
  f_twoback = 1
  f_oneback = 1
  for i = 3 to n {
    f = f_twoback + f_oneback
    f_twoback = f_oneback
    f_oneback = f
  }
  return f
}
```

Algorithm 8.1.3 also runs in time $\Theta(n)$.

The two algorithms for computing Fibonacci numbers that we have presented are iterative. However, recurrence relation (8.1.1) strongly suggests a *recursive* algorithm such as the following:

```
fibonacci_recurs(n) {
  if (n == 1)
    return 1
  if (n == 2)
    return 1
  return fibonacci_recurs(n − 2) + fibonacci_recurs(n − 1)
}
```

The preceding algorithm is obscenely inefficient. For example, to compute f_3 the algorithm recursively computes f_2 and f_1. In this case, each base case $n = 1, 2$ is computed once—for a total of two computations for the base cases. However, to compute f_4, the algorithm recursively computes f_3 and f_2. To compute f_3, two computations are required for the base cases. Since f_2 is computed again, to compute f_4, three computations are required for the base cases. The situation gets worse as n increases. To compute f_5, the algorithm recursively computes f_4 and f_3. To compute f_4, three computations are required for the base cases, and to compute f_3, two computations are required for the base cases. Thus, to compute f_5, five computations are required for the base cases. In general, when *fibonacci_recurs* computes f_n, f_n computations are required for the base cases (see Exercise 7). (Other subproblems are also recomputed.) Since

$$f_n > \left(\frac{3}{2}\right)^{n-1}$$

for $n \geq 6$ (see Exercise 8, Section 2.4), an unoptimized version of *fibonacci_recurs* runs in exponential time. (A clever *optimized* version of the algorithm might remove some or all of these redundant computations.) Comparing *fibonacci_recurs* to the two iterative versions points us to a potential problem in the divide-and-conquer approach: After division, we solve (conquer) each subproblem separately. When computing f_n as the sum of f_{n-1} and f_{n-2}, the recursive computation of f_{n-1} wastefully duplicates the computation of f_{n-2}. By contrast, the iterative version stores the value of f_{n-2} and reuses it in the computation of f_{n-1} and f_n without recomputing it. The dynamic-programming algorithms (Algorithms 8.1.1 and 8.1.3) gain efficiency by computing each subproblem only one time.

Dynamic programming should be considered if a problem (e.g., computing f_n) can be divided into subproblems that overlap, in the sense that information computed for one subproblem can be used for another subproblem as well (e.g., the value of f_{n-2} can be used in the computation of f_{n-1}). The essence of dynamic programming is a division of a problem into subproblems such that the subproblems have *substantial* overlap, which leads to a small number of subproblems. For example, *fibonacci_recurs*(n) generates an exponential number of recursive calls, whereas there are fewer than n subproblems to solve, namely the computations of $f_1, \ldots, f_{n-1}$.

Memoization

We will see several examples of how to use dynamic programming in the following sections. Here we want to discuss a general technique called **memoization** that attempts to relieve the potential inefficiency of recursion by using the basic idea of dynamic programming. Memoization does not obviate the need to find a good way to break a problem into subproblems, but if that has been achieved (or is immediate, as in the Fibonacci example), it allows us to write a recursive solution. We first add a table that is indexed by the possible inputs to the recursive function. We then change the code of the recursive function so that it first checks whether the value of the function for the requested input is already stored in the table. If the value is stored in the table, we simply return it (without recomputing it); otherwise, we call the function recursively and then add the value to the table for future reference. For example, a memoized version of *fibonacci_recurs* is:

```
memoized_fibonacci(n) {
    for i = 1 to n
        results[i] = −1 // −1 means undefined
    return memoized_fibonacci_recurs(results, n)
}

memoized_fibonacci_recurs(results, n) {
    if (results[n] != −1)
        return results[n]
    if (n == 1)
        val = 1
    else if (n == 2)
        val = 1
    else {
        val = memoized_fibonacci_recurs(results, n − 2)
        val = val + memoized_fibonacci_recurs(results, n − 1)
    }
    results[n] = val
    return val
}
```

Exercise 12 is to show that *memoized_fibonacci* runs in time $\Theta(n)$.

Functional programming languages and object-oriented programming languages would allow even more elegant solutions using higher-order functionals and classes.

Exercises

In Exercises 1–3, show the array computed by Algorithm 8.1.1 for the value given.

1S. $n = 6$ **2.** $n = 7$ **3.** $n = 8$

In Exercises 4–6, trace Algorithm 8.1.3 for the value given.

4S. $n = 4$ **5.** $n = 5$ **6.** $n = 6$

7S. Prove that when *fibonacci_recurs* computes f_n, $n \geq 3$, f_n computations are required for the base cases.

8. A robot can take steps of 1 meter or 2 meters. Let r_n denote the number of ways the robot can walk n meters. (Order is taken into account so that the 4-meter walk $1, 2, 1$ is considered distinct from the 4-meter walk $1, 1, 2$.) Prove that $r_n = f_{n+1}$ for all $n \geq 2$, where f_n is the nth Fibonacci number.

9. A robot can take steps of 1 meter or 2 meters. Write an algorithm to output all of the ways the robot can walk n meters (with order taken into account).

10S. A robot can take steps of 1 meter, 2 meters, or 3 meters. Write a dynamic-programming algorithm to calculate the number of ways the robot can walk n meters (with order taken into account).

11. A robot can take steps of 1 meter, 2 meters, or 3 meters. Write an algorithm to output all of the ways the robot can walk n meters (with order taken into account).

12. Show that *memoized_fibonacci* runs in time $\Theta(n)$.

13S. What is the running time of *memoized_fibonacci* if the lines

$$val = memoized\_fibonacci\_recurs(results, n - 2)$$
$$val = val + memoized\_fibonacci\_recurs(results, n - 1)$$

are changed to

$$val = memoized\_fibonacci\_recurs(results, n - 1)$$
$$val = val + memoized\_fibonacci\_recurs(results, n - 2)$$

8.2 Coin Changing Revisited

In Section 7.1, we developed a greedy algorithm for the coin-changing problem in which the goal was to make change for an amount A using the fewest number of coins, where the available denominations were

$$denom[1] > denom[2] > \cdots > denom[n] = 1.$$

We saw that whether the greedy algorithm produced the fewest number of coins depended on which denominations of coins were available. In this section, we develop a dynamic-programming algorithm for the coin-changing problem that produces the fewest number of coins no matter which denominations are available.

To break the given problem into subproblems, we vary the amount and restrict the denominations available. More precisely, we consider the problem of computing the minimum number of coins for an amount $j, 0 \leq j \leq A$, where the available denominations are

$$denom[i] > denom[i + 1] > \cdots > denom[n] = 1,$$

$1 \leq i \leq n$. We call this the i, j-*problem*. The original problem is $i = 1$ and $j = A$. We let $C[i][j]$ denote the solution to the i, j-problem; that is, $C[i][j]$ is the minimum number of coins to make change for the amount j, using coins i through n (see Figure 8.2.1). (We later address the problem of determining which coins achieve the minimum.)

		0	1	2	3	4	5	6	7	8	9	10	11	12
	1	0	1	2	3	4	5	1	2	3	4	1	2	2
i	2	0	1	2	3	4	5	1	2	3	4	5	6	2
	3	0	1	2	3	4	5	6	7	8	9	10	11	12

(column header label: j)

Figure 8.2.1 The array C for the denominations $denom[1] = 10$, $denom[2] = 6$, and $denom[3] = 1$ and amounts up to 12. The index i specifies that coins i through 3 are available, and j is the amount. When $i = 3$, only the coin of denomination 1 is available. Thus, in the last row, it takes j coins to make change for the amount j. When $i = 2$, the coins 6 and 1 are available. For example, the minimum number of coins to make change for the amount 8 is three—one coin of denomination 6 and two coins of denomination 1. When $i = 1$, all of the coins are available. For example, the minimum number of coins to make change for the amount 11 is two—one coin of denomination 10 and one coin of denomination 1.

To solve the i, j-problem, $i < n$, we must decide whether to use a coin of denomination $denom[i]$. If we do *not* use a coin of denomination $denom[i]$, in order to achieve the amount j, we must solve the $(i + 1), j$ problem. Since this is a subproblem (i.e., a smaller problem in the sense that fewer coins are available), we can design our algorithm so that this subproblem is already solved. Thus, given that we do not use coin i, the minimum number of coins to make change for the amount j is $C[i + 1][j]$.

On the other hand, if we use a coin of denomination $denom[i]$, we must complete the solution by making change for the amount $j - denom[i]$ using coins of denominations

$$denom[i] > denom[i + 1] > \cdots > denom[n] = 1.$$

If we use, say, k coins for the amount $j - denom[i]$, our solution to the problem of making change for the amount j uses $1 + k$ coins (since we already used one coin of denomination $denom[i]$). To minimize $1 + k$, we must choose k as small as possible. In other words, we must use the minimum number of coins to solve the subproblem of making change for the amount $j - denom[i]$ using coins i through n. (This is an example of the *optimal substructure property*, which we discuss thoroughly later in this section.) Therefore, we must solve the $i, (j - denom[i])$-problem. Since this is also a subproblem (i.e., a smaller problem in the sense that the amount is smaller than j), we can also design our algorithm so that this subproblem is already solved. Thus, given that we do use coin i, the minimum number of coins to make change for the amount j is $1 + C[i][j - denom[i]]$.

Now, either we use coin i or we don't! Thus, the solution to the i, j problem is

$$C[i][j] = \begin{cases} C[i+1][j] & \text{if } denom[i] > j \\ \min\{C[i+1][j], 1 + C[i][j - denom[i]]\} & \text{if } denom[i] \leq j. \end{cases}$$

(8.2.1)

Contrast the dynamic-programming algorithm outlined in the preceding paragraphs with the greedy algorithm in Section 7.1. When the greedy algorithm considers using a denomination d for an amount j, if $d \leq j$, it uses it—without regard to the consequences of solving the smaller problem of making change for the amount $d - j$. For example, if the available denominations are 10, 6, and 1 and the amount is 12, the greedy algorithm chooses one 10—without regard to the fact that the resulting problem of making change for the amount 2 requires two coins. The greedy algorithm thus chooses one 10 and two 1's. On the other hand, the dynamic-programming algorithm considers using denomination d and not using it and picks the better alternative. In this sense, dynamic programming can be considered an enhancement of the greedy technique. Again, if the available denominations are 10, 6, and 1 and the amount is 12, the dynamic-programming algorithm *considers* choosing a 10. Since this leaves the problem of making change for the amount 2, *if* the dynamic-programming algorithm chooses a 10, three coins will be required to make change for the amount 12: one 10 and two 1's. The dynamic-programming algorithm also considers not choosing a 10. In this case, the algorithm will make change for the amount 12 using only the denominations 1 and 6, and the optimal choice is to use two 6's. Since choosing two 6's results in fewer coins than using a 10, the dynamic-programming algorithm chooses two 6's.

Our dynamic-programming algorithm begins by computing $C[n][j]$ for $j = 0$ to the specified amount A. Since only the coin of denomination 1 is available,

$$C[n][j] = j \tag{8.2.2}$$

for $j = 0$ to A. After computing $C[i+1][j]$ for all j, it computes $C[i][j]$ in the order $j = 0$ to A using equation (8.2.1).

Algorithm 8.2.1 Coin Changing Using Dynamic Programming, Version 1.
This dynamic-programming algorithm computes the minimum number of coins to make change for a given amount. The input is an array *denom* that specifies the denominations of the coins,

$$denom[1] > denom[2] > \cdots > denom[n] = 1,$$

and an amount A. The output is an array C whose value, $C[i][j]$, is the minimum number of coins to make change for the amount j, using coins i through n, $1 \leq i \leq n$, $0 \leq j \leq A$.

Input Parameters: *denom, A*
Output Parameter: C

```
dynamic_coin_change1(denom, A, C) {
  n = denom.last
  for j = 0 to A
    C[n][j] = j
  for i = n − 1 downto 1
    for j = 0 to A
      if (denom[i] > j || C[i + 1][j] < 1 + C[i][j − denom[i]])
        C[i][j] = C[i + 1][j]
      else
        C[i][j] = 1 + C[i][j − denom[i]]
}
```

In Algorithm 8.2.1, the first for loop runs in time $\Theta(A)$ and the nested for loops run in time $\Theta(nA)$. Therefore, the run time of Algorithm 8.2.1 is $\Theta(nA)$.

As written, Algorithm 8.2.1 determines the minimum number of coins but does not tell us which coins to use to achieve the minimum. We can determine which coins to use by adding a statement to Algorithm 8.2.1 that records whether coin i is used to make change for the amount j. (We can determine which coins to use without an auxiliary array by examining the array C; see Exercise 7. Here we prefer to show how to use an auxiliary array since this method has wider applicability.)

Algorithm 8.2.2 Coin Changing Using Dynamic Programming, Version 2.
This dynamic-programming algorithm computes the minimum number of coins to make change for a given amount and tracks which coins are used. The input is an array *denom* that specifies the denominations of the coins,

$$denom[1] > denom[2] > \cdots > denom[n] = 1,$$

and an amount A. The output consists of arrays C and *used*. The value, $C[i][j]$, is the minimum number of coins to make change for the amount j, using coins i through n. The value, $used[i][j]$, is true or false to signify whether coin i appears in the smallest set of coins computed by Algorithm 8.2.1 for the amount j using only coins i through n. The values of i and j satisfy $1 \le i \le n$ and $0 \le j \le A$.

Input Parameters: *denom, A*
Output Parameters: *C, used*

```
dynamic_coin_change2(denom, A, C, used) {
  n = denom.last
  for j = 0 to A {
    C[n][j] = j
    used[n][j] = true
  }
```

```
    for i = n − 1 downto 1
      for j = 0 to A
        if (denom[i] > j || C[i + 1][j] < 1 + C[i][j − denom[i]]) {
          C[i][j] = C[i + 1][j]
          used[i][j] = false
        }
        else {
          C[i][j] = 1 + C[i][j − denom[i]]
          used[i][j] = true
        }
}
```

Example 8.2.3. The *used* array computed by Algorithm 8.2.2 for the denominations 10, 6, and 1 and amount $A = 12$ is shown in Figure 8.2.2.

								j						
		0	1	2	3	4	5	6	7	8	9	10	11	12
	1	F	F	F	F	F	F	F	F	F	F	T	T	F
i	2	F	F	F	F	F	F	T	T	T	T	T	T	T
	3	T	T	T	T	T	T	T	T	T	T	T	T	T

Figure 8.2.2 The *used* array computed by Algorithm 8.2.2 for the denominations 10, 6, and 1 and amount $A = 12$. $used[i][j]$ is true (T) or false (F) to signify whether coin i appears in the smallest set of coins computed by Algorithm 8.2.1 for the amount j using only coins i through n. For example, $used[1][11]$ is true because the minimum set of coins $\{10, 1\}$ for the amount 11 uses a coin of denomination 10. By contrast, $used[1][12]$ is false because the minimum set of coins $\{6, 6\}$ for the amount 12 does not use a coin of denomination 10. □

We can now write an algorithm to output a minimum size set of coins chosen from among coins i through n for an amount j. The algorithm inputs the index i, the amount j, the array *denom* of Algorithm 8.2.2, and the array *used* computed by Algorithm 8.2.2.

Algorithm 8.2.4 Computing a Minimum-Size Set of Coins for a Given Amount. This algorithm outputs a minimum-size set of coins to make change for an amount j using any of coins i through n with denominations specified by Algorithm 8.2.2. The algorithm inputs the index i, the amount j, the array *denom* of Algorithm 8.2.2, and the array *used* computed by Algorithm 8.2.2.

Input Parameters: i, j, *denom*, *used*
Output Parameters: None

```
optimal_coins_set(i, j, denom, used) {
  if (j == 0)
    return
```

```
    if (used[i][j]) {
        println("Use a coin of denomination " + denom[i])
        optimal_coins_set(i, j − denom[i], denom, used)
    }
    else
        optimal_coins_set(i + 1, j, denom, used)
}
```

Algorithm 8.2.4 terminates correctly. Each time the algorithm is called with $j > 0$, either i is incremented by 1 or j is decremented at least by 1. If j becomes 0 before $i = n$, the algorithm terminates correctly. If $i = n$ and $j > 0$, $used[i][j]$ is true so j continually decrements by 1 until it is 0, and the algorithm also terminates correctly.

When Algorithm 8.2.4 is called as

$$optimal\_coins\_set(1, A, denom, used)$$

j can be decremented at most A times and i can be incremented at most $n − 1$ times. Thus, the run time of Algorithm 8.2.4 with $i = 1$ and $j = A$, which outputs a minimum size set of coins chosen from among all available denominations to make change for the amount A, is $O(n + A)$.

Constructing a Dynamic-Programming Algorithm

To construct a dynamic-programming algorithm, the first step is to break the given problem into subproblems using *parameters* to characterize the subproblems. The solution to the original problem will be built from these subproblems. The parameters control the size of the subproblems, and small problem sizes *must* be included. The dynamic-programming algorithm will begin by solving small subproblems and end with a solution to the original problem. For example, to compute the nth Fibonacci number f_n (see Section 8.1), f_n is given in terms of smaller subproblems f_{n-1} and f_{n-2}. The parameter is the subscript. In this section, to compute the minimum number of coins, we broke the problem of making change for an amount A using the fewest number of coins, where the available denominations are

$$denom[1] > denom[2] > \cdots > denom[n] = 1,$$

into subproblems of making change for an amount j using the fewest number of coins, where the available denominations are

$$denom[i] > denom[2] > \cdots > denom[n] = 1.$$

The parameter i varies the number of coins available, and the parameter j varies the amount.

After defining the subproblems, we define the desired quantity to be computed in terms of the parameters. To compute the Fibonacci sequence, the quantity to compute was, in effect, already defined—namely f_n. For the coin-changing problem, we defined $C[i][j]$ to be the minimum number of coins for the i, j-problem.

The next step is to obtain initial conditions and a recurrence relation for the desired quantity. To compute the nth Fibonacci number, we used the recurrence relation

$$f_n = f_{n-1} + f_{n-2}$$

valid for $n \geq 3$, and initial conditions

$$f_1 = f_2 = 1.$$

To compute the minimum number of coins, $C[i][j]$, we used the recurrence relation (8.2.1) and initial conditions (8.2.2).

A dynamic-programming algorithm computes the values of the sequence defined by the recurrence relation and initial conditions. It does so bottom up; that is, it first uses the initial conditions to compute the trivial cases. It then uses the recurrence relation to compute the next easiest cases, then the next easiest cases, and so on, until it computes the solution to the original problem.

To compute the nth Fibonacci number, the dynamic-programming algorithm first computed f_1 and f_2. The algorithm then computed f_3, then f_4, and so on, until it computed the solution f_n to the original problem.

To compute the minimum number of coins, the dynamic-programming algorithm first computed $C[n][j]$ for all j using the initial conditions (one denomination available). The algorithm then computed the next easiest cases $C[n-1][j]$ for all j using the recurrence relation (two denominations available). It then computed the next easiest cases $C[n-2][j]$ for all j (three denominations available), and so on, until it computed the solution $C[1][A]$ to the original problem (all denominations available).

Dynamic programming is most often used to solve an optimization problem. An *optimization problem* is a problem that asks for the largest or smallest value meeting some specified criteria. To compute the instance that gives an optimal solution, the algorithm may track the indexes that lead to optimal solutions of subproblems. For example, to compute the minimum number of coins and to construct a set of coins that gives this minimum value, the dynamic-programming algorithm tracked the coins that gave the minimum values (see Algorithm 8.2.2).

The Optimal Substructure Property

The **optimal substructure property** is

> *If S is an optimal solution to a problem, then the components of S are optimal solutions to subproblems.*

In order for a dynamic-programming algorithm to solve an optimization problem correctly, the optimal substructure property *must* hold.

Example 8.2.5. The optimal substructure property holds for the coin-changing problem. Given available denominations of coins, if S is a minimum size set of coins for an amount A and we remove one coin of denomination d from S, then S, with this coin removed, is a minimum size set of coins for the amount $A - d$.   □

The optimal substructure property does *not* say that if S_1 and S_2 are optimal solutions to subproblems, then combining S_1 and S_2 gives an optimal solution to the original problem. This is the *converse* of the optimal substructure property.

Example 8.2.6. Suppose that the available denominations are 10, 6, and 1 for the coin-changing problem. One coin of denomination 1 and one coin of denomination 6 give an optimal solution for the amount 7. Five coins of denomination 1 give an optimal solution for the amount 5. Combining these solutions, which results in six coins of denomination 1 and one coin of denomination 6, does *not* yield an optimal solution for the amount 12. Thus, for the coin-changing problem, if S_1 and S_2 are optimal solutions to subproblems, combining S_1 and S_2 does not necessarily give an optimal solution to the original problem; the converse of the optimal substructure property does *not* hold for the coin-changing problem. As we observed earlier, the optimal substructure property *does* hold for this problem. □

We close with an example of a problem for which the optimal substructure property does *not* hold.

Example 8.2.7. We show that the optimal substructure property does *not* hold for the *longest-simple-path problem*: Given a connected, weighted graph G and vertices v and w in G, find a longest simple path in G from v to w (a *simple path* is a path with no repeated vertices). Assume that all of the weights in G are positive.

By inspection, a longest simple path in the graph of Figure 8.2.3 from vertex 1 to vertex 4 is $1, 3, 4$. *If* the optimal substructure property holds for the longest-simple-path problem, then $1, 3$ is a longest simple path from 1 to 3. But $1, 3$ is *not* a longest simple path from 1 to 4 because $1, 2, 4, 3$ is longer. Therefore, the optimal substructure property does not hold for the longest-simple-path problem.

Figure 8.2.3 A graph that shows that the optimal substructure property does not hold for the longest-simple-path problem. A longest simple path from vertex 1 to vertex 4 is $1, 3, 4$, but $1, 3$ is *not* a longest simple path from vertex 1 to vertex 3.

It can be shown that the longest-simple-path problem is **NP**-complete and is, therefore, unlikely to have a polynomial-time algorithm. □

Exercises

In Exercises 1–3, show the array C computed by Algorithm 8.2.1 for the given denominations and the amount A = 12.

1S. $10, 5, 1$ **2.** $10, 3, 1$ **3.** $10, 7, 1$

In Exercises 4–6, show the array used computed by Algorithm 8.2.2 for the given denominations and the amount A = 12.

4S. $10, 5, 1$ **5.** $10, 4, 1$ **6.** $10, 3, 1$

7S. Write an algorithm whose input is an index $i \leq n$, an amount $j \leq A$, the array *denom*, and the array C, and whose output is a minimal set of coins to make change for the amount j. Algorithm 8.2.1 describes i, n, A, *denom*, and C. What is the worst-case time of your algorithm?

8. Write a version of Algorithm 8.2.1 in which the output is a *one*-dimensional array C' in which $C'[j]$ is equal to the minimum number of coins for the amount j using all available coins (i.e., $C'[j] = C[1][j]$ for all j, where C is the output of Algorithm 8.2.1). Your algorithm must use only $O(n)$ storage cells. What is the worst-case time of your algorithm?

9. Show that the optimal substructure property holds for the shortest-path problem: Given a connected, weighted graph G and vertices v and w in G, find a shortest path in G from v to w. Assume that all of the weights in G are positive.

10S. Show that the converse of the optimal substructure property does not hold for the shortest-path problem.

11. Does the converse of the optimal substructure property hold for the longest-simple-path problem?

8.3 Multiplying Matrices

A large numeric application needs to calculate the product ABC, where A, B, and C are matrices. Matrix A is 300×200 (i.e., A has 300 rows and 200 columns); B is 200×100; and C is 100×300. We use the definition of matrix multiplication to compute the product of two matrices: If S is an $m \times k$ matrix and T is a $k \times n$ matrix, the entry in row i, column j, of the product U of S and T is

$$U[i][j] = \sum_{p=1}^{k} S[i][p] * T[p][j],$$

where $M[i][j]$ denotes the entry in row i, column j, of matrix M. We call the multiplication of entries in matrices such as $S[i][p] * T[p][j]$ **scalar**

multiplication. Thus, it takes k scalar multiplications to compute one entry in the product U. Since U is $m \times n$, the total number of scalar multiplications to compute the product is mkn.

We may compute the product ABC in two ways: $(AB)C$ or $A(BC)$. The result is the same (matrix multiplication is *associative*), but the number of scalar multiplications may differ substantially. For the grouping $(AB)C$, we first compute AB. Since A is 300×200 and B is 200×100, it takes

$$300 \cdot 200 \cdot 100 = 6{,}000{,}000$$

scalar multiplications to compute AB. Since AB is 300×100 and C is 100×300, it takes

$$300 \cdot 100 \cdot 300 = 9{,}000{,}000$$

scalar multiplications to compute $(AB)C$ after computing AB. Thus, it takes

$$6{,}000{,}000 + 9{,}000{,}000 = 15{,}000{,}000$$

scalar multiplications altogether to compute $(AB)C$.

For the grouping $A(BC)$, we first compute BC. Since B is 200×100 and C is 100×300, it takes

$$200 \cdot 100 \cdot 300 = 6{,}000{,}000$$

scalar multiplications to compute BC. Since A is 300×200 and BC is 200×300, it takes

$$300 \cdot 200 \cdot 300 = 18{,}000{,}000$$

scalar multiplications to compute $A(BC)$ after computing BC. Thus, it takes

$$6{,}000{,}000 + 18{,}000{,}000 = 24{,}000{,}000$$

scalar multiplications altogether to compute $A(BC)$. We see that computing the product as $(AB)C$ rather than $A(BC)$ reduces the number of scalar multiplications by 9,000,000—a significant improvement!

The general problem is: Given n matrices

$$M_{r_1,c_1}, M_{r_2,c_2}, \ldots, M_{r_n,c_n}$$

to be multiplied in this order, determine how to group the matrices so that the number of scalar multiplications is minimized. We denote a matrix with r_i rows and c_i columns as M_{r_i,c_i}.

We first note that to list all possible groupings and pick the one that uses the fewest scalar multiplications becomes highly inefficient when the number n of matrices grows. It can be shown that the number of groupings of n matrices is at least $4^{n-2}/(n-1)^2$ (see Exercise 11), so even for relatively small values of n, the number of groupings is large.

Suppose that we divide the original problem involving n matrices into two subproblems consisting of the first k matrices followed by the last $n-k$ matrices. We could then multiply the first k matrices to obtain a matrix M'

and then multiply the last $n - k$ matrices to obtain a matrix M''. Finally, we could multiply M' by M'' to obtain the solution.

While the preceding outline of an algorithm is promising, a couple of issues must be resolved. The first question is how to group the first k matrices and how to group the last $n - k$ matrices. The answer is that we should group the first k matrices optimally and we should also group the last $n - k$ matrices optimally—the optimal substructure property holds. (The final matrix multiplication $M'M''$ takes the same number of scalar multiplications regardless of how the matrices M' and M'' are computed, so the only way to optimize the total number of scalar multiplications is to optimize the calculation of M' and M''.) The optimal solutions to the subproblems will be readily at hand—we are using *dynamic programming*, and the solutions will have already been calculated and stored in a table.

A second question is how to determine k. The solution is to calculate the optimum number of scalar multiplications for *all* k and choose the minimum. It may seem as if we have come full circle and are calculating all possibilities, which requires exponential time. What saves us from exponential time is that, since we store solutions to subproblems, we do not repeatedly solve the same subproblems. As an example, for the problem

$$M_{5,3}M_{3,1}M_{1,4}M_{4,6},$$

using the dynamic-programming algorithm to compute the number of scalar multiplications for the grouping

$$((M_{5,3}M_{3,1})M_{1,4})M_{4,6},$$

we will need the number of scalar multiplications to compute $M_{5,3}M_{3,1}$. This value will have already been calculated *once* and stored. When we compute the number of scalar multiplications for the grouping

$$(M_{5,3}M_{3,1})(M_{1,4}M_{4,6}),$$

we again need to know the number of scalar multiplications to compute $M_{5,3}M_{3,1}$. Again we consult the table to obtain this value; we do *not* calculate it again.

To obtain our dynamic-programming algorithm, we let s_{ij} denote the minimum number of scalar multiplications to compute the product

$$M_{r_i,c_i}, M_{r_{i+1},c_{i+1}}, \ldots, M_{r_j,c_j}.$$

Notice that s_{1n}, the minimum number of scalar multiplications for the original problem, solves the problem. The earlier discussion shows that if $i < j$,

$$s_{ij} = \min_{i \le k < j}\{s_{ik} + s_{k+1,j} + r_i c_k c_j\}.$$

We group matrices i through k and compute this product, and we group matrices $k + 1$ through j and compute this product. To compute the product of matrices i through j, we multiply the two matrices that result. The term s_{ik} is the minimum number of scalar multiplications to multiply matrices i through k; the term $s_{k+1,j}$ is the minimum number of scalar multiplications to multiply matrices $k + 1$ through j; and the term $r_i c_k c_j$ is the number of scalar multiplications to compute the product of the two matrices that result. The optimum value s_{ij} is obtained by minimizing over all possible values of k. Initial values of s_{ij} are obtained by setting s_{ii} to zero for all i.

The dynamic-programming algorithm for matrix multiplication simply computes s_{ij} for all i and j using the formulas we have derived.

Algorithm 8.3.1 Optimal Matrix Multiplication. This algorithm computes the minimum number of scalar multiplications to multiply a sequence of n matrices. The input is the array *size* that contains the sizes of the matrices to be multiplied. The first matrix is $size[0] \times size[1]$; the second is $size[1] \times size[2]$; and so on. The nth matrix is

$$size[n - 1] \times size[n].$$

The output is the array s whose value, $s[i][j]$, is the minimum number of scalar multiplications to multiply matrices i through j. The value ∞ is the largest available integer value.

Input Parameter: *size*
Output Parameter: *s*

```
opt_matrix_mult(size, s) {
    n = size.last
    for i = 1 to n
        s[i][i] = 0
    // w = j − i
    for w = 1 to n − 1
        for i = 1 to n − w {
            j = w + i
            s[i][j] = ∞
            for k = i to j − 1 {
                q = s[i][k] + s[k + 1][j] + size[i − 1] * size[k] * size[j]
                if (q < s[i][j])
                    s[i][j] = q
            }
        }
}
```

Each for loop runs in time $O(n)$. Since the last three for loops are nested, the algorithm runs in time $\Theta(n^3)$.

Example 8.3.2. We trace Algorithm 8.3.1 for the matrices

$$M_{5,3}, M_{3,1}, M_{1,4}, M_{4,6}.$$

The array *size* is

$$size[0] = 5,\ size[1] = 3,\ size[2] = 1,\ size[3] = 4,\ size[4] = 6.$$

The first for loop sets $s[i][i]$ equal to zero for $i = 1, 2, 3, 4$ (see Figure 8.3.1).

	1	2	3	4
1	0	15	35	69
2		0	12	42
3			0	24
4				0

(with j labeling the columns and i labeling the rows)

Figure 8.3.1 The values of $s[i][j]$ for the matrices of Example 8.3.2.

Next w is set to 1, and the algorithm computes the values of $s[1][2]$, $s[2][3]$, and $s[3][4]$. To compute $s[1][2]$, the algorithm first sets $s[1][2]$ to ∞. The value of q is

$$s[1][1] + s[2][2] + size[0] * size[1] * size[2] = 0 + 0 + 5 \cdot 3 \cdot 1 = 15.$$

(Notice that the values $s[1][1]$ and $s[2][2]$ are obtained from the previous computations.) Since q is less than ∞, $s[1][2]$ is correctly reset to 15. Since $s[1][2]$ is the minimum number of scalar multiplications needed to multiply the first two matrices, it now has the correct value; there is only one way to multiply two matrices! Similarly, the algorithm sets $s[2][3]$ to 12 and $s[3][4]$ to 24.

Next w is set to 2, and the algorithm computes the values of $s[1][3]$ and $s[2][4]$. To compute $s[1][3]$, the algorithm first sets $s[1][3]$ to ∞. The first value of q is

$$s[1][1] + s[2][3] + size[0] * size[1] * size[3] = 0 + 12 + 5 \cdot 3 \cdot 4 = 72.$$

Since q is less than ∞, $s[1][3]$ is reset to 72. The second value of q is

$$s[1][2] + s[3][3] + size[0] * size[2] * size[3] = 15 + 0 + 5 \cdot 1 \cdot 4 = 35.$$

Since q is less than 72, $s[1][3]$ is reset to its correct value 35. The minimum number of scalar multiplications needed to multiply the first three matrices, $s[1][3]$, is 35. Similarly, the algorithm sets $s[2][4]$ to 42.

Finally w is set to 3, and the algorithm computes the value of $s[1][4]$. To compute $s[1][4]$, the algorithm first sets $s[1][4]$ to ∞. The first value of q is

$$s[1][1] + s[2][4] + size[0] * size[1] * size[4] = 0 + 42 + 5 \cdot 3 \cdot 6 = 132.$$

Since q is less than ∞, $s[1][4]$ is reset to 132. The second value of q is

$$s[1][2] + s[3][4] + size[0] * size[2] * size[4] = 15 + 24 + 5 \cdot 1 \cdot 6 = 69.$$

Since q is less than 132, $s[1][4]$ is reset to 69. The third value of q is

$$s[1][3] + s[4][4] + size[0] * size[3] * size[4] = 35 + 0 + 5 \cdot 4 \cdot 6 = 155.$$

Since q is not less than 69, $s[1][4]$ remains 69. The minimum number of scalar multiplications needed to multiply the given matrices is 69.   □

As written, Algorithm 8.3.1 determines the minimum number of scalar multiplications but does not tell us how to group the matrices to achieve the minimum. Using the method demonstrated in Section 8.2 for the coin-changing problem, the optimal grouping can be determined by adding a statement to Algorithm 8.3.1 that records the value of k that gives the minimum for matrices i through j (see Exercises 6 and 7).

Exercises

In Exercises 1–3, show how Algorithm 8.3.1 computes the minimum number of scalar multiplications for the given matrices. Give the values of the array s.

1S. $M_{4,3} M_{3,5} M_{5,2}$

2. $M_{6,6} M_{6,3} M_{3,4} M_{4,4}$

3. $M_{2,2} M_{2,3} M_{3,4} M_{4,2} M_{2,5}$

4S. Find five sets of values of i, j, k, l, and m to demonstrate that a grouping of the matrices

$$M_{ij} M_{jk} M_{kl} M_{lm}$$

that minimizes the number of scalar multiplications can occur in any one of the five possible ways.

5. Give a counterexample to show that the following conjecture is false: To minimize the number of scalar multiplications of the product $M_1 \cdots M_n$, the matrices should be grouped as

$$(M_1 \cdots M_k)(M_{k+1} \cdots M_n),$$

where M_k has the minimum number of columns, $1 \le k < n$.

6S. Modify Algorithm 8.3.1 by adding a statement that stores in an array *index* the value of k that gives the minimum for matrices i through j.

7. Write an algorithm that uses the array *index* of your algorithm in Exercise 6 to output an optimal grouping of matrices i through j with parentheses properly inserted. For example, for the matrices $M_{5,3}, M_{3,1}, M_{1,4}, M_{4,6}$, and $i = 1$, $j = 4$, the output should be $((1 * 2) * (3 * 4))$. What is the worst-case time of your algorithm?

$\mathcal{WWW}$ *Exercises 8-11 involve the* Catalan numbers, $C_0, C_1, \ldots$, *which are defined by the recurrence relation*

$$C_n = \sum_{k=1}^{n} C_{k-1} C_{n-k}$$

for all $n \geq 1$, and initial condition

$$C_0 = 1.$$

The Catalan numbers are named for the Belgian mathematician Eugène-Charles Catalan (1814–1894), who discovered an elementary derivation of the formula given in Exercise 9. Catalan published numerous papers in analysis, combinatorics, algebra, geometry, probability, and number theory. In 1844, he conjectured that the only consecutive positive integers that are powers (i.e., i^j, where $j \geq 2$) are 8 and 9. Over 150 years later, Preda Mihailescu announced a proof (in 2002).

8S. Compute $C_1, \ldots, C_5$.

9. It can be shown (see, e.g., Johnsonbaugh, 2001, 180–181) that

$$C_n = \frac{(2n)!}{(n+1)n!n!}.$$

Using this formula or otherwise, prove that

$$C_n \geq \frac{4^{n-1}}{n^2}$$

for all $n \geq 1$.

10. Prove that the number of ways to group the product $M_1 \cdots M_n$, $n \geq 2$, is equal to C_{n-1}.

11S. Prove that the number of groupings of n matrices is at least $4^{n-2}/(n-1)^2$.

8.4 The Longest-Common-Subsequence Problem

$\mathcal{WWW}$ Proteins are essentially linear chains of amino acids, of which 20 occur frequently in nature. The *primary structure* of a protein is a sequence of characters representing its amino acids. The primary structure is obtained through DNA, which encodes each amino acid by a triplet of DNA base pairs (genetic code). Large databases of protein sequences have been assembled without a corresponding understanding of the function of the proteins. One approach to understanding an unknown protein is to compare its amino acid sequence with proteins whose functions are known; frequently, two proteins with similar sequences of amino acids are similar. "Similar" sequences are defined as those having a *long common subsequence*, and the algorithm used to find a long common subsequence is described in this section. For example, the sequence *GVET* is a subsequence of both *GDVEGTA* and *GVCEKST*. By inspection, no other common subsequence of *GDVEGTA* and *GVCEKST* has length greater than four. Therefore, *GVET* is a longest common subsequence of *GDVEGTA* and *GVCEKST*. In practice, penalties are introduced for gaps, the number of characters in the original sequences that are omitted to obtain the subsequences. We begin by stating the problem precisely.

The **longest-common-subsequence problem** is: Given two sequences

$$a[1], \ldots, a[m], \qquad b[1], \ldots, b[n],$$

find a longest common subsequence; that is, find a subsequence

$$a[i_1], \ldots, a[i_k]$$

of a and a subsequence

$$b[j_1], \ldots, b[j_k]$$

of b, with the same length, such that

$$a[i_1] = b[j_1], \ldots, a[i_k] = b[j_k]$$

with k as large as possible.

To construct a dynamic-programming algorithm to solve the longest-common-subsequence problem, we begin by expressing the length of the longest common subsequence of the original problem in terms of lengths of longest common subsequences of subproblems of the original problem. Given sequences

$$a[1], \ldots, a[m], \qquad b[1], \ldots, b[n],$$

we define $c[i, j]$ to be the length of a longest common subsequence of

$$a[1], \ldots, a[i] \quad \text{and} \quad b[1], \ldots, b[j]$$

where $1 \le i \le m$ and $1 \le j \le n$. We also define

$$c[i, 0] = 0 = c[0, j]$$

for all $0 \le i \le m$ and $0 \le j \le n$. Next, we must obtain a recurrence relation for $c[i, j]$ in terms of $c[p, t]$, where p and t are "smaller" than i and j. We consider two cases.

In the first case, we suppose that $a[i] \ne b[j]$. Then, not both $a[i]$ *and* $b[j]$ are in a longest common subsequence of

$$a[1], \ldots, a[i] \quad \text{and} \quad b[1], \ldots, b[j]$$

(otherwise the subsequences chosen would not be *common*). Therefore, a longest common subsequence of

$$a[1], \ldots, a[i] \quad \text{and} \quad b[1], \ldots, b[j]$$

is a longest common subsequence of

$$a[1], \ldots, a[i] \quad \text{and} \quad b[1], \ldots, b[j-1]$$

or

$$a[1], \ldots, a[i-1] \quad \text{and} \quad b[1], \ldots, b[j].$$

Since we seek a *longest* common subsequence, in this case

$$c[i, j] = \max\{c[i, j-1], c[i-1, j]\}.$$

In the second case, we suppose that $a[i] = b[j]$. Let

$$d[1], \ldots, d[k]$$

be a longest common subsequence of

$$a[1], \ldots, a[i] \quad \text{and} \quad b[1], \ldots, b[j]$$

so that $c[i, j] = k$. Then

$$d[1], \ldots, d[k-1]$$

is a common subsequence of

$$a[1], \ldots, a[i-1] \quad \text{and} \quad b[1], \ldots, b[j-1].$$

In fact, we show that $d[1], \ldots, d[k-1]$ is a *longest* common subsequence of

$$a[1], \ldots, a[i-1] \quad \text{and} \quad b[1], \ldots, b[j-1];$$

that is, the optimal substructure property holds for the longest-common-subsequence problem. If there is a common subsequence of

$$a[1], \ldots, a[i-1] \quad \text{and} \quad b[1], \ldots, b[j-1]$$

of length k or greater, we can append $a[i] = b[j]$ to the common subsequence to obtain a common subsequence of

$$a[1], \ldots, a[i] \quad \text{and} \quad b[1], \ldots, b[j]$$

of length at least $k+1$. This is a contradiction. Therefore, $c[i-1, j-1] = k-1$ and

$$c[i, j] = c[i-1, j-1] + 1.$$

To summarize, the sequence $c[i, j]$ is defined by the following initial conditions and recurrence relation

$$c[i, j] = \begin{cases} 0 & \text{if } i = 0 \text{ or } j = 0 \\ c[i-1, j-1] + 1 & \text{if } i, j > 0 \text{ and } a[i] = b[j] \\ \max\{c[i-1, j], c[i, j-1]\} & \text{if } i, j > 0 \text{ and } a[i] \neq b[j]. \end{cases}$$

Example 8.4.1. Figure 8.4.1 shows the values of $c[i, j]$ for the sequence a defined as *GDVEGTA* and the sequence b defined as *GVCEKST*. We compute

		G	V	C	E	K	S	T
	0	1	2	3	4	5	6	7
0	0	0	0	0	0	0	0	0
G 1	0	1	1	1	1	1	1	1
D 2	0	1	1	1	1	1	1	1
V 3	0	1	2	2	2	2	2	2
E 4	0	1	2	2	3	3	3	3
G 5	0	1	2	2	3	3	3	3
T 6	0	1	2	2	3	3	3	4
A 7	0	1	2	2	3	3	3	4

Figure 8.4.1 The values of $c[i,j]$ for the sequence a defined as *GDVEGTA* and the sequence b defined as *GVCEKST*. The sequence a, indexed by i, appears beside the first column, and the sequence b, indexed by j, appears above the first row. The value 4 in the lower-right corner is the length of a longest common subsequence.

the table by first using the initial conditions to fill the first row and first column with zeros. We then use the recurrence relation to compute the rows from top to bottom and left to right. For example, to compute $c[1,1]$ we note that $a[1] = G = b[1]$, so the formula

$$c[1,1] = c[1-1, 1-1] + 1$$

applies. Since $c[0,0] = 0$, $c[1,1] = 1$.

To compute $c[1,2]$ we note that $a[1] = G \neq V = b[2]$, so the formula

$$c[1,2] = \max\{c[0,2], c[1,1]\}$$

applies. Since $c[1,1] = 1$ and $c[0,2] = 0$, $c[1,2] = 1$.

Notice that if $a[i] = b[j]$ where i and j are positive, $c[i,j]$ equals one plus the entry one row above and one column left of $c[i,j]$. If $a[i] \neq b[j]$ where i and j are positive, $c[i,j]$ equals the maximum of the entry above $c[i,j]$ and the entry to the left of $c[i,j]$.

The solution to the problem is found in the lower-right corner of the table. The value $c[7,7] = 4$ tells us that the length of a longest common subsequence is 4. □

The algorithm to compute $c[i,j]$ is directly derived from the initial conditions and recurrence relation.

Algorithm 8.4.2 Computing the Length of a Longest Common Subsequence. This dynamic-programming algorithm computes the length $c[i][j]$ of a longest common subsequence of

$$a[1], \ldots, a[i] \quad \text{and} \quad b[1], \ldots, b[j]$$

for $i = 0, \ldots, m$ and $j = 0, \ldots, n$.

Input Parameters: a, b
Output Parameter: c
$LCS(a, b, c)$ {
   $m = a.last$
   $n = b.last$
   for $i = 0$ to m
     $c[i][0] = 0$
   for $j = 1$ to n
     $c[0][j] = 0$
   for $i = 1$ to m
     for $j = 1$ to n
       if $(a[i] \mathrel{!=} b[j])$
         $c[i][j] = max(c[i-1][j], c[i][j-1])$
       else
         $c[i][j] = 1 + c[i-1][j-1]$
}

The first for loop runs in time $\Theta(m)$; the second for loop runs in time $\Theta(n)$; and the nested for loops run in time $\Theta(mn)$; therefore, the run time of Algorithm 8.4.2 is $\Theta(mn)$.

As with the coin-changing algorithm (Algorithm 8.2.2), we can add statements to Algorithm 8.4.2 to track how the array c is updated and then determine a longest common subsequence from the additional information provided (see Exercise 7). We can also determine a longest common subsequence directly from the array c.

Algorithm 8.4.3 Computing a Longest Common Subsequence. This algorithm uses the array c computed by Algorithm 8.4.2 to output a longest common subsequence. The array a of length m is the first sequence input to Algorithm 8.4.2, and n is the length of the second sequence input to Algorithm 8.4.2.

Input Parameters: a (first sequence), m (length of a), n (length of second sequence), c (contains lengths of longest common subsequences)
Output Parameters: None
$LCS\_print(a, m, n, c)$ {
   if $(c[m][n] == 0)$
     return
   if $(c[m][n] == c[m-1][n])$
     $LCS\_print(a, m-1, n, c)$
   else if $(c[m][n] == c[m][n-1])$
     $LCS\_print(a, m, n-1, c)$
   else {
     $LCS\_print(a, m-1, n-1, c)$
     $print(a[m])$
   }
}

Algorithm 8.4.3 begins by checking whether there is a common subsequence of positive length and, if not, it simply returns

```
if (c[m][n] == 0)
    return
```

If there is a common subsequence of positive length, the algorithm then checks if there is a common subsequence having the same length but from a shorter set of input sequences

```
if (c[m][n] == c[m − 1][n])
    LCS_print(a, m − 1, n, c)
else if (c[m][n] == c[m][n − 1])
    LCS_print(a, m, n − 1, c)
```

If so, it makes a recursive call to print a longest common subsequence. If the conditions

$$c[m][n] == c[m − 1][n]$$

and

$$c[m][n] == c[m][n − 1]$$

are both false, then $a[m]$ and $b[n]$ are equal and belong to a longest common subsequence. The algorithm makes a recursive call to print the first part of a longest common subsequence and then prints the value of $a[m]$ (it could just as well have printed $b[n]$).

Algorithm 8.4.3 always decrements either m or n or both so, in the worst case, its run time is $\Theta(m + n)$.

A Parallel Version

Although Algorithm 8.4.2 computes the c table row by row, the table can be computed in other ways. If multiple processors are available, there is an advantage to computing by diagonals as shown in Figure 8.4.2. The computation of the c table proceeds from the upper-left corner toward the lower-right corner. After all of the entries in the c table bounded by solid lines have been computed (see Figure 8.4.2), the entries in the diagonal indicated by the dotted lines can be computed. All of these entries can be computed *simultaneously* since the computation of each entry requires only the values above it, to the left of it, and to its upper-left, all of which have already been computed. Since there are $m + n − 1$ diagonals and it takes one unit of time to compute one diagonal, the parallel version takes time $\Theta(m + n)$. Notice the time savings: Algorithm 8.4.2 takes time $\Theta(mn)$. Computing that requires multiple processors to execute instructions simultaneously is called **parallel computing**, and the accompanying algorithms are called **parallel algorithms**. In Chapter 12, we explore parallel computing and parallel algorithms in detail. Dynamic programming can often be used to design parallel algorithms.

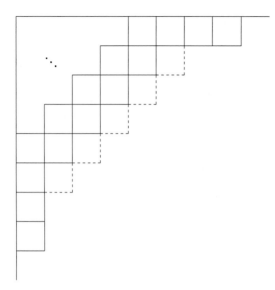

Figure 8.4.2 Computing the length of a longest common subsequence by diagonals. After all of the entries bounded by solid lines have been computed, the entries in the diagonal indicated by the dotted lines can be computed in parallel using multiple processors.

Exercises

In Exercises 1–4, find a longest common subsequence of the given sequences. Show the c table computed by Algorithm 8.4.2.

1S. *SLWOVNNDK, ALWGQVNBBK*   **2.** *SLWOVNNDK, SLWOVNNDK*

3. *SLWOVNNDK, KDNNVOWLS*   **4S.** *SLWOVNNDK, ABABCP*

5S. Professor Beavis has suggested that one can determine a longest common subsequence from the c table by scanning the far right column from the bottom to the top and noting at which characters (corresponding to the rows) the entries go down by one. Show that the professor is wrong by giving an example of sequences and the resulting c table for which the algorithm fails.

6. What is the best-case time of Algorithm 8.4.3?

7. Modify Algorithm 8.4.2 by inserting statements to track which of the conditions

$$a[i] == b[j]$$

or

$$a[i] \mathrel{!=} b[j] \mathbin{\&\&} c[i][j] == c[i][j-1]$$

or

$$a[i] \mathrel{!=} b[j] \mathbin{\&\&} c[i][j] == c[i-1][j]$$

holds. Use the output of the modified algorithm to write an algorithm that prints a longest common subsequence. What is the run time of your algorithm?

Determine whether each statement in Exercises 8–13 is true or false. If it is true, prove it; otherwise, provide a counterexample.

8S. If a and b are sequences that both begin with the character A, every longest common subsequence of a and b begins with A.

9. If a and b are sequences that both begin with the character A, some longest common subsequence of a and b begins with A.

10. If a and b are sequences that both end with the character A, every longest common subsequence of a and b ends with A.

11S. If a and b are sequences that both end with the character A, some longest common subsequence of a and b ends with A.

12. If a and b are sequences that both have the fourth character equal to A, every longest common subsequence of a and b contains A.

13. If a and b are sequences that both have the fourth character equal to A, some longest common subsequence of a and b contains A.

In Exercises 14 and 15, let

$$d[1], \ldots, d[k]$$

be a longest common subsequence of

$$a[1], \ldots, a[i] \quad and \quad b[1], \ldots, b[j].$$

14S. If $a[i] \neq b[j]$, is $d[1], \ldots, d[k-1]$ a common subsequence of

$$a[1], \ldots, a[i-1] \quad and \quad b[1], \ldots, b[j-1]?$$

15. If $a[i] \neq b[j]$, is $d[1], \ldots, d[k-1]$ a longest common subsequence of

$$a[1], \ldots, a[i-1] \quad and \quad b[1], \ldots, b[j-1]?$$

16S. Why can't a parallel algorithm compute all of the entries in a row simultaneously?

17. Write an algorithm to find a longest increasing subsequence in a sequence of numbers.

8.5 The Algorithms of Floyd and Warshall

In Section 7.4, we discussed Dijkstra's algorithm, which finds shortest-paths from a designated vertex to all other vertices in a graph. In the present section, we discuss the **all-pairs, shortest-path problem**—find a shortest path between *each* pair of vertices in a weighted graph—and a dynamic-programming algorithm due to Floyd that solves this problem. Essentially the same algorithm, known as *Warshall's algorithm*, solves the **transitive-closure problem**. The *transitive closure* of a relation R is the smallest transitive relation containing R. We begin with Floyd's algorithm.

Floyd's Algorithm

Throughout this subsection, we assume that G is a simple, undirected, weighted graph with vertices $1, \ldots, n$. We let $w(i, j)$ denote the weight of edge (i, j). We assume that $w(i, j) \geq 0$ for all i and j. We represent G using an adjacency matrix. If there is an edge incident on i and j, the entry in row i, column j, is $w(i, j)$. If no edge is incident on i and j, $i \neq j$, the entry in row i, column j, is ∞. If $i = j$, the entry in row i, column j, is zero.

Example 8.5.1. The adjacency matrix of the graph shown in Figure 8.5.1 is

$$
\begin{pmatrix}
0 & 8 & 3 & 1 & \infty \\
8 & 0 & 4 & \infty & 2 \\
3 & 4 & 0 & 1 & 1 \\
1 & \infty & 1 & 0 & 8 \\
\infty & 2 & 1 & 8 & 0
\end{pmatrix}.
$$

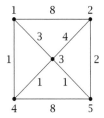

Figure 8.5.1 A graph to illustrate the all-pairs, shortest-path problem. □

A dynamic-programming algorithm to solve the all-pairs, shortest-path problem must begin by computing simple cases and end by solving the problem of computing a shortest path between each pair of vertices. In order to simplify the problem, we restrict the possible intermediate vertices on a path—starting by allowing *no* intermediate vertices (i.e., the path must go directly from the start vertex to the end vertex). In this case, the adjacency matrix gives the length of a shortest path between each pair of vertices. If no intermediate vertices are allowed, the shortest path from i to j, $i \neq j$, is the edge (i, j), whose length is $w(i, j)$, if such an edge exists. If there is no edge incident on i and j, $i \neq j$, there is no path from i to j, which is denoted ∞. Regardless of which intermediate vertices are allowed, the shortest path from i to i is always a path of length zero.

To explain Floyd's dynamic-programming algorithm, it is helpful to introduce some notation. For now, we concentrate on computing lengths of shortest paths rather than computing shortest paths themselves. We let $A^{(k)}$ denote the matrix whose ijth entry is the length of a shortest path from i to j, where the only intermediate vertices allowed are $1, \ldots, k$. Matrix $A^{(0)}$ is interpreted as allowing no intermediate vertices on paths, so $A^{(0)}$ is the adjacency matrix of the graph. The ijth entry in $A^{(n)}$ is the length of a shortest path from i to j, where the intermediate vertices allowed are $1, \ldots, n$; that is, *any* intermediate vertices may appear on a path from i to j. Since $A^{(n)}$ has no restrictions on the vertices that make up the paths, the ijth entry in $A^{(n)}$ *is* the length of a shortest path from i to j. Thus, $A^{(n)}$ is a solution to the all-pairs, shortest-path problem.

The algorithm begins with $A^{(0)}$, the adjacency matrix of the graph. It next computes $A^{(1)}$, then $A^{(2)}$, and so on, until it computes $A^{(n)}$, which solves the all-pairs, shortest-path problem.

Consider the problem of computing $A^{(k)}$ given that $A^{(k-1)}$ has already been computed. The only difference between $A^{(k)}$ and $A^{(k-1)}$ is that an additional vertex—namely k—may be used as an intermediate vertex to obtain a shortest path for $A^{(k)}$. Let P be a shortest path from i to j, where the only intermediate vertices allowed are $1, \ldots, k$. If P does *not* use k as an intermediate vertex, P is also a shortest path from i to j, where the only intermediate vertices allowed are $1, \ldots, k-1$. In this case,

$$A^{(k)}(i, j) = A^{(k-1)}(i, j).$$

If P *does* use k as an intermediate vertex, we have the situation shown in Figure 8.5.2. The part of P from i to k must be a shortest path from i to k that uses as intermediate vertices only $1, \ldots, k-1$. For, if there is a shorter path P' from i to k that uses as intermediate vertices only $1, \ldots, k-1$, we could replace the portion of P from i to k with P' to obtain a path shorter than P from i to j that uses as intermediate vertices only $1, \ldots, k$. We have shown that the optimal substructure property holds for shortest paths. Sim-

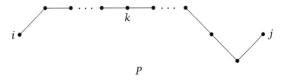

Figure 8.5.2 P is a shortest path from i to j in which k appears as an intermediate vertex. The only vertices allowed as intermediate vertices on P are $1, \ldots, k$. It follows that the part of P from i to k is a shortest path that uses as intermediate vertices only $1, \ldots, k-1$, and the part of P from k to j is a shortest path that uses as intermediate vertices only $1, \ldots, k-1$.

ilarly, the part of P from k to j is a shortest path from k to j that uses as intermediate vertices only $1,\dots,k-1$. We have shown that in this case,

$$A^{(k)}(i,j) = A^{(k-1)}(i,k) + A^{(k-1)}(k,j).$$

Either k is used on a shortest path or it is not; thus, in general,

$$A^{(k)}(i,j) = \min\{A^{(k-1)}(i,j),\, A^{(k-1)}(i,k) + A^{(k-1)}(k,j)\}. \qquad (8.5.1)$$

The preceding recurrence relation is precisely what is needed to compute the lengths of all shortest paths in a graph.

Example 8.5.2. We use the recurrence relation (8.5.1) to compute the lengths of all shortest paths in the graph of Figure 8.5.1. Since matrix $A^{(0)}$ is the adjacency matrix, we have

$$A^{(0)} = \begin{pmatrix} 0 & 8 & 3 & 1 & \infty \\ 8 & 0 & 4 & \infty & 2 \\ 3 & 4 & 0 & 1 & 1 \\ 1 & \infty & 1 & 0 & 8 \\ \infty & 2 & 1 & 8 & 0 \end{pmatrix}.$$

Sample computations of $A^{(1)}$ are

$$\begin{aligned} A^{(1)}(1,1) &= \min\{A^{(0)}(1,1),\, A^{(0)}(1,1) + A^{(0)}(1,1)\} \\ &= \min\{0,\, 0+0\} = 0 \end{aligned}$$

and

$$\begin{aligned} A^{(1)}(2,4) &= \min\{A^{(0)}(2,4),\, A^{(0)}(2,1) + A^{(0)}(1,4)\} \\ &= \min\{\infty,\, 8+1\} = 9. \end{aligned}$$

The latter equation shows that without using any intermediate vertices, there is no path from 2 to 4 $[A^{(0)}(2,4) = \infty]$. However, if 1 is allowed as an intermediate vertex, there is a shortest path $(2,1,4)$ from 2 to 4 of length 9 $[A^{(1)}(2,4) = 9]$.

Similar computations show that

$$A^{(1)} = \begin{pmatrix} 0 & 8 & 3 & 1 & \infty \\ 8 & 0 & 4 & 9 & 2 \\ 3 & 4 & 0 & 1 & 1 \\ 1 & 9 & 1 & 0 & 8 \\ \infty & 2 & 1 & 8 & 0 \end{pmatrix}, \qquad A^{(2)} = \begin{pmatrix} 0 & 8 & 3 & 1 & 10 \\ 8 & 0 & 4 & 9 & 2 \\ 3 & 4 & 0 & 1 & 1 \\ 1 & 9 & 1 & 0 & 8 \\ 10 & 2 & 1 & 8 & 0 \end{pmatrix},$$

$$A^{(3)} = \begin{pmatrix} 0 & 7 & 3 & 1 & 4 \\ 7 & 0 & 4 & 5 & 2 \\ 3 & 4 & 0 & 1 & 1 \\ 1 & 5 & 1 & 0 & 2 \\ 4 & 2 & 1 & 2 & 0 \end{pmatrix}, \qquad A^{(4)} = \begin{pmatrix} 0 & 6 & 2 & 1 & 3 \\ 6 & 0 & 4 & 5 & 2 \\ 2 & 4 & 0 & 1 & 1 \\ 1 & 5 & 1 & 0 & 2 \\ 3 & 2 & 1 & 2 & 0 \end{pmatrix},$$

$$A^{(5)} = \begin{pmatrix} 0 & 5 & 2 & 1 & 3 \\ 5 & 0 & 3 & 4 & 2 \\ 2 & 3 & 0 & 1 & 1 \\ 1 & 4 & 1 & 0 & 2 \\ 3 & 2 & 1 & 2 & 0 \end{pmatrix}. \qquad \square$$

Suppose that when we compute $A^{(k)}$ using $A^{(k-1)}$, instead of creating a new matrix, we overwrite the old values in $A^{(k-1)}$ with the new values of $A^{(k)}$. Such a computation is said to be done *in place* or, for lovers of Latin, *in situ*. When we compute $A^{(k)}(i,j)$, we use $A^{(k-1)}$ values:

$$A^{(k)}(i,j) = \min\{A^{(k-1)}(i,j),\, A^{(k-1)}(i,k) + A^{(k-1)}(k,j)\}.$$

If the values $A^{(k)}(i,k)$ and $A^{(k)}(k,j)$ have already been computed and have overwritten $A^{(k-1)}(i,k)$ and $A^{(k-1)}(k,j)$, there is a problem if the original values of $A^{(k-1)}(i,k)$ and $A^{(k-1)}(k,j)$ changed. However, these values *do not change*; that is,

$$A^{(k)}(i,k) = A^{(k-1)}(i,k) \quad \text{and} \quad A^{(k)}(k,j) = A^{(k-1)}(k,j).$$

The first equation follows from the fact that $A^{(k)}(i,k)$ is the length of a shortest path from vertex i to vertex k that uses as intermediate vertices only $1, \ldots, k$. However, such a path does not use vertex k as an intermediate vertex because k is the *end* vertex. Therefore,

$$A^{(k)}(i,k) = A^{(k-1)}(i,k).$$

Similarly,

$$A^{(k)}(k,j) = A^{(k-1)}(k,j).$$

[These equations also follow from recurrence relation (8.5.1); see Exercise 9.] Floyd's algorithm is given as Algorithm 8.5.3.

Algorithm 8.5.3 Floyd's Algorithm, Version 1. This algorithm computes the length of a shortest path between each pair of vertices in a simple, undirected, weighted graph G. All weights are nonnegative. The input is the adjacency matrix A of G. The output is the matrix A whose ijth entry is the length of a shortest path from vertex i to vertex j.

    Input Parameter: A
    Output Parameter: A

```
all_paths(A) {
    n = A.last
    for k = 1 to n // compute A^(k)
        for i = 1 to n
            for j = 1 to n
                if (A[i][k] + A[k][j] < A[i][j])
                    A[i][j] = A[i][k] + A[k][j]
}
```

Since each for loop in Algorithm 8.5.3 is executed n times, Floyd's algorithm runs in time $\Theta(n^3)$.

In order to find a shortest path between each pair of vertices, we introduce a second matrix *next*; $next[i][j]$ is the vertex that follows i on a shortest path from i to j. We initialize $next[i][j]$ to j for all i and j since, at the start of the algorithm, no vertices are allowed as intermediate vertices. Whenever we find a shorter path that results from introducing an intermediate vertex, we update $next[i][j]$:

```
if (A[i][k] + A[k][j] < A[i][j]) {
    A[i][j] = A[i][k] + A[k][j]
    next[i][j] = next[i][k]
}
```

The modified algorithm is Algorithm 8.5.4.

Algorithm 8.5.4 Floyd's Algorithm, Version 2. This algorithm computes the length of a shortest path between each pair of vertices in a simple, undirected, weighted graph G and stores the vertex that follows the first vertex on each shortest path. All weights are nonnegative. The input is the adjacency matrix A of G. The output is the matrix A whose ijth entry is the length of a shortest path from vertex i to vertex j and the matrix *next* whose ijth entry is the vertex that follows i on a shortest path from i to j.

```
    Input Parameter:    A
Output Parameters:    A, next

all_paths(A, next) {
    n = a.last
    // initialize next: if no intermediate
    // vertices are allowed next[i][j] = j
    for i = 1 to n
        for j = 1 to n
            next[i][j] = j
    for k = 1 to n
        for i = 1 to n
            for j = 1 to n
                if (A[i][k] + A[k][j] < A[i][j]) {
                    A[i][j] = A[i][k] + A[k][j]
                    next[i][j] = next[i][k]
                }
}
```

After using Algorithm 8.5.4 to compute the matrix *next*, we can use *next* to find a shortest path.

Algorithm 8.5.5 Finding a Shortest Path. This algorithm outputs a shortest path from vertex i to vertex j in a simple, undirected, weighted graph G. It assumes that matrix *next* has already been computed by Algorithm 8.5.4.

Input Parameters: *next, i, j*
Output Parameters: None

```
print_path(next, i, j) {
    // if no intermediate vertices, just print i and j and return
    if (j == next[i][j]) {
        print(i + " " + j)
        return
    }
    // output i and then the path from the vertex
    // after i (next[i][j]) to j
    print(i + " ")
    print_path(next, next[i][j], j)
}
```

Each time *print_path* is called, one or two vertices on a shortest path are output. Therefore, the time of *print_path* is proportional to the length of the path.

Example 8.5.6. For the graph of Figure 8.5.1, the matrix *next* computed by Algorithm 8.5.4 is

$$
\begin{pmatrix}
1 & 4 & 4 & 4 & 4 \\
5 & 2 & 5 & 5 & 5 \\
4 & 5 & 3 & 4 & 5 \\
1 & 3 & 3 & 4 & 3 \\
3 & 2 & 3 & 3 & 5
\end{pmatrix},
$$

and, row *i*, column *j*, of the matrix

$$
\begin{pmatrix}
1\,1 & 1\,4\,3\,5\,2 & 1\,4\,3 & 1\,4 & 1\,4\,3\,5 \\
2\,5\,3\,4\,1 & 2\,2 & 2\,5\,3 & 2\,5\,3\,4 & 2\,5 \\
3\,4\,1 & 3\,5\,2 & 3\,3 & 3\,4 & 3\,5 \\
4\,1 & 4\,3\,5\,2 & 4\,3 & 4\,4 & 4\,3\,5 \\
5\,3\,4\,1 & 5\,2 & 5\,3 & 5\,3\,4 & 5\,5
\end{pmatrix}
$$

shows the output of *print_path(i, j)*. □

Although our discussion of Floyd's algorithm was restricted to undirected graphs, the same algorithm can be applied to directed graphs. In this case, "path" means *directed* path, that is, a path of the form $(v_1, \ldots, v_k)$, where (v_i, v_{i+1}) is a directed edge from v_i to v_{i+1}, $i = 1, \ldots, k-1$.

Warshall's Algorithm

A relation R is *transitive* if, whenever (a, b) and (b, c) are in R, (a, c) is also in R. The **transitive closure** of a relation R is the smallest (in the sense of set containment) transitive relation containing R. Definition 8.5.7 gives the details.

Definition 8.5.7. Let R be a relation on X. The *transitive closure* of R is a relation R' on X satisfying

(a) $R \subseteq R'$.

(b) R' is transitive.

(c) If R'' is any transitive relation on X and $R \subseteq R''$, then $R' \subseteq R''$.

Consider constructing the transitive closure R' of a relation R. If

$$(x_1, x_2), (x_2, x_3), \ldots, (x_{k-1}, x_k) \in R,$$

in order for R' to be transitive, we must have $(x_1, x_k) \in R'$. Theorem 8.5.8 shows that R' is precisely the set of all such (x_1, x_k).

Theorem 8.5.8. *Let R be a relation on a set X. The transitive closure of R is the set*

$$R' = \{(x_1, x_k) \mid (x_1, x_2), (x_2, x_3), \ldots, (x_{k-1}, x_k) \in R\}. \tag{8.5.2}$$

Proof. Taking $k = 2$ in (8.5.2), we see that $R \subseteq R'$.

Next, we show that R' is transitive. Let $(a, b), (b, c) \in R'$. Then there are ordered pairs

$$(x_1, x_2), (x_2, x_3), \ldots, (x_{k-1}, x_k) \in R$$

and

$$(x_k, x_{k+1}), (x_{k+1}, x_{k+2}), \ldots, (x_{m-1}, x_m) \in R,$$

with $a = x_1$, $b = x_k$, and $c = x_m$. Since

$$(x_1, x_2), \ldots, (x_{k-1}, x_k), (x_k, x_{k+1}), \ldots, (x_{m-1}, x_m) \in R,$$

$(a, c) \in R'$. Therefore R' is transitive.

Let R'' be any transitive relation on X containing R. We must show that $R' \subseteq R''$. Let $(a, b) \in R'$. Then there are ordered pairs

$$(x_1, x_2), (x_2, x_3), \ldots, (x_{k-1}, x_k) \in R$$

with $a = x_1$ and $b = x_k$. Since $R \subseteq R''$,

$$(x_1, x_2), (x_2, x_3), \ldots, (x_{k-1}, x_k) \in R''.$$

Because R'' is transitive, $(a, b) = (x_1, x_k) \in R''$. Therefore, $R' \subseteq R''$ and the proof is complete. ∎

Theorem 8.5.8 states that the transitive closure of a relation R is the set of ordered pairs (a, b), where there is a path from a to b in the digraph of R.

Example 8.5.9. The transitive closure of the relation

$$R = \{(1, 2), (2, 3), (4, 5), (5, 4), (5, 5)\}$$

on $\{1, 2, 3, 4, 5\}$ is

$$R' = \{(1, 2), (1, 3), (2, 3), (4, 4), (4, 5), (5, 4), (5, 5)\}.$$

The digraphs of R and R' are shown in Figure 8.5.3. We see that $(1, 3) \in R'$ because there is a path $(1, 2, 3)$ from 1 to 3 in the digraph of R. Similarly, $(4, 4) \in R'$ because there is a path $(4, 5, 4)$ from 4 to 4 in the digraph of R.

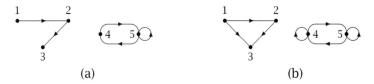

(a) $\qquad\qquad\qquad\qquad\qquad$ (b)

Figure 8.5.3 (a) The digraph of the relation R of Example 8.5.9. (b) The digraph of the closure R' of R. $\qquad$ □

Example 8.5.10. A telecommunications network has centers in Atlanta, Denver, Los Angeles, Miami, Philadelphia, and Seattle. There are direct, one-way links from Atlanta to Denver, from Atlanta to Philadelphia, from Denver to Los Angeles, from Los Angeles to Atlanta, and from Miami to Seattle. Consider the problem of determining whether there is a link, either direct or indirect (i.e., going through intermediate cities), from one city to another.

Define a relation R on the cities as $(c_i, c_j) \in R$ if there is a direct, one-way link from c_i to c_j. Then there is a direct or indirect link from c_i to c_j if and only if (c_i, c_j) is in the transitive closure of R, since a direct or indirect link from c_i to c_j is a path in the digraph of R. $\qquad$ □

To compute the transitive closure of a relation R, Warshall's algorithm uses the same logic as Floyd's algorithm. The adjacency matrix of Floyd's algorithm is replaced by the matrix of R, and instead of computing the length of a shortest path from i to j, Warshall's algorithm determines whether there are elements in R of the form

$$(i, x_1), (x_1, x_2), \ldots, (x_{m-1}, x_m), (x_m, j), \qquad (8.5.3)$$

that is, whether (i, j) is in the transitive closure of R. In order to compare Warshall's algorithm with Floyd's algorithm, we call (8.5.3) a *path from i to j*.

Example 8.5.11. The matrix of the relation R of Example 8.5.9 is

$$\begin{pmatrix} 0 & 1 & 0 & 0 & 0 \\ 0 & 0 & 1 & 0 & 0 \\ 0 & 0 & 0 & 0 & 0 \\ 0 & 0 & 0 & 0 & 1 \\ 0 & 0 & 0 & 1 & 1 \end{pmatrix}.$$

$\qquad$ □

Warshall's algorithm uses matrices $A^{(k)}$ similar to the ones used by Floyd's algorithm. In Warshall's algorithm, $A^{(k)}(i, j) = 1$ if there is a path from i to

j that uses as intermediate elements only $1, \ldots, k$, and 0 if there is no such path. Matrix $A^{(0)}$ is the matrix of the relation. If there is a path from i to j that uses as intermediate elements only $1, \ldots, k-1$, then this same path uses as intermediate elements only $1, \ldots, k$. In this case,

$$A^{(k)}(i, j) = A^{(k-1)}(i, j).$$

If there is no path from i to j that uses as intermediate elements only $1, \ldots, k-1$, there is a path from i to j that uses as intermediate elements only $1, \ldots, k$ if and only if there are paths from i to k and from k to j that use as intermediate elements only $1, \ldots, k-1$. In this case,

$$A^{(k)}(i, j) = A^{(k-1)}(i, k) \wedge A^{(k-1)}(k, j).$$

It follows that, in general,

$$A^{(k)}(i, j) = A^{(k-1)}(i, j) \vee [A^{(k-1)}(i, k) \,\&\, A^{(k-1)}(k, j)].$$

The matrices $A^{(k)}$ can be computed in place for exactly the same reason that they can be computed in place in Floyd's algorithm. Warshall's algorithm is given as Algorithm 8.5.12.

Algorithm 8.5.12 Warshall's Algorithm. This algorithm computes the transitive closure of a relation R on $\{1, \ldots, n\}$. The input is the matrix A of R. The output is the matrix A of the transitive closure of R.

    Input Parameter: A
    Output Parameter: A

```
transitive_closure(A) {
    n = A.last
    for k = 1 to n
        for i = 1 to n
            for j = 1 to n
                A[i][j] = A[i][j] ∨ (A[i][k] ∧ A[k][j])
}
```

Since each for loop in Algorithm 8.5.12 runs in time $\Theta(n)$, Warshall's algorithm runs in time $\Theta(n^3)$.

Exercises

Trace Floyd's algorithm for each graph in Exercises 1–3. Show each of the matrices $A^{(k)}$ and the matrix next of Algorithm 8.5.4. Show the output of Algorithm 8.5.5 for each pair of vertices.

1S.

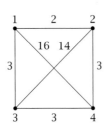

2.

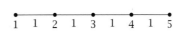

3.

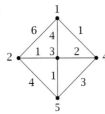

4S. What is the matrix of the relation R of Example 8.5.10?

5. What is the matrix of the transitive closure of the relation R of Example 8.5.10?

6. Define a relation R on a set of people as aRb if a is the parent of b. What is the transitive closure of R?

7S. Define a relation R on the set of integers as aRb if $a = b + 1$. What is the transitive closure of R?

8. Given an undirected graph G, define a relation R on the set of vertices of G as vRw if (v, w) is an edge. What is the transitive closure of R?

9. Use recurrence relation (8.5.1) to show that

$$A^{(k)}(i, k) = A^{(k-1)}(i, k) \quad \text{and} \quad A^{(k)}(k, j) = A^{(k-1)}(k, j)$$

for all i, j, and k.

10S. There are six permutations of the lines

```
for k = 1 to n
    for i = 1 to n
        for j = 1 to n
```

in Floyd's algorithm. Which ones give a correct algorithm?

11. Is the output of $print\_path(next, i, j)$ always the same as the output in reverse of $print\_path(next, j, i)$ for an undirected graph? Explain.

12. Suppose that A is a matrix whose ijth entry is the length of a shortest path from i to j in an undirected, weighted graph G with n vertices. Write an $O(n^2)$ algorithm that updates A when an additional edge is inserted into G.

13S. Give an example of a graph containing edges of negative weight and vertices i and j for which there is no shortest path from i to j, yet there is a path from i to j.

14. Suppose that G is a directed, weighted graph in which some weights are negative. Suppose further that G has no cycles of negative weight. Show that Floyd's algorithm still computes the length of a shortest path from vertex i to vertex j for all i and j.

15. Suppose that G is a directed, weighted graph in which some weights are negative. Write an algorithm that determines whether G contains a cycle of negative weight.

16S. Given a symmetric, $n \times n$ matrix A with nonnegative entries and a main diagonal of zeros, find a necessary and sufficient condition that there is a graph G such that when Floyd's algorithm computes $A^{(n)}$, $A^{(n)} = A$.

17. If a relation R is transitive, what is the transitive closure of R?

18. Let A and B be $n \times n$ matrices with positive entries off the diagonal and zero entries on the diagonal. Let $A \circ B$ be the matrix whose ijth entry is

$$[A \circ B](i, j) = \min \{A(i, k) + B(k, j) \mid 1 \le k \le n\}.$$

If A is an $n \times n$ matrix, define $A_1 = A$ and $A_{k+1} = A_k \circ A$. Show that $A_r \circ A_s = A_s \circ A_r$ for all r and s. This problem is due to Sung Soo Kim.

In Exercises 19–21, draw the digraph of the relation and show each of the matrices $A^{(k)}$ computed by Warshall's algorithm.

19S.
$$\begin{pmatrix} 1 & 0 & 1 & 1 \\ 0 & 1 & 0 & 0 \\ 1 & 0 & 1 & 0 \\ 0 & 0 & 1 & 1 \end{pmatrix}$$

20.
$$\begin{pmatrix} 1 & 0 & 1 & 1 & 0 \\ 0 & 1 & 0 & 0 & 1 \\ 1 & 0 & 1 & 0 & 0 \\ 0 & 0 & 1 & 1 & 0 \\ 1 & 0 & 0 & 0 & 1 \end{pmatrix}$$

21.
$$\begin{pmatrix} 1 & 1 & 0 & 1 & 0 \\ 0 & 1 & 0 & 1 & 0 \\ 0 & 0 & 1 & 0 & 0 \\ 0 & 0 & 1 & 1 & 0 \\ 1 & 1 & 0 & 1 & 1 \end{pmatrix}$$

22S. Explain why Warshall's algorithm can compute the matrices $A^{(k)}$ in place.

23. Let A be the matrix of a relation R on a set X containing n elements. Let A^k be the kth power of A, where $\vee$ replaces $+$ and $\wedge$ replaces $*$. Show that

$$A \vee A^2 \vee \cdots \vee A^n$$

is the matrix of the transitive closure of R.

24. Write an algorithm based on Exercise 23 to compute the transitive closure of a relation. What is the worst-case time of your algorithm?

Let R be a relation on a set X. The closure of *R with respect to property P is a relation R' on X such that R' has property P, $R \subseteq R'$, and if R'' is a relation on X containing R and having property P, then $R' \subseteq R''$.*

25S. State an algorithm to find the reflexive closure of a relation. What is the worst-case time of your algorithm?

26. State an algorithm to find the symmetric closure of a relation. What is the worst-case time of your algorithm?

27. A relation R on X is *irreflexive* if for every $x \in X$, $(x,x) \notin R$. Show that the irreflexive closure of a relation may not exist.

Notes

$\mathcal{WWW}$ Richard Bellman (1920–1984) gave the name "dynamic programming" to the technique discussed in this chapter. In Bellman's own words (see Bellman, 1984), here is the origin of the name:

> "In the first place I was interested in planning, in decision making, in thinking. But planning is not a good word for various reasons. I decided therefore to use the word, 'programming.' I wanted to get across the idea that this was dynamic, this was multistage, this was time-varying—I thought, let's kill two birds with one stone."

Although the method was known earlier (e.g., Massé, 1946, used a version of dynamic programming to solve a reservoir optimization problem), Bellman is acknowledged as the first person to develop dynamic programming in a mathematically precise way (see Bellman, 1957).

After receiving his undergraduate and master's degrees, serving in the U.S. Army, and working in theoretical physics at Los Alamos, he received his Ph.D. from Princeton in three months. In addition to his work on dynamic programming, he made many other significant contributions to both pure and applied mathematics.

Floyd's algorithm was published as Floyd, 1962 and based on Warshall's algorithm (Warshall, 1962), which was described in 1960. Warshall's algorithm is also known as the Roy-Warshall algorithm since it was also discovered by B. Roy. For more on the all-pairs, shortest-path algorithm see Lawler, 1976.

Chapter Exercises

8.1. Write a dynamic-programming algorithm to compute a^n based on the formulas

$$a^n = a^{n/2}a^{n/2}, \qquad n \text{ even}$$
$$a^n = a^{(n-1)/2}a^{(n-1)/2}a, \quad n \text{ odd}.$$

8.2. Define
$$F = \begin{pmatrix} 0 & 1 \\ 1 & 1 \end{pmatrix}.$$

Show that
$$F^n = \begin{pmatrix} f_{n-1} & f_n \\ f_n & f_{n+1} \end{pmatrix}, \quad n \geq 1,$$

where f_n is the nth Fibonacci number and f_0 is defined to be 0.

8.3. Using Exercises 8.1 and 8.2, or otherwise, write a dynamic-programming algorithm that calculates the nth Fibonacci number using at most $O(\lg n)$ arithmetic operations.

8.4. Write a dynamic-programming algorithm to calculate $C(n, k)$, the number of k-combinations (i.e., k-element subsets) of an n-element set. Use the formulas
$$C(n, k) = C(n - 1, k - 1) + C(n - 1, k)$$

valid for $1 \leq k \leq n - 1$, and

$$C(n, n) = 1 = C(n, 0)$$

valid for $n \geq 0$. What is the worst-case time of your algorithm?

8.5. Write a memoized dynamic-programming algorithm to calculate $C(n, k)$, the number of k-combinations (i.e., k-element subsets) of an n-element set (see Exercise 8.4). What is the worst-case time of your algorithm?

8.6. Use Algorithm 8.2.1 and the result of Exercise 7.1 to write an $O(nd)$ algorithm to determine whether the greedy coin-changing algorithm is optimal for all amounts; n is the number of coins, and d is the largest denomination.

Exercises 8.7–8.9 refer to Pearson's theorem, which can be used to construct a polynomial-time algorithm that determines whether the greedy coin-changing algorithm (Algorithm 7.1.1) is optimal for all amounts.

Assume that available denominations of coins are

$$d_1 > d_2 > \cdots > d_n = 1.$$

If we make change using v_k coins of denomination d_k, we denote the set of coins used by the vector

$$v = (v_1, v_2, \ldots, v_n).$$

If v and w are vectors of coins, we define $v < w$ to mean that v is lexicographically less than w; that is, for some i, $v_i < w_i$, and for all $j < i$,

$v_j = w_j$. *Among all minimal sets of coins for an amount x, we let $M(x)$ denote the greatest vector (in lexicographic order) that uses the minimum number of coins. Finally, we let $G(x)$ denote the vector of coins produced by the greedy algorithm (Algorithm 7.1.1) for an amount x. It can be shown (see Exercise 8.7) that Algorithm 7.1.1 is optimal for an amount x if and only if $G(x) = M(x)$.*

If Algorithm 7.1.1 is not optimal for all amounts, the following theorem due to David Pearson (see Pearson, 1994) characterizes the minimum amount for which it is not optimal, that is, the smallest amount x for which $G(x) \neq M(x)$.

Theorem. *Suppose that Algorithm 7.1.1 is not optimal for all amounts, and let x be the smallest amount for which $G(x) \neq M(x)$. Let*

$$v = M(x).$$

Let i be the first index for which $v_i \neq 0$, let j be the last index for which $v_j \neq 0$, and let

$$w = G(d_{i-1} - 1).$$

Then

- *$v_k = w_k$ for $k = 1, \ldots, j - 1$.*
- *$v_j = w_j + 1$.*
- *$v_k = 0$ for $k = j + 1, \ldots, n$.*

8.7. Show that Algorithm 7.1.1 is optimal for an amount x if and only if $G(x) = M(x)$.

8.8. The greedy algorithm is not optimal for the amounts 10, 6, and 1. Find x, v, i, j, and w as described in Pearson's theorem.

8.9. Write an algorithm, based on Pearson's theorem that runs in time $O(n^3)$, that determines whether the greedy algorithm is optimal for all amounts.

Exercises 8.10 and 8.11 are concerned with the longest-common-subsequence problem (see Section 8.4).

8.10. Let $M(n)$ be the maximum number of distinct longest common subsequences that two sequences, both of length n, can have. Show that $M(n) = \Omega(C^n)$, for some $C > 1$.

8.11. Extend Algorithm 8.4.3 to print *all* longest common subsequences of two sequences, both of length n. Exercise 8.10 tells us that the algorithm might take exponential time on some inputs. This does not mean, however, that it always takes exponential time. You should find an algorithm that runs in time $O(n^2 + nM'(n))$, where $M'(n)$ is the number of not necessarily distinct longest common subsequences. Algorithms such as this one, which run in polynomial time if we include the length of the output, are called *output-polynomial-time algorithms*.

8.12. Write a dynamic-programming algorithm to solve the activity-selection problem (see Exercise 7.5). How does your algorithm differ from a greedy algorithm that solves the problem? What is the worst-case time of your algorithm?

8.13. Write a dynamic-programming algorithm to solve the 0/1-knapsack problem (see Section 7.6). Your algorithm should *always* produce an optimal solution. What is the worst-case time of your algorithm?

8.14. Write a dynamic-programming algorithm to solve the subset-sum problem (see Exercise 7.10). Your algorithm should *always* produce an optimal solution. What is the worst-case time of your algorithm?

8.15. Write a dynamic-programming algorithm that, given a sequence $a_1, \ldots, a_n$ of real numbers, finds a subsequence $a_s, \ldots, a_t$ of consecutive elements of a so that the sum $\sum_{i=s}^{t} a_i$ is a maximum. If a_i is negative for all i, we define the maximum sum to be zero (which is obtained by selecting the empty subsequence).

8.16. Write a dynamic-programming algorithm to solve the *longest-common-substring problem*. What is the worst-case time of your algorithm?

8.17. Write an algorithm that finds a longest increasing subsequence *and* a longest decreasing subsequence in a sequence of numbers, and, thus, finds a longest monotone subsequence.

8.18. Using your algorithm of Exercise 8.17 or otherwise, show that the length of a longest monotone subsequence of a sequence of n numbers is at least $\sqrt{n}$. This result is due to Erdős and Szekeres.

8.19. Write an $O(n^2)$ algorithm that tests whether a relation on an n-element set is transitive. Your algorithm does not have to be a dynamic-programming algorithm.

8.20. Using the ideas of Section 5.4 and Exercise 8.1 or otherwise, write an $O(n^{\lg 7} \lg n)$ algorithm to compute the transitive closure of a relation on an n-element set. How does the time of your algorithm compare to the time required by Warshall's algorithm (Algorithm 8.5.12)?

8.21. Write a dynamic-programming algorithm to find a shortest cycle in a directed graph. What is the worst-case time of your algorithm?

8.22. Write a dynamic-programming algorithm to find the number of strings of length n accepted by a finite-state automaton. What is the worst-case time of your algorithm?

Exercises 8.23–8.25 are concerned with the following problem: Word processors and typesetting software attempt to make lines of text in a paragraph, except for the last line, as long as possible. (Even if the lines are ultimately right-justified as in this book, a paragraph looks best if lines of *text in a paragraph, except for the last line, are as long as possible.) This exercise is to write a dynamic-programming algorithm to place words in a paragraph into lines. The input is a list of word lengths $len_1, len_2, \ldots, len_n$, in the order the words appear in the paragraph, and a line length L. We assume that $len_i \leq L$ for all i so that each word fits on a line. If words i through j, $i \leq j$, are placed on a line so that they fit on the line with one space between the words, the gap g at the end of the line is*

$$g = L - j + i - \sum_{k=i}^{j} len_k.$$

If this is not the last line, the gap penalty is g^2. If this is the last line, the gap penalty is zero. The problem is to arrange the words on lines so that the sum of the gap penalties is minimized.

8.23. Explain why a power of g greater than one (e.g., g^2) is a better choice for the gap penalty than g.

8.24. Give an example to show that a greedy algorithm based on the heuristic, "If the next word fits on the line, place it on the line," is not always optimal.

8.25. Write a dynamic-programming algorithm that minimizes the sum of the gap penalties. What is the worst-case time of your algorithm?

8.26. A context-free grammar is in *Chomsky normal form* if every production is of the form

$$A \rightarrow BC \quad \text{or} \quad A \rightarrow a,$$

where A, B, and C are nonterminal symbols and a is a terminal symbol. (It is known that any context-free language not containing the null string is generated by a context-free grammar in Chomsky normal form.) Write a dynamic-programming algorithm that, given a context-free grammar G in Chomsky normal form, determines whether a given string is in the language generated by G. What is the worst-case time of your algorithm?

8.27. Write a parallel algorithm that, given a context-free grammar G in Chomsky normal form (see Exercise 8.26), determines whether a given string is in the language generated by G. What is the worst-case time of your algorithm?

8.28. Let T be a binary search tree that stores keys $K_1, \ldots, K_n$, and suppose that the probability of searching for key K_i is p_i. If c_i is the depth of key K_i in T, we define the *average search time for T* to be

$$\sum_{i=1}^{n} p_i c_i.$$

Write a dynamic-programming algorithm that, given keys and their probabilities of being searched, constructs an optimal binary search tree, that is, a binary search tree with minimum average search time. What is the worst-case time of your algorithm?

CHAPTER 9
Text Searching

Searching text is a ubiquitous problem, present wherever information is retrieved. Its applications range from using search engines on the web to locating words in files on your computer and to biologists searching sequence databases. The general form of the problem is to find within a text t a match for a pattern p, where *text*, *pattern*, and *match* can be interpreted in different ways. In the simplest case the text is a document in memory (in your word processor, for example), and the pattern is a word you want to locate within that document. This is the *classical version* of the text-searching problem, which can be solved by brute force sequential searching in time $O(|p| * |t|)$, where $|s|$ is the length of a string s. We discuss this algorithm in Section 9.1. In Section 9.2 we present the solution by Rabin-Karp, which runs in average time $O(|p| + |t|)$. For this algorithm, Rabin and Karp used the powerful notion of hashing (fingerprinting).

The classical problem can be solved in time $O(|p| + |t|)$. The two most famous algorithms achieving this time bound are Knuth-Morris-Pratt and Boyer-Moore. We explain Knuth-Morris-Pratt in detail in Section 9.3 and sketch the basic ideas behind Boyer-Moore in Section 9.4. Implementing Boyer-Moore is complicated, so instead we present an algorithm called Boyer-Moore-Horspool whose worst-case running time is $O(|p| * |t|)$, but which performs very well in practice and is easy to implement.

Stepping back from the classical problem, we find that there are multiple possible relaxations. For example, we can allow approximate matches. It is not immediately obvious what an approximate match should be, and we investigate that question in Section 9.5 discussing two very different approaches: edit distance and the don't-care wildcard.

Finally, in some situations we want to find a match of a particular form, for example when scanning a document for phone numbers or when verifying credit card information submitted by a web-form. These problems can be solved using regular expressions, an elegant technique that grew out of formal language theory (Section 9.6).

Before we start, we need to fix some terminology for the rest of this chapter. We usually denote the pattern to be searched for as p, and the text being searched as t. We also usually think of the underlying alphabet Σ as fixed.

You can think of it as containing all of the letters and punctuation symbols of the English language. For the Rabin-Karp algorithm we restrict ourselves to the binary alphabet $\Sigma = \{0, 1\}$. The set of all (finite) words on an alphabet Σ is denoted Σ^*, so $\{0, 1\}^*$ is the set of all binary strings.

The length of a string s is denoted by $|s|$. Within a program we write $s.length$ for $|s|$. We usually let $m = |p|$ and $n = |t|$ and assume that $m \leq n$. To simplify talking about strings, we write $p[i..j]$ for the substring of p starting at position i and ending at position j. Hence, $p = p[0..m - 1]$ (strings begin at position 0), and $p = [0..i]$ would be an arbitrary prefix of p. If $i > j$, we define $p[i..j]$ to be the empty string ε (the unique string of length 0). We also write $p[i]$ for $p[i..i]$, so $p[0]$ is the first and $p[m - 1]$ is the last letter of p. We write st for the concatenation of two strings s and t (programming languages usually use $s + t$ to denote the concatenation of the two strings).

9.1 Simple Text Search

Imagine a word-processor searching for a word (or phrase) in a document. The easiest approach to locating a word in a text is to compare the word letter by letter against the text, testing all possible locations in the text until a match is found.

Algorithm 9.1.1 Simple Text Search. This algorithm searches for an occurrence of a pattern p in a text t. It returns the smallest index i such that $t[i..i + m - 1] = p$, or -1 if no such index exists.

Input Parameters: p, t
Output Parameters: None

```
simple_text_search(p, t) {
    m = p.length
    n = t.length
    i = 0
    while (i + m ≤ n) {
        j = 0
        while (t[i + j] == p[j]) {
            j = j + 1
            if (j ≥ m)
                return i
        }
        i = i + 1
    }
    return −1
}
```

Example 9.1.2. Let us have a look at a run of *simple_text_search* searching for the pattern "001" in the text "010001". Figure 9.1.1 shows the progression of the algorithm.

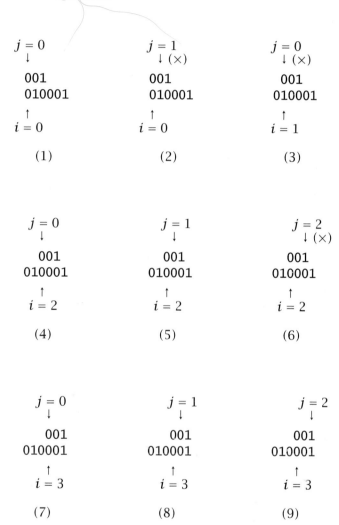

Figure 9.1.1 Searching for "001" in "010001" using *simple_text_search*. The cross ($\times$) in steps (2), (3), and (6) marks a mismatch. □

To convince ourselves that the algorithm works correctly, we have to verify only that the pattern is checked against all possible positions. Since the pattern contains $m = |p|$ characters, the last possible match for p in $t = t[0..n-1]$ would be $t[n-m..n-1]$, and, indeed, the outer while loop allows indexes i up to and including $n - m$.

In the worst case there is no match for the pattern, and the algorithm can take time $\Theta(m(n - m + 1))$ (Exercise 4 asks you to prove the lower bound).

The best case occurs if the pattern is found at the start of the text taking time $\Theta(m)$.

Theorem 9.1.3. *The algorithm simple_text_search solves the pattern-matching problem correctly in time* $O(m(n - m + 1))$.

In practice *simple_text_search* behaves better than $O(m(n - m + 1))$ because the inner while loop usually recognizes failure quite quickly. On random patterns and text, the running time of *simple_text_search* is $O(n - m)$ (see Exercise 9.1).

Exercises

1S. How many comparisons does *simple_text_search* perform when searching for the pattern "est" in the text "test"?

2. How many comparisons does *simple_text_search* perform when searching for the pattern "ita" in the text "itititit"?

3. Trace the algorithm *simple_text_search* on pattern "lai" and text "balalaika".

4S. Show that *simple_text_search* has a worst-case running time of $\Theta(m(n - m + 1))$. We proved only the upper bound $O(m(n - m + 1))$; the lower bound $\Omega(m(n - m + 1))$ still has to be proved.

5. Show that $m(n - m + 1)$ is $O(mn)$.

6. Show that $m(n - m + 1)$ is not $\Omega(mn)$. Together with Exercise 5 this implies that while $O(mn)$ is an upper bound on the running time of *simple_text_search*, it is not a *tight* upper bound.

7. Show that $m(n - m + 1)$ is not $O(m(n - m))$ even if we assume $m \le n$.

Exercises 8-10 investigate a variant of the simple text search algorithm that finds all occurrences of a pattern.

8S. Modify *simple_text_search* so that it prints out a list of locations of all matches for a pattern in a text.

9. Give an upper bound on the worst-case running time of your algorithm that finds all occurrences of a pattern.

10. Give a lower bound on the worst-case running time of your algorithm that finds all occurrences of a pattern.

Exercises 11-13 are about string matching with the don't-care *symbol "?" (sometimes called a* wildcard*). We assume that "?" is a special character that does not belong to the alphabet from which the text is made up. The* *don't-care symbol matches any letter in the text. For example, the first match for "?01?" in "1001110" is "0011" starting in the second position of the text. Note that "?" can match different characters in the same match.*

11S. Using the don't-care symbol "?", write a pattern that matches an American social security number.

12. Modify *simple_text_search* so that it returns the first match of a pattern possibly containing the don't-care symbol "?".

13. Extend the algorithm from Exercise 12 to also return the actual match that was found for the pattern.

9.2 The Rabin-Karp Algorithm

The simple text search we implemented in Section 9.1 can be ineffective for longer patterns, in particular if pattern and text contain repeated elements (see Exercise 4 in Section 9.1). The running time of the simple text search can be as bad as $\Theta(n^2)$ (for $m = n/2$, for example). Our ultimate goal is an algorithm running in linear time $O(n + m)$ in the worst case, a goal we will attain in the next section. Here we present an algorithm by Rabin and Karp that takes time $\Theta(n + m)$ on average.

The central idea of Rabin and Karp's algorithm is that, before we spend time checking for the match of a long pattern in a particular position (which might take m steps), it might pay to do some preliminary checking on whether to expect a matching pattern at that position. Suppose that a preliminary check could be implemented cheaply in time $O(1)$, say, and we could expect it to eliminate all but $1/m$th of the locations, that is $(n - m + 1)/m$ many. For these we would have to run the brute-force comparison, which takes time $O(m)$ for each location or time $O(m(n - m + 1)/m)$ altogether. Since the implementation requires $O(m)$ time for preprocessing, we get an overall average running time of $O(n + m)$.

How can we quickly exclude indexes from consideration? Suppose, for example, that we are searching for the pattern "000011" in

"0000010000100000".

The pattern has parity 0 (the number of ones in the string is even). Now consider the text we are searching: All substrings of length 6 have parity 1 (they contain an odd number of ones) with the exception of 100001. Out of $11 = 16 - 6 + 1$ positions in the text, we can rule out all but one, simply because they have the wrong parity. Rabin and Karp called this method *fingerprinting* because, instead of comparing the full pattern, we only compare a small aspect of it, its fingerprint.

Example 9.2.1. Let us see how the parity fingerprint helps in searching for $p =$ "010111" in $t =$ "0010110101001010011". The pattern p has parity 0, since it contains an even number of ones. We let $f[i]$ be the parity of the string $t[i..i+5]$. For example, $f[0] = 1$, since "001011" contains an odd number of ones. The following table lists all values of $f[i]$:

i	0	1	2	3	4	5	6	7	8	9	10	11	12	13	14	15	16	17	18
$t[i]$	0	0	1	0	1	1	0	1	0	1	0	0	1	0	1	0	0	1	1
$f[i]$	1	1	0	1	0	1	0	1	0	1	0	0	1	1					

The table tells us that the only positions in t we need to check are 2, 3, 4, 6, 8, 10, and 11, since all of the others have the wrong parity. Since p is different from all of the substrings found at these positions, we conclude that there is no match for p in t. □

We could extend our simple text search algorithm to first perform a parity check and then skip positions that have the wrong parity. A straightforward implementation will not lead to an improvement, because computing the parity of m bits takes m steps, and we need the check to be in constant time. However, we can do better. When we start the algorithm, we compute the parity of the first m bits of t [taking time $O(m)$ for preprocessing]. In Example 9.2.1 this gives us a parity of 1 for the six bits starting at index 0. When, in the next step, we need the parity of the m bits starting at index 1, we need to look only at the bits in positions 0 and m, because these are the only bits that change. In Example 9.2.1, both $t[0]$ and $t[6]$ are zero; hence the parity of $t[1..6]$ is the same as the parity of $t[0..5]$, namely 0. Using this trick we can update the parity in only two steps. In general, if the parity of the m bits starting at position i of the text is x, then the parity of the m bits starting at position $i+1$ is $x + t[i] + t[i+m] \bmod 2$.

Example 9.2.2. Consider again the string t in Example 9.2.1. Let us verify that $f[i+1] = f[i] + t[i] + t[i+6] \bmod 2$ for some sample values. By inspection (precomputation) we see that $f[0] = 1$. Now $f[1] = f[0] + t[0] + t[6] \bmod 2 = 1 + 0 + 0 \bmod 2 = 1$, and $f[2] = f[1] + t[1] + t[7] \bmod 2 = 1 + 0 + 1 \bmod 2 = 0$. And $f[13] = f[12] + t[12] + t[18] \bmod 2 = 1 + 1 + 1 \bmod 2 = 1$. □

On average we expect the parity check to reject half the inputs, so that the loop would take about $m(n-m+1)/2$ steps. Unfortunately, this is still $\Theta(m(n-m+1))$. While the basic idea is sound, parity is not good enough to give us the required speed-up because too many values share the same fingerprint. If we want to obtain a speed-up by a factor of q, we need a fingerprint function that

(a) maps m-bit strings to q different values (fingerprints),

(b) distributes the m-bit strings evenly across the q values, and

(c) is easy to compute sequentially, in the sense that if we change the string at the beginning and the end only, we can quickly (in time $O(1)$) compute the new value of the function.

A function fulfilling properties (a) and (b) is called a *hash function*. It distributes a large number of values evenly among a small number of fingerprints. Hash functions have found numerous applications in practice, for example in implementing hash tables for storing data or, more recently, to compute the message digests for digital signatures.

Parity fulfills all three properties for $q = 2$, which is why it gave us a speed-up by a factor of 2. Properties (a) and (b) are needed because they imply that on average $(q-1)/q$ of the inputs get rejected, and we need to run the brute-force algorithm on only $1/q$ of the inputs. Property (c) guarantees that we can find out whether an input can be eliminated in constant time. Eliminating positions therefore takes time $O((n-m+1)(q-1)/q)$, which is $O(n)$. This leaves us with approximately $(n-m+1)/q$ positions for which we need to compare the pattern to the text letter by letter. This might take m steps for each position, leading to a running time of $O(m(n-m+1)/q)$ on the positions that are not eliminated. If we choose q larger than m, this is $O(n)$. Since the algorithm needs time $O(m)$ for preprocessing, it takes time $O(n+m)$ on average.

How can we find a function with properties (a), (b), and (c) for $q > m$? Going back to the parity example, the first idea that comes to mind would be to simply take the sum of the m bits. This function fulfills (a) and (c). Unfortunately, it violates (b) badly (for example, there is only one input each that takes on values 0 or m).

Rabin and Karp suggested the following hash function: Consider the m bits as the binary expansion of a natural number and take the remainder after division by q. More precisely, if the m bits are $s_0 s_1 \ldots s_{m-1}$, use the value

$$\sum_{j=0}^{m-1} s_j 2^{m-1-j} \bmod q.$$

Example 9.2.3. Let us return to the text t we saw in Example 9.2.1, but instead of fingerprinting it with the parity function we use

$$f[i] = \sum_{j=0}^{5} t[i+j] 2^{5-j} \bmod 7.$$

The tables display the results. The third row shows the value $f[i]$.

i	0	1	2	3	4	5	6	7	8	9
$t[i]$	0	0	1	0	1	1	0	1	0	1
Σ	11	22	45	26	53	42	20	41	18	37
$f[i]$	4	1	3	5	4	0	6	6	4	2

i	10	11	12	13	14	15	16	17	18
$t[i]$	0	0	1	0	1	0	0	1	1
Σ	10	20	41	19					
$f[i]$	3	6	6	5					

Let us verify some entries in the table. For example, $t[0..5]$ ="001011" corresponds to the number $11 = 1 * 8 + 1 * 2 + 1 * 1$, and therefore $f[0] = 11 \bmod 7 = 4$. Similarly, $t[5..10]$ ="101010" corresponds to the number $32 + 8 + 2 = 42$, and therefore $f[5] = 42 \bmod 7 = 0$. □

The function $\sum_{j=0}^{m-1} s_j 2^{m-1-j} \bmod q$ fulfills property (a) because the remainder is always in the range $\{0, \dots, q-1\}$. Property (b) depends on the choice of q. For random texts and patterns, the value of q does not matter; but in practice values of q need to be avoided. Suppose, for example, you knew that your texts are binary and are made up of roughly 30% ones and 70% zeros, and you are using $q = 2$, and $m = 2$. In that case, we expect to see mostly substrings of the form 00 and a much smaller number of substrings 01, 10, and 11, implying that there is an imbalance between strings having fingerprints 0 and strings having fingerprint 1. In practice, it has turned out that choosing a prime number $q > m$ works very well and fulfills (b). We are left with verifying property (c), which we need for implementing the algorithm. Consider $m + 1$ bits $s_0 s_1 \dots s_{m-1} s_m$. The first m bits, $s_0 s_1 \dots s_{m-1}$, get assigned value $a = \sum_{j=0}^{m-1} s_j 2^{m-1-j} \bmod q$. The m bits starting in the next position $s_1 \dots s_m$ in turn get assigned

$$
\begin{aligned}
\sum_{j=0}^{m-1} s_{j+1} 2^{m-1-j} \bmod q &= s_m + \sum_{j=0}^{m-2} s_{j+1} 2^{m-1-j} \bmod q \\
&= s_m + 2 \sum_{j=0}^{m-2} s_{j+1} 2^{m-1-(j+1)} \bmod q \\
&= s_m + 2 \sum_{j=1}^{m-1} s_j 2^{m-1-j} \bmod q \\
&= s_m + 2(-2^{m-1} s_0 + \sum_{j=0}^{m-1} s_j 2^{m-1-j}) \bmod q \\
&= s_m + 2(a - 2^{m-1} s_0) \bmod q.
\end{aligned}
$$

This formula allows us to compute the next value from the previous in constant time. It pays to precompute $2^{m-1} \bmod q$, since it is used in every step.

Example 9.2.4. Returning to Example 9.2.3, we now see that there was no need to explicitly compute the values $\sum_{j=i}^{i+5} s_j 2^{5-1-j}$. Our new formula now gives us

$$f[i+1] = t[i+6] + 2(f[i] - 32t[i]) \bmod 7 = t[i+6] + 2f[i] - t[i] \bmod 7.$$

For example, $f[1] = t[6] + 2f[0] - t[0] \bmod 7 = 0 + 8 - 0 \bmod 7 = 1$, $f[8] = t[13] + 2f[7] - t[7] \bmod 7 = 0 + 12 - 1 \bmod 7 = 4$, and $f[10] = t[15] + 2f[9] - t[9] \bmod 7 = 0 + 4 - 1 \bmod 7 = 3$. □

Algorithm 9.2.5 Rabin-Karp Search. This algorithm searches for an occurrence of a pattern p in a text t. It returns the smallest index i such that $t[i..i + m - 1] = p$ or -1 if no such index exists.

Input Parameters: p, t
Output Parameters: None

$rabin\_karp\_search(p, t)$ {
   $m = p.length$
   $n = t.length$
   q = prime number larger than m
   $r = 2^{m-1} \bmod q$
   // computation of initial remainders
   $f[0] = 0$
   $pfinger = 0$
   for $j = 0$ to $m - 1$ {
      $f[0] = 2 * f[0] + t[j] \bmod q$
      $pfinger = 2 * pfinger + p[j] \bmod q$
   }
   $i = 0$
   while $(i + m \le n)$ {
      if $(f[i] == pfinger)$
         if $(t[i..i + m - 1] == p)$ // this comparison takes time $O(m)$
            return i
      $f[i + 1] = 2 * (f[i] - r * t[i]) + t[i + m] \bmod q$
      $i = i + 1$
   }
   return -1
}

Example 9.2.6. Let us look again at $p =$ "010101" in

$$t = \text{"00101101010010100011"}.$$

Running $rabin\_karp\_search$ for $q = 7$ gives us the table in Example 9.2.3. For example, the algorithm starts with $f[0] = 4$. In the next step it computes

$$f[i + 1] = 2 * (f[i] - r * t[i]) + t[i + m] \bmod q$$

with $r = 2^{m-1} \bmod q = 4$; hence we obtain $f[1] = 2(4 - 4t[0]) + t[6] \bmod 7 = 2(4 - 0) + 0 \bmod 7 = 1$. In the third step, we get $f[2] = 2(f[1] - 4t[1]) + t[7] \bmod 7 = 3$, in the fourth step $f[3] = 2(f[2] - 4t[2]) + t[8] \bmod 7 = 5$, and so on.

The value of $pfinger$ is $16 + 4 + 1 \bmod 7 = 0$; hence the only position we need to check in t is $i = 5$. Since $t[5 + 10] =$ "101010" $\ne$ "010101" $= p$, we know that p does not occur in t.

Let us try the same text t with another pattern $p =$ "001010". In this case, $pfinger$ is 3; hence we have to check only two positions, 2 and 10, and indeed $t[10..15] = p$.   □

Before we prove correctness, let us analyze the running time of *rabin_karp_search*. In the worst case, $f[i]$ equals *pfinger* for each location i and the main loop takes as much time as the simple text search, namely $O(m(n - m + 1))$. Together with the additional $O(m)$ time to compute the initial values of $f[0]$ and *pfinger*, we have a running time of $O(m(n-m+2))$, which is $O(m(n - m + 1))$. On average, however, we expect the test $(f[i] == pfinger)$ to succeed only about $1/q$th of the time because we assumed that our fingerprinting function distributes inputs evenly among the q possible output values. (We did not prove this, and a technical proof is beyond the scope of this book.) Hence, we expect to run the inner loop $(n - m + 1)/q$ times for $O(m)$ steps each. Since q was chosen larger than m, the expected running time for the loops is $O(n - m + 1)$. With the $O(m)$ preprocessing, this yields an expected running time of $O(n + m)$.

Theorem 9.2.7. *The algorithm rabin_karp_search correctly finds the first match for a pattern in a text (if it exists) in time $O(m(n - m + 1))$.*

Proof. We already did the running time analysis. We prove correctness by using the loop invariant

$$f[i] = \sum_{j=0}^{m-1} t_{i+j} 2^{m-1-j} \bmod q$$

for the while loop (see Section 2.2). We claim that the loop invariant is true every time the loop condition ($i + m \leq n$) is tested. The loop invariant states that $f[i]$ contains the correct fingerprint of $t[i..i + m - 1]$ during the ith iteration of the loop. Before we show that this is indeed correct, we show how to use the loop invariant to prove that the algorithm is correct.

In each iteration of the while loop, the algorithm checks whether $f[i]$ equals *pfinger*. If they are equal, it checks whether $t[i..i + m - 1] == p$; otherwise it continues to the next i. Since we assume that the loop invariant is true, we know that $f[i]$ is the correct fingerprint of $t[i..i + m - 1]$. If $f[i]$ is different from *pfinger*, we know that there cannot be a match of p starting at position i, since $p = t[i..i + m - 1]$ implies that

$$
\begin{aligned}
f[i] &= \sum_{j=0}^{m-1} t_{i+j} 2^{m-1-j} \bmod q &&\text{by the loop invariant} \\
&= \sum_{j=0}^{m-1} p_j 2^{m-1-j} \bmod q &&\text{because } p = t[i..i + m - 1] \\
&= pfinger &&\text{definition of } pfinger.
\end{aligned}
$$

Therefore, the algorithm behaves correctly by not comparing p to $t[i..i + m - 1]$ if $f[i]$ is different from *pfinger*. If, on the other hand, $f[i]$ and *pfinger* agree, the algorithm checks whether $t[i..i + m - 1]$ and p are the same, comparing letter by letter. If they are equal, it returns i; otherwise it continues with the next i. We conclude that *rabin_karp_search* does not miss a match for p in t if there is one. With this knowledge we can complete the argument that the algorithm works correctly. There are two ways of leaving the algorithm: because the loop condition $i + m \leq n$ fails or because a match $p = t[i..i + m - 1]$ is found. Since we argued that the algorithm did not miss any previous matches, we know that in the first case there is no match for p, and in the second case, the algorithm returns the first match for p.

We still need to verify that the loop invariant is true. Initially, the first time the loop condition is checked, $f[0]$ contains the correct value:

$$\sum_{j=0}^{m-1} t_j 2^{m-1-j} \bmod q,$$

because that is how we initialize $f[0]$. We earlier derived the formula

$$f[i + 1] = 2 * (f[i] - 2^{m-1} * t[i]) + t[i + m] \bmod q.$$

Since we use this formula to compute $f[i + 1]$ in the algorithm (with the difference that we have precomputed the value r of $2^{m-1} \bmod q$), $f[i+1]$ is computed correctly for the next iteration of the loop, and we have verified that the loop invariant is correct. ∎

We have ignored the problem of finding a prime number larger than q. Prime numbers are plentiful. Bertrand's postulate, for example, states that for any number m there is a prime number between m and $2m$, and better results are known. Hence we could find a prime larger than m in time $O(m^{3/2})$ (verifying primality by testing all possible factors). In practice, it is much faster to use randomized techniques to generate a large prime number. We would also choose q close to and smaller than the word-size of the computer since this speeds up the arithmetical computations that are at the heart of the algorithm.

Choosing the prime number at random has other advantages than just being faster. Compare the following algorithm to Algorithm 9.2.5, *rabin_karp_search.*

Algorithm 9.2.8 Monte Carlo Rabin-Karp Search. This algorithm searches for occurrences of a pattern p in a text t. It prints out a list of indexes such that with high probability $t[i..i + m - 1] = p$ for every index i on the list.

Input Parameters: p, t
Output Parameters: None

```
mc_rabin_karp_search(p, t) {
    m = p.length
    n = t.length
    q = randomly chosen prime number less than mn²
    r = 2^(m-1) mod q
```

```
// computation of initial remainders
f[0] = 0
pfinger = 0
for j = 0 to m − 1 {
    f[0] = 2 ∗ f[0] + t[j] mod q
    pfinger = 2 ∗ pfinger + p[j] mod q
}
i = 0
while (i + m ≤ n) {
    if (f[i] == pfinger)
        println("Match at position " + i)
    f[i + 1] = 2 ∗ (f[i] − r ∗ t[i]) + t[i + m] mod q
    i = i + 1
}
}
```

The algorithm $mc\_rabin\_karp\_search$ relies entirely on fingerprints to decide whether there is a match at position i. We removed the loop testing whether $t[i..i + m − 1] = p$ when the fingerprints of $t[i..i + m − 1]$ and p are the same. This makes the algorithm much faster; it now runs in time $O(n)$. However, it also makes the algorithm incorrect: Two strings could have the same fingerprint without being identical. Rabin and Karp observed that this is very unlikely to happen if q is a randomly chosen prime less than mn^2. Indeed, the probability of the algorithm making even a single wrong decision for a particular p and t is less than $2.53/n$, which is small when n is large. Furthermore, the algorithm only errs by listing wrong matches, also called *false positives*; the list will include all correct matches, since a position is only rejected if the fingerprints do not agree. Algorithms with these two properties are called *Monte-Carlo algorithms*.

Exercises

1S. Trace the algorithm $rabin\_karp\_search$ by hand on pattern "111" and text "011010011001110" with $q = 2$. How many comparisons between pattern and text symbols are made?

2. Trace the algorithm $rabin\_karp\_search$ by hand on pattern "111" and text "011010011001110" with $q = 5$. How many comparisons between pattern and text symbols are made?

3. Trace the algorithm $rabin\_karp\_search$ by hand on pattern "101" and text "011010011001110" with $q = 7$. How many comparisons between pattern and text symbols are made?

4S. Show that the worst-case running time of $rabin\_karp\_search$ is $\Theta(m(n − m + 1))$.

5. Implement *rabin_karp_search*. To find q, write a program searching for the smallest prime larger than m. *Hint:* By Bertrand's Postulate there is always a prime number between any m and $2m$, so the search takes time at most $O(m^{3/2})$; in practice, it is much faster.

6. Modify *rabin_karp_search* to print out a list of all matches for a pattern in a text. Your modified version should still run in average time $O(n + m)$.

9.3 The Knuth-Morris-Pratt Algorithm

In this section we present the algorithm of Knuth-Morris-Pratt that solves the pattern-matching problem in time $O(|p| + |t|)$. Let us look at an example to see why the simple text search can be inefficient. Suppose we have reached the following stage running *simple_text_search*:

```
Tweedledum
Tweedledee and Tweedledum
```

In the simple text search we would now move "Tweedledum" by one letter and start matching again. However, we see that "Tweedledum" cannot match in the second position of the text because we know that the text starts with "Tweedled" as we found out when comparing the pattern to the text. As a matter of fact, "Tweedled" does not contain any "T" after the first position; so we can shift the pattern to the first letter after "Tweedled" in "Tweedledee and Tweedledum" and continue matching.

```
        Tweedledum
Tweedledee and Tweedledum
```

Let us consider another example. We trace the simple text search with pattern p ="pappar", and text t ="pappappapparrassanuaragh"[†]

```
pappar
pappappapparrassanuaragh
```

After six comparisons, the simple text search encounters a mismatch between the final "r" of "pappar" and the "p" in the corresponding position of t. It then continues by trying to match "pappar" starting with $t[1]$ ="a" at position 1. Again, we know that there cannot be a match at this position. We know that we successfully matched "pappa" against the text; hence $t[0..4]$ = "pappa" and the next potential match for "pappar" could begin three positions over.

```
   pappar
pappa
```

[†]This word, of course, is not a complete English word. The full word is "Pappappapparrassannuaragheallachnatullaghmonganmacmacmacmwhackfalltheredebblenonthedubblandaddydoodled".

Hence, we can skip positions 1 and 2 of t altogether for matching p and align $p[0]$ with $t[3]$:

```
    pappar
pappappapparrassanuaragh
```

At this point we know that $p[0..1] = t[3..4]$ (this is why we shifted to that position), and we can continue comparisons at $t[5]$, the same position at which we encountered the mismatch. We conclude that whenever we match $p[0..4]$ against a text, but $p[5]$ does not match, we can shift the pattern by three positions and continue comparing in the same position at which the mismatch was found. More generally, given a search pattern p, we can compute a table that answers the following question for each k: If $p[0..k]$ matches the text, by how many positions can we shift the pattern if $p[k+1]$ does not match the text?

Example 9.3.1. Here is the table for p ="Tweedledum". We will see how to compute it later.

	T	w	e	e	d	l	e	d	u	m	
k	−1	0	1	2	3	4	5	6	7	8	9
$shift$	1	1	2	3	4	5	6	7	8	9	10

We notice that $shift[k] = \max\{1, k+1\}$. The reason is that if we have matched $p[0..k]$ against $t[i..i+k]$, but $p[k+1] \neq t[i+k+1]$, then there cannot be a match for p starting at positions i through $i+k$ in t. There cannot be a match at position i, because we just found out that $p[k+1] \neq t[i+k+1]$. Also, no matches are possible at $i+1$ through $i+k$, since these are the same as $p[1..k]$, and therefore do not contain a "T" with which a match for p must begin. Hence, we can shift the pattern to position $i+k+1$ and continue by comparing $p[0]$ to $t[i+k+1]$. In case $k = -1$ we know that $p[0] \neq t[i]$, so we have to move the pattern to the next position, giving us a shift of 1.

So when "Tweedledum" fails matching against "Tweedledee and Tweedledum" at $p[8]$ we look up $shift[7]$ to find that we can shift the pattern by 8 positions, so the next comparison is $p[0]$ ="T" against $t[8]$ ="e".   □

Example 9.3.2. For "pappar" we can use the following table:

	p	a	p	p	a	r
k	−1	0	1	2	3	4	5
$shift$| 1	1	2	2	3	3	6

Suppose, for example, that we are matching "pappar" against "panther". After failing to match $p[2]$ against the "n" in panther we can shift the pattern by $shift[1] = 2$ positions and continue by comparing "p" to "n" as shown:

$$j = 2 \qquad\qquad j = 0$$
$$\downarrow (\times) \qquad\qquad \downarrow (\times)$$

pappar   pappar
panther   panther

$$\uparrow \qquad\qquad\qquad \uparrow$$
$$i = 0 \qquad\qquad\quad i = 2$$

If we are matching "pappar" against "papaya tree" we can shift the pattern by $shift[2] = 2$ positions

$$j = 3 \qquad\qquad j = 0$$
$$\downarrow (\times) \qquad\qquad \downarrow$$

pappar   pappar
papaya tree   papaya tree

$$\uparrow \qquad\qquad\qquad \uparrow$$
$$i = 0 \qquad\qquad\quad i = 2$$

and continue by comparing $p[1] =$"a" to $t[3] =$"a".

As a final example, consider finding a match for "pappar" in "pappappap-parrassanuaragh".

$$j = 5$$
$$\downarrow (\times)$$

pappar
pappappapparrassanuaragh

$$\uparrow$$
$$i = 0$$

After six comparisons, we know that $p[0..4] = t[0..4]$, but $p[5] \neq t[5]$. Hence, we shift the pattern by $shift[4] = 3$ positions and continue by comparing $p[2]$ to $t[5]$.

$$j = 2$$
$$\downarrow$$

pappar
pappappapparrassanuaragh

$$\uparrow$$
$$i = 3$$

Four comparisons later we find another mismatch: $p[5]$ is different from $t[8]$. Again we shift the pattern by $shift[4] = 3$ positions and continue by comparing $p[2]$ to $t[8]$.

$$j = 2$$
$$\downarrow$$

pappar
pappappapparrassanuaragh

$$\uparrow$$
$$i = 6$$

We have found a match after four more comparisons. □

Why does the technique shown in Example 9.3.2 work? Suppose $p[0..k]$, the pattern up to position k, matches the letters in the search text starting in position i that is $p[0..k] = t[i..i + k]$. Consider shifting the pattern p by s positions. For the shift to be successful, the first $k - s + 1$ characters of p have to match in the new position:

p:			0	1	2	...	s	$s + 1$		...	k		...
t:	0 1 2...	i	$i + 1$	$i + 2$	...	$i + s$	$i + s + 1$		...	$i + k$		...
p:							0	1	2	...	$k - s$		...

Looking at the diagram, we see that for the shift to be successful we need $p[0..k - s] = t[i + s..i + k]$. However, we assumed that $t[i + s..i + k] = p[s..k]$, so we must have $p[0..k - s] = p[s..k]$. A successful shift has to fulfill this condition; also, we have to take the first such shift since otherwise we might miss a match, and therefore

$$shift[k] = \min\{s > 0 \mid p[0..k - s] = p[s..k]\}.$$

We require $s > 0$ since we do want to force a shift. The best case occurs if there is no match at all, and $s = k + 1$ (in that case both $p[0..k - s]$ and $p[s..k]$ are empty, hence equal).

Example 9.3.3. We can now justify the table in Example 9.3.1. For

$$p = \text{``Tweedledum''},$$

we know that $p[0] \neq p[j]$ for any $1 \leq j \leq 9$, and hence $shift[k] = k + 1$ for $k \geq 0$. □

Example 9.3.4. Let us return to a situation from Example 9.3.2:

$$j = 5$$
$$\downarrow (\times)$$

```
    pappar
pappappapparrassanuaragh
      ↑
    i = 3
```

In this situation, the current starting position of p in t is $i = 3$, and we are comparing $p[j]$ with $j = 5$ to $t[i + j] = t[8]$. The comparison fails, and hence we shift the pattern by $shift[j - 1]$, which is 3. That is, we add 3 to i and remove 3 from j to get $i = 8$ and $j = 2$ to continue:

$$j = 2$$
$$\downarrow$$

```
    pappar
pappappapparrassanuaragh
      ↑
    i = 6
```

In general, we have to be careful in the case that $shift[j-1] > j$:

$j = 0$
↓ (×)

```
    pappar
panther
```
↑
$i = 2$

Here $i = 2$ and $j = 0$, when a mismatch occurs. Now $shift[j-1]$ is 1; hence we change i to 3 to continue matching at $t[3]$, but we do not subtract 1 from j, since j is already 0. We continue with $i = 3$ and $j = 0$ as shown below:

$j = 0$
↓ (×)

```
    pappar
panther
```
↑
$i = 3$

This case always occurs when a mismatch is found for $j = 0$.   □

Suppose we know how to compute the table for a pattern p. The Knuth-Morris-Pratt algorithm then works as follows:

Algorithm 9.3.5 Knuth-Morris-Pratt Search. This algorithm searches for an occurrence of a pattern p in a text t. It returns the smallest index i such that $t[i..i + m - 1] = p$, or -1 if no such index exists.

Input Parameters: p, t
Output Parameters: None

```
knuth_morris_pratt_search(p, t) {
    m = p.length
    n = t.length
    knuth_morris_pratt_shift(p, shift) // compute array shift of shifts
    i = 0
    j = 0
    while (i + m ≤ n) {
        while (t[i + j] == p[j]) {
            j = j + 1
            if (j ≥ m)
                return i
        }
        i = i + shift[j - 1]
        j = max(j - shift[j - 1], 0)
    }
    return -1
}
```

Let us assume for the moment that *knuth_morris_pratt_shift* correctly computes the *shift* table in time $O(m)$ where m is the length of the pattern (we will see how to do this later). To prove correctness of *knuth_morris_pratt_search*, we need to show that our intuition about using the *shift* array is correct; that is, the shift array takes us to the next potential match without overlooking any intermediary matches. The following lemma justifies this intuition.

Lemma 9.3.6. *Assume $p[0..j-1] = t[i..i+j-1]$ and $p[j] \neq t[i+j]$; that is, we have a partial match of p starting at position i that failed at $i+j$. Let $i' = i + shift[j-1]$, and $j' = \max\{j - shift[j-1], 0\}$. Then*

(a) $p[0..j'-1] = t[i'..i'+j'-1]$, and

(b) $p \neq t[k..k+m-1]$ for $i \leq k < i'$.

That is, $p[0..j'-1]$ matches t starting at position i', and there are no matches for p in positions $i, i+1, \ldots, i'-1$.

Proof. By definition $shift[j-1]$ is an allowable shift, namely

$$p[0..j-1-shift[j-1]] = p[shift[j-1]..j-1].$$

Therefore,

$$
\begin{aligned}
p[0..j'-1] &= p[0..j-1-shift[j-1]] & \text{by definition of } j' \\
&= p[shift[j-1]..j-1] & \text{by definition of } shift[j-1] \\
&= t[i+shift[j-1]..j-1] & p[0..j-1] = t[i..i+j-1] \\
&= t[i'..i'+j'-1] & \text{by definition of } i' \text{ and } j',
\end{aligned}
$$

showing that (a) is true (note that in the case $j' = 0$ all of these strings are empty). Statement (b) follows, because $shift[j-1]$ is the smallest allowable shift; that is, we do not miss any matches by applying the shift. To prove this, assume, by way of a contradiction, that $p[0..m-1] = t[k..k+m-1]$ for some $i \leq k < i'$. Let $k' = k - i$. Then

$$
\begin{aligned}
p[0..j-1-k'] &= t[k..k+j-1-k'] & \text{by assumption} \\
&= t[k..i+j-1] & \text{by definition of } k' \\
&= p[k'..j-1] & \text{since we assumed that} \\
& & p[0..j-1] = t[i..i+j-1],
\end{aligned}
$$

and therefore $k' \geq shift[j-1]$ (by definition of $shift[j-1]$) contradicting $k' = k - i < i' - i = shift[j-1]$. ∎

Applying Lemma 9.3.6 to justify the use of shifting, we can now prove the algorithm correct.

Theorem 9.3.7. *The algorithm knuth_morris_pratt_search correctly computes the position of the first occurrence of pattern p in text t if there is one or returns -1 otherwise. The algorithm runs in time $O(m+n)$.*

Proof. We are assuming that *knuth_morris_pratt_shift*(p) correctly computes the *shift* table for p in time $O(m)$; that is,

$$shift[k] = \min\{s > 0 \mid p[0..k - s] = p[s..k]\} \quad \text{for } -1 \le k < m.$$

To reference the code, we assign line numbers:

```
(1)   while (i + m ≤ n) {
(2)       while (t[i + j] == p[j]) {
(3)           j = j + 1
(4)           if (j ≥ m)
(5)               return i
(6)       }
(7)       i = i + shift[j − 1]
(8)       j = max(j − shift[j − 1], 0)
(9)   }
```

We first verify that the algorithm runs in time $O(m + n)$. The outer loop (1) is performed at most n times, since i is increased in each iteration as the *shift* array contains only values greater than zero. The inner loop (2), however, might take $O(m)$ steps giving us an $O(mn)$ upper bound, which is not good enough. We try to extend the idea that i can be increased at most n times to the inner loop in which j gets increased. In a first attempt, we might trace the value of the expression $i + j$. However, that value remains constant if the inner loop fails for some $j > 0$ (if $j > 0$, then $shift[j - 1] \le j$; hence $i + j$ does not change in that case). A slight variation of this idea does work: Trace the value of $2i + j$ in line (2), where the condition of the inner while loop is checked. If the condition evaluates to true, j, and therefore $2i + j$, is increased. If it fails, the value $shift[j - 1]$ is added to i and at most $shift[j - 1]$ is subtracted from j. In consequence, $2i + j$ is increased by at least $shift[j - 1] \ge 1$. Hence, every time we return to line (2), the value of $2i + j$ has increased. Since $2i + j \le 2n + m$, this can happen at most $2n + m$ many times, giving us an upper bound of $O(m + n)$ for the running time of the loop. Since we assumed that the initialization takes time $O(m)$, we obtain an overall running time of $O(n + m)$.

To show that the algorithm is correct, we use a loop invariant. We claim that the following two statements are loop invariants for the inner loop in line (2); that is, both are true every time the algorithm performs line (2).

(a) $p[0..j - 1] = t[i..i + j - 1]$, and

(b) $p[0..m - 1] \ne t[k..k + m - 1]$ for $0 \le k < i$.

Intuitively, (a) claims that whenever we enter the loop we have a partial match of the first j letters of the pattern starting at position i of the text; (b) implies that the algorithm has not missed a match of the pattern at an earlier position.

Before we show that the two statements are indeed a loop invariant, we apply them to prove *knuth_morris_pratt_search* correct. We already showed that the algorithm terminates. Termination can happen in two ways: by leaving the if statement in line (4) or after having finished the outer loop. Let us consider the latter case first. For the algorithm to exit the outer loop, it must be true that $i + m > n$. Then (b) implies that there no matches for the pattern up to and including position $n - m$. However, there cannot be any matches starting after that position since there are less than m letters left, and the algorithm correctly returns -1. In the other case, the algorithm leaves through the return statement in line (5). When we entered the loop in line (2) we knew that $p[0..j - 1] = t[i..i + j - 1]$ from (a), and $p[j] = t[i + j]$ (otherwise we would not have entered the inner loop); hence we have $p[0..j] = t[i..i + j]$. We exit only if $j + 1$ is at least m, hence $j \geq m - 1$ and therefore $p = p[0..m - 1] = t[i..i + m - 1]$, which means we have found an occurrence of the pattern starting at position i. By (b) we know that there are no earlier occurrences we missed, so the algorithm correctly returns i at that point.

We conclude the proof by verifying that (a) and (b) are indeed a loop invariant. When we first test the loop condition, (a) is true because $j = 0$ and $p[0.. - 1]$ and $t[i..i - 1]$ are both the empty string; (b) is true because $i = 0$, which means that there are no previous positions k to consider.

We now need to show that, if (a) and (b) are true whenever we perform line (2), they are still true when we return to (2) the next time.

There are two cases, depending on whether the test in (2) fails or succeeds. If $t[i + j] = p[j]$, we increase j in line (3), so condition (a) will be true for the new j; (b) remains true, since i did not change at all. If, on the other hand, $t[i + j] \neq p[j]$, we do not enter the inner loop but continue with lines (7) and (8). This increases i by $shift[j - 1]$ and decreases j by the same value. Let us call the new values $i' = i + shift[j - 1]$, and $j' = \max\{j - shift[j - 1], 0\}$. Lemma 9.3.6 now tells us that

(a') $p[0..j' - 1] = t[i'..i' + j' - 1]$, and
(b') $p \neq t[k..k + m - 1]$ for $i \leq k < i'$.

Since (b) was true at the start of the loop, we know that $p \neq t[k..k + m - 1]$ for $0 \leq k < i$. Together with (b'), this implies that $p[0..m - 1] \neq t[k..k + m - 1]$ for $0 \leq k < i'$. Moreover, (a') tells us that $p[0..j' - 1] = t[i'..i' + j' - 1]$, so (a) and (b) are still true when we return to (2) and are therefore a loop invariant. ∎

We still have to show how to compute the shift table in time $O(m)$. The idea is the same as for finding the pattern in a string, with the difference that we try to locate the pattern within itself. Assume that $t = p$ and we run *knuth_morris_pratt_search*. Whenever we increase j in the inner loop, it is because we have found a partial match $p[0..j] = p[i..i + j]$, which implies that $shift[i + j] \leq i$ because

$$shift[i + j] = \min\{s > 0 \mid p[0..i + j - s] = p[s..i + j]\}.$$

On the other hand, we are making sure we are not missing any earlier matches; so, in fact, at that point $shift[i + j] = i$, and we can set this value in the *shift* table. This suggests that we just run *knuth_morris_pratt_search* with $t = p$ and set the values of *shift*[j] in the inner loop. However, we are actually using values from the *shift* table in *knuth_morris_pratt_search*, so how can this work? As it turns out, we only ever access values in the *shift* table that have already been computed earlier. We can therefore adapt *knuth_morris_pratt_search* to compute the shifts.

Algorithm 9.3.8 Knuth-Morris-Pratt Shift Table. This algorithm computes the shift table for a pattern p to be used in the Knuth-Morris-Pratt search algorithm. The value of *shift*[k] is the smallest $s > 0$ such that $p[0..k - s] = p[s..k]$.

> Input Parameter: p
> Output Parameter: *shift*

```
knuth_morris_pratt_shift(p, shift) {
    m = p.length
    shift[−1] = 1 // if p[0] ≠ t[i] we shift by one position
    shift[0] = 1 // p[0.. − 1] and p[1..0] are both the empty string
    i = 1
    j = 0
    while (i + j < m)
        if (p[i + j] == p[j]) {
            shift[i + j] = i
            j = j + 1;
        }
        else {
            if (j == 0)
                shift[i] = i + 1
            i = i + shift[j − 1]
            j = max(j − shift[j − 1], 0 )
        }
}
```

Example 9.3.9. The following table shows how *knuth_morris_pratt_shift* computes the shift table for "pappar":

$$shift[-1] = 1$$
$$shift[0] = 1$$

$i = 1, j = 0:$	$p[1] \neq p[0], j = 0 \quad \rightarrow$	$shift[1] = 2$
$i = 2, j = 0:$	$p[2] = p[0] \quad \rightarrow$	$shift[2] = 2$
$i = 2, j = 1:$	$p[3] \neq p[1], j \neq 0$	
$i = 3, j = 0:$	$p[3] = p[0] \quad \rightarrow$	$shift[3] = 3$
$i = 3, j = 1:$	$p[4] = p[1] \quad \rightarrow$	$shift[4] = 3$
$i = 3, j = 2:$	$p[5] \neq p[2], j \neq 0$	
$i = 5, j = 0:$	$p[5] \neq p[0], j = 0 \quad \rightarrow$	$shift[5] = 6$

This yields the table we used in Example 9.3.2. □

Example 9.3.10. As another example, we trace *knuth_morris_pratt_shift* on input "1010001":

$$
\begin{aligned}
& & & & shift[-1] = 1 \\
& & & & shift[0] = 1 \\
i = 1, j = 0: & \quad p[1] \neq p[0], j = 0 & \rightarrow & & shift[1] = 2 \\
i = 2, j = 0: & \quad p[2] = p[0], j = 0 & \rightarrow & & shift[2] = 2 \\
i = 2, j = 1: & \quad p[3] = p[1], j \neq 0 & \rightarrow & & shift[3] = 2 \\
i = 2, j = 2: & \quad p[4] \neq p[2], j \neq 0 & & & \\
i = 4, j = 0: & \quad p[4] \neq p[0], j = 0 & \rightarrow & & shift[4] = 5 \\
i = 5, j = 0: & \quad p[5] \neq p[0], j = 0 & \rightarrow & & shift[5] = 6 \\
i = 6, j = 0: & \quad p[6] = p[0], j = 0 & \rightarrow & & shift[6] = 7
\end{aligned}
$$

For example, $shift[2]$ and $shift[3]$ are both 2 since the initial part "10" of "1010001" repeats immediately.   □

†Correctness of Shift Table Computation

We need to show that *knuth_morris_pratt_shift* correctly computes the values

$$shift[k] = \min\{s > 0 \mid p[0..k - s] = p[s..k]\}$$

for $k = -1, 0, \ldots, m$ where $m = |p|$. We first prove a strengthening of Lemma 9.3.6.

Lemma 9.3.11. *Assume* $p[0..j - 1] = p[i..i + j - 1]$, *and* $p[j] \neq p[i + j]$. *Let* $i' = i + shift[j - 1]$, *and* $j' = \max\{j - shift[j - 1], 0\}$. *Then*

(a) $p[0..j' - 1] = p[i'..i' + j' - 1]$, *and*

(b) $p[0..i' + j' - 1 - s] \neq p[s..i' + j' - 1]$ *for* $i \leq s < i'$.

That is, $p[0..j' - 1]$ *matches* p *starting at position* i', *and either* $shift[i' + j' - 1] < i$ *or* $shift[i' + j' - 1] \geq i'$.

Proof. We prove the truth of (a) as in Lemma 9.3.6. Since $shift[j - 1]$ is an allowable shift, we have

$$
\begin{aligned}
p[0..j' - 1] & = & p[0..j - 1 - shift[j - 1]] & \quad \text{definition of } j' \\
& = & p[shift[j - 1]..j - 1] & \quad \text{by definition of } shift[j - 1] \\
& = & p[i + shift[j - 1]..j - 1] & \quad p[0..j - 1] = p[i..i + j - 1] \\
& = & p[i'..i' + j' - 1] & \quad \text{by definition of } i' \text{ and } j',
\end{aligned}
$$

showing that (a) is true (again, if $j' = 0$ all of the strings are empty). Suppose for a contradiction that (b) fails; that is, for some s we have

$$p[0..i' + j' - 1 - s] = p[s..i' + j' - 1],$$

---

†This subsection can be omitted without loss of continuity.

and $i \le s < i'$. Note that this implies that $p[0..i + j - 1 - s] = p[s..i + j - 1]$ since $i' + j' \ge i + j$. Let $s' = s - i$. Then

$$
\begin{aligned}
p[0..j - 1 - s'] &= p[0..i + j - 1 - s] && \text{by definition of } s' \\
&= p[s..i + j - 1] && \text{by assumption for contradiction} \\
&= p[s'..j - 1] && \text{since } p[0..j - 1] = p[i..i + j - 1]
\end{aligned}
$$

Hence $s' \ge shift[j - 1]$ (by definition of $shift[j - 1]$) contradicting $s' = s - i < i' - i = shift[j - 1]$. $\blacksquare$

Lemma 9.3.12. *The algorithm knuth_morris_pratt_shift correctly computes the shift array in time $O(m)$.*

Proof. Consider the values of the expression $i + j$ as we enter the while loop. Initially that value is 1, and we claim the value never decreases. If $p[i+j] = p[j]$, then j is increased, hence $i+j$ increases. If $p[i+j] \ne p[j]$, we add $shift[j - 1]$ to i and subtract the same value from j unless the difference becomes negative, in which case we let $j = 0$. In either case $i + j$ does not decrease.

We also note that the algorithm assigns a value to $shift[i + j]$ exactly when $i + j$ increases by one: if $p[i + j] = p[j]$, then $shift[i + j]$ is set, and j increased by one; if $p[i + j] \ne p[j]$, then $shift[i + j]$ is set if $j = 0$, and in that case i, and thus $i + j$, are increased by one. It follows that at any point of the algorithm, $shift[k]$ has been assigned a value for all $k < i + j$. Finally note that, if we set a value in the $shift$ array, we set it to i or $i + 1$, both of which are always at least one.

As in the case of the search algorithm, we can now prove termination by tracing the value of $2i + j$. This value is at most $3m$ and we claim it increases by at least one in each iteration of the loop, which implies that the loop is performed at most $3m$ times. Hence the running time is $O(m)$. There are two cases: If $p[i + j] = p[j]$ then j is increased, hence $2i + j$ increases. Otherwise, if $j \ne 0$, then $2i + j$ increases by a total of $shift[j - 1]$, which is always at least one. In the final case we have $j = 0$, and i is increased by 1 and j remains zero, which increases $2i + j$ by two.

The algorithm initializes both $shift[-1]$ and $shift[0]$ to 1. Since

$$shift[-1] = \min\{s > 0 \mid p[0.. - 1 - s] = p[s.. - 1]\} = 1,$$

and similarly $shift[0] = 1$, because $p[0.. - 1]$ and $p[0.. - 2]$ are empty, this is correct. Furthermore, since the while loop begins with $i + j$ having value 1, and $i + j$ never decreases, these two values are never overwritten, and hence remain correct.

The main part of the algorithm is the loop, which is captured by the following loop invariant:

(a) The values of $shift[k]$ are correct for all $-1 \le k < i + j$.

(b) $p[0..j - 1] = p[i..i + j - 1]$.

(c) $p[0..i + j - 1 - s] \neq p[s..i + j - 1]$ for $0 < s < i$.

We show that these three statements are indeed a loop invariant in Lemma 9.3.13. Intuitively, (a) says that we have computed all values of *shift* correctly so far, (b) says that for the current values of i and j we have a partial match of the pattern at positions i through $i + j - 1$ (which for $j = 0$ is always true), and (c) implies that $shift[i + j - 1] \geq i$.

The loop invariant immediately settles the correctness of the algorithm: As the loop terminates with $i + j = m$, (a) states that all of the values in the *shift* table are correct. ∎

Lemma 9.3.13. *The statements*

(a) The values of shift[k] are correct for all $-1 \leq k < i + j$,

(b) $p[0..j - 1] = p[i..i + j - 1]$, and

(c) $p[0..i + j - 1 - s] \neq p[s..i + j - 1]$ for $0 < s < i$,

are a loop invariant for our implementation of knuth_morris_pratt_shift; that is, all three conditions are true every time the loop condition is checked.

Proof. The first time the loop is entered we have $i = 1$ and $j = 0$, so (a) is true because we set $shift[-1]$ and $shift[0]$ correctly; (b) is true because both $p[0..j - 1]$ and $p[i..i + j - 1]$ are empty; and (c) is true because there is no s between 0 and i.

The next step is to show that if the loop invariant holds at the beginning of the execution of the loop, it still holds after the body has been executed.

We distinguish two cases.

First Case: $p[i + j] = p[j]$. In this case we execute

$$shift[i + j] = i$$
$$j = j + 1$$

We have to show that (a), (b), and (c) then hold for the new values. To distinguish between the values of i and j before and after the body of the loop is executed, call the new values $i' = i$, and $j' = j + 1$. We have to verify (a), (b), and (c) for i' and j'.

Let us begin with (b). We know that $p[0..j - 1] = p[i..i + j - 1]$. Since we assumed that $p[i + j] = p[j]$, we get $p[0..j' - 1] = p[0..j] = p[i..i + j] = p[i'..i' + j' - 1]$, which shows that (b) is true for i' and j'. Consider (c) next. We know that $p[0..i + j - 1 - s] \neq p[s..i + j - 1]$ for $0 < s < i$, which implies $p[0..i + j - s] \neq p[s..i + j]$ for $0 < s < i$ (we are adding a single letter to strings that are already different). This, however, is the same as $p[0..i' + j' - 1 - s] \neq p[s..i' + j' - 1]$ for $0 < s < i'$ (by definition of i' and j'). We are left with (a). We have to show that $shift[k]$ is correct for all $-1 \leq k < i' + j'$. By assumption, the values are correct for all $-1 \leq k < i + j$; so the only value we have to check is $shift[i + j]$, which was set to i. Because of (b), we know that $p[0..j] = p[i..i + j]$, and therefore $shift[i + j] \leq i$ (by definition

$shift[i + j] = \min\{s > 0 \mid p[0..i + j - s] = p[s..i + j]\})$. Assume for a contradiction that $0 < s = shift[i+j] < i$. Then $p[0..i+j-s] = p[s..i+j]$ for some s with $0 < s < i$, or (using i', j' instead), $p[0..i' + j' - 1 - s] = p[s..i' + j' - 1]$ for some $s < i$, contradicting (c) for i' and j', which we established earlier.

Second Case: $p[i + j] \neq p[j]$. In this case we execute

```
if (j == 0)
    shift[i] = i + 1
i = i + shift[j − 1]
j = max(j − shift[j − 1], 0)
```

The values of i and j after executing this code are $i' = i + shift[j - 1]$ and $j' = \max\{j - shift[j - 1], 0\}$. Lemma 9.3.11 tells us that (b) and (c) remain true for i' and j', so we are left with verifying (a). We assign $shift[i] = i + 1$ only if $j = 0$. However, $j = 0$ means that we must have had $p[i] \neq p[0]$, which immediately implies $shift[i] \neq i$. But $shift[i] \geq i$ by (c), and therefore $shift[i] = i + 1$ (because $shift[k] \leq k + 1$ for $k \geq 0$). ∎

Exercises

1S. Compute the *shift* table for the pattern "barbara".

2. Compute the *shift* table for the pattern "abracadabra".

3. Compute the *shift* table for the pattern "entente".

4S. Compute the *shift* table for the pattern "cancan".

5. Compute the *shift* table for the pattern "mathematics".

6S. Trace *knuth_morris_pratt_search* searching for an occurrence of "cancan" in "cacancacanccancanca". How many comparisons did the algorithm make?

7. Trace *knuth_morris_pratt_search* searching for an occurrence of "abracadabra" in "abrabracabracadabracadabracad". How many comparisons did the algorithm make?

8. Trace *knuth_morris_pratt_search* searching for an occurrence of "entente" in "tenttentetententen". How many comparisons did the algorithm make?

9S. Trace *knuth_morris_pratt_search* searching for an occurrence "mathematics" in "mathematicians and mathematics". How many comparisons did the algorithm make?

9.4 The Boyer-Moore-Horspool Algorithm

Boyer and Moore came up with a seemingly innocuous idea: Why not compare the pattern to the text from right to left instead of from left to right, while keeping the shift direction the same? For example, reimplementing the simple text search with this idea yields the following algorithm.

Algorithm 9.4.1 Boyer-Moore Simple Text Search. This algorithm searches for an occurrence of a pattern p in a text t. It returns the smallest index i such that $t[i..i + m - 1] = p$ or -1 if no such index exists.

Input Parameters: p, t
Output Parameters: None

```
boyer_moore_simple_text_search(p, t) {
    m = p.length
    n = t.length
    i = 0
    while (i + m ≤ n) {
        j = m - 1 // begin at the right end
        while (t[i + j] == p[j]) {
            j = j - 1
            if (j < 0)
                return i
        }
        i = i + 1
    }
    return -1
}
```

While this variant of our earlier *simple_text_search* still takes time $O(mn)$, it does lend itself to the implementation of two heuristics called the **occurrence** and the **match** heuristics, which speed it up significantly.

We first look at some examples of the occurrence heuristic.

Example 9.4.2. Suppose we are searching for the word "rum" in "conundrum". Running the Boyer-Moore version of the simple text search, we first compare the "m" of "rum" to the "n" of "conundrum":

```
rum
conundrum
```

The match fails. Now we know that "rum" does not contain the letter "n" at all, so we can actually shift the word over by three positions:

```
   rum
conundrum
```

This time "d" and "m" do not match and again we know that "rum" does not contain a "d", so we can move the pattern by another three positions:

```
      rum
conundrum
```

to finally find a match.   □

Example 9.4.3. As a second example of the occurrence heuristic, let us search for "drum" in "conundrum":

```
drum
conundrum
```

Again we have a mismatch, but this time the letter "u" actually occurs in the word "drum" so we can only move the pattern over by one letter, aligning the rightmost "u" in "drum" with the "u" from "conundrum":

```
 drum
conundrum
```

The mismatch between "m" and "n" here leads to a shift of four positions:

```
     drum
conundrum
```

giving us the final match.   □

Example 9.4.4. As a final example of the occurrence heuristic, let us try to match "natu" against "conundrum":

```
natu
conundrum
```

Matching "t" with "n" fails, so we shift the pattern over for the "n"s to match:

```
  natu
conundrum
```

Here "u" against "d" fails and "natu" does not contain a "d", so we need to shift the pattern beyond the "d"; and since there are only three letters of the text left after "d", the search fails.   □

We summarize the occurrence heuristic as follows: Match the pattern against the text from right to left. When encountering a mismatch with a letter α from the text, shift the pattern to align the rightmost occurrence of α in the pattern with the one in the text. If α does not occur in the pattern at all, move the pattern one position beyond α.

There is one subtle problem with this rule: It might make us shift the pattern back to the left rather than to the right if the rightmost occurrence of α has already moved beyond the current position. This situation is illustrated in the next example.

Example 9.4.5. We want to find a match for "date" in "detective":

```
date
detective
```

Using the occurrence heuristic the mismatch between "a" and "e" should lead to the following alignment:

```
date
  detective
```

This would mean moving the pattern back to a position dealt with earlier. □

Boyer and Moore's solution for this problem is to shift the pattern to the right by one position in case we would end up with a negative shift (a shift to the left).

Example 9.4.6. Applying the Boyer-Moore solution to

```
date
detective
```

we obtain

```
 date
detective
```

since the occurrence heuristic would lead to a negative shift, as seen in Example 9.4.5, and we therefore move the pattern by one position to the right.

□

The second technique, the match heuristic, is similar to the idea used in the Knuth-Morris-Pratt algorithm: If we fail halfway through a match, we can use the information about what we have seen of the text so far to shift the pattern to the next possible match. Since we are comparing from right to left, we need to compute the shift table for the reverse of the pattern.

Example 9.4.7. Let us use the match heuristic to find a match for $p =$ "banana" in $t =$ "a banana":

```
banana
a banana
```

We would match $p[3..5] =$ "ana" to $t[3..5] =$ "ana" in "a banana" and then find a mismatch of $p[2] =$ "n" against $t[2] =$ "b". A Knuth-Morris shift table for "ananab" yields $shift[3] = 2$; hence we shift p by two positions to the right:

```
  banana
a banana
```

at which point we have found a match.   □

The Boyer-Moore algorithm implements both of these heuristics, choosing whichever gives the larger shift. This makes it one of the fastest search algorithms in both theory and practice. The match heuristic guarantees a running time of $O(m+n)$ (as in Knuth-Morris-Pratt), and there are numerous improvements to reduce the actual number of comparisons. It is, however, a rather complex algorithm to implement, mostly because of the match heuristic. For this reason, we consider a variant suggested by Horspool, which is known as Boyer-Moore-Horspool. It implements a modification of the occurrence heuristic and is very fast in practice, although its worst-case running time is $\Theta(mn)$.

We earlier mentioned a subtle problem we can run into with the occurrence heuristic: It can potentially lead us to negative shifts (shifts to the left) because the rightmost occurrence of the letter is already to the right of the current position as in the example

```
date
detective
```

where the mismatched "e" in the text would lead to shifting the pattern to the left by two positions. This case occurs only if we have already matched parts of the pattern. Compare this to the case in which the last letter fails to match; we would always shift to the right. Horspool's solution is to always shift according to the last letter, not to the letter that actually fails. This eliminates negative shifts.

Example 9.4.8. In the case of

```
date
detective
```

we fail matching "a" against "e". We then shift the pattern to align the fourth letter in "detective" (the "e") with the next possible match in "date". Since "date" does not contain another "e", we can shift the entire pattern beyond the "e"

```
   date
detective
```

skipping three positions.   □

In summary, Horspool's version reacts to a mismatch by trying to align $t[i + m - 1]$ with the rightmost occurrence of that letter in the pattern to the left of $p[m - 1]$. This rule guarantees that the pattern is always shifted to the right. To perform the correct shift, we need to know for each letter of the alphabet what its rightmost occurrence is in the pattern to the left of $p[m - 1]$. More formally,

$$shift[w] = \begin{cases} m - 1 - \max\{i < m - 1 \mid p[i] = w\} & \text{if } w \text{ is in } p[0..m-2] \\ m & \text{otherwise.} \end{cases}$$

Example 9.4.9. For the word p ="kettle", we get the following shifts. If the letter in t aligned with the last letter of p is a "k", shift by 5; if it is an "e", shift by 4; if it is a "t", shift by 2; and if it is an "l", shift by 1. For any other letter, the shift is 6.

For example if t ="tea kettle", we initially align:

```
kettle
tea kettle
```

The mismatch of "l" and "k" leads to a shift of 4 because $t[5]$ = "e", and we find the match:

```
   kettle
tea kettle
```

Similarly, the mismatch of "e" and "t" in the following example leads to a shift of 2 because the last letter is a "t":

```
kettle
a kettle
```

Again, we find an immediate match.   □

Algorithm 9.4.10 Boyer-Moore-Horspool Search. This algorithm searches for an occurrence of a pattern p in a text t over alphabet Σ. It returns the smallest index i such that $t[i..i + m - 1] = p$ or -1 if no such index exists.

Input Parameters: p, t
Output Parameters: None

```
boyer_moore_horspool_search(p, t) {
    m = p.length
    n = t.length
    // compute the shift table
    for k = 0 to |Σ| − 1
        shift[k] = m
    for k = 0 to m − 2
        shift[p[k]] = m − 1 − k
    // search
    i = 0
    while (i + m ≤ n) {
        j = m − 1
        while (t[i + j] == p[j]) {
            j = j − 1
            if (j < 0)
                return i
        }
        i = i + shift[t[i + m − 1]] // shift by last letter
    }
    return −1
}
```

The *boyer_moore_horspool_search* algorithm runs in time $O(mn)$ if we assume that the alphabet Σ is fixed. Unlike the full Boyer-Moore algorithm and Knuth-Morris-Pratt algorithm, its space usage does not depend on p. Indeed, it uses only space $O(|\Sigma|)$, which is constant if we assume that the alphabet is fixed. In practice, the algorithm gives running times comparable to Boyer-Moore and is therefore quite useful, since it is much simpler to implement and uses less space.

Theorem 9.4.11. *The algorithm boyer_moore_horspool_search correctly computes the position of the first occurrence of pattern t in text t if there is one or returns −1 otherwise. The algorithm runs in time $O(mn)$.*

We leave the proof of the theorem to Exercise 9 (running time) and Exercises 9.13–9.15 (correctness).

Exercises

1S. In Example 9.4.5 we saw that the occurrence heuristic can lead to a negative shift. Give an example, where the pattern p is shifted by $|p| - 1$ positions to the left (the maximal possible).

2. In Example 9.4.5 we saw that the occurrence heuristic can lead to a negative shift. Is it possible that it leads to a zero shift?

3S. Compute the *boyer_moore_horspool_search* shift table for the pattern "banana".

4. Compute the *boyer_moore_horspool_search* shift table for the pattern "antenna".

5. Compute the *boyer_moore_horspool_search* shift table for the pattern "panpipe".

6S. Use *boyer_moore_horspool_search* to search for "banana" in "cananabananab". How many comparisons does the algorithm make? (Use the results from Exercise 3.)

7. Use *boyer_moore_horspool_search* to search for "pappar" in "pappappapparrassanuaragh".

8. Use the match heuristic to search for "banana" in "cananabananab".

9S. Show that *boyer_moore_horspool_search* runs in time $\Omega(mn)$ in the worst case (assume the alphabet is fixed).

10. Show that *boyer_moore_horspool_search* runs in time $O(n/m)$ in the best case (assume the alphabet is fixed). How does that compare to the best-case running times of the other algorithms we have seen?

11. We cannot always assume that the alphabet Σ is of a small, fixed size. What is the worst-case running time of *boyer_moore_horspool_search* if we take into account the size of the alphabet?

9.5 Approximate Pattern Matching

There are numerous variants of the approximate pattern-matching problem, reflecting the many situations in which a search has to be based on partial, imprecise information.

Think, for example, of comparing two files on your file system to find out how similar they are or what has changed in a new version of the file. The UNIX operating system supports the commands `diff` and `sdiff` to do that.

Example 9.5.1. We have files `prereq1.txt` containing CSC 225, CSC323, CSC343, CSC345, CSC415, CSC 416, and CSC 417 and `prereq2.txt` containing CSC 211, CSC 212, CSC 309, CSC 343, CSC 345, CSC 415, and CSC 416, each class name listed on a separate line of the file. Running the UNIX command `sdiff prereq1.txt prereq2.txt` yields:

```
CSC 225        |    CSC 211
CSC 323        |    CSC 212
               >    CSC 309
CSC 343             CSC 343
CSC 345             CSC 345
CSC 415             CSC 415
CSC 416             CSC 416
CSC 417        <
```

Here | means different, > denotes an additional line in the second file, and < denotes an additional line in the first file.   □

How does `sdiff` know whether it is actually pairing up the right text if there are several possibilities? The answer, of course, is, it does not and cannot know, because it does not know how the two files are related. One way to approach this problem is to define a measure of how different the two documents are by thinking of the differences as changes made by somebody starting with one file and editing it to become identical to the second file. The smallest number of changes necessary to turn one file into the other is called the **edit distance** between the two files; and associated with it we have the sequence of edits turning one file into the other, which we can use to distinguish between text that has changed, and text that has not changed.

Example 9.5.2. In the case of `prereq1.txt` and `prereq2.txt` from Example 9.5.1, four changes are sufficient to turn `prereq1.txt` into `prereq2.txt`: Change CSC 225 to CSC 211, CSC 323 to CSC 212, add CSC 309, and remove CSC 417. Three changes would not be enough to turn one file into the other, justifying the output of `sdiff`.   □

A seemingly different problem occurs when searching for a word in a text, but we are not entirely sure of the correct spelling. In that case, we want to tell the program that it should look for text similar to the one entered. It turns out that solving this problem is strongly related to comparing two texts.

A final variant we consider allows the pattern to contain wildcards such as "∗" for any sequence of symbols and "?" for any single symbol.

Example 9.5.3. In UNIX the command `ls *.html` lists all files in the current directory that end in `.html`, such as `index.html` and `default.html`. The command `ls page?.html` would list `page2.html` but not `page11.html`. □

Here we consider only the don't-care wildcard "?" matching a single letter. The "∗" wildcard can be handled using regular expressions, which we investigate in Section 9.6.

Edit Distance

We gave an intuitive definition of the edit distance of two texts s and t as the smallest number of editorial changes we would have to make to turn s into t. We need to specify what editorial changes are available. We allow three operations at unit cost:

(R)   Replace one letter with another letter.
(D)   Delete one letter.
(I)   Insert one letter.

Example 9.5.4. Let us see how to turn "ghost" into "house" using three operations:

g	h	o	s	t	delete g at position 0
h	o	s	t		insert u after position 1
h	o	u	s	t	replace t by e at position 4
h	o	u	s	e	

Note that we do not require the intermediary words to be correct English words. □

Of course, there might be several ways of turning one word into another, and some of them may take more operations than others. We define the *edit distance* dist(s, t) of two words s and t to be the smallest number of operations selected from (R), (D), and (I) that turns s into t. Note that we can always turn s into t; in the worst case we can delete all $|s|$ letters of s and then insert the $|t|$ letters of t in the right order. This shows that

$$\text{dist}(s, t) \leq |s| + |t|.$$

It turns out that the edit distance of two words can be computed very naturally using the dynamic-programming technique from Chapter 8. As subproblems of computing dist(s, t), we first compute the edit distance between prefixes of s and t, namely dist$(s[0..i], t[0..j])$, for $0 \leq i < |s|, 0 < j < |t|$.

Example 9.5.5. Here is the table of distances for the words $s = $ "presto", and $t = $ "peseta":

		0	1	2	3	4	5
		p	e	s	e	t	a
0	p	0	1	2	3	4	5
1	r	1	1	2	3	4	5
2	e	2	1	2	2	3	4
3	s	3	2	1	2	3	4
4	t	4	3	2	2	2	3
5	o	5	4	3	3	3	3

For example, $\text{dist}(s[0], t[0]) = 0$ because they are both the same letter, "p". Then $\text{dist}(s[0], t[0..j]) = j$ because the quickest way of turning "p" into $t[0..j]$, the prefixes of "peseta", is by appending the j letters $t[1..j]$. Similarly, $\text{dist}(s[0..1], t[0..j]) = j$ for $j \geq 1$ because we can replace "r" by "e" and append the remaining letters. Also, $\text{dist}(s[0..4], t[0..3])$ is 2 because we can delete the "r" from "prest" and replace the "t" by "e". Finally, we can turn "presto" into "peseta" by removing the "r", inserting an "e" before the "t", and replacing the "o" by an "a".   □

Let us define $d_{i,j} = \text{dist}(s[0..i], t[0..j])$. Then the edit distance of s and t is $\text{dist}(s, t) = d_{|s|-1,|t|-1}$. The question is, how do we compute the values in the table?

We need to compute $d_{i,j}$, the edit distance between $s[0..i]$, and $t[0..j]$. Let us begin at the end: How did $s[i]$, the last letter of $s[0..i]$, become $t[j]$, the last letter of $t[0..j]$? There are three operations we can use:

(R)   Replace $s[i]$ by $t[j]$ and turn $s[0..i - 1]$ into $t[0..j - 1]$.
      This takes at most $d_{i-1,j-1} + 1$ operations.

(D)   Delete $s[i]$ and turn $s[0..i - 1]$ into $t[0..j]$.
      This takes $d_{i-1,j} + 1$ operations.

(I)   Insert $t[j]$ at the end of $s[0..i]$ and turn $s[0..i]$ into $t[0..j - 1]$.
      This takes $d_{i,j-1} + 1$ operations.

However, there is one special case: If $s[i]$ and $t[j]$ are the same letter, then we do not actually have to replace $s[i]$ by $t[j]$ in (R), and it takes only $d_{i-1,j-1}$ steps to turn $s[0..i]$ into $t[0..j]$ by turning $s[0..i - 1]$ into $t[0..j - 1]$.

This discussion shows that we can turn $s[0..i]$ into $t[0..j]$ in at most

$$
\min \left\{ \begin{array}{l} d_{i-1,j-1} + \left\{ \begin{array}{ll} 0 & \text{if } s[i] = t[j] \\ 1 & \text{else} \end{array} \right. \\ d_{i-1,j} + 1 \\ d_{i,j-1} + 1 \end{array} \right\} \text{ steps.}
$$

Since we exhausted all of the possibilities of how $s[i]$ can turn into $t[j]$, this formula gives us the correct value of $d_{i,j}$. The formula shows that $d_{i,j}$ can be computed from the values of $d_{i-1,j}$, $d_{i-1,j-1}$ and $d_{i,j-1}$. In terms of the table containing the values, this means that $d_{i,j}$, the content of cell (i, j), can be computed from just three neighboring cells: cell $(i - 1, j)$ to the left, cell $(i - 1, j - 1)$ to the upper left, and cell $(i, j - 1)$ above. The easiest way to achieve this is to compute the table row by row starting in the upper left-hand corner.

Example 9.5.6. With our recursive formulas at hand, let us have another look at the table we computed in Example 9.5.5. How did we get started? In row 0 we were already applying our recursive formulas to an invisible row -1. Let us add a row and column -1 to the table. The value of $d_{-1,j}$ should be the smallest number of operations turning $s[0.. - 1]$ (the empty string) into $t[0..j]$. Since we can turn the empty string into $t[0..j]$ by inserting the $j + 1$ symbols of t and $j + 1$ operations are necessary, $d_{-1,j}$ has to be $j + 1$ and similarly, $d_{i,-1} = i + 1$.

Here then is the table of distances for the words $s =$ "presto", and $t =$ "peseta" including row -1:

		-1	0	1	2	3	4	5
			p	e	s	e	t	a
-1		0	1	2	3	4	5	6
0	p	1	0	1	2	3	4	5
1	r	2	1	1	2	3	4	5
2	e	3	2	1	2	2	3	4
3	s	4	3	2	1	2	3	4
4	t	5	4	3	2	2	2	3
5	o	6	5	4	3	3	3	3

Let us verify $d_{3,2}$. Since $s[3] = t[2]$, the value of $d_{3,2}$ is the minimum of $d_{2,2} + 1 = 3$, $d_{2,1} = 1$, and $d_{3,1} + 1 = 3$, which is 1. As a second example, consider $d_{5,3}$. Here $s[5] \neq t[3]$, so $d_{5,3}$ is the minimum of $d_{4,3} + 1 = 3$, $d_{4,2} + 1 = 3$, and $d_{5,2} + 1 = 4$, which is 3.

The table tells us more than just the distances. Going back from $d_{5,5}$ we can come up with a list of three operations that turn "presto" into "peseta". The value of $d_{5,5}$ is 3 because $d_{4,4}$ is 2. Hence, the last operation was replacing "o" at position 5 by "a". In turn, $d_{4,4}$ is 2 because $d_{3,3}$ is 2 (no operation). Next, $d_{3,3}$ equals 2 because $d_{3,2}$ equals 1 (insert "e" at position 3). The value of $d_{3,2}$ traces back to $d_{2,1}$ (no operation), which in turn goes back to $d_{1,0}$ (no operation). The value of $d_{1,0}$ is determined by $d_{0,0}$ (delete "r" at position 1), which in turn goes back to $d_{-1,-1}$ (no operation). Reading backwards tells us how to turn "presto" into "peseta": Delete "r" at position 1 to get "pesto", insert "e" at position 3 to get "peseto", replace "o" at position 5 to get "peseta". □

Algorithm 9.5.7 Edit-Distance. This algorithm returns the edit distance between two words s and t.

Input Parameters: s, t
Output Parameters: None

```
edit_distance(s, t) {
    m = s.length
    n = t.length
    for i = −1 to m − 1
        dist[i, −1] = i + 1 // initialization of column −1
    for j = 0 to n − 1
        dist[−1, j] = j + 1 // initialization of row −1
    for i = 0 to m − 1
        for j = 0 to n − 1
            if (s[i] == t[j])
                dist[i, j] = min(dist[i − 1, j − 1], dist[i − 1, j] + 1,
                                 dist[i, j − 1] + 1)
            else
                dist[i, j] = 1 + min(dist[i − 1, j − 1], dist[i − 1, j], dist[i, j − 1])
    return dist[m − 1, n − 1]
}
```

Theorem 9.5.8. *The algorithm edit_distance correctly computes the distance between two strings in time $O(mn)$.*

Proof. We have already verified correctness. The running time of $O(mn)$ is caused by the two nested loops. Preprocessing takes time $O(m+n)$ only. ∎

Best Approximate Match

In text searching, we are often interested in finding approximate rather than exact matches. In the general problem, we are given a pattern p and a text t, and we try to find a part of the text t that is as similar to p as possible. A solution depends on the measure of similarity employed. If we use edit distance, the problem becomes:

> Given a pattern p and a text t, find a subword $w = t[i..j]$ of t such that dist(p, w) is minimal.

The word w will then be considered an approximate match, and dist(p, w) is a measure of how good the match is.

Example 9.5.9. The best match for "retrieve" in "retreive, retreeve, retreev" is the subword "retreeve" starting at position 10, which has a distance 1 (replace i by e). ☐

A simple approach to finding the best approximate match would be to compute the edit distance between p and all subwords of t and look for the smallest one. Let $m = |p|$, and $n = |t|$. Since there are n^2 subwords of t and comparing each to p takes time $O(mn)$, this approach takes time $O(mn^3)$.

This simple approach violates the basic tenet of dynamic programming, namely not to recompute information that has already been computed. Consider running the edit-distance algorithm on p and t. The algorithm computes values $d_{i,j} = \text{dist}(p[0..i], t[0..j])$, the edit distances between $p[0..i]$ and $t[0..j]$, for all $0 \le i < m$ and $0 \le j < n$. In effect, it gives us the edit distance of p from all prefixes of t. This is already very close to what we need, the difference being that we are computing the edit distance between p and all $t[0..j]$ instead of also allowing suffixes of $t[0..j]$.

Let us define

$$ad_{i,j} = \min\{\text{dist}(p[0..i], t[\ell..j]) \mid 0 \le \ell \le j + 1\};$$

that is, $ad_{i,j}$ is the smallest edit distance between $p[0..i]$ and a subword of t ending in j (possibly the empty string if $\ell = j + 1$). The value we are looking for, then, is the minimum of $ad_{m-1,0}, ad_{m-1,1}, \ldots, ad_{m-1,n-1}$. The new array $ad_{i,j}$ looks more complicated than $d_{i,j}$, but it can actually be computed using the same formula as for d:

$$ad_{i,j} = \min \left\{ \begin{array}{l} ad_{i-1,j-1} + \left\{ \begin{array}{ll} 0 & \text{if } p[i] = t[j] \\ 1 & \text{else} \end{array} \right. \\ ad_{i-1,j} + 1 \\ ad_{i,j-1} + 1 \end{array} \right\}.$$

The formula can be justified using the same argument we used for $d_{i,j}$. If $p[i] = t[j]$, then we can extend the match found by $ad_{i-1,j-1}$. If $p[i] \ne t[j]$, then there are three possibilities of how the last letter of $p[0..i]$ and some $t[\ell..j]$ matched: replacing $p[i]$ by $t[j]$, deleting $p[i]$, or inserting $t[j]$ at the end of p. Since these are all possibilities, the formula is correct.

The computation of the ad array differs from the computation of the d array in the initialization. In the definition of $ad_{i,j}$, as an extreme case we allow $p[0..i]$ to be reduced to the empty string. Hence, $ad_{-1,j} = 0$ for all j (because the empty string is a substring of any string at any position j).

Algorithm 9.5.10 Best Approximate Match. This algorithm returns the smallest edit distance between a pattern p and a subword of a text t.

Input Parameters: p, t
Output Parameters: None

```
best_approximate_match(p, t) {
    m = p.length
    n = t.length
    for i = -1 to m - 1
        adist[i, -1] = i + 1  // initialization of column -1
    for j = 0 to n - 1
        adist[-1, j] = 0  // initialization of row -1
```

```
for i = 0 to m − 1
    for j = 0 to n − 1
        if (p[i] == t[j])
            adist[i, j] = min(adist[i − 1, j − 1], adist[i − 1, j] + 1,
                              adist[i, j − 1] + 1)
        else
            adist[i, j] = 1 + min(adist[i − 1, j − 1], adist[i − 1, j],
                                  adist[i, j − 1])
    differences = m
    for j = 0 to n − 1
        if (adist[m − 1, j] < differences)
            differences = adist[m − 1, j]
    return differences
}
```

As in the case of *edit_distance*, we have the following theorem.

Theorem 9.5.11. *The algorithm best_approximate_match correctly computes the smallest distance between p and a subword of t in time $O(mn)$.*

Example 9.5.12. Let us use *best_approximate_match* to search for "pierce" (misspelled) in the list "james, peirce, dewey":

		−1	0	1	2	3	4	5	6	7	8	9	10	11	12	13	14	15	16	17
			j	a	m	e	s	,	p	e	i	r	c	e	,	d	e	w	e	y
−1		0	0	0	0	0	0	0	0	0	0	0	0	0	0	0	0	0	0	0
0	p	1	1	1	1	1	1	1	0	1	1	1	1	1	1	1	1	1	1	1
1	i	2	2	2	2	2	2	2	1	1	1	2	2	2	2	2	2	2	2	2
2	e	3	3	3	3	2	3	3	2	2	2	2	3	2	3	3	2	3	2	3
3	r	4	4	4	4	3	4	4	3	3	3	2	3	3	3	4	4	4	3	3
4	c	5	5	5	5	4	4	5	4	4	4	3	2	3	4	4	5	5	4	4
5	e	6	6	6	6	5	5	5	5	4	5	4	3	2	3	4	4	5	5	5

The smallest value in the last row is 2, and we therefore have a match for "pierce" of that distance. Tracing the 2 back, we find out that the match is "peirce" in positions 6 to 11.   □

Call a match w in t a *k-approximate match for p*, if $dist(w, p) \leq k$. We can ask the question of whether, given p and t, a k-approximate match exists. Algorithm 9.5.10 solves the problem in time $O(mn)$. Using a data structure called *suffix trees*, some clever preprocessing improves the time to $O(kn)$.

Searching with Don't-Cares

For the purpose of this section, a pattern may contain—in addition to the letters from the alphabet—a special character, "?", called the don't-care symbol. We assume that "?" does not belong to Σ. For such a pattern p, a **(don't-care) match** in a text t is a position i such that $p[j] = t[i + j]$ or $p[j] = $ "?" for all $0 \leq j < |p|$.

In this section we present an algorithm due to Pinter to find such a match. This algorithm builds on an algorithm by Aho and Corasick, which in turn extends the Knuth-Morris-Pratt search. Aho and Corasick's algorithm solves the *multiple pattern* search problem: Given a text t and a set $P = \{p_1, \ldots, p_k\}$ of patterns (without the don't-care symbol), find all occurrences in t of every pattern in P. A simple solution would be to run the modified Knuth-Morris-Pratt algorithm from Exercise 9.10 separately for each pattern, which would give us a running time of $O(m + kn)$ where $m = |p_1| + \cdots + |p_k|$. For long texts this becomes too expensive. Aho and Corasick's algorithm solves the same problem in time $O(m + n)$ by looking at the set of patterns as a tree of patterns and implementing a shift table for that tree. Without going into further detail, we will just assume that we have an algorithm running in time $O(m + n)$ solving the multiple pattern search problem.

We return to the problem of matching don't-care patterns. We first split the pattern p into largest subpatterns not containing don't-care symbols.

Example 9.5.13. Consider the pattern "r?ss?ll". This pattern splits into three subpatterns: "r", "ss", and "ll". ☐

The splitting gives us a set of normal patterns $P = \{p_1, \ldots, p_k\}$, where p_j starts at index ℓ_j in p. Suppose t contains a don't-care match for p starting at position i. That means we have a normal match of p_j at position $i + \ell_j$ in t for $1 \le j \le k$.

Example 9.5.14. Assume we are searching the text "llssellrissulliss" for the pattern "r?ss?ll". $P = \{\text{"r"}, \text{"ss"}, \text{"ll"}\}$, and $\ell_1 = 0$, $\ell_2 = 2$, and $\ell_3 = 6$. The match of "r?ss?ll" starting at position 7 of the text corresponds to matches of "r" at position $7 + \ell_1 = 7$, "ss" at position $7 + \ell_2 = 9$, and "ll" at position $7 + \ell_3 = 13$. ☐

Let us reverse the viewpoint. Suppose that we find a match of pattern p_j starting at position i in t. This pattern potentially contributes to a don't-care match of p starting at position $i - \ell_j$. The idea of the algorithm now is to keep a counter $c[i]$ for each position i and increase the counter by one for each pattern p_j that contributes to a don't-care match of p starting in i. If there is a don't-care match of p starting in i, then $c[i]$ is increased k times, once for each p_j. Since the same pattern p_j cannot increase the same counter twice, a counter can become k only if all k patterns are present with the correct offset to form a don't-care match of p. In short, $c[i] = k$ if and only if there is a don't-care match of p starting at position i.

Algorithm 9.5.15 Don't-Care-Search. This algorithm searches for an occurrence of a pattern p with don't-care symbols in a text t over alphabet Σ. It returns the smallest index i such that $t[i + j] = p[j]$ or $p[j] = $ "?" for all j with $0 \le j < |p|$, or -1 if no such index exists.

Input Parameters: p, t
Output Parameters: None

```
don't_care_search(p, t) {
    m = p.length
    k = 0
    start = 0
    for i = 0 to m
        c[i] = 0
    // compute the subpatterns of p, and store them in array sub
    for i = 0 to m
        if (p[i] == "?") {
            if (start != i) {
                // found the end of a don't-care free subpattern
                sub[k].pattern = p[start..i − 1]
                sub[k].start = start
                k = k + 1
            }
            start = i + 1
        }
    if (start != i) {
        // end of the last don't-care free subpattern
        sub[k].pattern = p[start..i − 1]
        sub[k].start = start
        k = k + 1
    }
    P = {sub[0].pattern, . . . , sub[k − 1].pattern}
    aho_corasick(P, t) // we assume this algorithm is implemented
    for each match of sub[j].pattern in t starting at position i {
        c[i − sub[j].start] = c[i − sub[j].start] + 1
        if (c[i − sub[j].start] == k)
            return i − sub[j].start
    }
    return −1
}
```

The preprocessing in the algorithm takes time $O(m)$ (for determining the subpatterns) and $O(m + n)$ for running the Aho-Corasick algorithm. In each step of the main loop, a counter gets increased. There are n counters, each of which can be at most k. Hence, the body of the loop is performed at most kn times. Overall this gives us a running time of $O(m + kn)$. In case k is bounded (if we allow a limited number of don't-care symbols only, for example), then the running time is $O(m + n)$. Otherwise it could be as large as $O(mn)$. No better algorithms are currently known if k is not bounded.

Theorem 9.5.16. *The algorithm don't_care_search correctly performs a search with don't-cares in time $O(m + kn)$.*

Proof. We have already analyzed the running time of the algorithm. The correctness follows from the observation that $c[i]$ is k if and only if $sub[j].pattern$ matches t starting at position $i + sub[j].start$ for all $1 \le j \le k$. ∎

The reason we were using Aho-Corasick was that it performed in time $O(m + n)$ rather than $O(m + kn)$ (otherwise we could have just used Knuth-Morris-Pratt). Now it seems that this was unnecessary since *don't_care_search* ends up taking time $O(m + kn)$. However, the bottleneck in *don't_care_search* is incrementing the counters. Aho-Corasick in each step may find multiple matches of strings. If we can increase the counters for these matches simultaneously in constant time (on a parallel machine, for example), *don't_care_search* takes time $O(m + n)$ only.

Exercises

1S. Determine the edit distance between "center" and "centre" by computing the table of $d_{i,j}$ using *edit_distance*.

2. Determine the edit distance between "photographer" and "phonograph" by computing the table of $d_{i,j}$ using *edit_distance*.

3. Determine the edit distance between "banana" and "antenna" by computing the table of $d_{i,j}$ using *edit_distance*.

4S. Trace *best_approximate_match* to find the best match for "nite" in "tonight".

5. Trace *best_approximate_match* to find the best match for "specter" in "parerga et paralipomena".

6. Trace *best_approximate_match* to find the best match for "fudge" in "praeludium and fugue".

7S. Extend *best_approximate_match* to print the best approximate match it finds and the position of that match.

8. Write an algorithm that takes as input the matrix computed by *best_approximate_match* (like the matrix in Example 9.5.12), and from that matrix determines a best approximate match.

9S. Write a don't-care pattern for time and date.

10. Write a don't-care pattern for telephone numbers with area codes (assume the area code is within parentheses and groups are separated by dashes).

11. Write a don't-care pattern for IP-address, assuming all four blocks consist of three digits.

12S. Can appending a "?" to the end of a pattern change the results of a don't-care search?

13S. Trace *don't_care_search* on pattern "01?10" and text

"0110011110101010".

14. Trace *don't_care_search* on pattern "(?)" and text "(12),(2),(14)".

15. Trace *don't_care_search* on pattern "(??/??)" and text

"(1/99),(12/01),(10/8)".

16S. Trace *don't_care_search* on pattern "ind???nd?nt" and text

"Find, indented, independently."

Do not ignore spaces in the text.

9.6 Regular Expression Matching

Regular expressions are a very powerful technique for finding patterns with a given structure. In Perl (Practical Extracting and Reporting Language), for example, we could write

$$\text{if } (\$t =\sim /\backslash d\{3\}-\backslash d\{4\}/) \dots$$

to check whether variable *t* contains a local telephone number. The regular expression between the two forward slashes tells Perl that we are looking for three digits, followed by a dash, followed by another four digits. Most programming languages support regular expressions, including scripting languages such as JavaScript and VBScript for client- and server-side form validation and data extraction. The following JavaScript code could be used for verifying whether the variable *ccn* contains a correctly formatted American Express credit card number:

```
ccn.replace(/(\s|-)/,""); // remove spaces and dashes
valid = true;
if (!(ccn.match(/^3(4|7)\d{13}$/)))
    valid = false;
return valid;
```

The regular expression checks that *ccn* starts (^) with a 3 followed by either a 4 or a 7 followed by another thirteen digits before it ends ($).

Regular expressions as implemented by Perl and other programming languages are very rich, allowing features such as back-referencing in which a partial match of the pattern can be reused within the same pattern. Most of these features are there to simplify the pattern writing; but some features, such as back-referencing, make the problem more difficult. In this section we restrict ourselves to the three central constructs of regular expressions:

concatenation, **alternation**, and **repetition** (to be explained shortly). As basic symbols, we allow only symbols over some fixed alphabet Σ although implementing collections of symbols like $\backslash d$ for the class of digits would not be difficult. We assume that the symbols "$\cdot$" (concatenation), "$|$" (alternation), and "$*$" (repetition, called the *Kleene star*) are not part of the alphabet Σ, and neither are the parentheses "(", ")", which we use for grouping purposes.

The simplest pattern is a *concatenation* of letters, for example "html". We should really write "h$\cdot$t$\cdot$m$\cdot$l" to stress the fact that we are concatenating the letters, but we use the usual convention of dropping the "$\cdot$" when writing the pattern. It is understood implicitly.

Alternation allows us to offer options. For example, the pattern "jpg|gif" would match both "jpg" and "gif". If we wanted a pattern for image file extensions, we could use either ".jpg|.gif", or ".(jpg|gif)".[†] We use parentheses for grouping patterns (in this case to restrict the scope of the alternation symbol "$|$").

Finally the Kleene star allows us to match a pattern repeatedly. For example, "$0*$" matches any sequence of zeros (including the empty one). "$01*0$" matches any word that starts with a zero, ends with a zero, and has any number of ones between the two zeros.

Example 9.6.1. A pattern for binary strings would be "$(0|1)*$". Patterns are not unique. For example, "$0*(0|1)*$" is also a pattern for binary strings. The pattern

$$\text{``}\#(0|1|2|3|4|5|6|7|8|9|A|B|C|D|E|F)*\text{''}$$

is matched by hexadecimal numbers with an initial "#". □

Regarding precedence, note that $*$ binds more strongly than concatenation, and concatenation binds more strongly than alternation.

Example 9.6.2. "$01*$" describes all strings starting with a zero followed by any number of ones. The Kleene star applies only to "1", since it binds stronger than the concatenation between "0" and "1". If we wanted to describe strings that consist of arbitrarily long repetitions of "01", we would use "$(01)*$".

We saw earlier that concatenation binds more strongly than alternation. That is why ".jpg|.gif" matches both ".jpg" and ".gif". If alternation had precedence over concatenation, the pattern would match both ".jpggif" and ".jp.gif"; if that was our intention, we would write ".jp(g|.)gif". □

We need a more formal definition of what it means for a word w to match a pattern p. We define $L(p) \subseteq \Sigma^*$ as the set of all words over the alphabet Σ that match p by induction over the structure of p. There are four cases:

[†]For a regular expression in Perl or Javascript, we would have to escape the period, "$\backslash$.(jpg|gif)", because it is a special character.

$p = $"$a$", for some $a \in \Sigma$ $L(p) = \{$"a"$\}$,

$p = $"$q_1 | q_2$" $L(p) = L(q_1) \cup L(q_2)$,

$p = $"$q_1 \cdot q_2$" $L(p) = \{w_1 \cdot w_2 \mid w_1 \in L(q_1), w_2 \in L(q_2)\}$,

$p = $"$q*$" $L(p) = \{w_1 \cdot w_2 \cdots w_n \mid w_1, \ldots, w_n \in L(q), n \in \mathbb{N}\}$.

We say a text t **matches a pattern** p, if $t \in L(p)$. Patterns can be *ambiguous*; that is, there might be more than one way that a text can match a pattern as illustrated by the pattern "$(a * |ab)b*$" and the text "*abb*".

We work with a binary tree representation of the pattern. As an example, a binary tree representation of the pattern "$1(1 * |0*)1$", or "$1 \cdot (1 * |0*) \cdot 1$" to be more precise, is shown in Figure 9.6.1.

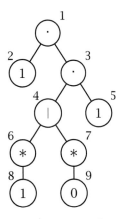

Figure 9.6.1 A binary tree representation of the pattern "$1(1 * |0*)1$".

Each internal node contains an operation ($\cdot$, $|$, or $*$) and each leaf contains an element from Σ. The operators $\cdot$ and $|$ are binary and $*$ is unary. Different binary trees can represent the same pattern (see Exercise 9.44).

A node in the tree determines a subpattern of the original pattern, namely the pattern described by the tree rooted in the node.

Example 9.6.3. Consider the binary tree representation of "$1(1 * |0*)1$" in Figure 9.6.1. Node 1 corresponds to the full pattern, which is the concatenation of the pattern "1" rooted in node 2 and "$(1 * |0*)1$" rooted in node 3. Node 4 corresponds to "$(1 * |0*)$", and node 7 corresponds to "$0*$".   □

Turning the regular expression into a binary tree requires some knowledge of parsing theory, a specialized task in the area of compiler construction. Exercise 9.43 asks for such an algorithm.

Before we attack the full problem of finding a match for a regular expression in a text, let us first see how to use the tree to find out whether a word w matches a pattern p, or, more formally, whether $w \in L(p)$.

The main idea is to keep track of which letters can be matched next. Consider, for example, the pattern "$0(0|1) * 0$". A corresponding tree is shown in Figure 9.6.2.

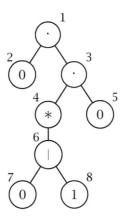

Figure 9.6.2 A binary tree representation of the pattern "0(0|1) ∗ 0".

Initially we expect to see the 0 in node 2. A 1 would lead to immediate failure. If w starts with a 0, we have matched the left subpattern of node 1, and we continue with the subpattern of node 3. The next symbol we expect could be any of the symbols in nodes 7, 8, and 5. We have to include node 5 because ∗ does allow multiplicity zero. In case w ="00", the second zero has to be the zero of node 5. If the second letter of w is a 1, we know we are in node 8. After that, again nodes 7, 8, and 5 are possible. If the second letter is a zero, we could be in node 7 or 5. Again, the next possible nodes are 7, 8, and 5. And so we continue. If we finish with the last letter of w matching node 5, then we know we have found a match. Otherwise, we know that w does not match because we considered all possibilities of how the pattern could match the word. We can therefore rephrase our basic idea more precisely: Keep track of the leaves of the pattern that can be matched next. We call these leaves the current **candidates**. With each new letter of w, we update the set of candidates to the set of leaves we could possibly match next. We still need to clarify some points. How do we find the candidates to start the process with? There might be several.

Example 9.6.4. The pattern "(0|1) ∗ 0" initially has three candidates for the first letter to match. Figure 9.6.3 shows the binary tree corresponding to the pattern. All leaves, nodes 5, 6, and 3, could be matched by the first letter of a text, and therefore make up the set of initial candidates. If w ="00", then the first zero is matched by node 5; if w ="10", the first "1" is matched by node 6, and, finally, if w ="0", then the zero is matched by node 3. □

We compute the initial set of candidates in a procedure *start*. Another procedure *match_letter* goes through the tree and determines which of the current candidates actually matches the next letter of w; it rejects the ones that do not match. After that, we apply the procedure *next_cand* that uses the information compiled by *match_letter* to compute the new set of candidates.

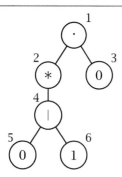

Figure 9.6.3 A binary tree representation of the pattern "$(0|1) * 0$".

In a simple implementation of these procedures, *next_cand* might take time $\Theta(n^2)$ because there could be $\Theta(n)$ candidates, each spawning $\Theta(n)$ new candidates. However, there are only n leaves to the tree, which suggests that a more sophisticated approach might lead to a better result. In fact, all three procedures can be implemented to run in time $O(n)$. To make this work, we need to precompute some information on the tree.

In Example 9.6.4 we had to allow node 3 as an initial candidate although it is the second part of a concatenation (node 1). The reason was that the pattern "$(0|1)*$", which corresponds to node 1, could match the empty word (because of the Kleene star in node 2). That is, to make the decision that node 3 had to be included in the initial set of candidates, we had to know that node 2 could match the empty string. We therefore store in each node of the tree a Boolean attribute to indicate whether the pattern corresponding to that node could match the empty word. Here is an algorithm using divide and conquer to compute this attribute that we call *eps* (for ε, the empty word). In practice we would compute this attribute while building the pattern tree.

Algorithm 9.6.5 Epsilon. This algorithm takes as input a pattern tree t. Each node contains a field *value* that is either $\cdot$, $|$, $*$ or a letter from Σ. For each node, the algorithm computes a field *eps* that is true if and only if the pattern corresponding to the subtree rooted in that node matches the empty word.

Input Parameter: t
Output Parameters: None

```
epsilon(t) {
   if (t.value == "·")
      t.eps = epsilon(t.left) && epsilon(t.right)
   else if (t.value == "|")
      t.eps = epsilon(t.left) || epsilon(t.right)
   else if (t.value == "*") {
         t.eps = true
         epsilon(t.left) // assume only child is a left child
   }
```

```
    else
        // leaf with letter in Σ
        t.eps = false
}
```

Example 9.6.6. If we run *epsilon* on the pattern "0(0 ∗ |1)1", we obtain the result shown in Figure 9.6.4.

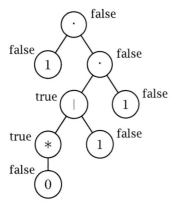

Figure 9.6.4 A binary tree representation of the pattern "0(0∗|1)1" together with the values of the *eps* attribute. □

With the help of the *eps* attribute, we can now compute the initial set of candidates (let us call them the *start positions*) in the tree. Again we use divide and conquer to traverse the tree. If the node is an alternation node, the start positions are the start positions of both subtrees (the match could start in either one). If the node is a multiplicity node, the start positions are the start positions in its subtree. If the node is a concatenation node, the start positions are the start positions of the left subtree. If the left subtree corresponds to a pattern that could be ε, we also need to add the start positions of the right subtree (remember Example 9.6.4). This gives us the following algorithm to compute the initial set of candidates.

Algorithm 9.6.7 Initialize Candidates. This algorithm takes as input a pattern tree *t*. Each node contains a field *value* that is either ·, |, ∗ or a letter from Σ and a Boolean field *eps*. Each leaf also contains a Boolean field *cand* (initially false) that is set to true if the leaf belongs to the initial set of candidates.

Input Parameter: *t*
Output Parameters: None

```
start(t) {
   if (t.value == ".") {
        start(t.left)
        if (t.left.eps)
           start(t.right)
   }
   else if (t.value == "|") {
        start(t.left)
        start(t.right)
   }
   else if (t.value == "*")
        start(t.left)
   else
      // leaf with letter in Σ
      t.cand = true
}
```

Example 9.6.8. For the pattern "$0(0 * |1)1$" of Example 9.6.6, there is only one starting position, as shown in Figure 9.6.5.

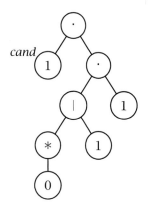

Figure 9.6.5 Only one starting position for the pattern "$0(0 * |1)1$".

The parse tree for the pattern "$(0|1) * 0$", as shown in Figure 9.6.3, contains three starting positions: 5, 6, and 3.   □

The *match_letter* procedure takes as input the tree t and the next letter a of the pattern to be processed. It prepares the tree for updating by the *next_cand* procedure by computing a Boolean attribute *matched* for each inner node of the tree that is true if the letter a successfully concludes a matching of the pattern corresponding to that node.

Example 9.6.9. We saw that the starting positions for the pattern "$(0|1) * 0$" (referring to the parse tree in Figure 9.6.3) are 5, 6, and 3. Suppose the next letter read is a 1. Since node 6 was a candidate, the pattern rooted at node 6, namely "1", is matched. So is the pattern at node 4, "(0|1)", and 2, "(0|1)∗". Similarly, reading the letter 0 would conclude matchings of the pattern "0" in node 5, the pattern "(0|1)" in node 4, the pattern "(0|1)∗" in node 2, the pattern "0" in node 3, and the full pattern, "(0|1) ∗ 0", in node 1. □

If *matched* is true for the root of the tree, we have found a match for the pattern. As before, we determine the *matched* attribute using divide and conquer. We have found a match for a concatenation node if we have completed matching its right child. An alternation node is matched if either of its children is matched, and a repetition node is matched if its child is matched. Finally, a leaf is matched if the value of the leaf (the corresponding letter in the pattern) is the same as the letter a, and the leaf is a candidate.

Algorithm 9.6.10 Match Letter. This algorithm takes as input a pattern tree t and a letter a. It computes for each node of the tree a Boolean field *matched* that is true if the letter a successfully concludes a matching of the pattern corresponding to that node. Furthermore, the *cand* fields in the leaves are reset to false.

Input Parameters: t, a
Output Parameters: None

```
match_letter(t, a) {
    if (t.value == "·") {
        match_letter(t.left, a)
        t.matched = match_letter(t.right, a)
    }
    else if (t.value == "|")
        t.matched = match_letter(t.left, a) || match_letter(t.right, a)
    else if (t.value == "*")
        t.matched = match_letter(t.left, a)
    else {
        // leaf with letter in Σ
        t.matched = t.cand && (a == t.value)
        t.cand = false
    }
    return t.matched
}
```

Example 9.6.11. We return to the pattern "0(0|1) ∗ 0" whose pattern tree is shown in Figure 9.6.2. The initial configuration of the tree, after running *epsilon* and *start*, is shown in Figure 9.6.6(a). If we run *match_letter* on the tree with "0" as the input letter, only the leaf node 2 is matched (since it was the only candidate). □

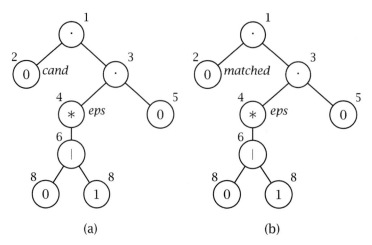

(a)   (b)

Figure 9.6.6 (a) The pattern tree of "0(0|1) ∗ 0" after running *epsilon* and *start*. Instead of displaying the values of all of the Boolean attributes *eps*, *matched*, and *cand*, we display the name of the attribute at the nodes for which the attribute is true. (b) The pattern tree from (a) after running *match_letter*(*t*,"0") on it.

With the *matched* information, we can now compute the new set of candidates. We implement the *next* algorithm with two inputs, the tree *t*, and a Boolean value *mark*, which allows us to specify whether start positions of the whole pattern should also be marked as candidates (in effect rerunning the *start* procedure). The second parameter allows us to compute the set of new candidates as the starting positions of appropriate subpatterns.

Example 9.6.12. We return to the pattern "(0|1) ∗ 0" and the corresponding pattern tree shown in Figure 9.6.3. Suppose the first letter of the text we read is a 1. The starting positions of the pattern are 5, 6, and 3. Hence the subpattern rooted in node 2 is matched. The new set of candidates then contains nodes 5 and 6, since node 2 is a Kleene star, and node 3, since node 2 was matched. □

We recursively run *next* on the whole tree. If the left child of a concatenation node has been matched, we select all of the start vertices of the right child as candidates. Also, if a repetition node has been matched, then all the start vertices of the left child are candidates.

As before, the start vertices of an alternation are the start vertices of both children nodes; the start vertices of a concatenation are the start vertices of the left child and, if the left child matches the empty pattern, the start vertices of the right node. The start vertices of a repetition node are the start vertices of its child.

Algorithm 9.6.13 New Candidates. This algorithm takes as input a pattern tree *t* that is the result of a run of *match_letter*, and a Boolean value *mark*.

It computes the new set of candidates by setting the Boolean field *cand* of the leaves.

Input Parameters: *t, mark*
Output Parameters: None

```
next(t, mark) {
    if (t.value == "·") {
        next(t.left, mark)
        if (t.left.matched)
            next(t.right, true) // candidates following a match
        else if (t.left.eps) && mark)
            next(t.right, true)
        else
            next(t.right, false)
    else if (t.value == "|") {
        next(t.left, mark)
        next(t.right, mark)
    }
    else if (t.value == "∗")
        if (t.matched)
            next(t.left, true) // candidates following a match
        else
            next(t.left, mark)
    else
        // leaf with letter in Σ
        t.cand = mark
}
```

We apply the *next* procedure by calling *next(t, false)* on the tree *t* whose candidates we want to compute.

Example 9.6.14. We continue Example 9.6.11 for pattern "0(0|1) ∗ 0". We test the pattern against the text "010". Figure 9.6.6 (b) showed the pattern tree after the application of *start* and *match_letter* for the letter "0". Figure 9.6.7 (a) shows the result of running *next* on that tree, computing the new set of candidates. We then run *match_letter* for the letter "1". Nodes 4, 5, and 6 are matched as shown in Figure 9.6.7(b). Updating the tree with *next* yields nodes 7, 8, and 5 as candidates [Figure 9.6.7(c)]. Running *match_letter* for letter "0" then yields Figure 9.6.7(d). Nodes 1, 3, 5, and 7 are matched. In particular, since node 1 is matched, we can conclude that "010" matches the pattern "0(0|1) ∗ 0", which, indeed, it does. □

We see that we could now eliminate the *start* algorithm, since it corresponds to a call of *next(t, true)* because initially all of the *matched* attributes are false.

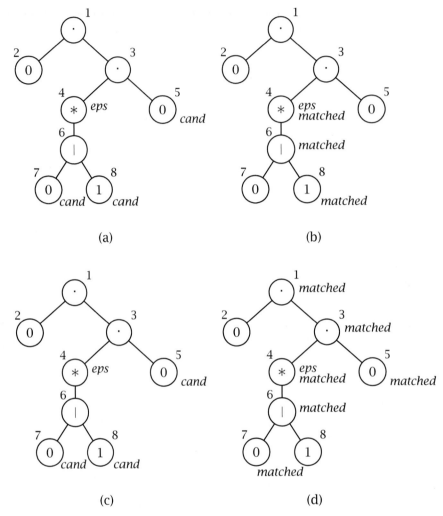

Figure 9.6.7 Matching the text "010" against the pattern "0(0|1) ∗ 0". The result of running *next* on the tree in Figure 9.6.6 (b) is shown in (a). Running *match_letter* for letter "1" on the tree from (a) yields the tree in (b). In turn, running *next* on the tree from (b) yields (c), and running *match_letter* for letter "0" on (c) gives us (d).

With these algorithms, we can finally implement the actual algorithm that tests whether a word w matches a regular expression p given as a tree with root t.

Algorithm 9.6.15 Match. This algorithm takes as input a word w and a pattern tree t and returns true if a prefix of w matches the pattern described by t.

```
   Input Parameters:    w, t
   Output Parameters:   None

match(w, t) {
  n = w.length
  epsilon(t)
  start(t)
  i = 0
  while (i < n) {
    match_letter(t, w[i])
    if (t.matched)
      return true
    next(t, false)
    i = i + 1
  }
  return false
}
```

Examples 9.6.11 and 9.6.14 trace this algorithm on pattern "0(0|1) ∗ 0" and text "010".

What is the run-time of this algorithm? The subprocedures *match, start,* and *match_letter* all take time $\Theta(m)$, where $m = |p|$, since they each traverse the pattern tree exactly once. Hence *match* takes time $O(mn)$.

However, *match* does not solve the problem we originally set out to settle, which was finding a match for a regular expression pattern in a piece of text. At first we might think of using *match* at each position of a piece of text. In the worst case this takes time $O(mn^2)$. We can do better than that, and only a simple modification to *match* is required. We need to substitute the call to *next(t,* false) by *next(t,* true), the idea being that in each step we not only continue matching the pattern but also restart the pattern by including all of its potential starting positions. The following algorithm implements these ideas.

Algorithm 9.6.16 Find. This algorithm takes as input a text *s* and a pattern tree *t* and returns true if there is a match for the pattern described by *t* in *s*.

```
   Input Parameters:    s, t
   Output Parameters:   None

find(s, t) {
  n = s.length
  epsilon(t)
  start(t)
  i = 0
  while (i < n) {
    match_letter(t, s[i])
    if (t.matched)
      return true
```

   next(t, true)
   $i = i + 1$
  }
  return false
}

The *find* algorithm runs in time $O(mn)$ as does *match*. The reason for the product is that for each letter from the text we might have to update as many as $\Omega(m)$ nodes in the pattern tree; that is, we might have to recompute $\Omega(m)$ candidates in each step. Let us have another look at what *match_letter* and *next* actually do. They take a set of candidates and a letter and compute a new set of candidates. That is, running *match_letter* followed by *next* is a function from sets of candidates and the alphabet to sets of candidates. Furthermore, it is a function we can precompute (without seeing any text), given the alphabet and the pattern. Since the pattern has length m, there are at most m leaves in the pattern tree; hence there are at most 2^m possible sets of candidates. For each such set and every letter in Σ, we can compute the next candidate set and store the information in a $2^m \times |\Sigma|$ table.

Example 9.6.17. In Examples 9.6.11 and 9.6.14 we computed, along the way, the following transitions:

Candidate Set	Letter	Candidate Set
$\varnothing$	"0"	$\varnothing$
$\varnothing$	"1"	$\varnothing$
$\{2\}$	"0"	$\{7,8,5\}$
$\{2\}$	"1"	$\varnothing$
$\{7,8,5\}$	"0"	$\{7,8,5\}$
$\{7,8,5\}$	"1"	$\{7,8,5\}$

Since there are four leaves in this example, the table should contain $2^4 \times 2$ rows; however, no other transitions can occur in *match*. When tracing *find* we would use the following rules:

Candidate Set	Letter	Candidate Set
$\{2\}$	"0"	$\{2,7,8,5\}$
$\{2\}$	"1"	$\{2\}$
$\{2,7,8,5\}$	"0"	$\{2,7,8,5\}$
$\{2,7,8,5\}$	"1"	$\{2,7,8,5\}$

Note that we automatically added node 2 to every candidate set to restart the pattern. □

After precomputing and storing the table of transitions, we can match each letter of the text in constant time, since we only have to look up the transition in the table instead of recomputing it. Hence running *match* or *find* with this method takes time at most $O(m2^m + n)$ (assuming the alphabet has fixed size). If we compare this to the $O(mn)$ running time of our first implementation, we see that the new implementation is advantageous if we have short patterns and long texts or if we have a single pattern that is matched against many different texts (in which case the $O(m2^m)$ steps for precomputing the transition table are well-spent).

Exercises

1S. What is $L(\text{``}0(0|1)*\text{''})$? Give a succinct answer.

2. What is $L(\text{``}(00|01|10|11)*\text{''})$? Give a succinct answer.

3. What is $L(\text{``}0*10*\text{''})$? Give a succinct answer.

4S. What is $L(\text{``}(0|10)*\text{''})$? Give a succinct answer.

5S. Write a pattern for octal numbers.

6. Write a pattern for decimal numbers.

7. Write a pattern for binary strings containing at least two ones.

8S. Write a pattern for binary strings containing at most two ones.

9. Write a pattern for binary strings with an odd number of ones.

10. Write a pattern for binary strings whose *weight* is a multiple of three (the weight of a binary string is the number of ones it contains).

11S. Write a pattern for binary strings of odd length.

★12. Write a pattern for binary strings that contain both an even number of ones and an even number of zeros.

13. Write a pattern for binary strings that contain the subword "111".

14S. Write a pattern for binary strings that do not contain the subword "111".

15. Write a pattern that matches both the American and the British spelling of theater. Make the pattern as succinct as possible.

16. On your web-form you have an input field for year of birth into which the user can enter four digits. Write a regular expression that verifies the input (only years in the range 1880 to 2004 should be accepted).

17S. Name at least five different programming languages that support regular expressions.

18. Show that no pattern is unique; that is, for every pattern p there is a pattern q different from p such that $L(p) = L(q)$.

19S. Find a binary tree representation for the pattern "$(0*|01*)(1|10*)$" and compute the *eps* attribute of each node using *epsilon*.

20. Find a binary tree representation for the pattern "$0*((0|1)(0|1*))$" and compute the *eps* attribute of each node using *epsilon*.

21. Find a binary tree representation for the pattern "$0*1*0$" and compute the *eps* attribute of each node using *epsilon*.

22S. Trace *match* on pattern "$0*1*0$" and text "0010" by drawing the parse tree for the pattern and listing the candidate sets that *match* computes.

23. Trace *match* on pattern "$0*1*0$" and text "0101" by drawing the parse tree for the pattern and listing the candidate sets that *match* computes.

24S. Trace *match* on pattern "$(01|0)(0|10)$" and text "010" by drawing the parse tree for the pattern and listing the candidate sets that *match* computes.

25. Trace *match* on pattern "$(0|(10*1))*$" and text "010010" by drawing the parse tree for the pattern and listing the candidate sets that *match* computes.

Notes

The first $O(m + n)$ algorithm for string matching was found independently by several authors around 1970. Knuth and Pratt based their algorithm on a theoretical result by Cook that showed that an $O(m + n)$ algorithm must exist. Independently of Cook's result, Morris had discovered a similar algorithm, and a joint paper by Knuth, Morris, and Pratt describing the algorithm was published in 1977, the same year that Rivest showed that $\Omega(n - m + 1)$ comparisons are necessary in the worst case.

Boyer and Moore found their algorithm in 1974. It was subsequently improved (and fixed) by many authors, including Knuth. Boyer-Moore-Horspool was described in Horspool, 1980. It is used in the UNIX `agrep` command. Stephen, 1994, discusses the algorithm.

In 1985 Pinter showed how to do don't-care searching using Aho-Corasick's algorithm for multiple pattern matches. Multiple pattern matches, and the related idea of suffix trees, are covered in detail by Gusfield, 1997.

The dynamic-programming algorithm for computing the edit distance between two strings was discovered independently by many authors in the early 1970s. Sellers observed in 1980 that this method could be used to find the best approximate match of a pattern in a string by simply changing the initial values of the problem. A fair amount of effort has been made to speed up these methods and reduce the space requirements. See the books by Stephen, 1994, and Gusfield, 1997.

The survey article by Aho, 1990, is a good, and short, introduction to the main problems in the field of text searching, with particular emphasis on the complexity of the problems. There are several good textbooks on these topics. Gusfield, 1997, comprehensively deals with text algorithms useful for computational biology. The emphasis is on practical algorithms with a detailed introduction to suffix trees. Crochemore and Rytter, 1994, cover more ground, including, for example, two-dimensional pattern matching and algorithms for parallel machines, neither of which Gusfield covers. The book by Stephen, 1994, is a comprehensive reference on several topics, including exact search, string distance, and approximate pattern matching. It is particularly valuable for its historical remarks and for material on comparing different algorithms.

Chapter Exercises

⋆**9.1.** [Requires probability theory.] Show that on random patterns and text the running time of *simple_text_search* is $O(n - m)$, assuming that the alphabet is fixed and each letter independently occurs with the same probability. *Hint:* Let $s = |\Sigma|$. The probability that index j in *simple_text_search* is increased k times is at most $(1/s)^k$. Show that this implies that the expected number of increases of j is at most $(s/(s - 1))^2$, and therefore the algorithm runs in time $O(n - m)$.

Exercises 9.2–9.4 investigate the actual running time of an implementation of simple_text_search.

9.2. Implement *simple_text_search* and run it on natural text inputs. Select ten different texts and ten different patterns of varying length (you can download whole books from the World Wide Web). Keep track of the running time $t(m, n)$ for the different values of m and n, and compute $t(m, n)/(m(n - m + 1))$. Do your examples show worst-case behavior?

9.3. Check whether the values $t(m, n)$ you obtained from running your implementation of *simple_text_search* meet the $O(n - m)$ upper bound predicted for random inputs.

9.4. Run your implementation of *simple_text_search* systematically on randomly generated patterns and texts for a range of values for m and n. Do your experiments bear out the $O(n - m)$ upper bound?

9.5. We implemented *rabin_karp_search* on a binary alphabet. Modify the algorithm so that it works on an arbitrary (but fixed) alphabet Σ containing d letters.

$\mathcal{WWW}$ **9.6.** Implement *mc_rabin_karp_search* and test how many errors it makes, that is, how many false matches it lists. Test with randomly chosen texts and patterns of lengths $n = 100, 200, 1000$ and $m = 3, 10, 50$ (giving you nine possible combinations). *Hint:* If you do not have any software to generate a random prime in the range from 2 to mn^2, pick one by hand from a list of prime numbers.

9.7. Show how to extend *rabin_karp_search* to work for patterns containing the don't-care symbol "?". *Hint:* Aim first for a $O(kn + m)$ algorithm, where k is the number of don't-care symbols in p. Then, modify the choice of q to make the algorithm work in time $O(n + m)$ for any k.

9.8. Extend *rabin_karp_search* to work with two-dimensional inputs. The input consists of two binary matrices, p of dimension $m \times m$ and t of dimension $n \times n$, and the algorithm should search for indexes $0 \le i, j < n$ such that $p[k, \ell] = t[i + k, j + \ell]$ for all $0 \le k, \ell < m$. What is the running time of your algorithm?

9.9. Implement *knuth_morris_pratt_search* and compare its performance to the simple text search.

9.10. Modify *knuth_morris_pratt_search* to print out all occurrences of a pattern, not just the first one. You need to be careful to keep the running time $O(m + n)$. The straightforward approach of shifting the pattern by one after a match is found leads to a running time of $\Theta(mn)$ as demonstrated by $p = 0^m$, and $t = 0^n$. This means you need to use the shift table in this case.

9.11. Implement *boyer_moore_horspool_search* and compare its performance to the simple text search.

9.12. Implement *boyer_moore_horspool_search* and compare its performance to the Knuth-Morris-Pratt search.

Exercises 9.13–9.15 contain the proof that boyer_moore_horspool_search is correct.

9.13. Show that *boyer_moore_horspool_search* correctly computes the shift of each letter; that is, $shift[w] = m - 1 - \max\{i < m - 1 \mid p[i] = w\}$ for all letters w that occur in $p[0..m - 2]$, and $shift[w] = m$ for all other letters.

9.14. Find a loop invariant for the inner loop in *boyer_moore_horspool_search* and use it to show that the algorithm works correctly. *Hint:* Use

   (a) $p[j + 1..m - 1] = t[i + j - 1..i + m - 1]$ and
   (b) $p[0..m - 1] \ne t[k..k + m - 1]$ for $0 \le k < i$

as the loop invariant.

9.15. Prove that the loop invariant from Exercise 9.14 is indeed a loop invariant.

9.16. Show that $dist(s, t) \le \max\{|s|, |t|\}$ for all words s and t.

9.17. Verify that the edit distance is really a distance function (metric); that is, it fulfills

$\mathrm{dist}(s,s) = 0$ for all $s \in \Sigma^*$ (Reflexivity),

$\mathrm{dist}(s,t) = 0 \Rightarrow s = t$ for all $s, t \in \Sigma^*$,

$\mathrm{dist}(s,t) = \mathrm{dist}(t,s)$ for all $s, t \in \Sigma^*$ (Symmetry),

$\mathrm{dist}(s,u) \leq \mathrm{dist}(s,t) + \mathrm{dist}(t,u)$ for all $s, t, u \in \Sigma^*$ (Triangle Inequality).

9.18. When computing the edit distance, we fill the table row by row. For computing the values in a particular row, we need only the values in the preceding row. Use this idea to modify the algorithm so it uses only linear space.

9.19. Extend the edit-distance algorithm to output a shortest sequence of operations transforming x into y. Add your code at the end of the algorithm after the full table has been computed. Your additional code should run in time $O(m + n)$. For example, $s =$"presto", $t =$"peseta" should output (see Example 9.5.5):

```
delete ''r'' at position 1
insert ''e'' at position 3
replace ''o'' by ''a'' at position 5
```

(*Note:* The problem of returning the shortest sequence of operations becomes much harder if you want to combine it with the space-saving idea of Exercise 9.18. A solution using divide-and-conquer was found by Hirschberg.)

9.20. A frequent error in written text is the transposition of adjacent letters, as in "witner" instead of "winter". Using two replaces, or one delete and an insert, assigns a cost of 2 to this error. To account for its frequency, we want to assign it unit cost. We do this by allowing an additional operation:

(T)   Transpose two adjacent letters.

Rewrite the recursive formula for computing $d_{i,j}$ to account for this new operation. *Hint:* Look two cells back.

9.21. Remember the sdiff UNIX command from Example 9.5.1. The difference between sdiff and computing the edit distance is that the edit distance works over letters whereas sdiff works over lines (where two lines are either equal or different). Implement sdiff (with graphical output as in Example 9.5.1) using the algorithm for computing the edit distance. Compare two lines until you find a mismatched symbol or the lines are equal.

Exercises 9.22–9.25 refer to the game of doublets invented by Lewis Carroll. In doublets you have to turn one word into another, replacing a single letter in each step. The problem becomes interesting by insisting that the intermediary words be real words. For example, "wet" turns into "dry" in the following sequence: "wet", "bet", "bey", "dey", "dry".

9.22. Turn "tea" into "hot".

9.23. Turn "more" into "less".

9.24. Turn "raven" into "miser".

9.25. Given a set of words L (our dictionary), we can define a distance $\text{dist}_L(x, y)$ to be the length of the shortest sequence of words from L that begins with x and ends with y, such that any two adjacent words in the sequence differ in one letter only. If no such sequence exists, let the distance be ∞. Show that dist_L is a metric (for any set L). (See Exercise 9.17 for the definition of a metric.)

9.26. If we restrict the edit operations to (R), the replacing of a letter, we obtain the *Hamming distance* d_H between two texts of the same length. Show that the *Hamming distance* is a metric (see Exercise 9.17), and is computable in time $O(n)$.

Exercises 9.27–9.29 concern a variant of the edit distance sometimes known as the Levenshtein distance. *For this variant we allow only insertions and deletions. Let us call the resulting variant of the edit distance* dist_{di}. *Since a replacement can be simulated by an insertion and a deletion,* dist_{di} *corresponds to a weighted version of the edit-distance problem where we charge twice the unit cost for replacement and unit cost for deletions and insertions.*

9.27. Show that $\text{dist}(x, y) \le \text{dist}_{di}(x, y) \le 2\,\text{dist}(x, y)$ for all x, y.

9.28. Show that dist_{di} is a metric (see Exercise 9.17).

9.29. Let $\text{lcs}(x, y)$ be the length of the longest common subsequence of x and y (see Section 8.4). Show that

$$2\,\text{lcs}(x, y) + \text{dist}_{di}(x, y) = n + m,$$

where $n = |x|$, and $m = |y|$. [*Note:* This relationship between dist_{di} and lcs has led to an algorithm computing dist_{di} by Hunt and Szymanski that can run as fast as $O(n \log n)$.]

9.30. How would you have to modify the code of Algorithm 9.5.15, *don't_care_search*, so that it finds all occurrences of a pattern, rather than just the first one? How does this modification affect the worst-case running time?

9.31. What is the difference between the patterns "$0 * | 1 *$", and "$(0|1) *$"?

9.32. What is $L(\text{"}0 * 1(0|1) *\text{"})$? Give a succinct answer.

9.33. What is $L(\text{"}(0|(10 * 1)) *\text{"})$? Give a succinct answer.

9.34. What is $L(\text{"}((0|1)(0|1)) *\text{"})$? Give a succinct answer.

9.35. Write a pattern for binary strings that contain the subword "101".

9.36. Write a pattern for binary strings that do not contain the subword "101".

9.37. Show that a pattern of length n can contain as many as $\Omega(n)$ starting positions (the positions computed by Algorithm 9.6.7).

Exercises 9.38–9.42 concern regular expressions as implemented in programming languages such as Perl or JavaScript and editors such as vi and emacs. The syntax of regular expressions in these languages and programs is similar to the syntax introduced in Section 9.6, the operators for concatenation, alternation, and multiplicity are the same, and we can use parentheses for grouping; for example, "(11|00)** " describes binary strings made up of pairs of ones and zeros. Writing regular expressions is simplified by having several classes of characters. For example, we can write "\d" for "(0|1|2|3|4|5|6|7|8|9)", that is, a digit. Similarly, "\w" is matched by a single word-character, that is, a character that can occur in a word; and "\s" is matched by any kind of space character (hardspace, tab, etc.). You can also write your own classes; for example, "[abc]" is matched by either "a", "b", or "c". A variant of this is "[^abc]", which is matched by any single character except for "a", "b", and "c". We also have several additional operations: We can use "?" to denote an optional match; for example, "*colou?r*" is matched by both "color" and "colour". The operator "+" is similar to the Kleene star, "***", except that it requires at least one match of the pattern; for example, "\d+" is a nonempty sequence of digits: a number. We can also require precise cardinalities using {a,b}, where a is the lower bound and b the upper bound on the matches required. For example, "\d{15,16}" is a 15- or 16-digit number, and "\w{3}" is a word on three letters.*

9.38. Write a regular expression pattern that is matched by both the British and the American spelling of the word "theater".

9.39. Write a regular expression pattern that is matched by a year, either in the two digit (YY) or in the four-digit format (YYYY).

9.40. Write a regular expression pattern that is matched by a time of day, as in "7am", or "12:55pm". Make sure your pattern is not matched by ill-formed times such as 32:72pm.

9.41. Write a regular expression pattern that is matched by phone numbers. *Hint:* Restrict yourself to phone numbers of a particular country. For example, US phone numbers could be written as follows: 1-(555)-123-4567 or (555)-123-4567 or 123-4567. The parentheses could be missing: 1-555-123-4567. Instead of dashes there could be spaces: 1 555 123 4567. Finally, there might be a one- to four-digit extension: 1-555-123-4567-1010.

9.42. Write a pattern that checks that if a text contains the word "Monty", it also contains the word "Python". By this specification, a text should also be accepted if it contains neither the word "Monty" nor "Python". Also, the exercise does not specify where the words occur in the text. They do not have to be next to each other or in any particular order. *Hint:* First simplify the problem by assuming that "Monty" occurs before "Python". Also, you need the "\b" special character that matches word boundaries in the text; for example, "\bPython\b" would be matched by "Monty Python's Flying Circus" but not by "Pythonesque".

9.43. [Requires knowledge of parsing.] Write an algorithm that takes as input a regular expression and returns a binary tree representing the expression. *Hint:* Assume that the regular expression is fully parenthesized and contains all occurrences of the concatenation operator · explicitly. Write a recursive function that translates a well-formed term into a tree.

9.44. There might be different trees associated with the same regular expression pattern. Give an example of a pattern with at least two (different) binary trees representing it.

★**9.45.** Can you write a regular expression pattern that matches binary strings containing the same number of ones and zeros?

CHAPTER 10
P and NP

Eventually you will encounter computational problems for which any algorithm you can think of has a prohibitive running time. Most likely this is not your fault. You will have stumbled across the class of **NP**-complete problems.

The problems we are concerned with in this chapter are problems such as frequency assignment in which we have to assign a small set of frequencies to a large number of base stations, in such a way that neighboring stations do not share too many frequencies, which causes interference. In this type of problem we would be able to recognize a good frequency assignment (we could check that there are no overlaps between neighboring stations), but finding the frequency assignment seems much harder; it seems that we have to try all possible solutions, of which there are exponentially many, making this approach infeasible in practice. Our goal in this chapter is to learn to distinguish between problems we can solve effectively on a computer—called feasible or tractable problems—and those problems for which we do not know or expect efficient solutions—also known as infeasible or intractable problems. Section 10.1 defines a feasible problem as one that can be solved in polynomial time. This includes most of the problems we have seen so far. In Section 10.2 we then introduce the notion of an **NP**-algorithm to capture the complexity of problems such as the frequency-assignment problem for which we can recognize a good solution. Section 10.3 introduces **reductions**, a tool to compare the difficulty of problems. With the help of reductions, we can identify the group of the most difficult **NP**-problems, the **NP**-complete problems. These, unfortunately, include problems of supreme practical interest such as the frequency-assignment problem, which is important for cellular phone networks. We discuss additional **NP**-complete problems of practical and theoretical interest in Sections 10.4 and 10.5. Chapter 11 surveys techniques to deal with **NP**-complete problems.

10.1 Polynomial Time

Decision and Acceptance

Reviewing the running times of the algorithms we have written so far, we see linear time, $\Theta(n)$; quadratic time, $\Theta(n^2)$; cubic time, $\Theta(n^3)$; and some intermediate time bounds, such as $\Theta(n \log n)$. All of these running times are bounded above by functions of the form n^k, in which the input size n appears as the base of a fixed exponent. A time bound of the form $O(n^k)$, for some fixed k, is called **polynomial time**. Algorithms running in polynomial running time are considered **efficient** in the sense that we could implement and run these algorithms for reasonably large inputs. Suppose that a computer can execute one step of an algorithm in 10^{-12} seconds. (Currently the fastest supercomputers can perform a single floating-point operation in 10^{-12} seconds.) Figure 10.1.1 shows the largest size problems that can be solved on such a machine for different durations and running times.

	n	n^2	n^3	n^{10}	2^n	$n!$	n^n
1 hour	3.6×10^{15}	6.0×10^7	1.5×10^5	35	51	17	13
10 hours ($\approx 1/2$ day)	3.6×10^{16}	1.8×10^8	3.3×10^5	45	54	18	14
100 hours (≈ 4 days)	3.6×10^{17}	6.0×10^8	7.1×10^5	56	58	19	14
1,000 hours (≈ 1 month)	3.6×10^{18}	1.8×10^9	1.5×10^6	71	61	20	15
10,000 hours (≈ 1 year)	3.6×10^{19}	6.0×10^9	3.3×10^6	90	64	20	16
100,000 hours (≈ 1 decade)	3.6×10^{20}	1.8×10^{10}	7.1×10^6	113	68	21	16

Figure 10.1.1 Largest size problems that can be solved for different durations and running times on a machine that can perform one operation in 10^{-12} seconds. The column heads (n, n^2, etc.) specify the number of steps required to solve a problem of size n. The first column (1 hour, 10 hours, etc.) specifies the time available. The entries in the table show the size of the largest problem that can be solved for inputs of size n for a given duration and running time.

Example 10.1.1. According to Figure 10.1.1, an algorithm that has running time n^{10} can solve only problem instances of size up to 56 in 100 hours. The reason is that the algorithm takes $56^{10} * 10^{-12} \approx 3.03 \times 10^5$ seconds, which is less than $100 * 60 * 60 = 3.6 \times 10^5$ seconds, the time available to it. On the other hand, $57^{10} * 10^{-12} \approx 3.62 \times 10^5$ is larger than 3.6×10^5. Therefore 56 is the largest problem size that can be handled. $\square$

The table in Figure 10.1.1 will change as computers become faster, but the asymptotic behavior of the values will remain the same. Additional time increases the largest problem size of a polynomial-time algorithm by a factor. For a linear-time algorithm, each additional factor of 10 in the maximum time allowed translates into a factor of 10 in the largest problem instance solved. For a quadratic algorithm, the factor is $10^{1/2} \approx 3.2$, and for a cubic algorithm $10^{1/3} \approx 2.2$. For exponential running times, an additional factor in the duration allowed translates into an additive constant: A 2^n-algorithm, for example, can solve problems larger by an additive constant $\log 10 \approx 3.3$ if we give it 10 times as much time.

Example 10.1.2. The reason that a factor of 10 in time implies an increase of $\log 10$ in size is the following: Suppose we run a 2^n-algorithm for time t on a machine that can perform one operation in 10^{-12} seconds, and the largest size we can solve is s. That is,

$$2^s = t * 10^{12}.$$

If we increase the time t by a factor of 10, we can solve instances s' with

$$2^{s'} = 10 * t * 10^{12} = 10 * 2^s.$$

Taking logarithms to the base 2 on both sides yields $s' = s + \log 10$. □

To formalize the notion of polynomial time, we need to explain what it means for an algorithm to solve a problem. Consider, for example, the string-matching problem with inputs p and t. If we are interested only in whether pattern p occurs within t, an algorithm returning "yes" or "no" on input p and t will do. We will concentrate on this type of problem that can be solved by answering "yes" or "no".

Definition 10.1.3. A *decision problem* consists of a set of instances that fall into two disjoint classes, the *positive instances* and the *negative instances*. An algorithm *accepts* an input if it returns "yes" on that input, and it *rejects* the input if it returns "no". An algorithm *decides* a problem by *accepting* all positive instances and *rejecting* all negative instances of the problem.

The outputs "yes" and "no" are special outputs encoding the decision of the algorithm. We sometimes use true and false or 0 and 1 to encode that decision.

Example 10.1.4 Primality Problem. Consider the problem of deciding whether a number is a prime number. The instances of the prime number problem are all of the natural numbers. The positive instances are the prime numbers, $\{2, 3, 5, 7, \ldots\}$, and the negative instances are the composite numbers and 1, $\{1, 4, 6, 8, 9, \ldots\}$. An algorithm deciding the primality of a number has to accept all prime numbers and reject all composites and 1. □

If we are interested in the position of a match in the string matching example, we are dealing with a **function problem**, since the algorithm needs to compute a value other than "yes" or "no" as an output. There are many important function problems, and we will investigate one particular class—optimization problems—in Section 11.3, but the present chapter focuses on decision problems.

Example 10.1.5 Factoring Problem. A function problem related to the primality problem from Example 10.1.4 is the *factoring problem*: Given a natural number, find the smallest divisor greater than 1. Solving the factoring problem solves the primality problem, since a number n is prime if and only if its smallest divisor greater than 1 is n itself. □

A decision problem is completely determined by the set of positive instances, that is, the set of instances on which an algorithm should answer "yes".

Example 10.1.6. As an example, let us consider the string-matching problem again. Suppose text and pattern are written over some (finite) alphabet Σ. In a first attempt we might want to define the set of positive instances as

$$L = \{pt \mid p \text{ matches } t\}.$$

For example, "01101" belongs to L, since the pattern "01" matches the word "101". However, "01101" also results from the pattern "011" and the text "01", which form a negative instance; hence "01101" should not be in L. We need a way to separate multiple inputs. The easiest solution is to introduce a separator symbol that does not belong to the alphabet. We choose "#" for that purpose and define

$$L = \{p\#t \mid p \text{ matches } t\}.$$

The Knuth-Morris-Pratt algorithm (see Section 9.3) can be used to accept set L in linear time.   □

Definition 10.1.7. We say that a decision problem L can be *decided in polynomial time* if there is an algorithm that on all inputs x runs in time $O(|x|^k)$, uses at most $O(|x|^k)$ binary cells of memory for storing variables, and returns "yes" for all $x \in L$ and "no" for all $x \notin L$. We say that the algorithm *decides L*. We define

$$\mathbf{P} = \{L \mid L \text{ can be decided in polynomial time}\},$$

the class of problems solvable in polynomial time.

An algorithm that decides L accepts all words in L and rejects all words in $\overline{L}$. For polynomial time something stronger is true, as we see from the following theorem.

Theorem 10.1.8. *A decision problem L can be decided in polynomial time if and only if there is an algorithm that accepts exactly the words in L in polynomial time.*

How could it happen that we have an algorithm that accepts exactly the words in L without deciding L? The problem is caused by inputs that are not instances or negative instances. On these the algorithm can give arbitrary outputs and take even longer than polynomial time. For example, let us consider the string-matching problem: On input $p\#t$ we accept if p matches t and reject if p does not match t. We did not specify any output for inputs not containing "#"; hence, the output for those inputs is undefined. While the algorithm accepts exactly the words in L, it does not decide L. We can modify the algorithm slightly to reject all inputs on which the algorithm does not commit to an output or outputs something different from the allowed output values.

Proof of Theorem 10.1.8. If there is an algorithm deciding L in polynomial time, that same algorithm accepts exactly the words in L in polynomial time. We have to work harder for the other direction. Suppose, then, that L can be accepted in polynomial time. Then there is an algorithm A accepting exactly the words in L in time $n^k + c$ for some $k, c \in \mathbb{N}$ (see Exercise 22). For inputs not from L, A might take longer or output a symbol other than "yes" or "no". We modify A as follows. We add a counter variable to the program, which counts how many instructions (the unmodified) A has performed so far. When A tries to output something other than "yes", we output "no" and halt. If A takes more than $|x|^k + c$ steps on input x, we also output "no" and halt. On an input $x \in L$, we know that A accepts in no more than $|x|^k + c$ steps; hence, the modified algorithm also accepts x. If $x \notin L$, then A either outputs a symbol other than "yes" or takes more than $|x|^k + c$. In either case the modified algorithm rejects it by outputting "no", thereby deciding L in time $|x|^k + c$, which is polynomial. ∎

Another look at the proof shows us that it depends on knowing that the algorithm has to terminate on the positive instances in a known number of steps. Indeed, if we remove the running time restriction, acceptability and decidability are no longer the same. An example of that is the Halting Problem:

$$K = \{A\#x \mid \text{program } A \text{ halts on input } x\}.$$

K models a particularly interesting problem: Does a program halt on a given input? If we could determine the answer, we could avoid infinite loops and system crashes. K can be accepted by an interpreter for the language the programs are written in (Java, say): Given A and x, run A on x and, if it halts, output "yes". However, there cannot be a program deciding K, as Alan Turing showed in 1936, building on work by Kurt Gödel.

Encodings

Example 10.1.6 alerted us that the encoding of inputs matters and, indeed, there is a more serious pitfall lurking here: How can we be sure that whether a problem can be decided in polynomial time does not depend on its encoding? Consider again the string-matching problem. With the particular encoding we chose, string matching could be solved in linear time. Would this still be true if, instead of "#", we used another separator symbol? The answer is yes, since the symbol does not change the length of the input. In general, however, the running time of an algorithm depends on the encoding chosen for the problem.

Example 10.1.9. Let us have another look at the problem of determining whether a number x is prime. A simple algorithm can test divisors from 2 to $x - 1$ (actually we need to test numbers up to $\sqrt{x}$ only). Assuming that we can perform each division in one step, the algorithm takes time $O(x)$. Does that mean *primality* can be decided in polynomial time?

The answer depends on the encoding. Remember that we measure the running time in the length of the input. What is the length of the input x? If we encode x in unary (as a sequence of x ones), then the preceding algorithm indeed shows that the set

$$L = \{1^p \mid p \text{ is prime}\}$$

can be decided in linear time (1^p is a sequence of p ones). However, if we use the more common encoding of numbers in binary, that is,

$$L = \{p \mid p \text{ is prime}\},$$

then the algorithm takes time $O(x) = O(2^{|x|})$, since the length $|x|$ of a binary string representing x is $\lceil \log x \rceil$. In this case, the running time is exponential in the length of the input x.   □

Examples 10.1.6 and 10.1.9 tell us that we need to worry about the encoding of a problem. We saw earlier examples of this behavior in the case of graph algorithms where it can make a difference whether we represent the graph using adjacency lists (see Section 3.3) or an adjacency matrix (see Section 2.5).

In general, there is no notion of a correct representation of a problem, but most problems we encounter have a standard representation that is understood implicitly. We usually choose the most **succinct** representation. For example, for graphs we would prefer the adjacency list representation over the adjacency matrix representation since it takes up less space. Similarly, numbers are usually encoded in binary rather than unary.

Note, however, that we do have some amount of freedom if we are interested only in whether a problem belongs to **P** or not. Returning to the primality problem, we could try to improve succinctness by using a decimal representation or a hexadecimal representation or settle on an even larger base. This, however, would not change the running time significantly, since these representations are **polynomially related**.

Theorem 10.1.10. *Let L_b and L_d contain encodings of the same set of integers, L_b in binary, and L_d in decimal. Then $L_b \in$ **P** implies that $L_d \in$ **P**.*

Proof. Suppose that L_b is in **P**. Then there is an algorithm A deciding L_b in time $n^k + c$ for some $k, c \in \mathbb{N}$ (see Exercise 22). We can write a linear-time algorithm B that converts decimal numbers into binary numbers. Consider a new algorithm that takes an input x and rejects it, if it is not a decimal number. Otherwise it uses B to convert x into its binary representation x_b and runs A on input x_b, returning the same answer that A gives. We claim that this new algorithm runs in polynomial time. The initial check for a correct decimal representation and the conversion to binary can both be done in polynomial time. This leaves us with running A on x_b. How long is x_b?

Since every decimal digit can be expressed using at most 4 bits, we certainly know that $|x_b| \leq 4|x|$. Therefore, this part of the algorithm takes time $|x_b|^k + c \leq (4|x|)^k + c = 4^k|x|^k + c = O(|x|^k)$; hence, the whole algorithm runs in polynomial time. ∎

The theorem rests on the fact that we can translate one representation in polynomial time into another for which we have an algorithm and then run the algorithm on that representation. We often encounter situations like this one, where we have to run a polynomial-time algorithm on the output of another polynomial-time algorithm. The next theorem assures us that the result is still a polynomial-time algorithm.

Theorem 10.1.11. *If A and B are polynomial-time algorithms with output, then $A(B(x))$, the* **composition** *of A and B, in which A is run on the output of B on x and the output of A is returned, can be computed in time polynomial in $|x|$.*

Proof. Suppose A runs in time $n^{k_a} + c_a$ and B in time $n^{k_b} + c_b$. Then, running B on x takes time $|x|^{k_b} + c_b$, resulting in some output y for which $|y| \leq |x|^{k_b} + c_b$ (since B is not allowed to use more than $|x|^{k_b} + c_b$ memory cells). Then, running A on y takes at most $|y|^{k_a} + c_a \leq (|x|^{k_b} + c_b)^{k_a} + c_a = O(|x|^{k_a k_b})$. This, together with the $|x|^{k_b} + c_b$ steps to compute y, is still $O(|x|^{k_a k_b})$; hence, $A(B(x))$ can be computed in polynomial time. ∎

Note that the exponents of the running times of A and B multiply. Hence, it is preferable that at least one of the algorithms runs in linear time (as in the converting bases example of Theorem 10.1.10), since in that case the running time does not increase unduly.

Exercises

1S. Name an algorithm we have seen that runs in linear time.

2. Name an algorithm we have seen that runs in quadratic time.

3. Give an example of an algorithm we have seen that does not run in polynomial time.

4S. What is the smallest integer k such that $\sqrt{n} = O(n^k)$?

5. What is the smallest integer k such that $n \log n = O(n^k)$?

6. Is there a smallest real $c > 0$ such that $n \log n = O(n^c)$? Prove your answer correct.

7. In Figure 10.1.1 we saw that a factor of 10 in the running time meant we could solve instances 10 times larger, if the algorithm is linear, and

$10^{1/2} \approx 3.2$ times larger, if the algorithm is quadratic. By what factor does the largest instance size we can solve increase for algorithms of running time n^{10}? Compute the value up to one decimal place.

Exercises 8-14 deal with solvable instance sizes. Let $s_f(t)$ be the largest instance size n on which we can run an algorithm with running time $f(n)$ in time t:

$$s_f(t) = \max\{n \mid f(n) \le t\}.$$

8S. Determine s_f for $f(n) = n^2$.

9. Determine s_f for $f(n) = n^3$.

10. Determine s_f for $f(n) = 2^n$.

11S. Determine s_f for $f(n) = \log n$.

12. Show that if $f(n) = n^n$, then $s_f(t) = \Theta(\log t / \log \log t)$.

13S. Assume that f is a polynomial. How does $s_f(t)$ relate to $s_f(2t)$? That is, how much larger are instances you can solve by allowing double the time?

14. Assume that $f(n) = c^n$. How does $s_f(t)$ relate to $s_f(2t)$? That is, how much larger are instances you can solve by allowing double the time?

Assume that a particular algorithm can solve instances of size n on a machine that takes 10^{-12} seconds per operation. What size instances can the same algorithm solve on a machine that takes 10^{-15} seconds per operation in the same time if the running time, $f(n)$, of the algorithm is that given in Exercises 15-19?

15S. $f(n) = n$

16. $f(n) = n^2$

17. $f(n) = n^3$

18S. $f(n) = \log n$

19. $f(n) = 2^n$

20. Consider the following piece of code:

```
power_2(k) {
    result = 2
    for i = 1 to k
        result = result * result
    return result
}
```

At first glance, this algorithm looks like a polynomial-time algorithm, but it is not. Why? Does it make a difference whether the input k is represented in unary or binary? *Hint:* What value does *power_2* compute? How much memory does it take to store that value?

21S. Show that if $f(n) = O(n^k)$, then there are $k', c \in \mathrm{N}$ such that $f(n) \le n^{k'} + c$ for all $n \in \mathrm{N}$.

22. From Exercise 21 conclude that if $L \in \mathbf{P}$, then there is an algorithm deciding L in time $n^k + c$ for some $k, c \in \mathrm{N}$. We often use this result when reasoning about polynomial-time algorithms and their running times.

23. Is it true that if $f(n) = O(n^k)$, then there is $c \in \mathrm{N}$ such that $f(n) \le cn^k$ for all $n \in \mathrm{N}$?

24S. Let x_b be the binary representation of a number x, and x_t the ternary representation of x. Then $|x_b| \le c|x_t|$ for some c. What is the smallest real number c for which this is true?

25. Let x_b be the binary representation of a number x, and x_d the decimal representation of x. Then $|x_b| \le c|x_d|$ for some c. What is the smallest real number c for which this is true?

10.2 Nondeterministic Algorithms and NP

Imagine yourself with the Sunday paper solving the crossword puzzle. Take the puzzle in Figure 10.2.1, for example.

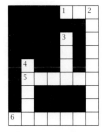

3	ERB, BAX, RAN
4	CAGE
5	BERIO, ELGAR, EWALD, REGER
6	LIGETI, EIMERT, ENESCU, WEBERN, COWELL, BRETAN
7	BORODIN, ARTIMOV, XENAKIS
8	HARRISON, SIBELIUS
9	BEETHOVEN, BALAKIREV, BERNSTEIN, BOULANGER

Figure 10.2.1 A crossword puzzle.

For each of the six entries, we need to select a name from the list on the right, which is ordered by the lengths of the names. Three down has to be Cage, since there is no other four-letter name available. Now that rules out Enescu and Bretan for five across, still leaving four choices. If we knew the first letter (L, E, W, or C) we would know which word to choose. The first letter depends on four down. At this point we need to guess and continue to work with that guess. It might turn out that our guess does not lead to a solution (W, for example, would force EWALD into the four down, leaving no choices for six across).

We formalize the guessing process by allowing an algorithm to invoke a library function *guess* that selects among different choices. Finding a solution for the crossword puzzle is then as easy—or as difficult—as guessing a correct letter whenever we have several choices with which to continue.

Example 10.2.1. We use *guess* on the alphabet $\Sigma = \{A, B, \ldots, Z\}$ to help us fill the puzzle in Figure 10.2.1. We know that three down has to be CAGE. At that point we are left with four choices for the five across. Using *guess* for the first letter of that word might give us L, so we would choose LIGETI for five across. This forces four down to become ELGAR, six across to become ARTIMOV, two down to become BALAKIREV, and one across to become ERB (see Figure 10.2.2).

Figure 10.2.2 A solution to the crossword puzzle of Figure 10.2.1.

Sometimes a single guess is not enough. If we had started in the upper-right corner, for example, guessing a B would have still left us with several choices for two down.   □

We can implement the idea of Example 10.2.1 as an algorithm. To make it simpler and more general, we guess a letter for every blank square. All we need to do then is to verify in the end that the guessed solution is correct. As the input to the puzzle problem, we have a Boolean matrix D of dimension $n \times n$ and a finite set of words W over an alphabet Σ ($W \subseteq \Sigma^*$). The entries of D encode whether a square is blank or blocked, and W is the set of words we can use to fill D. For simplicity we assume that a word can be used multiple times.

Algorithm 10.2.2 Crossword Puzzle. This algorithm solves a crossword puzzle, represented by a Boolean matrix $D[i, j]$, $1 \le i, j \le n$, and a finite set of words $W \subseteq \Sigma^*$. Σ is the alphabet, and $D[i, j]$ is true if the square is blank and false if it is blocked. We construct the solution in a new matrix $S[i, j]$, $1 \le i, j \le n$. The algorithm returns true if the crossword can be solved.

  Input Parameters: D, W
Output Parameters: None

puzzle(D, W) {
   for $i = 1$ to n
      for $j = 1$ to n

```
              if (D[i, j])
                  S[i, j] = guess(Σ)
              else
                  S[i, j] = blocked
          for each word w in S
            if (w ∉ W)
                return false
          return true
      }
```

Example 10.2.3. To obtain the solution shown in Figure 10.2.2, *puzzle* would guess letters

ERBACLAAEGKLIGETIGRAEARTIMOV.

It would then continue to verify that this is indeed a correct solution given the set of words W.   □

The running time of the algorithm is $\Theta(n^2)$ if we count a call to *guess* as a single step. If *guess* is not implemented correctly, it might make wrong guesses, and the algorithm could give a wrong answer. For example, if *guess* returns B for the square labeled 1 in Example 10.2.1, then there is no way to extend that guess to a correct solution. The only way the three squares of one across could be filled is using BAX, but there is no nine-letter name starting with X available.

Example 10.2.4. The sequence

ERBUCLAGHGONGAEMACMACMACMWHA

of guesses is not accepted by the algorithm. While it does lead to some correct words, for example ERB in one across and CAGE in three down, five across contains NGAEMA, which is not one of the words in W.   □

If we assume that we can implement *guess* so that it always chooses a good guess whenever there is one, then the algorithm will return the right result. If there is a solution, good guessing will find it, and the algorithm will recognize it; if there is no solution, it does not matter what we guess, the algorithm will reject any proposed solution because it is not correct.

Example 10.2.5. It is always possible that there is more than one good guess. For example, after guessing E, R, and B for the first squares of one across, the algorithm might guess E for the next square ($i = 2$, $j = 7$) instead of A as in Example 10.2.1. Figure 10.2.3 shows that there is a way of extending that guess to a correct solution.

This solution corresponds to the sequence

ERBECRANBGSEIMERTREIIBORODIN

of guesses.

Figure 10.2.3 A second solution to the crossword puzzle of Figure 10.2.1.□

We conclude that we can solve crossword puzzles in polynomial time if we allow guessing. Guessing is more formally known as **nondeterminism**. The algorithm *puzzle* is not deterministic because, whenever *guess* is called, there are different ways the computation can continue depending on which value *guess* selects. Any possible sequence of guesses, or **nondeterministic choices**, corresponds to a particular **computation path**, or **run**, of the nondeterministic algorithm. We argued previously that if the crossword puzzle (D, W) is solvable, then there is at least one successful run of the algorithm on (D, W), namely one guessing a correct solution of the crossword puzzle. The sequence of guesses along a successful run of the algorithm, that is, a run that ends with the algorithm accepting the input, is called a **witness** because it witnesses that the input is a positive instance. For the crossword puzzle of Figure 10.2.1, we saw two witnesses to its solvability using *puzzle*, one in Figure 10.2.2 and the other in Figure 10.2.3.

If, however, there is no solution to a crossword (D, W), then all runs will reject and return false on input (D, W) because *puzzle* checks a proposed solution obtained by guessing and rejects wrong solutions.

We use these two properties as the defining characteristics of a nondeterministic algorithm solving a problem.

Definition 10.2.6. A *nondeterministic algorithm* is an algorithm using the *guess* function. We say a nondeterministic algorithm runs in polynomial time if for every possible sequence of guesses the algorithm terminates in polynomial time. We allow the use of *guess* only on sets that the algorithm can explicitly construct in polynomial time.

Let L be a decision problem. We say that L can be solved in *nondeterministic polynomial time* if there is a nondeterministic algorithm that runs in polynomial time, and for all inputs x:

- If $x \in L$, then there is a sequence of guesses such that the algorithm returns true on input x (the algorithm *accepts* x).

- If $x \notin L$, then the algorithm returns false for all possible sequences of guesses (the algorithm *rejects* x).

A sequence of guesses that leads a nondeterministic algorithm to accept an input x is called a *witness* for that input.

The definition of a nondeterministic polynomial-time algorithm is unnatural in the sense that, as far as we know, there are no physical devices that implement nondeterministic guessing efficiently as required by the definition. We cannot, for example, substitute nondeterministic guesses by random guesses (which we can implement reasonably well in practice). If we randomly guessed a B for the square labeled 1 in Figure 10.2.1, we would not find a solution at all. The justification for the nondeterministic model of computation then is not its implementability. The model is justified by the definition of the language class **NP**, which precisely captures the computational complexity of many fundamental problems in computer science.

Definition 10.2.7. We define

$$\mathbf{NP} = \{L \mid L \text{ can be decided in nondeterministic polynomial time}\},$$

the class of problems solvable in nondeterministic polynomial time.

Since any deterministic polynomial-time algorithm is a nondeterministic polynomial-time algorithm (not making use of the *guess* function), any language decidable in polynomial time is decidable in nondeterministic polynomial time by the same algorithm.

Theorem 10.2.8. $P \subseteq NP$

Let CROSSWORD $= \{(D, W) \mid$ the crossword D can be solved using words from $W\}$. By writing *puzzle* we showed the following result.

Theorem 10.2.9. CROSSWORD $\in$ NP.

Often we will not define the set of positive instances of a problem explicitly, especially if the encoding does not play an important role. In that case, we present a problem in the following form:

Crossword Puzzle
Instance: Boolean matrix D, and a set $W \subseteq \Sigma^*$.
Question: Is the crossword puzzle described by D solvable using words from W?

We claimed that **NP** captures the complexity of several central problems in computer science. We present two such problems, graph coloring and the Hamiltonian-cycle problem.

Graph Coloring

How many colors do we need to color the map in Figure 10.2.4 if two adjacent regions are not allowed to have the same color? For this problem we call two regions **adjacent** if they share a boundary, that is, they overlap in a (curved) line.

Any two of Bolivia, Brazil, and Argentina share a border, forcing us to use three different colors for the three countries. Since Paraguay has a common

Figure 10.2.4 A map of South America.

border with all three of them, we need a fourth color for it. This means we need at least four colors to color the map of South America. Exercise 2 shows that the whole map can be colored using four colors.

If we kept coloring maps, we would soon discover that four colors were always sufficient. This experimental observation led several mathematicians to conjecture that all maps could be colored using at most four colors. The four-color conjecture was forty years old before the first serious attempt at a solution was published in 1879 by a mathematician named Kempe. It took another decade until Heawood found a mistake in Kempe's proof. Heawood managed to modify Kempe's proof to obtain the result that every map can be colored using at most five colors. It was only in 1976 that work by Appel and Haken finally turned the conjecture into a theorem.

Theorem 10.2.10 Four-Color Theorem, Appel and Haken, 1976. *Every map can be colored using at most four colors.*

All proofs of the four-color theorem given so far require a computer to verify the numerous cases into which the analysis splits and, because of that, have been a disappointment to many mathematicians. However, in the century it took to prove the four-color theorem, the conjecture influenced mathematical research. It was one of the roots of graph theory and the area of graph coloring in particular.

To translate the map problem into a question about graphs, we represent each region as a vertex and a shared boundary between two regions as an edge between the two vertices representing the regions.

Example 10.2.11. Figure 10.2.5 shows the South America map from Figure 10.2.4 with the corresponding graph. Note, that Bolivia, Brazil, Argentina, and Paraguay form a K_4.

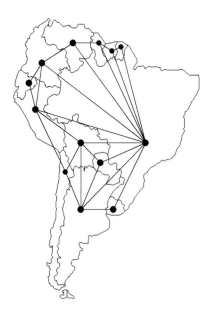

Figure 10.2.5 The South America graph.   □

Remember that a k-coloring of a graph $G = (V, E)$ is a function $c : V \to \{1, \ldots, k\}$ such that $c(u) \neq c(v)$ for every $(u, v) \in E$, and the chromatic number, $\chi(G)$, is smallest k such that there is a k-coloring of G (see Section 2.5).

The graphs corresponding to maps are those that can be drawn in the plane without edges intersecting. Such graphs are called **planar**. In our new terminology we can restate the Four-Color Theorem.

Theorem 10.2.12. *Every planar graph has chromatic number at most* 4.

Maps are not the only application of coloring graphs. Any situation in which resources (colors) are shared among multiple parties (vertices) while conflicts (edges) have to be avoided is naturally modeled as a graph-coloring problem.

Example 10.2.13 Register Allocation. Register allocation is a process occurring when running or compiling code. Variables that are needed by the interpreter or the runtime system of the compiler need to be loaded into a limited number of registers that are quickly accessible by the CPU. To simplify the problem, we assume that a variable gets assigned to a register for the duration of its lifetime during the execution of the program code. The lifetime of a variable can be determined from the scope of the variable. If the lifetimes of two variables overlap, the two variables have to be in memory at the same time and cannot be assigned to the same register. Hence, we can model the register-allocation problem as a graph: Each variable corresponds to a vertex, and an edge between two vertices means that the lifetimes of the two variables overlap. A **register allocation** for this graph is a coloring of the graph, each color corresponding to a register. Determining the smallest number of registers needed to run the code then is the same as determining the chromatic number of the graph of variable conflicts. □

The graph-coloring problem can be formally stated as follows.

Graph k-Colorability
Instance: Graph $G = (V, E)$, integer $k \leq |V|$.
Question: Is $\chi(G) \leq k$; that is, can the vertices of G be colored using at most k colors such that adjacent vertices have different colors?

Example 10.2.14. Figure 10.2.6 shows a graph with a 3-coloring.

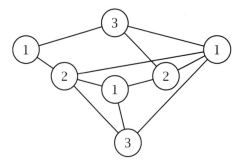

Figure 10.2.6 A graph with a 3-coloring. □

To show that we can decide graph k-colorability in **NP**, we need to write an **NP**-algorithm for it. We use the *guess* function to guess the colors of the vertices. We then need to verify that the coloring we guessed fulfills the condition that no edge has two endpoints of the same color. In the algorithm, we write $N(v)$ for the set of neighbors of v in $G = (V, E)$ (see Definition 2.5.7).

Algorithm 10.2.15 Graph k-Coloring. This algorithm finds a k-coloring of $G = (V, E)$, if there is one, and stores it in the array c. The algorithm returns true if a coloring is found.

Input Parameters: $G = (V, E), k$
Output Parameters: None

```
graph_coloring(G, k) {
    for each v in V
        c[v] = guess({1, 2, ..., k})
    for each v in V
        for each w in N(v)
            if (c[w] == c[v])
                return false
    return true
}
```

The algorithm runs in time $O(|V| + |E|)$ with $O(|V|)$ steps for guessing the colors and $O(|E|)$ steps for traversing the adjacency list of each vertex once to check the coloring.

We claim that the algorithm works correctly. If *graph_coloring* returns true, then each vertex v in V has been assigned a color $c(v) \in \{1, \ldots, k\}$. Suppose there are two adjacent vertices u and v of the same color. Let u be the vertex that is considered first in the second for each loop of *graph_coloring*. Since u is adjacent to v and $c(u) = c(v)$, the algorithm would have failed and returned false. On the other hand, if there is a k-coloring of the graph, then the algorithm can find it by guessing it correctly.

Theorem 10.2.16. *Graph k-colorability is in* **NP**.

Example 10.2.17. Figure 10.2.6 shows a graph with a 3-coloring, as it could have been guessed by *graph_coloring*. Figure 10.2.7 shows a possible outcome of trying to 2-color the same graph. This attempt failed, and indeed any attempt to 2-color this graph will fail, since it contains a K_3, which requires at least three different colors. Hence, any 2-coloring *graph_coloring* guesses will be rejected.

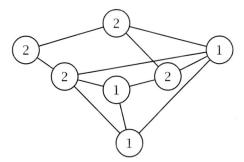

Figure 10.2.7 A failed 2-coloring.   ☐

Hamiltonian Cycles and the Traveling Salesperson

We want to visit the cities in Figure 10.2.8 using the available flight connections. Is there a tour that takes us to each city exactly once and then takes us back to the city we started from? Recall that such a tour is a **Hamiltonian**

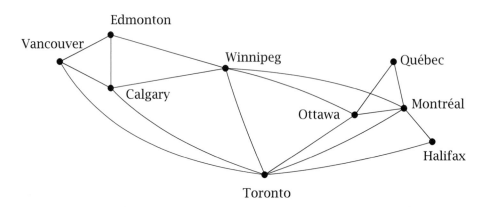

Figure 10.2.8 (Fictional) air routes in Canada.

cycle (see Definition 2.5.34), and a graph containing a Hamiltonian cycle is called **Hamiltonian**. We identify Hamiltonian cycles that use the same set of edges.

Formally, we can state the **Hamiltonian-cycle problem** as follows.

Hamiltonian Cycle
Instance: Graph $G = (V, E)$.
Question: Is G Hamiltonian?

Example 10.2.18. The subgraph of Figure 10.2.8 containing Vancouver, Edmonton, Calgary, and Winnipeg shown in Figure 10.2.9 is Hamiltonian.

Figure 10.2.9 Part of Figure 10.2.8.

For example, Vancouver, Edmonton, Winnipeg, Calgary, Vancouver is a Hamiltonian cycle of the graph. So is the tour Edmonton, Winnipeg, Calgary, Vancouver, Edmonton, but we would consider that to be the same Hamiltonian cycle (since it uses the same edges). Since no Hamiltonian cycle could use the connection from Edmonton to Calgary (it separates Winnipeg from Vancouver), the graph in Figure 10.2.9 has exactly one Hamiltonian cycle. □

To write an **NP**-algorithm for the Hamiltonian-cycle problem, we can guess the vertices in the cycle. We then have to verify that we traveled to every city and used only available connections. The following algorithm performs this task.

Algorithm 10.2.19 Hamiltonian Cycle. This algorithm finds a Hamiltonian cycle in $G = (V, E)$ if there is one and returns true in that case.

Input Parameter: $G = (V, E)$
Output Parameters: None

```
hamiltonian_cycle(G) {
    n = |V|
    for i = 1 to n
        visited[i] = false
    for i = 1 to n {
        c[i] = guess(V)
        visited[c[i]] = true
    }
    c[0] = c[n] // first node is the same as last
    // check that only edges of G are used
    for i = 0 to n − 1
        if ((c[i], c[i + 1]) ∉ E)
            return false
    // check that all vertices have been visited
    for i = 1 to n
        if (!(visited[i]))
            return false
    return true
}
```

Theorem 10.2.20. *The algorithm hamiltonian_cycle is an **NP**-algorithm deciding whether a graph is Hamiltonian.*

Proof. The algorithm guesses a sequence of n vertices and then checks that these vertices form a cycle. It then verifies that the sequence visits all vertices in V; hence, it returns true only if it has indeed found a Hamiltonian cycle. On the other hand, the algorithm accepts any Hamiltonian cycle. ∎

We obtain an important variant of the Hamiltonian-cycle problem by giving each edge a weight. We define the weight of any subgraph, including a Hamiltonian cycle, to be the sum of the weights of its edges. More formally, if $G' = (V', E')$ is a subgraph of the weighted graph $G = (V, E, weight)$, then the weight of G' is defined as:

$$weight(G') = \sum_{e \in E'} weight(e).$$

Our goal is to find a Hamiltonian cycle C meeting an upper bound w on $weight(C)$. This problem is known as the traveling-salesperson problem (TSP). The salesperson has to visit each city (vertex) once. The weights on the edges can correspond to distances or costs for traveling along that edge, and the goal is to minimize the traveled distance or overall cost of the tour.

Traveling Salesperson (TSP)
Instance: Weighted graph $G = (V, E, weight)$, w.
Question: Is there a Hamiltonian cycle C with $weight(C) \leq w$?

Example 10.2.21. Figure 10.2.10 contains some Indian cities with approximate road distances in miles. Is there a tour that would take us to all of these cities in less than 4500 miles? A Hamiltonian cycle avoiding the long route from Chennai to Kolkata would be Chennai, Nagpur, Kolkata, Agra, Delhi, Jaiselmer, Jaipur, Mumbai, Chennai. Adding the distances gives us a total of 4525 miles, which does not meet the given upper bound. In a second attempt, we might observe that Nagpur is farther from Kolkata and Chennai than it is from its other neighbors, so maybe we should try to take the cheapest route there leading through Agra and Jaipur (Agra and Mumbai would be even cheaper, but the route Agra, Nagpur, Mumbai cannot be extended to a Hamiltonian cycle, since it cuts the graph in two halves). For example, we could travel Chennai, Kolkata, Agra, Nagpur, Jaipur, Delhi, Jaiselmer, Mumbai, Chennai. This route is 4905 miles, hardly an improvement. Let us try a small variant: Chennai, Kolkata, Nagpur, Agra, Jaipur, Delhi, Jaiselmer, Mumbai, Chennai is only 4405 miles and therefore meets our upper bound.

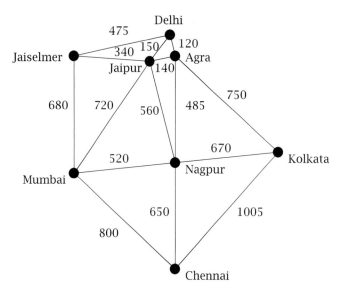

Figure 10.2.10 Road distances in India.   □

TSP can be solved in **NP** with an algorithm similar to the one for the Hamiltonian-cycle problem. We have only to add code to check whether the upper bound on the total weight is met.

Algorithm 10.2.22 TSP. This algorithm finds a Hamiltonian cycle in $G = (V, E, weight)$ of total weight at most w if there is one and returns true in that case.

Input Parameters: $G = (V, E, weight)$, w
Output Parameters: None

```
tsp(G, w) {
    n = |V|
    for i = 1 to n
        c[i] = guess(V)
    c[0] = c[n]
    // check that only edges of G are used,
    // and compute the total weight of the tour
    totalweight = 0
    for i = 1 to n - 1
        if ((c[i], c[i + 1]) ∉ E)
            return false
        else
            totalweight = totalweight + weight((c[i], c[i + 1]))
    // reject tours whose total weight is too large
    if (totalweight > w)
        return false
    // check that all vertices are visited
    for i = 1 to n
        visited[i] = false
    for i = 1 to n
        visited[c[i]] = true
    for i = 1 to n
        if (!(visited[i]))
            return false
    return true
}
```

Nondeterminism and Exponential Time

We introduced nondeterminism as a tool to capture the computational complexity of certain decision problems. Although we discussed nondeterministic *algorithms*, these are not algorithms that can be implemented efficiently. The reason is that we do not know of a physical equivalent of nondeterminism; we do not know how to make the right nondeterministic choice efficiently. Remember that we assumed that guessing would take only constant time. It seems that neither parallelism nor randomness nor quantum computers (all of which have claims to practical implementability) capture nondeterminism well. However, that does not mean that problems in **NP** are unsolvable. In this section we will show that all problems in **NP** can be decided by exponential-time algorithms, that is, algorithms running in time $O(2^{n^k})$ for some k.

Example 10.2.23. We can determine in time $O(n^{n+1})$ whether a graph G is k-colorable, where $n = |V| + |E|$ and we assume that $k \leq n$ (a graph on n vertices is always n-colorable; hence values larger than n are not of interest). For each vertex, try all k colors and check for each of the k^n resulting colorings whether it is a valid coloring, namely that no two adjacent vertices have the same color. Since we can check each coloring in time n, the overall runtime is $O(nk^n)$, which is $O(n^{n+1})$ since we assume that $k \leq n$. $O(n^{n+1})$ is exponential, since $n^{n+1} = 2^{(n+1)\log n} \leq 2^{n^2}$.   □

Observe the relationship between the nondeterministic polynomial-time algorithm for graph coloring, Algorithm 10.2.15, and the deterministic exponential-time solution of graph coloring in Example 10.2.23. We turned the guesses into an exhaustive search over all potential guesses. Since we apply *guess* only to sets of limited size (remember that the sets have to be constructed explicitly in polynomial time), and we apply *guess* only polynomially often along each path, we can turn every nondeterministic polynomial-time algorithm into an exponential-time algorithm.

Definition 10.2.24. Let

$$\mathbf{EXP} = \{L \mid L \text{ can be decided in exponential time}\},$$

where exponential time is any running time of the form $O(2^{n^k})$ for some k.

We have the following relationship between **NP** and **EXP**.

Theorem 10.2.25. $\mathbf{NP} \subseteq \mathbf{EXP}$.

We only sketch the proof, since the details are not of interest to us. The basic strategy of the proof is to turn the sequence of guesses into an exhaustive search.

Suppose we are given a nondeterministic algorithm A deciding a language L in nondeterministic time $n^k + c$. We now show how to turn A step by step into an exponential-time algorithm.

In a first step, we observe that we can restrict the function *guess* to the set $\{0, 1\}$; that is, we need only binary guesses, guesses between two possible choices. The reason is that we can simulate $guess(\{a_1, \ldots, a_\ell\})$ using at most $\lceil \log \ell \rceil$ binary guesses by guessing the digits of the binary representation of an index i between 1 and ℓ and then selecting a_i. Since we have only time $n^k + c$ to construct the set $\{a_1, \ldots, a_\ell\}$, we know that $\ell \leq n^k + c$, and therefore we need at most $\log(n^k + c)$ binary guesses to nondeterministically select an element from the set $\{a_1, \ldots, a_\ell\}$.

Translating arbitrary guesses to binary guesses, we now have a new algorithm B accepting the same language as A and running in time $O(n^{k+1})$, because A runs in time $O(n^k)$ and each step could be a guess that takes $\log(n^k + c) = O(n)$ steps to simulate using binary guesses.

In a second step, we move all of the guessing to the beginning of the algorithm. In the algorithms solving crossword puzzles and graph coloring (Algorithms 10.2.2 and 10.2.15), we already make all the guesses before verifying whether we have found a correct solution, but in general that need not be the case (see Example 10.2.26).

We know that algorithm B runs in time $n^{k+1} + c$ for some c. Hence, along each computation path, B can make at most $n^{k+1} + c$ binary guesses. Construct an algorithm C that first populates an array $guesses$ of size $n^{k+1} + c$ with $n^{k+1} + c$ binary guesses and then runs algorithm B with this modification: Every call to $guess$ in B is substituted by looking up $guesses[counter]$ and increasing the counter.

From A we have constructed a polynomial-time nondeterministic algorithm C that starts with making a polynomial number of binary guesses and then runs deterministically in polynomial time.

In a final step, we turn C into a deterministic algorithm D. Instead of guessing the $n^{k+1} + c$ cells in the array $guesses$ at the beginning of C, D tries all possible ways to assign binary values to the cells. There are $2^{n^{k+1}+c}$ such possibilities and checking each takes time $n^{k+1} + c$; hence, we obtain an overall runtime of $O(2^{n^{k+2}})$ for D, which is exponential.

Example 10.2.26. The following variant of the graph-coloring algorithm interleaves the guessing and the verification; each color is verified as it is added.

```
graph_coloring(G, k) {
    for each v in V
        c[v] = 0
    for each v in V {
        c[v] = guess({1, 2, ..., k})
        for each w in N(v)
            if (c[w] == c[v])
                return false
    }
    return true
}
```

If we moved the guessing to the beginning of the algorithm we would obtain Algorithm 10.2.15.   □

We have shown that **NP** $\subseteq$ **EXP** by transforming an **NP**-algorithm into an exponential-time algorithm. In Section 11.1 we will see several examples of how to find exponential-time solutions for nondeterministic algorithms with good exponents.

Exercises

1S. Color the different states in a map of Australia using three colors such that no two states that share a border have the same color.

2. Color the map of South America (Figure 10.2.4) using four colors such that no two countries that share a border have the same color.

3. Color a map of the United States using four colors such that no two states that share a border have the same color.

4S. Show that a map of the states of Australia cannot be colored with two colors if all states that share a border need to have different colors.

5. Prove that a map of the United States cannot be colored with three colors if all states that share a border need to have different colors.

6. Show that every graph $G = (V, E)$ is $|V|$-colorable.

7S. How many Hamiltonian cycles of the graph in Figure 10.2.10 contain both the connections Mumbai to Nagpur and Nagpur to Kolkata?

8. List all Hamiltonian cycles of the graph in Figure 10.2.8.

9. Does the graph in Figure 10.2.8 have a Hamiltonian cycle that uses the connection from Toronto to Montreal? If so, write it down; otherwise, prove that there is no such Hamiltonian cycle.

10S. Find a graph that has exactly three different Hamiltonian cycles.

11. Find a graph that has exactly two different Hamiltonian cycles.

12. The graph in Figure 10.2.5 has a unique Hamiltonian cycle. Find it and show that it is the only Hamiltonian cycle.

13S. What is the shortest tour through the eight cities in Figure 10.2.10?

14. What is the longest tour through the eight cities in Figure 10.2.10?

15. How many tours are there through the eight cities in Figure 10.2.10?

10.3 Reducibility and NP-Completeness

To determine that the Eiffel tower is taller than the Musée d'Orsay we do not have to know the height of either building. We can, assuming we are in Paris, compare them by looking at them. Similarly, we might be able to determine the complexity of a problem relative to other problems, even if we cannot determine its absolute complexity precisely.

Example 10.3.1. Consider the following two instances of coloring a graph and solving a crossword puzzle.

2 | RG, RB, GR, GB, BR, BG
3 | RRR, GGG, BBB
5 | RRRRR, GGGGG, BBBBB

The vertices in the graph have been translated into the four pairs of 3-letter words in the four corners of the crossword puzzle. The words connecting these four corners correspond to the edges in the graph. Note that all 3- and 5-letter words contain only the same letter, whereas the 2-letter words always contain two different letters. Hence, we could fill the top part of the crossword as follows:

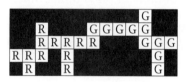

which leads to a coloring in which the upper-left vertex in the graph is red and the upper-right vertex is green. The 2-letter words guarantee that adjacent vertices have different colors. For example, using all R's,

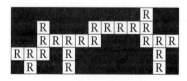

which would correspond to coloring the two upper vertices red, is not a correct solution of the crossword puzzle since the word RR is not allowed.

The crossword-puzzle instance has been constructed in such a way from the graph problem that the graph can be colored using three colors if and only if the crossword problem is solvable. Someone good at solving crossword problems could in this way help to solve graph-coloring problems.

In our particular example, the crossword puzzle can be solved, yielding a 3-coloring of the original graph.   □

Example 10.3.1 illustrates the idea at the root of comparing the complexity of problems. We have two problems A and B, 3-colorability and crossword puzzle, for example, and we assume that any instance a of A can be translated into an instance $f(a)$ of B such that the translation turns positive instances of A into positive instances of B and negative instances of A into negative instances of B. If this is the case, we say that A **reduces** to B. We think of A as being easier than B (or at most as difficult) because, if we can solve B, we can also solve A, by first translating A instances into B instances, then solving B and returning the answer.

Example 10.3.2. In Example 10.3.1 we translated a particular instance of the 3-coloring problem into a particular instance of the crossword-puzzle problem. It turned out that there was a solution to the crossword puzzle, and hence we knew that there was also a solution to the 3-coloring problem: The positive crossword puzzle instance translated back into a positive instance of 3-coloring. If we built a crossword puzzle corresponding to K_4 in a similar fashion, then that crossword puzzle would not be solvable since a solution would correspond to a 3-coloring of K_4, which does not exist. □

We need to be careful in the definition of translation. The definition of reducibility is justified through the principle that if A reduces to B and B can be solved easily, then A can be solved easily. For the principle to work, the translation must itself be computationally easy. For our purposes that means the translation has to be computable in polynomial time.

Definition 10.3.3. We say that problem A *reduces* to problem B, and we write $A \leq_p B$, if there is a function f that can be computed by an algorithm in polynomial time such that for all instances x,

$$x \in A \Leftrightarrow f(x) \in B.$$

We also say that A reduces to B *via* f, if we want to emphasize the function f that witnesses the reduction.

The next theorem shows why we use the symbol $\leq_p$ to compare the complexity of problems.

Theorem 10.3.4. *If $A \leq_p B$ and $B \in$ **P**, then $A \in$ **P**.*

Proof. Suppose $A \leq_p B$ via a polynomial-time reduction f, and B is decided by an algorithm M running in polynomial time. Consider the following algorithm N:

Input Parameter: Instance x of A
Output Parameters: None

```
N(x) {
    y = f(x)
    return M(y)
}
```

Then algorithm N decides A. If $x \in A$, then $y = f(x) \in B$ and $M(y)$ returns true, since M decides B. Otherwise it returns false. By Theorem 10.1.11, algorithm N runs in polynomial time since N is the composition of M and f. ∎

There are two ways to read Theorem 10.3.4. The first interpretation is immediate: If A reduces to B and B is computationally easy, then so is A. The other interpretation is that if A reduces to B and A is not computationally easy, then neither is B (if it was, so would be A). In the current section we are mainly concerned with the second interpretation, but we also want to include some examples showing that the idea behind Theorem 10.3.4 is a very practical one: If we can efficiently solve some problem that other problems reduce to, then the other problems can also be solved efficiently (see also Exercises 10.21–10.27).

Example 10.3.5. The game of NIM is played by two players, call them players I and II. In the version of the game we are interested in, there are two piles of cards on the table. Alternately, beginning with player I, the players remove cards from the two piles according to the following rules: (i) At least one card has to be removed in each move. (ii) A player can remove cards from only one of the piles during each move. The player who removes the last card wins the game. See Figure 10.3.1 for an example of a game.

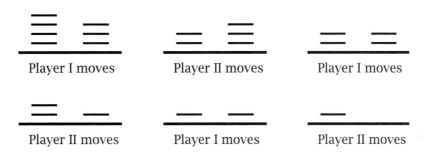

| Player I moves | Player II moves | Player I moves |
| Player II moves | Player I moves | Player II moves |

Figure 10.3.1 A game of NIM.

In the game in Figure 10.3.1, player II wins, taking the last remaining card. We can write the game as a sequence of pairs of numbers, $(4, 3)$, $(2, 3)$, $(2, 2)$, $(2, 1)$, $(1, 1)$, $(1, 0)$, $(0, 0)$, where $(4, 3)$, for example, means that there are four cards in the first pile and three cards in the second pile. Player II wins the game by making the move $(0, 0)$.

Since ties are not possible in NIM, one of the players can force a win from a particular starting position. In Figure 10.3.1, player I could have won if he had removed only one card in the first move, turning $(4, 3)$ into $(3, 3)$. Player I has the following winning strategy for each starting position (m, n) where $m \neq n$: Reduce the larger pile to the same size as the smaller pile. Following this strategy, player I wins (note that player II has to remove a card, so after player II has moved, the piles have different sizes again, so that player I can continue his strategy). If the starting position is of the form (n, n), then player II can win using the same strategy. We can therefore easily determine (in polynomial time) which player can force a win starting from an arbitrary position.

Now consider the following game played on a board. A rook is positioned somewhere on the board. Alternately players I and II can move the rook any number of squares vertically or horizontally, with the restriction that the rook can be moved only west and south, not east and north, and it must be moved. The player who moves the rook into the lower-left square wins the game.

A closer look at the second game shows that it is just a rephrasing of NIM. The size of the first pile corresponds to the vertical and the size of the second pile to the horizontal position of the rook on the board. For example, the winning configuration $(0, 0)$ in NIM corresponds to the final square $(1, 1)$ on the board. Figure 10.3.2 shows the game of NIM we played in Figure 10.3.1 with cards on a table.

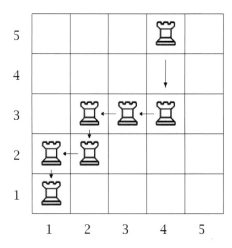

Figure 10.3.2 The moves of the rook corresponding to the game of NIM played in Figure 10.3.1.

If we let

NIM = $\{(n, m) \mid$ Player I can force a win in NIM starting in $(n, m)\}$,

and

ROOK = $\{(n, m) \mid$ Player I can force a win if the rook is located in $(n, m)\}$,

then $(n, m) \in$ ROOK if and only if $(n - 1, m - 1) \in$ NIM. We conclude that ROOK $\leq_p$ NIM via the reduction f that maps (x, y) to $(x - 1, y - 1)$. Since NIM can be decided in polynomial time, ROOK can also be decided in polynomial time. As a matter of fact, we can determine the set ROOK explicitly, namely ROOK = $\{(n, m) \mid n \neq m\}$. $\qquad\square$

In the preceding example it was not difficult to see that both the NIM and the ROOK problems can be solved in polynomial time, so one might argue that it was not necessary to use a reduction. The next example shows that this is not always the case. It introduces *linear programming,* which is a very general problem that can be solved efficiently and which can be used to solve many different types of problems.

Example 10.3.6. In Section 7.6 we first encountered the *continuous-knapsack problem* in which we are given n objects, a knapsack of capacity C, and a profit goal of P. Each object has associated with it a weight w_i and a profit p_i. The objects are arbitrarily divisible; so, for example, we can decide to pack 35% of the first object for a profit of $0.35p_1$ and adding weight $0.35w_1$ to the knapsack. The question is whether we can pack the knapsack to obtain a profit of at least P without exceeding the capacity C. More formally, we are asking whether there are $0 \le x_i \le 1$, $1 \le i \le n$, such that

$$\sum_{i=1}^{n} x_i w_i \le C,$$

and

$$\sum_{i=1}^{n} x_i p_i \ge P.$$

We solved this problem using a greedy approach, but we could instead have used linear programming. A **linear program** is a set of linear inequalities:

$$
\begin{array}{ccccccc}
a_{1,1}x_1 & + & a_{1,2}x_2 & + & \dots & a_{1,n}x_n & \ge & b_1 \\
a_{2,1}x_1 & + & a_{2,2}x_2 & + & \dots & a_{2,n}x_n & \ge & b_2 \\
\vdots & & \vdots & & & \vdots \quad \vdots \\
a_{m,1}x_1 & + & a_{m,2}x_2 & + & \dots & a_{m,n}x_n & \ge & b_m.
\end{array}
$$

The coefficients $a_{i,j}$ are rational numbers. The *linear-programming problem* asks whether there is a rational solution to the linear program. Linear programming can be solved in polynomial time (using decidedly nontrivial methods) and there are many software packages to do so. The knapsack problem and the linear-programming problem are very similar except that in a linear program we allow only $\ge$. This can easily be dealt with by multiplying a $\le$-equation by -1. There is a solution to the continuous-knapsack problem if and only if there is a solution to the linear program

$$
\begin{array}{ccccccc}
(-w_1)x_1 & + & (-w_2)x_2 & + & \dots & (-w_n)x_n & \ge & -C \\
p_1x_1 & + & p_2x_2 & + & \dots & p_nx_n & \ge & P \\
x_1 & & & & & & \ge & 0 \\
-x_1 & & & & & & \ge & -1 \\
\vdots & & \vdots & & & \vdots \quad \vdots \\
& & & & & x_n & \ge & 0 \\
& & & & & -x_n & \ge & -1.
\end{array}
$$

In other words, the continuous-knapsack problem reduces to the linear-programming problem, which we know to be solvable in polynomial time.

Hence, we can conclude that the continuous-knapsack problem is solvable in polynomial time without writing any algorithm at all.   □

We have measured complexity using the classes **P**, **NP**, and **EXP**. Figure 10.3.3 outlines our current view of the world of computational complexity. The inclusions **P** ⊆ **NP** and **NP** ⊆ **EXP** are from Theorems 10.2.8 and 10.2.25.

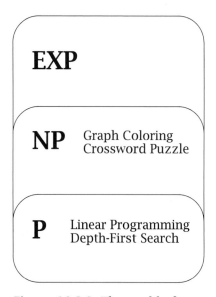

Figure 10.3.3 The world of computational complexity.

Figure 10.3.3 suggests knowledge we do not have. The actual location of **NP** between **P** and **EXP** is not known, and we do not know that graph coloring, for example, cannot be solved in polynomial time. The only known relationships between these classes are the inclusions and the fact that **P** ≠ **EXP** (see Exercise 10.3). It could be that all **NP**-problems can be solved in polynomial time; that is, **P** = **NP**. On the other hand, it could be that every problem in exponential time can be solved in **NP**; that is, **NP** = **EXP**. Neither of these alternatives is considered likely by experts. Computer scientists believe that the world looks as shown in Figure 10.3.3 with **P** ⊂ **NP** ⊂ **EXP**, the inclusions being proper. However, the proper inclusions have not been established and are considered difficult. Proving that nondeterministic polynomial-time algorithms are strictly more powerful than deterministic ones, namely that **P** ≠ **NP**, remains the main open research problem in computer science.

Why is this question of interest to us? During the 1970s it became increasingly clear that **NP** contains a large group of problems that are of practical importance, but for which polynomial-time algorithms are not known. Graph coloring is one of the early examples. In the meantime many more problems have been added to the list from diverse areas such as biology, physics, and others. We cannot expect to show that these problems are not solvable in polynomial time (since this would settle the difficult **P** $\neq$ **NP** problem), so we aim for a more modest goal: We show that these problems are difficult *relatively* speaking. Namely, we show that these problems are as hard as any other problem in the class **NP**. We will show, for example, that any **NP**-problem reduces to graph coloring; that is, any **NP**-problem can be rephrased as a graph-coloring problem. This shows that graph coloring is as hard as any **NP**-problem; hence, in a sense it is a hardest problem in **NP**.

Definition 10.3.7. We say that a problem B in **NP** is **NP**-*complete*, if for all **NP**-problems A we have $A \leq_p B$.

The following theorem formalizes our intuition of **NP**-complete problems as hard problems.

Theorem 10.3.8. *If any* **NP**-*complete problem is in* **P**, *then* **NP** = **P**.

Proof. Let B be an **NP**-complete problem that is in **P**. Let A be an arbitrary **NP**-problem. Because B is **NP**-complete, we know that $A \leq_p B$. By assumption, B is in **P**, and Theorem 10.3.4 implies that A is in **P**. Since A was an arbitrarily chosen **NP**-problem, we have shown that all **NP**-problems are in **NP**; and, hence, **P** = **NP**. ■

There are thousands of **NP**-complete problems spread over all areas of science. Theorem 10.3.8, together with the fact that no researcher has found a polynomial-time algorithm for any of them, is taken as empirical evidence that **P** $\neq$ **NP**.

The reduction $\leq_p$ has some properties we would expect of an *ordering* relation. In particular, we can show that it is transitive.

Lemma 10.3.9. *If* $A \leq_p B$ *and* $B \leq_p C$, *then* $A \leq_p C$.

Proof. Suppose $A \leq_p B$ via a polynomial-time reduction f, and $B \leq_p C$ via a polynomial-time reduction g. Then, by virtue of f and g being reductions, we obtain

$$x \in A \Rightarrow f(x) \in B \Rightarrow g(f(x)) \in C, \text{ and}$$

$$x \notin A \Rightarrow f(x) \notin B \Rightarrow g(f(x)) \notin C,$$

which says that $h(x) = g(f(x))$, the composition of g and f, reduces A to C. Furthermore, the function h can be computed in polynomial time, since it is the composition of two functions computable in polynomial time (Theorem 10.1.11). Hence, $A \leq_p C$. ■

To prove that a problem A is **NP**-complete using the definition, we have to show that every **NP**-problem reduces to A, which is difficult. Instead, we use the following theorem to show **NP**-completeness.

Theorem 10.3.10. *If* A *and* B *are problems in* **NP**, A *is* **NP**-*complete, and* $A \leq_p B$, *then* B *is* **NP**-*complete.*

Proof. To show that B is **NP**-complete, by definition, we have to show that any **NP**-problem reduces to it. So let C be an arbitrary **NP**-complete problem. Since A is **NP**-complete, $C \leq_p A$. By assumption $A \leq_p B$, and therefore, by transitivity of $\leq_p$ (Lemma 10.3.9), we have $C \leq_p B$, which is what we had to show. ∎

Theorem 10.3.10 allows us to prove that a new problem B is **NP**-complete by reducing a known **NP**-complete problem A to it. This is a popular sport among computer scientists; however, before we can apply Theorem 10.3.10, we need an *initial* **NP**-complete problem, the satisfiability problem to which we devote the next subsection. Section 10.4 will then show the **NP**-completeness of some fundamental problems by reducing the satisfiability problem to them.

Satisfiability

The first problem to be shown **NP**-complete is the satisfiability problem from logic. Since it was the first **NP**-complete problem, it had to be shown **NP**-complete from the definition. We start with Boolean variables $x_1, x_2, \ldots$ that can be connected using Boolean operators such as disjunction ($\vee$), conjunction ($\wedge$), negation ($\bar{\ }$), implication ($\rightarrow$), and equivalence ($\leftrightarrow$). For example, x_1, $\overline{x}_1$, $x_1 \rightarrow (\overline{x}_2 \vee \overline{x}_3)$, and $(x_1 \wedge x_2) \leftrightarrow (x_2 \vee x_3)$ are Boolean formulas (see Section 2.1). A **truth assignment** assigns a truth value to each variable in a formula.

Example 10.3.11. Let

$$\varphi = (x_1 \wedge x_2) \leftrightarrow (x_2 \vee x_3).$$

If x_1 and x_3 are false, and x_2 is true, then φ is false. However, under the truth assignment that makes all variables false, φ is true. □

In the most general form of the satisfiability problem, we are given a Boolean formula over Boolean variables and are asked whether there is an assignment of truth values to the variables that makes the formula true. A formula that is true for some assignment of truth values to its variables is called **satisfiable**. A formula that is false for all assignments of truth values to its variables is **unsatisfiable**.

Example 10.3.12. Consider the formula

$$\varphi = (x_1 \leftrightarrow (\overline{x}_2 \vee x_3)) \wedge (\overline{x}_1 \vee (x_2 \wedge \overline{x}_3)) \wedge (x_2 \rightarrow x_3).$$

The following truth table shows that φ is false for all truth assignments and is therefore unsatisfiable.

x_1	x_2	x_3	$(x_1 \leftrightarrow (\overline{x}_2 \vee x_3))$	$(\overline{x}_1 \vee (x_2 \wedge \overline{x}_3))$	$(x_2 \rightarrow x_3)$	φ
T	T	T	T	F	T	F
T	T	F	F	T	F	F
T	F	T	T	F	T	F
T	F	F	T	F	T	F
F	T	T	F	T	T	F
F	T	F	T	T	F	F
F	F	T	F	T	T	F
F	F	F	F	T	T	F

□

We concentrate on Boolean formulas in conjunctive normal form (CNF). Recall that a Boolean formula is in CNF, if it is the conjunction of disjunctions of literals (see Section 2.1). The disjunctions are called the clauses of the formula. In a clause, a literal is either **positive**, such as x_1 or x_4 in $(x_1 \vee \overline{x}_2 \vee x_4)$, or **negative**, such as $\overline{x}_2$ in $(x_1 \vee \overline{x}_2 \vee x_4)$. We assume that a clause does not contain the same literal twice. For example, we do not allow $x_1 \vee \overline{x}_2 \vee \overline{x}_2$. It would have to be written as $x_1 \vee \overline{x}_2$. We say a formula is in k-**CNF**, if every clause contains exactly k literals.

Example 10.3.13. The CNF formula

$$(x_1 \vee \overline{x}_5 \vee x_7 \vee x_9) \wedge (\overline{x}_2 \vee \overline{x}_6 \vee x_7 \vee x_8 \vee x_9) \wedge (x_3 \vee x_4) \wedge (x_1 \vee x_3 \vee \overline{x}_9)$$

has four clauses, and the last clause contains three literals, two of them positive and one negative. The formula is not k-CNF for any k, since the clauses contain different numbers of literals.

The formula $(x_1 \vee \overline{x}_2) \wedge (\overline{x}_1 \vee x_2)$ is in 2-CNF.

It is possible for a clause to contain only one literal, so $(x_1 \vee x_2) \wedge x_3$ is a CNF formula, as is $\overline{x}_1 \wedge x_3$. It is also possible that there is only one clause in a CNF formula, as in the case $x_1 \vee x_2$.   □

The problem we are interested in is the satisfiability problem for Boolean formulas in CNF.

Satisfiability (SAT)
Instance: A Boolean formula φ in CNF.
Question: Is φ satisfiable?

Satisfiability is in **NP**, since we can guess a truth assignment using non-determinism and then verify that it satisfies the formula in polynomial time (see Exercise 10.29). Satisfiability was shown to be **NP**-complete by Cook (Cook, 1971). Independently, and at roughly the same time, Levin showed that a certain tiling problem is **NP**-complete (Levin, 1973). These two problems are probably the only two problems to have been shown **NP**-complete from the definition.

Theorem 10.3.14 Cook-Levin Theorem. SAT *is* NP-*complete.*

We will not prove the Cook-Levin theorem since the technical details are not of interest to us here. The proof shows that the computation of any **NP**-algorithm on any input can be translated into a Boolean formula that is satisfiable if and only if the algorithm accepts the input.

In the following sections we will use the satisfiability problem to prove **NP**-completeness of other problems. For that purpose, it is often helpful to know that we can assume that φ is not only in CNF but also that each clause contains only a small number of variables. Indeed, it is possible to show that the satisfiability problem for formulas in 3-CNF is **NP**-complete.

3-**Satisfiability** (3SAT)
Instance: A Boolean formula φ in 3-CNF.
Question: Is φ satisfiable?

Theorem 10.3.15. 3SAT *is* **NP**-*complete*.

Proof. We show that SAT $\leq_p$ 3SAT. The result then follows from Theorem 10.3.10. We have to show how to translate an arbitrary CNF formula φ into a 3-CNF formula $\varphi' = f(\varphi)$ such that φ is satisfiable if and only if φ' is satisfiable. To this end, we want to replace clauses that do not contain exactly three literals with a set of new clauses that do, in such a way that satisfiability is retained. Consider a clause containing a single literal: ℓ_1. We can replace it by four clauses:

$$\ell_1 \vee y_1 \vee y_2, \quad \ell_1 \vee \overline{y}_1 \vee y_2, \quad \ell_1 \vee y_1 \vee \overline{y}_2, \quad \ell_1 \vee \overline{y}_1 \vee \overline{y}_2,$$

where y_1, and y_2 are new variables. A truth assignment making ℓ_1 true makes all four of the new clauses true. On the other hand, consider a truth assignment that satisfies the four new clauses. Then, in one of the clauses, the two literals different from ℓ_1 are false, and therefore ℓ_1 has to be true to make that clause true. Therefore, the original clause containing just ℓ_1 is made true by this truth assignment.

We leave the case in which the original clause contains two literals as an exercise (Exercise 7). Since clauses containing three literals do not need to be changed, this leaves us with the clauses containing at least four literals. Consider a single clause containing $k \geq 4$ literals

$$\ell_1 \vee \ell_2 \vee \cdots \vee \ell_k.$$

We select $k-3$ new variables $y_1, \ldots, y_{k-3}$ and build the $k-2$ clauses

$$
\begin{array}{ccccc}
\ell_1 & \vee & \ell_2 & \vee & \overline{y}_1 \\
y_1 & \vee & \ell_3 & \vee & \overline{y}_2 \\
& & \vdots & & \\
y_{i-2} & \vee & \ell_i & \vee & \overline{y}_{i-1} \\
& & \vdots & & \\
y_{k-4} & \vee & \ell_{k-2} & \vee & \overline{y}_{k-3} \\
y_{k-3} & \vee & \ell_{k-1} & \vee & \ell_k.
\end{array}
$$

A truth assignment satisfying the original clause $\ell_1 \vee \ell_2 \vee \cdots \vee \ell_k$ has to make some ℓ_i true. We can extend this truth assignment to satisfy all of the $k-2$ new clauses by making all y_j with $j < i-1$ false and all y_j with $j \geq i-1$ true:

$$
\left.
\begin{array}{ccccc}
\ell_1 & \vee & \ell_2 & \vee & \overline{y}_1 \\
y_1 & \vee & \ell_3 & \vee & \overline{y}_2 \\
& & \vdots & & \\
y_{i-3} & \vee & \ell_{i-1} & \vee & \overline{y}_{i-2}
\end{array}
\right\} \quad \text{true, since } y_1, \ldots, y_{i-2} \text{ are false}
$$

$$
\left.
\begin{array}{ccccc}
y_{i-2} & \vee & \ell_i & \vee & \overline{y}_{i-1}
\end{array}
\right\} \quad \text{true, since } \ell_i \text{ is true}
$$

$$
\left.
\begin{array}{ccccc}
y_{i-1} & \vee & \ell_{i+1} & \vee & \overline{y}_i \\
& & \vdots & & \\
y_{k-4} & \vee & \ell_{k-2} & \vee & \overline{y}_{k-3} \\
y_{k-3} & \vee & \ell_{k-1} & \vee & \ell_k
\end{array}
\right\} \quad \text{true, since } y_{i-1}, \ldots, y_{k-3} \text{ are true.}
$$

Conversely assume that there is a truth assignment making all of the k new clauses true. If all ℓ_i, $1 \leq i \leq k$, were false in that truth assignment, then y_1 has to be false because the first clause is true. Then y_2 has to be false to make the second clause true. We can continue to argue that all of the y_i have to be false, but then the last clause is false, which is a contradiction. Therefore, at least one ℓ_i is true, and the original clause is satisfied by the truth assignment we considered.

Hence, we can substitute each clause in φ with several clauses of three literals (as described in the preceding paragraphs) to obtain a new formula φ' in 3-CNF such that φ is satisfiable if and only if φ' is satisfiable.

Building φ' from φ takes only polynomial time, since each clause is replaced by fewer than k clauses and $k \leq |\varphi|$. Since φ can contain at most $|\varphi|$ clauses, we conclude that $|\varphi'| \leq |\varphi|^2$. ∎

Example 10.3.16. Applying the substitutions in the proof of Theorem 10.3.15, the formula

$$\varphi = x_1 \wedge (\overline{x}_1 \vee x_2 \vee \overline{x}_3 \vee x_4)$$

becomes

$$
\begin{aligned}
\varphi' &= (x_1 \vee y_0 \vee y_1) \wedge (x_1 \vee \overline{y}_0 \vee y_1) \wedge (x_1 \vee y_0 \vee \overline{y}_1) \wedge (x_1 \vee \overline{y}_0 \vee \overline{y}_1) \\
&\quad \wedge (\overline{x}_1 \vee x_2 \vee \overline{y}_2) \wedge (y_2 \vee x_2 \vee \overline{y}_3) \wedge (y_3 \vee \overline{x}_3 \vee x_4).
\end{aligned}
$$

Formula φ is satisfied, for example, by letting x_1 be true and x_2, x_3, and x_4 be false. We can extend this to a satisfying assignment of φ' by letting y_0, y_1, y_2, and y_3 be false. □

Often we are interested in determining not only whether φ is satisfiable, but in a satisfying assignment if φ is satisfiable—a task which at first might seem harder than the decision problem we have considered so far. However, it turns out that being able to solve the decision problem is enough to also find a satisfying assignment. Suppose we have an algorithm A that correctly decides the general satisfiability problem, for example, the exponential-time algorithm we know exists by Theorem 10.2.25. How can we use A to find a satisfying assignment for a formula φ? First we can use A to check that φ is indeed satisfiable. Consider a variable x of φ. There are two possibilities: There is a satisfying assignment of φ in which x is true, or x is false in all satisfying assignments of φ. Using A, we can decide which is the case by letting x be true in φ and running A on the resulting formula to find out whether it is still satisfiable. If the resulting formula is satisfiable, we set x and continue; otherwise set x to false and continue.

Example 10.3.17. Consider the formula

$$\varphi = (x_1 \vee \overline{x}_2 \vee x_4) \wedge (\overline{x}_1 \vee x_2) \wedge (\overline{x}_1 \vee \overline{x}_2 \vee x_3) \wedge \overline{x}_3,$$

which is satisfiable. If we set x_1 to true in φ, the first clause is true, so we can drop it; the second clause becomes x_2, the third clause becomes $(\overline{x}_2 \vee x_3)$, and the last clause remains $\overline{x}_3$. We obtain the formula

$$x_2 \wedge (\overline{x}_2 \vee x_3) \wedge \overline{x}_3,$$

which is unsatisfiable. Therefore, setting x_1 to true will not lead to a satisfying assignment of φ; hence, x_1 has to be false in any satisfying assignment.

If we set x_1 to false in φ, we obtain

$$(\overline{x}_2 \vee x_4) \wedge \overline{x}_3,$$

which is satisfiable. Letting x_2 be true leads to

$$x_4 \wedge \overline{x}_3,$$

which is satisfiable. Setting x_3 to true leads to an unsatisfiable formula; hence, we try setting x_3 to false. We obtain the formula

$$x_4,$$

which is satisfiable, and we continue by letting x_4 be true. This gives us the following satisfying assignment: x_1 and x_3 are false, and x_2 and x_4 are true. The only information we needed in the process of determining this truth assignment was whether a formula was satisfiable or not. □

To simplify the algorithm, let us write $\varphi[x \to \text{true}]$ ($\varphi[x \to \text{false}]$) to denote the formula obtained from φ by setting all occurrences of variable x to true (false, respectively), all occurrences of the negation of x to false (true), and simplifying the resulting formula.

Algorithm 10.3.18 Satisfiability Witness. This algorithm takes as input a CNF formula φ on variables $x_1, \ldots, x_n$, and either returns a satisfying assignment for φ in the array x or false if there is no such assignment. It assumes that we have an algorithm A that decides whether a formula is satisfiable or not.

Input Parameter: φ
Output Parameter: x

```
satisfiability_witness(φ, x) {
    if (!(A(φ))
        return false
    for i = 1 to n {
        ψ = φ[x_i → true]
        if (A(ψ)) {
            x[i] = true
            φ = ψ
        }
        else {
            x[i] = false
            φ = φ[x_i → false]
        }
    }
    return true
}
```

A formula φ can contain at most $|\varphi|$ variables; hence, *satisfiability_witness* takes time $n f(n)$ if A takes time $f(n)$ on formulas of length n, which proves the next theorem.

Theorem 10.3.19. *If SAT is in* **P***, then witnesses for satisfiable formulas can be found in polynomial time.*

The algorithm for *satisfiability_witness* showed how to solve a search problem (finding a satisfying assignment) given an algorithm for the decision problem. Results of this type are true for all known **NP**-complete problems: We can always find a witness, if we can decide whether there is one.

Exercises

1S. Find a solution to the crossword puzzle in Example 10.3.1 and the coloring of the original graph to which the solution corresponds.

2. Construct a crossword problem corresponding to the 3-colorability of K_4 in a fashion similar to Example 10.3.1.

3. Construct a crossword problem for k-coloring the simple cycle C_5 on five vertices for $k = 2$ and $k = 3$. What is the difference between the two?

Recall the rook game from Example 10.3.5. In Exercise 4 we explicitly compute the set of winning positions of Player I, and Exercise 5 considers a variant of the game. We keep the restriction that in each move the piece has to be moved, that it cannot be moved east or north, and that the player who moves it to the lower-left square wins.

4S. Show formally that the set ROOK = $\{(n, m) \mid$ Player I can force a win with the rook starting in $(n, m)\}$ equals $\{(n, m) \mid n \neq m\}$. *Hint:* Find a winning strategy for player I.

5. Assume instead of a rook we use the king (who can move one square in any direction). Determine the set KING = $\{(n, m) \mid$ Player I can force a win with the king starting in $(n, m)\}$. What is the winning strategy for player I?

6. Show that, if we extend our notion of a linear program (see Example 10.3.6) to also include equalities $(a_{i,1}x_1 + a_{i,2}x_2 + \ldots + a_{i,n}x_n = b_n)$, the problem can still be solved in polynomial time.

7S. Complete the proof of Theorem 10.3.15 by showing what to do with a clause $\ell_1 \vee \ell_2$ containing two literals.

8. Let CYCLE = $\{(G, k) \mid G$ contains a simple cycle of length at least $k\}$. Show that the Hamiltonian-cycle problem reduces to CYCLE.

10.4 NP-Complete Problems

Using the **NP**-completeness of SAT and 3SAT as a starting point, we show that finding an independent set or a clique or coloring a graph are hard tasks to solve. These are fundamental problems, which have been used in the **NP**-completeness proofs of many other problems.

Independent Sets and Cliques

A set of vertices U is **independent** in a graph $G = (V, E)$ if there is no edge incident on two vertices of U. The size of a maximal independent set in G is called the **independence number** of G and written $\alpha(G)$.

Example 10.4.1. Consider the graph in Figure 10.4.1. It contains an independent set of size 3 consisting of nodes 1, 3, and 6. The set is independent, since no two of the nodes are adjacent in the graph. To show that the independence number of the graph is 3, we have to show that there is no independent set of 4 vertices. If there were a set of four independent vertices, it could contain at most one of the vertices 1 and 2; hence three vertices from the set $\{3, 4, 5, 6\}$ need to be independent, which is not possible.

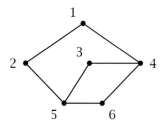

Figure 10.4.1 A graph of independence number 3. □

The independent-set decision problem can be phrased as follows:

Independent Set
Instance: Graph $G = (V, E)$, integer $k \le |V|$.
Question: Is $\alpha(G) \ge k$; that is, does G contain an independent set of size at least k?

Theorem 10.4.2. *The independent-set problem is* **NP**-*complete.*

Proof. We leave it to Exercise 10.31 to show that the independent-set problem is in **NP**. By Theorem 10.3.10, we can show that the independent-set problem is **NP**-complete by reducing the **NP**-complete problem 3SAT to it.

Suppose that we are given a Boolean formula φ in 3-CNF with clauses $C_1, \ldots, C_m$. We build a graph $G = (V, E)$ such that φ is satisfiable if and only if G contains an independent set of size m, the number of clauses. For each clause C_i we draw a triangle (three vertices connected by three edges) and label the vertices of each triangle with the literals in the corresponding clause. We call two literals **contradictory** if they are the positive and negative versions of the same variable. For example, $\overline{x}_3$ and x_3 are contradictory, but $\overline{x}_3$ and x_1 are not. To the triangles, we add edges between pairs of vertices if they are labeled by contradictory literals. We claim that the resulting graph G contains an independent set of size m if and only if φ is satisfiable.

For example, Figure 10.4.2 shows the graph G resulting from

$$\varphi = (x_1 \vee \overline{x}_2 \vee x_3) \wedge (x_2 \vee x_3 \vee x_4) \wedge (\overline{x}_1 \vee x_2 \vee x_4) \wedge (x_2 \vee \overline{x}_3 \vee \overline{x}_4) \wedge (\overline{x}_1 \vee \overline{x}_3 \vee x_4).$$

The graph G contains an independent set on five vertices as shown by the circles in Figure 10.4.2: $\overline{x}_2$ from C_1, x_3 from C_2, $\overline{x}_1$ from C_3, $\overline{x}_4$ from C_4, and $\overline{x}_1$ from C_5. This corresponds to the truth assignment that makes x_1, x_2, and x_4 false and x_3 true. That truth assignment satisfies φ, since each clause is satisfied.

To prove the claim that G contains an independent set of size m if and only if φ is satisfiable, we first assume that G contains an independent set of size m. Fix such an independent set U of m vertices. Then, U can contain at most one vertex from each triangle, since there are edges between any two vertices of the same triangle. Since there are only m triangles altogether, U must contain exactly one vertex from each triangle. Consider the labels

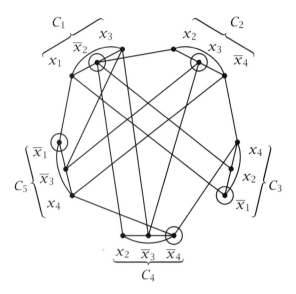

Figure 10.4.2 The graph G for $\varphi = (x_1 \vee \overline{x}_2 \vee x_3) \wedge (x_2 \vee x_3 \vee \overline{x}_4) \wedge (\overline{x}_1 \vee x_2 \vee x_4) \wedge (x_2 \vee \overline{x}_3 \vee \overline{x}_4) \wedge (\overline{x}_1 \vee \overline{x}_3 \vee x_4)$. Each clause corresponds to a (flattened) triangle. The five nodes within circles form a maximal independent set.

associated with the vertices in U. Since U is an independent set, no two of these labels are contradictory. Therefore, if we assign the value "true" to the literals associated with a vertex in U, we obtain a partial truth assignment to the variables in φ. This truth assignment satisfies φ, since it makes at least one literal in each clause true. The truth assignment still satisfies φ after we assign arbitrary truth values to any remaining variables.

It remains to show that if φ is satisfiable, then G contains an independent set of size at least m. Assume then that φ is satisfiable and fix a truth assignment that satisfies φ. With this truth assignment, at least one literal in each clause of φ has to be made true by what it means to be satisfiable. Choose one such literal from each clause and collect the corresponding vertices in a set U. Then U contains m vertices, since we picked one vertex for each clause (from each triangle). We claim that there cannot be any edge between two vertices of U. Such an edge would connect to two contradictory literals, which is not possible because we chose the vertices according to a truth assignment and it is not possible for both a variable and its negation to be true. Therefore, U is an independent set of size m. ∎

A property related to being an independent set is that of being a clique. A set of vertices U is a **clique** in $G = (V, E)$ if all edges between any two vertices in U belong to E. The size of a maximal clique is called the **clique number** of the graph and written $\omega(G)$.

Clique

Instance: Graph $G = (V, E)$, integer $k \leq |V|$.

Question: Is $\omega(G) \geq k$; that is, does G contain a clique of size at least k?

Cliques are areas of high connectivity in a graph. Depending on the context, high connectivity can be desirable or undesirable. When we think of the graph as a network, cliques are highly connected subgroups of the network, very robust against server or network failures and, therefore, desirable. If, on the other hand, the graph models conflicts and we have to find a coloring of the graph, then large cliques are undesirable since they force us to use many colors: Each vertex of a clique requires a different color (resource). In either case, it is often important to know the size of a maximal clique in a graph.

Solving the clique problem is as hard as solving the independent-set problem, since an independent set in G is a clique in $\overline{G}$, the complement of G (for the definition of $\overline{G}$, see Section 2.5).

Theorem 10.4.3. *The clique problem is NP-complete.*

Proof. We leave it to Exercise 10.32 to show that the clique problem is in **NP**. Because of Theorem 10.3.10, we can prove that the clique problem is **NP**-complete by reducing any **NP**-complete problem to it. We show how to reduce the **NP**-complete independent-set problem to the clique problem. The reduction maps an instance G, k of the independent-set problem to the instance $\overline{G}$, k. To show that this function is indeed a reduction, assume that G contains an independent set U on at least k vertices. Since U is an independent set in G, G does not contain any edges between any pair of vertices in U. Then, by definition, $\overline{G}$ contains all edges between any two vertices of U; hence, U is a clique on k vertices in $\overline{G}$ (Figure 10.4.3).

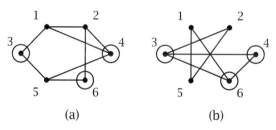

(a)   (b)

Figure 10.4.3 A graph G in (a) and its complement $\overline{G}$ in (b) with independent set $\{3, 4, 6\}$ in G and the corresponding clique $\{3, 4, 6\}$ in $\overline{G}$.

It remains to show that if $\overline{G}$ contains a clique on k vertices, then G has an independent set of size k. Assume that $\overline{G}$ contains a clique U on k vertices. Then $\overline{G}$ contains all edges between any two vertices of U. Again, by definition of the complement of a graph, G does not contain any edges between any two vertices of U and therefore U is an independent set of size at least k in G. In summary, we have shown that G contains an independent set of size at least k if and only if $\overline{G}$ contains a clique of size at least k, showing that the function that maps G, k to $\overline{G}, k$ is a reduction from the independent-set problem to the clique problem. Therefore, the clique problem is **NP**-complete. ∎

Graph Coloring

In Theorem 10.2.16 we showed that graph k-colorability is in **NP**. In case $k = 2$, we can actually solve the problem in polynomial time using breadth-first search (see Exercise 10.1). The problem turns out to be **NP**-complete for any $k \geq 3$.

Theorem 10.4.4. *Graph 3-colorability is* **NP**-*complete.*

Proof. Since we already know that graph 3-colorability is in **NP**, it is sufficient to show how to reduce 3SAT to 3-colorability. We translate the elements of the 3SAT problem, variables and clauses, into components in the graph that simulate the satisfiability behavior in the context of graph coloring. Such components are usually called *gadgets*, and this type of construction is called a *gadget construction*.

We are given a formula φ in 3-CNF with clauses $C_1, \ldots, C_m$. Our goal is to construct a graph G that is 3-colorable if and only if φ is satisfiable. We build G step by step. We start with a triangle on three vertices that we name $b, t,$ and f as shown in Figure 10.4.4. Since there are only three colors available, $b, t,$ and f have to be assigned those three different colors.

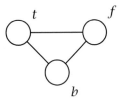

Figure 10.4.4 The base triangle $\{b, t, f\}$.

The colors of t and f correspond to true and false, while the third color, the color of b, is used for encoding purposes. For each variable x in φ, we take two new vertices v_x and $v_{\overline{x}}$ to build another triangle with b at the base (see Figure 10.4.5).

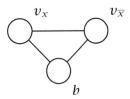

Figure 10.4.5 The triangle $\{v_x, v_{\overline{x}}, b\}$. The vertex b is the same vertex we saw in Figure 10.4.4.

This triangle forces v_x and $v_{\overline{x}}$ to be colored with the colors of t and f, and since the colors of v_x and $v_{\overline{x}}$ have to be different (because of the edge between them), we can read a coloring as a truth assignment to x; namely, if v_x has the same color as t, we can call x true and false otherwise. In this way, a 3-coloring of the graph induces a truth assignment to the variables, and we therefore speak about a coloring satisfying φ.

For each clause $C_i = \ell_{i,1} \lor \ell_{i,2} \lor \ell_{i,3}$, we build a gadget that guarantees that at least one literal in each clause is satisfied by the coloring. The gadget is displayed in Figure 10.4.6. We call the six vertices in a row the *baseline* of the gadget and the outer two vertices of the baseline its *endpoints*. The three labeled vertices are the tops of the triangles. This completes the construction of G.

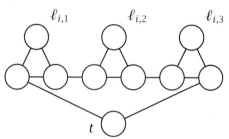

Figure 10.4.6 The clause gadget for 3-colorings. The vertex t is the same vertex we saw in Figure 10.4.4, and the vertices labeled $\ell_{i,j}$ are the vertices we created for each variable.

Figure 10.4.7 shows G for the formula $\varphi = (x_1 \lor x_2 \lor \overline{x}_3) \land (\overline{x}_1 \lor \overline{x}_2 \lor x_3) \land (x_1 \lor \overline{x}_2 \lor x_3)$.

We first argue that a 3-coloring of G translates to a satisfying assignment of φ. The vertices t, f, and b have to be colored with the three different colors; so without loss of generality let us assume that t is red, f is green, and b is blue. Now v_x and $v_{\overline{x}}$ have to be colored red and green, or green and red, since there is an edge between them, and both are connected to the blue b. From this information we construct a truth assignment as follows. If v_x is red, we let x be true, and false otherwise. Fix this truth assignment. We show that this assignment satisfies φ. Consider a clause $C_i = \ell_{i,1} \lor \ell_{i,2} \lor \ell_{i,3}$ and its corresponding gadget. Assume that $\ell_{i,1}$, $\ell_{i,2}$, and $\ell_{i,3}$ are all false under the truth assignment we fixed. Then the tops of all three triangles in the gadgets are green. This forces the vertices in the baseline of the gadget to be alternately blue and red; since there are six vertices in the baseline, one of the endpoints has to be red, which is not possible since it is connected to t, which is colored red (see Figure 10.4.8).

Hence, one of the tops is colored red, meaning that the corresponding literal is true in the truth assignment we fixed, and therefore clause C_i is satisfied. Since this argument is true for all clauses, all clauses are satisfied and therefore φ is satisfied by the truth assignment, implying that φ is satisfiable.

In the other direction, we have to argue that if φ is satisfiable, then G can be 3-colored. Fix a satisfying assignment of G. Color vertices t, f, and b with colors red, green, and blue in that order. Red signifies true and green

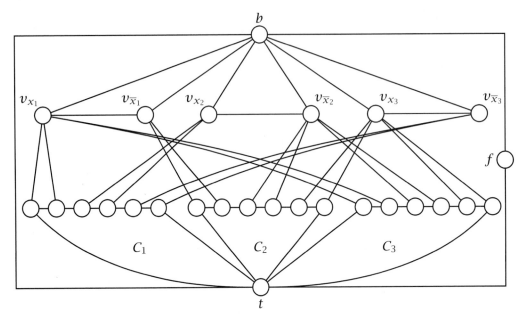

Figure 10.4.7 The graph G for the formula $\varphi = (x_1 \vee x_2 \vee \overline{x}_3) \wedge (\overline{x}_1 \vee \overline{x}_2 \vee x_3) \wedge (x_1 \vee \overline{x}_2 \vee x_3)$. On top are the three triangles for x_1, x_2, x_3; below are the three clause gadgets, one for each clause. For example, the top of the middle triangle of the C_2 gadget is $v_{\overline{x}_2}$ because the second clause contains the literal $\overline{x}_2$. Finally, the triangle $\{b, f, t\}$ surrounds the rest of the graph, the edge b to t on the left side and edges t to f and f to b on the right side.

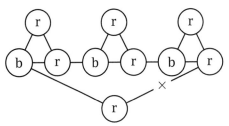

Figure 10.4.8 Color conflict in the clause gadget: If all tops are green, then the colors in the baseline have to alternate between red and blue. Consequently, one of the endpoints of the baseline is red, conflicting with the red t.

signifies false. For each variable x in φ, color vertex v_x red and $v_{\overline{x}}$ green, if x is true, and v_x green and $v_{\overline{x}}$ red, if x is false. Finally, we have to show how to color the gadgets. Since we chose a satisfying assignment, at least one of the three top vertices of the triangles has to be red. Figure 10.4.9 shows how to color the gadget in each of these cases. For example, if all of the tops are red, we color the nodes of the baseline alternately with colors green and blue.

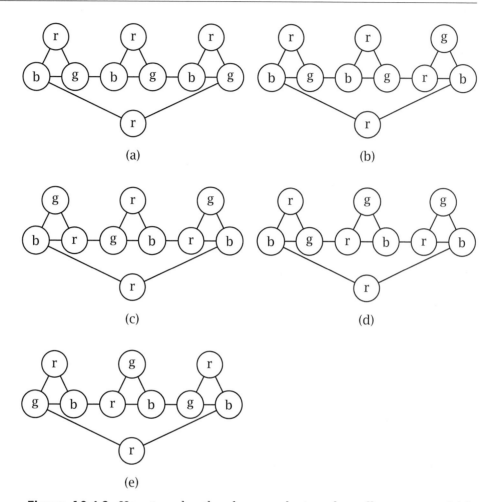

Figure 10.4.9 How to color the clause gadgets: when all tops are red (a), when one of the outer tops is green (b), when both of the outer tops are green (c), when one of the outer tops is red (d), when both of the outer tops are red (e).

We have shown that G is 3-colorable if and only if φ is satisfiable. This establishes that satisfiability reduces to graph 3-colorability, which, therefore, is **NP**-complete. ■

The result can be strengthened to show that deciding whether a planar graph is 3-colorable is **NP**-complete, although we know that all planar graphs are 4-colorable by the four-color theorem. From the **NP**-completeness of the planar case, it also follows that CROSSWORD is **NP**-complete, since we can make the construction of Example 10.4.1 work for general planar graphs.

Exercises

1S. Show that $\omega(G) = \alpha(\overline{G})$.

2. Show that a graph G can have two different maximal independent subsets, that is, independent subsets of size $\alpha(G)$. Can the two sets be disjoint?

3. Give an example of a graph with two different maximal cliques of size 3.

4S. List all maximal independent sets for the graph in Figure 10.4.2 that contain the vertex labeled $\overline{x}_2$ in C_1 and the corresponding truth assignments.

5. Construct G for $\varphi = (x_1 \vee x_2 \vee x_3) \wedge (\overline{x}_1 \vee x_2 \vee \overline{x}_3) \wedge (\overline{x}_1 \vee \overline{x}_2 \vee x_3) \wedge (\overline{x}_1 \vee x_2 \vee x_3)$ as in the proof of Theorem 10.4.2. List all maximal independent sets and the corresponding truth assignments to φ.

6. Construct G for $\varphi = (x_1 \vee \overline{x}_2 \vee x_3) \wedge (\overline{x}_1 \vee x_3 \vee x_4) \wedge (x_1 \vee \overline{x}_3 \vee x_4) \wedge (\overline{x}_1 \vee x_2 \vee \overline{x}_4) \wedge (x_1 \vee \overline{x}_2 \vee \overline{x}_4) \wedge (\overline{x}_1 \vee x_2 \vee \overline{x}_3)$ as in the proof of Theorem 10.4.2. List all maximal independent sets and the corresponding truth assignments to φ.

7. Can a graph be isomorphic to its own complement? If so, give an example; otherwise show that it is not possible.

8S. Give a 3-coloring of the graph in Figure 10.4.7 and write down the corresponding truth assignment to φ.

9. Construct G for $\varphi = (x_1 \vee x_2 \vee x_3) \wedge (\overline{x}_1 \vee x_2 \vee \overline{x}_3) \wedge (\overline{x}_1 \vee \overline{x}_2 \vee x_3) \wedge (\overline{x}_1 \vee x_2 \vee x_3)$ as in the proof of Theorem 10.4.4. Give a 3-coloring of G, and write down the corresponding truth assignment to φ.

10. Construct G for $\varphi = (x_1 \vee \overline{x}_2 \vee x_3) \wedge (\overline{x}_1 \vee x_3 \vee x_4) \wedge (x_1 \vee \overline{x}_3 \vee x_4) \wedge (\overline{x}_1 \vee x_2 \vee \overline{x}_4) \wedge (x_1 \vee \overline{x}_2 \vee \overline{x}_4) \wedge (\overline{x}_1 \vee x_2 \vee \overline{x}_3)$ as in the proof of Theorem 10.4.4. Give a 3-coloring of G, and write down the corresponding truth assignment to φ.

10.5 More on NP-Completeness

Determining whether a problem is **NP**-complete is a difficult task and requires experience. Nevertheless, recognizing the **NP**-completeness of a problem is important since it tells us that we have to use new techniques to tackle the problem. We discuss some of these techniques in Chapter 11. If a problem has resisted several serious attempts at a solution by a polynomial-time algorithm, we should investigate the possibility that it is **NP**-complete. The best strategy is to look for known **NP**-complete problems that have a similar structure and attempt to establish a reduction from the **NP**-complete problem to the unsolved problem. We include some general tips on how to find such a reduction and then conclude with descriptions of some **NP**-complete problems of different flavors.

There are different types of reductions, reflecting the degree of structural similarity between two problems. Garey and Johnson (Garey and Johnson, 1979) distinguished three types of reductions: **restriction**, **local replacement**, and **component design** (also known as gadget proofs).

If a problem contains a well-known **NP**-complete problem as a special case, then the problem is **NP**-complete. For example, we saw that SAT, the satisfiability problem of Boolean formulas in CNF, is **NP**-complete. From that, it immediately follows that the satisfiability of arbitrary Boolean formulas is **NP**-complete since SAT is a special case restricted to formulas in conjunctive normal form (see Exercise 10.71). In these cases, the reduction is often the identity function or some other simple function.

Example 10.5.1. The Hamiltonian-cycle problem is a special case of the traveling-salesperson problem (TSP), since $G = (V, E)$ has a Hamiltonian cycle if and only if $G' = (V, E, weight)$, where $weight(e) = 1$ for all $e \in E$, contains a tour of weight at most $|V|$. The Hamiltonian-cycle problem therefore is a restriction of the TSP; hence, knowing that it is **NP**-complete allows us to conclude that TSP is **NP**-complete. □

Proofs by local replacement work by modifying the inputs locally. For example, we saw that $f(G, k) = (\overline{G}, k)$ reduced the clique problem to the independent-set problem and vice versa (see Theorem 10.4.3). The local replacement consisted of flipping the presence and absence of edges in the graph G; the parameter k remained unchanged. We saw another proof by local replacement, the reduction from SAT to 3SAT (see Theorem 10.3.15), in which we locally replaced clauses by sets of other clauses.

In some cases the encoding of the original problem cannot be done locally, since the problem we are trying to reduce to has a different structure. In that case, we need more complex constructions to encode the original problem. We saw several examples of this type: the independent-set problem, the graph 3-colorability problem, and even Example 10.3.1 where we showed how to translate a graph coloring into a crossword puzzle. The translations in these examples are not immediate. For each element of the original problem, we came up with elements in the new problem, and we designed additional **components** (gadgets) to restrict solutions to the new problem in such a way that they could be translated into solutions of the original problem.

Example 10.5.2. Let us have a closer look at the reduction from 3SAT to 3-colorability given in Theorem 10.4.4. Parts of this reduction seem local: We create vertices whose color we interpret as true and false, for each variable we create a triangle, and for each clause we add the graph depicted in Figure 10.4.6. However, the components we designed to encode the satisfiability of a formula in terms of the coloring of a graph are not purely local, since they interact: The base vertex is used in the variable and the clause components; and the variable components overlap with the clause components, reflecting the occurrence of a variable in a clause. □

The distinction between the different types of reductions is not strict. One could, for example, argue that the **NP**-completeness proof for the independent-set problem is a replacement proof, since the additional edges between contradictory edges are not complex enough to be considered components on their own.

Cellular Networks, Packing, and Scheduling

When you turn on your cell phone to make a call, your cell phone tries to connect to the nearest available base transceiver station to reserve a frequency for the call. A base station operates several transceivers (transmitters and receivers), each of which has a channel of frequencies assigned to it. To avoid interference, there are rules on how channels may be assigned. For example, transceivers in the same base station may not operate on the same or even on adjacent channels, while transceivers belonging to base stations that are close to each other should not operate on the same channel. Typically a phone company owns a radio spectrum consisting of about 50 channels, and a large metropolitan area needs on the order of 100,000 base stations. How can the company best assign its channels to the base stations? This problem, known as the frequency-assignment problem (or, more accurately, the channel-assignment problem), exists in many versions, reflecting the technologies involved and the parameters that have to be optimized to maximize profit. These problems tend to be **NP**-complete, since they are thinly-disguised variants of the graph-coloring problem. Much effort is being invested in finding heuristics to solve frequency-assignment problems.

The frequency-assignment problem is the latest in a series of **NP**-complete problems concerning resource management. There are the packing problems, in which items of different sizes have to be arranged to fit local storage restrictions; allocation problems, in which storage space has to be reserved for a set of entities (memory for storing data objects, for example); and scheduling problems, which are storage problems with the additional dimension of time. As we mentioned earlier, allocation problems, such as the frequency-assignment problem, are often related to graph-coloring problems. Many packing and scheduling problems derive from the seemingly innocuous, but **NP**-complete, partition problem:

Partition
Instance: Sizes $s_1, s_2, \ldots, s_n$.
Question: Can the sizes be partitioned into two sets such that their total weight is the same; that is, is there an $I \subseteq \{1, \ldots, n\}$ such that $\sum_{i \in I} s_i = \sum_{i \notin I} s_i$?

The partition problem is also related to the subset-sum problem, which is at the root of the knapsack cryptosystem we discuss later.

Minesweeper and Other Games and Puzzles

Games such as Go and chess are played on small boards of fixed size. Since there is no varying input size for these games, an asymptotic complexity does not seem to make sense. However, the situation changes if we can generalize the problem to inputs of arbitrary size. For chess and similar games such a generalization hardly makes sense, but there is no problem playing games such as minesweeper, checkers, or Sokoban on boards of arbitrary size. Imagine minesweeper on an $n \times n$ board. Squares with numbers indicate how many mines are in the neighboring eight squares. We call a square *safe* if we can be sure that there is no mine beneath it. For example, in Figure 10.5.1, the square in the upper-right corner is not safe. As a matter of fact, we can be certain that there is a mine beneath it. Squares that have already been uncovered are always safe (otherwise the mine would have exploded and the game would have been over). The objective of minesweeper is to find, in each step, a safe square to uncover if there is one. As it turns out, it is **NP**-complete to decide whether a particular square is unsafe in a given stage of the game.

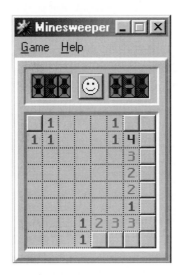

Figure 10.5.1 Where are the mines? Is the square in the lower-right corner safe?

For games in general, questions of interest include whether a particular player can win in a given situation, and, if so, what the winning move is, or—in a two-player game—whether the opponent can force a draw. With puzzles, we are usually interested in whether they are solvable and, if so, what a solution is.

Example 10.5.3 Generalized Instant Insanity. In the generalized version of instant insanity, we are given n cubes whose six sides are colored with colors chosen from a set of n colors. Can the n cubes be stacked in a column so that each color occurs exactly once on each side of the column?   □

NP-algorithms are not powerful enough for settling many game problems. This means we cannot apply our notion of **NP**-completeness directly since an **NP**-complete problem has to be in **NP**. However, the hardness part in the definition of **NP**-completeness does not require the problem to be in **NP**, and we can isolate this notion. We call a problem **NP-hard** if some **NP**-complete problem reduces to it. By this definition an **NP**-hard problem is at least as hard as any problem in **NP**, and possibly harder.

Among the **NP**-hard game problems are

- deciding whether a puzzle can be solved and, if so, how (generalized instant insanity, crossword puzzle, Tetris, Sokoban),

- deciding whether a move is unsafe (minesweeper), and

- deciding whether a player can force a win in a given situation (checkers, Go, hex).

The reason these problems are typically not within **NP** is that they involve players making moves alternately. **NP** can guess what one player would do, but it is beyond **NP** to then check all of the possible moves the other player could make in response. For that, we have to go to beyond **NP**, occasionally all the way up to **EXP**. Most games can be solved in exponential time by a brute force search. One-player games and puzzles, however, do often have decision problems in **NP** (for example, minesweeper, generalized instant insanity, Tetris, and crossword puzzles). Sokoban is an exception.

Knapsacks and Cryptography

Cryptographers might be the only people you will ever encounter that are actually happy about **NP**-completeness results. To make public-key cryptography work, cryptographers need trapdoor functions, that is, functions that are easy to compute, but whose inverses are hard to compute without knowledge of some secret value (the private key). While we know—theoretically—that such functions exist (under certain assumptions), it is hard to construct them explicitly. One source cryptographers have tried to tap is **NP**-complete problems, in particular, a variant of the knapsack problem known as the subset-sum problem. The resulting cryptosystems have been (mis)named knapsack cryptosystems. The subset-sum problem is the following:

Subset Sum
Instance: Sizes $s_1, s_2, \ldots, s_n$, number k.
Question: Is there a subset of the sizes that sums to k; that is, is there an $I \subseteq \{1, \ldots, n\}$ such that $\sum_{i \in I} s_i = k$?

The subset-sum problem is **NP**-complete, as is finding the set I for a given k. Hence, we can use the map taking I to $\sum_{i \in I} s_i$ as an encryption function (since computing its inverse is difficult). This encryption function takes sets to numbers, which does not seem useful. This is easily remedied for the output since we can think of the number written in binary. Similarly for the input we can think of I as a binary string, the n bits of the string encoding which elements belong to i.

Example 10.5.4. Let $s_1 = 2$, $s_2 = 5$, $s_3 = 10$, $s_4 = 21$. We interpret the binary string 1010 as the subset $I = \{2, 4\}$, which we encrypt as $5 + 21 = 26$, or 11010 in binary. Similarly, the string 1110 would be encrypted as $5 + 10 + 21 = 36$, which is 100100.   □

Unfortunately, we have forgotten to build a trapdoor into our encryption function; reversing the encryption (decryption) is as difficult for us as it is for our opponent. To introduce a trapdoor, we start with a set of sizes of a special form for which the subset-sum problem is easy to solve (this system is our private key). We then multiply all sizes by a factor using some fixed modulus, which gives us a new set of sizes that is our public key. For this new set, the subset-sum problem is no longer obviously easily solvable, but we can still solve it since we hold the private key—the original system in which decryption is easy.

Example 10.5.5. Consider the system $s_1 = 2$, $s_2 = 5$, $s_3 = 10$, $s_4 = 21$. We claim that in this system decryption is easy. Since $s_4 > s_1 + s_2 + s_3$, we know that to get any value larger than s_4, we need s_4. For example, if we know that the sum is 36 (100100 in binary), we know immediately that s_4 has to be present, reducing the problem to $36 - s_4 = 15$. Since $s_1 + s_2 < s_3 = 10$, again we can conclude that $s_3 = 10$ has to be present to obtain a sum of 15, leaving us with 5, which is s_2. In this case, it is simple to reconstruct the string 1110 from the sum 36, since the set of sizes has the particular property of being *superincreasing*: Each size is larger than the sum of the preceding sizes. For these sizes the problem can be solved in polynomial time using the greedy approach. However, this means our opponent could also solve the problem in polynomial time if we made the system $s_1 = 2$, $s_2 = 5$, $s_3 = 10$, $s_4 = 21$ public. Instead, we multiply the whole system by a factor and take the result modulo a fixed number. Choose, for example, the factor 11 and the modulus 41. Multiplying each of 2, 5, 10, and 21 by 11 and taking the result modulo 41 gives us the system 22, 14, 28, and 26. This new sequence is no longer superincreasing; hence, an opponent trying to decrypt $27 = 36 \times 11 \bmod 41$ would have a hard time doing so. We, however, having access to the original system, can translate 27 into 36 and then decrypt 36 in the superincreasing system $s_1 = 2$, $s_2 = 5$, $s_3 = 10$, $s_4 = 21$ to obtain 1110. Since *all* numbers were multiplied by 11, we know that $27 = 14 + 28 + 26 \bmod 41$; that is, 1110 is also the result of decrypting 27 in the new system. In summary, we can use 22, 14, 28, and 26 in public to do the encryption, and use 2, 5, 10, 21 in private for decryption.   □

The original encryption algorithm based on the idea in Example 10.5.5 was successfully attacked and so were several more recent cryptosystems based on the subset-sum problem. The problem is to build a trapdoor into an **NP**-complete problem that does not open a door for the opponent as well. Cryptographers have used other problems believed to be computationally hard to build public-key cryptosystems, for example, factoring (RSA) and the discrete logarithm (ElGamal). With these systems, the problem is generally not the trapdoor but the hardness of the original problem. While we think that both factoring and computing the discrete logarithm are difficult problems, there are currently no proofs to this effect.

Protein Folding and Computational Biology

Protein folding is the problem of determining the geometric shape a protein will take in space. Proteins are sequences of amino acids and can be described as strings over a 20-letter alphabet (one letter for each acid). Determining the complexity of protein folding is hard, partially because we do not know exactly why proteins fold the way they do. This has led to simplified models of protein folding, including the *two-dimensional hydrophilic-hydrophobic model*. In this model we distinguish only two elements, encoded as 0 and 1, and we want to embed the sequence in the two-dimensional mesh (grid) by placing adjacent elements of the sequence into neighboring positions in the mesh. Ones are hydrophobic and try to cluster. An embedding in the grid is assigned a score counting the number of pairs of ones that are adjacent in the embedding without appearing consecutively in the sequence.

Example 10.5.6. Figure 10.5.2 shows a possible embedding of the sequence

10110111010110100001010.

The dashes connect neighboring elements in the sequence. The squiggly lines show pairs of adjacent ones that clustered successfully. For this embedding the score is 7 as the squiggly lines show.

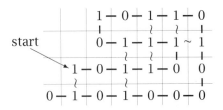

Figure 10.5.2 Embedding a hydrophilic-hydrophobic sequence in the grid. □

In this model we are looking for an embedding that maximizes the score. Experiments show that this model seems to capture aspects of the full protein-folding problem. It was recently proved that deciding whether a given string can be embedded such that it meets a given lower bound on the score is **NP**-complete.

Computational biology is rooted in the observation that proteins and DNA can be considered as sequences, that is, as words over an alphabet. DNA, for example, is a sequence of four bases, A, C, G, and T; and we can therefore think of it as a string over the alphabet $\{A, C, G, T\}$. Solving basic biological tasks, such as sequencing DNA, relies heavily on sophisticated string matching techniques. Two problems that play a role here are the longest-common-subsequence and the shortest-common-supersequence problems.

For two sequences, these problems can be solved in polynomial time (see Section 8.4 for a polynomial-time algorithm that solves the two-sequence longest-common-subsequence problem); but for an arbitrary number of sequences, the problems are **NP**-complete.

Exercises

1S. Can you partition $\{1, 2, 3, 4, 9, 11, 12\}$ into two subsets that have equal sum?

2. Can you partition $\{1, 2, 4, 8, 12, 14\}$ into two subsets that have equal sum?

3. Can you partition $\{1, 2, 5, 7, 8, 9\}$ into two subsets that have equal sum?

4S. Find an optimal folding of the sequence 011000010110110 in the grid. What is its score?

5. Find an optimal folding of the sequence 0100000100101001001 in the grid. What is its score?

6. Where are the mines in the configuration shown in Figure 10.5.1? Is the square in the lower-right corner safe?

Notes

The notion of polynomial-time decidability crystallized in the 1960s in papers by Cobham, Edmonds, and Rabin, capturing feasible computation as opposed to brute-force algorithms traversing exponential search spaces. In the early 1970s, the introduction of the class **NP** and the notion of **NP**-completeness by Cook and Levin made possible a refined classification of many problems of practical interest and explained the absence of efficient solutions.

WWW   By the end of the 1970s, the fast growth of the field led Garey and Johnson to publish their monograph on the theory of **NP**-completeness, which is still the standard reference on the subject (Garey, Johnson, 1979). The study of **NP** led to deeper investigations into the complexity of computational problems, resulting in a branch of computer science known as complexity theory (Fortnow, Homer, 2003). Papadimitriou's book on *Computational Complexity* gives a good introduction to the field (Papadimitriou, 1994). (Sipser, 1992) provides an account of the history of **NP**. The **P** = **NP** problem is now recognized as a central problem in mathematics and computer science. It is one of the seven problems for which the Clay Institute of Mathematics offers a prize of $1,000,000.

The crossword-puzzle problem was shown to be **NP**-complete by Lewis and Papadimitriou in 1978. Both the graph-colorability problem and the clique problem were shown to be **NP**-complete in a famous paper by Karp (Karp, 1972). Karp's paper also contains many other fundamental **NP**-completeness results including proofs that the Hamiltonian cycle, vertex cover, 3-dimensional matching, partition, subset sum, and 0/1-knapsack problems are **NP**-complete.

Example 10.3.5 is from a column by Martin Gardner for the *Scientific American* (Gardner, 1996).

The history of the four-color theorem is told in the book (Fritsch, Fritsch, and Peschke, 1998), including a detailed presentation of the ideas behind the original proof by Appel and Haken, and the improved version by Robertson, Sanders, Seymour, and Thomas.

There have been many results on protein folding. For the three-dimensional hydrophilic-hydrophobic model, **NP**-completeness was shown in (Berger and Leighton, 1998). The two-dimensional case was settled in (Creszenci, Goldmann, Papadimitriou, Piccolboni, and Yannakakis, 1998). The first knapsack cryptosystem was introduced by Merkle and Hellmann in (Merkle, Hellmann, 1978). Many variants of it have appeared since then. For more information on the frequency-assignment problem, see the recent survey (Eisenblätter, Grötschel, and Koster, 2000). Minesweeper was shown **NP**-complete in (Kaye, 1998).

Chapter Exercises

10.1. Write an algorithm that decides in linear time whether a graph, represented as an adjacency list, is 2-colorable.

10.2. How does the solution to Exercise 10.1 help you to decide whether a graph is bipartite?

10.3. Suppose we have a list P_k, $k = 0, 1, \ldots$, of computer programs with the following properties:

- Given an input x and an index k, we can run P_k on x in time $|x|^k + k$.
- Every P_k is a decision algorithm; that is, it returns 0 or 1 on all inputs.
- Let M be an arbitrary polynomial-time decision algorithm. Then there is a k such that $M(x) = P_k(x)$ for all x.

In short, P_k, $k = 0, 1, \ldots$, lists all polynomial-time decision algorithms in such a way that we can efficiently simulate every P_k on any input. Such a listing can be obtained from any programming language interpreter, but the details are too technical to go into here. Consider the following algorithm:

```
diag_p(k) {
    if (P_k(k) == true)
        return false
    else
        return true
}
```

Argue that *diag_p* is an exponential-time decision algorithm, and the language it decides is different from any language decided by a P_k. From that, conclude that **P** ≠ **EXP**.

10.4. Find a planar graph not containing a triangle that needs at least three colors in a coloring.

10.5. We need four colors for coloring South America, since the associated graph contains a K_4, a complete graph on four vertices. Find a planar graph not containing a K_4 as a subgraph that cannot be colored with three colors. Draw a map that would be represented by that graph. (Does your map correspond to an actual geographical location?)

10.6. Characterize the graphs $G = (V, E)$ that are not $(|V| - 1)$-colorable.

10.7. Show that being composite (the opposite of being prime) is in **NP**. *Hint:* You can guess an integer digit by digit.

10.8. Show that testing whether a graph G contains a simple path on k vertices is in **NP**.

10.9. Show that testing whether a graph G is a subgraph of a graph H is in **NP**.

10.10. Show that testing whether two graphs G and H are isomorphic is in **NP**.

⋆**10.11.** [Requires number theory.] Show that primality is in **NP**. *Hint:* Use the fact that there is a primitive root in F_p of order p if and only if p is prime. You will need to apply this criterion recursively to construct a valid witness of primality.

10.12. Show that, if any **NP**-complete problem is not in **P**, then no **NP**-complete problem is in **P**.

10.13. Show that $\leq_p$ is reflexive; that is, $A \leq_p A$.

10.14. Show that, if A can be decided in **P**, then $A \leq_p B$ (unless B or $\overline{B}$ is empty).

In Exercises 10.5.15 and 10.5.16, we consider variants of the rook game from Example 10.3.5 for several chess pieces. We keep the restriction that in each move the piece has to be moved, it cannot be moved east or north, and that the player who moves it to the lower-left square wins.

10.15. In fairy chess there is a piece called a chancellor, which can move like a rook (vertically or horizontally) or a knight (one square in any direction and two squares in an orthogonal direction). Determine the set CHANCELLOR $= \{(n, m) \mid$ Player I can force a win with the chancellor starting in $(n, m)\}$.

10.16. Instead of the rook, let us consider the queen, which can move horizontally, vertically, and diagonally. Write an algorithm that determines in linear time whether player I can win if the queen starts in position (n, m). *Hint:* Use dynamic programming.

10.17. In the *game of 15*, two players alternate naming one of the nine numbers between 1 and 9. Once a number has been named, it cannot be named again. The first player to name three numbers that sum to 15 wins. For example, if the players name the numbers $7, 2, 3, 8, 4, 6, 5$ in this order, then the first player wins, having named $7, 3,$ and 5. Show that the first player can always force a tie (that is, neither player wins), by rephrasing the game of 15 as a game of tic-tac-toe (for which we know that the first player can force a tie).

10.18. Show that, if we can solve the longest-common-subsequence problem for two sequences of length n in time $O(f(n))$, then we can find the longest increasing subsequence of a sequence in time $O(f(n) + n \lg n)$.

Exercises 10.19 and 10.20 are about the linear-programming *problem we encountered in Example 10.3.6. The problem consists of determining whether a set of linear inequalities has a solution. It is known to be solvable in polynomial time, and you can use this fact in the following two exercises.*

10.19. Show that the variant of the linear-programming problem in which we allow both linear inequalities and equalities can be solved in polynomial time. *Hint:* Show that this variant can be reduced to the linear-programming problem without equalities.

★**10.20.** The solution to a linear-programming problem is an array $(x_1, \ldots, x_n)$ of real values. It is known that if there is a solution to a linear program, then there is one of at most polynomial size; that is, the decimal expansions of $x_1, \ldots, x_n$ have at most polynomial length in the input. Use this fact to show that we can compute a solution $(x_1, \ldots, x_n)$ to the linear program explicitly, if it exists. *Hint:* Search for the solution by specifying it partially. Remember that you can assume that *some* solution to the linear program has at most polynomial size. That does not mean that *all* solutions have at most polynomial size.

Exercises 10.21–10.23 show how to solve the minimum-range query problem *efficiently. In the minimum-range query problem, we are given an array a and have to answer requests of the form: Find a smallest element in a between indexes i and j; that is, given i and j, find an index k such* *that $a[k] = \min\{a[\ell] \mid i \le \ell \le j\}$. We are interested in an offline solution to the minimum-range query problem. An offline algorithm is allowed to preprocess the input to be able to answer requests and queries more quickly. Offline algorithms are useful if many queries must be answered.*

10.21. Show that minimum-range queries can be answered in time $\Theta(1)$ by using preprocessing time $\Theta(n^3)$.

10.22. Show that minimum-range queries can be answered in time $\Theta(1)$ by using preprocessing time $\Theta(n^2)$. *Hint:* Use dynamic programming.

10.23. Show that minimum-range queries can be answered in time $\Theta(1)$ by using preprocessing time $\Theta(n \log n)$. *Hint:* Since there is no time to precompute the answers for all possible queries, you have to restrict the preprocessing to a smaller subset of all queries. Consider using the regions whose length is a power of 2. When answering a query, the query region $[i..j]$ has to be reconstructed from the regions in this smaller set.

Exercises 10.24–10.26 show how to solve the least-common-ancestor problem in polynomial time by reducing it to the minimum-range query problem that we solved in Exercises 10.21–10.23. Exercise 10.27 in turn shows how to improve the solution to the minimum-range query problem by using the least-common-ancestor problem. The least common ancestor of two nodes u and v in a rooted tree is the vertex w, which is an ancestor of both u and v; and none of its children is an ancestor of both u and v. Equivalently, it is the node of smallest depth (distance from the root) on the unique simple path from u to v.

10.24. Given a tree T, show that for a suitable choice of an array a (depending on T), if we define

$$A = \{(u, v, w) \mid w \text{ is the least common ancestor of } u \text{ and } v\}$$
$$B = \{(i, j, k) \mid a[k] = \min\{a[\ell] \mid i \le \ell \le j\}\},$$

we have $A \le_p B$. *Hint:* Record the depth of every node in a depth-first traversal of T. The depth of each inner node will be recorded twice, since an inner node is traversed twice: once when first encountered and, again, after the subtree in it has been processed.

10.25. Show how to answer queries for the least common ancestor of two nodes in time $\Theta(1)$ using preprocessing time $\Theta(n \log n)$. *Hint:* Use the result from Exercise 10.23.

⋆**10.26.** Show how to answer queries for the least common ancestor of two nodes in time $\Theta(1)$ using preprocessing time $\Theta(n)$. *Hint:* The result from Exercise 10.23 can be improved in the case of the special array a obtained from T, since depths in adjacent cells of the array differ by 1. Consider splitting a into blocks of length $(\log n)/2$.

⋆⋆ **10.27.** Assume you can solve the least-common-ancestor problem in preprocessing time $\Theta(n)$ with each query taking time $\Theta(1)$ (see Exercise 10.26). Show how to use this solution to solve the general minimum-range query problem (from Exercises 10.21–10.23), using preprocessing time $\Theta(n)$ with each query taking time $\Theta(1)$. *Hint:* From the array a, construct a binary tree T, called the *Cartesian tree*, in linear time. The Cartesian tree of an array a is defined recursively as follows: The root of a Cartesian tree is the index i of a smallest element in the array. The left child is a Cartesian tree of the subarray $a[1..i-1]$, and the right child is a Cartesian tree of the subarray $a[i+1..n]$. The construction of T does not follow the recursive definition.

10.28. Why is it not possible that both **P** = **NP** and **NP** = **EXP**?

10.29. Show that SAT is in **NP**.

10.30. Show that a k-CNF formula on k variables containing at most $2^k - 1$ clauses is satisfiable. *Hint:* Each clause must contain all variables since we do not allow repetition of a literal in a clause. Without that restriction, the claim is false.

10.31. Show that the independent-set problem is in **NP**.

10.32. Show that the clique problem is in **NP**.

10.33. What do graphs G with $\chi(G) = 1$ look like?

10.34. Show that $\omega(G) \leq \chi(G)$; that is, the clique number is a lower bound on the chromatic number. Give an example of a graph G for which this bound is not tight; that is, $\omega(G) < \chi(G)$.

10.35. Show that $\alpha(G) + \omega(G) \leq |V|$ for any graph $G = (V, E)$.

Exercises 10.36 and 10.37 concern the 2-satisfiability problem, in which we are given a formula φ in 2-CNF and have to decide its satisfiability.

10.36. Show that 2SAT reduces to 2-colorability.

10.37. Write a polynomial-time algorithm deciding 2-satisfiability.

10.38. Show that we can find maximal independent sets of graphs in polynomial time if and only if we can compute the independence number in polynomial time. *Hint:* See the proof of Theorem 10.3.19 (which precedes the statement of the theorem).

10.39. Show that if CROSSWORD ∈ **P**, then we can find solutions to crossword puzzles in polynomial time. *Hint:* See the proof of Theorem 10.3.19.

10.40. Show that the satisfiability problem for k-CNF formulas is **NP**-complete for any fixed $k \geq 3$.

10.41. A formula is in 3-DNF if it is the disjunction of conjunctive clauses, where each clause contains exactly three literals. Show that deciding whether there is an assignment of truth values to variables in φ that makes it false is **NP**-complete.

10.42. Show that deciding whether a graph is k-colorable is **NP**-complete for any fixed $k \geq 3$ by giving a reduction from 3-colorability.

$\star$ **10.43.** Show that we can find 3-colorings of graphs in polynomial time if we can decide whether any graph is 3-colorable in polynomial time.

Exercises 10.44–10.46 concern the vertex-cover problem (see Exercise 7.8). A vertex cover of a graph $G = (V, E)$ is a set U of vertices of G such that at least one endpoint of each edge of G is in U.

10.44. Define a decision version of the vertex-cover problem.

10.45. Show that the decision version of the vertex-cover problem is in **NP**.

10.46. Show that the decision version of the vertex-cover problem is **NP**-complete. *Hint:* Reduce from the independent-set problem.

Exercises 10.47 and 10.48 are about Hamiltonian paths and cycles. A Hamiltonian path in a graph $G = (V, E)$ is a path $v_0, \ldots, v_m$ containing every vertex in V exactly once.

10.47. Give a direct reduction from the Hamiltonian-path problem to the Hamiltonian-cycle problem.

10.48. Give a direct reduction from the Hamiltonian-cycle problem to the Hamiltonian-path problem.

$\star$ **10.49.** A *Boolean circuit* consists of and gates, or gates, not gates, a set of input gates (accepting values 0 and 1), and a designated output gate that contains the value computed by the circuit. We call the circuit *planar* if it can be drawn in the plane such that none of the wires between the gates intersect. This notion gives rise to the planar satisfiability problem: Given a planar Boolean circuit, is there an assignment of 0 and 1 to the inputs of the circuit such that it computes 1? Show that the planar satisfiability problem is **NP**-complete by reducing SAT to it. *Hint:* Any satisfiability problem can be interpreted as a Boolean circuit in the plane; however, wires between the gates will intersect. You have to show that an intersection can be replaced by a planar circuit such that the resulting circuit is satisfiable if the original circuit is.

10.50. Show that CROSSWORD is **NP**-complete by reducing planar satisfiability to it (see Exercise 10.49). *Hint:* You need to build gadgets for selecting inputs and computing only and gates, or gates, and not gates.

10.51. In the *subgraph-isomorphism problem*, we are given two graphs G and H and have to decide whether H is isomorphic to a subgraph of G. Show that the subgraph-isomorphism problem is **NP**-complete.

10.52. A *degree-constrained spanning tree* of a graph is a spanning tree of maximum degree k for some fixed k. Show that deciding whether a graph G contains a spanning tree with degree constrained by k is **NP**-complete.

10.53. In the $0/1$-knapsack problem, we are given sizes $s_1, \ldots, s_n$, values $v_1, \ldots, v_n$, and integers c and r. Intuitively, we have n items each having a size and a value. Our goal is to pack items into the knapsack without exceeding the capacity c and maximizing the value r. More formally, we want to decide whether there is an $I \subseteq \{1, \ldots, n\}$ such that $\sum_{i \in I} s_i \le c$ and $\sum_{i \in I} s_i \ge r$. Show that the $0/1$-knapsack problem is **NP**-complete.

Exercises 10.54–10.56 concern the longest-path problem *that asks for the longest simple path in a graph.*

10.54. Formulate a decision version of the longest-path problem.

10.55. Show that the decision version of the longest-path problem is in **NP**.

10.56. Prove that the decision version of the longest-path problem is **NP**-complete.

$\star\star$**10.57.** Recall that the complete bipartite graph $K_{m,m}$ consists of two disjoint sets of m vertices each such that each edge is incident on one vertex in one set and one vertex in the other set (see Section 2.5). Show that deciding whether a graph contains $K_{m,m}$ as a subgraph is **NP**-complete. *Hint:* Reduce from the clique problem.

10.58. The *Euclidean traveling salesperson* is the variant of the traveling-salesperson problem in the plane where the distance between two cities is the Euclidean distance. We also assume that the salesperson can travel between any pair of cities. Show that a Hamiltonian cycle of shortest length does not intersect itself. *Hint:* Some elementary geometry is needed.

$\star$**10.59.** In Section 9.6 we introduced regular expressions for text matching (with concatenation, alternation, and repetition) and showed that we can decide in polynomial time whether a text matches a regular expression pattern. Suppose we extend the language for regular expressions to include back references: Whenever we use parentheses in a regular expression, the part of the word that matches the pattern within the parentheses can be referred to in the expression itself by using the expression "$\backslash n$" (where n is the number identifying the parenthesized expression; they are numbered in the order that they appear in the expression). For example, "$(a*)b\backslash 1$" would match "b", "aba", "$aabaa$", and so on. Show that deciding whether a pattern with back references matches a word is **NP**-complete.

Exercises 10.60–10.63 deal with the coin-changing problem *(see Section 7.1). In this version of the coin-changing problem, we are given a set of denominations $d_1, \ldots, d_n$ and an amount k and are asked whether we can give change for k using denominations $d_1, \ldots, d_n$, that is, whether there* *are natural numbers $q_1, \ldots, q_n$ such that $\sum_{i=1}^{n} q_i d_i = k$. The denominations and k are represented in binary. We do not assume that the smallest denomination is 1.*

10.60. Show that the coin-changing problem is in **NP**. *Hint:* You need to be careful when guessing the q_i, since their values might be exponentially large.

10.61. Show that the coin-changing problem reduces to the subset-sum problem.

★**10.62.** Show that the coin-changing problem is **NP**-complete by reducing the subset-sum problem to it.

10.63. Exercise 10.62 showed that the coin-changing problem is **NP**-complete. In Section 8.2 we presented an algorithm that can be modified to solve the coin-changing problem in time $O(k(|d_1| + \cdots + |d_n|))$. Is there a contradiction, or does this imply that **P** = **NP**?

WWW   *Exercises 10.64–10.69 deal with the* paint by numbers puzzle *invented by Tetsua Nishio. As a computer game it is also known as* picross. *The game is played on a rectangular board. Every square of the board can be black (1) or white (0). Each row and column has assigned to it a sequence of numbers that describes the lengths of consecutive sequences of dark squares in a row or column. The following picture gives an example:*

The problem is to find the picture, given the numbers. Computationally we are interested in the solvability of a puzzle; that is, how hard is it to determine whether, for a given board with numbers, there is a picture corresponding to those numbers.

10.64. Find the picture in the following paint by numbers puzzle.

10.65. Show that determining whether there is a picture corresponding to the numbers is in **NP**.

10.66. Give an example that shows that it possible that there is more than one solution to a paint by number puzzle.

10.67. Show that determining whether there is more than one solution to a paint by number puzzle is in **NP**.

10.68. If you were trying to find a polynomial-time algorithm for determining whether a given paint by number puzzle is solvable, what programming technique would you use?

10.69. If you were trying to show that determining whether a paint by number puzzle is solvable is **NP**-complete, from which **NP**-complete problem would you reduce?

⋆⋆**10.70.** Determine the complexity of deciding whether a paint by number puzzle is solvable.

10.71. In Section 10.5 we claimed that the set BOOLEAN = {φ | φ is a satisfiable Boolean formula} is **NP**-complete, since SAT is a restriction of it. Give the reduction that shows BOOLEAN $\leq_p$ SAT. *Hint:* It is tempting to think that the reduction is the identity, but φ can be a satisfiable Boolean formula without being a satisfiable formula in 3-CNF.

10.72. Give an informal **NP**-algorithm that shows that deciding whether a square in minesweeper is unsafe is in **NP**.

Exercises 10.73 and 10.74 deal with the longest-common-subsequence problem. In that problem, we are given a set $W \subseteq \Sigma^*$ of words and are asked to find the length of a longest string that occurs as a subsequence in all strings of W. (Remember that in a subsequence, as opposed to a subword, the string can occur with gaps: "cog" is a subsequence of "crossing".)

10.73. Formulate a decision version of the longest-common-subsequence problem.

10.74. Show that the decision version of the longest-common-subsequence problem is in **NP**.

Exercises 10.75 and 10.76 concern the shortest-common-supersequence problem. In that problem, we are given a set $W \subseteq \Sigma^*$ of words and are asked to find the length of a shortest string that contains all words in W as subsequences. For example, for "red" and "bad", the shortest-common-supersequence must contain five letters, since there are five different letters, and "bread" is a supersequence on five letters.

10.75. Formulate a decision version of the longest-common-subsequence problem.

10.76. Show that the decision version of the shortest-common-supersequence problem is in **NP**.

10.77. Show that the subset-sum problem is **NP**-complete by reducing the partition problem to it.

10.78. Show that, given a string w and a number k, we can decide in **NP** whether w can be embedded in the two-dimensional grid in such a way that there are at least k pairs of ones in w that are adjacent in the embedding without being consecutive in w.

10.79. Find the article that shows that the minesweeper problem is **NP**-complete. Which **NP**-complete problem does the author use to prove **NP**-completeness of the minesweeper problem?

10.80. Find the article that shows that Tetris is **NP**-complete. State precisely one of the Tetris-related problems that the article shows to be **NP**-complete. Which **NP**-complete problem do the authors use to prove **NP**-completeness of Tetris?

10.81. Find the article that shows that the protein-folding problem in the two-dimensional hydrophilic-hydrophobic model is **NP**-complete. Which **NP**-complete problem do the authors use for the **NP**-completeness reduction?

10.82. Find an article that proves that verifying the correctness of a sorting network is **NP**-complete. Give a full reference (author, title, journal, hyperlink, if available). Which problem does the author use for the reduction?

10.83. Find an **NP**-complete problem in a natural science. Give a short, formal description of the problem and a full reference to the paper proving it **NP**-complete. Which problem is used in the reduction for the **NP**-completeness proof?

*It is usually easy to see that a problem lies in **NP**. One notable exception is the knotting problem: Given a piece of string in three-dimensional space, can you unknot it (without imitating Alexander the Great)? The string can be represented as a sequence of coordinates connected by lines. Exercises 10.84–10.86 are about the unknotting problem. Hint: A piece of string will help.*

10.84. Can the following string be unknotted?

10.85. Can the following string be unknotted?

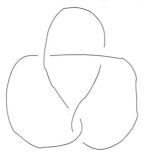

10.86. Can the following string be unknotted?

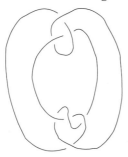

10.87. Find an article that shows that recognizing whether a piece of string can be unknotted is in **NP**. Give a full reference, including the names of the authors, title, and journal.

CHAPTER 11

Coping with NP-Completeness

Chapter 10 alerted us to the fact that many practical problems are **NP**-complete and therefore intractable. How do we solve such problems when we encounter them in real life? This question has received attention from many different research groups and, consequently, many different approaches have been tried, some of which we survey in the present chapter.

Some of the approaches are based on modifying the problem to simplify it (approximation, problem restriction, heuristics), while others search exact solutions (brute force), sometimes by extending the computational model to allow additional resources.

Brute Force. The most direct attack on an **NP**-complete problem is by brute force. Since **NP** is contained in **EXP**, every **NP**-complete problem can be solved by an exponential-time algorithm. We saw, for example, that the k-colorability problem can be solved in time n^{n+1}. In Section 11.1 we show that for many problems, such as satisfiability and independent set, we can obtain running times that, although still exponential, are much better.

Resources. We can also consider extending the computational model by allowing additional *resources* other than time or space. If we could build efficient nondeterministic computers, we could allow nondeterminism in our algorithms, since then nondeterministic polynomial time would really be polynomial time in practice. As we do not know how to implement nondeterminism efficiently at the physical level, nondeterminism is only a theoretical resource, and we have to look for other, more realistic choices. A random number generator often helps, as we saw in the case of randomized quicksort (Section 6.2). *Randomized algorithms*, algorithms using randomness, have become very popular in algorithm design and have been especially successful in the areas of computational geometry and cryptography. We investigate some examples of randomized algorithms in Section 11.2.

Parallel processors can be considered an additional resource. Chapter 12 is entirely devoted to *parallel algorithms*. Recently, computer scientists have explored methods from biomolecular chemistry for massively parallel computations.

More recently, computer scientists discovered *quantum computation*, the use of quantum effects in computation. It is known that quantum computers, if we could build them, could break the popular cryptosystem RSA in polynomial time (with high probability), a task that is not known to be efficiently solvable on classical computers. Unfortunately, only very small prototypes of quantum computers exist so far, not having more than seven quantum bits. However, quantum techniques have already been successful in cryptography, and the area of quantum computation holds promise for the future.

Approximation. *Approximation algorithms* are used for solving optimization problems such as finding a largest independent set. Instead of trying to find an optimal solution, that is, solving the problem exactly, it might be sufficient to find a near-optimal solution that approximates the optimal solution. We discuss approximation algorithms in Section 11.3.

Problem Restriction. We can also modify the problem by restricting it. For example, instead of trying to solve coloring problems for general graphs, for our purposes it might be sufficient to color planar graphs or graphs of bounded degree. Sometimes restricted problems turn out to be as difficult as the original problem (satisfiability of a planar circuit is still **NP**-complete), but often the problem becomes easier. For example, if we restrict the satisfiability problem to Horn formulas, that is, formulas in conjunctive normal form in which every clause contains at most one negative literal, satisfiability can be decided in polynomial time. This particular example led to the programming language Prolog, which solves an extended version of the satisfiability problem for Horn formulas (for details, see Nerode and Shore, 1993).

A particular type of restricted problem is systematically studied in the area of *parameterized complexity*. Consider the problem of finding an optimal move in a chess game. There are at most $16 * 28 = 448$ possible moves in each step (there are sixteen pieces, and the queen can move to 7 squares in each of 4 directions). So, if we wanted to predict all possibilities for n steps, we might have to trace as many as 448^n different branches of the game tree. This is impossible for a normal chess game, but if we are interested only in the endgame, where n might be as small as 5 or 6 (problems of the type "mate in three"), a solution might be realistic. Parameterized complexity starts with the observation that in practice some parameters tend to be small, and we can therefore assume that they are fixed. This leads to a more detailed view of computational complexity presented in Section 11.4.

Average-case complexity studies algorithms that run well on most inputs, but not necessarily on all. If we focus on the inputs on which an average-case algorithm works well, we could consider this approach a special case of the restricted problem approach. We will not discuss average case complexity in this book. Jie Wang's 1997 survey article is a good start for learning about average case complexity.

Heuristics. What can we do, if a problem does not yield under the attacks described previously? Take, for example, the chess problem. We do not know how to write a program playing chess in real time based solely on the ideas described above. Nevertheless, there are now computers that can beat the human world chess champion. Chess players have accumulated a lot of experiential data that can be used in programming a chess program.

We call techniques arising from experiments rather than theoretical analysis *heuristics*. As chess computers show, heuristic techniques can be remarkably powerful. We will see a randomized heuristic for solving the Hamiltonian-path problem in the second part of Section 11.2.

Heuristics do not have to be problem specific. How do humans solve difficult problems, for example? Every time you win a game of minesweeper, you have solved an **NP**-complete problem, albeit a small one, as we saw in Chapter 10. Artificial intelligence investigates techniques used by humans or found in nature and tries to apply them to hard computational problems. *Neural networks* try to capture brain processes, *genetic algorithms* mimic evolution, *fuzzy logic* imitates human reasoning, and *simulated annealing* and *taboo search* are similar to physical processes encountered in nature. One problem with using these general approaches is the gap between the problem and its solution, which makes it hard to determine performance and quality of these solutions analytically. Typically, the best we get in these cases is empirical data, which is quite acceptable for some applications. For example, training a neural network to recognize letters would be appropriate, whereas using it to maintain your bank account information would probably not be. We investigate *local search* and *simulated annealing*, two of the main general problem solving heuristics, in Section 11.5.

11.1 Brute Force

Independent Set

In Section 10.2 we saw that **NP** $\subseteq$ **EXP**, since polynomially many guesses of a nondeterministic algorithm can be simulated by searching a search space of exponential size. As an application of the results, we showed in Example 10.2.23 that k-colorability can be decided in time $O(n^{n+1})$.

Example 11.1.1. In Section 10.3 we defined an *independent set* of vertices of a graph $G = (V, E)$ as a set of vertices of G such that there is no edge between any two of them. The *independence number* $\alpha(G)$ is the size of a largest independent set in the graph G. We claim that we can compute $\alpha(G)$ in time $\Theta(n^2 2^n)$, where $n = |V|$, the number of vertices. For a given subset U of the vertices V of the graph, we can check in time n^2 whether U is an independent set by verifying that there are no edges between any two vertices in U. An algorithm that tests all 2^n subsets of V consecutively and keeps track of the largest independent set found so far can thus compute $\alpha(G)$ in time $\Theta(n^2 2^n)$. $\qquad\square$

It seems that since there are 2^n subsets to check, we should not be able to compute $\alpha(G)$ in time less than $\Theta(2^n)$, but, surprisingly, we can do much better.

Suppose I is a largest independent set in G. By definition, I consists of $\alpha(G)$ vertices. Consider a vertex v of G. There are two possibilities: v

belongs to I or it does not. If it does not, then I is an independent set of $\alpha(G)$ vertices in $G - \{v\}$, the graph obtained from G by removing the vertex v.

Example 11.1.2. Figure 11.1.1 shows a graph G with a maximal independent set I and a vertex v not belonging to I.

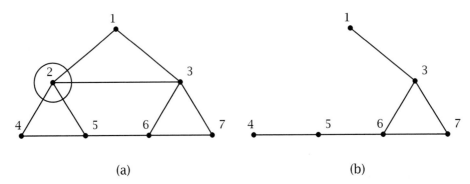

(a)   (b)

Figure 11.1.1 (a) Graph G with independent set $I = \{1, 4, 7\}$ and vertex $v = 2$ not belonging to I. Note that I is also an independent set in $G - \{v\}$, displayed in (b), the graph obtained from G by removing v and the edges adjacent to it. □

If v does belong to I, then no vertex adjacent to it can belong to I (since I is independent). The set of vertices adjacent to v is called $N(v)$, the *neighborhood of v*. In this case, we can conclude that $I - \{v\}$ is an independent set on $\alpha(G) - 1$ vertices in $G - \{v\} - N(v)$, the graph obtained from G by removing v, the vertices in $N(v)$, and all edges incident on v or a vertex in $N(v)$.

Example 11.1.3. Consider again the graph G and the maximal independent set I from Figure 11.1.1. This time, v was chosen to belong to the set I. Figure 11.1.2 illustrates the situation. □

In both cases, v belonging to I or not belonging to I, we reduce the size of the graph in which we are searching for a largest independent set. We can use this idea to write a recursive algorithm that pursues both possibilities.

Algorithm 11.1.4 Largest Independent Set. This algorithm returns $\alpha(G)$, the size of a largest independent set in $G = (V, E)$.

    Input Parameter: $G = (V, E)$
Output Parameters: None

```
largest_independent_set(G) {
    if (E == ∅)
        return |V|
```

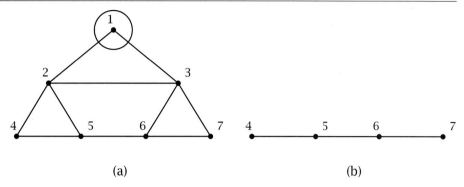

(a)   (b)

Figure 11.1.2 (a) Graph G with independent set $I = \{1, 4, 7\}$ and vertex $v = 1$ belonging to I. Note that, since v belongs to I, no neighbor of it does; hence, $I - \{v\} = \{4, 7\}$ is an independent set in the graph $G - \{v\} - N(v)$, pictured in (b).

```
    else {
        pick first v ∈ V such that N(v) ≠ ∅
        G₁ = G - {v}
        G₂ = G - {v} - N(v)
        k₁ = largest_independent_set(G₁) // assume v not in independent set
        k₂ = largest_independent_set(G₂) // assume v in independent set
        return max(k₁, k₂ + 1)
    }
}
```

Example 11.1.5. Figure 11.1.3 shows a sample run of *largest_independent_set* on the graph from Example 11.1.2. □

Theorem 11.1.6. *The algorithm largest_independent_set computes $\alpha(G)$, the size of a largest independent set of G, in time $O(1.62^n)$, where n is the number of vertices of G.*

Proof. We first prove that the algorithm is correct. If G has no edges, then the set V of all its vertices is an independent set, and $\alpha(G) = |V|$. On the other hand, if G does contain at least one edge, there has to be a vertex v with at least one neighbor, which the algorithm can therefore pick. Since an independent set of G_1 is also an independent set in G, we know that $\alpha(G_1) \leq \alpha(G)$. If we have an independent set in G_2, we can add v to it to obtain an independent set in G (because v is not adjacent to any vertex in G_2); hence, $\alpha(G_2) + 1 \leq \alpha(G)$. This implies that $\max(\alpha(G_1), \alpha(G_2) + 1) \leq \alpha(G)$. To show equality we consider two cases: Either v does belong to a largest independent set or it does not. In the first case $\alpha(G) \leq \alpha(G_2) + 1$; in the second case $\alpha(G) \leq \alpha(G_1)$. Hence, $\alpha(G) = \max(\alpha(G_1), \alpha(G_2) + 1)$, which is what the algorithm computes.

For the running time analysis, let a_n be the largest number of steps taken by the algorithm on any graph G with n vertices. Checking whether E is

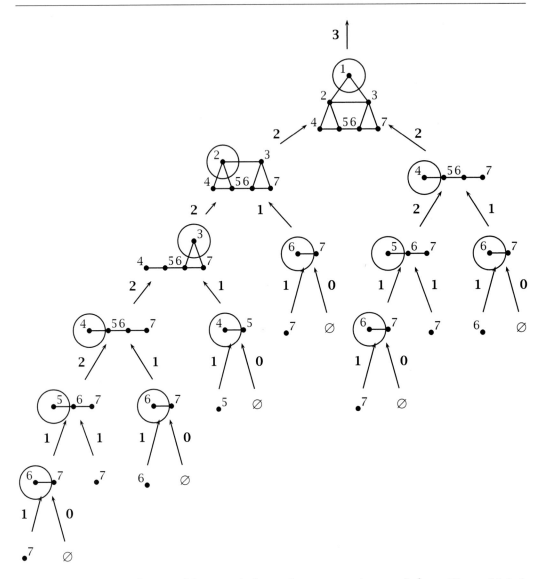

Figure 11.1.3 Sample run of *largest_independent_set* on the graph from Figure 11.1.1. The circled nodes represent the next choice of v; the left child is $G - \{v\}$ and the right child $G - \{v\} - N(v)$. The bold number is the value returned by *largest_independent_set*.

empty and finding a vertex with non-empty neighborhood can be done in time $O(n)$ (by traversing the list of vertices). Constructing G_1 also takes time $O(n)$ because we have to remove one vertex (and the edges adjacent to it). Constructing G_2, however, might take as long as $\Theta(n^2)$ because v might have $\Theta(n)$ neighbors, each one of which might have $\Theta(n)$ edges attached to it. Let $f(n)$ be the number of steps taken by the algorithm to compute G_1 and G_2. We have argued that $f(n) = \Theta(n^2)$. Now G_1 has at most $n - 1$

vertices, and G_2 has at most $n - 2$ vertices (since $N(v) \neq \emptyset$). This leads us to the following recurrence relation:

$$
\begin{aligned}
a_0 &= 0 \\
a_n &= f(n) + a_{n-1} + a_{n-2}.
\end{aligned}
$$

Then a_n is of order $\Theta(\Phi^n)$, where $\Phi = (\sqrt{5}+1)/2 = 1.61803\ldots$, which is less than 1.62. Let us show that a_n is of order $O(1.62^n)$; we leave the stronger statement that $a_n = \Theta(\Phi^n)$ to Exercise 8. We assume that $f(n) \leq cn^2$ for some $c > 0$. We have to show that $a_n \leq d1.62^n$ for some constant $d > 0$. We claim that any $d > 3000c$ will do. For the base step, we have to verify that $a_0 = 0 < d1.62^0 = d$, which is true, since $d > 0$. For the induction step, we can therefore assume that $a_m \leq 1.62^m$ for all $m < n$. We conclude that

$$
\begin{aligned}
a_n &= f(n) + a_{n-1} + a_{n-2} \\
&\leq cn^2 + d1.62^{n-1} + d1.62^{n-2} \\
&\leq d1.62^n(cn^2/(d1.62^n) + 1/1.62 + 1/1.62^2).
\end{aligned}
$$

Now $m^2 < 3 * 1.62^m$ for all $m \geq 0$ (this can be proved by induction), and therefore

$$
\begin{aligned}
cn^2/(d1.62^n) + 1/1.62 + 1/1.62^2 &\leq c/(3d) + 1/1.62 + 1/1.62^2 \\
&\leq 1/1000 + 1/1.62 + 1/1.62^2 \\
&< 1,
\end{aligned}
$$

implying $a_n \leq d1.62^n$, which is what we had to show. ∎

We will see how to improve this algorithm to run in time $O(1.39^n)$ in Exercises 11.1–11.3. Currently, the best running time of algorithms computing the independence number is achieved by Robson's algorithm, which runs in time $O(1.2108^n)$. Robson's algorithm builds on earlier work by Tarjan and Trojanowksi.

We can use Robson's result to derive exponential-time algorithms for other **NP**-complete problems. This works particularly well when we have a reduction to largest independent set that generates instances with a small vertex set.

Theorem 11.1.7. *The size of a largest clique can be computed in time $O(1.2108^n)$ where n is the number of vertices of G.*

Proof. Remember that G has a clique of size k if and only if $\overline{G}$, the complement of G (having exactly those edges that G does not have), contains an independent set of size k. Since $\overline{G}$ has the same number of vertices as the original graph, we can run Robson's algorithm on $\overline{G}$ to solve the original problems without any loss of efficiency. ∎

Satisfiability

Another problem that is often attacked by brute-force methods is the satisfiability problem. One explanation of the importance of the satisfiability problem is that many other problems can be very *parsimoniously* encoded in the satisfiability problem; that is, the translation does not enlarge problem instances very much.

Example 11.1.8. The reduction from the problem of finding the largest clique to the problem of finding the largest independent set we saw in Theorem 11.1.7 is very parsimonious: The number of vertices does not change at all. Since we measured the running time of these algorithms in the number of vertices, the same running time estimate applies to both problems. □

A parsimonious encoding makes it possible to use algorithms for satisfiability to solve other problems without a large loss of efficiency. This observation has led to several so-called SAT solvers, including successful commercial implementations.

Here we concentrate on how to solve 3SAT, the variant of satisfiability in which we are given a Boolean formula in conjunctive normal form such that each clause contains three literals. As a matter of fact, we solve the slightly more general case in which every clause contains at most three literals.

Example 11.1.9. Consider the formula

$$\varphi = (x_1 \vee \overline{x}_2 \vee x_3) \wedge (x_1 \vee \overline{x}_2 \vee \overline{x}_3) \wedge (x_1 \vee x_2) \wedge (\overline{x}_1 \vee x_2 \vee x_3) \wedge (\overline{x}_1 \vee \overline{x}_2 \vee x_3).$$

We see that φ is in conjunctive normal form, since it is the conjunction of disjunctions of literals. It is not a 3-CNF formula, since the third clause contains only two literals. Is the formula satisfiable? Let us try; to satisfy φ we have to satisfy all clauses simultaneously. If x_1 is false and x_2 is true, then, because of the first clause, x_3 has to be true to make φ true; but then the second clause is false. So, it cannot be that x_1 is false and x_2 is true in a satisfying assignment. Hence, if x_1 is false, x_2 has to be false as well. That, however, would leave the third clause unsatisfied. Therefore, x_1 must be true in a satisfying assignment. Letting x_1 be true satisfies the first three clauses. The last two clauses are then satisfied by setting x_3 to true, allowing us to let x_2 be either true or false. □

We assume that no variable occurs twice in the same clause; if, for example, we have a clause $(x_2 \vee x_1 \vee x_2)$, we can simply remove one of the x_2's. If a variable occurs both positively and negatively in the same clause, as in $(x_1 \vee \overline{x}_2 \vee \overline{x}_1)$, we can remove the whole clause, since it is always true and therefore has no impact on satisfiability.

How can we decide whether a formula φ is satisfiable or not? If we measure the complexity in the number of variables occurring in the formula, then we can solve the problem in time $O(|\varphi|2^n)$ by testing all possible 2^n assignments of truth-values to the n variables (it takes time $O(|\varphi|)$ to compute the truth-value of φ for a particular assignment). Example 11.1.9 suggests that we can do better with a different approach. Select a clause C with three elements a, b, c from φ, that is, $C = (a \vee b \vee c)$. (In Example 11.1.9 we selected $a = x_1$, $b = \overline{x}_2$, and $c = x_3$.) If both a and b are false, then c has to be true to make C true. Furthermore, if this partial assignment cannot be extended to a satisfying truth assignment of all clauses in φ, then if a is false, b has to be true. If this assumption still does not lead to a satisfying truth assignment of φ, then a has to be true (this is precisely what happened in Example 11.1.9). Instead of checking all eight possible truth assignments to a, b and c, in this way we check at most seven—by excluding the one that makes all three of them false. We can use this idea for an algorithm that improves on the $O(|\varphi|2^n)$ running time. Let us write $\varphi[a \to \text{true}]$ to denote the formula obtained from φ by setting all occurrences of a to true and all occurrences of the negation of a to false and simplifying the formula by simplifying the clauses and removing true clauses (and letting the formula be false if there is a clause that evaluates to false). Similarly, $\varphi[a \to \text{false}]$ results from φ by substituting a by false and the negation of a by true and simplifying the formula.

Example 11.1.10. If we let φ be the formula from Example 11.1.9,

$$(x_1 \vee \overline{x}_2 \vee x_3) \wedge (x_1 \vee \overline{x}_2 \vee \overline{x}_3) \wedge (x_1 \vee x_2) \wedge (\overline{x}_1 \vee x_2 \vee x_3) \wedge (\overline{x}_1 \vee \overline{x}_2 \vee x_3),$$

then $\varphi[x_1 \to \text{true}] = (x_2 \vee x_3) \wedge (\overline{x}_2 \vee x_3)$ (the remains of the last two clauses). As another example,

$$\varphi[\overline{x}_2 \to \text{false}] = (x_1 \vee x_3) \wedge (x_1 \vee \overline{x}_3) \wedge (\overline{x}_1 \vee x_3).$$

In Example 11.1.9 we started the search for a satisfying truth assignment by assuming that both x_1 and $\overline{x}_2$ are false and got

$$\varphi[x_1 \to \text{false}][\overline{x}_2 \to \text{false}] = x_3 \wedge \overline{x}_3,$$

which told us that this assumption would not lead us to a satisfying truth assignment, since we cannot satisfy that formula. We then tried letting x_1 be false and $\overline{x}_2$ be true, yielding

$$\varphi[x_1 \to \text{false}][\overline{x}_2 \to \text{true}] = \text{false}$$

because of the third clause. This led us to the conclusion that x_1 has to be true in a satisfying assignment, and we obtained

$$\varphi[x_1 \to \text{true}] = (x_2 \vee x_3) \wedge (\overline{x}_2 \vee x_3),$$

which could be satisfied by letting x_3 be true.   □

Algorithm 11.1.11 3-Satisfiability. This algorithm takes as an input a formula φ in CNF in which every clause contains at most three literals and returns true if and only if φ is satisfiable.

Input Parameter: φ
Output Parameters: None

```
3_satisfiability(φ) {
    if (φ does not contain any clauses)
        return φ // φ has to be the logical constant true or false
    if (φ contains a clause with one literal a) {
        φ = φ[a → true] // a has to be true
        return 3_satisfiability(φ)
    }
    if (φ contains a clause with two literals a, b) {
        φ₁ = φ[a → false][b → true]
        φ₂ = φ[a → true]
        return 3_satisfiability(φ₁) || 3_satisfiability(φ₂)
    }
    if (φ contains a clause with three literals a, b, c) {
        φ₁ = φ[a → false][b → false][c → true]
        φ₂ = φ[a → false][b → true]
        φ₃ = φ[a → true]
        return 3_satisfiability(φ₁) || 3_satisfiability(φ₂) || 3_satisfiability(φ₃)
    }
}
```

Let a_n be the largest number of recursive calls made by *3_satisfiability* on a formula with n variables. We have $a_0 = 0$, since a formula without variables does not contain any clauses, therefore triggering no recursive calls. Also, $a_1 = 1$, since a formula with one variable evaluates to true or false after one recursive call; and $a_2 = a_1 + a_0 = 3$, since a formula with two variables is reduced to two formulas, one with one variable and one with no variable.

In general, we have $a_n = a_{n-1} + a_{n-2} + a_{n-3}$, since in the worst case φ contains a clause with three literals and we make three recursive calls with formulas containing at most $n - 3$, $n - 2$, and $n - 1$ variables. In summary, we have

$$
\begin{aligned}
a_0 &= 0 \\
a_1 &= 1 \\
a_2 &= 3 \\
a_n &= a_{n-1} + a_{n-2} + a_{n-3}.
\end{aligned}
$$

The solution to the recurrence relation is $O(1.84^n)$ (see Exercise 10), showing that *3_satisfiability* has a running time of $O(|\varphi|1.84^n)$, since we can compute the operation $\varphi[x \to y]$ in time $O(|\varphi|)$.

Theorem 11.1.12.   *3_satisfiability solves the 3SAT problem in time* $O(|\varphi|1.84^n)$.

Exercise 11.5 shows how to modify *3_satisfiability* to run in time $O(|\varphi|1.77^n)$. The current best upper bound for 3SAT is $O(|\varphi|1.481^n)$, due to Dantsin, Goerdt, Hirsch, and Schöning.

Exercises

1S. Trace the run of *largest_independent_set* on the following graph and determine its independence number:

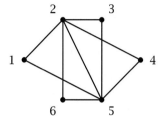

2. Trace the run of *largest_independent_set* on the following graph and determine its independence number:

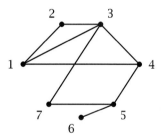

3S. Trace the run of *3_satisfiability* on

$$\varphi = (x_1 \vee \overline{x}_2) \wedge (x_1 \vee x_2 \vee x_4) \wedge (x_2 \vee x_3 \vee \overline{x}_4) \wedge (x_2 \vee x_4) \wedge (\overline{x}_3 \vee \overline{x}_4).$$

4. Trace the run of *3_satisfiability* on

$$\varphi = (x_1 \vee \overline{x}_2) \wedge (x_2 \vee \overline{x}_3) \wedge (x_3 \vee \overline{x}_4) \wedge (x_4 \vee \overline{x}_1).$$

5. Modify *3_satisfiability* so it lists all satisfying assignments of φ.

In Example 11.1.1 we claimed that given a graph $G = (V, E)$ and a subset U of the vertices, we can test in time n^2 whether U is an independent set ($n = |V|$). This is true for both the adjacency matrix and the adjacency list representation of G as we will see in Exercises 6 and 7.

6S. Show that, if G is represented by an adjacency matrix, we can verify independence of a set U of vertices in time $|U|^2$.

7. Show that, if G is given in the adjacency list representation, we can verify independence of a set U of vertices in time $|U|n$.

8. In Theorem 11.1.6 we showed that the running time of *largest_independent_set* is of order $\Theta(a_n)$, where a_n is the solution to the recurrence relation

$$a_0 = 0$$
$$a_n = f(n) + a_{n-1} + a_{n-2}.$$

Show by induction that a_n is of order $\Theta(\Phi^n)$, where $\Phi = (\sqrt{5}+1)/2$, and we assume that $f(n) = \Theta(n^2)$. *Hint:* For the upper bound, show that $a_n \le a\Phi^n - bn^2$ for appropriately chosen a and b (depending on f).

9S. Write an algorithm deciding whether a formula φ is satisfiable (SAT) in time $O(|\varphi|2^n)$, where n is the number of variables in φ.

10. Let a_n be defined by the recurrence relation

$$a_0 = 0$$
$$a_1 = 1$$
$$a_2 = 3$$
$$a_n = a_{n-1} + a_{n-2} + a_{n-3}.$$

Show by induction that a_n is of order $O(1.84^n)$.

11. Modify *largest_independent_set* so that it returns a largest independent set of the graph.

12S. Describe a deterministic algorithm deciding the Hamiltonian-cycle problem. What is its asymptotic running time? Assuming that you have a machine that takes time 10^{-12} for a single operation, what is the largest instance of the Hamiltonian-cycle problem you can solve on that machine in a day (using reasonable estimates for the constants in your asymptotic running time)?

13. Describe a deterministic algorithm deciding the TSP. What is its asymptotic running time? Assuming that you have a machine that takes time 10^{-12} for a single operation, what is the largest instance of the TSP you can solve on that machine in a day (using reasonable estimates for the constants in your asymptotic running time)?

11.2 Randomness

We discuss two applications of randomness. First, we show that, in a sense, we can trade memory for randomness when traversing mazes. The second application is a heuristic randomized solution to the Hamiltonian-path problem.

Navigating Mazes

What is the best method to get out of a maze? Well-known techniques such as the right-hand rule (place your right hand on the wall and follow the wall) or dropping pebbles at intersections to mark corridors that have already been investigated have certain disadvantages. The right-hand rule, for example, does not succeed in all cases (see Exercise 1). The pebbling technique is always successful if there is a solution. The pebbles allow us to use backtracking (see Exercise 4.21), but a large number of pebbles might be necessary. The problem of finding a path from an entrance to an exit in a maze can be modeled by graphs; vertices correspond to special points in the maze, such as the exit and entry points, dead ends, and intersection points, and edges model the connections between these points. Figure 11.2.1 shows a maze and the graph corresponding to it.

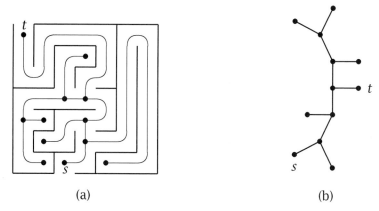

(a)   (b)

Figure 11.2.1   (a) A maze with paths. (b) The graph corresponding to the maze.

The task is to find a path between two special vertices s, the entrance, and t, the exit, of a given a graph G. This problem is known as st-connectivity. From Sections 4.2 and 4.3 we conclude that both a breadth-first search and a depth-first search solve the problem in linear time in the size of G. How could we possibly improve on these algorithms?

Let us have a closer look at a depth-first search starting at s. In terms of searching a maze, the depth-first search corresponds to moving from one intersection to the next and marking the intersections we have already seen by a pebble. In the worst case, the graph G is a path with n vertices between s and t, and we need n pebbles to complete the search. Using a breadth-first search, we always find the shortest path from s to t, but we might waste a lot of time investigating dead ends close to s when t might be just around the next corner.

The pebbles in the maze correspond to the memory of a search algorithm. In the breadth-first search, the queue might contain as many as $\Theta(n)$ vertices (see Figure 11.2.2) at a time. Similarly, in the depth-first search we might have

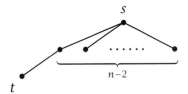

Figure 11.2.2 A bad case for breadth-first search. Initially, the queue contains s; in the next step it contains the $n - 2 \in \Theta(n)$ neighbors of s.

to call the algorithm recursively $\Theta(n)$ times, requiring that $\Theta(n)$ vertices be placed on the stack (see Figure 11.2.3).

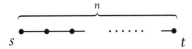

Figure 11.2.3 A bad case for depth-first search. At the end of the depth-first search, the algorithm has to remember all $n - 1 = \Theta(n)$ predecessors.

Here we have something tangible to improve on, the memory requirements of the algorithms or, figuratively speaking, the number of pebbles needed to solve the maze. Why do we need pebbles? If we ran a depth-first search on the graph without marking the vertices we have already visited, the algorithm could run into an infinite loop by following an edge to a vertex visited earlier.

Surprisingly, we can trade memory for randomness. The randomized algorithm for solving a maze is simple. Begin at vertex s; in each step continue to one of the neighbors of the current vertex, selecting each neighbor with equal probability at random; stop when t is reached. Visualize this as a person walking through the maze, randomly picking one of the choices at each intersection to continue. This approach is called taking a **random walk** on the graph.

Algorithmically, we can write the randomized search as follows.

Algorithm 11.2.1 Randomized st-Connectivity. This algorithm takes as an input a graph $G = (V, E)$ and two vertices $s, t \in V$. It returns true with probability one if there is a path from s to t; if there is no path from s to t, it fails to terminate.

   Input Parameters: G, s, t
Output Parameters: None

randomized_st_connectivity(G, s, t) {
   vertex = s
   while (*vertex* != t)
      vertex = random vertex from $N(vertex)$
   return true
}

Example 11.2.2. Let us see how the algorithm performs on a very small graph, in which s and t are connected by one additional vertex to form a path on three vertices (Figure 11.2.4).

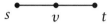

$s \qquad v \qquad t$

Figure 11.2.4 Path on three vertices s, v, t with endpoints s and t.

Initially the algorithm is located in s. In the first step, the only neighbor of s is v; hence, the algorithm moves to v. At that point there are two neighbors, s and t, and the algorithm chooses one of them, each with probability $1/2$. Hence, after two steps, the algorithm has already found its way out of the maze with probability $1/2$. With probability $1/2$, it has returned to s after two steps.

If the algorithm does not move to t, it has to move back to s. Then, in the next step, it has to relocate to v again; and it gets another chance to move to t which, again, happens with probability $1/2$. The probability that the algorithm misses both chances is $1/2 * 1/2 = 1/4$; that is, with probability $1 - 1/4 = 3/4$, the algorithm reaches t in the first four steps.

More generally, we observe that if the algorithm does not reach t within the first $2k$ steps, it must have moved back and forth between s and v during those steps. In particular, in steps $2, 4, \ldots, 2k$, it must have always moved back to s. The probability of one such move is $1/2$; hence, the probability of k such moves is $(1/2)^k = 2^{-k}$. Therefore, with probability $1 - 2^{-k}$, the algorithm reaches t within $2k$ moves.

In Exercise 4 we show that we expect the algorithm to find the exit t of the maze in four steps.   □

In Exercises 5 and 6 we investigate the case that G is the complete graph on n vertices; even in that case the randomized algorithm finds the exit rather quickly.

However, *randomized_st_connectivity* does not only work well for these special types of graphs, it works well for any kind of graph. We state this result without proof.

Theorem 11.2.3. *If we are given a graph G on n vertices with two special vertices s and t, Algorithm 11.2.1, randomized_st_connectivity, finds a path from s to t with probability at least $1/2$ in less than $2n^3$ steps if such a path exists.*

In particular, we expect *randomized_st_connectivity* to find a path out of the maze in at most $2n^3$ steps if there is such a path. If there is no such path, the algorithm runs forever; we have written an algorithm that does not necessarily terminate. One way to avoid this is by stopping the algorithm after it has performed the loop a certain number of times. For example, we could stop the algorithm after $2n^3$ steps. If it has not found t by that time, we return false. This algorithm has the following properties: If it returns true, it has found a path from s to t; and if there is such a path, it finds it with probability at least $1/2$. However, it is possible that the algorithm returns false, even though there is a path from s to t. Such an algorithm is called a **Monte-Carlo algorithm** (with one-sided error). One advantage of a Monte-Carlo algorithm is that we can make the error probability arbitrarily small by running the algorithm repeatedly: If we run *randomized_st_connectivity* k times, the probability that we will not find a path from s to t, if there is one, is less than 2^{-k}, since each run of the algorithm has a chance of at least $1/2$ of finding the exit.

The main difference between *randomized_st_connectivity* and its variants on the one hand and the deterministic searches on the other hand is that the randomized algorithms do not need to memorize any history of their movements. As a consequence, *randomized_st_connectivity* might not terminate since it could run into an infinite loop, and the Monte-Carlo variant we saw could give wrong answers (albeit with small probability). On the positive side, however, the memory requirements have been reduced drastically from $\Theta(|G|)$ for the deterministic algorithm to $\Theta(\log|G|)$ to store a single node of the graph (the current location).

Finding Hamiltonian Paths

Computer scientists do not expect that randomness will help us to solve **NP**-complete problems such as finding a Hamiltonian cycle for all inputs. However, random techniques might help in solving a large number of inputs. Of this type is a heuristic suggested by Pósa to find a Hamiltonian path (or cycle). The idea is similar to the one used in traversing a maze. We try to build a Hamiltonian path vertex by vertex. Let G be the graph and assume that it has n vertices. Since a Hamiltonian path has to traverse every vertex exactly once, we can start with an arbitrary vertex of G, call it v_0. In the next step, we randomly select one of the neighbors of v_0 to get a path v_0, v_1. We continue in this manner. At the ith step, we have a path $v_0, v_1, \ldots, v_i$. If the path already contains all vertices of G (i.e., if $i = n-1$), we are done, since we have found a Hamiltonian path. Otherwise we check if v_i has neighbors that are not already on the path. If so, we randomly select one of those neighbors, call it v_{i+1} and extend the path by adding the edge from v_i to v_{i+1} to obtain $v_0, v_1, \ldots, v_i, v_{i+1}$. If, on the other hand, all of the neighbors of v_i are already on the path, we pick one of them, v_j, say, and change the path from $v_0, v_1, \ldots, v_j, v_{j+1}, \ldots, v_i$ to $v_0, v_1, \ldots, v_j, v_i, v_{i-1}, \ldots, v_{j+1}$ (see Figure 11.2.5). Finally, keeping v_0 the same, we rename the vertices along the new path (for example, v_i turns into v_{j+1}, and v_{j+1} into v_i).

In case $j = i - 1$, this move does not change the path; in that case, we have run into a dead end, and stop.

Algorithm 11.2.4 Randomized Hamiltonian Path. This algorithm takes as an input a graph $G = (V, E)$ and searches for a Hamiltonian path. It returns true if it finds a Hamiltonian path and false otherwise.

> Input Parameter: $G = (V, E)$
> Output Parameters: None

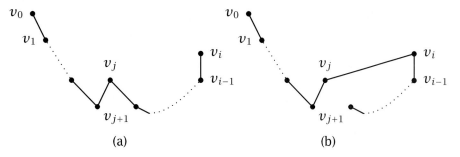

Figure 11.2.5 Given a path $v_0, \ldots, v_j, v_{j+1}, \ldots, v_i$, as shown in (a), such that v_i is a neighbor of v_j, we can change the path to $v_0, \ldots, v_j, v_i, \ldots, v_{j+1}$, as illustrated in (b).

randomized_hamiltonian_path(G) {
    v_0 = random vertex in G
    $i = 0$
    do {
       $N = N(v_i) - \{v_0, \ldots, v_{i-1}\}$
       // N contains those neighbors of v_i (the current last vertex
       // of the path) that are not already on the path
       if ($N \neq \varnothing$) {
          $i = i + 1$
          v_i = random vertex in N
       }
       else if ($v_j \in N(v_i)$ for some $0 \leq j < i - 1$)
          $(v_0, \ldots, v_i) = (v_0, \ldots, v_j, v_i, \ldots, v_{j+1})$
       else
          return false
    } while ($i\ != |V| - 1$)
    return true
}

If *randomized_hamiltonian_path* returns true, it has indeed found a Hamiltonian path, which is stored in variables $v_0, \ldots, v_{|V|-1}$. However, it is possible that the algorithm runs into a dead end and fails to find a Hamiltonian path, although such a path exists. Experiments with the algorithm show that it is very good at finding Hamiltonian paths in large graphs, and there are theoretical results proving that it is almost always successful for graphs of sufficiently large minimum degree.

Exercises

1S. Draw an example of a maze, together with an entry point and an exit point, in which there is a path from the entry to the exit, but the right-hand rule does not find it.

2. Give an example of a maze, together with an entry and an exit point in which there is a path from the entry to the exit, but neither the right-hand rule nor the left-hand rule finds it. (In the left-hand rule we use our left hand instead of our right hand.)

3. Figure 11.2.2 shows a graph for which breadth-first search requires $\Theta(n)$ pebbles (memory locations). Similarly, depth-first search requires $\Theta(n)$ pebbles for the graph in Figure 11.2.3. However, if we swapped the algorithms and applied breadth-first search to Figure 11.2.3 and depth-first search to Figure 11.2.2, both algorithms perform very well, using only a single pebble. Show that there are graphs on which *both* depth-first search and breadth-first search require $\Theta(n)$ pebbles.

4S. [Requires basic probability theory.] Show that the expected number of steps that *randomized_st_connectivity* needs to find t in the graph from Example 11.2.2 is 4. *Hint:* Use the geometric distribution.

   In Exercises 5 and 6 we analyze randomized_st_connectivity on $G = K_n$, where s and t are two arbitrary vertices of K_n.

5. [Requires basic probability theory.] Determine the probability that the algorithm reaches t for the first time in the kth step.

6. [Requires basic probability theory.] Determine the expected number of steps the algorithm takes to reach t.

   Exercises 7–9 concern the st-connectivity problem: Given a graph G and two vertices s and t in the graph, is there a path in G from s to t?

7S. Write a linear-time algorithm that solves the st-connectivity problem. The algorithm takes as input a graph G, and two vertices s and t. It returns true if there is a path and false otherwise. *Hint:* Use depth-first or breadth-first search.

8. Modify the algorithm from Exercise 7 so that it returns a path from s to t.

9. Modify the algorithm from Exercise 7 so that it returns a *shortest* path from s to t.

10S. Write out the Monte Carlo version of *randomized_st_connectivity* described after Theorem 11.2.3.

11. Modify Algorithm 11.2.4 for finding a Hamiltonian path to search for a Hamiltonian cycle instead.

12. Show that there is a graph G containing a Hamiltonian path for which Algorithm 11.2.4, *randomized_hamiltonian_path*, fails if it starts with a bad choice of v_0.

13S. Is there a graph G containing a Hamiltonian path for which Algorithm 11.2.4, *randomized_hamiltonian_path*, always fails; that is, whatever the sequence of random guesses made by the algorithm, the Hamiltonian path is not found?

11.3 Approximation

Several of the problems we have encountered come in two flavors. Remember, for example, the independent-set problem. We saw that the decision version of that problem, deciding whether a graph G contains an independent set of size at least k, is **NP**-complete. Compare that to the problem we solved in Section 11.1 when we showed how to compute $\alpha(G)$, the size of a largest independent set in G, in exponential time. A problem that asks for a largest, or smallest, solution is called an *optimization problem*.

Example 11.3.1. The decision version of the traveling-salesperson problem asks whether a weighted graph G contains a Hamiltonian cycle of weight at most w. The optimization version looks for a Hamiltonian cycle of smallest weight (if it exists). □

The decision and optimization versions of a problem are usually related; in the decision problem, we are interested in a particular kind of object (an independent set in a graph, a Hamiltonian cycle in a weighted graph). Associated with this object, we have a measure (size of the independent set, total weight of the Hamiltonian cycle) that tells us about some resource used by the solution. In the decision variant, we are asked to decide whether we can meet a given bound on the resource ($\alpha(G) \geq k$, total weight $\leq k$). In the optimization version, we are asked to optimize the solution (an independent set of size $\alpha(G)$, or the Hamiltonian cycle of smallest weight).

Example 11.3.2. In the graph-coloring problem, a solution is a coloring of the graph. The smaller the number of colors needed in the solution the better the solution; hence, we can measure the quality of the solution as the number of colors it uses. In the decision version of the graph-coloring problem, we ask whether there is a coloring using at most k colors. In the optimization version, we are asked to find a coloring with the smallest number of colors. That number is the chromatic number, $\chi(G)$, of the graph. □

For some decision problems, it is not immediately obvious whether they have an optimization variant. Take, for example, satisfiability. What is a measure of how satisfiable a formula is? One possible answer is: Measure the satisfiability of a formula by how many clauses can be satisfied simultaneously. In the decision version, we ask for all of the clauses to be satisfied; in the optimization version, we ask for the largest number of clauses that can be satisfied simultaneously. If we think of the clauses as constraints specified for the solution of a practical problem, this makes sense; if we cannot satisfy all the constraints at once, we can at least try to meet as many as we can.

Let us try to formalize these ideas. In an **optimization problem**, we are given a set I of instances of the problem. For each instance $x \in I$, there is a set of candidates $C(x)$ that solves problem I. We also have a function m from the set of all candidates to $\mathbb{R}_{\geq 0}$ that measures the aspect of the solution to be optimized. An **optimal solution** to an instance $x \in I$ is a $c \in C(x)$ such that $m(c') \geq m(c)$ for all $c' \in C(x)$ (for a **minimization problem**), or $m(c') \leq m(c)$ for all $c' \in C(x)$ (for a **maximization problem**).

For a maximization problem we define $opt_I(x) = \max\{m(c) \mid c \in C(x)\}$, and $opt_I(x) = \min\{m(c) \mid c \in C(x)\}$ for a minimization problem.

Example 11.3.3. In the independent set example the instances are all graphs, $I = \{G \mid G \text{ is a graph}\}$. For $G \in I$ we let $C(G)$ be the set of all independent sets in G. The function m is the number of vertices in the independent set. Since we are looking for a largest independent set,

$$opt(G) \quad = \quad \max\{m(c) \mid c \in C(x)\}$$
$$= \quad \max\{|U| \mid U \text{ is an independent set in } G\}.$$

That is, $opt(G) = \alpha(G)$, the largest number of vertices in an independent subgraph of G. □

The decision problem asks: Given $x \in I$ and $k \in \mathbb{R}_{\geq 0}$, is there a $c \in C(x)$ such that $m(c) \leq k$ (for a minimization problem), or $m(c) \geq k$ (for a maximization problem)? This shows that, if we can solve the optimization problem, we can also solve the decision problem since we only have to compare the optimal value to the value k given in the decision problem. In the other direction, we can often solve the optimization problem using the decision problem by using a binary search tactic, assuming that the value $opt(x)$ is not too large compared to x (see Exercise 11.17).

In this section we talk about approximation algorithms, algorithms that try to find a solution $c \in C(x)$ to x with measure $m(c)$ as close as possible to $opt(c)$. Suppose we have an algorithm A that produces a solution $A(x)$ on input x. The **performance ratio** of A on input x is $R_A(x) = opt(x)/m(A(x))$ for a maximization problem, and $R_A(x) = m(A(x))/opt(x)$ for a minimization problem. The definition guarantees that $R_A(x) \geq 1$. The **absolute worst-case performance ratio** of the algorithm is defined as

$$R_A = \sup\{R_A(x) \mid x \in I\};$$

that is, R_A is the least upper bound of all $R_A(x)$, $x \in I$ (see Section 2.1).

Example 11.3.4. In the next section we will discuss approximation algorithms for the bin-packing problem; the goal is to pack items of varying sizes into bins of a fixed size. An algorithm should try to minimize the number of bins needed to pack the items. We will see an algorithm *next_fit* whose performance ratio is $R_{next\_fit} = 2$. What does that mean? Since bin packing is a minimization problem, we know that $R_{next\_fit}(x) = m(next\_fit(x))/opt(x)$. Now $R_{next\_fit}(x) \leq R_{next\_fit} = 2$ because R_{next_fit} is an upper bound on all $R_{next\_fit}(x)$ (the smallest upper bound, actually). Hence,

$$m(next\_fit(x))/opt(x) \leq 2$$

and

$$m(next\_fit(x)) \leq 2opt(x).$$

This expresses the fact that the algorithm *next_fit* never uses more than twice the number of bins necessary to solve the problem. □

The example shows that the performance ratio of an algorithm tells us to within what factor the approximation algorithm can approximate $opt(x)$ for any input x. We conclude that the closer R_A is to 1, the better the algorithm performs.

Some algorithms perform better for larger instances; and, in that case, R_A could be an unfair measure since small instances could distort the picture. This is solved by the *asymptotic worst-case performance ratio* defined as

$$R_A^\infty = \limsup_{opt(x) \to \infty} R_A(x)$$

$$= \inf_{n} \sup_{opt(x) \geq n} R_A(x).$$

Example 11.3.5. Suppose we have an algorithm A for which $R_A(x) = 1 + 1/|x|$, for $x > 0$. Then $R_A = 2$ since $R_A(1) = 2$ and $R_A(x) \leq 2$ for all x. However, this is hardly fair, since already for $|x| > 1$, the approximation ratio is always at most 1.5. In this example $R_A^\infty = 1$, better reflecting the performance of algorithm A for large instances x. □

Bin Packing

In the bin-packing problem, we are given n items having sizes $s_1, s_2, \ldots, s_n \in (0, 1]$ and are asked to pack those items into bins of capacity 1. More formally, a packing of the n items into k bins is a function $b : \{1, \ldots, n\} \to \{1, \ldots, k\}$, assigning bin numbers to items such that $c_i = \sum_{j:b(j)=i} s_j \leq 1$ for all i; that is, c_i, the accumulated size of the items in bin i, is at most 1. The decision version of the bin-packing problem asks whether the n given items can be placed into at most k bins.

Bin Packing
Instance: Sizes $s_1, s_2, \ldots, s_n \in (0, 1]$, integer k.
Question: Is there a packing of $s_1, s_2, \ldots, s_n$ into at most k bins?

We are not allowed to cut items into smaller pieces. If we were allowed this, a solution would be simple: We could fit the items into $\lceil \sum_{i=1}^{n} s_i \rceil$ bins. Bin packing is used to model cases where items cannot be split, such as packing books into crates (size corresponds to volume), music tracks onto multi-volume CD sets (size equals length), or TV commercials into movies (again size equals length).

Example 11.3.6. Suppose we want to release a CD box set with recordings of some Haydn symphonies. We have selected symphonies No. 6 ("Le Matin," 22 mins), 7 ("Le Midi," 22 mins), 8 ("Le Soir," 23 mins), 17 (15 mins), 19 (12 mins), 22 ("The Philosopher," 18 mins), 30 ("Alleluja," 12 mins), 31 ("Hornsignal,"

25 mins). We can write up to 78 minutes of music on a single CD, and we are not allowed to split a symphony across multiple CDs. If we follow the order of the symphonies, we put symphonies 6, 7, and 8 on the first CD (67 mins), symphonies 17, 19, 22, and 30 on the second CD (57 mins), and symphony 31 on the third CD (25 mins).

We can rephrase this problem as a bin-packing problem since the only difference is the capacity of the bins. We can normalize the lengths by dividing all of them by 78. The sizes of the Haydn symphonies then become

$$s = [22/78, 22/78, 23/78, 15/78, 12/78, 18/78, 12/78, 25/78],$$

and the packing derived above fills the first bin up to 67/78, the second to 57/78, and the third to 25/78.   □

In the optimization version we want to minimize the number of bins used. For sake of brevity, we write $s = (s_1, \ldots, s_n)$. We have

$$opt(s) = \min\{k \mid \text{ the items in } s \text{ can be fit into at most } k \text{ bins}\}.$$

Since there has to be room for all items in the k bins, we know that $opt(s) \geq \lceil \sum_{i=1}^{n} s_i \rceil$. On the other hand, $opt(s) \leq n$ since we could put each item into its own bin, yielding

$$\left\lceil \sum_{i=1}^{n} s_i \right\rceil \leq opt(s) \leq n.$$

If all of the items are small, $opt(s)$ is close to the lower bound; if they are all large, it is close to the upper bound. What happens when the item sizes are mixed?

Example 11.3.7. In Example 11.3.6, we have

$$s = [22/78, 22/78, 23/78, 15/78, 12/78, 18/78, 12/78, 25/78],$$

and therefore

$$\left\lceil \sum_{i=1}^{n} s_i \right\rceil = \lceil 149/78 \rceil = 2.$$

Hence we know that we need at least two CDs for the symphonies. We also saw in Example 11.3.6 that three CDs are sufficient. That packing is not optimal; we can fit all symphonies on just two CDs as follows: The first CD contains symphonies 6, 17, 19, and 31 (for a total of 74/78), and the second CD contains symphonies 7, 8, 22, and 30 (with a total size of 75/78).   □

Since the bin-packing problem is **NP**-complete (implying that its optimization version is also hard), we might not expect fast algorithms to find solutions close to $opt(s)$; as it turns out, however, we can approximate $opt(s)$ remarkably well. Bin packing was one of the first problems investigated for approximability in the early seventies, and it has been one of the most popular problems since, with a host of literature on its numerous variants, including multi-dimensional bin packing and others.

The simplest strategy for solving the bin-packing problem is the **Next-Fit algorithm** developed by Johnson in 1973. In the Next-Fit algorithm, we always have one bin we are currently filling with items. We process the list of items one by one. As long as we can add the current item to the current bin, we do so. If the current item does not fit into the remaining space of the current bin, we close the bin and continue with a new bin.

Algorithm 11.3.8 Next Fit. This algorithm computes an assignment b of n items with sizes $s[1], \ldots, s[n] \in (0, 1]$ into bins and returns the number k of bins it used.

Input Parameter: s
Output Parameters: None

```
next_fit(s) {
    n = s.last
    k = 1 // current bin
    size = 0 //accumulated size of items in current bin
    for i = 1 to n
        if (size + s[i] ≤ 1) {
            b[i] = k // enough room to add item i to bin k
            size = size + s[i]
        }
        else {
            k = k + 1
            b[i] = k
            size = s[i]
        }
    return k
}
```

Example 11.3.9. Let us see what *next_fit* does with the Haydn symphonies from Example 11.3.6. Since we assume that the bin size is 1 rather than 78, we divide all numbers by 78 to obtain

$$s = [22/78, 22/78, 23/78, 15/78, 12/78, 18/78, 12/78, 25/78].$$

The Next-Fit strategy puts the first three symphonies into the first bin and then closes it at $c[1] = 22/78 + 22/78 + 23/78 = 67/78$. The next four symphonies fit into the second bin, which is closed at $c[2] = 15/78 + 12/78 + 18/78 + 12/78 = 57/78$. Finally, the last symphony goes into the third bin, which finishes with $c[3] = 25/78$. We see that *next_fit* finds the solution we described in Example 11.3.6 of putting the symphonies on the CDs in order.

□

The running time of *next_fit* is $\Theta(n)$, which is optimal because we have to assign a bin to each item. In spite of its simplicity, the algorithm performs remarkably well.

In the sample run of the algorithm in Example 11.3.9, notice that the content of two adjacent bins always adds up to more than 1. This is true in general and leads to a performance ratio of 2 as first shown by Johnson in 1973.

Theorem 11.3.10. $next\_fit(s) \leq 2opt(s) - 1$

Proof. Assume, for a contradiction, that *next_fit* at some point opens a bin numbered $2opt(s)$; that is, $2opt(s) \leq next\_fit(s)$. Let $c_1, \ldots, c_{2opt(s)-1}$ be the levels to which bins 1 through $2opt(s) - 1$ have been filled at that point. Since the algorithm reached bin $2opt(s)$, all preceding bins were closed. A bin is closed if we encounter an item that does not fit into the remaining space of that bin. The bin is closed, and the item placed into the next bin. This implies that $c_i + c_{i+1} > 1$ for all $i < 2opt(s)$; that is, the sum of the sizes of two adjacent bins has to be greater than one, since otherwise we could have placed the contents of bin $i + 1$ into bin i.

We conclude that

$$
\begin{aligned}
\sum_{i=1}^{n} s_i \;&\geq\; \sum_{i=1}^{next\_fit(s)} c_i \quad \text{since } next\_fit(s) \leq n \\
&\geq\; \sum_{i=1}^{2opt(s)} c_i \quad \text{by assumption, } 2opt(s) \leq next\_fit(s) \\
&=\; (c_1 + c_2) + (c_3 + c_4) + \cdots + (c_{2opt(s)-1} + c_{2opt(s)}) \\
&>\; opt(s) * 1 \quad \text{since } c_i + c_{i+1} > 1 \text{ for all } i < 2opt(s) \\
&=\; opt(s).
\end{aligned}
$$

This contradicts our earlier observation that $\sum_{i=1}^{n} s_i \leq opt(s)$. ∎

Example 11.3.11. The upper bound in Theorem 11.3.10 is asymptotically optimal; the factor of 2 cannot be improved. Consider the input

$$ s = \underbrace{[1/2, 1/(2n), 1/2, 1/(2n), \ldots, 1/2, 1/(2n)]}_{4n} $$

of $4n$ items. The *next_fit* algorithm uses $next\_fit(s) = 2n$ bins, whereas we can pack the n items optimally in $opt(s) = n + 1$ bins, as shown in Figure 11.3.1 (see next page). □

Corollary 11.3.12. $R_{nf} = 2$

Proof. By Theorem 11.3.10 we know that $R_{nf}/opt(s) \leq 2$, and Example 11.3.11 shows that $R_{nf}/opt(s) \geq 2n/(n + 1)$ for all n, implying the claim. ∎

There are two important features of the *next_fit* algorithm worth taking note of. First, *next_fit* deals with each item as it encounters it; that is, no

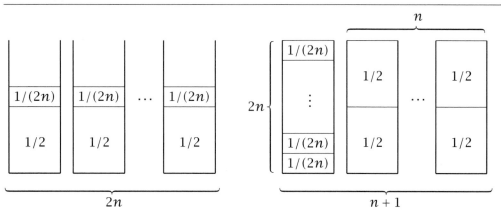

Figure 11.3.1 If *next_fit* is run on the $4n$ items in

$$s = [1/2, 1/(2n), 1/2, 1/(2n), \ldots, 1/2, 1/(2n)],$$

it packs the items as shown on the left, using $2n$ bins. An optimal packing of the same items that uses only $n + 1$ items is shown on the right.

preprocessing of the items is necessary. This makes *next_fit* a good choice in situations where we are presented with items one at a time and have to place them instantaneously without knowing what items we will see in the future. Algorithms working under this condition are called **online algorithms**. The second important feature of *next_fit* is that it works with only one open bin at a time, making *next_fit* a **bounded-space algorithm**. For example, if the bins are shipping containers, trucks, or magnetic tapes, this is a desirable property.

We have seen that the Next-Fit strategy gives us a linear-time, bounded-search online algorithm with a performance ratio of 2. The performance ratio can be improved by using another strategy, First Fit. **First Fit** is similar to Next Fit, with the difference that we do not close bins; in each step we look for the first bin into which we can fit the current item. We open a new bin only if none of the bins has enough space left for the item. First Fit is not a bounded-space algorithm (since bins are never closed), but it still is an online algorithm since it processes items as they are encountered.

Algorithm 11.3.13 First Fit. This algorithm computes an assignment b of n items with sizes $s[1], \ldots, s[n] \in (0, 1]$ into bins and returns the number k of bins it used.

Input Parameter: s
Output Parameters: None

first_fit(s) {
    $n = s.last$
    $k = 1$ // number of bins used
    $c[k] = 0$ // $c[i]$ is the total size of items in bin i

```
for i = 1 to n {
    j = 1
    while (c[j] + s[i] > 1) {
        j = j + 1
        if (j > k) {
            // open new bin
            k = j
            c[k] = 0
        }
    }
    // add item i to bin j
    b[i] = j
    c[j] = c[j] + s[i]
}
return k
}
```

The algorithm as shown here runs in time $O(n^2)$, although it can be improved to $O(n \log n)$, which is optimal (see Exercise 11.9). Garey, Graham, Johnson and Yao showed that $first\_fit(s) \leq \lceil 17/10 opt(s) \rceil$.

Theorem 11.3.14. $R_{\text{ff}}^{\infty} = 17/10$

Since the proof is rather involved we do not discuss it here.

Example 11.3.15. Proving the lower bound of $17/10$ on the asymptotic approximation ratio is also complicated, but we can show that the lower bound is at least $5/3$. Fix $0 < \varepsilon < 1/126$, and consider the following list s of items: $n/3$ items of size $a = 1/7 + \varepsilon$, followed by $n/3$ items of size $b = 1/3 + \varepsilon$, followed by $n/3$ items of size $c = 1/2 + \varepsilon$. Observe that 6 items of size a fit into a bin, since $6a < 6/7 + 6/126 < 1$. Similarly, 2 items of size b fit into a bin, and one item of size c fits into a bin. Hence, $first\_fit$ fills $(n/3)/6$ bins with items of size a, $(n/3)/2$ bins with items of size b, and $n/3$ bins with items of size c using a total of $n/18 + n/6 + n/3 = 5n/9$ bins as shown on the left in Figure 11.3.2. However, we could pack the items using only $n/3$ bins by putting into each bin an item of each size as shown on the right in Figure 11.3.2. This is possible, since $a + b + c = 1/7 + 1/3 + 1/2 + 3\varepsilon < 1/42 + 3/126 = 1$.

In summary, $opt(s) \leq n/3$, but $first\_fit(s) = 5n/9$. Since this example can be constructed for arbitrarily large n, we see that $R_{\text{ff}}^{\infty} \geq (5/9)/(1/3) = 5/3$. □

First Fit would behave much better in Example 11.3.15 if the sizes of items would not increase. As a matter of fact, it would find the optimal solution. This suggests that we first order the items in descending order and then apply First Fit. This strategy is called First Fit Decreasing (interpreting decreasing as $\geq$ rather than $>$).

Algorithm 11.3.16 First Fit Decreasing. This algorithm computes an assignment b of n items with sizes $s[1], \ldots, s[n] \in (0, 1]$ into bins and returns the number k of bins it used.

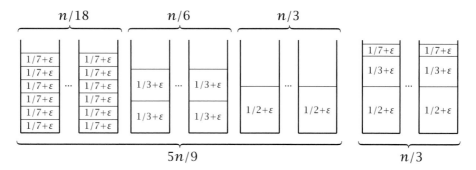

Figure 11.3.2 Applying the First-Fit strategy to $n/3$ items of size $1/7 + \varepsilon$, followed by $n/3$ items of size $1/3 + \varepsilon$, followed by $n/3$ items of size $1/2 + \varepsilon$ yields the packing shown on the left, using $5n/9$ bins. On the right, we show how the same items could be packed into $n/3$ bins, showing that the asymptotic performance ratio is at least $5/3$.

Input Parameter: s
Output Parameters: None

```
first_fit_decreasing(s) {
    s.sort(>) // sort s in decreasing order
    return first_fit(s)
}
```

Example 11.3.17. Let us see whether *first_fit_decreasing* can improve on *next_fit* in distributing the Haydn symphonies onto CDs (see Example 11.3.9). Rearranging the input in decreasing order yields

$$s = [25/78, 23/78, 22/78, 22/78, 18/78, 15/78, 12/78, 12/78].$$

The first three symphonies are put onto the first CD, which then is filled to $c[1] = 70/78$. The next four symphonies then go onto the second CD, which is then filled to $c[2] = 57/78$, forcing the next symphony onto the third CD, since there is no room for it on either the first or the second CD. The final fillsizes are $c[1] = 70/78$, $c[2] = 57/78$, and $c[3] = 12/78$, and we needed three CDs, not improving on the performance of *next_fit*. □

Note that *first_fit_decreasing* is not an online algorithm since the preprocessing step assumes that we know all items. Like *first_fit*, it can be made to run in time $\Theta(n \log n)$.

In general, the improvement in performance over *first_fit* is quite dramatic; *first_fit_decreasing* comes within an 11/9 factor of an optimal solution for sufficiently large inputs: $R_{\mathrm{ffd}}^{\infty} = 11/9$ (Johnson, 1973). We show a weaker result.

Theorem 11.3.18. $first\_fit\_decreasing(s) \le 3/2\,opt(s)$

Proof. Analyzing $first\_fit\_decreasing$ amounts to investigating how $first\_fit$ works on inputs s that are decreasing. Hence, we can assume that $s[1] \ge s[2] \ge \cdots s[n]$. Let us consider items that do not get placed into any of the first $opt(s)$ bins. Such an item cannot have size greater than $1/2$. If it did, all items preceding it would also have size greater than $1/2$ (since we sorted the sequence), meaning that we have $opt(s) + 1$ items of size greater than $1/2$. These would require at least $opt(s) + 1$ bins in any packing, since no two could fit into the same bin. That contradicts the definition of $opt(s)$ as the number of bins necessary for an optimal packing.

We have shown that all items placed into bins numbered $opt(s) + 1$ or higher have size at most $1/2$. How many such items are there? That is, how many items are placed into bins beyond $opt(s)$? Suppose, for a contradiction, that there are at least $opt(s)$ items $i_1, \ldots, i_{opt(s)}$ that get placed into bins numbered $opt(s) + 1$ or higher. Let $c[j]$ be the filling-level of bin j at the end of the algorithm. Since i_j was not placed into bin j ($j \le opt(s)$), we must have $c[j] + s[i_j] > 1$ for all $1 \le j \le opt(s)$. This implies

$$
\begin{aligned}
opt(s) \;\ge\; & \sum_{j=1}^{n} s_j \\
=\; & \sum_{i=1}^{k} c[i] \\
=\; & \sum_{i=1}^{opt(s)} c[i] + \sum_{i=opt(s)+1}^{k} c[i] \\
\ge\; & \sum_{i=1}^{opt(s)} c[i] + \sum_{j=1}^{opt(s)} s[i_j] \\
=\; & \sum_{j=1}^{opt(s)} (c[j] + s[i_j]) \\
>\; & opt(s) * 1 = opt(s),
\end{aligned}
$$

which is a contradiction.

We have shown that $first\_fit\_decreasing$ places at most $opt(s) - 1$ items, each of size at most $1/2$, beyond bin number $opt(s)$. To do this, it needs at most $\lceil (opt(s) - 1)/2 \rceil \le opt(s)/2$ additional bins (since at least two items will fit into each bin), which makes a total of at most $3/2\,opt(s)$ bins. ∎

There are numerous other fitting strategies for solving the bin-packing problem ranging from best-fit, to worst-fit, and almost worst-fit, which, strangely enough, is just as good as first-fit. It can be shown that, among online fitting strategies that only start new bins when the current item does not fit into any other bin, $first\_fit$ is optimal in the sense that for any such algorithm A, its asymptotic performance ratio satisfies $r_A^{\infty} \ge 17/10$.

For online algorithms in general, Van Vliet showed in 1996 that $r_A^\infty \geq 1.54$. The currently best online algorithm, Harmonic+1 by Richey, achieves $r_A^\infty \leq 1.589$.

If we do not insist on online algorithms, we can still improve the performance ratio. If we want to keep the running time within $O(n \log n)$, then we can use Modified First Fit Decreasing, suggested in 1985 by Garey and Johnson, which has an asymptotic performance ratio of less than 1.19. Without the time restriction, there are polynomial-time algorithms achieving an asymptotic performance ratio of 1 (see the chapter by Coffmann, Garey, and Johnson in Hochbaum, 1997 for all of these results on bin tracking).

Graph Coloring

If we consider graph coloring as an optimization problem, we are asking for the *chromatic number $\chi(G)$* of G, the smallest number of colors needed to color the vertices of a given graph so that no two adjacent vertices have the same color. In Chapter 10 we saw that deciding whether $\chi(G) \leq k$ is **NP**-complete; as a matter of fact, even deciding $\chi(G) \leq 3$ is **NP**-complete.

As a first approach to approximating $\chi(G)$, we try a greedy algorithm. We color the vertices one by one, making sure that, when we select a color for a vertex v, we make it different from the colors chosen for any of its neighbors, the vertices adjacent to v. Remember that $N(v)$ is the neighborhood of v in G.

Algorithm 11.3.19 Greedy Coloring. This algorithm takes as an input a graph $G = (V, E)$ and constructs a coloring of the vertices of the graph such that no two adjacent vertices have the same color.

Input Parameter: $G = (V, E)$
Output Parameters: None

```
greedy_coloring(G) {
    n = |V|
    C = {1,...,n} // set of colors
    for each v ∈ V
        color v with smallest color in C not used by any vertex in N(v)
}
```

Since C certainly contains sufficiently many colors (one for each vertex), the algorithm finds a coloring of the graph in which no two adjacent vertices have the same color. Let $\Delta(G)$ be the largest degree of a vertex in G; that is, $\Delta(G) = \max\{|N(v)| \mid v \in V\}$.

Theorem 11.3.20. *The algorithm greedy_coloring colors a graph G in time $O(n^2)$ such that no two adjacent vertices have the same color using at most $\Delta(G) + 1$ colors.*

Proof. To prove correctness, consider two adjacent vertices u and v. The algorithm processes u and v in some order; let us assume it picks u before

v. When it selects a color for v, it ensures that this color is different from the color chosen for u, since $u \in N(v)$.

The running time is determined by the while loop that potentially has to search through a list of $O(n)$ neighbors for each vertex.

We claim that the algorithm uses only colors $\{1, \ldots, \Delta(G) + 1\}$. The reason is that each vertex has at most $\Delta(G)$ neighbors, so one of the colors in $\{1, \ldots, \Delta(G) + 1\}$ is not in use by the neighbors of the vertex; and, since we choose the smallest unused color, that color can be found in the set $\{1, \ldots, \Delta(G) + 1\}$. ∎

Theorem 11.3.20 shows that *greedy_coloring* is a good choice for graphs with small maximum degree, and in Exercise 11.15 we will show how to exploit this in the case of planar graphs. Unfortunately, in general, $\Delta(G) + 1$ is too generous an upper bound for $\chi(G)$: *greedy_coloring* does not get within a factor of $n/2$ of the correct chromatic number for some graphs (see Exercise 13). Since a factor of n is an easy upper bound on the performance ratio (assign each vertex its own separate color), a factor of $n/2$ seems rather disappointing.

There are very strong indications, however, that we will not be able to do much better. A result by Feige and Killian shows that we cannot approximate $\chi(G)$ to within a factor of n^c for any $c < 1$ unless something very unlikely happens (similar to **P** = **NP**). The techniques for proving this result are beyond the scope of this book. As a matter of fact, stating the result precisely is beyond the scope of this book (see Hochbaum, 1997, for details). Instead, we present a weaker inapproximability result due to Johnson.

Theorem 11.3.21. *For every polynomial-time algorithm A approximating the graph-coloring problem, we have*

$$R_A \geq 4/3,$$

unless **P** = **NP**.

Proof. Suppose we had a polynomial-time algorithm A with $R_A < 4/3$. We show that $A(G) \leq 3$ if and only if $\chi(G) \leq 3$ for all graphs G. Since we are assuming that A runs in polynomial time, this implies that we can decide whether $\chi(G) \leq 3$ in polynomial time, a problem we know to be **NP**-complete (see Chapter 10). Therefore, **P** = **NP** (using Theorem 10.3.8 from Chapter 10).

By the definition of R_A, we have $A(G) \leq R_A * \chi(G)$, namely $A(G)$ is within an R_A factor of the optimal value $\chi(G)$. If $\chi(G) \leq 3$, then $A(G) \leq R_A * \chi(G) \leq 3R_A < 3 * (4/3) = 4$. On the other hand, $R_A(G) \geq \chi(G)$ since $\chi(G)$ is optimal, and therefore $R_A(G) \geq 4$ implies that $A(G) \geq 4$. In summary, $\chi(G) \leq 3$ if and only if $A(G) \leq 3$, completing the proof. ∎

Since we cannot expect performance ratios of order n^c with $c < 1$, the next question to ask is whether we can achieve performance ratios of the form n/k for some natural number $k > 0$. Johnson showed that this is indeed possible for any $k > 0$.

Theorem 11.3.22. *For every fixed $k > 0$, there is a polynomial-time algorithm that approximates $\chi(G)$ to within a factor of n/k, where n is the number of vertices of G.*

Proof. Fix $k > 0$. Suppose we are given a graph $G = (V, E)$ on n vertices. If $n = |V|$ is less than $2k$, we can use a brute-force algorithm to find $\chi(G)$ in time $O((2k)^{2k+1})$ (see Example 10.2.23 in Chapter 10), which is $O(1)$ since k is a fixed number. If $n \geq 2k$, we can partition the vertices of G into at most $\lfloor n/k \rfloor$ sets of size at most $2k$, since $\lfloor n/k \rfloor * 2k \geq (n/k - 1) * 2k = n + (n - 2k) \geq n$. The partition of the vertices results in at most $\lfloor n/k \rfloor$ subgraphs of G containing at most $2k$ vertices each. For every subgraph, we compute an optimal coloring by brute force using a different set of colors for each subgraph. As subgraphs of G, each of these graphs can be colored using at most $\chi(G)$ colors.

This gives us a coloring of G using at most $\chi(G)\lfloor n/k \rfloor$ colors, which is within a factor of n/k of $\chi(G)$. ∎

Since we cannot improve on the general problem, we investigate stronger initial assumptions on the problem. Suppose we know that a graph can be colored with k colors. Can we find a coloring not using too many additional colors? The simplest case occurs if G is 2-colorable. Then we can traverse the graph in a breadth-first search and assign alternating colors to alternating layers of the search. Hence, a 2-colorable graph can be 2-colored in linear time.

What about 3-colorable graphs? It turns out that this problem is much harder. We present an algorithm by Avi Wigderson that solves this problem.

Suppose we are given a graph $G = (V, E)$, and we know that it is 3-colorable. Pick an arbitrary vertex $v \in V$ and consider the vertices connected to it, its neighborhood $N(v) = \{u \mid (u, v) \in E\}$. Since all vertices in $N(v)$ are adjacent to v, and we know that G can be colored by three colors, one of which must be assigned to v, it follows that for any v we can color $N(v)$ using only two colors.

This suggests the following approach: Pick a vertex of large degree and color its neighborhood with two colors in linear time using breadth-first search. Remove the colored vertices from the graph and repeat the process with new colors until all of the remaining vertices have small degree. At that point, run the greedy algorithm on the remaining graph with a new set of colors to complete the coloring of G.

For the following algorithm, we assume that we have implemented a linear-time algorithm $two\_color(G, c)$ that colors a 2-colorable graph G using colors c and $c + 1$ only (see Exercise 10.1). As we did earlier, we write $G - N(v)$ for the graph that results from G after removing from G the vertices in $N(v)$ and all edges incident on vertices in $N(v)$.

Algorithm 11.3.23 Wigderson Coloring. This algorithm takes as input a 3-colorable graph $G = (V, E)$ and constructs a coloring of the vertices of the graph such that no two adjacent vertices have the same color.

Input Parameter: $G = (V, E)$
Output Parameters: None

```
wigderson_coloring(G) {
    n = |V|
    color_count = 0
    while (V contains a vertex of degree at least √n) {
        pick v of degree at least √n
        G' = (N(v), E)
        two_color(G', color_count)
        color_count = color_count + 2 //move on to next set of colors
        G = G − N(v)
    }
    greedy_coloring(G, color_count) // see new implementation below
}

greedy_coloring(G, c) {
    n = |V|
    C = {c, ..., c + n} // set of colors
    for each v ∈ V
        color v with smallest color in C not used by any vertex in N(v)
}
```

The algorithm works correctly. It uses a new set of two colors for each neighborhood coloring and another new set for the final coloring of the remaining graph. Since we observed that we can 2-color neighborhoods and that the greedy algorithm works correctly, *wigderson_coloring* does find a coloring of the graph G.

How many colors does the algorithm use? Let us have a closer look at the while loop. In each iteration we pick a vertex of degree at least $\sqrt{n}$ and 2-color its neighborhood, which is then removed from the graph. Since G contains only n vertices, this can happen at most $n/\sqrt{n} = \sqrt{n}$ many times. After that we have a graph of largest degree less than $\sqrt{n}$, which can be colored by the greedy algorithm using at most $\sqrt{n}$ additional colors. Since each of the $\sqrt{n}$ neighborhoods took two colors, we used at most $3\sqrt{n}$ colors overall.

This algorithm was found by Wigderson in 1983. In Exercise 11.16 we show how to improve the number of colors to $\sqrt{8n}$.

Theorem 11.3.24. *A 3-colorable graph can be colored in polynomial time using at most $O(\sqrt{n})$ colors.*

This result seems disappointingly weak, but since its discovery it has been improved only slightly. The current best polynomial-time algorithm due to Blum and Karger, 1997, still uses $O(n^{3/14} \log^k n)$ colors (for some $k > 0$). For this problem there are no strong lower bounds. While it is known that 4-coloring a 3-colorable graph is **NP**-hard, it is an open question whether 5-coloring a 3-colorable graph is **NP**-hard.

Exercises

1S. Describe bin packing as a minimization problem according to the definition we gave at the beginning of the section. What are I, $C(x)$, and m for the bin-packing problem?

2. Describe graph coloring as a minimization problem according to the definition we gave at the beginning of the section. What are I, $C(x)$, and m for the graph-coloring problem?

3. Describe satisfiability as a maximization problem according to the definition we gave at the beginning of the section. What are I, $C(x)$, and m for the satisfiability problem?

4S. Assume that we have implemented an algorithm computing $\alpha(G)$, the independence number of a graph. Using that algorithm, show how to write an algorithm that decides, given G and k, whether G contains an independent set of size at least k.

Exercises 5–8 deal with the problem of how to distribute Vaughan Williams' nine symphonies across multiple CDs of a box set. We assume that each CD can hold 78 minutes of music and that we are not allowed to split a symphony across multiple CDs. The symphonies have the following lengths: No. 1, "A Sea Symphony" (67 mins), No. 2, "A London Symphony" (45 mins), No. 3, "A Pastoral Symphony" (37 mins), No. 4 (31 mins), No. 5 (38 mins), No. 6 (34 mins), No. 7, "Sinfonia Antartica" (45 mins), No. 8 (27 mins), No. 9 (34 mins).

5S. Compute a lower bound on the number of CDs needed.

6S. Show how *next_fit* arranges the nine symphonies. How many CDs does *next_fit* need for all nine symphonies?

7. Show how *first_fit* arranges the nine symphonies. How many CDs does *first_fit* need for all nine symphonies?

8. Show how *first_fit_decreasing* arranges the nine symphonies. How many CDs does *first_fit_decreasing* need for all nine symphonies?

In Exercises 9–11 run different bin-packing strategies on the input

$$s = [1/2, 1/3, 1/5, 1/3, 1/2, 1/5, 1/3, 1/5, 1/6, 1/2].$$

9S. Show how *next_fit* arranges the items in s. How many bins does *next_fit* use on input s?

10. Show how *first_fit* arranges the items in s. How many bins does *first_fit* use on input s?

11. Show how *first_fit_decreasing* arranges the items in *s*. How many bins does *first_fit_decreasing* use on input *s*?

12S. Show that for every n there is a graph G for which $\Delta(G) = n - 1$ and $\chi(G) = 2$.

13. Show that for every n there is a graph G such that $\chi(G) = 2$, but *greedy_coloring* uses $\lceil n/2 \rceil$ colors to color G if the vertices are presented in a bad order.

14. Show that for every graph G it is possible that *greedy_coloring* uses only $\chi(G)$ colors to color G if the vertices are presented in the right order.

15S. Show that $R_{greedy\_coloring}(G) \leq n/2$, where $G = (V, E)$ and $n = |V|$.

11.4 Parameterization

The parameterized complexity view is based on the observation that, for many practical occurrences of **NP**-complete problems, some parameters remain small, even if the instances we have to solve are large. Consider, for example, the problem of finding cliques in graphs. This is a problem of interest to ranking algorithms of search engines on the world wide web. While the world wide web (the instance) is huge, the size of the cliques the ranking algorithms are interested in (the parameter) is small. We can find out whether a graph $G = (V, E)$ contains a clique of size k in time $O(k^2|V|^k)$ by listing all k-element subsets of V, of which there are $\binom{|V|}{k} \in O(|V|^k)$ many, and testing each for whether it is a clique in time $O(k^2)$. While a running time of $O(k^2 n^k)$ looks good, we need to remember that, although k is small, it is not going to be 2 or 3 but rather 50 or 100. With a running time of the form $O(k^2 n^k)$, we could not expect even instances of size $n = 10$ to be solvable on a computer. The problematic term is n^k. Our goal is to remove k from the exponent of n, where it severely restricts the size of instance we can solve, and find solutions running in time $O(f(k)n^c)$ for some small constant c not depending on k and some function f. Problems that can be solved in time $O(f(k)n^c)$, with c independent of k, are called **fixed parameter tractable (FPT)**.

Let us compare the two exponential running times $2^k n$ and n^k. The table in Figure 11.4.1 shows the largest value of the parameter k for which we can solve instances of size n on a machine that takes 10^{-12} for a single operation if we run that machine for an hour. It illustrates that, if our objective is to solve problem instances with small values of k, then a running time of the form $2^k n$ is preferable to one of the form n^k.

Example 11.4.1. In Example 10.2.13 we saw that the problem of register allocation can be understood as a graph-coloring problem. In Section 11.3 we saw that graph coloring is a problem that is very hard to approximate. However, compilers seem to manage quite well in solving the register-allocation problem using heuristics. A technical explanation of this behavior was given

largest k	for $2^k n$	for n^k
$n = 10$	48	15
$n = 10^2$	45	7
$n = 10^3$	41	5
$n = 10^6$	31	2
$n = 10^9$	21	1

Figure 11.4.1 Largest parameter size handled by a 1-teraflop machine in an hour for different values of n. A 1-teraflop machine takes time 10^{-12} for a single operation.

recently by Mikkel Thorup. Structured imperative programming languages, such as Basic, Pascal, C++, or Java, can be assigned a parameter called tree-width, which measures how tree-like the control-flow diagrams of these languages are. Programs without goto have a tree-width of at most 6. Thorup also showed that a performance ratio of $\lfloor tree\text{-}width + 1 \rfloor$ can be achieved in polynomial time (for the number of registers used). Hence, for most structured programming languages, at most 4 times the optimal number of registers is used. For languages with goto, however, the tree-width is not bounded, and the problem remains hard to solve. □

Vertex Cover

A **vertex cover** for a graph $G = (V, E)$ is a subset U of the vertices V such that every edge of the graph has at least one endpoint in U.

Vertex Cover
Instance: Graph $G = (V, E)$, integer k.
Question: Is there a vertex cover U of G containing at most k vertices?

Example 11.4.2. Imagine, for example, a museum with corridors hung with expensive paintings. A guard positioned at the end of a corridor can overlook a whole corridor (we assume that the corridors are straight). By turning regularly, the guard can overlook any number of corridors that end in his location. If we model the corridors as edges and the endpoints of corridors as vertices, then a vertex cover corresponds to a placement of guards such that every corridor is watched over (covered) by at least one guard. Since guards are expensive, we want to find a small vertex cover. For example, the graph in Figure 11.4.2 has a vertex cover of size 4. □

There is another useful way of viewing a vertex cover. Think of a vertex as an event and an edge between two vertices as a conflict between the two events. In this view, a vertex cover is a set of events that we can remove to obtain a conflict-free set of events.

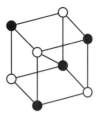

Figure 11.4.2 The solid vertices of the graph form a vertex cover.

Example 11.4.3. Biologists face the problem of determining the evolutionary history of related genetic sequences. Consider the following four sequences α, β, γ, and δ.

α: QAVTAQ___VTAQQCQIIAQCTAAIIQCQCT
β: RAUTAQ___VTAQQCQIIAQ__AAIIQCCCT
γ: RAVTAQIUQVTIQQCQINAQ__AAIIUCQCT
δ: QAVTAQIVQVTAQQCQIIAQ__AAII__QCT

Aligning the sequences as shown here by introducing gaps (written as "_") to minimize mismatches is known as *multiple sequence alignment*, an interesting problem in its own right. We are interested in the evolutionary development of the four sequences instead. While local mutations (corresponding to changing a letter, a Q to an R, for example) can occur frequently, events that lead to the removal or addition of letters or sequences of letters are much rarer and are considered major events in the evolutionary history. Compare, for example, sequences α and β with sequences γ and δ. α and β show a gap in positions 7 through 9, where γ and δ have a sequence IUQ (or IVQ). There are two ways this gap could have arisen: The original sequence began RAVTAQIUQVTI... (or similarly), and α and β lost three letters; or the original sequence began RAVTAQVTI..., and γ and δ added a sequence IUQ (or IVQ). Figure 11.4.3 shows *a* possible evolutionary history of the four sequences.

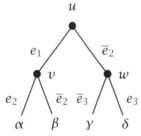

Figure 11.4.3 Possible evolution of sequences α, β, γ, and δ.

This particular solution assumes that there is an original sequence (at u and w).

```
u: RAVTAQIUQVTIQQCQINAQ  AAIIQCQCT
------------------------------------
α: QAVTAQ___VTAQQCQIIAQCTAAIIQCQCT
β: RAUTAQ___VTAQQCQIIAQ__AAIIQCCCT
γ: RAVTAQIUQVTIQQCQINAQ__AAIIUCQCT
δ: QAVTAQIVQVTAQQCQIIAQ__AAII__QCT
```

Event e_1 led to the loss of IUQ in sequences α and β, and event e_3 led to the loss of QC in δ (QC mutated to UC in γ). Furthermore, to explain the difference between α and the remaining sequences, α added a sequence CT in event e_2.

Now imagine we had a fifth sequence ε:

```
u: RAVTAQIUQVTIQQCQINAQ  AAIIQCQCT
------------------------------------
α: QAVTAQ___VTAQQCQIIAQCTAAIIQCQCT
β: RAUTAQ___VTAQQCQIIAQ__AAIIQCCCT
γ: RAVTAQIUQVTIQQCQINAQ__AAIIUCQCT
δ: QAVTAQIVQVTAQQCQIIAQ__AAII__QCT
ε: QAVTAQ___VTAQQCQIIAQCTAAII__QCT
```

It looks as if ε underwent both event e_1 and e_3; however, that is not possible if we adhere to the tree in Figure 11.4.3: There is no place ε can be located in the tree (since e_1 and e_3 are on different branches). Reordering the events in the tree does not resolve the problem because the addition of ε has caused a *conflict* between events e_1 and e_3: For ε to result from u, both events e_1 and e_3 must have occurred. Hence, if there was a tree explaining the evolution of all sequences $\alpha, \ldots, \varepsilon$ from u, it would have to contain e_1 and e_3 on the same branch. If e_1 occurs before e_3 in the tree (that is, closer to the root), then sequence δ, in which event e_3, but not e_1, occurred, cannot be explained. If, on the other hand, e_3 occurs before e_1, then α and β, in which e_1, but not e_3, occurred, cannot be explained. Hence, in either case there is an unresolvable conflict between e_3 and e_1. We could say that e_3 is causing the problem because of sequence ε; indeed, if we go back and change the alignment of ε with u, we see that the problem can be removed by introducing a new event (the removal of the final CT).

```
u: RAVTAQIUQVTIQQCQINAQ  AAIIQCQCT
------------------------------------
α: QAVTAQ___VTAQQCQIIAQCTAAIIQCQCT
β: RAUTAQ___VTAQQCQIIAQ__AAIIQCCCT
γ: RAVTAQIUQVTIQQCQINAQ__AAIIUCQCT
δ: QAVTAQIVQVTAQQCQIIAQ__AAII__QCT
ε: QAVTAQ___VTAQQCQIIAQCTAAIIQCT__
```

Since realigning sequences is expensive, we want to identify a small set of events to reconsider. To use the vertex-cover idea, we set up a graph on the set of all events with an edge between two events if they conflict (see Exercise 11.28 for a formal definition of conflict). Then the size of a smallest vertex cover is the smallest number of events we have to reconsider to obtain a conflict-free graph.   □

The vertex-cover problem is **NP**-complete, even if we restrict ourselves to planar graphs (as in the museum case). Exercise 11.20 shows that a vertex cover can be approximated to within a factor of 2.

Our question is whether we can find vertex covers efficiently if we are interested only in *small* covers. What makes deterministic simulations of **NP**-complete problems expensive in the general case is that we have to deal with search trees of a size that is exponential in the input (the graph). For some problems, such as vertex cover, we can construct a search tree whose size depends on k alone and not on the size of the whole graph. So, even if the search tree has exponential size 2^k, say, we can solve the problem for arbitrarily large graphs if we know k to be small. We call this the method of **bounded search trees**.

Suppose we are given a graph $G = (V, E)$ and a parameter k. We want to answer the question whether there is a vertex cover for G containing at most k vertices. We call such a vertex cover a k-**vertex cover**. Pick an arbitrary edge e of G. Then a vertex cover for G has to contain at least one of the endpoints of e, call them u and v. Consider the case that u is in a vertex cover of G of size at most k. Then all the edges incident on u are covered by u, and we can remove them from the graph. The remaining graph G' then has a $(k-1)$-vertex cover. Since we do not know which endpoint of e, u or v, belongs to the vertex cover, we have to investigate both cases; but in either case we have managed to reduce the parameter k by 1. For an example, see Figure 11.4.4.

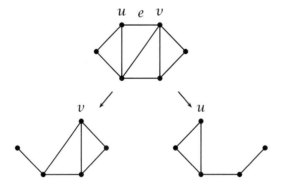

Figure 11.4.4 For a vertex cover to cover edge e, it must contain either u or v, possibly both.

This leads us to the following algorithm:

Algorithm 11.4.4 Vertex Cover. This algorithm determines whether a graph $G = (V, E)$ has a vertex cover of size at most k.

```
    Input Parameter:    G = (V, E)
    Fixed Parameter:    k
  Output Parameters:    None

vertex_cover(G, k) {
  if ((k == 0) || (E == ∅))
    return E == ∅
  else {
    pick first e = (u, v) in E
    G₁ = (V − {u}, E − {(u, w) | w ∈ V})
    G₂ = (V − {v}, E − {(v, w) | w ∈ V})
    return vertex_cover(G₁, k − 1) || vertex_cover(G₂, k − 1)
  }
}
```

Example 11.4.5. Figure 11.4.5 shows a sample run of *vertex_cover* on the graph from Figure 11.4.4 searching for a vertex cover of size at most 3. This implies that we need to perform the search only down to the third level (if we call the topmost level 0); that is, the depth of the search tree is bounded by the size of the vertex cover we are looking for.

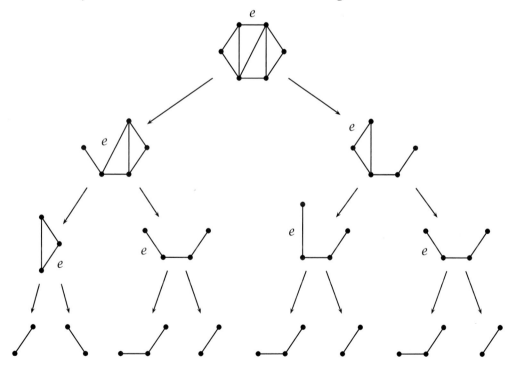

Figure 11.4.5 Bounded search tree for a run of *vertex_cover(G, 3)* with *G* from Figure 11.4.4. Since none of the graphs at the last level is empty, there is no vertex cover of *G* using at most 3 vertices.   □

Before we show that Algorithm 11.4.4 is correct, let us analyze its running time. We are given $G = (V, E)$ as an adjacency list of size $n = |V| + |E|$. In this representation we can check whether E is empty in time $O(|V|)$ and compute G_1 and G_2 in time $O(|E|)$. Therefore, the processing in each recursive step takes at most time $O(n)$. Since we make two recursive calls, and the recursion stops after k steps (bounded search tree), the whole algorithm takes time $O(2^k n)$.

If the algorithm returns true, then the test

return $E == \emptyset$

must have returned true; that is, after removing at most k vertices from G, the remaining graph must have been empty. In other words, G has a vertex cover of size at most k (since an edge is only removed if it is covered; if all edges have been removed, then all edges are covered). For the other direction, we note that, if there is a vertex cover of size at most k, it is discovered by the algorithm. Consider the recursive call

return $vertex\_cover(G_1, k - 1)$ || $vertex\_cover(G_2, k - 1)$

If u belongs to the vertex cover, follow the recursive call to

$vertex\_cover(G_1, k - 1)$

If u does not belong to the vertex cover, follow

$vertex\_cover(G_2, k - 1)$

After at most k recursive steps, E is empty and true is returned.

Theorem 11.4.6. *The k-vertex-cover problem can be solved in time* $O(2^k(|V| + |E|))$.

We have shown that the vertex-cover problem is fixed-parameter tractable, since for every fixed k the running time is $O(|V| + |E|)$. While we can hardly expect to improve on the linear time dependence on $n = |V| + |E|$, it is reasonable to ask whether 2^k can be improved upon. Indeed, this is possible using a technique called **reduction to a problem kernel**, which is a preprocessing technique that reduces the problem to another problem whose size depends only on the parameter.

Again, we are given $G = (V, E)$ and a parameter k, and we are looking for a k-vertex cover. Algorithm 11.4.4 is based on the observation that at least one endpoint of each edge has to be in a vertex cover. More is true; for each vertex v, either v or its entire neighborhood $N(v)$ has to be in the vertex cover. If v is not in the vertex cover, the only way edges incident on it can be covered is if all its neighbors belong to the vertex cover.

How does this help us? Consider a vertex v of degree greater than k. Since we are interested only in vertex covers of size at most k, we can exclude the case that all vertices in $N(v)$ belong to the vertex cover; hence, v has to belong to every k-vertex cover (to cover all edges incident on it). This leads us to the following approach: In a preprocessing step, we determine how many vertices of degree greater than k the graph contains. Suppose the number is m. We know that all these m vertices have to belong to a k-vertex cover of G; hence, if $m > k$ we can reject the input because there cannot be a k-vertex cover in that case. If $m \leq k$, we remove from G all the vertices of degree greater than k (and the edges incident on them); we also remove all isolated vertices (vertices that are not incident on any edges do not play a role in a vertex cover). This leaves $k - m$ vertices for a vertex cover of the remaining graph G'. We can now run Algorithm 11.4.4 on the graph G' with parameter $k - m$ and return the result it computes.

In the implementation of the improved vertex-cover algorithm, we assume that we have a procedure $larger\_degree(G, v, k)$ that returns true if the degree of v in G is larger than k and a procedure $isolated(G, v)$ that returns true if v is isolated in G, meaning it has degree 0.

Algorithm 11.4.7 Vertex Cover, Improved Version. This algorithm determines whether a graph $G = (V, E)$ has a vertex cover of size at most k.

Input Parameter: $G = (V, E)$
Fixed Parameter: k
Output Parameters: None

```
improved_vertex_cover(G, k) {
    m = 0
    V' = ∅
    for each v in V
        if (larger_degree(G, v, k))
            m = m + 1
        else
            V' = V' ∪ {v} // collect vertices of degree at most k in V'
    if (m > k)
        return false
    // compute G'
    E' = {(u, v) | (u, v) ∈ E and u, v ∈ V'}
    G' = (V', E')
    // remove isolated vertices from G'
    for each v in V'
        if (isolated(G', v))
            G' = G' - {v}
    if (|V'| > 2k(k - m))
        // in this case there cannot be a k - m vertex cover
        return false
    return vertex_cover(G', k - m)
}
```

We have to show that Algorithm 11.4.7 is correct. The first loop counts the number m of vertices in G of degree larger than k. We have already argued that each of these m vertices has to be contained in any k-vertex cover of G; hence, if $m > k$, the algorithm is justified in rejecting the input. Otherwise, we can restrict G to the vertices V' that have degree at most k to obtain the graph $G' = (V', E')$ and look for a $k - m$ vertex cover of G'. We remove vertices of degree 0 (isolated vertices), since they are irrelevant for a vertex cover (not being incident on an edge). A $(k - m)$-vertex cover in G' can cover at most $k(k - m)$ edges because each vertex in G' has degree at most k. Since G' does not contain any isolated vertices, G' can contain at most $2k(k - m)$ vertices (two for each edge) if it has a $(k - m)$-vertex cover. Hence, the algorithm can reject G' if it contains more than $2k(k - m)$ vertices. Finally, we use our previous *vertex_cover* algorithm to look for a $(k - m)$-vertex cover of G'.

The problem kernel in this algorithm is G', after the isolated vertices have been removed, with parameter $k - m$. That is, we are claiming that the size of G' depends on the parameter k only, not on n. This is true, since we know that G' can have at most $2k(k - m) \leq 2k^2$ vertices, a number not depending on G but just on the fixed parameter k. On the problem kernel G', we can even run a brute-force algorithm, since n is no longer part of the input size. However, we do better by running our previous implementation of the vertex-cover algorithm.

Let us analyze the running time of *improved_vertex_cover*. The running time of the first loop

```
for each v in V
    if (larger_degree(G, v, k))
        m = m + 1
    else
        V' = V' ∪ {v} // collect vertices of degree at most k in V'
```

depends on the running time of *larger_degree*. A straightforward implementation would determine the degree of v in G and compare it to k. This would take time $\Theta(|V|)$; hence, the loop would take time $\Theta(|V|^2)$. However, in the adjacency-list representation we can do better than that. We need only check whether the linked list for vertex v contains more than k neighbors or not. This can be done in time $O(k)$; hence, the loop takes time $O(|V|k)$ altogether. To compute E', we take all of the edges incident on vertices in V'. Since every vertex in V' has degree at most k, we can construct E' in time $O(|V'|k)$, which is $O(|V|k)$ since $|V'| \leq |V|$. The isolated vertices can be removed in time $O(|V|)$, since we can recognize an isolated vertex by its empty adjacency list, which can be done in time $O(1)$. By the correctness analysis, G' now has at most $2k^2$ vertices and k^2 edges. Therefore, *vertex_cover*, Algorithm 11.4.4, takes time $O(2^k(k^2 + 2k^2))$ on G'. Totaling the running times, we have shown that the k-vertex-cover problem can be solved in time $O(|V|k + 2^k k^2)$.

Theorem 11.4.8. *The k-vertex-cover problem can be solved in time $O(|V|k + 2^k k^2)$.*

Comparing this result to Theorem 11.4.6, we have improved in two respects: We have removed the dependency on $|E|$, leaving only $|V|$; and, more importantly, we have reduced the factor of $|V|$ from 2^k to k. Since in applications we imagine $|V|$ to be large, this makes a significant difference. In comparison, the additive constant of $2^k k^2$ we introduced is negligible if k is small, which is what we are assuming.

Three-Dimensional Matching

One of the six core **NP**-complete problems listed in Garey and Johnson is three-dimensional matching. It asks for a matching of objects from three different domains.

Example 11.4.9. The following table contains a list of possible courses a student wants to schedule.

Teacher	Course	Time
Dr. T	CSC 319	Monday evening
Dr. T	CSC 321	Wednesday evening
Dr. T	CSC 491	Thursday evening
Dr. X	CSC 240	Monday evening
Dr. X	CSC 321	Thursday evening
Dr. M	CSC 447	Wednesday evening
Dr. M	CSC 491	Thursday evening
Dr. Q	CSC 321	Tuesday evening
Dr. Q	CSC 491	Wednesday evening
Dr. Q	CSC 321	Thursday evening

The student plans to enroll for four classes. Students cannot take two classes that are taught at the same time, and they are not allowed to enroll for the same course twice. Let us also assume that the student does not want to take two classes with the same instructor. Under these conditions, can the student enroll full time, that is, for four classes? The answer is yes: The student can take CSC 240 with Dr. X on Mondays, CSC 321 with Dr. Q on Tuesdays, CSC 447 with Dr. M on Wednesdays, and CSC 491 with Dr. T on Thursdays.   □

Formally, we are given a set of triples $T \subseteq X \times Y \times Z$, where X, Y, and Z are pairwise disjoint sets. A **three-dimensional matching** M of T is a subset of T such that no two elements of M agree in any coordinate.

Three-Dimensional Matching (3DM)
Instance: $T \subseteq X \times Y \times Z$
Parameter: Integer k
Question: Is there a set $M \subseteq T$ containing at least k triples such that no two of the triples agree in any coordinate?

We can solve the problem by a brute-force approach in time $O(|T|^{k+1})$ by testing all $\binom{|T|}{k} \leq |T|^k$ possible sets containing k triples. We use the technique of **color-coding** (or **hashing**) to show that 3DM is fixed-parameter tractable; that is, we can move k out of the exponent of T to get a running time of the form $O(f(k)|T|^c)$ for some constant c independent of k.

Color coding is based on the observation that we do not always need the full information about a problem (the set T in our case). It is often sufficient to have simplified information obtained by coloring the original elements and then distinguishing only the color classes.

Example 11.4.10. The following example from recreational mathematics illustrates the idea of color coding. Consider the 8×8 board in Figure 11.4.6 with two opposite corner squares removed. The goal is to place domino tiles (tiles consisting of two squares) on this board in such a way that all squares of the board are covered, the tiles do not overlap, and they do not stick out over the boundaries of the board. This is called *tiling the board*.

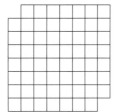

Figure 11.4.6 The modified chessboard.

It turns out that this is impossible, and there is an elegant proof using color-coding: Color the squares of the board like a chessboard as shown in Figure 11.4.7.

Figure 11.4.7 The colored chessboard.

Every domino tile, because of its shape, covers one black and one white square. However, the board has 32 black and only 30 white squares, so we cannot tile the board using dominos. The point of this example is that by choosing the coloring properly, we could reduce the problem to two sets—the black and the white squares—and argue about their cardinality.   □

For the parameterized 3DM problem we need k tuples, each with 3 coordinates; hence, in total we need $3k$ distinct elements. We guarantee distinctness by using color-coding. Suppose there is a set M of k triples with distinct coordinates. Assume that we could color the elements of $X \cup Y \cup Z$ using $3k$ colors such that the $3k$ coordinates of M have different colors.

Example 11.4.11. Let X be the set of uppercase Roman letters, Y the set of lowercase Roman letters, and Z the set of Greek letters. Let the set T consist of the 8 triples shown in the following table.

Tuple	X	Y	Z
1.	A	a	δ
2.	A	c	β
3.	B	c	α
4.	B	d	γ
5.	C	a	α
6.	C	c	γ
7.	D	b	γ
8.	D	c	α

There is a three-dimensional matching of size 3, namely triples 2, 5, and 7; that is, $M = \{(A, c, \beta), (C, a, \alpha), (D, b, \gamma)\}$. Let us color the elements as follows, using numbers as color names: $h(A) = 4$, $h(B) = 8$, $h(C) = 5$, $h(D) = 7$, $h(a) = 3$, $h(b) = 8$, $h(c) = 2$, $h(d) = 7$, $h(\alpha) = 9$, $h(\beta) = 1$, $h(\gamma) = 6$, and $h(\delta) = 9$. If we color the triples accordingly, we get the following table.

Tuple	Colors		
1.	4	3	9
2.	4	2	1
3.	8	2	9
4.	8	7	6
5.	5	3	9
6.	5	2	6
7.	7	8	6
8.	7	2	9

Note that we chose the coloring so that triples 2, 5, and 7 still form a matching, even as colored triples. □

Since we use only $3k$ colors, there are at most $3k * 3k * 3k = (3k)^3$ possible color triples. Not all of these triples may correspond to real triples in the set T. In Example 11.4.11, for example, we do not have a triple in T corresponding to the color triple $(5, 5, 1)$. We say a color triple is *realized* if it corresponds to some triple in T. (In Example 11.4.11, $(4, 3, 9)$ is realized by (A, a, δ).)

We now search for a three-dimensional matching of the realized color triples using brute force. Since there are at most $(3k)^3$ color triples, we need to investigate at most $\binom{(3k)^3}{k} \leq (3k)^{3k}$ possible sets of k color triples, and we can check whether each set's color coordinates conflict.

Example 11.4.12. We continue Example 11.4.11. Since the third coordinate contains only three colors, 1 (in tuple 2), 6 (in tuples 4, 6, and 7), and 9 (in tuples 1, 3, 5, and 8), each has to occur exactly once in a matching of size 3. This reduces the number of possibilities to $1 * 3 * 4 = 12$. Checking all of them leaves us with two sets of triples—$\{2, 5, 4\}$ and $\{2, 5, 7\}$—and, indeed, if we go back to the original triples, both of these are matchings. On the other hand, we observe that the color triples $\{1, 3, 7\}$ do not form a matching (9 occurs multiple times); however, the corresponding triples from T do form a matching. That is, a coloring can lose important information about the original problem.   □

We see that, if the $3k$ coordinates of a three-dimensional matching of T are assigned $3k$ different colors, then the color triples corresponding to the matching are themselves a matching in the color space. The advantage of looking at colors is that the color space is much smaller than the original space. We saw that we have to investigate at most $(3k)^{3k}$ potential matchings in the color space, a number that depends only on the fixed parameter k and not on $|T|$, as opposed to $\binom{|T|}{k}$, the number of potential matchings in the brute-force approach on the full set T.

We assumed that we could color the elements of $X \cup Y \cup Z$ with $3k$ colors in such a way that the $3k$ coordinates of a matching would be assigned different colors. This we cannot do in general, since it assumes that we already know where the coloring is. Moreover, as Example 11.4.12 shows, matches of the original set T can disappear in the colored version. However, we do not need to restrict ourselves to look at a single coloring. Suppose we had a set of colorings $\mathcal{H}$ of $X \cup Y \cup Z$ with the following property: For every subset S of $X \cup Y \cup Z$ containing $3k$ elements, there is a coloring $h \in \mathcal{H}$ such that all elements of S are assigned different colors under h. We could color T consecutively using all colorings in $\mathcal{H}$ and search for a three-dimensional matching of size k in the set of color triples. In pseudocode we would write this as follows:

```
for each h ∈ ℋ {
    C = h(T)
    using brute force, search for k triples in C that form a matching
    if there are k such triples
        return true
}
```

Under the assumption that for each set of $3k$ elements there is a coloring in $\mathcal{H}$ that gives a different color to each of the $3k$ elements, this pseudocode algorithm works correctly. Assume that T contains k triples that form a three-dimensional matching. Eventually, the algorithm considers the coloring $h \in \mathcal{H}$ that gives different colors to the $3k$ coordinates involved in that matching. It computes $C = h(T)$. By assumption, C is a set of color triples containing k triples that form a matching that is then found by the brute-force algorithm. Furthermore, since we consider only realized triples, every matching found in the color space translates back into a matching in T. Therefore the algorithm is correct.

How long does it take? We argued earlier that C has size at most $(3k)^3$, and we therefore need to consider at most $\binom{(3k)^3}{k} \le (3k)^{3k}$ possible sets, each taking time $3k$ to check. Hence, the brute-force search takes at most $(3k)^{3k+1}$ steps. Assuming we can compute the function h in $t_{\mathcal{H}}$ steps, we have to apply it to all triples in T taking time $O(|T| * t_{\mathcal{H}})$. Finally, we have to repeat the procedure at most $|\mathcal{H}|$ many times, leading to an overall running time of

$$O((3k)^{3k+1} * t_{\mathcal{H}} * |T| * |\mathcal{H}|).$$

We note that the running time depends on the choice of $\mathcal{H}$.

Example 11.4.13. We could let $\mathcal{H} = \{h \mid X \cup Y \cup Z \to \{1, \dots, 3k\}\}$, that is, the set of *all* colorings of $X \cup Y \cup Z$ with $3k$ colors. This guarantees that, for every $3k$-element subset S of $X \cup Y \cup Z$, there is a function in $\mathcal{H}$ that assigns a different color to each element of S. We can describe every function in $\mathcal{H}$ as a string over the alphabet $\{1, \dots, 3k\}$ of length $n = |X \cup Y \cup Z|$; hence we can compute every function in time $\Theta(n)$ by looking up its value in the string (table look-up). We also conclude that $|\mathcal{H}| = (3k)^n$. This yields a running time of

$$O((3k)^{3k+1}(3k)^n n|T|),$$

which even for fixed k is exponential, because of the factor $(3k)^n$. $\square$

Example 11.4.13 showed that simply taking all possible colorings does not lead to an acceptable running time since there are too many colorings. However, we do not *need* all possible colorings, since we need only ensure that for every $3k$ subset there is a coloring that gives a different color to each element of the subset.

Example 11.4.14. Let us have another look at the coloring shown in Example 11.4.11. We used it to discover the matching $\{2, 5, 7\}$. The same coloring, however, also reveals that $\{2, 4, 5\}$ is a matching. We conclude that a single coloring can cover more than one matching. $\square$

A smaller set of colorings $\mathcal{H}$ is supplied by families of *hash functions*. These can be constructed effectively as the following theorem shows. The proof is based on ideas from modular arithmetic.

Theorem 11.4.15. *Given m and ℓ, there is a set $\mathcal{H}$ of colorings, that is, functions $h : \{1, \dots, m\} \to \{1, \dots, \ell\}$ such that for every k-element subset $S \subseteq \{1, \dots, m\}$ there is a coloring $h \in \mathcal{H}$ such that h is one-to-one on S. Furthermore, $\mathcal{H}$ contains at most $2^{O(\ell)} \log m$ functions, and each function can be computed in time $O(\log m)$.*

In our case we want to color the coordinates in T. There are $m = 3|T|$ elements to color with $\ell = 3k$ colors. By Theorem 11.4.15, there is a set $\mathcal{H}$

of functions such that for *every* set of $3k$ coordinates (including the ones in a matching), there is a coloring $h \in \mathcal{H}$ that assigns a different color to each coordinate, and $\mathcal{H}$ has size at most $2^{O(k)} \log(3|T|)$. In summary, the overall running time is

$$(3k)^{3k+1} * \log(3|T|) * |T| * 2^{O(k)} \log(3|T|),$$

which is $2^{O(k \log k)} |T| \log^2 |T|$, and this shows that the three-dimensional matching problem can be solved in time $O(|T| \log^2 |T|)$ for fixed k.

Theorem 11.4.16. *The three-dimensional matching problem is fixed parameter tractable.*

Exercises

Exercises 1–5 deal with klam *values. Klam values are the largest parameter values for which problem instances can be solved in reasonable time. For a given running time $f(n, k)$ depending on instance size n and parameter size k, we define $klam_f(n)$ to be the largest value of k such that $f(n, k) < t$, where we think of the value of t as fixed:*

$$klam_f(n) = \max\{k \mid f(n, k) \leq t\}.$$

1S. Determine $klam_f(n)$ for $f(n, k) = nk$.

2. Determine $klam_f(n)$ for $f(n, k) = n^k$.

3S. Determine $klam_f(n)$ for $f(n, k) = k^n$.

4. Determine $klam_f(n)$ for $f(n, k) = 2^k n$.

5. Determine $klam_f(n)$ for $f(n, k) = 2^k n^2$.

6S. Show that the number of edges in a simple path in G is at most twice the size of a vertex cover of G.

7. Compare the largest parameters we can handle by Algorithms 11.4.4 and 11.4.7. To simplify, assume that Algorithm 11.4.4 has running time $2^k n$ and Algorithm 11.4.7 has running time $nk + 2^k k^2$. Also, assume that the computer we are using can perform a single operation in 10^{-12} seconds. Compute the largest value of k each algorithm can handle in an hour for $n = 10, 100, 1000, 10^6, 10^9, 10^{12}$, and present your findings in a table.

8. Modify algorithm 11.4.4 so that it outputs a vertex cover of size at most k if there is one.

9S. Write a procedure *larger_degree*(G, v, k) that takes as an input a vertex in an adjacency-list representation of a graph $G = (V, E)$ and returns true if its degree is larger than k and false otherwise. The algorithm should run in time $O(k)$.

10. Write a procedure *isolated*(G, v) that takes as an input a vertex in an adjacency-list representation of a graph $G = (V, E)$ and returns true if its degree is 0 and false otherwise. The algorithm should run in time $O(1)$.

11. Is there another schedule that the student in Example 11.4.9 can choose?

12S. Show that the figure

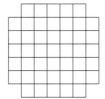

cannot be tiled using trominoes of the form ▢▢▢ .

Exercises 13–15 are about the set T of triples defined in Example 11.4.11.

13S. Find all matchings in T of size 3.

14. Does T contain a matching of size 4?

15. What is the smallest number of colorings that are sufficient to discover all matchings from Exercise 13. *Hint:* Since we are looking for matchings of size 3, we have $9 = 3 * 3$ colors.

11.5 Heuristics

Local Search

The philosophy of local search is to start with an attempted solution of the problem and keep modifying it locally to improve it as a solution to the problem. To implement this idea for a particular problem we need two things: a measure of goodness of a solution and a way to modify a solution locally that can lead to improvements.

Let us have another look at the n-queens problem for which we wrote a backtracking solution in Section 4.5. We can describe an attempted solution as a permutation $f : \{1, \ldots, n\} \to \{1, \ldots, n\}$; that is, there is a queen in column i and row $f(i)$ for all $i \in \{1, \ldots, n\}$.

Example 11.5.1. Figure 11.5.1 shows a (rather unsuccessful) attempt at solving the 5-queens problems. We can describe the position displayed in Figure 11.5.1 as $f(1) = 5$, $f(2) = 2$, $f(3) = 3$, $f(4) = 4$, and $f(5) = 1$. □

By requiring f to be a permutation, we automatically fulfill the requirement that no two queens are in the same row or column. However, as the example $f(i) = i$ (for $i \in \{1, \ldots, n\}$) shows, there can be many collisions

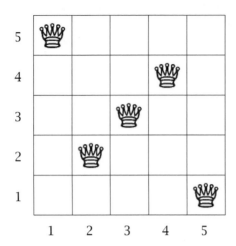

Figure 11.5.1 Five queens on a 5 × 5 board.

in the diagonals. We can use the number of collisions in the diagonals as a measure of the goodness of a solution. If we interpret a collision as a pair of queens that attack each other, we can count collisions as follows: $k \geq 1$ queens in the same diagonal count for $k - 1$ collisions. For example, the board in Figure 11.5.1 has four collisions (two collisions in each of the main diagonals).

Example 11.5.2. A single queen can be attacked by at most four other queens, namely at most two on each diagonal that the queen is on, one on either side of it. Hence, a board with n queens can result in at most $4n$ collisions. For an improvement of this result, see Exercise 11.37.   □

Now that we can measure how good a solution is, we still need a local way to change a current solution (represented by f) to a (hopefully) better solution. We want to keep f a permutation, so we do not have to worry about collisions in columns and rows. Consequently, we cannot simply change the location of a single queen, but we have to move at least two queens at once. Furthermore, we have to move the two queens in such a way that no column or row collisions arise. The easiest way to do this is to exchange two columns of the solution.

Example 11.5.3. Swapping the first two columns of the board pictured in Figure 11.5.1 reduces the number of collisions to 2. On the other hand, swapping columns 1 and 3 still results in four, albeit different, collisions.   □

We say, a bit imprecisely, that we swap the queens in column i and j when talking about exchanging columns i and j. Such a swap might, or might not, decrease the number of collisions as we have just seen. We therefore have to look for swaps that reduce the number of collisions. It is possible that we will run into a situation in which no swap will reduce the number of collisions.

Example 11.5.4. Consider the 6×6 board in Figure 11.5.2.

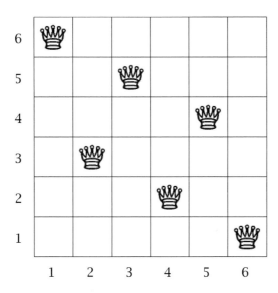

Figure 11.5.2 Six queens on a 6×6 board.

This configuration has only one collision; however, every swap, with the exception of swapping columns 1 and 6, leads to two collisions. Swapping columns 1 and 6 leaves the number of collisions the same but leads to a situation that is (up to symmetry) the same as the original one; hence, no possible swap will lead us closer to a solution. $\square$

If we run into a dead end, as in Example 11.5.4, without having found a solution, we restart the search with a new initial permutation. This leads to the question of what permutation to start with. Since we are not just interested in *a* solution (we know how to build one from Section 4.5), but in many solutions of different types, we begin with an arbitrary permutation. In algorithmic terms we start with a randomly chosen permutation.

For implementing the algorithm, we assume that we have an array method *random_permutation* that generates a random permutation of the numbers 1 through n in the array (see Section 1.3) and a method $swap(i, j)$ that swaps the values with indexes i and j of the array.

Algorithm 11.5.5 Queens. This algorithm finds a solution to the n-queens problem, which is stored in the array q.

Input Parameter: n
Output Parameter: q

```
queens(n, q) {
  do {
    q.random_permutation()
    do {
      swaps = 0 // initialize counter
      for each i, j ∈ {1, ..., n}
        if (queen in column i or j under attack)
          if (swapping queens in column i and j reduces collisions) {
            q.swap(i, j)
            swaps = swaps + 1
          }
    } while (swaps > 0)
  } while (there are collisions in q)
}
```

The outcome of the algorithm depends on the initial randomized permutation and the order in which we check the columns for swapping.

Example 11.5.6. Let us run the algorithm for a 7×7 board with the initial permutation being the identity, as shown in Figure 11.5.3.

If we perform comparisons in the order $(1, 2), \ldots, (1, 7), (2, 3), \ldots, (6, 7)$, the algorithm makes the changes shown in the figure. After only 18 steps, a solution is found. □

We did not go into the details of how the algorithm determines whether a swap is advantageous. This decision can be made in constant time for each potential swap (see Exercise 11.33).

Let us analyze the running time of the algorithm. The innermost loop, the for loop, takes $\Theta(n^2)$ steps. In the inner do loop, the number of collisions is reduced by at least one in each step, unless we fail to find an advantageous swap, in which case we leave the inner do loop. Since there can be at most $4n$ initial collisions (as we saw in Example 11.2), the inner do loop takes at most $O(n^3)$ steps to either find a solution or abort. Test runs with the algorithm suggest that for large enough n the algorithm finds a solution based on the first random permutation, in which case the outer do loop only runs once. Based on these experiments, we anticipate a running time of at most $O(n^3)$. The absence of a formal analysis, even a probabilistic one, of how often the outer do loop runs makes this algorithm a heuristic algorithm.

We can summarize the characteristics of the local search approach using a pseudocode template. The variable c contains the current solution. By $\mathcal{T}$ we denote the set of local transformation; in the n-queens example this is the set of all column swaps (i, j). For a particular $T \in \mathcal{T}$ we denote by $T(c)$ the result of applying T to c, corresponding to $q.swap(i, j)$ in the n-queens example. Finally, *eval* is a method evaluating the quality of the solution, whose value we want to maximize.

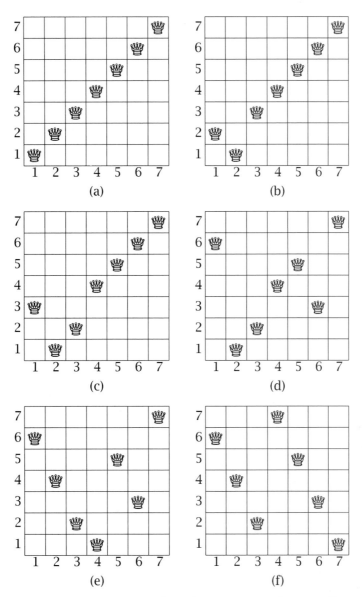

Figure 11.5.3 The initial configuration, (a), has 6 collisions. Swapping the first two columns improves this to 5, (b). Swapping column 1 and 3 reduces the number of collisions to 4 as seen in (c). Since swapping 1 and 4 would yield in a configuration with 4 collisions, we do not perform that swap. Similarly we would not reduce collisions by swapping 1 and 5. However, exchanging columns 1 and 6 reduces the number of collisions to 3, (d). Swapping 1 and 7 does not change the number of collisions. We do not exchange 2 and 3, since this would increase collisions. However, swapping 2 and 4 brings us down to two collisions, (e). The next swap that reduces the number of collisions is column 4 and 7, which, in one move, yields the solution (f).

```
local_search() {
    c = random element of the search space
    do {
        changed = false
        for each T ∈ 𝒯 {
            c' = T(c)
            Δ = eval(c) − eval(c')
            if (Δ < 0) {
                c = c'
                changed = true
            }
        }
    } while (changed)
    output c
}
```

If we set

$$eval(q) = -\text{number of collisions in } q,$$

this code corresponds to the inner do loop of the n-queens problem, since $\Delta < 0$ means that $eval(c) < eval(c')$; that is, c' has a smaller number of collisions than c. In Example 11.5.4 we saw that local modifications can get us stuck at a suboptimal solution since there might not be a way to improve the current solution locally, and there is a better solution located elsewhere. This scenario is sometimes described figuratively using mountains and valleys. The height of a mountain reflects the goodness of the solution. A climber who starts in some valley and climbs upward eventually reaches a peak, an optimal solution within the close neighborhood. However, the peak could be the peak of a hill, and there could be a larger mountain farther off; but the climber would have to pass through some deep valley to get there and would therefore not consider it. This is the problem of *local optima* illustrated in Figure 11.5.4.

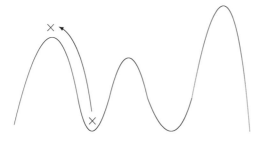

Figure 11.5.4 The climber finds a close-by peak and misses a higher peak farther off.

Several techniques, such as *simulated annealing* and *taboo search*, have been developed to deal with this problem. We have already seen one in the n-queens problem: Keep restarting the local search at a different location until a satisfactory solution is found. By selecting the starting position randomly, we hope that we will eventually come close enough to a real mountain for the climber to scale. This approach is sometimes called the *iterated hill climber*.

```
iterated_local_search() {
    do {
        changed = false
        c = random element of the search space
        do {
            for each T ∈ T {
                c' = T(c)
                Δ = eval(c) − eval(c')
                if (Δ < 0) {
                    c = c'
                    changed = true
                }
            } while (changed)
        } while (eval(c) is not acceptable)
        output c
}
```

Another solution would be to relax the definition of what it means for a solution c to be acceptable. In the n-queens example, we required there to be no collisions at all; but we could have allowed any number of collisions to be acceptable in a solution.

Other famous problems that can be solved well using the iterated local-search approach are the traveling-salesperson problem and satisfiability.

Simulated Annealing

Let us write a local-search algorithm for finding a largest independent set. We use $\triangle$, the symmetric difference operator, defined by $A \triangle B = (A-B) \cup (B-A)$. With that, we can write $A \triangle \{v\}$, which is $A - \{v\}$ if $v \in A$ and $A \cup \{v\}$ if $v \notin A$.

Algorithm 11.5.7 Independent Set Search. This algorithm searches for a large independent set in the input graph $G = (V, E)$.

    Input Parameter: $G = (V, E)$
Output Parameters: None

```
independent_set_search(V, E) {
    do {
        I = random subset of V
```

```
        do {
          changed = false
          for each v ∈ V {
            I' = I △ {v}
            Δ = eval(I) − eval(I')
            if (Δ < 0) {
              I = I'
              changed = true
            }
          }
        } while (changed)
      } while (eval(I) is not acceptable)
      output I
}
```

We have not yet defined *eval*. In an initial attempt, we could let $eval(I) = |I|$ if I is an independent set in G and 0 otherwise. Then $\Delta < 0$ would mean that $|I| < |I'|$, and I' is an independent set; that is, we have found a larger independent set than I, the current independent set. While this definition of *eval* works, it does not lead to good results. The reason is that, if we start with a set I that is not independent (which is very likely to happen), we are probably stuck with it since *eval* does not measure how far away I is from being an independent set. Therefore, it is unlikely that we will find the right vertices to remove from I to turn it into an independent set.

The solution is to relax the independence condition: We do not require I to be an independent set, but we do want to steer the search away from sets I with too many edges. To achieve this, we penalize the algorithm for choosing sets I with too many edges between vertices in I. For example, we can let $eval(I) = |I| − |E(I)|$, where $E(I) = E \cap (I \times I)$ is the set of edges of G between vertices in I; we can think of edges in $E(I)$ as bad edges. Note that, with this definition, we know that there is an independent set of size at least $eval(I)$ in G. We can take the set I and remove one endpoint of each edge in $E(I)$. The result is an independent set, and its size is at least $|I| − |E(I)| = eval(I)$.

There is one problem with *independent_set_search* we have not addressed yet. Like the hill climber, *independent_set_search* might get stuck in a local optimum. In the context of independent sets, a local optimum is an independent set that is maximal—it cannot be extended anymore by adding vertices to it—without being maximum (of largest size). Our goal is to modify the algorithm so it can, by itself, without restarting, get out of a local optimum. We take inspiration from physics. To transform matter into a lowest energy state, a procedure called *annealing* is applied in the laboratory. The matter is heated, and then the temperature is lowered slowly to the freezing point. If the temperature changes are performed carefully, the system will, with high probability, enter a lowest energy point (a single crystal, for example). We take this as a metaphor for solving optimization problems: The high temperature at the beginning puts the system into an initial state, from which the optimal state is reachable. By lowering the temperature, we reduce the range of solutions, hoping that the optimal solution is still within reach. To apply this idea to an optimization problem, we need to introduce a new parameter we call **temperature**. This parameter controls how strictly we insist on only changing to a better solution. At very high temperatures the system should be allowed to change to any neighboring state, be it better or worse. As the temperature cools, we restrict this freedom to keep the changes more local. This is the basic strategy of **simulated annealing**.

To turn the independent set search into a simulated annealing process, we have to add to the algorithm a parameter corresponding to temperature. We need a function $p(T, \Delta)$ that, based on the temperature and the change Δ to the evaluation function, computes a probability with which we want to accept local modifications that make the solution worse (for which $\Delta > 0$). We also need a schedule according to which we change the temperature. We keep a counter n for each local modification we test and use $T(n)$ as the temperature at step n. We assume that the function *random* returns a pseudorandom real number between 0 and 1. With this, we can write the following procedure:

```
sa_independent_set_search(V, E) {
    I = random subset of V
    n = 0
    do {
        n = n + 1
        T = T(n) // set current temperature
        for each v ∈ V {
            I' = I △ {v}
            Δ = eval(I) − eval(I')
            if ((Δ < 0)||(random() < p(T, Δ))
                I = I'
        }
    } while (eval(I) is not acceptable)
    output I
}
```

Since *random*() returns a pseudorandom real number between 0 and 1, the algorithm will, with probability $p(T, \Delta)$, change to a set I' whose evaluation is worse than I. The function $T(n)$ controls the temperature schedule.

We have not talked about the choice of p and T. For p the Boltzman distribution from thermodynamics is popular: $p(T, \Delta) = \exp(-\Delta/T)$. When choosing the Boltzman distribution, the probability $p(T, \Delta)$ is close to 1 for large temperatures, which means that for large temperatures the algorithm is likely to make any change from I to I'. As T becomes smaller, p drops to zero. The dependence of p on Δ is as we would expect. The larger the value of Δ (threatening to make the current solution much worse), the smaller the probability of acceptance, and vice versa.

Example 11.5.8. Figure 11.5.5 tabulates some values of the function

$$p(T, \Delta) = \exp(-\Delta/T).$$

For example, the entry $p(5, 10) = 0.14$ means that, in one out of seven cases (roughly speaking), we accept a solution that worsens the evaluation function by 10 at a temperature of 5 degrees. Note that, as we mentioned earlier, p goes to 0 as T decreases or Δ increases.

$p(T, \Delta)$	$\Delta = 0$	$\Delta = 1$	$\Delta = 2$	$\Delta = 5$	$\Delta = 10$
$T = 100$	1.00	0.99	0.98	0.95	0.90
$T = 50$	1.00	0.98	0.96	0.90	0.82
$T = 20$	1.00	0.95	0.90	0.78	0.61
$T = 10$	1.00	0.90	0.82	0.61	0.37
$T = 5$	1.00	0.82	0.67	0.37	0.14
$T = 1$	1.00	0.37	0.14	0.01	0.00
$T = 0$	?	0.00	0.00	0.00	0.00

Figure 11.5.5 Values of the function $p(T, \Delta) = \exp(-\Delta/T)$ for different inputs. □

The choice of a schedule for T is usually more difficult and involves running experiments for different schedules. Typically, one starts with a large temperature T and, splitting the schedule into one or two stages, linearly decreases T in each stage until the temperature has reached the freezing point $T = 0$.

Implementations of this algorithm (with slight modifications to the evaluation function) show that it performs very well compared to other methods, even on graphs with 10,000 to 70,000 vertices.

Exercises

1S. How does Algorithm 11.5.5, *queens*, behave if it is started on a 3×3 board for which there is no solution?

2. Trace Algorithm 11.5.5, *queens*, on a 4×4 board on which the queens are initially positioned along the main diagonal (ignore the initial randomized permutation and the restart).

3. Can we improve Algorithm 11.5.5, *queens*, by also allowing rows to be swapped?

4S. How many solutions are there to the 4-queens problem? Positions that can be obtained from each other by rotating the board or mirroring it are counted as being the same.

Notes

Hromkovič's *Algorithms for Hard Problems* gives a general overview of approaches for dealing with intractable problems, covering techniques ranging from brute force and parameterized complexity to randomization and heuristics (Hromkovič, 2001).

WWW   Exponential-time algorithms for finding a largest independent set go back to a paper by Tarjan and Trojanowski that contains an $O(2^{n/3})$ algorithm. In 1986, Mike Robson found the currently best largest-independent-set algorithm, which takes time $O(2^{0.276n})$. He has recently announced that the constant factor in the exponent can be reduced to less than $1/4$. The variants of the *largest_independent_set* algorithm presented here as exercises are taken from Herbert Wilf's book, *Algorithms and Complexity*, whose text is available online (Wilf, 1994).

The idea of randomness has influenced computer science at many different levels, from the most theoretical to the most practical, and consequently there is a wide range of literature on randomness in computer science. For our purposes, the two most interesting aspects of randomness are how to generate randomness and how to exploit it in the writing of algorithms. True randomness cannot be generated (that is part of the definition of randomness); however, we can build good pseudorandom number generators that work well in practice. A comprehensive survey of this area can be found in Knuth's *Seminumerical Algorithms*, the second volume in his series *The Art of Computer Programming* (Knuth, 1998a). The book *Randomized Algorithms* by Motwani and Raghavan is a comprehensive introduction to the topic of writing algorithms that use randomness (Motwani, Raghavan, 1995). In particular, it contains more information on random walks, which have turned out to be a very useful tool in many areas. Our presentation of Pósa's algorithm is based on (Kučera, 1990).

Forcing the truth-value of variables in 3SAT to reduce the running time was initiated in a paper by Monien and Speckenmeyer from 1985, an earlier report by Juan Bulnes of 1973 having gone unnoticed. This approach culminated in a $O(1.505^n)$ algorithm by Kullmann (Kullmann, 1999). Recently Dantsin, Goerdt, Hirsch and Schöning have improved that bound to $O(1.481^n)$ by showing how to derandomize (remove the randomness) from a randomized algorithm for 3SAT; the algorithm they derandomized used a random walk technique on the graph of possible assignments (Dantsin, Goerdt, Hirsch, Schöning, 2002).

WWW   A recent survey of approximation results for bin packing by Coffmann, Garey, and Johnson can be found in Dorit Hochbaum's *Approximation Algorithms for NP-hard problems* (Hochbaum, 1997). There is a recent monograph by Vijay Vazirani on Approximation Algorithms (Vazirani, 2001). The lecture notes by Rajeev Motwani on approximation algorithms are available online (Motwani, 1992).

Example 11.4.3 is based on the paper (Korostensky and Gonnet, 1999). A parameterized algorithm for solving the vertex-cover problem is implemented in the DARWIN system at the University of Zürich. Parameterized complexity is a recent area studying the computational complexity of problems with fixed or small parameters. For an introductory survey of the area, see the article "Computational Tractability: The View From Mars" (Downey, Fellows, and Stege, 1999b). The book by Downey and Fellows (Downey, Fellows, 1999a) gives a comprehensive treatment of the area, in particular containing references for Theorem 11.4.8, due to Balasubramanian, Downey, Fellows, and Raman (1992), Theorem 11.4.16, due to Downey, Fellows, and Koblitz, and Theorem 11.4.15 due to Alon, Yuster, and Zwick (1994).

Michalewicz and Fogel's *How to Solve It* gives an engaging general overview of modern heuristic methods (Michalewicz and Fogel, 2000). The local search solution to the n-queens problem is from (Sosič and Gu, 1990). Using simulated annealing to solve the independent-set (or clique) problem was first suggested by (Aarts, and Korst, 1989). (Homer and Peinado, 1996) compared different algorithms for finding cliques, including the simulated-annealing algorithm, which did very well. The method of simulated annealing traces back to the paper (Metropolis, et al, 1953). It was discovered as a general method for solving optimization problems by (Kirkpatrick, Gelatt, and Vecchi, 1983), and (Cerny, 1985).

Chapter Exercises

Exercises 11.1–11.3 improve the running time of largest_independent_set.

11.1. Show that, if $G = (V, E)$ is a graph that does not contain any vertices of degree at least 2, then the size of a largest independent set is $|V| - |E|$. *Hint:* What does such a graph look like?

11.2. Show that we can compute $\alpha(G)$ in time $O(1.47^n)$. Do this by modifying the *largest_independent_set* algorithm as follows. First check whether G contains a vertex of degree at least 2. If it does not, we can use the result from the previous exercise to compute the size of a largest independent set. Otherwise, we pick a vertex of degree 2 in G and perform the recursion as in *largest_independent_set*. Show (using induction) that the resulting recurrence relation $a_n = cn^2 + a_{n-1} + a_{n-3}$ has a solution a_n of order $O(1.47^n)$.

11.3. Show that we can compute $\alpha(G)$ in time $O(1.39^n)$. *Hint:* Distinguish between graphs that have a vertex of degree at least 3 and graphs that do not. Based on this distinction, improve the recursive algorithm and show that the resulting recurrence relation has a solution of order $O(1.39^n)$.

11.4. Remember that a vertex cover of a graph $G = (V, E)$ is a set U of vertices of G such that at least one endpoint of each edge of G is in U. Use a reduction from the vertex-cover problem to the independent-set problem to derive a deterministic algorithm computing the size of a smallest vertex cover in time $O(1.2108^n)$. You can assume that we can determine the size of a largest independent set in time $O(1.2108^n)$.

11.5. Improve *3_satisfiability* by adding the following heuristic: A variable is called *pure* if it occurs only positively or negatively in φ. We can eliminate pure variables by setting them to true (if they appear positively) or false otherwise. When *3_satisfiability* encounters a clause with three elements a, b, c and a is not pure, then $\varphi_3 = \varphi[a \rightarrow \text{true}]$ contains a clause with at most two literals. Show how this idea can be used to reduce the running time of the algorithm to $O(|\varphi|1.76923^n)$.

Exercises 11.6–11.8 deal with the problem of how to distribute Haydn's 104 numbered symphonies across multiple CDs. We assume that each CD can hold 78 minutes of music and that we are not allowed to split a symphony across multiple CDs. The following table lists the symphonies by length.

length (mins)	9	11	12	13	14	15	16	17	18	19
# symphonies	1	1	1	6	3	4	5	7	7	7
length (mins)	20	21	22	23	24	25	26	27	28	29
# symphonies	2	7	10	10	9	7	8	3	1	5

11.6. Compute a lower bound on the number of CDs needed.

11.7. How many CDs does *first_fit_decreasing* need for all 104 symphonies?

11.8. Try to improve on *first_fit_decreasing*.

⋆**11.9.** Show that First Fit always takes time $\Omega(n \log n)$. *Hint*: Reduce sorting to First Fit, and then use the lower bound for comparison-based sorting.

⋆**11.10.** Implement First Fit so it runs in time $O(n \log n)$. *Hint*: A good choice of a data structure for representing the bins is essential.

11.11. Show that the First-Fit strategy always gives results at least as good as the Next-Fit strategy; that is, *next_fit*$(s) \leq$ *first_fit*(s) for all possible inputs s.

11.12. Give an example that shows that the First Fit Decreasing strategy can lead to a solution that is worse than the one found by the First-Fit strategy; that is, find an s for which *first_fit*$(s) <$ *first_fit_decreasing*(s).

11.13. Show that there is a factor $\alpha > 1$ such that the First Fit Decreasing strategy uses α times as many bins as the First-Fit strategy; that is, for every n construct an s such that α *first_fit*$(s) <$ *first_fit_decreasing*(s). *Note:* The α you find is also a lower bound on R^{∞}_{ffd} (why?), which has a value of $11/9$.

Exercises 11.14 and 11.15 concern the problem of coloring planar graphs, that is, graphs that can be drawn in the plane without edges intersecting.

11.14. Euler's formula states that for a planar graph on n vertices and m edges we have $n + f = 2 + m$, where f is the number of faces the plane is separated into by the graph (counting the unbounded outer face). Use this formula to show that every planar graph contains a vertex of degree at most 5.

11.15. Show how to modify *greedy_coloring* so it colors planar graphs using at most six colors. What is the running time of your algorithm? *Hint:* Use Exercise 11.14.

11.16. Change the degree cut-off of $\sqrt{n}$ in Wigderson's algorithm so that the algorithm uses only $\sqrt{8n}$ colors altogether.

11.17. Assume that we have an algorithm that decides whether a graph G contains an independent set of size at least k. Use that algorithm to compute $\alpha(G)$ quickly, that is, if the decision algorithm runs in polynomial time, then your algorithm should also run in polynomial time. *Hint:* What are the largest and smallest possible values of $\alpha(G)$ for G? Use binary search.

Exercises 11.18–11.20 investigate the following algorithm:

```
approx_vertex_cover(G = (V,E)) {
    while (E != ∅) {
        pick first (u, v) in E
        println("Add edge (" + u + "," + v + ") to vertex cover.")
        G = G − {u, v} // remove u and v, and all adjacent edges from G
    }
}
```

11.18. Determine the running time of *approx_vertex_cover*.

11.19. Show that *approx_vertex_cover* computes a vertex cover.

11.20. Show that the size of the vertex cover computed by *approx_vertex_cover* is at most twice as large as an optimal vertex cover. Together with Exercises 11.18 and 11.19 this implies that we can approximate the size of a vertex cover to within a factor of 2 in polynomial time.

Exercises 11.21 and 11.22 show that we can approximate the length of an optimal tour for the Euclidean traveling-salesperson problem to within a factor of 2. In the Euclidean traveling-salesperson problem we are given n ≥ 3 points (cities) in the plane and are asked to find a Hamiltonian cycle of shortest length. There are connections between every pair of two points, and the distance between them is measured by the usual Euclidean metric.

11.21. Show that a minimum spanning tree on the n points (where the weight of an edge is its length) has weight less than the length of an optimal Hamiltonian cycle.

⋆**11.22.** Show how to construct a Hamiltonian cycle in polynomial time whose length is at most twice the length of an optimal Hamiltonian cycle. *Hint:* You cannot simply traverse the minimum spanning tree and follow its edges, since that would result in a tour that visits each vertex twice. All you need to know about the Euclidean metric $d(x, y)$ between two points is that the triangle inequality holds; that is, for any number of points $d(p_1, p_n) \le \sum_{i=1}^{n-1} d(p_i, p_{i+1})$.

11.23. In Exercise 4.10 we saw that the girth (the length of a smallest cycle) in a graph $G = (V, E)$ can be computed in time $O(nm)$, where $n = |V|$, $m = |E|$. Show that in time $O(n^2)$ we can compute the girth to within an additive constant of 1; that is, the actual girth of G and the value you compute may not differ by more than 1. Include a careful analysis showing that your algorithm really runs in time $O(n^2)$ rather than $O(mn)$. Give an example of a graph for which your algorithm does not find the correct girth but is off by 1.

11.24. Show that the k-vertex-cover problem can be solved in time $O(|E| + 2^k k^2)$. *Hint: improved_vertex_cover* realizes this time bound with a reasonable implementation of procedure *larger_degree*.

Exercises 11.25–11.27 show how to write a k-vertex-cover algorithm running in time $O(|V|k + (5^{1/4})^k k^2)$.

11.25. Write an algorithm to solve the k-vertex-cover problem on graphs G whose maximum degree is 2 running in time $O(|V|)$.

11.26. Modify *vertex_cover* using the following idea: If G contains a vertex v of degree at least 3, then either v or all of its three neighbors have to be in the vertex cover. Recursively investigate both cases. If G contains only vertices of degree at most 2, run the algorithm from Exercise 11.25. Write a recurrence relation for the running time of the algorithm and use it to show that the algorithm runs in time $O((5^{1/4})^k (|V| + |E|))$.

11.27. Use Exercise 11.26 to derive an algorithm solving the k-vertex-cover problem in time $O(|V|k + (5^{1/4})^k k^2)$.

11.28. Remember the setting of Example 11.4.3. An event adds or removes gaps from a sequence. We are given a sequence u (the original sequence), a set of events E, and a set of sequences S, all of which can be derived from u by applying different combinations of events in E. With an event e we associate the set $S(e)$ of all sequences in which that event took place. We say that e_1 and e_2 conflict, if none of the following hold: $S(e_1) \subseteq S(e_2)$, $S(e_1) \subseteq \overline{S(e_2)}$, $\overline{S(e_1)} \subseteq S(e_2)$, or $\overline{S(e_1)} \subseteq \overline{S(e_2)}$. Show that there is no evolutionary tree with root u containing all sequences in S at the leaves, if there are two events in E that conflict. *Hint:* Assume there is such a tree, and two events e_1 and e_2 that conflict. If a sequence is associated with an event, it has to appear in a leaf below the event. There are only four ways in which e_1 and e_2 can appear on the tree: e_1 below e_2, e_2 below e_1, e_1 below $\overline{e}_2$, or e_2 below $\overline{e}_1$.

11.29. Given an $n \times n$ matrix of zeros and ones, we can try to compress it by representing it as the union of at most k rectangles of ones. For example, the matrix

```
0000000000000
0000011100000
0011111111100
0011111111100
0000011100000
0000011100000
0011111111100
0011111111100
0000011100000
0000000000000
```

can be represented as the union of three rectangles. The question whether a given matrix can be compressed to at most k rectangles is **NP**-complete. Show that, if we consider k a fixed parameter, then the problem is fixed parameter tractable. *Hint:* Show that if two consecutive rows, or columns, are different, then there must be a border of a rectangle between them. Use this property to reduce the matrix to a problem kernel.

Exercises 11.30–11.32 are about polyominoes, connected sets of squares. A particular type of polyomino is the domino tile, which consists of two adjacent squares. Increasing the number of squares to six, we get hexominoes, three of which are shown.

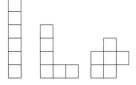

11.30. There are 35 different hexominoes (hexominoes that are congruent are considered to be the same). Give a list of all of them.

11.31. Show how to tile the following pattern using every hexomino once.

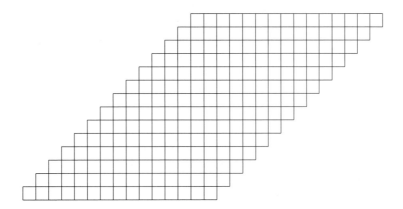

11.32. The 35 hexominoes consist of $35 * 6 = 210$ squares. There are five rectangles with the same number of squares: $210 = 3 * 70 = 6 * 35 = 14 * 15 = 5 * 42 = 10 * 21$. Show that none of these can be tiled using every hexomino exactly once. *Hint:* Remember Example 11.4.10.

Exercises 11.33–11.36 are about implementing and testing the local search n-queens algorithm.

11.33. Rewrite the algorithm so it includes the details of how to test in constant time whether a swap of two columns reduces the collisions. *Hint:* You need to do some preprocessing.

11.34. Implement the n-queens algorithm and find a solution for $n = 20$. *Hint:* See Section 1.3 on how to generate a random permutation.

11.35. Use your implementation of the n-queens algorithm and run it for large values of n. How often do you need to restart the local search from a new random initial permutation depending on n?

11.36. Use your implementation of the n-queens algorithm and run it for large values of n. What is its experimental asymptotic run-time behavior?

11.37. In the analysis of the local search n-queens algorithm, we claimed that there can be at most $4n$ collisions for any given permutation. Improve the upper bound to $2n$.

11.38. Show that the upper bound from Exercise 11.37 is tight in the sense that there can be as many as $2n - o(n)$ collisions on an $n \times n$ board generated from a permutation.

11.39. Use a local search heuristic to solve the satisfiability problem. *Hint:* A solution is a randomly chosen truth assignment. As a local modification, use the flipping of a variable, that is, changing its truth value from true to false or from false to true. Measure the quality of a solution by how many clauses are satisfied by the current truth assignment.

11.40. Use a local search heuristic to solve the following variant of the traveling-salesperson problem: The input is a weighted complete graph K_n; that is, every pair of vertices has a cost associated with them (the cost of traveling from one to the other). The output should be a cheapest Hamiltonian path in the graph. *Hint:* As in the n-queens problem, changing a single piece of a Hamiltonian path does not make sense. Think about a local move involving two edges.

11.41. Implement Algorithm 11.5.7, *independent_set_search*, with the evaluation function $eval(I) = |I| - |E(I)|$ and test it on large randomly-chosen graphs. To generate a random graph on n vertices, start with the empty graph and add each possible edge (independently) with probability $1/2$. In such a graph, the largest independent set has size roughly $2 \log n$ (with high probability). Compare this to your results.

CHAPTER 12

Parallel and Distributed Algorithms

In this chapter we investigate how to speed up computations by using multiple processors instead of a single processor. Algorithms designed to run on a network of processors are called **parallel** or **distributed algorithms** depending on the nature of the network. Processors in distributed networks are usually much more independent than processors in a parallel network (think, for example, of computers in the Internet, compared to the processors in a vector machine such as the Cray supercomputers). We survey different models of parallel computation in Section 12.1 and introduce basic terminology. In Section 12.2, we introduce the Parallel Random Access Machine model (PRAM) and show how to write algorithms on the PRAM for some fundamental problems. For example, we show how to solve the **broadcasting problem** of distributing a piece of data to all processors in the network. We also present **semigroup algorithms** that allow us to quickly compute certain expressions such as $\sum_{i=1}^{n} x_i$ in parallel and **parallel-prefix algorithms** that, for example, can compute all partial sums $\sum_{i=1}^{k} x_i$ $(1 \leq k \leq n)$ simultaneously on a parallel machine. We isolate a technique called **pointer jumping** and apply it to the **list-ranking problem** of finding the ordinal number of an element in a linked list. Closer to the hardware level, we consider **circuits**, which are gates connected by wires. As an example of circuits, Section 12.3 presents a sorting network that sorts n inputs in parallel time $O(\lg^2 n)$. Section 12.4 introduces different parallel architectures such as trees, meshes, and hypercubes. We show how to sort on a mesh and how to use a mesh for component labeling, an important image-processing task. Finally, Section 12.5 shows how to solve some fundamental problems of **distributed computing**.

12.1 Introduction

Suppose we have to print n copies of a report, and each copy takes one unit of time to print. If we have access to only one printer, it takes time n to print all reports (or longer if the printer breaks down). If we have two printers, the job could be finished in time $\lceil n/2 \rceil$ by sending $\lceil n/2 \rceil$ print requests to the first printer and $\lfloor n/2 \rfloor$ to the second printer. More generally, if we had p printers, we could do the job in time $\lceil n/p \rceil$.

Printing multiple copies of a report is an example of a task that can be performed well by multiple machines. Different instances of the task do not depend on each other, so we can assign them freely to p different machines (printers). If we have as many machines as there are reports to print, we can solve the problem in parallel time 1, the time it takes to print a single report on a single machine. If we compare the running times of the two solutions, p steps on one printer (sequential solution) and 1 step on p printers (parallel solution), we see that the parallel version with p printers is faster by a factor of p. We say that the parallel solution gives us a **speed-up** of p over the sequential solution.

In this chapter we ask to what extent computational tasks can be sped up by using more than one processor or machine; that is, to what extent can we **parallelize** the task? In the printing example, we had a sequential algorithm—namely printing n reports, one report at a time, using a single printer—that solved the problem in time $f(n) = n$. Given p printers, we could solve the task in parallel time $\lceil f(n)/p \rceil$. We cannot expect p processors to do better than that, since otherwise we could improve the sequential running time to less than $f(n)$ by running the parallel processes one after the other on a single processor; the best speedup we can expect using p processors is a factor of p.

In designing a parallel algorithm, we are trading the resource of hardware (processors) for time. Adding additional hardware may result in reduced running time over a sequential algorithm up to a factor of p, for p processors, as we saw previously. If time is a priority and we can afford additional hardware, then we should look for parallel algorithms.

One approach to finding a parallel algorithm is to start with a sequential algorithm and see whether we can parallelize it or, at least, certain parts of it. In general, we should not expect as dramatic a speedup as in the printing example. We will see some cases where we get a smaller speedup even if the number of processors p is larger than the input size n. There are also problems for which no parallel algorithm is known that is faster than the best sequential algorithm. Computer scientists have developed a tool similar to **NP**-completeness, called **P**-completeness, to identify such problems that are inherently sequential. As we do not expect to find polynomial-time algorithms for **NP**-complete problems, we do not expect **P**-complete problems to parallelize. We will not deal with the theory of **P**-completeness here but instead concentrate on problems that do parallelize. Before we begin, we present another example.

Suppose we were asked to write a function that computes the maximum value in an array. We would probably come up with an algorithm similar to the following one.

Algorithm 12.1.1 Maximum. This algorithm returns the maximum value in array $a[0], \ldots, a[n-1]$. The value of $a.length$ is the number of elements in the array.

Input Parameter: *a*
Output Parameters: None

```
maximum(a) {
   n = a.length
   current_max = a[0]
   for i = 1 to n − 1
      if (a[i] > current_max)
         current_max = a[i]
   return current_max
}
```

Figure 12.1.1, which displays the comparisons made by this algorithm, shows us that the algorithm is inherently sequential. Each comparison depends on all the previous comparisons.

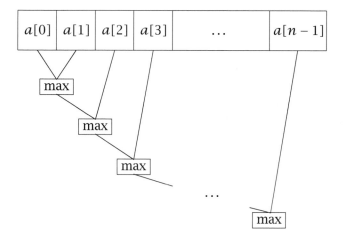

Figure 12.1.1 Comparisons made by *maximum*.

Assume we have an unlimited number of processors at our disposal. How could we improve on the *maximum* algorithm? Figure 12.1.1 shows that we are wasting parallel time: In the first step we use one processor to find the maximum of two elements. Using $\lfloor n/2 \rfloor$ processors we could find the maxima of $\lfloor n/2 \rfloor$ pairs in one step. In the next step, we could then use $\lfloor n/4 \rfloor$ processors to compute the maxima of these maxima, and so on.

Example 12.1.2. We trace the improved algorithm on the 8 inputs

$$21, 11, 23, 17, 48, 33, 22, 41.$$

Figure 12.1.2 shows the sequence of comparisons.

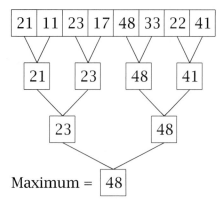

Figure 12.1.2 Comparisons made by an improved version of *maximum* illustrated on the sequence $(21, 11, 23, 17, 48, 33, 22, 41)$. We perform as many comparisons in parallel as we can: 4 in the first step, 2 in the second step, and 1 in the third step. In three parallel steps we have computed the maximum of 8 elements using 7 processors.   □

How much time does this parallel algorithm take in general? In each step we halve the number of elements whose maximum we have to compute; thus there are at most $\lceil \lg n \rceil$ steps performed by this algorithm, which is a substantial improvement over the sequential running time $\Theta(n)$. Furthermore, we need only $\lceil n/2 \rceil$ processors to achieve the parallel running time of $O(\lg n)$. At a first glance, our new solution looks very good; with a linear number of processors, we can solve a problem that requires sequential time $\Theta(n)$ in parallel time $O(\lg n)$. However, we are overlooking something in our reckoning. In the first step, we use roughly $n/2$ processors, in the second step $n/4$ processors, in the kth step $n/2^k$ processors. After the first step, half of the (potentially expensive) hardware is idle and will remain idle for the rest of the program. After the second step, three quarters of the processors are idle, and during the last few steps most of the hardware is idle. We would have a hard time justifying this waste of hardware to our business manager. This is why parallel algorithms are also measured by the work they perform. The **work** of a parallel algorithm is the product of the number of processors needed by the number of steps the algorithm performs. Our parallel algorithm has work $\Theta(n \lg n)$. This time is worse than the sequential algorithm, which has work $\Theta(n)$ (since it runs for n steps on a single processor). We say that the parallel algorithm is not **work-optimal** since there is another algorithm (albeit sequential) with lower work. We will present a technique called **accelerated cascading**, which is often helpful in making parallel algorithms work-optimal. Exercise 12.4 applies this technique to the maximum problem to show that it can be solved in time $O(\lg \lg n)$ and work $O(n)$.

Several different models of parallel computation are used in practice. We can, for example, limit the complexity of the processors involved. If an algorithm is implemented at the hardware level, we might not want each processor to correspond to a general-purpose processor. In computing the maximum, we needed only a small specialized gate that computes the maximum of two inputs. This type of gate does not even need local memory; it simply has to pass on the larger input. Models of parallel computation at this fine level of granularity are called **circuits**, since we can think of them as being similar to electrical circuits with very simple local gates. Circuits can be used to implement basic arithmetic and logical tasks in processors. In Section 12.3 we will see how to sort using circuits.

At a lower level of granularity we can think of each processor as a complete computer, able to run its own sequential algorithm. At this level, we distinguish between different models depending on how the processors communicate. In the **PRAM model**, which we will study in more detail in Section 12.2, all processors share a common memory that is used for communication (modern operating systems allow you to set up processes with shared memory; threads also share common memory). Particular tasks can be solved well by special types of networks, such as rings, trees, or grids. Section 12.4 studies PRAM algorithms on several well-known **parallel architectures**.

On the other hand, processors could be very loosely coupled:

- Memory may be **distributed** rather than shared (every processor has its own local memory, and there is no global memory),

- The processors may not share a common clock, forcing them to work asynchronously, and

- We might have little knowledge or control over the particular network that exists between the processors (think, for example, of the Internet and mobile computing).

The area of **distributed computing**, which deals with algorithms for loosely coupled networks of processors, has become increasingly important with the advent of local area networks and wide area networks (such as the Internet). We will cover some of the algorithms at the root of distributed computation in Section 12.5 on **distributed algorithms**.

12.2 The Parallel Random Access Machine (PRAM)

To explain how a parallel algorithm works, we need a machine model on which the parallel algorithm can run. The **Parallel Random Access Machine (PRAM)** has become the standard model for that purpose. It generalizes the *Random Access Machine (RAM)* model for sequential algorithms. We describe both models here without giving a precise formal definition.

The RAM model consists of a central processing unit (CPU) with random-access memory attached to it. The central processing unit can perform arithmetic and logical operations on a set of registers whose contents can be loaded from and stored into memory using random-access addressing. Each operation takes unit time.

The PRAM model consists of several RAM processors with one additional shared random-access memory to which all processors have access. The processors are **synchronized** by a global clock, each processor performing one step during each clock cycle.

We write algorithms for a PRAM as we do for a RAM, with one difference: We add a **parallel loop** that allows us to perform a block of code in parallel on several processors. We write

for $i = 1$ to n in parallel {
    Block of code
}

to mean that we perform the block of code on several processors in parallel. Since i runs from 1 to n, we need n processors to perform this parallel loop. The time needed to perform this loop is the maximum time taken by any of the n processors, rather than the sum (as it would be on a sequential machine).

Example 12.2.1. Initializations often assign the same, or easily computable values, to the elements of an array. Using multiple processors we can speed up that process by a factor of n:

for $i = 1$ to n in parallel
    $a[i] = 0$

This segment of code initializes each element of an array a of size n to zero, using n processors, in parallel time $O(1)$. The work is $\Theta(n)$, which is optimal. □

Next, consider searching an unordered array in parallel. The sequential algorithm takes time $\Theta(n)$.

Algorithm 12.2.2 Parallel Search. Given an array a of size n and a number x, this algorithm searches for x in a and returns true if there is an i such that $a[i] = x$ and false otherwise.

Input Parameters: a, x
Output Parameters: None

```
parallel_search(a, x) {
    n = a.length
    found = false
    for i = 0 to n − 1 in parallel
        if (a[i] == x)
            found = true
    return found
}
```

Algorithm 12.2.2 runs on n processors in constant parallel time. The work is $\Theta(n)$, which is optimal. The algorithm assumes that the processors have concurrent access to memory resources. First, the condition $a[i] == x$ has to be checked in parallel by n processors requiring that we assume that all n processors can simultaneously access the value in the same variable x. Second, all processors for which the condition $a[i] == x$ is true write to the variable *found*. If the entire array is filled with x, all processors try to write a value to the same variable.

Assuming that our computer supports this degree of concurrent activity might not be warranted in practice. Implementing concurrent reads and writes is expensive, and in the case of concurrent writing we also run into the problem of conflicts: What happens if different processors try to write different values to the same location? We deal with this issue by distinguishing different variants of the PRAM model based on what kind of concurrency we allow in reading and writing variables.

Exclusive Read (ER) The value of a variable can be read by only one processor at a time.

Concurrent Read (CR) The value of a variable can be read by multiple processors at the same time.

Exclusive Write (EW) A variable can be written by only one processor at a time.

Concurrent Write (CW) Multiple processors can write a value to the same variable at the same time.

We obtain four different PRAM models: EREW, the most restrictive; CRCW, the most generous; and the mixed models, CREW and ERCW, of which CREW is by far the more common, allowing concurrent reading but prohibiting concurrent writing.

Example 12.2.3. The algorithm *parallel_search* is a CRCW algorithm. It is CR because of concurrent access to x and CW because of concurrent access to *found*. On the other hand, the parallel maximum algorithm depicted in Figure 12.1.2 can be implemented on an EREW PRAM since in every step each variable is read and written by at most one processor.

Every sequential algorithm is an EREW algorithm since there is only one processor, so no concurrency occurs. □

Reconsider the code from Example 12.2.1:

for $i = 1$ to n in parallel
    $a[i] = 0$

Should this code be considered a CR or an ER algorithm? It seems that we should call it a CR algorithm since the processors are simultaneously accessing the variable i. This, however, is not what is really happening since each processor gets a different value of i. The value of i is stored locally by the processor with the program it has to execute, so it does not lead to read conflicts with the other processors.

When running a CW algorithm, it can happen that several processors write different values to the same variable. For example, this occurs when we try to modify *parallel_search* to return a location where x is found. Consider the following CRCW algorithm that returns a location in parallel time $O(1)$.

Algorithm 12.2.4 Locate. Given an array a and a value x, the algorithm returns an index i such that $a[i] = x$ if there is one and -1 otherwise.

Input Parameters: a, x
Output Parameters: None

```
locate(a, x) {
    n = a.length
    location = -1
    for i = 0 to n - 1 in parallel
        if (a[i] == x)
            location = i
    return location
}
```

If x occurs more than once in the array, then the statement *location = i* is executed in parallel by different processors for different values of i. We distinguish between several models of how to resolve conflicts. In **priority CW**, the processors are assigned priorities; the processor with highest priority successfully writes in case of a conflict. In **common CW**, all processors that write a value to the same variable have to write the same value; otherwise the algorithm fails. There are also models in which the value is chosen arbitrarily or all values are combined in some way.

Algorithm 12.2.2 is a common CRCW algorithm, since all processors try to write the same value. However, Algorithm 12.2.4 works only in the arbitrary CW and the priority CW model since it might try to write different values to the variable *location*. It works in the EW model if all the elements in the array are distinct.

Even when we restrict the model to exclusive writes, there can be problems with concurrent reads. Consider the following piece of code:

```
n = a.length
x = 0
for i = 0 to n in parallel
    if (i == n)
        x = 1
    else
        a[i] = x
```

What values does the array $a[i]$ contain after executing this code? Although only processor n writes to x, all other processors try to read from it. If processors 0 through $n - 1$ use local copies of x, the array will contain only zeros, although processor n might have changed the value of x in the global memory. This is called the *cache coherence problem*. If all processors access x in global memory, the outcome will depend on the random order in which the processors access x. These problems are serious and have to be dealt with in practice; we circumvent them by writing code that avoids them.

It is often simpler to design algorithms that allow concurrent reading and writing than to write programs for the more restrictive EREW model. In practice, however, we probably need an EREW or a CREW algorithm. It is therefore helpful to know that we can always remove the concurrent reading and writing at a cost of a logarithmic factor. Suppose we are given a CR algorithm that we want to turn into an ER algorithm. Instead of having multiple processors access the same variable in parallel, we create a local copy of the variable for each processor. In order to do this, we have to make the value of the variable known to all processors. This is known as the **broadcasting problem**. More precisely, we are looking for a parallel ER algorithm that initializes all elements in an array a of n elements with the value of a variable x. Suppose we had already filled the first half of the array with x; that is, $a[0] = a[1] = \cdots = a[n/2 - 1] = x$. We could then use $n/2$ processors to copy the contents of the first half into the second half in one parallel step: Processor j copies the content of $a[j]$ into $a[j + n/2]$. To fill the first half of a, we apply the same idea recursively $\lg n$ times; in this way, we can broadcast a piece of data in parallel time $\lg n$. We implement this idea iteratively to make it more transparent which processors are used in the parallel step.

Algorithm 12.2.5 ER Broadcast. This algorithm takes as input a value x and an array a and assigns x to all elements of the array.

Input Parameters: a, x
Output Parameters: None

```
er_broadcast(a, x) {
    n = a.length
    a[0] = x
    for i = 0 to ⌈lg n⌉ - 1
        for j = 0 to 2^i - 1 in parallel
            if (2^i + j < n)
                a[2^i + j] = a[j]
}
```

Example 12.2.6. Let $x = 0$, and $n = 10$. *er_broadcast* starts by writing x to $a[0]$. For each value of i it then doubles the number of cells containing x until all cells are filled.

	$a[0]$	$a[1]$	$a[2]$	$a[3]$	$a[4]$	$a[5]$	$a[6]$	$a[7]$	$a[8]$	$a[9]$
start	0									
$i = 0$	0	**0**								
$i = 1$	0	0	**0**	**0**						
$i = 2$	0	0	0	0	**0**	**0**	**0**	**0**		
$i = 3$	0	0	0	0	0	0	0	0	**0**	**0**

For example, when $i = 2$ we use four processors to copy the values in $a[0]$, $a[1]$, $a[2]$, $a[3]$ to $a[4]$, $a[5]$, $a[6]$, $a[7]$ in one parallel step.   □

Why is *er_broadcast* an ER algorithm? Each processor reads from a different location $a[j]$, and we know that each processor obtains its own value of j, but what about i and n? It seems that all processors have to access i and n simultaneously. However, we can eliminate access to i by keeping a counter for it in each processor, and we eliminate access to n by running the outer for loop only up to $\min\{2^i - 1, n - 2^i - 1\}$.

The outer for loop is sequential and runs for $\Theta(\lg n)$ iterations. The inner loop is parallel and takes only $O(1)$ parallel time; hence, *er_broadcast* runs in parallel time $\Theta(\lg n)$. In the inner loop, j takes on values of order $\Theta(n)$; hence, we need $\Theta(n)$ processors to implement the algorithm, implying that the work is $\Theta(n \lg n)$, which is not optimal since the sequential algorithm has work $\Theta(n)$ only.

Theorem 12.2.7. *er_broadcast is an ER algorithm that initializes an n-element array in parallel time $\Theta(\lg n)$.*

Proof. We have already analyzed work and running time of *er_broadcast* leaving the proof of correctness. The algorithm works by doubling, in each step, the number of array cells that contain x. We picture the step from i to $i + 1$:

	$a[0]$	...	$a[2^i - 1]$	$a[2^i]$	...	$a[2^{i+1} - 1]$	$a[2^{i+1}]$	...	$a[n]$
i	x	...	x						
$i+1$	x	...	x	**x**	...	**x**			

This means that during the execution of the outer for loop, we always have $a[0] = \ldots = a[2^i - 1] = x$, implying that eventually all cells are filled with x.   ∎

Using *er_broadcast*, we can turn every CR algorithm into an ER algorithm by substituting concurrent reads with a broadcast of the variable to all processors.

Corollary 12.2.8. *Any CR algorithm on p processors running in parallel time $O(f(n))$ can be turned into an equivalent ER algorithm on p processors running in parallel time $O(f(n) \lg p)$.*

Example 12.2.9. Algorithm 12.2.2, the CR parallel-search algorithm that runs in parallel time $O(1)$ on n processors, can be turned into an ER parallel search algorithm running in time $O(\lg n)$ on n processors.   □

Using a similar idea, we can turn CW algorithms into EW algorithms. The details depend on which CW model we have. Again, we get a factor of $\lg p$, where p is the number of processors. We state this result and leave the proof to Exercise 12.1.

Theorem 12.2.10. *Any CRCW algorithm on p processors running in parallel time $O(f(n))$ can be turned into an equivalent EREW algorithm on p processors running in parallel time $O(f(n) \lg p)$, assuming we know how to resolve write conflicts efficiently.*

Note that we have only one $\lg p$ factor instead of two (one from CR, one from CW) since a CRCW algorithm never writes and reads at the same time. Hence, in a transformation from CRCW to EREW, we substitute concurrent reads by exclusive reads and concurrent writes by exclusive writes, slowing down the running time by a factor of $\lg p$.

Semigroup Algorithms and Accelerated Cascading

How fast can we sum n numbers on an EREW PRAM; that is, given an array a of size n, how fast can we compute $\sum_{i=0}^{n-1} a[i]$? This problem belongs to a family of problems that all have the same form. For a fixed binary associative relation $\otimes$, we want to compute $\otimes_{i=0}^{n-1} a[i]$ on an array a. This problem is known as the **semigroup problem** since a set of elements together with an associative binary relation is called a **semigroup**. Other problems of this form include computing the maximum, where $\otimes = \max$, and computing the product of n numbers, where $\otimes = \times$.

In the introductory section, we presented two algorithms for computing the maximum: one sequential, the other parallel. The sequential algorithm took time $O(n)$. The parallel algorithm took time $O(\lg n)$ and work $O(n \lg n)$. Both algorithms can be made to work for any associative binary relation $\otimes$ that can be computed in constant time (such as max, $+$, or $\times$).

Algorithm 12.2.11 Sequential $\otimes$-Sum. This algorithm computes $\otimes_{i=0}^{n-1} a[i]$ given an array a as input.

Input Parameter: a
Output Parameters: None

```
sequential_⊗_sum(a) {
  n = a.length
  current_sum = a[0]
  for i = 1 to n − 1
    current_sum = current_sum ⊗ a[i]
  return current_sum
}
```

We can also adapt the approach shown in Figure 12.1.2 to compute the $\otimes$-sum on a parallel machine. We computed the maximum by first computing the maximum of each pair in parallel and then the maximum of each pair of maxima of pairs and so on. To compute the $\otimes$-sum, we pursue the same strategy. We start by splitting the input into blocks of size 2 and compute the $\otimes$-sum of each block and then repeat doubling the size of the blocks until we have computed the full $\otimes$-sum, as shown in Figure 12.2.1.

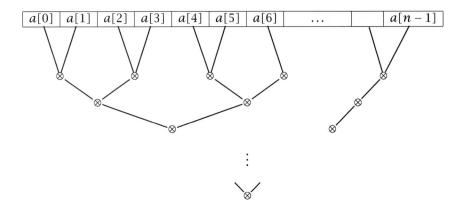

Figure 12.2.1 Computing the $\otimes$-sum on a parallel machine.

We have to convert Figure 12.2.1 into a parallel algorithm. To keep the results of each parallel step, we store the $\otimes$-sum of each block in the first element of that block. Initially the block size is 1; that is, each block consists of a single element, which, therefore, is its own $\otimes$-sum. In the ith phase of the algorithm, the blocksize is 2^{i+1}. The first elements of the blocks are at positions $j \times 2^{i+1}$, where j ranges from 0 to $\lceil n/2^{i+1} \rceil - 1$. For example, for $i = 0$ (blocksize $2 = 2^{i+1}$), the blocks start at 0, 2, 4, 6, and so on; for $i = 1$, they begin at 0, 4, 8, and so on.

Algorithm 12.2.12 Parallel $\otimes$-sum. This EREW algorithm computes $\otimes_{i=0}^{n-1} a[i]$, given an array a as input.

    Input Parameter: a
Output Parameters: None

```
parallel_ ⊗ _sum(a) {
   n = a.length
   for i = 0 to ⌈lg n⌉ − 1
      for j = 0 to ⌈n/2^{i+1}⌉ − 1 in parallel
         if (j × 2^{i+1} + 2^i < n)
            a[j × 2^{i+1}] = a[j × 2^{i+1}] ⊗ a[j × 2^{i+1} + 2^i]
   return a[0]
}
```

Example 12.2.13. We trace $parallel\_ \otimes \_sum$ on the array

$$a = [10, 3, 6, 17, 24, 13, 7, 23, 42, 12],$$

where $\otimes$ is the maximum operator. We begin with a blocksize of 1, each element being its own block.

	$a[0]$	$a[1]$	$a[2]$	$a[3]$	$a[4]$	$a[5]$	$a[6]$	$a[7]$	$a[8]$	$a[9]$
start	10	3	6	17	24	13	7	23	42	12

When $i = 0$ the blocksize is $2^{i+1} = 2$. The parallel loop becomes

for $j = 0$ to $\lceil n/2 \rceil - 1$ in parallel
   if $(j \times 2 + 1 < n)$
      $a[j \times 2] = a[j \times 2] \otimes a[j \times 2 + 1]$,

which means that we compute the maximum of each pair and write the result into the cell containing the first element of the pair.

	$a[0]$	$a[1]$	$a[2]$	$a[3]$	$a[4]$	$a[5]$	$a[6]$	$a[7]$	$a[8]$	$a[9]$
start	10	3	6	17	24	13	7	23	42	12
$i = 0$	10	3	17	17	24	13	23	23	42	12

We boxed the first element of each block. In the next step, $i = 1$ and the blocksize becomes 4. We pair the blocks of size 2 from the previous step, compute the maximum of their first elements, and write the result into the first element of the blocks of length 4.

	$a[0]$	$a[1]$	$a[2]$	$a[3]$	$a[4]$	$a[5]$	$a[6]$	$a[7]$	$a[8]$	$a[9]$
$i = 0$	10	3	17	17	24	13	23	23	42	12
$i = 1$	17	3	17	17	24	13	23	23	42	12

For $i = 2$ we repeat the process to get two blocks of size (at most) 8.

	$a[0]$	$a[1]$	$a[2]$	$a[3]$	$a[4]$	$a[5]$	$a[6]$	$a[7]$	$a[8]$	$a[9]$
$i = 1$	17	3	17	17	24	13	23	23	42	12
$i = 2$	24	3	17	17	24	13	23	23	42	12

Finally as i becomes 3 we have reduced the array to one block.

	$a[0]$	$a[1]$	$a[2]$	$a[3]$	$a[4]$	$a[5]$	$a[6]$	$a[7]$	$a[8]$	$a[9]$
$i = 2$	24	3	17	17	24	13	23	23	42	12
$i = 3$	42	3	17	17	24	13	23	23	42	12

The first element of the only remaining block, $a[0] = 42$, is the maximum of the array. □

Example 12.2.14. Let us trace *parallel_ ⊗ _sum* for the array

$$a = [10, 3, 6, 17, 24, 13, 7, 23, 42, 12]$$

of Example 12.2.13, this time with ⊗ being addition. We show only the results with the first element of each block being boxed.

	$a[0]$	$a[1]$	$a[2]$	$a[3]$	$a[4]$	$a[5]$	$a[6]$	$a[7]$	$a[8]$	$a[9]$
start	10	3	6	17	24	13	7	23	42	12
$i = 0$	13	3	23	17	37	13	30	23	56	12
$i = 1$	36	3	23	17	67	13	30	23	56	12
$i = 2$	103	3	23	17	67	13	30	23	56	12
$i = 3$	159	3	23	17	67	13	30	23	56	12

Hence, the sum of all elements in the array is $a[0] = 159$. □

Theorem 12.2.15. *Algorithm 12.2.12 is an EREW algorithm computing the $\otimes$-sum of an array correctly in parallel time $O(\lg n)$ and work $O(n \lg n)$ if $\otimes$ is associative.*

Proof. The outer for loop repeats the inner for loop $O(\lg n)$ times. Since the inner loop takes only $O(1)$ parallel time, the algorithm takes parallel time $O(\lg n)$. The index of the inner for loop is always bounded by n, so we never need more than n processors, which shows that the work is $O(n \lg n)$.

The algorithm works correctly since, in each parallel step, the first element of every block contains the $\otimes$-sum of the elements of the block. When we double the blocksize, we add the $\otimes$-sums of the two old blocks within the new block, giving us the correct sum for the new block. We need $\otimes$ to be associative since we are applying the operator $\otimes$ in a particular order (as determined by the block structure). ∎

Our parallel $\otimes$-sum algorithm is not work-optimal since it has work $O(n \lg n)$, whereas the sequential algorithm has work $O(n)$ only. We can reduce the work of *parallel_ $\otimes$ _sum* to $O(n)$ by a popular technique called **accelerated cascading**. In accelerated cascading we combine two algorithms: one that is slow, but work-optimal (*sequential_ $\otimes$ _sum* in our case), with one that is fast, but not work-optimal (*parallel_ $\otimes$ _sum*). In the first phase, we run the slow algorithm on small instances of the problem to reduce the overall problem size, and then, in the second phase, we run the fast algorithm.

To achieve work $O(n)$ in our case, we should use only $O(n/\lg n)$ processors in each of the $O(\lg n)$ steps. That is possible if we can reduce the input size from n to $O(n/\lg n)$. We do this by beginning with blocks of size $\lg n$. Using $n/\lg n$ processors, one for each block, we compute the $\otimes$-sum of each block by running the slow *sequential_ $\otimes$ _sum*. This takes the $n/\lg n$ processors time $O(\lg n)$. We are left with $n/\lg n$ elements whose $\otimes$-sum we have to compute for which we can now use the fast *parallel_ $\otimes$ _sum*. Figure 12.2.2 shows the two phases of the work-optimal parallel $\otimes$-sum algorithm.

Algorithm 12.2.16 Optimal $\otimes$-Sum. This algorithm computes $\otimes_{i=0}^{n-1} a[i]$ given an array a as input.

Input Parameter: a
Output Parameters: None

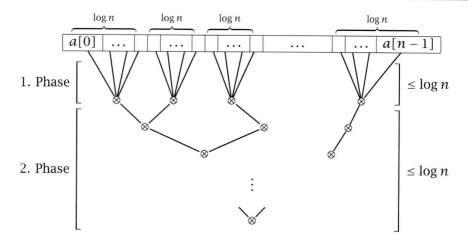

Figure 12.2.2 Making ⊗-sum work-optimal using accelerated cascading. The processors work in two phases. In the first phase, $n/\lg n$ processors implement the sequential ⊗-sum algorithm on blocks of $\lg n$ inputs each. This phase takes $\lg n$ parallel steps since each processor has to access $\lg n$ elements one by one. After the first phase, we use the parallel ⊗-sum algorithm to compute the ⊗-sum of the $n/\lg n$ elements left after the first phase. This takes $\lg n$ parallel steps. Every step of the algorithm, both in the first and the second phase, needs at most $n/\lg n$ processors; hence, the work is $\Theta(n)$.

$optimal\_\otimes\_sum(a)$ {
  $n = a.length$
  $blocksize = 2^{\lceil \lg \lg n \rceil}$
  // first compute ⊗ sum of all blocks of size $blocksize \approx \lg n$
  for $i = 0$ to $\lfloor n/blocksize \rfloor$ in parallel {
    $base = i \times blocksize$
    for $j = 1$ to $blocksize - 1$
      if $(base + j < n)$
        $a[base] = a[base] \otimes a[base + j]$
  }
  // second compute the ⊗ sum of the remaining $\lfloor n/blocksize \rfloor$ elements
  for $i = \lg blocksize$ to $\lceil \lg n \rceil - 1$
    for $j = 0$ to $\lceil n/2^{i+1} \rceil - 1$ in parallel
      if $(j \times 2^{i+1} + 2^i < n)$
        $a[j \times 2^{i+1}] = a[j \times 2^{i+1}] \otimes a[j \times 2^{i+1} + 2^i]$
  return $a[0]$
}

Example 12.2.17. Let us trace $optimal\_\otimes\_sum$ for

$$a = [1, 2, 3, 4, 5, 6, 7, 8, 9, 10, 11]$$

and $\otimes = +$. We have $n = 11$, and therefore *blocksize* is 4 ($\lg\lg 11$ is roughly 1.8). The first part of the algorithm splits the array into blocks of size 4 and in parallel computes the sum of each block sequentially. In the table we have boxed the first element of each block.

	$a[0]$	$a[1]$	$a[2]$	$a[3]$	$a[4]$	$a[5]$	$a[6]$	$a[7]$	$a[8]$	$a[9]$	$a[10]$
start	1	2	3	4	5	6	7	8	9	10	11
$j = 1$	3	2	3	4	11	6	7	8	19	10	11
$j = 2$	6	2	3	4	18	6	7	8	30	10	11
$j = 3$	10	2	3	4	26	6	7	8	30	10	11

At this point, the first element of each block contains the sum of the original elements in that block: $10 = 1 + 2 + 3 + 4$, and $30 = 9 + 10 + 11$, for example. The algorithm now continues by running *parallel_$\otimes$_sum*, with the difference that we can now start out i as $2 = \lg\ blocksize$ since we have already summed the blocks of size 4.

	$a[0]$	$a[1]$	$a[2]$	$a[3]$	$a[4]$	$a[5]$	$a[6]$	$a[7]$	$a[8]$	$a[9]$	$a[10]$
start	10	2	3	4	26	6	7	8	30	10	11

For $i = 2$ we combine blocks of size 4 to obtain blocks of size 8.

	$a[0]$	$a[1]$	$a[2]$	$a[3]$	$a[4]$	$a[5]$	$a[6]$	$a[7]$	$a[8]$	$a[9]$	$a[10]$
start	10	2	3	4	26	6	7	8	30	10	11
$i = 2$	36	2	3	4	26	6	7	8	30	10	11

For $i = 3$ we combine the remaining two blocks to get one block.

	$a[0]$	$a[1]$	$a[2]$	$a[3]$	$a[4]$	$a[5]$	$a[6]$	$a[7]$	$a[8]$	$a[9]$	$a[10]$
$i = 2$	36	2	3	4	26	6	7	8	30	10	11
$i = 3$	66	2	3	4	26	6	7	8	30	10	11

At this point $a[0] = 66$ is the sum of the original elements of a.   □

Theorem 12.2.18. *The EREW algorithm optimal_$\otimes$_sum computes the $\otimes$-sum of an array in parallel time $O(\lg n)$ and work $O(n)$.*

Proof. Since $blocksize = 2^{\lceil \lg\lg n \rceil} \geq 2^{\lg\lg n} = \lg n$, we know that the first parallel loop (which implements the first phase) needs at most $n/\lg n$ processors. Also, $blocksize = 2^{\lceil \lg\lg n \rceil} \leq 2^{1+\lg\lg n} = 2\lg n$ and therefore, the inner for loop takes time $O(\lg n)$. Since the inner loop is executed in parallel, the first phase of the algorithm takes parallel time $O(\lg n)$ and work $O(n)$.

The outer loop of the second phase of the algorithm runs $O(\lg n)$ times; hence, it takes parallel time $O(\lg n)$ since the inner loop is performed in parallel. How many processors do we need for the inner loop? The index runs only up to $\lceil n/2^{i+1} \rceil - 1$, which is less than $n/\lg n$ since i starts at $\lg$ *blocksize*; therefore,

$$\lceil n/2^{i+1} \rceil - 1 \le n/2^{i+1} \le n/2^{1+\lg blocksize} \le n/blocksize \le n/\lg n.$$

Again this gives us parallel time $O(\lg n)$ and work $O(n)$.

We conclude that the algorithm runs in parallel time $O(\lg n)$ and work $O(n)$. Since the algorithm is a combination of two EREW algorithms, it is itself an EREW algorithm. The correctness follows from the correctness of its two constituent algorithms. ∎

Corollary 12.2.19. *If the best sequential algorithm for $\otimes$-sum takes time $\Theta(n)$, then optimal_$\otimes$_sum is work-optimal.*

The corollary applies to most tasks, including computing the maximum and summing n values since a sequential algorithm has to look at all inputs to determine the output, and this takes time $\Omega(n)$.

In some cases, the running time can still be improved. For example, Exercise 12.2 asks you to implement a CRCW algorithm computing the maximum of n elements in constant parallel time using n^2 processors. With that number of processors, the algorithm is not work-optimal. A slightly different approach gives a CRCW algorithm for computing the maximum running in time $\Theta(\lg \lg n)$ and work $\Theta(n)$. For EREW machines it can be argued that any parallel algorithm for finding the maximum of n elements has to take time $\Omega(\lg n)$. More surprisingly, Cook, Dwork, and Reischuk in 1986 showed that this $\Omega(\lg n)$ lower bound still holds for CREW models.

The technique of accelerated cascading can be applied to our broadcasting algorithm, Algorithm 12.2.5. The task is to write an ER algorithm to assign the value of a variable x to all elements of an array a. Our algorithm *er_broadcast* solved the problem in parallel time $O(\lg n)$ and work $O(n \lg n)$. This is not work-optimal since a sequential algorithm solves the problem in time—and therefore work—$O(n)$. At this point we apply accelerated cascading. We use the fast, suboptimal *er_broadcast* to broadcast x to the first $n/(\lg n)$ elements of the array and then use $n/(\lg n)$ processors to fill $\lg n$ copies of each element into the remaining positions.

Algorithm 12.2.20 Optimal ER Broadcast. This algorithm takes as input a value x and an array a and assigns x to all elements of the array.

    Input Parameters: a, x
Output Parameters: None

```
optimal_er_broadcast(a, x) {
    n = a.length
    n' = ⌈n/ lg n⌉
    a[0] = x
```

```
// Use er_broadcast to fill the first n' cells of a with x
for i = 0 to ⌈lg n'⌉ − 1
    for j = 0 to 2^i − 1 in parallel
        if (2^i + j < n')
            a[2^i + j] = a[j]
// Spread the contents using n' processors
// each performing the sequential algorithm
for i = 1 to ⌈lg n⌉
    for j = 0 to n' − 1 in parallel
        if (i × n' + j < n)
            a[i × n' + j] = a[j]
}
```

Example 12.2.21. Let us trace *optimal_er_broadcast* for $x = 0$, and $n = 20$. Then $n' = 5$. The first pair of nested for loops fills the first five elements of the array with zeros using the recursive doubling technique of *er_broadcast* as illustrated by Figure 12.2.3.

	$a[0]$	$a[1]$	$a[2]$	$a[3]$	$a[4]$	$a[5]$	$a[6]$	$a[7]$	$\cdots$	$a[19]$
start	0								$\cdots$	
$i = 0$	0	**0**							$\cdots$	
$i = 1$	0	0	**0**	**0**					$\cdots$	
$i = 2$	0	0	0	0	**0**				$\cdots$	

Figure 12.2.3 Filling the first $n' = 5$ cells of x.

The second pair of for loops now duplicates the block of five zeros into each of the remaining 3 blocks as shown in Figure 12.2.4.

	$a[0]$	$a[1]$	$a[2]$	$a[3]$	$a[4]$	$a[5]$	$a[6]$	$a[7]$	$a[8]$	$a[9]$
start	0	0	0	0	0					
$i = 1$	0	0	0	0	0	**0**	**0**	**0**	**0**	**0**
$i = 2$	0	0	0	0	0	0	0	0	0	0
$i = 3$	0	0	0	0	0	0	0	0	0	0

	$a[10]$	$a[11]$	$a[12]$	$a[13]$	$a[14]$	$a[15]$	$a[16]$	$a[17]$	$a[18]$	$a[19]$
start										
$i = 1$										
$i = 2$	**0**	**0**	**0**	**0**	**0**					
$i = 3$	0	0	0	0	0	**0**	**0**	**0**	**0**	**0**

Figure 12.2.4 Distributing the contents of the initialized $n' = 5$ cells.   □

Let us analyze *optimal_er_broadcast*. The first part of the algorithm takes parallel time $O(\lg n')$, which is $O(\lg n)$, using at most $2^{\lceil \lg n' \rceil - 1} \le n' \le n/\lg n$ processors. The second part also takes time $O(\lg n)$ using at most $n' \le n/\lg n$ processors. Hence, the algorithm takes parallel time $O(\lg n)$ and work $O(n)$. Correctness follows from the correctness of the two algorithms we combined, the parallel and the sequential one. The algorithm is an EREW algorithm since in both parts the variables we read and write to the array are unique to the processor.

Theorem 12.2.22. *optimal_er_broadcast is a work-optimal EREW algorithm solving the broadcasting problem in $O(\lg n)$ time.*

Parallel Prefix

Imagine we are analyzing market data and we want to track the highs of a particular stock. We are given a list of daily closing values of the stock. For every day we want to know the highest price the stock has reached up to that day.

Example 12.2.23. Here is a history of a fictional stock with the highest closing prices up to each day.

	6/1	6/2	6/3	6/4	6/5	6/6	6/7	6/8	6/9
close	11.89	14.10	14.59	15.75	15.01	16.20	15.86	14.95	14.08
max	11.89	14.10	14.59	15.75	15.75	16.20	16.20	16.20	16.20

$\square$

We can use Algorithm 12.2.12 to compute the maximum up to each particular day; but since we would have to run the algorithm separately for every day, this approach is inefficient. We can imagine other problems in which, instead of one final result, we also want partial results up to each point. Examples include partial sums or averages (see Exercise 12.5), and precomputing the carries when adding two numbers (see Exercise 12.8). As in the case of semigroup algorithms, we have a binary associative operator $\otimes$ on a fixed set. The **parallel-prefix problem** is to compute all values $\otimes_{i=0}^{k} a[i]$ for $0 \le k < n$, where $\otimes_{i=0}^{k} a[i]$ is called the $(k+1)$**st prefix**. The problem is also known as the **prefix-sum problem**.

Example 12.2.24. In the stock market Example 12.2.23, we can let $\otimes = \max$; hence $\otimes_{i=0}^{k} a[i]$ is the maximum of the values $a[0]$ through $a[k]$. $\square$

If $\otimes$ can be computed efficiently, as will be the case in most natural examples, then we can compute the prefixes in sequential time $O(n)$.

Algorithm 12.2.25 Sequential Prefix. This algorithm computes the prefixes $sum[k] = \otimes_{i=0}^{k} a[i]$ for all $0 \le k < n$ given an n-element array a as input.

Input Parameter: a
Output Parameters: None

```
sequential_prefix(a) {
    n = a.length
    sum[0] = a[0]
    for i = 1 to n − 1
        sum[i] = sum[i − 1] ⊗ a[i]
}
```

To explain how we can parallelize the computation of the prefixes, let us go back to Algorithm 12.2.2 in which we computed the $\otimes$-sum of an array. Example 12.2.14 shows how the algorithm in each step doubles the length of the blocks whose $\otimes$-sum it computes. We use this idea of doubling the block length to compute the parallel prefixes fast. Figure 12.2.5 shows how we can use this idea to compute prefixes.

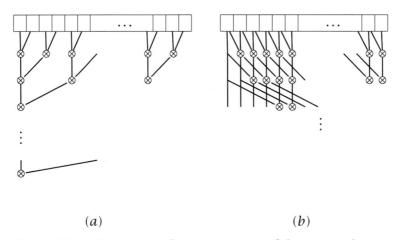

(a)   (b)

Figure 12.2.5 Comparing the computation of the $\otimes$-sum shown in (a) to the computation of all prefixes shown in (b).

The following algorithm implements this idea: In phase i we compute $a[j − 2^i] \otimes \cdots \otimes a[j]$ for each position j ($2^i \le j < n$). When i is larger than $\lg n$, every array element will contain the correct prefix-sum.

Algorithm 12.2.26 Parallel Prefix. This algorithm computes the prefixes $sum[k] = \otimes_{i=0}^{k} a[i]$ for all $0 \le k < n$ given an n-element array a as input.

Input Parameter: a
Output Parameters: None

```
parallel_prefix(a) {
    n = a.length
    for j = 0 to n − 1 in parallel
        sum[j] = a[j]
```

> for $i = 0$ to $\lceil \lg n \rceil$
>   for $j = 0$ to $n - 1$ in parallel
>   if $(j + 2^i < n)$
> $sum[j + 2^i] = sum[j] \otimes sum[j + 2^i]$
> }

Example 12.2.27. Let us trace *parallel_prefix* for

$$a = [10, 2, 13, 7, 32, 11, 3, 5]$$

and $\otimes = +$.

	$a[0]$	$a[1]$	$a[2]$	$a[3]$	$a[4]$	$a[5]$	$a[6]$	$a[7]$
start	10	2	13	7	32	11	3	5

For $i = 0$ we perform

$$sum[j + 1] = sum[j] + sum[j + 1]$$

for all $j < n - 1$ *in parallel.* It is important that the processors act simultaneously. For example, $sum[2] = sum[1] + sum[2] = 2 + 13 = 15$; that is, $sum[1]$ equals 2, although at the end of this stage it will be $12 = 10 + 2$.

	$sum[0]$	$sum[1]$	$sum[2]$	$sum[3]$	$sum[4]$	$sum[5]$	$sum[6]$	$sum[7]$
start	10	2	13	7	32	11	3	5
$i = 0$	10	12	15	20	39	43	14	8

For $i = 1$ we perform

$$sum[j + 2] = sum[j] + sum[j + 2]$$

giving us

	$sum[0]$	$sum[1]$	$sum[2]$	$sum[3]$	$sum[4]$	$sum[5]$	$sum[6]$	$sum[7]$
$i = 0$	10	12	15	20	39	43	14	8
$i = 1$	10	12	25	32	54	63	53	51

and finally, $i = 2$ yields

	$sum[0]$	$sum[1]$	$sum[2]$	$sum[3]$	$sum[4]$	$sum[5]$	$sum[6]$	$sum[7]$
$i = 1$	10	12	25	32	54	63	53	51
$i = 2$	10	12	25	32	64	75	78	83

and the algorithm stops. Figure 12.2.6 shows the original array together with the final results.

	0	1	2	3	4	5	6	7
a	10	2	13	7	32	11	3	5
sum	10	12	25	32	64	75	78	83

Figure 12.2.6 Array a together with its partial prefix sums.

Let us trace the computation of a single element, say $sum[6]$.

$$
\begin{aligned}
sum[6] &= sum[2] + sum[6] & \text{for } i = 2 \\
&= sum[0] + sum[2] + sum[4] + sum[6] & \text{for } i = 1 \\
&= sum[0] + sum[1] + sum[2] + sum[3] \\
&\quad + sum[4] + sum[5] + sum[6] & \text{for } i = 0 \\
&= a[0] + a[1] + a[2] + a[3] + a[4] + a[5] + a[6],
\end{aligned}
$$

which is the correct value. □

Example 12.2.28. As another example, let us work with the data from the stock market Example 12.2.23. Here we choose $\otimes$ = max. The algorithm proceeds as shown in Figure 12.2.7.

	6/1	6/2	/6/3	6/4	6/5	6/6	6/7	6/8	6/9
close	11.89	14.10	14.59	15.75	15.01	16.20	15.86	14.95	14.08
$i = 0$	11.89	14.10	14.59	15.75	15.75	16.20	16.20	15.86	14.95
$i = 1$	11.89	14.10	14.59	15.75	15.75	16.20	16.20	16.20	16.20
$i = 2$	11.89	14.10	14.59	15.75	15.75	16.20	16.20	16.20	16.20
$i = 3$	11.89	14.10	14.59	15.75	15.75	16.20	16.20	16.20	16.20

Figure 12.2.7 The computation of Algorithm 12.2.26 computing partial prefix maximums. □

Theorem 12.2.29. *The EREW algorithm parallel_prefix solves the parallel-prefix problem in parallel time $O(\lg n)$ and work $O(n \lg n)$.*

Proof. The initialization loop takes parallel time $O(1)$ using n processors. The nested loops run in parallel time $O(\lg n)$ also using n processors. Hence, the algorithm runs in parallel time $O(\lg n)$ and work $O(n \lg n)$.

The correctness of the algorithm follows from the fact that, in each step of the second for loop, $sum[k]$ contains the $\otimes$-sum of the 2^i elements up to $a[k]$ (or the first k elements if $2^i > k$). Hence, when 2^i becomes larger than n, each $sum[k]$ contains the sum of the first k elements. We leave a formal proof with loop invariant to Exercise 23. ∎

As in the case of semigroup algorithms, we can use accelerated cascading to reduce the work to $O(n)$, which is optimal. We use the slow but work-optimal sequential algorithms for blocks up to length $\lg n$ and then the fast, suboptimal *parallel_prefix* algorithm on the $n/\lg n$ last elements of those blocks. Finally, we have to distribute the prefixes over these blocks. We leave the implementation to Exercise 24, but we present a sample run in the following example.

Example 12.2.30. Assume that $a = [24, 32, 10, 11, 7, 16, 9, 45, 2, 19, 31, 5]$ and $\otimes = +$. We have $n = 11$; let us split a into blocks of length $\lfloor \lg 12 \rfloor = 3$. In the first phase, we use the sequential algorithm on each block in parallel to compute the prefixes for each block. We have boxed the first element of each block.

	$a[0]$	$a[1]$	$a[2]$	$a[3]$	$a[4]$	$a[5]$	$a[6]$	$a[7]$	$a[8]$	$a[9]$	$a[10]$	$a[11]$
start	24	32	10	11	7	16	9	45	2	19	31	5
$i = 0$	24	56	10	11	18	16	9	54	2	19	50	5
$i = 1$	24	56	66	11	18	34	9	54	56	19	50	55

In the second phase, we run *parallel_prefix* on the last elements of these blocks: 66, 34, 56 and 55. For readability we do not display the elements that are not affected in this phase.

	$a[0]$	$a[1]$	$a[2]$	$a[3]$	$a[4]$	$a[5]$	$a[6]$	$a[7]$	$a[8]$	$a[9]$	$a[10]$	$a[11]$
start	24	56	66	11	18	34	9	54	56	19	50	55
$i = 0$			66			100			90			101
$i = 1$			66			100			156			201

The array now looks as follows:

	$a[0]$	$a[1]$	$a[2]$	$a[3]$	$a[4]$	$a[5]$	$a[6]$	$a[7]$	$a[8]$	$a[9]$	$a[10]$	$a[11]$
start	24	56	66	11	18	100	9	54	156	19	50	201

During the last phase, we now use the prefixes we have just computed in the second phase to compute the prefixes within the blocks. For this, we use the sequential algorithm.

	$a[0]$	$a[1]$	$a[2]$	$a[3]$	$a[4]$	$a[5]$	$a[6]$	$a[7]$	$a[8]$	$a[9]$	$a[10]$	$a[11]$
start	24	56	66	11	18	100	9	54	156	19	50	201
$i = 0$	24	56	66	77	18	100	109	54	156	165	50	201
$i = 1$	24	56	66	77	84	100	109	154	156	165	206	201

Here is the result displayed together with the original array:

	$a[0]$	$a[1]$	$a[2]$	$a[3]$	$a[4]$	$a[5]$	$a[6]$	$a[7]$	$a[8]$	$a[9]$	$a[10]$	$a[11]$
a	24	32	10	11	7	16	9	45	2	19	31	5
sum	24	56	66	77	84	100	109	154	156	165	206	201

$\square$

Pointer Jumping

When processing a linked list node by node, it is sometimes useful to know how many nodes remain to be processed. This task is easy to solve for an array since we know the size of an array. A linked list, however, changes dynamically, making it expensive to keep information about how far each node is from the end of the list up to date. This leads us to the following task that is known as **list ranking**: Given a linked list, compute for each node in the list how far it is from the end of the list. The distance of a node from the end of the list is known as its **rank**. More formally, for a node u we can define its rank recursively as follows: If u is the last node in the linked list, then $rank(u) = 1$; otherwise, u is followed by a node $u.next$, and we can let $rank(u) = rank(u.next) + 1$.

To compute the rank sequentially, we first read through the whole list to determine its length and then traverse the list a second time to assign the ranks. This algorithm takes time $\Theta(n)$, where n is the length of the linked list.

Algorithm 12.2.31 Sequential List Ranking. This algorithm takes as an input the first node u of a linked list. Each node has fields *next*, the next node of the list or null for the last node in the list, and *rank*, which is assigned the distance of the node from the end of the list.

```
    Input Parameter:     u
Output Parameters:     None

sequential_list_ranking(u) {
    n = 0 // counter for total number of nodes
    node = u
    while (node ! = null) {
        n = n + 1
        node = node.next
    }
    node = u // start again at the beginning
    while (node ! = null) {
        node.rank = n
        n = n - 1
        node = node.next
    }
}
```

On a parallel computer, we might try to have a processor for each node that computes the distance from the end by waiting for the result from the processor belonging to the next node. This leads to a $\Theta(n)$ solution since each processor has to wait for all of its successors. In particular, the first processor has to wait $\Theta(n)$ time, which is no improvement on *sequential_list_ranking*; as a matter of fact it is worse, since it needs n processors.

The solution is a trick we have seen in a different guise when computing parallel prefixes. There we also had to compute a value for each element, namely the sum of all preceding elements. We can look at the list-ranking problem in the same way: If each node contains the value 1 initially, then list ranking is the same as solving a parallel-suffix problem (suffix, rather than prefix, since we sum from the end). The strategy of recursive doubling we used for parallel prefixes is called **pointer jumping** in the context of lists. A look at the algorithm shows why this name is appropriate.

For the list-ranking algorithm we assume that each node is assigned to a unique processor. This allows us to write code working on all nodes of the list in parallel. For a node u, let $L(u)$ be the list that starts with u. We write

    for each *node* in $L(u)$ in parallel
      node.rank = 1

to mean that we initialize the field *rank* of each node in $L(u)$ to the value 1 in constant parallel time. In other words, each processor writes the value 1 into the field *rank* of the node it holds. The code might suggest the following solution to the list-ranking problem:

    for $i = 1$ to n in parallel
      node.rank = i

This code would be hard to implement, however, since we cannot guarantee that processor i is assigned to the node of rank i. While we might make such a guarantee when the linked list is first created, it would be very expensive to reassign processors as the linked list changes dynamically.

Algorithm 12.2.32 List Ranking. This algorithm takes as an input the first node u of a linked list $L(u)$. Each node has fields *next*, the next node of the list or null for the last node in the list, and *rank*, which is assigned the distance of the node from the end of the list.

   Input Parameter: u
  Output Parameters: None

```
list_ranking(u) {
    for each node in L(u) in parallel
        node.rank = 1
    done = false
    do {
        for each node in L(u) in parallel
            if (node.next == null)
                done = true
```

```
        else {
            node.rank = node.rank + node.next.rank
            node.next = node.next.next
        }
    } while (!done)
}
```

The assignment *node.next = node.next.next* explains the name pointer jumping for this technique of computing the list ranks. The following example shows how the pointers jump.

Example 12.2.33. Let us trace the algorithm on a linked list of 14 elements. In the first parallel step we initialize the rank of each node to 1.

In the main loop, we add to the rank of each element the rank of the element it is pointing to and change its successor to the successor of that element. The first step results in

Only three more steps are sufficient to compute the rank of each element.

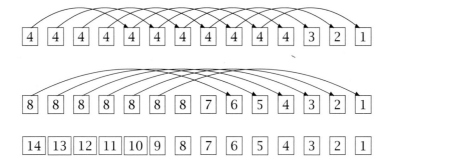

Theorem 12.2.34. *The EREW algorithm list_ranking computes the rank of each node in a linked list of length n in time $O(\lg n)$ and work $O(n \lg n)$.*

Proof. After each node in $L(u)$ has been assigned rank 1, each list $L(v)$ (the list starting at v) contains $rank(v)$ nodes. Since each node has a rank value of 1, the sum of the rank values in $L(v)$ is the same as $rank(v)$. More succinctly,

$$rank(v) = \sum_{w \in L(v)} w.rank.$$

Performing the pointer jump corresponds to taking the first two elements out

$$rank(v) \quad = \quad \sum_{w \in L(v)} w.rank$$

$$= \quad v.rank + v.next.rank + \sum_{w \in L(v.next.next)} w.rank.$$

Hence, to compute $rank(v)$, the algorithm adds $v.next.rank$ to $v.rank$ and removes the node $v.next$ from $L(v)$ by changing $v.next$ to $v.next.next$.

After at most $\lceil \lg n \rceil$ steps the algorithm terminates since all next pointers are null. ∎

Exercises

1S. Show that the variable j in *er_broadcast* takes on values of order $\Theta(n)$.

2. Trace *er_broadcast* for $x = 2$ and $n = 19$.

3. Modify *er_broadcast* so that the loop over j runs up to $\min\{2^i - 1, n - 2^i - 1\}$. Why does the modified algorithm still work correctly?

4S. Example 12.2.9 claims that there is an ER $O(\lg n)$ parallel-time algorithm for parallel search. Write out such an algorithm. What is its work?

5. Write an $\Theta(\lg n)$ algorithm computing the maximum of an array of n numbers in the EREW model.

6. Modify *locate* to run on a CREW PRAM in parallel time $\Theta(\lg n)$. The algorithm should return the first location at which x was found or -1 if x is not contained in the array.

7S. Trace *parallel_$\otimes$_sum* for $\otimes = +$ and $a = [31, 24, 71, 3, 12, 28]$.

8. Trace *parallel_$\otimes$_sum* for $\otimes = \min$ and $a = [9, 8, 7, 6, 5, 4, 3, 2, 1]$.

9. Trace *parallel_$\otimes$_sum* for $\otimes = \times$ and $a = [5, 2, 3, 1, 4]$.

10S. Does *parallel_$\otimes$_sum* still work correctly if i runs from 0 to $\lfloor \lg n \rfloor - 1$ instead of $\lceil \lg n \rceil - 1$? If so, prove it; otherwise give a counterexample.

11. Does *parallel_$\otimes$_sum* still work correctly if j runs from 0 to $\lfloor n/2^{i+1} \rfloor - 1$ instead of $\lceil n/2^{i+1} \rceil - 1$? If so, prove it; otherwise give a counterexample.

12. Give an example of an operator $\otimes$ and an array a for which *parallel_$\otimes$_sum* fails to compute the correct $\otimes$-sum of the array. *Hint:* Because of Theorem 12.2.15, the operators $\otimes$ cannot be associative in this case.

13S. Trace *optimal_$\otimes$_sum* for $\otimes = *$ and

$$a = [2,2,2,2,2,2,2,2,2,2].$$

14. Trace *optimal_$\otimes$_sum* for $\otimes = +$ and

$$a = [1,2,3,4,5,6,7,8,9,10,11,12,13,14].$$

15. Trace *optimal_$\otimes$_sum* for $\otimes = \max$ and

$$a = [23,1,34,55,4,11,91,4,12,3,30,2,1,20].$$

16S. Trace *optimal_er_broadcast* for $x = 3$ and $n = 25$.

17. Trace *optimal_er_broadcast* for $x = 3$ and $n = 32$.

18. Professor Curly suggests that we can reduce the number of processors used by *optimal_er_broadcast* by one if we let $n' = \lfloor n/\log n \rfloor$ and change the first for loop so that i runs up to $\lceil n' \rceil$ instead of $\lceil n' \rceil - 1$. Does this modified algorithm still work correctly? If not, give a counterexample.

19S. Trace *parallel_prefix* on

$$a = [1,2,3,4,5,6,7,8,9,10]$$

and $\otimes = *$.

20. Trace *parallel_prefix* on

$$a = [19,61,12,31,23,24,54,91,23,41,93,12]$$

and $\otimes = +$.

21. Trace *parallel_prefix* on

$$a = [93,15,1,4,2,67,43,12,89,71,23,47,19,12,33,87]$$

and $\otimes = \min$.

22S. Simple graphics programs usually allow us to change the orientation of pictures by flipping horizontally (h) and rotating by 90 degrees (r). This leads to eight possible positions the picture can be in, namely $1, r, r^2, r^3, h, hr, hr^2, hr^3$. For example, 1 is the original position (which is the same as h^2 and r^4), and hr^2 is the same as flipping the picture vertically. Define a table for $\otimes$ that corresponds to performing the operations sequentially; for example, $r \otimes r = r^2$ and $hr^3 \otimes hr^2 = r$. Using this table for $\otimes$, trace *parallel_prefix* on $a = [r,r,h,r,h,h,r,r,h,r,h,r,r,r,h,r,h,r]$.

23. Show that *parallel_prefix* is correct using the loop invariant

$$sum[k] = \otimes_{\ell=\max\{k-2^i+1,0\}}^{k} a[\ell] \text{ for all } 0 \le k < n.$$

(See Section 2.2 for information on loop invariants.)

24S. Write pseudocode for a work-optimal $O(\lg n)$ parallel-time EREW algorithm to solve the parallel-prefix problem.

25. Trace the work-optimal version of *parallel_prefix* on

$$a = [19, 61, 12, 31, 23, 24, 54, 91, 23, 41, 93, 12]$$

and $\otimes = +$ (as in Example 12.2.30).

26. Trace the work-optimal version of *parallel_prefix* on

$$a = [13, 23, 41, 15, 12, 43, 15, 1, 14, 42, 67, 43]$$

and $\otimes = \max$ (as in Example 12.2.30).

27S. Trace *list_ranking* on a linked list containing 18 nodes.

28. Trace *list_ranking* on a linked list containing 26 nodes.

29. Modify *list_ranking* so that it computes the distance of each node from the beginning of the list. Your new algorithm should still take time $\Theta(\lg n)$.

30S. Professor Gomer Pyle suggests that, in our implementation of *list_ranking*, it is possible that in the last parallel iteration of the for each loop, no more pointer jumping occurs since all of the next fields are already null. If this is true, show an example where this happens and improve the algorithm to eliminate this behavior. Otherwise prove the professor wrong.

12.3 Sorting Networks

Sorting networks are circuits built from a single type of gate, the **comparator gate**. The comparator gate takes as input two numbers and outputs them in order. We draw a comparator as an edge between the two **wires** that are compared.

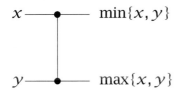

$$x \quad\longrightarrow\quad \min\{x, y\}$$

$$y \quad\longrightarrow\quad \max\{x, y\}$$

A **sorting network** is a circuit of comparator gates that outputs its input in ascending order. We draw a sorting network as a set of wires, one for each input with the comparator gates added between the wires. Before a gate can act, it has to wait until all of its inputs are available. Comparator gates whose wires do not overlap can perform in parallel. When visually presenting a sorting network, we group comparator gates that can perform in parallel together. They form a **layer** of the network. Each layer takes one step to perform (since all comparators in a layer can perform in parallel).

Example 12.3.1. The following network correctly sorts four numbers using five gates in three steps.

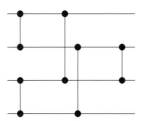

The network consists of three layers: The first and the second layer contain two gates each; the final, third layer contains a single gate. Running the network on inputs 17, 42, 23, and 7 produces:

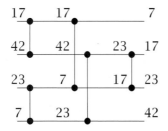

The number of gates used in a network is called the **size** of the network. The **depth** of the network is the number of steps it takes until every comparator gate has computed its output. The sorting network in Example 12.3.1 has size 5 and depth 3, meaning that the numbers are sorted after three steps.

How can we solve the sorting problem for n numbers in general? Let us first solve a simpler problem: How can we find the largest input element? We could first compare the first two inputs, then compare the larger input to the third input, and so on, always comparing the previous result to next input, until we reach the last wire. For eight elements, we obtain the following network of size and depth 7:

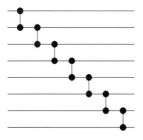

The 7 comparators in the diagonals assure that the largest element makes its way to the lowest wire, where it must go. The idea of the **odd-even transposition network** is to introduce many such diagonals as illustrated in Figure 12.3.1 for $n = 10$.

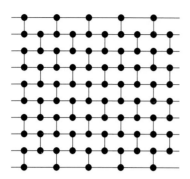

Figure 12.3.1 The odd-even transposition network for $n = 10$ wires. The network has depth 10 and size 45.

An odd-even transposition network on n wires is built from two pairings of the wires. To describe the pairings, we label the wires with numbers 1 through n. The first pairing, which is used during the odd steps, adds comparators between wires 1 and 2, 3 and 4, 5 and 6, etc. The second pairing, used during the even steps, starts with the second wire adding gates between 2 and 3, 4 and 5, and so on. We alternate these pairings $n - 2$ times to get a network of depth n.

Example 12.3.2. Let us run the odd-even transposition network on the array $a = [17, 51, 21, 17, 23, 56, 15, 10, 19, 45]$. To make it easier to read the example, we do not display the wires and comparators but simply present in the columns a snapshot of the array after each step of the network. Column 0 is the input to the network.

0	1	2	3	4	5	6	7	8	9	10
17	17	17	17	17	17	17	10	10	10	10
51	51	17	17	17	17	10	17	15	15	15
21	17	51	21	21	10	17	15	17	17	17
17	21	21	51	10	21	15	17	17	17	17
23	23	23	10	51	15	21	19	19	19	19
56	56	10	23	15	51	19	21	21	21	21
15	10	56	15	23	19	51	23	23	23	23
10	15	15	56	19	23	23	51	45	45	45
19	19	19	19	56	45	45	45	51	51	51
45	45	45	45	45	56	56	56	56	56	56

□

Theorem 12.3.3. *The odd-even transposition network sorts n numbers in n steps using $\Theta(n^2)$ processors.*

We leave the proof of correctness for Exercise 12.12.

While the odd-even transposition network is faster than our best sequential algorithms, the speed-up of a factor of $\lg n$ is bought at the expense of $\Theta(n^2)$ processors. The question is whether we can improve the network, both in depth and in size. This turns out to be a difficult problem. We did not discuss sorting in the PRAM model, where a rather sophisticated parallel version of mergesort solves the problem in time $O(\lg n)$ and work $O(n \lg n)$. It was long conjectured (by Knuth, for example) that these bounds could not be achieved with a sorting network. It came as a surprise then, when Ajtai, Komlós and Szemerédi presented a sorting network of depth $O(\lg n)$ and size $O(n \lg n)$ (Ajtai, Komlós, Szemerédi, 1983). Their construction is very complicated, and, unfortunately, not of practical interest. Our goal in this section is to present a sorting network due to Batcher that has depth $O(\lg^2 n)$ and size $O(n \lg^2 n)$. Batcher used a divide-and-conquer approach to the sorting problem: An input sequence is split into two halves, sorted recursively, and then the halves are merged. The task of efficiently merging two sorted sequences into a single sorted sequence turns out to be more difficult for sorting networks than it is for general algorithms. To solve this problem, we first show how to build a sorting network for special sequences called bitonic sequences. We then apply this sorting network to merge two sorted sequences and finally use that network to construct a general sorting network of depth $O(\lg^2 n)$ and size $O(n \lg^2 n)$.

Bitonic Sort

We approach the sorting problem by first solving it for simple input sequences. The simplest possible input would be a sequence that is already sorted in ascending order in which case there is no work to do. In a next step, we consider sequences that are rotations of increasing sequences. We call a sequence $a_0, \ldots, a_{n-1}$ **cyclically increasing** if there is an index i such that $a_i, \ldots, a_{n-1}, a_0, \ldots a_{i-1}$ is increasing (for $i = 0$ this means the sequence itself is increasing). For example, $(92, 78, 92)$, and $(12, 23, 31, 4, 7)$ are cyclically increasing, whereas $(1, 3, 1, 3)$ and $(12, 3, 2)$ are not. We can visualize a cyclically increasing sequence by writing its numbers on the perimeter of a circle (see Figure 12.3.2).

To simplify the presentation, we assume for the rest of this section that n is a power of 2. We build a network D_n that considers its input as being made up of two halves and compares each element from the first half with an element of the second half; more precisely, every element a_i is compared to $a_{i+n/2}$, where $0 \le i < n/2$. Figure 12.3.3 shows D_{16}. In general D_n has size $n/2$ and depth 1 (since all comparators can work in parallel).

Example 12.3.4. If we give D_8 the sequence $(4, 5, 6, 7, 8, 9, 12, 3)$ it produces as output $(4, 5, 6, 3, 8, 9, 12, 7)$. On $(5, 6, 7, 8, 9, 12, 3, 4)$ the output is $(5, 6, 3, 4, 9, 12, 7, 8)$. For $(6, 7, 8, 9, 12, 3, 4, 5)$ we obtain $(6, 3, 4, 5, 12, 7, 8, 9)$. □

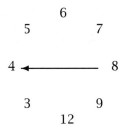

Figure 12.3.2 The cyclically increasing sequence $(4, 5, 6, 7, 8, 9, 12, 3)$ visualized on the perimeter of a circle. The arrow points to the first element in the sequence.

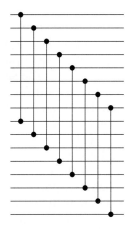

Figure 12.3.3 The D_{16} network.

Consider the two halves of the outputs of D_8 in Example 12.3.4. It appears that D_8 splits a cyclically increasing input sequence into two cyclically increasing output sequences such that all elements of the first half of the output sequence are smaller than the elements in the second half. Before we show that this is true in general, let us see why it is true in a small example.

Example 12.3.5. Let us use the sequence $a = (4, 5, 6, 7, 8, 9, 12, 3)$. The output sequence is $b = (b_0, \ldots, b_7)$. Each element a_i gets compared with a_{i+4}. We visualize this on a circle:

Initially, the arrow points to $a_0 = 4$. Comparing a_0 to a_4 in D_8 corresponds to letting b_0 be the smaller of the two ends of the arrow and a_4 the larger. Hence $b_0 = 4$ and $b_4 = 8$. Rotating the arrow clockwise by one position gives us (ignore the extra line for the moment):

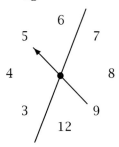

Therefore, $b_1 = 5$ and $b_5 = 9$. Continuing in this manner, we obtain $b = (4, 5, 6, 3, 8, 9, 12, 7)$. We divide the circle into two halves by drawing a line through its center such that maximum and minimum are in opposite halves of the circle. Now observe that the minimum is always on the same side of the arrow (at its head) until the arrow jumps over the line through the center that separates the maximum from the minimum. The reason is that the line separates the cycle into two halves such that every number in the half containing the minimum (3, 4, 5 and 6) is smaller than any number in the other half (7, 8, 9, and 12). As a matter of fact if we look at b, we see that each half of b corresponds to the numbers in one half of the cycle, $(4, 5, 6, 3)$ to $(3, 4, 5, 6)$ and $(8, 9, 12, 7)$ to $7, 8, 9, 12$. This explains why all elements in the first half are smaller than all elements in the second half. It also explains why both halves are cyclically increasing: They are rotations of subsequences of the original sequence.   □

Lemma 12.3.6. *If the input to D_n is a cyclically increasing sequence, then the output $(b_0, \ldots, b_{n-1})$ consists of two cyclically increasing sequences*

$$(b_0, \ldots, b_{n/2-1}) \quad and \quad (b_{n/2}, \ldots, b_{n-1})$$

such that $b_i \leq b_j$ for $0 \leq i < n/2 \leq j < n$; that is, every element of $(b_0, \ldots, b_{n/2-1})$ is smaller than any element of $(b_{n/2}, \ldots, b_{n-1})$.

Proof. Since a is cyclically increasing, we know that there is an index m such that $a_m, \ldots, a_{n-1}, a_0, \ldots, a_{m-1}$ is increasing (possibly $m = 0$). Imagine the sequence arranged on a circle with a line through the center separating the minimum and the maximum element, as shown in Figure 12.3.4.

The line splits the circle into two halves, and we observe that each element in the half containing the minimum is at most as large as each element in the half containing the maximum, since the elements increase as we move clockwise from the minimum to the maximum.

The network D_n calculates

$$b_i = \min\{a_i, a_{i+n/2}\} \quad and \quad b_{i+n/2} = \max\{a_i, a_{i+n/2}\}.$$

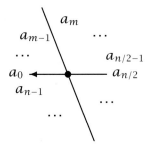

Figure 12.3.4 A sequence $(a_0, \ldots, a_{n-1})$ arranged on a cycle. The arrow initially points to a_0, the first element of the sequence. The line through the center separates a_m, the smallest element, from a_{m-1}, the largest element.

In Figure 12.3.4, for example, b_0 is the smaller and $b_{n/2}$ the larger of the two elements at the two ends of the arrow, and the same is true for b_i and $b_{i+n/2}$ if we rotate the arrow clockwise by i positions. Hence, we can think of computing the output as rotating the arrow step by step $n/2 - 1$ times from its initial position. Note that the two ends of the arrow always lie in opposite halves of the circle. Since all elements in one half are at most as large as all elements in the other half that means that the $b_i = \min\{a_i, a_{i+n/2}\}$ are always picked from the half containing the minimum, while the $b_{i+n/2} = \max\{a_i, a_{i+n/2}\}$ are always picked from the half containing the maximum. This implies that all elements of $(b_0, \ldots, b_{n/2-1})$ are smaller than all elements of $(b_{n/2}, \ldots, b_{n-1})$. Also, these two subsequences are cyclically increasing, since each is the rotation of a subsequence of the original sequence. ∎

In summary, the network D_n divides a cyclically increasing sequence into two cyclically increasing sequences of size $n/2$ such that each element in the first sequence is smaller than each element of the second sequence. We can now use $D_{n/2}$ on each half to further process the two subsequences. If we continue this process recursively, we get a network B_n that sorts cyclically increasing sequences, see Figure 12.3.5 for B_{16}. Note that B_n has depth $\lg n$. Each of the $\lg n$ layers contains $n/2$ comparators; hence B_n has size $n \lg n/2$.

Lemma 12.3.7. B_n is a sorting network for cyclically increasing sequences. B_n has depth $\lg n$ and size $n \lg n/2$.

Proof. We prove correctness by induction on n. The statement is true for $n = 1$ since B_1 is a wire without any comparators. Now let n be a proper power of 2. By the inductive hypothesis, we can assume that $B_{n/2}$ correctly sorts cyclically increasing sequences of length $n/2$. Consider a cyclically increasing sequence as input to B_n. By Lemma 12.3.6, D_n divides this sequence into two cyclically increasing sequences such that each element of the first sequence is smaller than each element of the second sequence. Hence, since

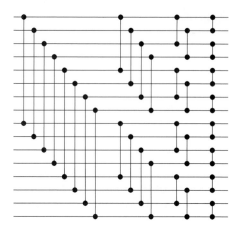

Figure 12.3.5 The B_{16} network.

both sequences are sorted correctly by $B_{n/2}$, the whole sequence is sorted correctly. ∎

Example 12.3.8. We trace B_8 on input $(4, 5, 6, 7, 8, 9, 12, 3)$. After running D_8 on this input, we get the sequence $(4, 5, 6, 3, 8, 9, 12, 7)$. We now run D_4 on both halves, giving us $(4, 3, 6, 5)$ and $(8, 7, 12, 9)$. Running D_2 on all four halves yields $(3, 4, 5, 6, 7, 8, 9, 12)$. □

Network B_n does more than sort cyclically increasing sequences; it also correctly sorts bitonic sequences. A **bitonic sequence** is a sequence that is a rotation of a sequence that is first increasing and then decreasing. More formally, $a_0, \ldots, a_{n-1}$ is **bitonic** if there is an m and a c such that $a_m \leq \ldots \leq a_{(m+c) \bmod n} \geq a_{(m+c+1) \bmod n} \ldots \geq a_{m-1}$.

Example 12.3.9. For example, $(1, 2, 3, 2, 1)$ is bitonic with $m = 0$ and $c = 2$. $(5, 12, 34, 56, 49, 8, 6, 3, 4)$ is bitonic with $m = 7$, and $c = 5$ since $3 \leq 4 \leq 5 \leq 12 \leq 34 \leq 56 \geq 49 \geq 8 \geq 6$. On the other hand, $(12, 6, 8, 4)$ is not bitonic. □

We can restate Lemma 12.3.6 for bitonic sequences.

Lemma 12.3.10. *If the input to D_n is a bitonic sequence, then the output $b_0, \ldots, b_{n-1}$ consists of two bitonic sequences*

$$(b_0, \ldots, b_{n/2-1}) \quad and \quad (b_{n/2}, \ldots, b_{n-1})$$

such that $b_i \leq b_j$ for $0 \leq i < n/2 \leq j < n$; that is, all elements of

$$(b_0, \ldots, b_{n/2-1})$$

are less than or equal to the elements of

$$(b_{n/2}, \ldots, b_{n-1}).$$

The proof is similar, if a bit more elaborate, than the proof of Lemma 12.3.6, and the reader is invited to skip it on a first reading. With Lemma 12.3.10 we can now show that B_n correctly sorts bitonic sequences. The proof is identical to the proof of Lemma 12.3.7 with the exception that we use Lemma 12.3.10 instead of Lemma 12.3.6.

Theorem 12.3.11. *B_n is a sorting network for bitonic sequences of depth* $\lg n$ *and size* $O(n \lg n)$.

We conclude this section with a proof of Lemma 12.3.10. The main idea is that, as in the case of cyclically increasing sequences, we can separate the sequence into two halves (on the circle) such that one half contains only elements that are at most as large as the elements of the other half.

Proof. Fix m and c such that $a_m \leq \ldots \leq a_{(m+c) \bmod n} \geq a_{(m+c+1) \bmod n} \ldots \geq a_{m-1}$. Again, visualize the sequence $(a_0, \ldots, a_{n-1})$ arranged on a circle.

We claim that there is a line through the center of the cycle that splits the circle into two halves in such a way that every element of one half is at most as large as every element of the other half. Before proving this claim, we take a look at some examples.

Example 12.3.12. Let $a = (3, 4, 5, 6, 7, 3, 1, 2)$. If we arrange the numbers on a cycle, we get the following picture with the separating line crossing between 3 and 4, and 7 and 3.

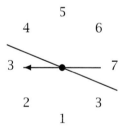

□

We now use an argument similar to the one in Lemma 12.3.6. The arrow pointer rotating through the cycle always has one end in one half of the circle and the other end in the other half. Hence, every element in the sequence of minima is smaller than every element in the sequence of maxima. Furthermore, both sequences are rotations of the sequences making up their half of the sequence; hence, as rotations of subsequences of a bitonic sequence, they have to be bitonic.

Example 12.3.13. In Example 12.3.12 let us first look at the sequence of minima. Initially the head of the arrow points into the half with the smaller numbers; hence the sequence starts with 3. If we rotate the arrow by one step, it jumps across the separating line, and it is now the tail that points to the smaller element.

Therefore, the sequence of minima continues with 3, 1, and 2, and therefore the full sequence of minima is $(3, 3, 1, 2)$. Note that this is a subsequence of the original sequence. The sequence of maxima starts with 7. After rotating the arrow by one position, its head will point to the larger value; hence, the sequence continues 4, 5, 6, to give us $(7, 4, 5, 6)$ as the sequence of maxima. Again, note that this is a subsequence of a rotation of the original sequence. □

We still have to prove the claim that there is a line separating the circle into a "larger" and a "smaller" half. To see this, start with the arrow pointing to a smallest element in the array. Then the element at the head of the arrow is smaller than, or equal to the element at the tail of the arrow. Now rotate the arrow step by step until the element at its head is larger than or equal to the element at its tail. (This will happen eventually, in the worst case, after we have rotated the arrow by 180 degrees and its tail comes to rest on the smallest element we started with.)

The two steps between which the switch occurs are illustrated in the following diagram:

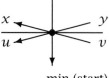

min (start)

In this situation we know that $x \geq v$ and $u \leq y$. We draw the separating line between the two arrows to separate the half containing x and y from the half containing u and v. We know that the smallest element we started with is in the same half as u and v since the tail of the arrow could not have moved over it. We also know that a largest element is in the other half since we would not have moved the head of the arrow over it. A bitonic sequence has to increase between the minimum and the maximum in both directions; hence, the situation looks as follows:

max

min

Now, for an element w in the half containing the minimum and an element z in the half containing the maximum, we have $w \leq \max\{u, v\} \leq \min\{x, y\} \leq z$, which is what we had to prove to verify the claim. ∎

Merging and Sorting

How does sorting bitonic sequences get us closer to building a general sorting network? The answer, a bit surprising at first, is that it helps us merge two sorted sequences. Remember that mergesort works by splitting sequences into two equal halves, sorting each sequence recursively and then merging the two sorted sequences. The usefulness of our bitonic sorter B_n emerges when observing that two sorted sequences back to back form a bitonic sequence; that is, if $a_0 \leq \ldots \leq a_{n/2-1}$ and $b_0 \leq \ldots \leq b_{n/2-1}$ are two increasing sequences, then $a_0, \ldots, a_{n/2-1}, b_{n/2-1}, \ldots, b_0$ is a bitonic sequence of length n. Hence, applying B_n to this sequence, sorts it. This allows us to use B_n to build a merging network M_n that merges two increasing sequences. All we have to do is reverse the second sequence before we submit the input to B_n. For example, Figure 12.3.6 shows M_8, and Figure 12.3.7 shows what M_4 looks like explicitly.

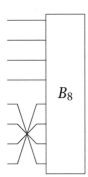

Figure 12.3.6 The structure of the M_8 merging network.

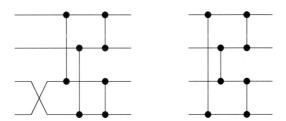

Figure 12.3.7 The M_4 merging network. The left diagram shows M_4 with wire intersections, and the right diagram shows M_4 after removing the wire intersections.

Example 12.3.14. Let us see how M_8 merges sequences $(12, 18, 23, 34)$ and $(7, 14, 29, 81)$. It first reverses the second sequence to obtain

$$(12, 18, 23, 34, 81, 29, 14, 7),$$

which is a bitonic sequence. It then applies B_8 to that sequence. This first means running D_8 to get $(12, 18, 14, 7, 81, 29, 23, 34)$, then two D_4 to get $(12, 7, 14, 18)$ and $(23, 29, 81, 34)$, and finally four D_2 that yield

$$(7, 12, 14, 18, 23, 29, 34, 81). \qquad \square$$

Theorem 12.3.15. *We can build a network to merge two sorted sequences in depth* $\lg n$ *and size* $n \lg n / 2$.

Using the merging networks, we can now build a sorting network S_n that works for all sequences by using the idea of mergesort. We let S_1 be a single wire. Then S_1 correctly sorts a single input. From S_1 we build S_2 by applying M_2 to the two wires. Since a single input is a sorted sequence, S_2 correctly sorts sequences of length 2. Similarly, we build S_4 by using two copies of an S_2 to sort the two halves of the input and then merge the sorted halves using M_4 (see Figure 12.3.8).

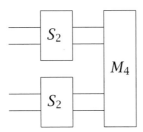

Figure 12.3.8 The structure of the S_4 sorting network.

Example 12.3.16. Let us see how S_4 works on an example. If we unravel the definition of M_4 (using the drawing in Figure 12.3.7), we obtain the following picture of S_4:

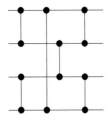

If we run S_4 on input $(4, 1, 3, 2)$ we get $(1, 4, 2, 3)$ after the first layer containing the two S_2, then $(1, 2, 4, 3)$ after the second layer, and finally $(1, 2, 3, 4)$ after the last layer. $\qquad \square$

As we built S_4 from two S_2 and one M_4, we can build S_n from two $S_{n/2}$ and one M_n (see Figure 12.3.9).

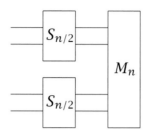

Figure 12.3.9 The structure of the S_n sorting network.

Example 12.3.17. S_8 looks as follows (identify the components of S_8: M_8 and the two S_4; in turn, note how each of the two S_4 is made up of one M_4 and two S_2).

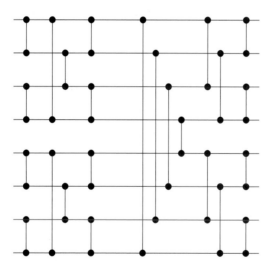

S_8 has depth 6 and size 24. Using S_8 to sort

$$(10, 7, 2, 12, 9, 31, 5, 17),$$

we get

$$(2, 7, 10, 12, 5, 9, 17, 31)$$

after the first part of the network, which consists of two S_4 in parallel. Then, after the next layer (the four comparators of the D_8 after the wires are disentangled), we have

$$(2, 7, 9, 5, 12, 10, 17, 31).$$

After the two D_4, we have

$$(2, 5, 9, 7, 12, 10, 17, 31),$$

which turns into

$$(2, 5, 7, 9, 10, 12, 17, 31)$$

through the final four D_2.   □

Theorem 12.3.18. *S_n is a sorting network of depth $\Theta(\lg^2 n)$ and size $\Theta(n \lg^2 n)$ that correctly sorts input sequences of length n.*

Proof. We prove the theorem by induction on n. S_1 is correct since it has only one input. Let n be a proper power of 2. As the induction hypothesis, we assume that $S_{n/2}$ sorts $n/2$ inputs correctly. Then the network S_n first sorts each half of its input using $S_{n/2}$ correctly and then uses M_n to sort the two sequences, yielding a sorted sequence of length n.

The depth of S_n is the sum of the depth of $M_n, M_{n/2}, M_{n/4}, \ldots, M_1$, which is $\lg n + \lg(n/2) + \lg(n/4) + \ldots = \Theta(\lg^2 n)$ (see Exercise 26, Section 2.3). Let s_n denote the size of S_n. Then s_n is the size of M_n plus $2s_{n/2}$, the size of two $S_{n/2}$. Since M_n has size $n \lg n/2$, we get the following recurrence on s_n:

$$s_n = n \lg n/2 + 2s_{n/2}.$$

From the result of Exercise 2.14 we can conclude that s_n is of order $\Theta(n \lg^2 n)$ (let $t_n = 2s_n$ and apply Exercise 2.14 to t_n).   ■

The Zero-One Principle of Sorting Networks

To emphasize the ideas behind the constructions of sorting networks, we have shown correctness of our sorting networks directly. The zero-one principle for sorting networks is a tool that often simplifies such correctness proofs.

Theorem 12.3.19. *If a sorting network works correctly on all inputs consisting only of zeros and ones, it works correctly on arbitrary inputs.*

Theorem 12.3.19 allows us to verify sorting networks by testing them only on sequences of zeros and ones. For a network with n inputs, this means we need to verify at most 2^n inputs, as opposed to infinitely many.

Proof. Assume there is a sorting network that correctly sorts all sequences of zeros and ones but does not sort correctly some sequence of numbers $a_0, \ldots, a_{n-1}$.

Let $b_0, \ldots, b_{n-1}$ be the output produced by the sorting network on sequence $a_0, \ldots, a_{n-1}$. Since the output is not correctly sorted, there must be $s < t$ such that $b_s > b_t$. We associate a sequence of zeros and ones with $a_0, \ldots, a_{n-1}$: Label each a_i that is less than b_s with a zero and all the other a_i with a one. We claim that, if we run the sequence $a_0, \ldots, a_{n-1}$ and the sequence of its labels simultaneously through the sorting network, all of the a_i keep their labels. This implies that b_s is labeled with a 1 and b_t with a zero. Since $s < t$, the sorting network does not correctly sort the sequence of labels, which is a contradiction since the labels are zeros and ones.

We still need to verify the claim that the labels of the input elements remain the same. Consider a comparator gate. If both inputs are labeled zero or both inputs are labeled one, the same is true for the output. This leaves us with the case that we have inputs $a < a'$ and a is labeled with a 0 and a' with a 1, in which case the comparator gate will not do anything to either a and a' or the labels. The other possibility is that we have inputs $a > a'$ and a is labeled 1 and a' is labeled 0. In this case, the comparator gate will switch both a and a' and 0 and 1, and again the labels stay with their original elements. ∎

We can now use the zero-one principle to show that the odd-even transposition network (Figure 12.3.1) we introduced at the beginning of this section works correctly.

Theorem 12.3.20. *The odd-even transposition network sorts sequences of length n in depth n and size n^2.*

Proof. Fix n and consider the odd-even sorting network for sequences of length n. Because of Theorem 12.3.19, we only have to show that the network correctly sorts all binary sequences. Fix an arbitrary binary sequence $a_0, \ldots, a_{n-1}$ of length n. Let a_i be the first 0 in this sequence; that is, $a_i = 0$ and $a_k = 1$ for all $k < i$. If i is even, then a_i will be compared to a_{i+1} in the first layer of the network, and nothing happens. However, in the second layer, a_i is compared to $a_{i-1} = 1$, and the two elements change place. Since all elements before a_i are zero, from that point on a_i moves until it has reached the first wire. If i is odd, a_i will start moving towards the first wire immediately and settle there. Both situations are illustrated in Figure 12.3.10.

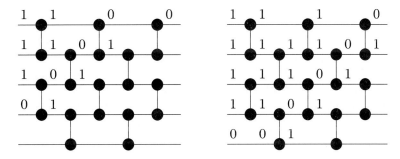

Figure 12.3.10 The left network shows the first 0 starting to move immediately. In the right network, there is a delay of one step before the first 0 starts moving to the first wire.

More generally, we distinguish three states for each 0 in the sequence: "obstructed", "moving", and "arrived". There are two kinds of obstructions to a 0 getting closer to its final position: being in the wrong phase (as the first

0 in Figure 12.3.10) or being held up by a 0 before it that is not moving yet. By induction, we can show that the kth zero in the sequence starts moving (at the latest) in the $(k + 1)$st layer until it has arrived at its final position. We earlier showed that the first zero (a_i) begins moving in either the first or second layer and then moves straight to its final position (since there are no zeros to the left of it). The second zero can only be obstructed by the first zero when the first zero is not moving yet. Since the first zero starts moving in the second layer at the latest, the second zero will start moving in the second or third layer (when it is in the right phase). In general, the kth zero can be obstructed only by the preceding zeros all of which are moving by the kth layer. Hence, the kth zero will start moving either in the kth or the $(k + 1)$st layer (depending on the phase). The kth zero can be at most $n - k$ positions from its final position. Since it starts moving towards that position in layer $k + 1$ at the latest, there are $n - k$ layers left for it to move to its final position.   ■

Example 12.3.21. Let us see how the odd-even transposition network sorts the sequence $(1, 1, 0, 1, 0, 0)$.

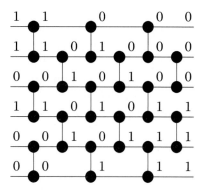

The first zero, a_2, starts moving with a delay of one since it is in the wrong phase; but from that point on, it keeps moving to the first wire. The second zero, a_4, is delayed for the same reason. The third zero, a_5, is delayed since the second zero is not moving yet. However, after the second step, when the second zero has started moving, the third zero also starts its way to the correct wire without any further interruptions.   □

Exercises

1S. Prove that the sorting network shown in Example 12.3.1 sorts all sequences of four numbers correctly (without using the zero-one principle).

2. Prove that there cannot be a sorting network using only four gates that sorts all sequences of four numbers correctly.

3. Show that there cannot be a sorting network of depth two that sorts all sequences of four numbers correctly (whatever the number of gates may be).

4S. Show that, if we construct a network with comparators in the diagonal, that is, at step i we have a comparator between wire i and wire $i + 1$ ($1 \le i < n$), then the largest element of the input is output on wire n.

5S. Draw the odd-even transposition network for $n = 10$ and show how the network runs on inputs $10, 9, 8, 7, 6, 5, 4, 3, 2, 1$.

6. Draw the odd-even transposition network for $n = 7$ and show how the network runs on inputs $17, 32, 19, 17, 9, 19, 11$.

7. Draw the odd-even transposition network for $n = 12$ and show how the network runs on inputs $1, 1, 1, 0, 0, 1, 0, 0, 0, 1, 1, 0$.

8S. Calculate the exact size of the odd-even transposition network on n wires.

9. Construct a sorting network of size $\lfloor n/2 \rfloor$ that correctly sorts sequences that are monotone (increasing or decreasing).

10. Give an example showing that B_4 does not correctly sort all input sequences.

11S. Show how B_8 sorts $(8, 7, 6, 5, 4, 3, 2, 1)$.

12. Show how B_8 sorts $(32, 11, 13, 19, 23, 29, 40, 35)$.

13. Show how B_8 sorts $(6, 5, 4, 3, 2, 1, 8, 7)$.

14S. Use B_{16} to sort $(9, 10, 11, 12, 13, 14, 15, 16, 1, 2, 3, 4, 5, 6, 7, 8)$.

15. Use B_{16} to sort $(9, 12, 23, 26, 29, 28, 25, 21, 19, 17, 13, 10, 4, 3, 5, 7)$.

16. Use B_{16} to sort $(9, 10, 11, 12, 13, 14, 15, 16, 8, 7, 6, 5, 4, 3, 2, 1)$.

17S. Show that the rotation of a subsequence of a cyclically increasing sequence is still cyclically increasing.

18. Show that every sequence of three elements is bitonic.

19. Show that the rotation of a subsequence of a bitonic sequence is bitonic.

20S. Draw M_8 explicitly and use it to merge $(7, 9, 12, 13)$ and $(1, 5, 11, 15)$.

21. Draw M_8 explicitly and use it to merge $(2, 5, 6, 9)$ and $(3, 7, 10, 11)$.

22. Draw M_{16} explicitly and use it to merge

$$(3, 5, 9, 12, 17, 22, 27, 31) \text{ and } (1, 2, 7, 11, 21, 23, 37, 51).$$

23S. Draw M_8 without wire crossings (as we did for M_4 in Figure 12.3.7).

24. Draw M_{16} without wire crossings (as we did for M_4 in Figure 12.3.7).

25S. Show how S_8 sorts $(7, 7, 1, 11, 9, 3, 2, 4)$.

26. Draw S_{16} explicitly and use it to sort

$$(1, 19, 4, 5, 3, 11, 3, 9, 2, 3, 17, 9, 10, 9, 3, 13).$$

27. Draw S_{16} without wire crossings (as we did for S_8 in Example 12.3.17).

28S. Show that S_n has depth $\lg n (\lg n + 1)/2$ if n is a power of 2.

29. Derive an explicit formula for s_n, the size of S_n. *Hint:* Try with s_n being of the form $\alpha n \log^2 n + \beta n \log n$ and determine α and β.

30. Our sorting network S_n assumes that the number n of inputs is a power of 2. Show that we can remove this restriction as follows: Given n inputs, build a sorting network for $2^{\lceil \lg n \rceil}$ inputs and remove the superfluous wires. Show that this gives us a correct sorting network of depth $O(\lg^2 n)$ and size $O(n \lg^2 n)$.

31S. Use the odd-even transposition network to sort the sequence

$$(12, 23, 4, 7, 6, 1, 17, 19, 3, 2)$$

simultaneously with the sequence $(1, 1, 0, 0, 0, 0, 1, 1, 0, 0)$ of labels (every element less than 10 was labeled 0, the others 1).

32. Consider the sequence $(1, 4, 3, 6, 2, 5)$. We can associate different binary sequences of labels with this sequence. For example, choosing 4 as the cut-off number would result in the labeling $(0, 1, 0, 1, 0, 1)$. List all seven possible labelings that can arise from $(1, 4, 3, 6, 2, 5)$. Then use the odd-even transposition network to order $(1, 4, 3, 6, 2, 5)$ and one of its labelings simultaneously.

12.4 Parallel Architectures

If we have a set of processors with prescribed (and static) communication channels, we speak of a **parallel architecture** or an **interconnection network**. We can picture the communication channels as edges in a graph whose vertices are the processors. We talk about network **topologies** to mean particular families of graphs. For example, we could arrange the processors in the star topology, in which all processors are connected to one central processor (see Figure 12.4.1).

In the star topology, every processor is at most two steps away from every other processor. We call the largest distance between any two processors the **diameter** of the network. The star topology has a diameter of 2. A small diameter in a network generally means fast communication. Also, the star

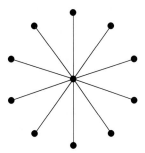

Figure 12.4.1 The star topology. One central processor is directly connected to all other processors.

topology uses only n communication channels to connect $n + 1$ processors, which is the minimum (see Exercise 3). On the downside, the star topology has very low connectivity: Removing a single vertex (the central vertex) disconnects the whole network and makes communication between any two computers impossible. This behavior is unacceptable in many situations; imagine the Internet going down because of a single machine outage.[†] Another serious problem arises when too many processors try to communicate at once. Since all communications have to go through the central processor, the speed of this single processor is a bottleneck for the whole network. Hence, vertices of large degree (number of incident channels) can be disadvantageous.

Another way to connect n processors using a small number of connections is the linear array and its variant, the ring (see Figure 12.4.2). Both occur in practice; for example, an Ethernet is a linear array and a token ring a ring.

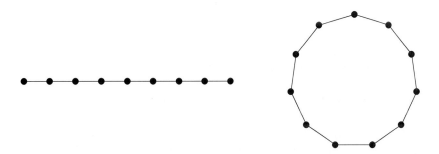

Figure 12.4.2 The linear array on the left and the ring topology on the right.

The connectivity of the ring is slightly higher than that of the star and the linear array; after removing a single processor from a ring, the network is still

---

[†]Maybe not surprisingly the ARPANET, the grandfather of the Internet, was sponsored by the Department of Defense to investigate the possibilities of distributed computing.

connected; that is, every processor can still communicate with every other processor. However, if we remove two processors that are not neighbors from the network, the ring will be disconnected. A disadvantage of both the linear array and the ring is their diameter, which is $\Theta(n)$, making them mostly useful for small values of n, as in local area networks (Ethernet and token ring are typical LAN technologies).

If we want better connectivity, we have to add communication channels. If we add all possible channels, we obtain a topology that corresponds to the complete graph K_n (see Figure 12.4.3).

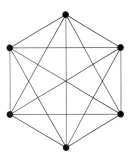

Figure 12.4.3 A network of six processors with all possible communication channels.

The main advantage of K_n is its small diameter of 1, and, thereby, the absence of any bottleneck in the communication between processors. However, we pay a high price for connecting the network: We use $n(n-1)/2$ channels to connect n processors. It is worthwhile to look at intermediate architectures such as trees, meshes, and hypercubes.

Linear arrays and stars are trees, and it is natural to base networks on trees, as we did when we computed the maximum using a binary tree (see Figure 12.1.2). Trees are connected by the minimum number of edges, meaning that removal of a vertex or an edge immediately disconnects them. On the positive side, we can have trees with vertices of small degree and small diameter. For example, a binary tree, in which every vertex has degree at most 3, allows us to connect n vertices with a diameter of $2 \lg n$.

A generalization of the linear array is the $n \times m$ mesh, which lays out nm processors on an $n \times m$ orthogonal grid such that each processor is connected to its immediate neighbors as in Figure 12.4.4. In the early 1980s, Inmos designed a chip called the transputer with four links that make it ideal for use in the mesh topology.

Another popular topology is the **hypercube**. The zero-dimensional hypercube is a single processor. A d-dimensional hypercube, $d > 0$, is constructed from two copies of a $(d-1)$-dimensional hypercube by connecting the two copies of each vertex. Figure 12.4.5 shows all hypercubes up to dimension 4.

The vertices in a d-dimensional hypercube can be labeled using d-bit binary strings as follows: The two vertices of the one-dimensional hypercube

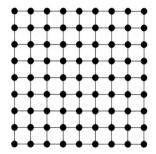

Figure 12.4.4 A 9×9 mesh.

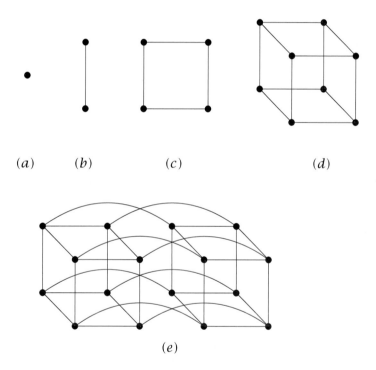

Figure 12.4.5 Hypercubes of dimensions zero through four. (a) Dimension 0. (b) Dimension 1. (c) Dimension 2. (d) Dimension 3. (e) Dimension 4.

are labeled 0 and 1. Recursively, we build labels for the d-dimensional hypercube. Assume we have already labeled every vertex of the $(d-1)$-dimensional hypercube with a $(d-1)$-bit binary string. The d-dimensional hypercube consists of two copies of the $(d-1)$-dimensional hypercube. Assign one of the copies the label 0 and the other the label 1. Now, a vertex in the d-dimensional hypercube can be labeled by concatenating a 0 or 1, depending on which copy it is in, with its label in the $(d-1)$-dimensional hypercube.

Example 12.4.1. In the one-dimensional case, the vertices are simply labeled 0 and 1. In the two-dimensional case, we take two copies of the one-dimensional hypercube and prefix a 0 or a 1 to their labels, depending on which copy the vertex belongs to (see Figure 12.4.6). In this way, we can label the vertices of the two-dimensional hypercube with labels 00, 01, 10, and 11. Figure 12.4.7 shows the names of the vertices in the three-dimensional hypercube.

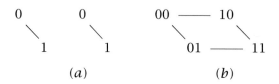

(a) (b)

Figure 12.4.6 Labeling the two-dimensional hypercube. (a) We start with two labeled copies of the one-dimensional hypercube. (b) When connecting these two copies to form the two-dimensional hypercube, we prefix the label of each vertex with a 0 or 1, depending on which copy the vertex belongs to.

```
000——— 010
|    \        \
|     001——+——011
|          |
100——+——110   |
     \        \ |
      101 ——— 111
```

Figure 12.4.7 Labeling the three-dimensional hypercube. It is made up of two copies of the two-dimensional hypercube. The first copy, which becomes the top layer, we label with 0; the other, the bottom layer, with 1.   □

Since different names correspond to different vertices, we conclude that the d-dimensional hypercube contains 2^d vertices. The degree of each vertex in the d-dimensional hypercube is d (all vertices have exactly d neighbors; we also say the hypercube is a *regular* graph of degree d). The diameter of the hypercube is d, implying that we can route a message from any vertex to any other vertex in at most d steps. There even is a very simple routing algorithm based on the following observation: Two nodes whose labels differ in exactly one coordinate are directly connected by a channel (see Exercise 11). This allows us to send a message from vertex v to vertex w by changing the label of v to the label of w one coordinate at a time.

Example 12.4.2. To send a message from 01010 to 11101 in the five-dimensional hypercube, we can route the message through 01010, 11010, 11110, 11100, 11101.   □

This simple routing algorithm can lead to congestion if multiple messages are routed at the same time.

Example 12.4.3. Assume there are two messages being sent in the five-dimensional hypercube, one from 01010 to 11101, as in Example 12.4.2, and one from 10010 to 11110. The first is routed along 01010, 11010, 11110, 11100, 11101 and the second along the path 10010, 11010, 11110. We see that in the second step there are two messages at 11010. If, as we usually assume, only one message can be sent along an edge, one of the messages has to be delayed, causing congestion. □

In practice, more sophisticated techniques are needed to deal with packet routing on hypercubes.

One reason for the popularity of the hypercube network is that it can simulate other networks efficiently. Some of them, such as linear arrays, can be found as subgraphs of the hypercube; others, such as trees, can be efficiently embedded in the hypercube if we allow edges to be dilated and we permit vertices of the hypercube to simulate several vertices of the original network. Hence, algorithms written for the hypercube can often be adapted to work on other architectures as well. A disadvantage of the hypercube network is that it is expensive to extend, since new connections have to be added to every node if we increase the dimension of the hypercube. Hence, hypercubes are in turn embedded in other networks that are easier to implement in hardware.

We present algorithms for the linear array and the square mesh: We solve the sorting problem on both topologies and show how to solve the component-labeling problem on the square mesh.

Sorting

We show how to sort on two topologies: the linear array and the mesh. On a linear array, we can implement the odd-even transposition network we saw in Section 12.3. Each processor keeps a counter so it knows whether the system is currently in the odd or the even phase. To implement a comparator gate, two adjacent processors have to work together and possibly exchange their elements. In an even phase, the even processors team up with their right neighbors; that is, we pair $(0, 1), (2, 3), (4, 5)$, and so on, and the even processors receive the smaller element.

Example 12.4.4. We show how to do the first phase of the odd-even transposition network on the sequence $a = [18, 42, 31, 56, 12, 11, 19, 34, 11]$. Since the first phase is an even phase, we pair $(0, 1), (2, 3), (4, 5)$, and $(6, 7)$; 8 does not have a partner and is therefore idle in this step.

	$a[0]$	$a[1]$	$a[2]$	$a[3]$	$a[4]$	$a[5]$	$a[6]$	$a[7]$	$a[8]$
start	18	42	31	56	12	11	19	34	11
0	18	42	31	56	11	12	19	34	11

□

In an odd phase the even processors team up with their left neighbors, yielding the pairings $(1, 2)$, $(3, 4)$, $(5, 6)$, and so on. Again each pair implements a comparator gate.

Example 12.4.5. We continue Example 12.4.4. After the first step (an even phase), we have obtained $[18, 42, 31, 56, 11, 12, 19, 34, 11]$. The second step is an odd phase, so now we pair processors in pairs $(1, 2)$, $(3, 4)$, $(5, 6)$, and $(7, 8)$. Processor 0 is idle in this step.

	$a[0]$	$a[1]$	$a[2]$	$a[3]$	$a[4]$	$a[5]$	$a[6]$	$a[7]$	$a[8]$
start	18	42	31	56	12	11	19	34	11
0	18	42	31	56	11	12	19	34	11
1	18	31	42	11	56	12	19	11	34

After n steps, all processors stop. At this point, they have simulated all n phases of the odd-even transposition network.

Example 12.4.6. Figure 12.4.8 shows a complete run of the algorithm on the input sequence $a = [18, 42, 31, 56, 12, 11, 19, 34, 11]$.

	$a[0]$	$a[1]$	$a[2]$	$a[3]$	$a[4]$	$a[5]$	$a[6]$	$a[7]$	$a[8]$
start	18	42	31	56	12	11	19	34	11
0	18	42	31	56	11	12	19	34	11
1	18	31	42	11	56	12	19	11	34
2	18	31	11	42	12	56	11	19	34
3	18	11	31	12	32	11	56	19	34
4	11	18	12	31	11	32	19	56	34
5	11	12	18	11	31	19	32	34	56
6	11	12	11	18	19	31	32	34	56
7	11	11	12	18	19	31	32	34	56
8	11	11	12	18	19	31	32	34	56

Figure 12.4.8 A simulation of the odd-even transposition network on a linear-array structure. Processors pair up with a different neighbor in each alternating step to implement the comparator gates.

The correctness of this algorithm follows from the correctness of the odd-even transposition network, which we proved in Theorem 12.3.20.

Theorem 12.4.7. *We can sort n numbers on a linear array in time n using odd-even transposition sort.*

This algorithm gives us a speedup of a factor of $\lg n$ over the sequential algorithm. We cannot expect to do better on a linear array, since in the worst case the smallest element has to travel the whole length of the array, which takes $n - 1$ steps.

The second example shows how to sort on a mesh. The algorithm called **Shearsort** sorts in two phases that are repeated $\lceil \lg n \rceil + 1$ times. In the row sort phase, all rows of the mesh are sorted using the odd-even-transposition algorithm for linear arrays. The rows are alternatingly sorted in increasing and decreasing order (this is important). In the column sort phase we sort all columns in ascending order. Repeating the two phases at most $\lceil \lg n \rceil + 1$ times sorts the elements in the mesh.

Example 12.4.8. Let us use Shearsort to sort the sequence

$$a = [15, 4, 10, 6, 1, 5, 7, 11, 12, 14, 13, 8, 9, 16, 2, 3].$$

We assign the numbers to the processors in the mesh row by row.

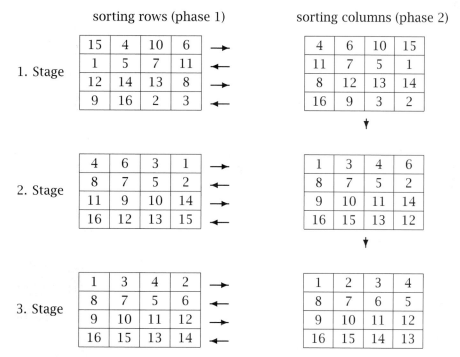

After the last row sort, the elements are sorted "as the ox plows" (boustrophedon), that is, alternatingly in ascending and descending order. □

We want to use the zero-one principle to show that Shearsort works in general. The zero-one principle was stated for sorting networks, not for general algorithms (and, as a matter of fact, it fails for arbitrary algorithms). However, Shearsort is a rather restricted kind of algorithm. It is a **comparison-exchange algorithm** in that it can be implemented using comparators only. Second, it is **oblivious**, meaning that the outcome of a comparator does not influence which comparisons are made later on. An oblivious, comparison-exchange algorithm can be implemented as a sorting network, and therefore the zero-one principle applies to it.

Theorem 12.4.9. *Shearsort sorts n^2 elements in $2n(\lg n + 1)$ steps on the $n \times n$ mesh.*

Proof. Since Shearsort is an oblivious, comparison-exchange algorithm we can apply the zero-one principle; hence, we have to check only that it works for binary inputs. Let us have a look at two rows $2i$ and $2i + 1$ after the row sort phase. Since row $2i$ has been sorted in increasing order, it starts with a block of zeros and ends with a block of ones. Similarly, row $2i + 1$ begins with a block of ones and ends with a block of zeros. If the number of ones in the two rows is at least n, the two rows will result in at least one row full of ones after the column sort phase. Similarly, if the number of zeros in the two rows is at least n, then we will get a row full of zeros after the column sort phase.

Example 12.4.10. Let us see what happens on input

0	1	0	0	1	0	0	1	→
0	1	1	1	0	1	1	1	←
0	0	1	0	1	0	0	1	→
1	0	0	1	0	0	1	0	←
1	1	1	0	1	0	1	0	→
0	0	0	0	1	1	0	1	←
0	0	1	1	1	1	0	1	→
1	1	0	0	1	1	1	1	←

The arrows on the right indicate the order in which we sort in the row sorting phase during the first stage. After the row sort, the first two rows look as follows:

0	0	0	0	0	1	1	1
1	1	1	1	1	1	0	0

The blocks of ones overlap, so after the upcoming column sort phase, these two rows account for one complete row of ones. In rows three and four, the zeros outnumber the ones:

0	0	0	0	0	1	1	1
1	1	1	0	0	0	0	0

Hence, these two rows result in a row of zeros at the top after the column sort. Rows five and six together have eight zeros and eight ones:

| 0 | 0 | 0 | 1 | 1 | 1 | 1 | 1 |
| 1 | 1 | 1 | 0 | 0 | 0 | 0 | 0 |

Hence, they result in one row of zeros at the top and one row of ones at the bottom. The last two rows have a majority of ones and hence result in a row of ones. Overall, this guarantees us at least four all-zero or all-one rows after the column sort (five, actually, because of row five and six). The result of the column sort is

0	0	0	0	0	0	0	0
0	0	0	0	0	0	0	0
0	0	0	0	0	1	0	0
0	0	0	0	0	1	0	0
1	1	1	1	1	1	1	1
1	1	1	1	1	1	1	1
1	1	1	1	1	1	1	1
1	1	1	1	1	1	1	1

After one more row and column sort we obtain

0	0	0	0	0	0	0	0
0	0	0	0	0	0	0	0
0	0	0	0	0	0	0	0
1	0	0	0	0	0	0	1
1	1	1	1	1	1	1	1
1	1	1	1	1	1	1	1
1	1	1	1	1	1	1	1
1	1	1	1	1	1	1	1

One more row sort yields a sorted array. □

Since a pair of rows has to contain either n zeros or n ones, we know that each pair of rows results in at least one row of all zeros or one row of all ones. These rows are not affected by further row or column sorts; hence, we can ignore them from that point onwards. This means that applying a row sort followed by a column sort halves the number of rows that contain elements that have not yet reached their final position. Therefore, after $\lg n + 1$ repetitions, all elements have reached their final position. Since the row sort and the column sort each take n steps, the overall running time is $2n(\lg n + 1)$. ■

Component Labeling

Component labeling is a fundamental problem of image processing in which different components of an image need to be identified. We restrict ourselves to the simplest case of an $n \times n$ image made up of black and white pixels, which we represent as 1 and 0. Figure 12.4.9(a) shows an example.

0	1	1	0	0	0	0	1	0	1
0	1	0	0	1	0	0	1	0	1
0	1	1	0	1	0	1	1	0	1
0	1	0	0	0	0	1	0	0	1
0	1	1	1	1	1	1	0	0	1
0	1	0	0	0	0	0	0	0	1
0	1	1	1	1	1	1	1	1	1
1	0	0	0	0	0	0	0	0	0
0	1	0	0	1	1	1	0	0	1
0	0	1	0	0	0	0	1	1	0

(a)

0	a	a	0	0	0	0	a	0	a
0	a	0	0	c	0	0	a	0	a
0	a	a	0	c	0	a	a	0	a
0	a	0	0	0	0	a	0	0	a
0	a	a	a	a	a	a	0	0	a
0	a	0	0	0	0	0	0	0	a
0	a	a	a	a	a	a	a	a	a
a	0	0	0	0	0	0	0	0	0
0	a	0	0	b	b	b	0	0	b
0	0	a	0	0	0	0	b	b	0

(b)

Figure 12.4.9 (a) A picture with two gray values 0 and 1. (b) The picture from (a) with labeled components.

Two ones that are immediate neighbors, horizontally, vertically, or diagonally, are said to belong to the same **component** of the picture. A **maximal component** is a component that cannot be extended; that is, for any two neighboring ones, a maximal component contains either both or neither. The **component-labeling problem** asks us to assign each maximal component a different label, so we can tell to which component a particular black pixel belongs (see Section 4.2). The picture in Figure 12.4.9(a) contains three maximal components, which are labeled a, b, and c in Figure 12.4.9(b).

A natural network for approaching the component-labeling problem on a parallel machine is the mesh. We assign to each pixel (i, j) a processor $P_{i,j}$ that is connected to its four immediate neighbors: above, below, to the left, and to the right ($P_{i-1,j}$, $P_{i+1,j}$, $P_{i,j-1}$, and $P_{i,j+1}$). We let the indexes of the processors range from 1 to n, and we assume that there are rows and columns indexed 0 and $n + 1$ that contain only zeros. In the figures we do not display this white border since it is there only to simplify the algorithm.

Any algorithm solving the general component-labeling problem on the mesh takes at least time $\Omega(n)$ since it takes $\Omega(n)$ parallel steps for a message to traverse the whole mesh. For example, in Figure 12.4.10 pixels $(1, 1)$ and $(1, 3)$ should have the same label if and only if pixel $(n - 1, n)$ is black, and it takes at least $2n - 3$ steps for a message from $(n - 1, n)$ to get to $(1, 1)$.

Most labeling algorithms work by propagating a component label within each component. This leads to conflicts when two different labels meet. One of the simplest algorithms to solve the conflict works as follows:

1	0	1	1	1	...	1	0
1	0	0	0	0	...	0	1
1	0	0	0	0	...	0	1
.							.
.							.
.							.
1	0	0	0	0	...	0	1
1	0	0	0	0	...	0	?
0	1	1	1	1	...	1	0

Figure 12.4.10 A picture for which the component-labeling problem takes $\Omega(n)$ steps. The labels of pixels $(1, 1)$ and $(1, 3)$ depend on whether pixel $(n - 1, n)$ contains 0 or 1.

1. Label each pixel with a unique number; for example, pixel (i, j) gets assigned label $in + j$.

2. Each processor containing a black pixel looks at its own label and at all the labels of black pixels neighboring it and changes its label to the smallest label it sees. Perform this second step n^2 times.

For a more formal version of the algorithm, we assume that the picture is stored in a two-dimensional array a. Each element of a has a field *color*, which is either 0 or 1, and a field *label*, which is set by the algorithm and, eventually, contains a unique label for the component to which the pixel belongs.

Algorithm 12.4.11 Minimum Label. This algorithm takes as input a two-dimensional array a with indexes ranging from 0 to $n + 1$. Every element of the array contains fields *color* and *label*. The color field of elements in rows and columns with indexes 0 or $n + 1$ is assumed to be zero. The algorithm computes a component labeling for a and stores it in the label field.

Input Parameters: a, n
Output Parameters: None

```
minimum_label(a, n) {
    // initialize the label field of
    // every black pixel to a unique value
    for i, j ∈ {1, ..., n} in parallel
        if (a[i, j].color == 1)
            a[i, j].label = i × n + j
        else
            a[i, j].label = 0
    // perform the second step on
    // every label n² times
```

```
for k = 1 to n²
    for i, j ∈ {1, ..., n} in parallel
        for x = i - 1 to i + 1
            for y = j - 1 to j + 1
                if (a[x, y].color == 1)
                    a[i, j].label = min(a[i, j].label, a[x, y].label)
}
```

Note that $P_{i,j}$ needs to look at the labels not only of the four processors it is connected to but also at the labels of the four processors diagonally surrounding it. In the mesh, however, it does not have direct access to these processors. Hence, when we implement the minimum-label algorithm on the mesh, we have to wait two steps until the color and label information from the diagonal neighbors has reached a processor. Since every processor has to do this, it slows down the algorithm by a factor of two, overall.

We claim that, after *minimum_label* has run, all black pixels that belong to the same component have the same label; and black pixels that belong to different components have different labels. Therefore, each maximal component has a unique label. All white pixels are labeled with 0.

Example 12.4.12. Figure 12.4.11 (next page) illustrates how *minimum_label* works on the following input:

1	0	0	1	0
0	1	0	1	1
1	0	0	0	0
1	1	0	1	1
1	1	1	1	1

In the first step, each black pixel is labeled with a unique number. Six more steps are sufficient in this example to find the unique labeling.   □

Why does *minimum_label* work? First of all, we note that two black pixels that belong to different components are never assigned the same label. The reason is that initially all black pixels have different labels, and in the code we only propagate a label within a component. It remains, then, to show that once the algorithm terminates, all pixels in the same component have the same label. Define the **diameter** of a component to be largest distance between two pixels of the component *within* the component.

Example 12.4.13. In the original picture of Example 12.4.12, the distance between pixel $(1, 1)$ and $(4, 5)$ is six; the shortest connection between the two pixels is $(1, 1)$, $(2, 2)$, $(3, 1)$, $(4, 2)$, $(5, 3)$, $(4, 4)$, $(4, 5)$. Since all other pixels in the same component have distance at most 6 from each other, the diameter of that component is 6. The diameter of the other component (labeled 9) is 1.   □

1	0	0	1	0
0	1	0	1	1
1	0	0	0	0
1	1	0	1	1
1	1	1	1	1

(0)

6	0	0	9	0
0	12	0	14	15
16	0	0	0	0
21	22	0	24	25
26	27	28	29	30

(1)

6	0	0	9	0
0	6	0	9	14
12	0	0	0	0
16	16	0	24	24
21	21	22	24	24

(2)

6	0	0	9	0
0	6	0	9	9
6	0	0	0	0
12	12	0	22	24
16	16	16	22	24

(3)

6	0	0	9	0
0	6	0	9	9
6	0	0	0	0
6	6	0	16	22
12	12	12	16	22

(4)

6	0	0	9	0
0	6	0	9	9
6	0	0	0	0
6	6	0	12	16
6	6	6	12	16

(5)

6	0	0	9	0
0	6	0	9	9
6	0	0	0	0
6	6	0	6	12
6	6	6	6	12

(6)

6	0	0	9	0
0	6	0	9	9
6	0	0	0	0
6	6	0	6	6
6	6	6	6	6

(7)

Figure 12.4.11 Running *minimum_label* on the input displayed in (0). In step (1) each pixel is assigned a unique label. In step (3), the component in the upper-right corner is labeled. Finally, in step (7), the number 6 (the smallest label in the other component) has spread throughout the whole component.

Since there are only n^2 pixels, the diameter of a component is certainly at most n^2 (and there can be components with diameter $\Omega(n^2)$, see Exercise 20). Within each component, consider the pixel with the smallest label. After k iterations of the loop, each pixel that has distance at most k from the pixel with the smallest label will also have been labeled with that smallest label if it belongs to the same component. Since all components have diameter at most n^2, after n^2 steps every pixel in every component shares the original smallest label in that component.

Theorem 12.4.14. *We can solve the component-labeling problem in parallel time $\Theta(n^2)$ using n^2 processors.*

This result appears less impressive if we compare it to the sequential algorithm, which also solves the problem in time $\Theta(n^2)$ (see Section 4.2). A second look at the parallel algorithm suggests one possible improvement: The correctness proof showed that the algorithm is actually done after d

steps, where d is the maximum of the diameters of any of the components in the image. Unfortunately, we usually do not have any a priori bounds on the value of d other than n^2; so, in general, we cannot hardcode d into the algorithm. However, we can establish a messaging system that checks whether there have been any changes in the labels. If not, messages can be sent to all processors to stop. We leave the details to Exercise 12.30. Where d is of lesser order than n^2, this leads to an improved running time.

We now turn to an algorithm due to Levialdi that solves the problem in time $O(n)$ regardless of the diameters of the components. Levialdi's approach is to shrink each component step by step to a single pixel. At that point a unique label can be assigned to the pixel. Finally, the shrinking operation is undone, propagating the label throughout the whole component.

The shrinking operation is local. There are two rules: If your neighbors to the right, below, and the lower right are all zero, you turn to zero; if your neighbor to the right and the neighbor below are one, you turn to one; in all other cases you do not change. We can visualize the two rules as follows:

First Rule

x	0
0	0

$\rightarrow$

0	?
?	?

Second Rule

x	1
1	?

$\rightarrow$

1	?
?	?

The rules are applied simultaneously to all pixels.

Example 12.4.15. Consider labeling components in the image

1	0	1	1	0
1	0	1	0	1
1	0	1	0	1
1	0	0	0	1
0	0	1	1	1

Remember that the image is invisibly surrounded by a border of zeros.

No rule applies to pixel $(1, 1)$; hence it remains unchanged. Pixel $(3, 3)$, however, falls under the first rule, and the 1 turns to 0. The first rule also applies to pixels $(4, 1)$ and $(5, 5)$ [in the case of $(5, 5)$ because of the border of zeros]. The second rule applies only twice in the picture, namely to pixels $(1, 3)$ and $(4, 4)$. Pixel $(1, 3)$ is already 1; hence we see no change there, but $(4, 4)$ does change from 0 to 1. In all other positions neither of the rules apply; hence they remain unchanged. The result after the first step is:

1	0	1	1	0
1	0	1	0	1
1	0	0	0	1
0	0	0	1	1
0	0	1	1	0

It is instructive to observe how the components evolve. It looks as if they are rolled up like a carpet from the lower-right corner. In the next step, the rules continue to roll up that component: Pixels $(4, 5)$ and $(5, 4)$ change to 0 (first rule), and pixels $(4, 3)$ and $(3, 4)$ change to 1 (second rule). The other end of the component and the other component get frayed: $(3, 1)$ and $(2, 3)$ both turn to 0. The only other application of a rule in this image is of the second rule to position $(1, 3)$, which, however, does not make a change.

1	0	1	1	0
1	0	0	0	1
0	0	0	1	1
0	0	1	1	0
0	0	1	0	0

In the next step, the carpet rolls up one more diagonal and starts becoming smaller. One of the two components has been reduced to a single pixel at this point. In the algorithm we would now assign it the label $1 \times 5 + 1 = 6$.

1	0	1	1	0
0	0	0	1	1
0	0	1	1	0
0	0	1	0	0
0	0	0	0	0

In the next step, the component that was just labeled vanished entirely, while the other component is still being reduced.

0	0	1	1	0
0	0	1	1	0
0	0	1	0	0
0	0	0	0	0
0	0	0	0	0

The two lowest elements now vanish.

0	0	1	1	0
0	0	1	0	0
0	0	0	0	0
0	0	0	0	0
0	0	0	0	0

In the next step, the last component is finally reduced to a single pixel.

0	0	1	0	0
0	0	0	0	0
0	0	0	0	0
0	0	0	0	0
0	0	0	0	0

At this point in the algorithm, we would label the last remaining black pixel with $1 \times 5 + 3 = 8$. In the next step, this pixel also vanishes, and we are done.

0	0	0	0	0
0	0	0	0	0
0	0	0	0	0
0	0	0	0	0
0	0	0	0	0

□

In Example 12.4.15, each component is reduced to a single pixel before it vanishes entirely. This is true in general.

Lemma 12.4.16. *Applying the shrinking rules at most $2n - 1$ times yields a square of zeros.*

Example 12.4.17. In Example 12.4.15 we had to apply the shrinking rules 7 times, which is less than $2 \times 5 - 1$. □

Proof. To show that it is sufficient to apply the shrinking rules $2n - 1$ times, we show that after the ith application, the diagonal D_i from pixel $(n, n - i + 1)$ to $(n - i + 1, n)$ consists of zeros only. (You can visually check this in Example 12.4.15.) This is true for $i = 1$ since the pixels below, to the right, and to the lower right of pixel (n, n) are all 0. Let us see what the diagonal D_i looks like after the ith application of the shrinking rules. The neighbors below, to the right, and to the lower right of any of the pixels in D_i belong to D_{i-1} and D_{i-2}, both of which contain 0 after the $(i - 1)$st application of the shrinking rules. Hence, all the pixels of D_i turn to 0 after the ith step (by the first rule). ∎

Our next goal is to show that the shrinking rules do not break up a component or merge two different components. This guarantees that the algorithm works correctly since all components remain intact and separate.

Lemma 12.4.18. *Applying the shrinking rules cannot merge two different components.*

Proof. The only way two components could merge is by the introduction of a new 1, which happens only through the second rule. Let us look at an application of the second rule:

a	b	c
d	x	1
e	1	?

By the second rule, x turns to 1 in this situation. How could this connect two components that were not connected before? It cannot be through b, c, d, or e, since these (if they are 1) are already connected by the two 1's to the left and below x. Hence, x must connect the component to which a belongs to the component to which the two 1's belong. This means that a has to be 1. If either b or d is a 1, a would already belong to the same component as the two 1's, so we can assume that both b and d are 0, in which case a turns into 0 in the next step and can therefore no longer establish a connection between two components. ∎

Lemma 12.4.19. *Applying the shrinking rules does not disconnect a component.*

Proof. Let us say that a 1 causes another 1 if it is either the same 1, which is not affected by the shrinking rules, or if the second shrinking rule is applied to it, resulting in the other 1. That is, a 1 can cause 1's in three positions: above itself, to its left, and at its own position.

We want to show that if two 1's belong to the same component, then all of the 1's they cause belong to the same component. This means that the shrinking rules do not disconnect a component. We first observe that it is sufficient to prove the claim for two 1's that are immediate neighbors: If two 1's belong to the same component, we can connect them by a series of neighbors. If the claim is true for each pair of neighbors, it is then true for the two 1's at the end of the series.

To prove the claim, consider how it could happen that two neighboring 1's cause two 1's that are not connected. There are only four ways two 1's can be neighbors to each other. Let us investigate them separately. First, consider two horizontally neighboring 1's:

a	b	c
d	1	1

These two 1's can cause b, c, and d to turn into 1's. The middle 1 in the lower row remains (the first rule does not apply because there is a 1 to the right) and therefore connects all of b, c, and d.

A similar argument applies in the case of two 1's that are vertical neighbors:

a	b
c	1
d	1

Again, the two 1's can cause b, c, and d to turn to 1's, and the 1 in the middle row remains connecting them.

This leaves us with the two diagonal cases. For

a	b	c
d	e	1
f	1	g

we have a simple argument: e turns to 1 connecting all 1's that could possibly be caused by the two 1's. Similarly, considering

a	b	c
d	1	e
f	g	1

we see that the central 1 remains (since the first rule does not apply) connecting all 1's possibly caused by these two 1's. ∎

Lemma 12.4.20. *In the step before a component vanishes, it consists of a single pixel.*

Proof. Suppose there is a component containing at least two points that vanishes in a single step. Since the component is connected, it must contain two adjacent 1's; that is, the component must contain one of the following:

1	1
?	?

1	?
1	?

1	?
?	1

?	1
?	1

In all four cases at least one 1 is left after applying the shrinking rule, contradicting the assumption that the component vanishes. ∎

We can now put the lemmas together to construct a labeling algorithm. A good time to decide on a label for a component is when it consists of a single pixel. That this must happen is guaranteed by Lemma 12.4.16 and Lemma 12.4.20. When a processor finds an isolated 1 at position (i, j), it labels it with value $in + j$. After $2n - 1$ steps, we have reduced the whole image to zeros (Lemma 12.4.16). At this point we run the shrinking process backwards. Each processor undoes the shrinking rules in parallel step by step. The components come into being as single pixels that have a unique label assigned to them. As we then undo the shrinking rules, we propagate that label to the new 1's that are generated. Lemma 12.4.18 tells us that we reach only pixels that belong to the same component, and Lemma 12.4.19 says that we reach all points that belong to that component. After at most $2n - 1$ steps of unraveling, we are done.

Example 12.4.21. We trace backwards the run of Levialdi's algorithm in Example 12.4.15, assigning the labels as we undo the shrinking rules.

0	0	0	0	0
0	0	0	0	0
0	0	0	0	0
0	0	0	0	0
0	0	0	0	0

(1)

0	0	8	0	0
0	0	0	0	0
0	0	0	0	0
0	0	0	0	0
0	0	0	0	0

(2)

0	0	8	8	0
0	0	0	0	0
0	0	0	0	0
0	0	0	0	0
0	0	0	0	0

(3)

0	0	8	8	0
0	0	0	8	0
0	0	8	0	0
0	0	0	0	0
0	0	0	0	0

(4)

6	0	8	8	0
0	0	0	8	8
0	0	8	8	0
0	0	8	0	0
0	0	0	0	0

(5)

6	0	8	8	0
6	0	0	0	8
0	0	0	8	8
0	0	8	8	0
0	0	8	0	0

(6)

6	0	8	8	0
6	0	8	0	8
6	0	0	0	8
0	0	0	8	8
0	0	8	8	0

(7)

6	0	8	8	0
6	0	8	0	8
6	0	8	0	8
6	0	0	0	8
0	0	8	8	8

(8)

Image (8) is a component-labeling of the original picture. □

Theorem 12.4.22. *We can solve the component-labeling problem in parallel time $\Theta(n)$ using n^2 processors arranged on a mesh.*

The algorithm is not work-optimal since we can solve the problem sequentially in time $O(n^2)$. There are algorithms for other network topologies (meshes of trees) that achieve a running time of $\Theta(\lg^2 n)$ using $\Theta(n^2)$ processors.

An even more serious objection to the algorithm is that it needs to keep track of the history of the shrinking process: Once we have reduced the whole image to zeros, we could have gotten there from any initial image. To make Levialdi's algorithm work, each processor must, in each step, store the contents of all of its eight immediate neighbors to be able to undo the shrinking rules. Since the shrinking phase runs for $2n - 1$ steps, this means that each processor has to store roughly $16n$ bits of information. The algorithm can be modified to run using only $\Theta(\lg n)$ bits of storage, but the running time increases to $\Theta(n \lg n)$ (Cypher, Sanz, Snyder; 1990). A more complicated algorithm using pipelining achieves a running time of $\Theta(n)$ using only $\Theta(\lg n)$ storage bits (Shi, Ritter; 1994).

Exercises

1S. What is the diameter of a linear array on n vertices?

2. What is the diameter of a ring on n vertices?

3. A network of processors is *connected* if any two processors in the network can communicate with each other. Show that a connected network on n processors contains at least $n - 1$ communication channels between processors. *Hint:* Rephrase the problem in graph-theoretic terms and then use a result from graph theory.

4S. Show how to embed the linear array on eight vertices in the three-dimensional hypercube; that is, map the eight vertices to vertices in the hypercube so that adjacent vertices in the array are mapped to adjacent vertices in the hypercube.

5. Draw a four-dimensional hypercube with labeled vertices, as we did for the three-dimensional hypercube in Figure 12.4.7.

6. Draw the five-dimensional hypercube.

7S. Show that two vertices in the hypercube whose labels agree in all but one coordinate are adjacent.

8. Show that the distance between two vertices in the hypercube is the same as the Hamming distance of their labels. (The *Hamming distance* of two binary sequences is the number of positions in which they disagree.)

9. Show that for any vertex in the d-dimensional hypercube there is another vertex that has distance d from it.

10S. Show that the diameter of the d-dimensional hypercube is d (upper and lower bound).

11. Write an algorithm that takes as input the labels of two vertices v and w in a d-dimensional hypercube and prints a shortest list of vertices that can take a message from v to w. (See Example 12.4.2.)

12. Show that the d-dimensional hypercube has connectivity at most d; that is, it is possible to remove d vertices and disconnect the hypercube.

13S. Trace Shearsort on input

16	3	2	13
5	10	11	8
9	6	7	12
4	15	14	1

14. Trace Shearsort on input

16	12	20	2
6	14	4	8
7	13	3	9
15	5	11	1

15. Trace Shearsort on input

1	0	1	0	1
0	1	1	0	0
1	1	0	1	1
0	0	0	1	0
1	1	1	0	1

16S. Trace Shearsort on input

4	19	3	1	12	14
9	36	5	10	35	6
18	2	31	7	32	29
20	33	21	8	26	30
11	25	22	13	27	16
34	24	23	15	17	28

17. How often does Shearsort have to repeat its two phases to sort a decreasing input sequence of length n?

18. Show that the zero-one principle is not true for non-oblivious comparison-exchange algorithms. *Hint:* If we do not have to be oblivious, we can tell how many different inputs there are.

19S. Give an example that shows that Shearsort fails to sort its input if, instead of sorting the rows alternately in ascending and descending order, we sort them all in ascending order.

20S. Show that an $n \times n$ black and white image can contain components of diameter $\Omega(n^2)$.

21. Trace *minimum_label* on input

1	0	0	1	1
0	1	0	0	1
1	0	0	0	1
0	1	0	1	0
1	0	1	0	1

22. Trace *minimum_label* on input

1	1	1	1	1	1
0	0	0	0	0	1
1	1	1	1	0	1
1	0	0	1	0	1
1	0	0	0	0	1
1	0	1	1	1	1

23S. Trace Levialdi's component-labeling algorithm on input

1	1	1	1	1
1	0	0	0	1
1	0	1	0	1
1	0	0	0	1
1	1	1	1	1

24. Trace Levialdi's component-labeling algorithm on input

1	0	0	1	1
0	1	0	0	1
0	0	1	0	1
1	0	0	1	1
1	1	1	1	1

25. Trace Levialdi's component-labeling algorithm on input

1	0	1	1	0	1
1	0	0	0	1	0
1	1	1	0	1	1
1	0	0	0	1	0
1	0	1	1	0	1
1	0	1	1	1	0

12.5 Distributed Algorithms

WWW In early 1999, a network of nearly 100,000 PCs on the Internet decrypted a DES-encrypted message in less than a day, sealing the fate of the 25-year old government standard for encryption (DES is an abbreviation for Data Encryption Standard; it has now been superseded by AES, the Advanced Encryption Standard). The attack was not based on sophisticated mathematical properties of the DES encryption scheme, but on brute force. DES uses a 56-bit key; that is, there are only 2^{56} possible keys to check. A typical PC at the time could check about 2 million keys in a second, so one PC would take about $2^{56}/(2 * 10^6)$ seconds, or roughly 1000 years. 100,000 PCs working in parallel reduce that time to about 4 days.

Similar distributed projects have been set up for tasks such as factoring large numbers (another activity of interest to cryptanalysts), finding large twin primes, and even searching for extraterrestrial intelligence (the famous SETI project). All of these projects exhibit a typical feature of distributed computation: The task to be solved parallelizes well. The task breaks into highly independent subtasks with little communication between the tasks necessary. In the DES project, for example, keys were separated into large blocks and handed to different processors to work on. Similarly, all the SETI screen savers perform the same analysis, each on a different dataset.

We conclude that the core question in distributed computing is not whether, or how, the problem parallelizes, but how the multitude of processors establish and maintain a distributed computation in a potentially unreliable or even hostile environment. What should be done if a PC that has been working on a particular block of keys does not return any results? Was the communication lost or was the computer shut down? Do we reassign the block of keys or do we wait? What if one of the PCs has been hacked and is now maliciously returning wrong results? Can we recognize whether this happens? And, who is "we"? In all of the examples mentioned previously, there is one central processor that farms out the tasks to available clients and administers the whole computation. However, in general, we do not want to assume that there is necessarily one dedicated leader. Remember that the ARPANET, the forerunner of the Internet, was created by the US Department of Defense in 1969 as a *decentralized* communication network to guard against potential nuclear attacks. Even if some of the hosts in the Internet are taken out, communication is still possible. If the main computer in a centralized network is removed, the whole network collapses.

Example 12.5.1. Natural scientists and computer scientists are working on building software and toolkits for PVDGs (Petascale Virtual Data Grids).[†] Virtual data grids are distributed systems (built on computer networks) that analyze distributed data: Data may be received by any machine in the network and might have to be available to any other machine for analysis. The software has to simulate a virtual data space for storage and retrieval of experimental data. Potential applications range from studying particle collisions and supernovas to studying the human brain and the human genome, all of which require handling huge datasets. □

We see that the study of distributed algorithms is driven by questions that concern the basic communication between the processors forming the distributed network. At lower levels, communication involves protocols such as TCP/IP for packet routing on the Internet, and CORBA for remote method invocation. Here, we concentrate on a less technical view; that is, we assume that basic communication tools between processors are available. We then

---

[†]A petabyte is 10^{15} bytes.

want to solve problems such as broadcasting a piece of information to every processor in the network (the *broadcasting problem*) or selecting a processor for performing a particular task, (the *leader-election problem*).

There are many models of distributed computation. It is generally assumed that processors are loosely coupled; that is, there are information channels between certain pairs of processors, but no other information is shared. In particular, there is no notion of a global state, as there is in a centralized algorithm. However, occasionally it does make sense to assume that all processors can work synchronously, through access to a *global clock*. Such networks are called *synchronous*. If we do not assume the existence of a global clock, we call the network computation *asynchronous*. For the algorithms in this section, we make several further assumptions. For example, we require that channels between processors be reliable, so no messages are lost. We also usually require that every machine has a unique ID (such as an IP address) and that the network does not change during the execution of the algorithm (which is certainly not true in general). Each machine is assumed to know its local neighborhood, that is, which machines it is connected to directly by which channels. We add to our programming language the ability to send and receive messages along these channels as follows:

> send $\langle M \rangle$ to p
> receive $\langle M \rangle$ from p

The first line of code sends a message M to processor p, which must be a neighbor of the processor on which the send command is run; the second line receives a message M from p, which, again, must be a neighbor of the processor running the receive command. We drop the "to p" or the "from p" part if there is a unique channel for the message.

Sending a message is an active process, but receiving a message is inherently passive: The processor enters a waiting loop until the message arrives (in practice this would be handled by an interrupt). In this case, we say that the processor is in a **waiting** state. If it never receives the message, it will remain waiting forever without terminating.

We also add a command

> terminate

to our language that allows an algorithm to terminate execution. This usually means that the algorithm has successfully completed its task.

Broadcasting

Given a distributed network of machines, we want to write a distributed algorithm that broadcasts to all processors in the network that some event has occurred. In a distributed algorithm we distinguish between **initiators** and **noninitiators**. In the broadcasting problem, one of the machines wants to inform all of the other machines in the network that some event has occurred. That machine is the initiator of the broadcasting process; the other machines are noninitiators. Let us first investigate the special case of a directed ring topology; that is, the machines are arranged in a cycle, and every machine has a successor and predecessor corresponding to the order in which the machines appear on the cycle.

To broadcast in a ring, the initiator sends a special message called the **token** to its next neighbor, which in turn passes it on along the ring until the token returns to the initiator. At that point, the initiator knows that every machine in the ring has seen the token and that the information has been broadcast. We do not include any actual message with the token; in a particular application, messages could be appended to the token.

Algorithm 12.5.2 Ring Broadcast. This algorithm is run on a ring network. The initiator runs *init_ring_broadcast*, and the noninitiators run *ring_broadcast*. All processors terminate successfully after having received a message from the initiator.

```
init_ring_broadcast() {
    send token to successor
    receive token from predecessor
    terminate
}
```

```
ring_broadcast() {
    receive token from predecessor
    send token to successor
    terminate
}
```

If the ring consists of n machines, then the distributed-broadcast algorithm takes $\Theta(n)$ steps, and n messages get sent. The number of messages sent is known as the **message complexity**, and in a distributed algorithm it is as important a measure as the number of steps the algorithm takes. An algorithm that blocks the network by flooding it with messages is useless.

Theorem 12.5.3. *Algorithm 12.5.2 solves the broadcasting problem on a directed ring of n machines using time and message complexity $\Theta(n)$.*

In an actual implementation of the ring-broadcasting algorithm, we would put a time limit on how long the initiator waits for the token. If the initiator did not receive the token by the time-out, it would assume the token was lost and would have to rerun the broadcasting algorithm.

We can extend the idea of the ring broadcast to arbitrary, connected networks as follows:

Algorithm 12.5.4 Broadcast. This algorithm works on any (fixed) connected network. The initiator runs *init_broadcast* and the noninitiators *broadcast*. All processors terminate successfully after having received a message from the initiator. In the algorithms we assume that the current machine we are running the code on is called p.

```
init_broadcast() {
    N = {q | q is a neighbor of p}
    for each q ∈ N
        send token to neighbor q
    terminate
}
```

```
broadcast() {
    receive token from neighbor q
    N = {q | q is a neighbor of p}
    for each q ∈ N
        send token to neighbor q
    terminate
}
```

There is one feature of the ring-broadcasting algorithm (Algorithm 12.5.2) that is not implemented by Algorithm 12.5.4: the acknowledgment of success. In the ring-broadcasting algorithm, the initiator terminated only after it knew that all processors in the network had received its message; that is, we implemented a broadcast algorithm with acknowledgment. In Algorithm 12.5.4, by comparison, the initiator terminates immediately after sending messages to all of its neighbors, and the broadcast could fail without the initiator being aware of it. Failure would be a serious problem in an actual implementation since without acknowledgment we would not know whether the algorithm had failed, and we would not know whether we would have to rerun the broadcast algorithm.

Our goal then is to write a broadcasting algorithm with acknowledgment for an arbitrary connected network of n machines. The initiator may terminate only after all processors in the network have received its message.

The basic idea of the ring algorithm was to pass a message around the ring until it returns to the initiator. In an arbitrary network this becomes more complicated: A message might return to the initiator without having traversed the entire network. Another problem is that messages could start cycling, since we do not allow any assumptions on the structure of the network. The two problems suggest a graph theory tool we have seen earlier: the spanning tree. It does not contain any cycles (since it is a tree), and it does reach all machines, since it is spanning. We know that a spanning tree exists since we assumed that the network is connected. If we had a spanning tree of the network, we could send out messages along its edges to reach each machine in the network and then receive acknowledgments in return. However, since we do not have a spanning tree, we need to build one. This is achieved by the *echo algorithm*. The echo algorithm builds a tree vertex by vertex until it has exhausted the network (turning the tree into a spanning tree), at which point messages are sent back to the initiator to acknowledge success. The initiator starts the computation by sending messages to all of its neighbors. It then waits until it has obtained a reply from all of the neighbors. All other nodes wait until they get a message from one of their neighbors. That neighbor becomes their *parent* in the spanning tree. Once a node has received a message, it becomes part of the tree (through its parent) and then sends messages to all of its neighbors except its parent. It then waits until it has received acknowledgments for each of the messages it sent. At this point, it sends a message to its parent to signal that the traversal of the subtree of the spanning tree of which it is the root is complete.

Algorithm 12.5.5 Echo. This algorithm works on any (fixed) connected network. The initiator runs *init_echo* and the noninitiators *echo*. All processors terminate successfully after having received a message from the initiator. The initiator terminates after all processors have received its message. The machine on which we are running the code is called p.

```
init_echo() {
    N = {q | q is a neighbor of p}
    for each q ∈ N
        send token to neighbor q
    counter = 0
    while (counter < |N|) {
        receive token
        counter = counter + 1
    }
    terminate
}

echo() {
    receive token from neighbor q
    parent = q
    N = {q | q is a neighbor of p} − {parent}
    for each q ∈ N
        send token to neighbor q
    counter = 0
    while (counter < |N|) {
        receive token
        counter = counter + 1
    }
    send token to neighbor parent
    terminate
}
```

Example 12.5.6. We show a possible sample run of Algorithm 12.5.5 on the network in Figure 12.5.1(a). We draw a token as a full disc with an arrow indicating the direction it is traveling along an edge. Whenever the algorithm adds an edge to the spanning tree by choosing a parent for a machine, we indicate that by turning the corresponding edge into a directed edge pointing from the parent to the child. Within each node, we keep track of the *counter* variable of the machine. Initially, the value is $\perp$ to denote that it is undefined; once the machine has terminated, we indicate this by changing the value to $\top$. Figure 12.5.1(a) depicts the initial state of the network, when machine 2 decides to initiate the broadcasting process. It sends out tokens to machines 1, 6, and 3, and its counter turns to 0.

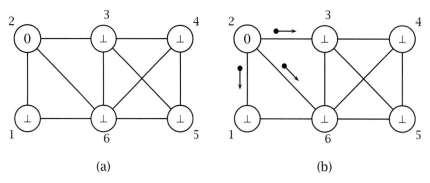

(a)   (b)

Figure 12.5.1 (a) Initial state of the network. (b) Machine 2 has initiated the broadcasting process.

The result of machine 2 initializing the broadcasting process is seen in Figure 12.5.1(b).

In Figure 12.5.2(c), the first message, sent from 2 to 1, has reached its destination, adding the edges from 2 to 1 to the tree; and node 1 has initialized its counter to 0 and sent a message to its neighbor 6. The message from 2 to 6 is still on its way. The snapshot of the network in Figure 12.5.2(d) shows that several things have happened. The message from machine 2 to 3 has arrived in 3, making 2 the parent of 3. Machine 3 has initialized its counter to 0 and in turn sent messages to 4, 5, and 6.

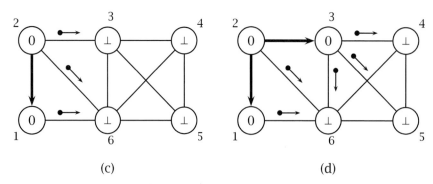

(c)   (d)

Figure 12.5.2 (c) The first edge of the tree, 2 to 1, is found. (d) The tree extends to node 3.

In the next stage [Figure 12.5.3(e)], the message from 1 has reached 6, extending the tree to include 6, and messages have been sent from 6 to its neighbors 2, 3, 4, and 6. None of the other messages have made any progress in the meantime.

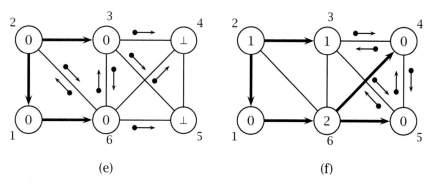

(e)   (f)

Figure 12.5.3 (e) The tree contains nodes 2, 3, 1, and 6. (f) The tree spans the entire network.

Figure 12.5.3(e) shows several messages being received by machines that already belong to the tree, namely machine 2 receiving the message from 6, and machine 6 receiving the messages from 2 and 3. The counters are updated correspondingly. Also, the two messages from 6 to 4 and 5 have resulted in new edges of the tree (turning it into a spanning tree, although the algorithm is not aware of that yet). Messages are sent from 4 to 3 and 5, and from 5 to 3 and 4.

In Figure 12.5.4(g) processors 3, 4, and 5 have received messages from all of their children, so they now return messages to their respective parents.

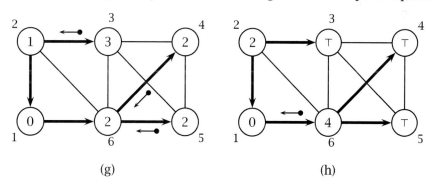

(g)   (h)

Figure 12.5.4 (g) Nodes 4, 5, and 3 have received messages from all of their children. (h) Node 6 has received messages from all of its children, and nodes 3, 4, and 5 have terminated successfully.

In the next step [Figure 12.5.4(h)], machine 6 has received messages from all of its children and therefore sends a message to its parent, processor 1. Furthermore, processors 3, 4, and 5 have terminated. Figures 12.5.5(i) and (j) show how this message is passed on to processor 2, the root of the spanning

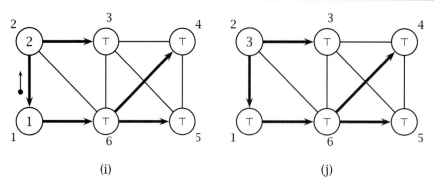

(i)   (j)

Figure 12.5.5 (i) Node 6 has terminated successfully. (j) Node 2 is about to terminate successfully, completing the computation.

tree, which terminates in the next step since it has received messages from all of its children.

In conclusion, we note the sample run described here is only one of several possible runs of the algorithm. For example, if after the initial step shown in Figure 12.5.1, the message from processor 2 to 6 had reached 6 before the message from 1, we would have obtained a different spanning tree of the network. ☐

Note that every machine p sends at most one message to each neighbor. Therefore, every edge of the network is traversed by at most two messages, one in each direction, implying that the overall message complexity is at most twice the number of edges in the network. Consequently, the algorithm stops performing after a while; but it could be that at that point some, or all, of the machines are still waiting for messages and have not terminated. In that case, we say the algorithm is in a *deadlock*. We have to verify that the algorithm cannot run into a deadlock; that is, the only way the algorithm can stop performing is after all machines have terminated. Let us consider a potential deadlock state in which the machines that have not yet terminated are permanently deadlocked in a waiting state. We first observe that in such a state every machine in the network has received a message from a neighbor: If there was a machine that had not received a message, then there is such a machine q adjacent to a machine p that has received a message (since the network is connected). Now since q is not a parent of p (since it has not received any message at all), p must have sent a message to q, contradicting the assumption. We can therefore conclude that the algorithm successfully builds a spanning tree of the network (encoded in the *parent* relation). Now assume that the algorithm halts without all machines having terminated successfully. Select a non-terminating machine p at a maximum distance in the spanning tree from the initiator (which is the root of the spanning tree). Machine p has two types of neighbors: first, those neighbors that are at most as far away from the initiator as p, and second, those that have larger distance from the initiator than p. Since we assumed that p was the farthest distance from the initiator at which a machine did not terminate successfully, all machines farther away than p did terminate successfully and, if they were neighbors of p, sent a message to p. Now consider the first type of neighbors of p. Any neighbor q of p that has the same distance or less from the initiator as p must already be part of the spanning tree when it receives a message from p. (Otherwise p would become its parent, and q would be farther away from the initiator than p.) Therefore, any neighbor q of the second type must have already sent a message to p (unless, of course, it is the parent of p). In either case, p obtains messages from all neighbors (with the exception of its parent if it has one) and therefore either sends a message to its parent and terminates successfully, or, in case p is the initiator, terminates successfully.

Theorem 12.5.7. *The echo algorithm (Algorithm 12.5.5) broadcasts a message to all processors in an arbitrary (fixed) connected network using time $\Theta(d)$ and message complexity $\Theta(m)$, where m is the number of edges in the network and d the diameter.*

We leave the proof that the number of steps performed by the echo algorithm is $\Theta(d)$ to Exercise 5.

Leader Election

In the broadcasting problem there is one processor initiating the broadcasting process. How was this processor selected? In some circumstances the processor might be determined before the algorithm runs, for example, if it is the printer server in a local area network and the task is a print request. However, in a distributed computing environment, there usually is no significant difference between the processors; every processor could perform every task. And since the network might change over time, it is often preferable to select a processor for a certain task when the task has to be performed, rather than using a predetermined processor, which might not be available when it is needed. Think, for example, about a processor coordinating recovery after a partial system failure. Only the processors that are still active can participate.

Example 12.5.8. In the 1970s IBM developed the token ring network, a special local area network topology. In a token ring, the processors are arranged in a ring along which a single token gets passed. When a processor wants to send a message to another machine, it first needs to obtain the token. It then appends its message to the token and sends the new token to the receiver, which takes the token off the network, reads the message, and then puts the token (without the message) back on the network. The main advantage of token rings is that they avoid message collisions, since at any one time at most one token is in the ring. One problem this architecture encounters is that tokens can get lost, possibly in transmission from one processor to another, or because a processor is holding on to it longer than it is allowed to. In these cases, it becomes necessary for the processors in the ring that notice the loss of the token to generate a new token. Since several processors might notice the problem, they need to agree on which processor will generate the new token for the ring.   □

How then can a group of processors that recognize that a certain task has to be performed select a processor to perform it? Phrased differently, we want to write a distributed algorithm in which a group of processors, the initiators, select one of the initiators (to perform or coordinate some task). This problem is known as **leader election**.

We are assuming that the distributed environment is asynchronous, and that every processor p has its own unique (numerical) ID $p.ID$. We also assume that the processors pass messages in order; that is, multiple messages on a channel cannot overtake each other. Furthermore, we solve the problem only for one particular architecture, the unidirectional ring, a ring on which messages can be sent in only one direction; that is, every processor p has exactly one next neighbor, $p.next$, to which it can send messages, and one previous neighbor from which it can receive messages (see Figure 12.5.6).

Figure 12.5.6 A unidirectional ring on eleven processors.

As a leader, we decide to elect the processor with the smallest ID, which belongs to the group of initiators (we used a similar idea for labeling components of an image on a square grid of processors in Section 12.4). With this idea, we can solve the leader-election problem using the broadcasting algorithm: Every initiator broadcasts its ID along the ring, and every initiator keeps track of the smallest ID it has seen. Consequently, the processor with the smallest ID recognizes that it is the processor with the smallest ID and becomes the leader.

Algorithm 12.5.9 Leader Election. This algorithm runs on the unidirectional ring. The initiators run *init_election* and the noninitiators run *election*. All processors terminate successfully, and exactly one initiator has its *leader* attribute set to true. In the algorithms, we assume that the current machine we are running the code on is called p. Every processor has a next neighbor, $p.next$, to which it can send messages.

```
init_election() {
    send ⟨token, p.ID⟩ to p.next
    min = p.ID
    receive ⟨token, I⟩
    while (p.ID ≠ I) {
        if (I < min)
            min = I
        send ⟨token, I⟩ to p.next
        receive ⟨token, I⟩
    }
    if (p.ID == min)
        p.leader = true
    else
        p.leader = false
    terminate
}


election() {
    p.leader = false // noninitiator is never chosen as leader
    do {
        receive ⟨token, I⟩
        send ⟨token, I⟩ to p.next
    } while (true)
}
```

Let us show that the algorithms work correctly. We claim that *p.leader* can be true for at most one processor. The noninitiators automatically set the attribute *leader* to false, so we need to consider only the initiators. For an initiator p with ID I to set its attribute *p.leader* to true, it must have received the message ⟨token, I⟩ it sent out initially. Since we assume that the messages in the ring do not change order, this also means that p must have processed the message of all the other initiators at that point, since an initiator will send on messages only after it has sent out a token with its own ID. Therefore, the variable *min* of p contains the smallest ID of any initiator, which is unique. Therefore, at most one processor (the initiator with the smallest ID) can set its attribute *leader* to true. Furthermore, the initiator with the smallest ID *does* set its attribute *leader* to true when its original messages return. Hence, the algorithm is correct and terminates.

If the ring consists of n processors, each initiator stops after n steps, having sent at most a total of n^2 messages.

Theorem 12.5.10. *Algorithm 12.5.9 solves the leader-election problem on the unidirectional ring in n steps with a message complexity of $O(n^2)$.*

In Exercises 12.36–12.38 we show that an easy modification of Algorithm 12.5.9 solves the leader-election problem with an average message complexity of $O(n \log n)$. There are more complicated algorithms that solve the leader-election problem on the unidirectional ring with a worst-case message complexity of $O(n \log n)$, which is known to be optimal (even in the average case). On an arbitrary graph $G = (V, E)$, the leader-election problem can be solved in time $\Theta(n)$ and message complexity $\Theta(n \log n + m)$, where $n = |V|$ and $m = |E|$, a result that is known to be optimal.

Exercises

1S. Write a broadcasting algorithm (with a single initiator and acknowledgment) for the complete network K_n. What is the time complexity of your algorithm? What is the message complexity of your algorithm?

2. Give a sample run of the echo algorithm (Algorithm 12.5.5) in the style of Example 12.5.6 on the following graph.

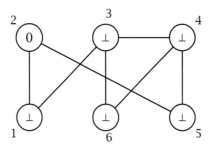

3. Give a sample run of the echo algorithm (Algorithm 12.5.5) in the style of Example 12.5.6 on the following graph.

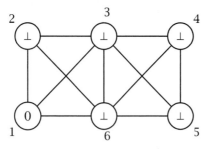

4S. Solve the *synchronization problem* on a ring. A processor wants to run a piece of code p, but it has to make sure that all of the other processors on the ring are ready for the code to be performed. That is, in each processor q, some event e_q must occur before p may be performed. *Hint:* The problem can be solved with a distributed algorithm in $\Theta(n)$ steps and message complexity $\Theta(n)$.

5. Show that the echo algorithm (Algorithm 12.5.5) runs in time $\Theta(d)$, where d is the diameter of the network. (The *diameter* of a graph is the largest distance between any two vertices.)

6. In the leader-election algorithm, we assumed that messages do not overtake each other on the ring. Show that this assumption is essential by providing an example where the outcome is not acceptable (no leader, or multiple leaders) if the messages are allowed to overtake each other. Is it possible that no leaders get elected? Is it possible that multiple leaders get elected?

7S. Only the initiators in the leader-election algorithm terminate since the noninitiators run infinite loops. Modify the code so that all processors terminate after a leader has been elected.

Notes

$\mathcal{WWW}$ The PRAM as a model for parallel computation generalizing the RAM model emerged in the late 1980s, and it has since become the standard model for shared memory SIMD (single instruction stream, multiple data stream) computers. Jájá's *Introduction to Parallel Algorithms* (Jájá, 1992) and Akl's *Design and Analysis of Parallel Algorithms* (Akl, 1989) are good introductory textbooks on PRAM programming. Although the PRAM is a theoretical model, there have been attempts at building a PRAM computer, and there even is a recent book on practical PRAM programming.

A wealth of material on sorting networks, including information on networks for small values of n can be found in Knuth's *Sorting and Searching*, the third volume in his series *The Art of Computer Programming* (Knuth, 1998b). The idea of building a sorting network using bitonic sorters is due to Batcher who patented it in 1969. Earlier, Batcher had designed the odd-even merging network, a sorting network based on mergesort. The zero-one principle (Theorem 12.3.19) was discovered by Knuth. Detecting whether a sorting network is incorrect is an **NP**-complete problem, a result due to Rabin, 1980 (according to Knuth,1998b). Exercises 12.23 and 12.24 on primitive sorting networks are from Knuth, 1998b.

Leighton's *Introduction to Parallel Algorithms and Architectures* is the standard reference for parallel architectures (Leighton, 1992). The book covers parallel algorithms for arrays, trees, hypercubes, and related network topologies. Shearsort was discovered independently in 1986 by Sado and Igarishi, and Scherson, Sen, and Shamir. There are several $O(n)$ time sorting algorithms for the mesh, beginning with one based on Batcher's odd-even merging network (Thompson, Kung, 1977). The basic component-labeling algorithm is due to Levialdi. It has been modified and improved to reduce the amount of space used within each processor and the amount of communication necessary between processors. The currently best algorithm runs in time $O(n)$ on n^2 processors using $O(\lg n)$ local space and is due to Shi and Ritter (Shi, Ritter, 1994).

$\mathcal{WWW}$ The theory of **P**-completeness identifies problems that we do not expect to parallelize. The book *Limits of Parallel Computation* covers this material in detail (Greenlaw, Hoover, and Ruzzo, 1995).

Distributed algorithms and distributed computation are dealt with in books by (Tel, 2000), (Lynch, 1996), and (Attiya and Welch, 1998). The echo algorithm is due to Chang (Chang, 1982). The leader-election algorithm was published even earlier, by LeLann (LeLann, 1977).

Chapter Exercises

12.1. Prove Theorem 12.2.10 for the common CW model.

Exercises 12.2–12.4 concern the problem of computing the maximum of an array of n numbers in the CRCW model.

12.2. Show how to compute the maximum of an array of n numbers in parallel time $O(1)$ on a CRCW (common) PRAM using n^2 processors. *Hint:* See how concurrency helped in the parallel-search algorithm.

12.3. Show how to compute the maximum of an array of n numbers in parallel time $O(\lg \lg n)$ and $O(n \lg \lg n)$ processors on a CRCW PRAM. *Hint:* Instead of a binary tree of depth $\lg n$, use a tree of depth $\lg \lg n$ in which each node at level $1 \le i \le \lg \lg n$ has $2^{2^{(\lg \lg n) - i}}$ children. For example, the root has $2^{2^{\lg \lg n - 1}} = \sqrt{n}$ children.

12.4. Design a work-optimal algorithm that computes the maximum of an array of n numbers in parallel time $O(\lg \lg n)$ and work $O(n)$ on a CRCW PRAM. *Hint:* Use accelerated cascading. As a slow, work-optimal algorithm, use the maximum algorithm from Section 12.2 and as the fast, suboptimal algorithm, use the algorithm from Exercise 12.3.

12.5. You are given an array a of n numbers and want to compute all partial averages, that is, the averages of $a[0], \ldots, a[k]$ for all $0 \le k < n$. Write an $O(\lg n)$ parallel-time EREW algorithm. The algorithm does not have to be work-optimal.

12.6. Use accelerated cascading to implement a work-optimal algorithm for parallel search.

12.7. Write a work-optimal $O(\lg n)$ parallel-time algorithm that computes the maximum of an array of n numbers in the EREW model *Hint:* You can model this algorithm after *optimal_ $\otimes$ _sum.*

12.8. Show how to add two n-bit binary numbers in $O(\lg n)$ parallel time using n processors. *Hint:* You could add the two numbers in constant time if you knew ahead of time where the carries occur. This can be done in $O(\lg n)$ time using a parallel-prefix computation over three elements: g (generate carry), k (kill carry), p (pass on carry). Two ones generate a carry (g), a one and a zero pass it on (p), and two zeros kill a carry (k).

12.9. In Exercise 8.15 we saw how to solve the maximum-sum-subsequence problem using dynamic programming. Given an array a of n integers, possibly negative, we want to find two indexes i and j such that $\sum_{k=i}^{j} a[k]$ is as large as possible. Show how to solve this problem using parallel-prefix computation in time $O(\lg n)$. *Hint:* You need to perform a series of two prefix computations followed by a semigroup algorithm for different operators $\otimes$.

12.10. Write an $O(\lg n)$ time EREW algorithm to find the middle element of a linked list. The middle element is the element of rank $\lfloor n/2 \rfloor$ assuming the list contains n nodes. *Hint:* Use pointer jumping.

12.11. Write an $O(\lg n)$ time EREW algorithm that counts how many nodes in a linked list contain a given value. *Hint:* Use pointer jumping.

12.12. Show that the odd-even transposition network presented in Figure 12.3.1 sorts n numbers. *Hint:* Trace some small examples and see what route the numbers take.

12.13. Show how to sort five inputs on a sorting network of size 9. Prove that your network is correct.

12.14. Show how to sort five inputs on a sorting network of depth 5. Prove that your network is correct.

12.15. Show how to sort six inputs on a sorting network of depth 6. Prove that your network is correct.

Exercises 12.16–12.19 are about a triangular sorting network T_n. We define T_n recursively. T_1 is a single wire, and T_2 is two wires with a comparator. Recursively, we construct T_n from T_{n-1} by adding a new wire for the first input and $n-1$ new comparators between wires 1 and 2 such that there is a comparator before and after every comparator between wires 2 and 3. T_5 would look like this:

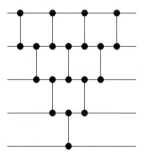

12.16. Show how T_5 sorts $(5, 4, 3, 2, 1)$.

12.17. Draw T_{10} and use it to sort $(12, 4, 5, 9, 2, 4, 3, 1, 7, 10)$.

12.18. Determine the size and depth of T_n exactly.

12.19. Show that T_n correctly sorts n inputs.

> *In Exercises 12.21 and 12.22 we give another proof of correctness for the sorting network S_n constructed from the bitonic sorter in Section 12.3. Using the zero-one principle simplifies several parts of that proof.*

12.20. Show that the bitonic sorter B_n correctly sorts bitonic input sequences consisting of zeros and ones only.

12.21. Show that M_n correctly merges two bitonic sequences of zeros and ones.

12.22. Show that S_n sorts any sequence of n numbers.

> *Exercises 12.23–12.26 develop a tool for proving correctness for primitive sorting networks. A sorting network is primitive if comparators are allowed only between neighboring wires. For example, the odd-even transposition network and the triangular sorting network (described before Exercise 12.16) are primitive.*

12.23. Show that every primitive sorting network on n elements needs to have at least $\binom{n}{2}$ comparators.

12.24. [R. W. Floyd.] Show that a primitive sorting network works correctly if and only if it sorts the sequence $(n, n - 1, \ldots, 1)$.

12.25. Use Exercise 12.24 to show that the odd-even transposition network works correctly.

12.26. Use Exercise 12.24 to show that the triangular sorting network described before Exercise 12.16 works correctly.

12.27. Show how to embed a ring on n processors in a linear array of n processors such that any algorithm running on the ring can be simulated on the array with at most a slow-down of a constant factor. What is the factor?

12.28. Show that for $d \geq 2$, the linear array of length 2^d is a subgraph of the d-dimensional hypercube. *Hint:* Show, by induction, that the d-dimensional hypercube contains a Hamiltonian cycle.

12.29. Show that the d-dimensional hypercube does not contain the complete binary tree of depth d as a subgraph for $d \geq 3$. *Hint:* The vertices containing the leaves all have the same Hamming weight modulo 2.

12.30. Let d be the maximum diameter of any component in the image. Modify the first component algorithm we saw, Algorithm 12.4.11, to run in time $O(n + d)$ without assuming that the algorithm knows the value of d. *Hint:* On top of the labeling algorithm install a messaging system. Every time the label of pixel (i, j) changes, we send a message to processor $(1, 1)$ that a change has happened. If processor $P_{1,1}$ has not received a change-of-label message in more than $2n$ steps (the time it would take a message from processor $P_{n,n}$ to reach processor $P_{1,1}$), then it sends out a message to all processors to stop.

12.31. Show how to modify Levialdi's algorithm for component labeling to work for components that are connected horizontally or vertically (we do not allow diagonal connections in this version). *Hint:* Substitute each pixel in the image by an appropriate 3×3 square of pixels and run Levialdi's algorithm.

12.32. Show how to modify Levialdi's algorithm to count the number of maximal components in an image in time $O(n)$ and using only $O(\lg n)$ bits of storage in each processor.

12.33. Suppose we have a ring of processors each holding a Boolean value. Write a distributed algorithm that allows one processor, the initiator, to compute the conjunction (the "and") of all the values in $\Theta(n)$ steps and message complexity $\Theta(n)$.

Exercises 12.34–12.35 extend Exercise 12.33. Again, suppose we have a ring of processors each storing a Boolean value. This time we want every processor in the ring to know the value of the conjunction.

12.34. Show how to solve the problem in $\Theta(n)$ steps and message complexity $\Theta(n^2)$.

12.35. Suppose the ring is synchronized; that is, the processors have access to a global clock so that they can perform actions in perfect synchronization. Show that the problem can be solved in $\Theta(n)$ steps with message complexity $\Theta(n)$.

Exercises 12.36–12.38 deal with an improved version of the leader-election algorithm due to Chang and Roberts. It is based on the following observation: If initiator p receives a message $\langle \mathbf{token}, I \rangle$ for which $p.ID < I$, there is no need for p to pass on this message since the processor with ID I will not get chosen over p.

12.36. Write out the Chang-Roberts version of the leader-election algorithm.

12.37. Show that the Chang-Roberts leader-election algorithm still has a worst-case message complexity of $\Theta(n^2)$. *Hint:* The lower bound is the interesting part.

⋆**12.38.** [Requires probability theory.] Show that in the average case, the Chang-Roberts algorithm has a message complexity of $O(n \log n)$. *Hint:* Assume that the IDs of the n processors along the ring are a permutation of the numbers $\{1, \ldots, n\}$, and that each such permutation has equal probability of occurring. First show that we can assume that all processors are initiators. For a particular message $\langle \textbf{token}, I \rangle$, where $I \in \{1, \ldots, n\}$, compute the probability that the message is passed k times in the ring. Then, show that you would expect the message $\langle \textbf{token}, I \rangle$ to be passed $\sum_{k=1}^{i-1} 1/k$ times in the ring. The inequality $\sum_{i=1}^{k} 1/i \le \log k$ will come in handy at this point.

12.39. Develop a leader-election algorithm for a (bidirectional) tree. Bidirectional here means that messages can be passed in both directions along any channel (edge of the tree). Your algorithm should run in time $\Theta(h)$ and have message complexity $\Theta(n)$, where n is the number of processors in the tree and h is the height of the tree.

12.40. Professor Alicia Dribbler suggests the following approach to selecting a leader in an arbitrary (connected) graph $G = (V, E)$: Use the echo-broadcasting algorithm (Algorithm 12.5.5) to build a spanning tree of G, and then use the result from Exercise 12.39 to select a leader on that spanning tree. Professor Dribbler's algorithm has time and message complexity $\Theta(|E|)$. As we mentioned earlier, a message complexity of $\Theta(|V| \log |V| + |E|)$ is optimal for this task. What is the professor confused about?

References

AARTS, E., and J. KORST, *Simulated Annealing and Boltzman Machines: A Stochastic Approach to Combinatorial Optimization and Neural Computing*, Wiley, New York, 1989.

ADLEMAN, L. M., "Molecular computation of solutions to combinatorial problems," *Science*, 266 (1994), 1021–1024.

AHO, A. V., J. E. HOPCROFT, and J. D. ULLMAN, *Data Structures and Algorithms*, Addison-Wesley, Reading, Mass., 1983.

AHO, A. V., "Algorithms for finding patterns in strings," in *Handbook of Theoretical Computer Science*, Vol. A: *Algorithms and Complexity*, J. van Leeuwen, ed., Elsevier, Amsterdam, 1990.

AJTAI, M., J. KOMLÓS, and E. SZEMERÉDI, "An $O(n \log n)$ sorting network," *Proc. 15th ACM Symp. Theory of Comp.*, (1983), 1–9.

AKL, S. G., *The Design and Analysis of Parallel Algorithms*, Prentice Hall, Englewood Cliffs, N.J., 1989.

ATTIYA, H., and J. WELCH, *Distributed Computing: Fundamentals, Simulations, and Advanced Topics*, McGraw-Hill, New York, 1998.

BELLMAN, R., *Dynamic Programming*, Princeton University Press, Princeton, N.J., 1957.

BELLMAN, R., *Eye of the Hurricane*, World Scientific Publishing, Singapore 1984.

BENTLEY, J., *Programming Pearls*, 2nd ed., Addison-Wesley, Reading, Mass., 2000.

BERGER, B., and T. LEIGHTON, "Protein folding in the hydrophobic-hydrophilic (HP) model is NP-complete," in *Proceedings of the Second Annual International Conference on Computational Molecular Biology (RECOMB98)*, S. Istrail, P. Pevzner, and M. Waterman, eds., ACM Press, (1998), 30–39.

BLUM, A., and D. KARGER, "An $\tilde{O}(n^{3/14})$-coloring algorithm for 3-colorable graphs," *Inf. Proc. Let.*, 61 (1997), 49–53.

BLUM, M., R. W. FLOYD, V. PRATT, R. L. RIVEST, and R. E. TARJAN, "Time bounds for selection," *Jour. Comp. Sys. Sci.*, 4 (1973), 448–461.

BRASSARD, G., and P. BRATLEY, *Fundamentals of Algorithmics*, Prentice Hall, Englewood Cliffs, N.J., 1996.

CARMONY, L., "Odd pie fights," *Math. Teacher*, 72 (1979), 61–64.

CERNY, V., "A thermodynamical approach to the traveling saleman problem: An efficient simulation algorithm," *Jour. Opt. Theory and Applications*, 45 (1985), 41–51.

CHANG, E. J. H., "Echo algorithms: depth parallel operations on general graphs," *IEEE Trans. on Software Engineering*, SE-8 (1982), 391–401.

CHEN, P. C., "Heuristic sampling: A method for predicting the performance of tree searching programs," *SIAM J. Comput.*, 21 (1992), 295–315.

CHEN, P. C., "Heuristic sampling on DAGs," *Algorithmica*, 12 (1994), 458–475.

CHRYSTAL, G., *Textbook of Algebra*, Vol. II, 7th ed., Chelsea, New York, 1964.

CHU, I. P., and R. JOHNSONBAUGH, "Tiling deficient boards with trominoes," *Math. Mag.*, 59 (1986), 34–40.

COOK, S., "The complexity of theorem-proving procedures," *Proc. 3rd ACM Symp. Theory of Comp.*, (1971), 151–158.

COOK, S., C. DWORK, and R. REISCHUK, "Upper and lower time bounds for parallel random access machines without simultaneous writes," *SIAM J. Comput.*, 15 (1986), 87–97.

COPPERSMITH, D., and S. WINOGRAD, "Matrix multiplication via arithmetic progressions," *Proc. 19th ACM Symp. Theory of Comp.*, (1987), 1–6.

CRESCENZI, P., D. GOLDMAN, C. H. PAPADIMITRIOU, A. PICCOLBONI, and M. YANNAKAKIS, "On the complexity of protein folding." *Jour. of Comp. Biology*, 5 (1998), 423–466.

CROCHEMORE, M., and W. RYTTER, *Text Algorithms*, Oxford University Press, New York, 1994.

DANTSIN, E., A. GOERDT, E. A. HIRSCH, and U. SCHÖNING, "Deterministic algorithms for k-SAT based on covering codes and local search," *Proc. ICALP '00*, Springer Verlag, (2000), 236–243.

DE BERG, M., M. VAN KREVELD, M. OVERMARS, and O. SCHWARZKOPF, *Computational Geometry*, Springer-Verlag, Berlin, 1997.

DIJKSTRA, E. W., "A note on two problems in connexion with graphs," *Numer. Math.*, 1 (1959), 260–271.

DOWNEY, R. G., and M. R. FELLOWS, *Parameterized Complexity*, Springer-Verlag, New York, 1999a.

DOWNEY, R. G., M. R. FELLOWS, and U. STEGE, "Computational tractability: The view from Mars," *Bull. European Assn. Theor. Comput. Sci.*, 69 (1999b), 73–97.

DRISCOLL, J. R., H. N. GABOW, R. SHRAIRMAN, and R. E. TARJAN, "Relaxed heaps: An alternative to Fibonacci heaps with applications to parallel computation," *Commun. ACM*, 31 (1988), 1343–1354.

EDELSBRUNNER, H., *Algorithms in Combinatorial Geometry*, Springer-Verlag, New York, 1987.

EISENBLÄTTER, A., M. GRÖTSCHEL, and A. M. C. A. KOSTER, "Frequency planning and ramifications of coloring," citeseer.nj.nec.com/401496.html.

FLOYD, R. W., "Algorithm 97 (SHORTEST PATH)," *Commun. ACM*, 5 (1962), 345.

FLOYD, R. W., and R. L. RIVEST, "Expected time bounds for selection," *Commun. ACM*, 18 (1975), 165–172.

FORTNOW, L., and S. HOMER, "A short history of computational complexity," in *The History of Mathematical Logic*, D. van Dalen, J. Dawson, and A. Kanamori, eds., North-Holland, Amsterdam, 2003.

FREDMAN, M. L., and R. E. TARJAN, "Fibonacci heaps and their uses in improved network optimization algorithms," *Jour. ACM*, 34 (1987), 596–615.

FRITSCH, R., G. FRITSCH, and J. PESCHKE, *The Four-Color Theorem: History, Topological Foundations, and Idea of Proof*, Springer-Verlag, New York, 1998.

GARDNER, M., *Penrose Tiles to Trapdoor Ciphers ... and the Return of Dr. Matrix*, revised reprint of the 1989 original, Mathematical Association of America, Washington, D.C., 1996.

GAREY, M. R., and D. S. JOHNSON, *Computers and Intractability: A Guide to the Theory of NP-Completeness*, W.H. Freeman, San Francisco, 1979.

GOLOMB, S., "Checker boards and polyominoes," *Amer. Math. Monthly*, 61 (1954), 675–682.

GOLOMB, S., and L. BAUMERT, "Backtrack programming," *Jour. ACM*, 12 (1965), 516–524.

GRAHAM, R. L., D. E. KNUTH, and O. PATASHNIK, *Concrete Mathematics*, Addison-Wesley, Reading, Mass., 1989.

GREENLAW, R., H. J. HOOVER, and W. L. RUZZO, *Limits to Parallel Computation: P-Completeness Theory*, Oxford University Press, New York, 1995.

GROVER, L. K., "A fast quantum mechanical algorithm for database search," *Proc. 28th Annual ACM Symp. Theory of Comp.*, (1996), 212.

GUDDER, S., "Quantum computation," *Amer. Math. Monthly*, 110 (2003), 181–201.

GUSFIELD, D., *Algorithms on Strings, Trees, and Sequences: Computer Science and Computational Biology*, Cambridge University Press, 1997.

HOARE, C. A. R., "Algorithm 63 (PARTITION) and algorithm 65 (FIND)," *Commun. ACM*, 7 (1961), 321–322.

HOCHBAUM, D., ed., *Approximation Algorithms for NP-Hard Problems*, PWS, 1997.

HOLTON, D. A., and J. SHEEHAN, *The Petersen Graph*, Cambridge University Press, 1993.

HOMER, S., and M. PEINADO, "On the performance of polynomial-time CLIQUE algorithms on very large graphs," in *Cliques, Coloring, and Satisfiability: 2nd DIMACS Implementation Challenge*, D. S. Johnson and M. Trick, eds., DIMACS Series in Discrete Mathematics and Theoretical Computer Science, Amer. Math. Soc., Providence, R.I., 1996.

HOPCROFT, J. E., and R. E. TARJAN, "Efficient planarity testing," *Jour. ACM*, 21 (1974), 549–568.

HORSPOOL, R. N., "Practical fast searching in strings," *Software Practice and Experience*, 10 (1980), 501–506.

HROMKOVIČ, J., *Algorithmics for Hard Problems: Introduction to Combinatorial Optimization, Randomization, Approximation, and Heuristics*, Springer-Verlag, New York, 2001.

HUANG, B. C, and M. A. LANGSTON, "A simple algorithm for merging two disjoint linearly ordered sets," *Commun. ACM*, 31 (1988), 348–352.

HUFFMAN, D. A., "A method for the construction of minimum-redundancy codes," *Proc. IRE*, 40 (1952), 1098–1101.

ITAI, A., and M. RODEH, "Finding a minimum circuit in a graph," *SIAM J. Comput.*, 7 (1978), 413–423.

JÁJÁ, J., *An Introduction to Parallel Algorithms*, Addison-Wesley, Reading, Mass., 1992.

JOHNSONBAUGH, R., *Discrete Mathematics*, 5th ed., Prentice Hall, Upper Saddle River, N.J., 2001.

KARP, R., "Reducibility among combinatorial problems," in *Complexity of Computer Computations*, R. E. Miller and J. W. Thatcher, eds., Plenum Press, New York, 1972, 85–103.

KATAJAINEN, J., T. PASANEN, and J. TEUHOLA, "Practical in-place mergesort," *Nordic Jour. Comp.*, 3 (1996), 27–40.

KIRKPATRICK, S., C. D. GELATT, and M. P. VECCHI, "Optimisation by simulated annealing," *Science*, 220 (1983), 671–680.

KNUTH, D. E., "Estimating the efficiency of backtrack programs," *Math. Comp.*, 29 (1975), 121–136. Also in *Selected Papers on Analysis of Algorithms*, D. E. Knuth, CSLI Publications, Stanford, Calif., 2000.

KNUTH, D. E., "Algorithms," *Sci. Amer.* (April 1977), 63–80.

KNUTH, D. E., "Algorithmic thinking and mathematical thinking," *Amer. Math. Mo.*, 92 (1985), 170–181.

KNUTH, D. E., *The Art of Computer Programming*, Vol. 1: *Fundamental Algorithms*, 3rd ed., Addison-Wesley, Reading, Mass., 1997.

KNUTH, D. E., *The Art of Computer Programming*, Vol. 2: *Seminumeric Algorithms*, 3rd ed., Addison-Wesley, Reading, Mass., 1998a.

KNUTH, D. E., *The Art of Computer Programming*, Vol. 3: *Sorting and Searching*, 2nd ed., Addison-Wesley, Reading, Mass., 1998b.

KOROSTENSKY, C., and G. GONNET, "Gap heuristics and tree construction using gaps," Technical Report, ETH Zuerich, 312, (1999). ftp://ftp.inf.ethz.ch/pub/publications/tech-reports/3xx/321.ps.gz

KOZEN, D., and S. ZAKS, "Optimal bounds for the change-making problem," *Theor. Comput. Sci.*, 123 (1994), 377–388.

KRUSKAL, J. B., "On the shortest spanning subtree of a graph and the traveling salesman problem," *Proc. Amer. Math Soc.*, 7 (1956), 48–50.

KUCERA, L., *Combinatorial Algorithms*, Adam Hilger, Briston, 1990.

KULLMANN, O., "New methods for 3-SAT decision and worst-case analysis," *Theor. Comput. Sci.*, 223 (1999), 1–72.

LAWLER, E. L., *Combinatorial Optimization: Networks and Matroids*, Holt, 1976.

LEIGHTON, F. T., *Introduction to Parallel Algorithms and Architectures*, Morgan Kaufman, San Mateo, Calif., 1992.

LELANN, G., "Distributed systems—towards a formal approach," *Proc. IFIP Congress on Information Processing*, (1977), 155–160.

LEVIN, L. A., "Universal sorting problems," *Problemy Peredaci Informacii*, 9 (1973) (in Russian), 115–116. English translation in *Problems of Information Transmission*, 9, 265–266.

LIU, C. L., *Elements of Discrete Mathematics*, 2nd ed., McGraw-Hill, New York, 1985.

LUCAS, É., *Récréations Mathématiques*, Vol. 1, Gauthier-Villars, Paris, 1882.

LYNCH, N., *Distributed Algorithms*, Morgan Kaufmann, San Francisco, 1996.

MARTIN, G. E., *Polyominoes: A Guide to Puzzles and Problems in Tiling*, Mathematical Association of America, Washington, D.C., 1991.

MASSÉ, P., *Les Reserves et la Regulation de l'Avenir dans la vie Economique*, Herman, Paris, 1946.

MERKLE, R. C., and M. E. HELLMAN, "Hiding information and signatures in trapdoor knapsacks," *IEEE Trans. on Information Theory*, IT-24 (1978), 525–530.

METROPOLIS, N., A. W. ROSENBLUTH, M. N. ROSENBLUTH, A. H. TELLER, and E. TELLER, "Equations of state calculations by fast computing machines," *Jour. Chem. Phys.*, 21 (1953), 1087–1091.

MICHALEWICZ, Z., and B. F. FOGEL, *How to Solve It: Modern Heuristics*, Springer-Verlag, New York, 2000.

MOORE, E. F., "The shortest path through a maze," in *Proc. Int. Symp. on Theory of Switching*, Harvard Univ. Press, 1959, 285–292.

MOTWANI, R., "Lecture notes on approximation algorithms: Volume I," CS-TR-92-1435", 82. http://theory.stanford.edu/people/rajeev/postscripts/approximations.ps.gz

MOTWANI, R., and P. RAGHAVAN, *Randomized Algorithms*, Cambridge University Press, Cambridge, 1995.

NERODE, A., and R. A. SHORE, *Logic for Applications*, Springer-Verlag, New York, 1993.

NEWMAN, J. R., "Leonhard Euler and the Koenigsberg bridges," *Sci. Amer.* (July 1953), 66–70.

PAPADIMITRIOU, C. H., and K. STEIGLITZ, *Combinatorial Optimization: Algorithms and Complexity*, Prentice Hall, Englewood Cliffs, N.J., 1982.

PAPADIMITRIOU, C. H., *Computational Complexity*, Addison-Wesley, Reading, Mass., 1994.

PEARSON, D., "A polynomial-time algorithm for the change-making problem," Cornell CS Tech. Report 94-1433, (1994).

PREPARATA, F. P., and M. I. SHAMOS, *Computational Geometry*, Springer-Verlag, New York, 1985.

PRIM, R. C., "Shortest connection networks and some generalizations," *Bell. Sys. Tech. Jour.*, 36 (1957), 1389–1401.

ROBERTS, F. S., *Applied Combinatorics*, Prentice Hall, Englewood Cliffs, N.J., 1984.

SEDGEWICK, R., "Implementing quicksort programs," *Commun. ACM*, 10 (1978), 847–857.

SHI, H., and G. X. RITTER, "A fast algorithm for image component labeling with local operators on mesh connected computers," *Jour. of Parallel and Distributed Computing*, 23 (1994), 455–461.

SHOR, P. W., "Polynomial-time algorithms for prime factorization and discrete logarithms on a quantum computer," *SIAM Jour. of Comp.*, 26 (1997), 1484-1509.

SIPSER, M., "The history and status of the P versus NP question," *Proc. 24th ACM Symp. Theory of Comp.*, (1992), 603-618.

SOSIC, R. and J. GU, "A polynomial time algorithm for the N-queens problem," *SIGARTN: SIGART Newsletter (ACM Special Interest Group on Artificial Intelligence)*, 1 (1990), 7–11.

STANDISH, T. A., *Data Structures in Java*, Addison-Wesley, Reading, Mass., 1998.

STEPHEN, G. A., *String Searching Algorithms*, Lecture Notes Series on Computing, World Scientific Publishing, 1994.

STRASSEN, V., "Gaussian elimination is not optimal," *Numerische Mathematik*, 3 (1969), 354–356.

TARJAN, R. E., "Finding dominators in directed graphs," *SIAM J. Comput.*, 3 (1974), 62–89.

TARJAN, R. E., "Efficiency of a good but not linear set union algorithm," *Jour. ACM*, 22 (1975), 215–225.

TARJAN, R. E., *Data Structures and Network Algorithms*, Society for Industrial and Applied Mathematics, Philadelphia, 1983.

TARJAN, R. E., and J. VAN LEEUWEN, "Worst-case analysis of set union algorithms," *Jour. ACM*, 31 (1984), 245–281.

TARRY, G., "Le problème des labyrinthes," *Nouvelles Ann. de Math.*, 3 (1895), 187–190.

TEL, G., *Introduction to Distributed Algorithms*, 2nd ed., Cambridge University Press, 2000.

THOMPSON, C. D., and H. T. KUNG, "Sorting on a mesh-connected parallel computer", *Commun. ACM*, 20 (1977), 263–271.

TUCKER, A., *Applied Combinatorics*, 3rd ed., Wiley, New York, 1995.

VAZIRANI, V., *Approximation Algorithms*, Springer Verlag, New York, 2001.

WALKER, R. J., "An enumerative technique for a class of combinatorial problems," *Proc. Symp. Applied Math.*, 10 (1960), 91–94.

WANG, J., "Average-case computational complexity theory," in *Complexity Theory Retrospective II*, L. A. Hemaspaandra and A. L. Selman, eds., (2) 1997, 295–328.

WARSHALL, S., "A theorem on boolean matrices," *Jour. ACM*, 9 (1962), 11–12.

WEISS, M. A., *Data Structures and Problem Solving Using Java*, 2nd ed., Addison-Wesley, Reading, Mass., 2001.

WELLS, M. B., *Elements of Combinatorial Computing*, Pergamon Press, New York, 1971.

WEST, D., *Introduction to Graph Theory*, 2nd ed., Prentice Hall, Upper Saddle River, N.J., 2000.

WILF, H. S., *Algorithms and Complexity*, http://www.cis.upenn.edu/~wilf/AlgComp2.html, 1994. Also available as *Algorithms and Complexity*, Prentice Hall, Upper Saddle River, N.J., 1986.

WILLIAMS, J. W. J., "Algorithm 232 (HEAPSORT)," *Commun. ACM*, 7 (1964), 347–348.

WILSON, R. J., *Introduction to Graph Theory*, 4th ed., Addison-Wesley, Reading, Mass., 1996.

WONG, D. F., and C. L. LIU, "A new algorithm for floorplan design," *23rd Design Automation Conference*, (1986), 101–107.

Solutions to Selected Exercises

Chapter 1: Introduction

Section 1.1

1. 1. $x = a$

    2. If $b < x$, then $x = b$.

    3. If $c < x$, then $x = c$.

4. If the set S is an infinite set, the algorithm will not terminate, so it lacks the finiteness and output properties. Line 1 is not precisely stated since *how* to list the subsets of S and their sums is not specified; thus the algorithm lacks the precision property. The order of the subsets listed in line 1 depends on the method used to generate them, so the algorithm lacks the determinism property. Since line 2 depends on the order of the subsets generated in line 1, the determinism property is lacking here as well.

Section 1.2

1.   Input Parameter: s
        Output Parameters: None

```
array_min(s) {
   small = s[1]
   i = 2
   while (i ≤ s.last) {
      if (s[i] < small) // smaller value found
         small = s[i]
      i = i + 1
   }
   return small
}
```

4.   Input Parameter: s
        Output Parameters: *smallest, 2nd_smallest*

```
find_two_smallest(s, smallest, 2nd_smallest) {
    if (s[1] > s[2]) {
        smallest = s[2]
        2nd_smallest = s[1]
    }
    else {
        smallest = s[1]
        2nd_smallest = s[2]
    }
    for i = 3 to s.last
        if (s[i] < 2nd_smallest)
            if (s[i] < smallest) {
                2nd_smallest = smallest
                smallest = s[i]
            }
            else
                2nd_smallest = s[i]
}
```

7. Input Parameter: s
    Output Parameters: None

```
find_last_largest(s) {
    index = 1
    for i = 2 to s.last
        if (s[i] ≥ s[index])
            index = i
    return index
}
```

10. Input Parameter: s
     Output Parameters: None

```
find_out_of_order(s) {
    for i = 2 to s.last
        if (s[i] < s[i − 1])
            return i
    return 0
}
```

13. Input Parameter: s
     Output Parameter: s

```
sort_bits(s) {
    i = 1
    j = s.last
```

```
    while (i < j) {
        while (i < j && s[i] == 0)
            i = i + 1
        while (i < j && s[j] == 1)
            j = j - 1
        swap(s[i], s[j])
    }
}
```

Section 1.3

1. Input Parameter: n
    Output Parameter: a

```
random_permutation(n, a) {
    for i = 1 to n
        a[i] = i
    for i = 1 to n - 1
        swap(a[i], a[rand(i, n)])
}
```

Chapter 2: Mathematics for Algorithms

Section 2.1

1. degree = 3; coefficients: $7, 1, 0, -3$

4. [$p(x) + q(x)$ only.] Suppose that $p(x) = \sum_{i=1}^{m} c_i x^i$ and $q(x) = \sum_{i=1}^{n} d_i x^i$. If $m < n$, define $c_i = 0$ for $m < i \le n$. If $m > n$, define $d_i = 0$ for $n < i \le m$. Then $p(x) + q(x)$ is the polynomial $\sum_{i=1}^{\max\{m,n\}} (c_i + d_i) x^i$.

7. The degree of $p(x) - q(x)$ is 5.

10. $\{3, 4\}$

13. $\{4\}$

14. The nonempty intersection of two closed intervals is always a closed interval.

17. The intersection can be a closed interval, for example, $[2, 3] = (1, 3] \cap [2, 4]$. The intersection cannot be an open interval. The intersection can be a half-open interval, for example, $(1, 3] = (1, 3] \cap [0, 4]$.

18. False. A counterexample is $2, 6, 3$.

20. Those consisting of one element

22. Increasing, nondecreasing

25. None

28. Nonincreasing, nondecreasing

29. Not in conjunctive normal form, and not in disjunctive normal form

32. In conjunctive normal form, and in disjunctive normal form

34. The following table

p	q	$p \leftrightarrow q$	$(\overline{p} \vee q) \wedge (\overline{q} \vee p)$
T	T	T	T
T	F	F	F
F	T	F	F
F	F	T	T

shows that $p \leftrightarrow q$ and $(\overline{p} \vee q) \wedge (\overline{q} \vee p)$ are equivalent.

37. $\overline{p \wedge \overline{q}}$

39. 6

42. 10

44. 2.584962501

47. −0.736965594

49. 2.392231208

52. 0.480415248

53. 1.489896102

56. Let $u = \log_b y$ and $v = \log_b x$. By definition, $b^u = y$ and $b^v = x$. Now

$$x^{\log_b y} = x^u = (b^v)^u = b^{vu} = (b^u)^v = y^v = y^{\log_b x}.$$

59. Set

$$a = 1 - \frac{1}{n} \quad \text{and} \quad b = 1 - \frac{1}{n+1}$$

to prove that $\{(1 - 1/n)^n\}_{n=1}^{\infty}$ is increasing. Set

$$a = 1 - \frac{1}{2n} \quad \text{and} \quad b = 1$$

to prove that $\{(1 - 1/n)^n\}_{n=1}^{\infty}$ is bounded above by 4/9.

62. Suppose that a and b are least upper bounds of a set X. Since a is a least upper bound of X, and b is an upper bound of X, by the definition of "least upper bound," $a \leq b$. Reversing the roles of a and b, we have $b \leq a$. Therefore, $a = b$.

Section 2.2

1. Basis Step: $1 = 1^2$

Inductive Step: Assume true for n. Then

$$\sum_{i=1}^{n+1} (2i - 1) = \sum_{i=1}^{n} (2i - 1) + (2n + 1) = n^2 + (2n + 1) = (n + 1)^2.$$

4. Basis Step: $1^2 = (1 \cdot 2 \cdot 3)/6$

Inductive Step: Assume true for n. Then

$$\sum_{i=1}^{n+1} i^2 = \sum_{i=1}^{n} i^2 + (n + 1)^2 = \frac{n(n + 1)(2n + 1)}{6} + (n + 1)^2 = \frac{(n + 1)(n + 2)(2n + 3)}{6}.$$

7. Basis Step: $\dfrac{1}{1 \cdot 3} = \dfrac{1}{3}$

Inductive Step: Assume true for n. Then

$$\sum_{i=1}^{n+1} \frac{1}{(2i - 1)(2i + 1)} = \sum_{i=1}^{n} \frac{1}{(2i - 1)(2i + 1)} + \frac{1}{(2n + 1)(2n + 3)}$$
$$= \frac{n}{2n + 1} + \frac{1}{(2n + 1)(2n + 3)} = \frac{n + 1}{2n + 3}.$$

8. Take $r = 1/2$ in Theorem 2.2.3.

11. Basis Step: $1! \geq 2^{1-1}$

Inductive Step: Assume true for n. Then

$$(n + 1)! = (n + 1)n! \geq (n + 1)2^{n-1} \geq 2 \cdot 2^{n-1} = 2^n,$$

since $n + 1 \geq 2$ for $n \geq 1$.

14. Basis Steps ($n = 6, 7$): We can make six cents postage by using three 2-cent stamps. We can make seven cents postage by using one 7-cent stamp.

Inductive Step: We assume that $n \geq 8$ and postage of k cents can be achieved by using only 2-cent and 7-cent stamps for $6 \leq k < n$. By the inductive assumption, we can make postage of $n - 2$ cents. We may add a 2-cent stamp to make n cents postage.

17. Basis Step ($n = 6$): Use three 2-cent stamps.

Inductive Step: Assume that we can make postage for n cents. If there is at least one 7-cent stamp, replace it by four 2-cent stamps to make $n + 1$ cents postage. If there are no 7-cent stamps, there are at least three 2-cent stamps (because $n \geq 6$). Replace three 2-cent stamps by one 7-cent stamp to make $n + 1$ cents postage.

19. We prove that $pow = a^{i-1}$ is a loop invariant for the while loop. Just before the while loop begins executing, $i = 1$ and $pow = 1$, so $pow = a^{1-1}$. We have proved the Basis Step.

Assume that $pow = a^{i-1}$. If $i \leq n$ (so that the loop body executes again), pow becomes

$$pow * a = a^{i-1} * a = a^i,$$

and i becomes $i + 1$. We have proved the Inductive Step. Therefore $pow = a^{i-1}$ is an invariant for the while loop.

The while loop terminates when $i = n + 1$. Because $pow = a^{i-1}$ is an invariant, at this point $pow = a^n$, which is the value the algorithm returns. Therefore, the algorithm correctly computes a^n.

Section 2.3

1. $\Theta(n)$

4. $\Theta(n^2)$

7. $\Theta(n^2)$

10. $\Theta(n)$

13. $\Theta(n)$

16. $\Theta(n^3)$

19. $\Theta(n \lg n)$

20. $\Theta(\lg \lg n)$

23. First note that

$$\sum_{i=1}^{n} i \lg i \leq \sum_{i=1}^{n} n \lg n \leq n(n \lg n) = n^2 \lg n.$$

Therefore, $\sum_{i=1}^{n} i \lg i = O(n^2 \lg n)$. Now

$$
\begin{aligned}
\sum_{i=1}^{n} i \lg i \; &\geq \; \sum_{i=\lceil n/2 \rceil}^{n} i \lg i \\
&\geq \; \sum_{i=\lceil n/2 \rceil}^{n} \lceil n/2 \rceil \lg \lceil n/2 \rceil \\
&= \; \lceil (n+1)/2 \rceil \lceil n/2 \rceil \lg \lceil n/2 \rceil \\
&\geq \; (n/2)^2 \lg(n/2) \\
&\geq \; \frac{n^2 \lg n}{8},
\end{aligned}
$$

since $\lg n \geq 2$ for $n \geq 4$. Thus, $\sum_{i=1}^{n} i \lg i = \Omega(n^2 \lg n)$. Therefore, $\sum_{i=1}^{n} i \lg i = \Theta(n^2 \lg n)$.

26. $\displaystyle\sum_{i=0}^{k} \lg(n/2^i)$ $= (k+1)\lg n - (1 + 2 + \cdots + k)$

$= (k+1)k - \dfrac{k(k+1)}{2}$

$= \dfrac{(k+1)k}{2}$

$= \dfrac{(1 + \lg n)\lg n}{2} = \Theta(\lg^2 n)$

28. False. If the statement were true, we would have $n^n \leq C2^n$ for some constant C and for all sufficiently large n. The preceding inequality may be rewritten as

$$\left(\frac{n}{2}\right)^n \leq C,$$

for some constant C and for all sufficiently large n. Since $(n/2)^n$ becomes arbitrarily large as n becomes large, we cannot have $n^n \leq C2^n$ for some constant C and for all sufficiently large n.

31. False. A counterexample is $f(n) = n$ and $g(n) = 2n$.

34. True. If $f(n) = O(g(n))$, then there exist constants $C > 0$ and N such that $f(n) \leq Cg(n)$ for all $n \geq N$. Now $f(n)/C \leq g(n)$ for all $n \geq N$. Therefore $g(n) = \Omega(f(n))$.

37. False. A counterexample is $f(n) = n$, $g(n) = n^2$.

38. The Θ-notation ignores constants that are present in the formula for the *actual* time.

40. True. Since $\lim_{n\to\infty} f(n)/g(n) = 0$, taking $\varepsilon = 1$, there exists N such that

$$\frac{f(n)}{g(n)} < 1, \quad \text{for all } n \geq N.$$

Therefore, for all $n \geq N$, $f(n) < g(n)$ and $f(n) = O(g(n))$.

43. True. Since $\lim_{n\to\infty} f(n)/g(n) = c > 0$, taking $\varepsilon = c/2$, there exists N such that

$$\left| \frac{f(n)}{g(n)} - c \right| < c/2, \quad \text{for all } n \geq N.$$

This last inequality may be written

$$-\frac{c}{2} < \frac{f(n)}{g(n)} - c < \frac{c}{2}, \quad \text{for all } n \geq N,$$

or

$$\frac{c}{2} < \frac{f(n)}{g(n)} < \frac{3c}{2}, \quad \text{for all } n \geq N,$$

or

$$\frac{c}{2}g(n) < f(n) < \frac{3c}{2}g(n), \quad \text{for all } n \geq N.$$

Therefore, $f(n) = \Theta(g(n))$.

46. We have

$$1^k + 2^k + \cdots + n^k \leq n^k + n^k + \cdots + n^k = n \cdot n^k = n^{k+1}$$

for $n \geq 1$; hence

$$1^k + 2^k + \cdots + n^k = O(n^{k+1}).$$

Also,

$$
\begin{aligned}
1^k + 2^k + \cdots + n^k &\geq \lceil n/2 \rceil^k + \cdots + (n-1)^k + n^k \\
&\geq \lceil n/2 \rceil^k + \cdots + \lceil n/2 \rceil^k + \lceil n/2 \rceil^k \\
&= \lceil (n+1)/2 \rceil \lceil n/2 \rceil^k \geq (n/2)(n/2)^k = n^{k+1}/2^{k+1}.
\end{aligned}
$$

Therefore,

$$1^k + 2^k + \cdots + n^k = \Omega(n^{k+1}).$$

We conclude that

$$1^k + 2^k + \cdots + n^k = \Theta(n^{k+1}).$$

Section 2.4

1. After one month, there is still just one pair because a pair does not become productive until after one month. Therefore, $a_1 = 1$. After two months, the pair alive in the beginning becomes productive and adds one additional pair. Therefore, $a_2 = 2$. The increase in pairs of rabbits $a_n - a_{n-1}$ from month $n - 1$ to month n is due to each pair alive in month $n - 2$ producing an additional pair. That is, $a_n - a_{n-1} = a_{n-2}$. Since $a_1 = f_2$ and $a_2 = f_3$ and $\{a_n\}$ satisfies the same recurrence relation as $\{f_n\}$, we conclude that $a_n = f_{n+1}$, $n \geq 1$.

4. Basis Step ($n = 2$): $f_2^2 = 1^2 = 1 = 1 \cdot 2 - 1 = f_1 f_3 + (-1)^3$

Inductive Step:

$$
\begin{aligned}
f_n f_{n+2} + (-1)^n &= f_n(f_n + f_{n+1}) + (-1)^n \\
&= f_n^2 + f_n f_{n+1} + (-1)^n \\
&= f_{n-1} f_{n+1} + (-1)^{n+1} + f_n f_{n+1} + (-1)^n \\
&= f_{n+1}(f_{n-1} + f_n) = f_{n+1}^2
\end{aligned}
$$

7. Basis Steps ($n = 1, 2$): $f_1 = 1$ is odd, and the subscript, 1, is not divisible by 3. $f_2 = 1$ is odd, and the subscript, 2, is not divisible by 3.

Inductive Step: First, assume that n is divisible by 3. Then, $n - 1$ and $n - 2$ are not divisible by 3; so, by the inductive assumption, f_{n-1} and f_{n-2} are odd. Therefore, $f_n = f_{n-1} + f_{n-2}$ is even.

Now assume that n is not divisible by 3. Then, exactly one of $n - 1$, $n - 2$ is divisible by 3; so, by the inductive assumption, one of f_{n-1}, f_{n-2} is odd and the other is even. Therefore, $f_n = f_{n-1} + f_{n-2}$ is odd.

10. Basis Steps: $(n = 1)$ $f_2 = 1 = 2 - 1 = f_3 - 1$, and $f_1 = 1 = f_2$.

$(n = 2)$ $f_2 + f_4 = 1 + 3 = 5 - 1 = f_5 - 1$, and $f_1 + f_3 = 1 + 2 = 3 = f_4$.

Inductive Step:

$$\sum_{k=1}^{n+1} f_{2k} = \sum_{k=1}^{n} f_{2k} + f_{2n+2}$$

$$= f_{2n+1} - 1 + f_{2n+2} = f_{2n+3} - 1$$

$$\sum_{k=1}^{n+1} f_{2k-1} = \sum_{k=1}^{n} f_{2k-1} + f_{2n+1}$$

$$= f_{2n} + f_{2n+1} = f_{2n+2}$$

13. $\begin{aligned} a_n &= a_{n-1} + 3 \\ &= a_{n-2} + 3 + 3 = a_{n-2} + 2 \cdot 3 \\ &= a_{n-3} + 3 \cdot 3 \\ &\quad\vdots \\ &= a_{n-k} + k \cdot 3 \\ &\quad\vdots \\ &= a_1 + (n-1)3 \\ &= 2 + (n-1)3 = 3n - 1 \end{aligned}$

16. $\begin{aligned} a_n &= 2na_{n-1} \\ &= 2n[2(n-1)a_{n-2}] = 2^2 n(n-1)a_{n-2} \\ &= 2^2 n(n-1)[2(n-2)a_{n-3}] = 2^3 n(n-1)(n-2)a_{n-3} \\ &\quad\vdots \\ &= 2^n n(n-1)\cdots 2 \cdot 1 a_0 \\ &= 2^n n(n-1)\cdots 2 \cdot 1 \cdot 1 = 2^n n! \end{aligned}$

19. If $n = 1$, $a^n = a$; thus, a is returned. For $n > 1$, the algorithm uses the formula $a^n = a^m a^{n-m}$.

22. $c_n = n - 1$

24. If $n = 1$, $a^n = a$; thus, a is returned. For $n > 1$, if n is even, $m = n/2$ and $a^n = a^m a^m$. If n is odd, $m = (n-1)/2$ and $a^n = a^m a^m a$.

27. Assume that $n = 2^k$. Now

$$c_n = c_{2^{k-1}} + 1 = c_{2^{k-2}} + 2 = \cdots = c_1 + k = 0 + k = \lg n.$$

30. (Basis Step): $c_2 = 2 + c_1 > c_1$

(Inductive Step): Assume that $c_k > c_{k-1}$ for all k, $2 \le k < n$. Suppose that $n > 2$. We use the inductive assumption to conclude that $c_{\lfloor n/2 \rfloor} \ge c_{\lfloor (n-1)/2 \rfloor}$. Now

$$c_n = n + c_{\lfloor n/2 \rfloor} > n - 1 + c_{\lfloor (n-1)/2 \rfloor} = c_{n-1}.$$

31. $T(n) = \Theta(n^2)$

34. $T(n) = \Theta(n^2 \log n)$

37. $T(n) = \Theta(n^2)$

38. We use induction to prove that $T(n)$ is well-defined for all n. $T(0)$ is well-defined since its value is given as an initial condition. Thus, the Basis Step ($n = 0$) is proved.

Assume that $T(k)$ is well-defined for all $k < n$. Suppose that $n > 0$. Now $n < 2n \le bn$. Thus, $n/b < n$. Therefore, $\lfloor n/b \rfloor < n$. By the inductive assumption $T(\lfloor n/b \rfloor)$ is well-defined. It follows that

$$T(n) = aT(\lfloor n/b \rfloor) + cn^k$$

is well-defined. The Inductive Step is complete.

41. For $n \ge m$,

$$
\begin{aligned}
f(mn) &= (mn)^k \log_b(mn) \\
&= m^k n^k (\log_b m + \log_b n) \\
&\le m^k n^k (\log_b n + \log_b n) \\
&= 2m^k n^k \log_b n \\
&= 2m^k f(n).
\end{aligned}
$$

Also,

$$f(n + 1) = (n + 1)^k \log_b(n + 1) \ge n^k \log_b n = f(n)$$

for all n. Therefore, f is a smooth function.

44. In case a/b denotes the floor, define

$$
T_{u,v}(n) = \begin{cases} u & \text{if } n = 0 \\ aT_{u,v}(n/b) + vn^k & \text{if } n > 0. \end{cases}
$$

In case a/b denotes the ceiling, define

$$
T_{u,v}(n) = \begin{cases} u & \text{if } n = 1 \\ aT_{u,v}(n/b) + vn^k & \text{if } n > 1. \end{cases}
$$

By Lemma 2.4.15,

$$
T_{u,v}(n) = \begin{cases} \Theta(n^k) & \text{if } a < b^k \\ \Theta(n^k \log n) & \text{if } a = b^k \\ \Theta(n^{\log_b a}) & \text{if } a > b^k. \end{cases}
$$

Since $f(n) = \Omega(n^k)$, there exist N and C_2 such that

$$f(n) \ge C_2 n^k, \quad \text{for } n \ge N.$$

Let

$$x = \min\{T(n)/T_{1,1}(n) \mid 1 \le n \le N\},$$
$$y = \min\{x, C_2\}.$$

For $n \le N$,

$$T(n) \ge xT_{1,1}(n) = T_{x,x}(n) \ge T_{x,y}(n).$$

As in the proof of the case $T(n) \le aT(n/b) + f(n)$, we can use induction to show that

$$T(n) \ge T_{x,y}(n)$$

for all n. If $a < b^k$, by Lemma 2.4.15, $T_{x,y}(n) = \Theta(n^k)$. Since $T(n) \ge T_{x,y}(n)$, it follows that $T(n) = \Omega(n^k)$. The cases $a = b^k$ and $a > b^k$ are handled similarly.

Section 2.5

1. $V = \{1, 2, 3, 4\}$; $E = \{e_1, e_2, e_3, e_4, e_5, e_6\}$; e_1 and e_6 are parallel edges; e_5 is a loop; there are no isolated vertices; G is not a simple graph; e_1 is incident on vertices 1 and 2.

4. $N(1) = \{1, 2, 3\}$, $N(2) = \{1, 3\}$, $N(3) = \{1, 2, 4\}$, $N(4) = \{3\}$.

7. The degree of vertex 1 is 3. The degree of vertex 2 is 4. The degree of vertex 3 is 3. The degree of vertex 4 is 3. The degree of vertex 5 is 3.

10.

Vertex	Indegree	Outdegree
1	2	0
2	2	1
3	1	1
4	0	1
5	1	0
6	0	2
7	1	2

13.

$K_{2,3}$ $K_{3,3}$

15. $\begin{pmatrix} 0 & 0 & 0 & 1 & 0 \\ 0 & 0 & 0 & 0 & 1 \\ 0 & 0 & 0 & 0 & 1 \\ 1 & 0 & 0 & 0 & 0 \\ 0 & 1 & 1 & 0 & 0 \end{pmatrix}$

18. $\begin{pmatrix} 0 & 1 & 0 & 1 & 0 \\ 1 & 0 & 1 & 0 & 1 \\ 0 & 1 & 0 & 1 & 0 \\ 1 & 0 & 1 & 0 & 1 \\ 0 & 1 & 0 & 1 & 0 \end{pmatrix}$

19. Bipartite. $V_1 = \{1, 2, 5\}$, $V_2 = \{3, 4\}$.

22. Not bipartite

25. Not bipartite

28. Not bipartite

31. Not bipartite

34. 3

37. Cycle, simple cycle

40. Cycle, simple cycle

43. Simple path

46. Cycle

47. $(1, 1)$, $(2, 3, 7, 2)$, $(2, 3, 4, 6, 7, 2)$, $(2, 3, 4, 5, 6, 7, 2)$, $(3, 7, 6, 4, 3)$, $(3, 7, 6, 5, 4, 3)$, $(4, 6, 5, 4)$

49. 12

52.

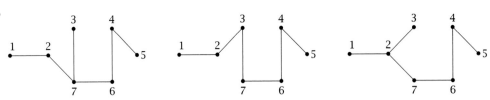

The second is a simple path. None is a cycle or a simple cycle.

53. No. The graph is not connected.

56. Yes. A Hamiltonian cycle is $(1, 2, 4, 6, 5, 3, 1)$.

59. No. Suppose by way of contradiction that $K_{3,4}$ has a Hamiltonian cycle

$$(v_1, v_2, v_3, v_4, v_5, v_6, v_7, v_1).$$

We assume that the seven vertices are partitioned as $\{1, 3, 5, 7\}, \{2, 4, 6\}$ and that $v_1 = 1$. Notice that each of v_1, v_3, v_5, v_7 is odd, and each of v_2, v_4, v_6 is even. Thus, edge (v_7, v_1) is incident on odd vertices, which is a contradiction. Therefore, $K_{3,4}$ does not have a Hamiltonian cycle.

61. When $n \geq 3$

64. Yes

66. No. The graph is not connected.

69. Yes. We assume that the vertices are $1, 2, 3, 4, 5$. An Euler cycle is

$$(1, 2, 3, 4, 5, 1, 3, 5, 2, 4, 1).$$

72. When n is odd, the degree of every vertex is even; so, K_n contains an Euler cycle. When n is odd, the degree of every vertex is odd; so, in this case, K_n does not contain an Euler cycle. (See Exercise 74.)

75. The vertices represent the islands and river banks, and the edges represent the bridges:

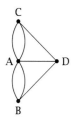

This graph has no Euler cycle because all the vertices have odd degree (see Exercise 74); thus, the bridge problem has no solution.

76.

79. Suppose that G is not connected. Let C be a component of G, and let V_1 be the set of vertices in C. Let V_2 be the set of vertices in G that are not in V_1. Since G is not connected, $V_2 \neq \emptyset$. In $\overline{G}$, for every $v_1 \in V_1$ and $v_2 \in V_2$, there is an edge e incident on v_1 and v_2. Thus, in $\overline{G}$ there is a path from v to w if $v \in V_1$ and $w \in V_2$. Suppose that v and w are in V_1. Choose $x \in V_2$. Then (v, x, w) is a path from v to w. Similarly, if v and w are in V_2, there is a path from v to w. Thus $\overline{G}$ is connected.

81. The graphs are isomorphic. Ordering for G_1: 1, 2, 3, 4, 5; ordering for G_2: 3, 4, 1, 5, 2.

84. The graphs have the equal adjacency matrices if we order the vertices of the first graph in Figure 2.5.18 as $1, 2, 3, 4, 5, 6, 7, 8, 9, 10$, and we order the vertices of the graph in this exercise as $1, 2, 3, 4, 7, 6, 10, 9, 5, 8$.

87. The chromatic number is 3. We can color this graph using three colors. On the other hand, three colors are necessary because the graph contains K_3 as a subgraph.

90. The chromatic number is 2. We can color this graph using two colors. On the other hand, two colors are necessary because the graph contains K_2 as a subgraph.

Section 2.6

1. This graph is not a tree because it is not connected.

4. This graph is a tree because it is a simple graph and, if v and w are vertices, there is a unique simple path from v to w.

5. If either m or n, or both, equals 1

8. 4

11. If T consists of the root and no edges, the diameter and height are both zero, so the statement is true. Thus, suppose that T has at least one edge. Let P be a shortest path of maximum length. Then, the length of P is the diameter of T. Now one end vertex of P must be a terminal vertex (otherwise, P is not a *longest* shortest path). We may assume that P begins at a terminal vertex. Notice that P moves along edges toward the root (we call these *Up* edges) and then along zero or more edges away from the root (we call these *Down* edges). Now the number of Up edges is less than or equal to the height of the tree, and the number of Down edges is also less than or equal to the height of the tree. Therefore, the diameter of T is less than or equal to twice the height of T.

14. 5

17. $1, 2, 3, 4, 6, 7, 8, 9, 10$

20. They are siblings.

23. One is an ancestor of the other.

26. Let G be a graph with n vertices and fewer than $n - 1$ edges, and suppose, by way of contradiction, that G is connected. Add parallel edges until the resulting graph G^* has $n - 1$ edges. Since G^* is connected and has $n - 1$ edges, by Theorem 2.6.5, G^* is acyclic. But adding an edge in parallel introduces a cycle. Contradiction.

Chapter 3: Data Structures

Section 3.1

1.

After	Stack (Top at Right)	b	i
$b = s.empty()$		true	
$s.push(-3)$	−3		
$b = s.empty()$	−3	false	
$i = s.top()$	−3		−3
$s.pop()$			
$b = s.empty()$		true	
$s.push(38)$	38		
$s.push(88)$	38 88		
$s.push(70)$	38 88 70		
$b = s.empty()$	38 88 70	false	
$i = s.top()$	38 88 70		70
$s.pop()$	38 88		
$i = s.top()$	38 88		88

Section 3.2

1. 54 100 630 60 100

4. *push(val)* {
    if ($t == SIZE - 1$)
      return false
    $t = t + 1$
    $data[t] = val$
    return true
}

7. *is_full()* {
    return $(r + 1) \bmod SIZE == f$
}

10. *dequeue()* {
    if ($r == -1$)
      return false
    if ($r == f$)
      $r = f = -1$

```
    else {
        f = f + 1
        if (f == SIZE)
            f = 0
    }
    return true
}
```

13. *one(q)* {
```
    if (q.empty())
        return false
    val = q.front()
    q.dequeue()
    flag = q.empty()
    q.insert_front(val)
    return flag
}
```

Section 3.3

1. null

4. *count(start)* {
```
    numb_nodes = 0
    while (start != null) {
        numb_nodes = numb_nodes + 1
        start = start.next
    }
    return numb_nodes
}
```

The worst-case time is $\Theta(n)$, where n is the number of nodes in the list.

7. *mergelists(p1, p2)* {
```
    if (p1 == null)
        return p2

    if (p2 == null)
        return p1
    if (p1.data ≤ p2.data) {
        p = p1
        swap(p1, p2)
    }
    else
        p = p2
    while (p1 != null) {
        // Here neither p1 nor p2 is null, and p1.data > p2.data
        swap(p1, p2)
```

```
    // Here p1.data ≤ p2.data
    while (p1 != null && p1.data ≤ p2.data) {
        p1tr = p1
        p1 = p1.next
    }
    p1tr.next = p2
}
return p
}
```

The worst-case time is $\Theta(n)$, where n is the total number of nodes in the two lists.

9. *init*() {
```
    head = new node
    tail = new node
    head.next = tail
    tail.prev = head
}
```

12. *queue_init*() {
```
    r = f = null
}
```

empty() {
```
    return r == null
}
```

enqueue(*val*) {
```
    temp = new node
    temp.data = val
    temp.next = null
    if (rear = null)
        front = rear = temp
    else
        rear = rear.next = temp
}
```

dequeue() {
```
    front = front.next
    if (front = null)
        rear = null
}
```

front() {
```
    return front.data
}
```

15.

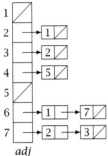

adj

Section 3.4

1. We use induction to prove that if a binary tree has n nodes, the conditional line,

> if ($root$!= null) {

is executed $2n + 1$ times.

The proof is by induction on n. The basis step is $n = 0$. In this case, the conditional line is executed $1 = 2 \cdot 0 + 1$ time, which verifies the basis step.

Now assume that $n > 0$ and if a binary tree has $m < n$ nodes, the conditional line is executed $2m + 1$ times.

Let T be an n-node binary tree with root $root$. Suppose that T's left subtree contains n_l nodes and T's right subtree contains n_r nodes. When inorder is called with input $root$, first the line

> if ($root$!= null) {

is executed, which accounts for one execution of the conditional line.

Next, inorder is called with input $root.left$. The tree rooted at $root.left$ has $n_l < n$ nodes; so, by the inductive assumption, the conditional line is executed a total of $2n_l + 1$ times while processing T's left subtree. Similarly, the tree rooted at $root.right$ has $n_r < n$ nodes; so, by the inductive assumption, the conditional line is executed a total of $2n_r + 1$ times while processing T's right subtree. The total number of times the conditional line is executed is, therefore,

$$1 + (2n_l + 1) + (2n_r + 1) = 2(n_l + n_r + 1) + 1 = 2n + 1.$$

The inductive step is complete.

4. *terminals*($root$) {
    if ($root$ == null) {
      return 0
    if ($root.left$ == null && $root.right$ == null)
      return 1
    return *terminals*($root.left$) + *terminals*($root.right$)
}

7.   Input Parameter: *root* (never null)
     Output Parameters: None

expr_tree(*root*) {
   if (*root.left* == null)
      print(*root.data*)
   else
      print("(" + *expr_tree*(*root.left*) + *root.data* + *expr_tree*(*root.right*) + ")")
}

10. We begin at the root. Since 10 < 40, the algorithm moves to 40's left child (13). Since 10 < 13, the algorithm moves to 13's left child (7). Since 10 > 7, the algorithm would move to 7's right child except that there is none. Therefore, 10 is inserted as 7's right child.

13. Since 57 has two children, we move to 57's right child, and then we repeatedly move to a left child until we reach node 60. We then replace 57 by 60 and delete the original node containing 60. The result is

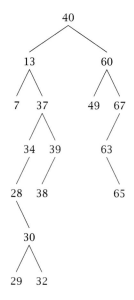

16. *BSTinsert*(*root*, *val*) {
       // set up *node* to be added to tree
       temp = new *node*
       temp.data = *val*
       temp.left = *temp.right* = null
       if (*root* == null) // special case: empty tree
          return *temp*
       where = *root*

```
    while (true)
      if (val < where.data)
        if (where.left == null) {
          where.left == temp
          return root
        }
        else
          where = where.left
      else
        if (where.right == null) {
          where.right == temp
          return root
        }
        else
          where = where.right
}
```

19. This algorithm returns true if the binary tree rooted at *root* is a binary search tree, or false if it is not a binary search tree. The algorithm also sets *minval* to the smallest value in the tree, and *maxval* to the largest value in the tree. These values are used internally in the algorithm.

Input Parameters:	*root* (assumed not null)
Output Parameters:	*minval, maxval*

```
check_BST(root, minval, maxval) {
    minvalL = ∞ // to avoid special case
    maxvalR = −∞ // also to avoid special case
    if (root.left != null)
        if (check_BST(root.left, minvalL, maxvalL) == false || maxvalL > root.data)
            return false
    if (root.right != null)
        if (check_BST(root.right, minvalR, maxvalR) == false || minvalR < root.data)
            return false
    minval = min(minvalL, root.data)
    maxval = max(maxvalR, root.data)
    return true
}
```

Section 3.5

1. The array is *a*, and *e* is the index of the last item stored. The index of the first element is 0.

```
init() {
    e = −1
}
```

```
delete() {
    index = 0
    // find largest
    for i = 1 to e
        if (a[i] > a[index])
            index = i
    // remove largest
    for i = index + 1 to e
        a[i − 1] = a[i]
    e = e − 1
}

largest() {
    val = a[0]
    // find largest
    for i = 1 to e
        if (a[i] > val)
            val = a[i]
    return val
}

insert(val) {
    e = e + 1
    a[e] = val
}
```

4. The section showed that the time is $O(n^2)$, so it suffices to construct an example that takes time $\Theta(n^2)$.

Suppose that we insert the values $n, n − 1, \ldots, 1$, in this order, and then perform n deletions. When $n − 1$ is inserted, n must move one cell to make room for $n − 1$, which takes time at least 1. When $n − 2$ is inserted, $n − 1$ and n must each move one cell, which takes time at least 2; and so on. When 1 is inserted, each of $2, 3, \ldots, n − 1$ must move one cell, which takes time at least $n − 1$. The total time is at least

$$1 + 2 + \cdots + n − 1 = \frac{(n − 1)n}{2} = \Theta(n^2).$$

7. The following figures show how siftdown works:

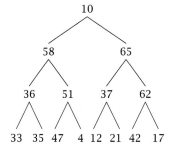
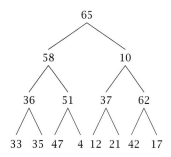

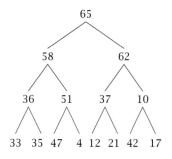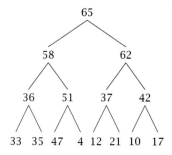

10. The following figures show how insert works:

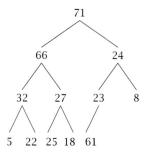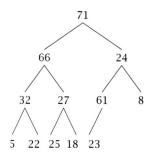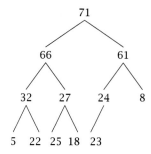

14. *into*

11	3	1	8	9	6	2	4	7	10	5

outof

3	7	2	8	11	6	9	4	5	10	1

18.

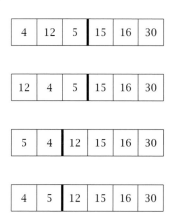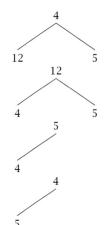

21. Make $|x_1| + |x_2|$ the parent of x_1 and x_2; make $|x_3| + |x_4|$ the parent of x_3 and x_4; and so on. Make $|x_1| + |x_2| + |x_3| + |x_4|$ the parent of $|x_1| + |x_2|$ and $|x_3| + |x_4|$; and so on. Continue until a root is constructed.

24. The second-largest element must be a child of the root.

27. *largest*() {
    return *key*[*outof*[1]]
  }

30.   Input Parameters: s, the index in the *key* array where the value
                                          to insert is located, and n (the size of the heap)
    Output Parameters: None

```
insert(s, n) {
    i = n = n + 1
    val = key[s]
    // i is the child and i/2 is the parent.
    while (i > 1 && val > key[outof[i/2]]) {
        // copy parent value to child
        outof[i] = outof[i/2]
        into[outof[i]] = i
        // move i to parent
        i = i/2
    }
    // insert val at index i
    outof[i] = s
    into[s] = i
}
```

In the worst case, the value added travels all the way from the last level to the root; thus, the worst-case time is $\Theta(\lg n)$.

33. $\Theta(n \lg n)$

Section 3.6

1. After the for loop executes, there are eight single-node trees. The following pictures show the changes that result as *union* executes:

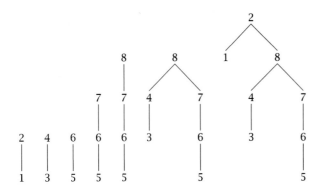

4. The trees are unchanged. Since *findset1*[*i*] will be equal to *findset1*[*j*], *mergetrees1* will be called with both arguments equal to the root of the tree. Thus, *mergetrees1* will set the parent of the root equal to the root. But this was *already* the value of the parent of the root.

7. When union executes, the height of the tree that results can be at most 1 more than the maximum height of the two trees that were merged. Since union is called at most *m* times and all trees began with height 0, the maximum height of a tree is *m*.

10. *find*(*i*) {
    if (*i* == *parent*[*i*])
      return *i*
    return *parent*[*i*]
}

Chapter 4: Searching

Section 4.1

1. The algorithm first compares 6 with $L[2] = 6$. Since the values are equal, the algorithm returns the index 2.

4. The algorithm first compares 24 with $L[2] = 6$. Since $24 > 6$, the algorithm repeats by searching the second part of the array $L[3], L[4]$.

   The algorithm next compares 24 with $L[3] = 8$. Since $24 > 8$, the algorithm repeats by searching the second part of the array $L[4]$.

   The algorithm next compares 24 with $L[4] = 11$. Since $24 > 11$, the algorithm repeats by considering searching the second part of the array. Since the array to search is now empty, the algorithm concludes by returning -1 to signal that the *key* was not found.

5. *bsearch*(L, i, j, key) {
    if $(i \leq j)$ {
        $k = (i + j)/2$
        if $(key == L[k])$
           return k
        if $(key < L[k])$
           return *bsearch*$(L, i, k - 1, key)$
        else
           return *bsearch*$(L, k + 1, j, key)$
    }
    return -1
}

8. Yes. Consider $L[1] = 10$, $L[2] = 8$, $L[3] = 9$ and $key = 8$.

11. The algorithm is not correct. The input $L[1] = 10$ and $key = 8$ results in infinite recursion.

14. First key is compared with $L[1]$. Since $3 < 6$, we follow the left edge where key is compared with $L[0]$. Since $3 = 3$, we follow the middle edge, which indicates that key was found.

17.

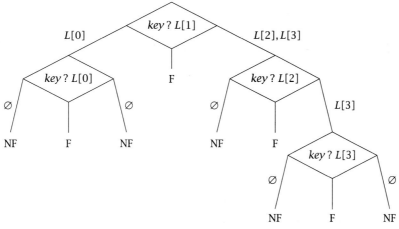

20. 5

21. Denote the coins $C_1, \ldots, C_5$. We define $C_i > C_j$ to mean that coin i weighs more than coin j.

    if $(C_1 > C_2)$
      if $(C_1 > C_5)$
        C_1 is the heavy coin
      else
        C_2 is the light coin

else if ($C_1 == C_2$)
  if ($C_3 > C_4$)
    if ($C_3 > C_5$)
      C_3 is the heavy coin
    else
      C_4 is the light coin
  else if ($C_3 == C_4$)
    if ($C_1 > C_5$)
      C_5 is the light coin
    else
      C_5 is the heavy coin
  else
    if ($C_3 == C_5$)
      C_4 is the heavy coin
    else
      C_3 is the light coin
else
  if ($C_1 == C_5$)
    C_2 is the heavy coin
  else
    C_1 is the light coin

24. Suppose that there is an algorithm that can solve the four-coin problem in two weighings in the worst case. Then the decision tree for the algorithm has height 2. The first weighing either compares two coins against two coins or one coin against one coin. The following figure shows that if the algorithm begins by weighing two coins against two coins, the decision tree can account for at most six outcomes; however, eight outcomes are possible:

An edge from a node to a left child means that the left pan weighs less than the right pan. An edge from a node to a right child means that the left pan weighs more than the right pan. A middle edge means that the pans balance. Notice that when the algorithm weighs two coins against two coins, they cannot balance. Therefore, no algorithm can begin by weighing two coins against two coins.

Similarly, the following figure shows that if the algorithm begins by weighing one coin against one coin and they balance, the decision tree can account for at most three outcomes; however, four outcomes are possible:

Therefore, no algorithm can begin by weighing one coin against one coin, and there is no algorithm that can solve the four-coin problem in two weighings in the worst case.

27. A decision tree that solves the 12-coin problem in two weighings in the worst case would have height 2. However, such a tree has at most nine terminal nodes. Since the 12-coin problem has 24 possible outcomes, there is no such decision tree (i.e., algorithm) for the 12-coin problem.

Section 4.2

1. $1, 2, 3, 4, 5$

4. $3, 2, 1, 4, 5$

7. $1, 4, 5, 3, 2$

10. $4, 7, 10, 11, 12, 9, 8, 5, 6, 3, 2$

13.

				trav	
(a) *start* = 5	*visit*	f f f f t	$adj[5] \rightarrow 4$		5 calls 4
(b) *start* = 4	*visit*	f f f t t	$adj[4] \rightarrow 2 \rightarrow 3 \rightarrow 5$		4 calls 2
(c) *start* = 2	*visit*	f t f t t	$adj[2] \rightarrow 1 \rightarrow 4$		2 calls 1
(d) *start* = 1	*visit*	t t f t t	$adj[1] \rightarrow 2 \rightarrow 3$		1 calls 3
(e) *start* = 3	*visit*	t t t t t	$adj[3] \rightarrow 1 \rightarrow 4$		3 returns to 1
(f) *start* = 1	*visit*	t t t t t	$adj[1] \rightarrow 2 \rightarrow 3$		1 returns to 2
(g) *start* = 2	*visit*	t t t t t	$adj[2] \rightarrow 1 \rightarrow 4$		2 returns to 4
(h) *start* = 4	*visit*	t t t t t	$adj[4] \rightarrow 2 \rightarrow 3 \rightarrow 5$		4 returns to 5
(i) *start* = 5	*visit*	t t t t t	$adj[5] \rightarrow 4$		5 returns to *dfs*

16.

(a) *start* = 3   *visit* | f | f | t | f | f | $adj[3] \to 5 \to \overset{\underset{\downarrow}{trav}}{4} \to 2$ 3 calls 5

(b) *start* = 5   *visit* | f | f | t | f | t | $adj[5] \to \overset{\underset{\downarrow}{trav}}{4} \to 3 \to 2$ 5 calls 4

(c) *start* = 4   *visit* | f | f | t | t | t | $adj[4] \to 5 \to 3 \to \overset{\underset{\downarrow}{trav}}{1}$ 4 calls 1

(d) *start* = 1   *visit* | t | f | t | t | t | $adj[1] \to 4 \to \overset{\underset{\downarrow}{trav}}{2}$ 1 calls 2

(e) *start* = 2   *visit* | t | t | t | t | t | $adj[2] \to 5 \to 3 \to \overset{\underset{\downarrow}{trav}}{1}$ 2 returns to 1

(f) *start* = 1   *visit* | t | t | t | t | t | $adj[1] \to 4 \to \overset{\underset{\downarrow}{trav}}{2}$ 1 returns to 4

(g) *start* = 4   *visit* | t | t | t | t | t | $adj[4] \to 5 \to 3 \to \overset{\underset{\downarrow}{trav}}{1}$ 4 returns to 5

(h) *start* = 5   *visit* | t | t | t | t | t | $adj[5] \to 4 \to 3 \to \overset{\underset{\downarrow}{trav}}{2}$ 5 returns to 3

(i) *start* = 3   *visit* | t | t | t | t | t | $adj[3] \to 5 \to 4 \to \overset{\underset{\downarrow}{trav}}{2}$ 3 returns to *dfs*

20. *dfs*(*adj*, *start*) {

```
dfs(adj, start) {
    n = adj.last
    for i = 1 to n
        visit[i] = false
    visit[start] = true
    println(start)
    // s is an initially empty stack
    s.push(adj[start])
    while (!s.empty()) {
        trav = s.top()
        s.pop()
        while (trav != null) {
            v = trav.ver
            if (!visit[v]) {
                s.push(trav.next)
                visit[v] = true
                println(v)
                trav = adj[v]
            }
```

```
        else
           trav = trav.next
      }
    }
  }
```

Section 4.3

1. $1, 2, 4, 3, 5$ **4.** $8, 5, 7, 9, 10, 11, 12, 1, 2, 3, 4, 6$

7. $1, 4, 2, 5, 3$ **10.** $4, 7, 5, 1, 10, 8, 9, 6, 3, 2, 11, 12$

13.

(a)   *front rear* q | 5 | *visit* | f | f | f | f | t |

(b) *current* = 5   *front rear* q | 4 | *visit* | f | f | f | t | t |

(c) *current* = 4   *front rear* q | 2   3 | *visit* | f | t | t | t | t |

(d) *current* = 2   *front rear* q | 3   1 | *visit* | t | t | t | t | t |

(e) *current* = 3   *front rear* q | 1 | *visit* | t | t | t | t | t |

(f) *current* = 1   *front rear* q | | *visit* | t | t | t | t | t |

16.

(a)   *front rear* q | 3 | *visit* | f | f | t | f | f |

(b) *current* = 3   *front rear* q | 5 4 2 | *visit* | f | t | t | t | t |

(c) *current* = 5   *front rear* q | 4   2 | *visit* | f | t | t | t | t |

(d) *current* = 4   *front rear* q | 2   1 | *visit* | t | t | t | t | t |

(e) *current* = 2   *front rear* q | 1 | *visit* | t | t | t | t | t |

(f) *current* = 1   *front rear* q | | *visit* | t | t | t | t | t |

20. *bfs*(*adjm*, *start*) {
    n = *adjm.last*
    for *i* = 1 to *n*
      visit[*i*] = false
    visit[*start*] = true
    println(*start*)
    // *q* is an initially empty queue
    q.enqueue(*start*)
    while (!*q.empty*()) {
      current = *q.front*()
      q.dequeue()
      for *i* = 1 to *n*
        if (*adjm*[*current*][*i*] == 1 && !*visit*[*i*]) {
          visit[*i*] = true
          println(*i*)
          q.enqueue(*i*)
        }
      }
    }
}

The worst-case time is $\Theta(n^2)$.

Section 4.4

1. 7, 5, 8, 2, 1, 3, 6, 9, 10, 4

4. 10, 6, 4, 7, 1, 2, 3, 5, 8, 9

7. 10, 6, 4, 7, 1, 2, 3, 5, 8, 9

8. First, *top_sort* calls *top_sort_recurs* with $i = 1$. Vertex 1 is marked as visited, and we begin traversing 1's adjacency list. The only vertex on the list is 2. Since 2 is not visited, *top_sort_recurs* is called with $v = 2$.

Vertex 2 is marked as visited, and we begin traversing 2's adjacency list. The first vertex on the list is 5. Since 5 is not visited, *top_sort_recurs* is called with $v = 5$.

Vertex 5 is marked as visited, and we begin traversing 5's adjacency list. The only vertex on the list is 8. Since 8 is not visited, *top_sort_recurs* is called with $v = 8$.

Vertex 8 is marked as visited, and we begin traversing 8's adjacency list. The only vertex on the list is 9. Since 9 is not visited, *top_sort_recurs* is called with $v = 9$.

Vertex 9 is marked as visited. Since 9's adjacency list is empty, 9 is placed last in the topological sort, and *top_sort_recurs* with *start* = 9 returns to its caller *top_sort_recurs* with *start* = 8.

Execution of *top_sort_recurs* with *start* = 8 resumes by attempting to move to the next node on 8's adjacency list. Since there are no more nodes on 8's list, 8 is placed before 9 in the topological sort, and *top_sort_recurs* with *start* = 8 returns to its caller *top_sort_recurs* with *start* = 5.

Execution of *top_sort_recurs* with *start* = 5 resumes by attempting to move to the next node on 5's adjacency list. Since there are no more nodes on 5's list, 5 is placed before 8 in the topological sort, and *top_sort_recurs* with *start* = 5 returns to its caller *top_sort_recurs* with *start* = 2.

Execution of *top_sort_recurs* with *start* = 2 resumes by moving to the next node on 2's adjacency list, which contains vertex 3. Since 3 is not visited, *top_sort_recurs* is called with $v = 3$.

Vertex 3 is marked as visited. Since 3's adjacency list is empty, 3 is placed before 5 in the topological sort, and *top_sort_recurs* with *start* = 3 returns to its caller *top_sort_recurs* with *start* = 2.

Execution of *top_sort_recurs* with *start* = 2 resumes by attempting to move to the next node on 2's adjacency list. Since there are no more nodes on 2's list, 2 is placed before 3 in the topological sort, and *top_sort_recurs* with *start* = 2 returns to its caller *top_sort_recurs* with *start* = 1.

Execution of *top_sort_recurs* with *start* = 1 resumes by attempting to move to the next node on 1's adjacency list. Since there are no more nodes on 1's list, 1 is placed before 2 in the topological sort, and *top_sort_recurs* with *start* = 1 returns to its caller *top_sort*.

Since 2 and 3 are visited, but 4 is not visited, *top_sort* next calls *top_sort_recurs* with $i = 4$. Vertex 4 is marked as visited, and we begin traversing 4's adjacency list. Since 1 is visited, but 7 is not visited, *top_sort_recurs* is called with *start* = 7.

Vertex 7 is marked as visited. The only vertex, 8, on 7's adjacency list is visited; so, 7 is placed before 1 in the topological sort, and *top_sort_recurs* with *start* = 7 returns to its caller *top_sort_recurs* with *start* = 4.

Execution of *top_sort_recurs* with *start* = 4 resumes by attempting to move to the next node on 4's adjacency list. Since there are no more nodes on 4's list, 4 is placed before 7 in the topological sort, and *top_sort_recurs* with *start* = 4 returns to its caller *top_sort*.

Since 5 is visited, but 6 is not visited, *top_sort* next calls *top_sort_recurs* with $i = 6$. Vertex 6 is marked as visited. The vertices, 3 and 9, on 6's adjacency list are visited; so, 6 is placed before 4 in the topological sort, and *top_sort_recurs* with *start* = 6 returns to its caller *top_sort*.

Since 7, 8, and 9 are visited, but 10 is not visited, *top_sort* next calls *top_sort_recurs* with $i = 10$. Vertex 10 is marked as visited. The only vertex, 8, on 10's adjacency list is visited; so, 10 is placed first in the topological sort, and *top_sort_recurs* with *start* = 10 returns to its caller *top_sort*. The algorithm then terminates.

11. First, *top_sort* calls *top_sort_recurs* with $i = 1$. Vertex 1 is marked as visited, and we begin traversing 1's adjacency list. The only vertex on the list is 3. Since 3 is not visited, *top_sort_recurs* is called with $v = 3$.

Vertex 3 is marked as visited, and we begin traversing 3's adjacency list. The first vertex on the list is 6. Since 6 is not visited, *top_sort_recurs* is called with $v = 6$.

Vertex 6 is marked as visited, and we begin traversing 6's adjacency list. The first vertex on the list is 9. Since 9 is not visited, *top_sort_recurs* is called with $v = 9$.

Vertex 9 is marked as visited, and we begin traversing 9's adjacency list. The only vertex on the list is 10. Since 10 is not visited, *top_sort_recurs* is called with $v = 10$.

Vertex 10 is marked as visited. Since 10's adjacency list is empty, 10 is placed last in the topological sort, and *top_sort_recurs* with *start* = 10 returns to its caller *top_sort_recurs* with *start* = 9.

Execution of *top_sort_recurs* with *start* = 9 resumes by attempting to move to the next node on 9's adjacency list. Since there are no more nodes on 9's list, 9 is placed before 10 in the topological sort, and *top_sort_recurs* with *start* = 9 returns to its caller *top_sort_recurs* with *start* = 6.

Execution of *top_sort_recurs* with *start* = 6 resumes by moving to the next node, 4, on 6's adjacency list. Since 4 is not visited, *top_sort_recurs* is called with $v = 4$.

Vertex 4 is marked as visited. Since 4's adjacency list is empty, 4 is placed before 9 in the topological sort, and *top_sort_recurs* with *start* = 4 returns to its caller *top_sort_recurs* with *start* = 6.

Since there are no more nodes on 6's list, 6 is placed before 4 in the topological sort, and *top_sort_recurs* with *start* = 6 returns to its caller *top_sort_recurs* with *start* = 3.

Since the next and last node, 4, on 3's list, is visited, 3 is placed before 6 in the topological sort, and *top_sort_recurs* with *start* = 3 returns to its caller *top_sort_recurs* with *start* = 1.

Since there are no more nodes on 1's list, 1 is placed before 3 in the topological sort, and *top_sort_recurs* with *start* = 1 returns to its caller *top_sort*.

Since 2 is not visited, *top_sort* next calls *top_sort_recurs* with $i = 2$. Vertex 2 is marked as visited, and we begin traversing 2's adjacency list. The vertex, 3, on 2's adjacency list is visited; so, 2 is placed before 1 in the topological sort, and *top_sort_recurs* with *start* = 2 returns to its caller *top_sort*.

Since 3 and 4 are visited, *top_sort* next calls *top_sort_recurs* with $i = 5$. Vertex 5 is marked as visited, and we begin traversing 5's adjacency list. The first vertex on the list is 8. Since 8 is not visited, *top_sort_recurs* is called with $v = 8$.

Vertex 8 is marked as visited. The only vertex, 9, on 8's adjacency list is visited; so, 8 is placed before 2 in the topological sort, and *top_sort_recurs* with *start* = 8 returns to its caller *top_sort_recurs* with *start* = 5.

Execution of *top_sort_recurs* with *start* = 5 resumes by moving to the next node on 5's adjacency list, which contains vertex 6. Since 6 is visited and this is the last node on 5's adjacency list, 5 is placed before 8 in the topological sort, and *top_sort_recurs* with *start* = 5 returns to its caller *top_sort*.

Since 6 is visited, but 7 is not visited, *top_sort* next calls *top_sort_recurs* with $i = 7$. Vertex 7 is marked as visited. Since the vertices, 10 and 4, on 7's list are visited, 7 is placed before 5 in the topological sort, and *top_sort_recurs* with *start* = 7 returns to its caller *top_sort*.

Since 8, 9, and 10 are visited, the algorithm then terminates.

14.

17. $\Theta(m + n)$

20.
```
top_sort(adjm, ts) {
    n = adjm.last
    // k is the index in ts where the next vertex is to be stored in the
    // topological sort. k is assumed visible in top_sort_recurs.
    k = n
    for i = 1 to n
        visit[i] = false
    for i = 1 to n
        if (!visit[i])
            top_sort_recurs(adjm, i, ts)
}


top_sort_recurs(adjm, start, ts) {
    visit[start] = true
    for i = 1 to adjm.last
        if (adjm[start][i] == 1 && !visit[i])
            top_sort_recurs(adjm, i, ts)
    ts[k] = start
    k = k - 1
}
```

Section 4.5

1. By symmetry, we need only consider the situation in which the first queen is placed in the first column and the first row. Since this queen conflicts with every position in the second column, there is no solution to the 2-queens problem.

4.

7. In the first column, the algorithm only searches rows 1 through $(n + 1)/2$, that is, the upper half of the rows. However, if there is a solution that places a queen in the first column and in the lower half of rows, by rotating the board through a middle, horizontal line, we obtain a solution that places a queen in the first column and in the upper half of rows. Therefore, if there is a solution, there is one that places a queen in the first column and in the upper half of rows, and the algorithm will find it.

10. Using the $n \bmod 3 = 0$ or 1 formula for placing the queens on an 8×8 board yields

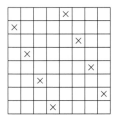

which is not a solution. Note that $8 \bmod 3 = 2$.

13. 1

16. 4

19. 4

22. 6

23. We begin by analyzing the worst-case time t_k, for fixed n, required by

rhamilton(adj, k, x).

We *define* the time required to be the number of times that *path_ok* is called.

Suppose that $2 \le k < n$. The for loop in *rhamilton* runs at most $n - 1$ times, so

path_ok(adj, k, x)

is called at most $n - 1$ times. Since $k - 1$ vertices are used, *path_ok* returns true at most $n - k + 1$ times. Thus,

rhamilton$(adj, k + 1, x)$

is called at most $n - k + 1$ times. Therefore,

$$t_k \le (n - 1) + (n - k + 1)t_{k+1}.$$

When $k = n$, there is no recursive call, so that

$$t_n \le (n - 1).$$

We can use inequality $t_k \le (n - 1) + (n - k + 1)t_{k+1}$ to estimate t_2 as follows:

$$
\begin{aligned}
t_2 \;&\le\; (n - 1) + (n - 1)t_3 \\
&\le\; (n - 1) + (n - 1)[(n - 1) + (n - 2)t_4] \\
&=\; (n - 1) + (n - 1)^2 + (n - 1)(n - 2)t_4 \\
&\le\; (n - 1) + (n - 1)^2 + (n - 1)(n - 2)[(n - 1) + (n - 3)t_5] \\
&=\; (n - 1) + (n - 1)^2 + (n - 1)^2(n - 2) + (n - 1)(n - 2)(n - 3)t_5
\end{aligned}
$$

$$\vdots$$

$$
\begin{aligned}
\leq\ & (n-1) + (n-1)^2 + (n-1)^2(n-2) + (n-1)^2(n-2)(n-3) \\
& + \cdots + (n-1)^2(n-2)(n-3)\cdots 4\cdot 3 \\
& + (n-1)(n-2)(n-3)\cdots 3\cdot 2t_n \\
\leq\ & (n-1) + (n-1)^2 + (n-1)^2(n-2) + (n-1)^2(n-2)(n-3) \\
& + \cdots + (n-1)^2(n-2)(n-3)\cdots 4\cdot 3 \\
& + (n-1)^2(n-2)(n-3)\cdots 3\cdot 2.
\end{aligned}
$$

The last inequality follows from the fact that $t_n \leq n-1$. Factoring out $(n-1)(n-1)!$ gives

$$
t_2 \leq (n-1)(n-1)!\left[\frac{1}{(n-1)!} + \frac{1}{(n-2)!} + \cdots + \frac{1}{2!} + 1\right].
$$

A result from calculus tells us that

$$
e = \sum_{i=0}^{\infty} \frac{1}{i!},
$$

where e is the base of the natural logarithm. It follows that

$$
t_2 \leq (n-1)(n-1)!\sum_{i=1}^{\infty} \frac{1}{i!} = (n-1)(n-1)!(e-1) \leq (e-1)n!;
$$

and, so,

$$
t_2 = O(n!).
$$

The for loop in *hamilton* runs in time $\Theta(n)$, so the time for Algorithm 4.5.4 is $O(n!)$.

26. When $k = 2$, *path_ok* is called one time—when $x[k] = 2$ and *path_ok* returns true. When $k = 3$, *path_ok* is called two times—once when $x[k] = 2$ and *path_ok* returns false, and once when $x[k] = 3$ and *path_ok* returns true—and so on. Thus, the total number of times that *path_ok* is called is

$$
1 + 2 + \cdots + (n-1) = \frac{(n-1)n}{2}.
$$

29. The solution array x contains 0's and 1's. If $x[k] = 0$, k is not included in the subset. If $x[k] = 1$, k is included in the subset.

```
all_subsets(n) {
   rall_subsets(n, 1)
}
rall_subsets(n, k) {
   for x[k] = 0 to 1
      if (k == n) {
         for i = 1 to n
            if (x[i] == 1)
               print(i + " ")
```

```
        println()
    }
    else
        rall_subsets(n, k + 1)
}
```

Chapter 5: Divide and Conquer

Section 5.1

1. First, the board is divided into four 2×2 subboards as shown in (a). The subboard that contains the missing square is recursively tiled; in this case, the deficient 2×2 board is a tromino. Next, we place a tromino as shown in (b) so that each of its 1×1 squares lies in one of the three remaining subboards. Each of these 1×1 squares is considered as missing in the remaining subboards. We can then recursively tile these deficient subboards. Again, each of the deficient 2×2 boards is a tromino, so the problem is solved.

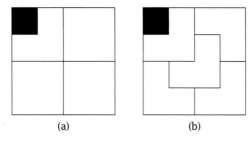

    (a)   (b)

4. First, the board is divided into four 4×4 subboards as shown in (a). The subboard that contains the missing square is recursively tiled as shown in (b). Next, we place a tromino as shown in (c) so that each of its 1×1 squares lies in one of the three remaining subboards. Each of these 1×1 squares is considered as missing in the remaining subboards. We can then recursively tile each of these deficient 4×4 subboards as shown in (d). The problem is solved.

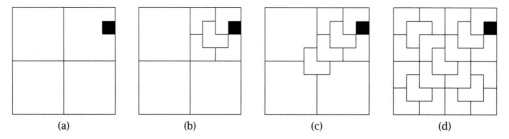

    (a)   (b)   (c)   (d)

5. $c_n = 4c_{n/2} + 1$. By the Main Recurrence Theorem, Theorem 2.4.7, $c_n = \Theta(n^2)$.

8. Such a board can be tiled with ij 2×3 rectangles of the form

11. Exercise 9 gives a solution if $n = 7$.

If $n = 11$, enclose the missing square in a corner 7×7 subboard (see the following figure). Tile this subboard using the result of Exercise 9. Tile the two 6×4 subboards using the result of Exercise 8. It is straightforward to tile the 5×5 subboard with a corner square missing. Thus the 11×11 board is tiled.

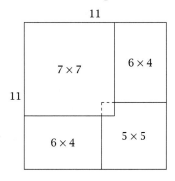

Suppose that $n > 11$. Enclose the missing square in a corner $(n - 6) \times (n - 6)$ subboard. Recursively tile this board. Tile the two $6 \times (n - 7)$ subboards using the result of Exercise 8. Tile the deficient 7×7 subboard using the result of Exercise 9. The $n \times n$ board is tiled.

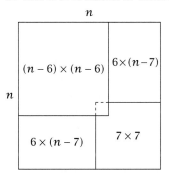

14. Only those 4×4 deficient boards in which the missing square is in a corner can be tiled. The following figure shows a tiling:

To see that no other deficient 4×4 board can be tiled, first number the squares of a 4×4 board as follows:

1	2	3	1
2	3	1	2
3	1	2	3
1	2	3	1

Notice that each tromino covers a 1, a 2, and a 3. Since five trominoes are required, if there is a tiling, all five 2's are covered. Therefore, the missing square cannot be a 2. Similarly, the missing square cannot be a 3.

Now number the squares as follows:

1	3	2	1
2	1	3	2
3	2	1	3
1	3	2	1

An argument similar to that for the other numbering shows that the missing square cannot be a 2 or a 3. Therefore, the missing square must be a corner square.

17. For $n = 0$, the $2^n \times 2^n$ L-shape is a tromino and, so, it is tiled.

For $n > 0$, divide the $2^n \times 2^n$ L-shape into four $2^{n-1} \times 2^{n-1}$ L-shapes:

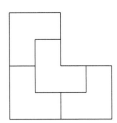

Recursively tile each of the four $2^{n-1} \times 2^{n-1}$ L-shapes.

Section 5.2

1. We begin by examining the first element in each array:

$$\boxed{14 \mid 24 \mid 27} \qquad \boxed{17 \mid 26 \mid 54} \;.$$

$$\quad\uparrow\qquad\qquad\qquad\uparrow$$

Since $14 < 17$, 14 is copied into the output array

$$\boxed{14 \mid \cdots} \;,$$

and we move to the next item in the first array

$$\boxed{14 \mid 24 \mid 27} \qquad \boxed{17 \mid 26 \mid 54} \;.$$

$$\qquad\uparrow\qquad\qquad\qquad\uparrow$$

Since 24 > 17, 17 is copied into the output array

14	17	$\cdots$

,

and we move to the next item in the second array

14	24	27
↑

17	26	54
↑

.

Since 24 < 26, 24 is copied into the output array

14	17	24	$\cdots$

,

and we move to the next item in the first array

14	24	27
↑

17	26	54
↑

.

Since 27 > 26, 26 is copied into the output array

14	17	24	26	$\cdots$

,

and we move to the next item in the second array

14	24	27
↑

17	26	54
↑

.

Since 27 < 54, 27 is copied into the output array

14	17	24	26	27	$\cdots$

,

and we attempt to move to the next item in the first array. Since we have now reached the end of the first array, we copy the end of the second array to the output. The result is

14	17	24	26	27	54

.

4. We begin by examining the first element in each array:

7	10	11	29	31
↑

9	28	71	79	101
↑

.

Since 7 < 9, 7 is copied into the output array

$$\boxed{7} \quad \cdots \quad ,$$

and we move to the next item in the first array

| 7 | 10 | 11 | 29 | 31 | | 9 | 28 | 71 | 79 | 101 | .

   ↑   ↑

Since $10 > 9$, 9 is copied into the output array

$$\boxed{7 \quad 9} \quad \cdots \quad ,$$

and we move to the next item in the second array

| 7 | 10 | 11 | 29 | 31 | | 9 | 28 | 71 | 79 | 101 | .

   ↑   ↑

Since $10 < 28$, 10 is copied into the output array

$$\boxed{7 \quad 9 \quad 10} \quad \cdots \quad ,$$

and we move to the next item in the first array

| 7 | 10 | 11 | 29 | 31 | | 9 | 28 | 71 | 79 | 101 | .

     ↑   ↑

Since $11 < 28$, 11 is copied into the output array

$$\boxed{7 \quad 9 \quad 10 \quad 11} \quad \cdots \quad ,$$

and we move to the next item in the first array

| 7 | 10 | 11 | 29 | 31 | | 9 | 28 | 71 | 79 | 101 | .

       ↑   ↑

Since $29 > 28$, 28 is copied into the output array

$$\boxed{7 \quad 9 \quad 10 \quad 11 \quad 28} \quad \cdots \quad ,$$

and we move to the next item in the second array

| 7 | 10 | 11 | 29 | 31 | | 9 | 28 | 71 | 79 | 101 | .

       ↑   ↑

Since $29 < 71$, 29 is copied into the output array

| 7 | 9 | 10 | 11 | 28 | 29 | $\cdots$ | , |

and we move to the next item in the first array

| 7 | 10 | 11 | 29 | 31 | | 9 | 28 | 71 | 79 | 101 | .
          ↑   ↑

Since $31 < 71$, 31 is copied into the output array

| 7 | 9 | 10 | 11 | 28 | 29 | 31 | $\cdots$ | , |

and we attempt to move to the next item in the first array. Since we have now reached the end of the first array, we copy the end of the second array to the output. The result is

| 7 | 9 | 10 | 11 | 28 | 29 | 31 | 71 | 79 | 101 | .

5. The array is first divided into two equal parts

| 14 | 40 | 31 | 28 | | 3 | 15 | 17 | 51 | .

Each part is then sorted by mergesort. The process begins by dividing each part into equal parts

| 14 | 40 | | 31 | 28 | | 3 | 15 | | 17 | 51 | ,

and then each of these parts into equal parts

| 14 | | 40 | | 31 | | 28 | | 3 | | 15 | | 17 | | 51 | .

This subdividing process now ends because each part contains only one item. Each pair is then merged

| 14 | 40 | | 28 | 31 | | 3 | 15 | | 17 | 51 | .

Each of these pairs is then merged

| 14 | 28 | 31 | 40 | | 3 | 15 | 17 | 51 | .

Finally these pairs are merged

| 3 | 14 | 15 | 17 | 28 | 31 | 40 | 51 |

to obtain the sorted array.

8. The array is first divided into two equal parts

| 23 | 23 | 23 | 23 | | 23 | 23 | 23 | 23 | .

Each part is then sorted by mergesort. The process begins by dividing each part into equal parts

| 23 | 23 | | 23 | 23 | | 23 | 23 | | 23 | 23 | ,

and then each of these parts into equal parts

| 23 | | 23 | | 23 | | 23 | | 23 | | 23 | | 23 | | 23 | .

This subdividing process now ends because each part contains only one item. Each pair is then merged

| 23 | 23 | | 23 | 23 | | 23 | 23 | | 23 | 23 | .

Each of these pairs is then merged

| 23 | 23 | 23 | 23 | | 23 | 23 | 23 | 23 | .

Finally these pairs are merged

| 23 | 23 | 23 | 23 | 23 | 23 | 23 | 23 |

to obtain the sorted array.

9. This nonrecursive version of mergesort sorts the array $a[1], \ldots, a[n]$. It first merges subarrays of size 1, then subarrays of size 2, then subarrays of size 4, and so on. The variable *size* is the size of the current subarrays to merge. The expression $min(i + 2 * size - 1, n)$ is the index of the last element in the last subarray in the merge. The last subarray's size may be less than *size*, because we have reached the end of the array and *size* is not an exact divisor of n.

The algorithm merges from a to an auxiliary array b, then from b back to a, then from a back to b, and so on. This reduces the extra copying that was done in the original mergesort algorithm. The variable *parity* controls the source and destination arrays for the merge.

The merge algorithm is essentially the same as Algorithm 5.2.2, except that there is an extra parameter to indicate the destination of the merge. The result is *not* copied back to the original array.

```
mergesort(a) {
    n = a.last
    size = 1
    parity = 1
    while (size ≤ n − 1) {
        i = 1
```

```
    if (parity == 1)
       while (i ≤ n − size) {
          merge(a, i, i + size − 1, min(i + 2 * size − 1, n), b)
          i = i + 2 * size
       }
    else
       while (i ≤ n − size) {
          merge(b, i, i + size − 1, min(i + 2 * size − 1, n), a)
          i = i + 2 * size
       }
    size = 2 * size
    if (parity == 0)
       parity = 1
    else
       parity = 0
  }
 if (parity == 0)
    for i = 1 to n
       a[i] = b[i]
}
```

12. We use strong induction to show that for all $n > 1$, $t_n \geq t_k$ for all $k < n$. The basis step is $t_2 = 2t_1 + 2 > t_1$.

Now assume that $n > 2$ and if $m < n$, $t_m \geq t_k$ for all $k < m$. We show that $t_n \geq t_k$ for all $k < n$. Notice that it suffices to show that $t_n \geq t_{n-1}$ since $t_{n-1} \geq t_k$ for all $k \leq n - 1$ by the inductive assumption.

Now

$$
\begin{aligned}
t_n &= t_{\lceil n/2 \rceil} + t_{\lfloor n/2 \rfloor} + 2n \\
&\geq t_{\lceil (n-1)/2 \rceil} + t_{\lfloor (n-1)/2 \rfloor} + 2(n-1) = t_{n-1}.
\end{aligned}
$$

The inductive assumption justifies the inequality.

Section 5.3

1. The 16 points sorted by x-coordinate are $(1, 2)$, $(1, 5)$, $(1, 9)$, $(3, 7)$, $(3, 11)$, $(5, 4)$, $(5, 9)$, $(7, 6)$, $(8, 4)$, $(8, 7)$, $(8, 9)$, $(11, 3)$, $(11, 7)$, $(12, 10)$, $(14, 7)$, $(17, 10)$, so the dividing point is $(7, 6)$. We next find $deltaL = \sqrt{8}$, the minimum distance among the left-side points, and $deltaR = 2$, the minimum distance among the right-side points. Thus $delta = 2$. The points, sorted by y-coordinate in the vertical strip, are $(8, 4)$, $(7, 6)$, $(8, 7)$, $(8, 9)$. In this case, we compare each point in the strip to all the following points. The distances from $(8, 4)$ to $(7, 6)$, $(8, 7)$, $(8, 9)$ are not less than 2, so $delta$ is not updated at this point. The distance from $(7, 6)$ to $(8, 7)$ is $\sqrt{2}$, so $delta$ is updated to $\sqrt{2}$. The distances from $(7, 6)$ to $(8, 9)$ and from $(8, 7)$ to $(8, 9)$ are greater than $\sqrt{2}$, so $delta$ remains $\sqrt{2}$. Therefore, the distance between the closest pair is $\sqrt{2}$.

3. If we replace "three" by "two," when there are three points, the algorithm would be called recursively with inputs of sizes 1 and 2. But a set consisting of one point has no pair—let alone a closest pair.

6. $(8, 4)$, $(8, 7)$, $(8, 9)$, $(8, 20)$

9. $\Theta(n(\lg n)^2)$

12. The input is $p_0 = (20, -\sqrt{399})$, $p_1 = (19, 0)$, $p_2 = (39.5, 0.5)$, $p_3 = (1, 18)$, $p_4 = (21.5, 19.5)$, $p_5 = (59.5, 0.5)$ (see the following figure).

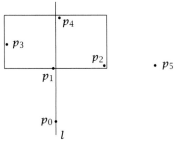

When the points are divided, the line l is at $x = 20$. The left-side points are p_0, p_1, p_3, and the right-side points are p_2, p_4, p_5. Also, $\delta = \delta_L = \delta_R = 20$.

The points in the strip are p_0, p_1, p_2, p_3, p_4. When we compare p_0 with the next two points in the strip, we compare p_0 with p_1 and p_2. Since

$$\text{dist}(p_0, p_1) = \delta, \qquad \text{dist}(p_0, p_2) > \delta,$$

the value of δ does not change.

We next compare p_1 with p_2 and p_3. The figure shows the $\delta \times 2\delta$ box. Since

$$\text{dist}(p_1, p_2) > \delta, \qquad \text{dist}(p_1, p_3) > \delta,$$

again the value of δ does not change.

We next compare p_2 with p_3 and p_4. Since

$$\text{dist}(p_2, p_3) > \delta, \qquad \text{dist}(p_2, p_4) > \delta,$$

again the value of δ does not change.

We next compare p_3 and p_4. Since

$$\text{dist}(p_3, p_4) > \delta,$$

again the value of δ does not change. The algorithm returns $\delta = 20$ as the distance between a closest pair. However,

$$\text{dist}(p_1, p_4) < \delta,$$

so the value computed is incorrect.

15. Let B be either of the left or right $\delta \times \delta$ squares that make up the $\delta \times 2\delta$ rectangle (see Figure 5.3.3). We argue by contradiction and assume that B contains four or more points. We partition B into four $\delta/2 \times \delta/2$ squares as shown in Figure 5.3.4. Then each of the four squares contains at most one point, and therefore exactly one point. Subsequently, we refer to these four squares as the subsquares of B.

The figure

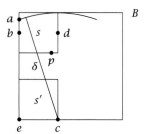

shows the following construction. We reduce the size of the subsquares, if possible, so that

- Each subsquare contains one point.
- The subsquares are the same size.
- The subsquares are as small as possible.

Since at least one point is not in a corner of B, the subsquares do not collapse to points and so at least one point is on a side of a subsquare s interior to B. We choose such a point and call it p. We select a subsquare s' nearest p. We label the two corner points of s' on the side farthest from p, e and c. We draw a circle of radius δ with center at c and let a be the (noncorner) point where this circle meets the side of s. Note that this circle meets a side of s in a noncorner point. Choose a point b in s on the same side as a between a and e. Let d be the corresponding point on the opposite side of s. Now the length of the diameter of rectangle $R = bdce$ is less than δ; hence, R contains at most one point. This is a contradiction since R contains p and the point in s'. Therefore, B contains at most three points.

Section 5.4

1. We let A_{ij} denote the entry in row i, column j, in matrix A, and similarly for B. Notice that

$$\mathbf{a}_{11} = \begin{pmatrix} A_{11} & A_{12} & \cdots & A_{1,n/2} \\ \vdots & \vdots & & \vdots \\ A_{n/2,1} & A_{n/2,2} & \cdots & A_{n/2,n/2} \end{pmatrix},$$

$$\mathbf{b}_{11} = \begin{pmatrix} B_{11} & B_{12} & \cdots & B_{1,n/2} \\ \vdots & \vdots & & \vdots \\ B_{n/2,1} & B_{n/2,2} & \cdots & B_{n/2,n/2} \end{pmatrix},$$

$$
\mathbf{a}_{12} = \begin{pmatrix} A_{1,n/2+1} & A_{1,n/2+2} & \cdots & A_{1,n} \\ \vdots & \vdots & & \vdots \\ A_{n/2,n/2+1} & A_{n/2,n/2+2} & \cdots & A_{n,n} \end{pmatrix},
$$

$$
\mathbf{b}_{21} = \begin{pmatrix} B_{n/2+1,1} & B_{n/2+1,2} & \cdots & B_{n/2+1,n/2} \\ \vdots & \vdots & & \vdots \\ B_{n,1} & B_{n,2} & \cdots & B_{n,n/2} \end{pmatrix}.
$$

Therefore, for $1 \leq i, j \leq n/2$, the entry in row i, column j, of $\mathbf{a}_{11}\mathbf{b}_{11} + \mathbf{a}_{12}\mathbf{b}_{21}$ is

$$
\sum_{k=1}^{n/2} A_{ik}B_{kj} + \sum_{k=n/2+1}^{n} A_{ik}B_{kj} = \sum_{k=1}^{n} A_{ik}B_{kj},
$$

which is equal to the entry in row i, column j, of AB. Thus, $\mathbf{a}_{11}\mathbf{b}_{11} + \mathbf{a}_{12}\mathbf{b}_{21}$ properly computes the upper quarter of the product AB.

The other computations can be verified in a similar manner.

4. Since $a_{11} = 3$, $a_{12} = 1$, $a_{21} = 4$, $a_{22} = -1$, $b_{11} = 2$, $b_{12} = -5$, $b_{21} = 6$, $b_{22} = -3$, we obtain

$$
q_1 = (a_{11} + a_{22}) * (b_{11} + b_{22}) = (3 + -1) * (2 + -3) = -2.
$$

Similarly, $q_2 = 6$, $q_3 = -6$, $q_4 = -4$, $q_5 = -12$, $q_6 = -3$, and $q_7 = 6$. We obtain

$$
\begin{pmatrix} 3 & 1 \\ 4 & -1 \end{pmatrix} \begin{pmatrix} 2 & -5 \\ 6 & -3 \end{pmatrix} = \begin{pmatrix} q_1 + q_4 - q_5 + q_7 & q_3 + q_5 \\ q_2 + q_4 & q_1 + q_3 - q_2 + q_6 \end{pmatrix}
$$

$$
= \begin{pmatrix} 12 & -18 \\ 2 & -17 \end{pmatrix}.
$$

7. We use induction on k, and let M_{ij} denote the entry in matrix M in row i, column j. If $k = 1$, $A^1 = A$. A_{ij} is 1 if there is an edge from i to j, which is a path of length 1, and 0 otherwise. Thus the assertion is true if $k = 1$. The basis step is proved.

Assume that the assertion is true for k. Now $A^{k+1} = A^k A$. By the inductive assumption, A_{it}^k gives the number of paths of length k from i to t. If A_{tj} is 0, there is no edge from t to j, so there are $A_{it}^k A_{tj} = 0$ paths of length $k+1$ from i to j, where the last edge is (t, j). If A_{tj} is 1, there is an edge from t to j, so there are $A_{it}^k A_{tj} = A_{it}^k$ paths of length $k+1$ from i to j, where the last edge is (t, j). Summing over all t, we count all paths of length $k+1$ from i to j. Thus the number of paths of length $k+1$ is

$$
\sum_{t=1}^{n} A_{it}^k A_{tj} = A_{ij}^{k+1}
$$

as desired.

Chapter 6: Sorting and Selection

Section 6.1

1. First 40 is inserted into 14 giving 14 40. Next 31 is inserted into 14 40 giving 14 31 40. Next 28 is inserted into 14 31 40 giving 14 28 31 40. Next 3 is inserted into 14 28 31 40 giving 3 14 28 31 40. Next 15 is inserted into 3 14 28 31 40 giving 3 14 15 28 31 40. Next 17 is inserted into 3 14 15 28 31 40 giving 3 14 15 17 28 31 40. Finally 51 is inserted into 3 14 15 17 28 31 40 giving 3 14 15 17 28 31 40 51.

4. Since all the values are equal, each element remains in its original position.

5. 1 2 3 4 5

7. $(1,5), (2,3), (2,4), (2,5), (2,6), (2,7), (3,4), (3,5), (3,6), (3,7), (4,5), (4,6), (4,7)$

10. There are zero inversions.

13. Let $p_1, p_2, \ldots, p_{n!}$ denote the $n!$ distinct permutations, and let $I(p_i)$ denote the number of inversions in p_i. Let p'_i denote the permutation obtained by reversing p_i. Note that

$$I(p_i) + I(p'_i) = \frac{n(n-1)}{2},$$

since each inversion appears in either p_i or p'_i, but not both, and the total number of inversions is $\binom{n}{2} = n(n-1)/2$. Therefore,

$$\sum_{i=1}^{n!} I(p_i) = \frac{n!}{2} \cdot \frac{n(n-1)}{2}.$$

Therefore, the average number of inversions is equal to

$$\frac{1}{n!} \left(\frac{n!}{2} \cdot \frac{n(n-1)}{2} \right) = \frac{n(n-1)}{4}.$$

16. Swapping adjacent elements removes at most one inversion. Since there are $\binom{n}{2} = n(n-1)/2$ inversions in a decreasing sequence, an algorithm that swaps only adjacent elements must remove $\Theta(n^2)$ inversions when the input is a decreasing sequence. Such an algorithm requires worst-case time $\Omega(n^2)$.

Section 6.2

1. Since 40, 31, and 28 are greater than 14, k simply increments giving

14	40	31	28	3	15	17	51

   ↑   ↑
   h k

Since $3 < 14$, h increments and we swap $a[h]$ and $a[k]$ giving

| 14 | 3 | 31 | 28 | 40 | 15 | 17 | 51 |

           $\uparrow$ $\uparrow$
           h k

Next k increments giving

| 14 | 3 | 31 | 28 | 40 | 15 | 17 | 51 |

           $\uparrow$ $\uparrow$
           h k

Since 15, 17 and 51 are greater than 14, k simply increments and the for loop ends. After swapping $a[i]$ and $a[h]$, we obtain

| 3 | 14 | 31 | 28 | 40 | 15 | 17 | 51 |

           $\uparrow$
           h

The value $h = 2$ is returned.

4. Since all the values in the array are equal, the condition $a[k] < val$ is always false. Therefore, k simply increments, and no values are swapped in the for loop. After the for loop ends, $i = h = 1$; so, when $a[i]$ and $a[h]$ are swapped the array is still unchanged. The value $h = 1$ is returned.

5. First the partition algorithm is called. The result is

| 3 | 14 | 31 | 28 | 40 | 15 | 17 | 51 |

and $p = 2$ (see Exercise 1).

Quicksort is then called recursively on each of the two sides

| 3 | | 31 | 28 | 40 | 15 | 17 | 51 |

The result is the sorted array

| 3 | 14 | 15 | 17 | 28 | 31 | 40 | 51 |

8. First the partition algorithm is called. The result is

| 23 | 23 | 23 | 23 | 23 | 23 | 23 | 23 |

and $p = 1$ (see Exercise 4).

Quicksort is then called recursively on each of the two sides. The left side is empty, and the right side is

| 23 | 23 | 23 | 23 | 23 | 23 | 23 |

The result is the sorted array

23	23	23	23	23	23	23	23

.

9. Quicksort begins by calling partition. Since the first element in the array is less than all of its successors, the condition $a[k] < val$ is always false. Therefore, k simply increments, and no values are swapped in the for loop. After the for loop ends, $i = h = 1$; so, when $a[i]$ and $a[h]$ are swapped the array is still unchanged. The value $h = 1$ is returned, which means that the partition element is placed at the beginning of the array.

Quicksort is then called on an empty left side, and a right side that is the original array with the first element removed. Thus quicksort operates on *another* increasing array. Again, the partition element is placed at the beginning of the array. The process continues in this fashion.

12. 12 2 10 10

15. Yes

17. We assume that after finding the partition element, median-of-three partitioning swaps the partition element with the first element and then proceeds as in the original partition algorithm (Algorithm 6.2.2).

Median-of-three partitioning begins by choosing 28—the median of 14, 28, and 51. After swapping the first element, 14, and 28, the array becomes

28	40	31	14	3	15	17	51

.

Since 40 and 31 are greater than 28, k simply increments giving

28	40	31	14	3	15	17	51

.

$\quad\uparrow\qquad\qquad\qquad\uparrow$
$\quad h\qquad\qquad\qquad\ k$

Since $14 < 28$, h increments and we swap $a[h]$ and $a[k]$ giving

28	14	31	40	3	15	17	51

.

$\qquad\uparrow\qquad\qquad\uparrow$
$\qquad h\qquad\qquad\ k$

Next k increments giving

28	14	31	40	3	15	17	51

.

$\qquad\uparrow\qquad\qquad\qquad\uparrow$
$\qquad h\qquad\qquad\qquad\ k$

Since $3 < 28$, h increments and we swap $a[h]$ and $a[k]$ giving

| 28 | 14 | 3 | 40 | 31 | 15 | 17 | 51 |

  ↑   ↑
  h   k

Next k increments giving

| 28 | 14 | 3 | 40 | 31 | 15 | 17 | 51 |

  ↑   ↑
  h   k

Since $15 < 28$, h increments and we swap $a[h]$ and $a[k]$ giving

| 28 | 14 | 3 | 15 | 31 | 40 | 17 | 51 |

    ↑   ↑
    h   k

Next k increments giving

| 28 | 14 | 3 | 15 | 31 | 40 | 17 | 51 |

    ↑   ↑
    h   k

Since $17 < 28$, h increments and we swap $a[h]$ and $a[k]$ giving

| 28 | 14 | 3 | 15 | 17 | 40 | 31 | 51 |

      ↑   ↑
      h   k

Next k increments giving

| 28 | 14 | 3 | 15 | 17 | 40 | 31 | 51 |

      ↑   ↑
      h   k

Since $51 > 28$, the for loop concludes. After swapping $a[i]$ and $a[h]$, we obtain

| 17 | 14 | 3 | 15 | 28 | 40 | 31 | 51 |

      ↑
      h

The value $h = 5$ is returned. Notice the even division in this case.

20. Since all the values are equal, partition operates the same as in the original case (see Exercise 4).

23. $\Theta(n \lg n)$

Section 6.3

1. Since $6 \le 3$ is false, we follow the right edge. The array becomes $3, 6, 12$. Since $6 \le 12$ is true, we follow the left edge. The array remains $3, 6, 12$, and the array is sorted.

4. $sort4(a)$ {
    // sort $a[1], a[2]$
    if $(a[1] > a[2])$
      $swap(a[1], a[2])$
    // sort $a[3], a[4]$
    if $(a[3] > a[4])$
      $swap(a[3], a[4])$
    // find largest
    if $(a[2] > a[4])$
      $swap(a[2], a[4])$
    // find smallest
    if $(a[1] > a[3])$
      $swap(a[1], a[3])$
    // sort $a[2], a[3]$
    if $(a[2] > a[3])$
      $swap(a[2], a[3])$
}

7. In the worst case, three comparisons are required to sort three items using an optimal sort.

If $n = 4$, the algorithm sorts three items (three comparisons—worst case) and then inserts the fourth item in the sorted three-item array (two comparisons—worst case) for a total of five comparisons in the worst case.

If $n = 5$, the algorithm sorts four items (five comparisons—worst case) and then inserts the fifth item in the sorted four-item array (three comparisons—worst case) for a total of eight comparisons in the worst case.

If $n = 6$, the algorithm sorts five items (eight comparisons—worst case) and then inserts the sixth item in the sorted five-item array (three comparisons—worst case) for a total of 11 comparisons in the worst case.

The decision tree analysis shows that any algorithm requires at least five comparisons in the worst case to sort four items. Thus the algorithm uses the minimum number of comparisons when $n = 4$.

The decision tree analysis shows that any algorithm requires at least seven comparisons in the worst case to sort five items. It is possible, in fact, to sort five items using seven comparisons in the worst case. Thus the algorithm does not use the minimum number of comparisons when $n = 5$.

The decision tree analysis shows that any algorithm requires at least 10 comparisons in the worst case to sort six items. It is possible, in fact, to sort six items using

10 comparisons in the worst case. Thus the algorithm does not use the minimum number of comparisons when $n = 6$.

Section 6.4

1. After initializing the array c to zero, the next for loop sets $c[k]$ to the number of occurrences of value k in the array input array a:

$$c[2] = c[3] = c[8] = c[9] = c[10] = c[15] = c[17] = 1.$$

The next for loop modifies c so that $c[k]$ is equal to the number of elements in a less than or equal to k:

$$c[2] = 1, \quad c[3] = 2, \quad c[8] = 3, \quad c[9] = 4, \quad c[10] = 5, \quad c[15] = 6, \quad c[17] = 7.$$

The next for loop copies the items from a into the array b, which will be sorted. Copying begins with the last element in a.

The last element in a is 8. Since $c[8] = 3$, 8 is copied to the third cell of b:

| | | 8 | | | | |

The predecessor of 8 in a is 10 and $c[10] = 5$, so 10 is copied to the fifth cell of b:

| | | 8 | | 10 | | |

The predecessor of 10 in a is 9 and $c[9] = 4$, so 9 is copied to the fourth cell of b:

| | | 8 | 9 | 10 | | |

The predecessor of 9 in a is 2 and $c[2] = 1$, so 2 is copied to the first cell of b:

| 2 | | 8 | 9 | 10 | | |

The predecessor of 2 in a is 17 and $c[17] = 7$, so 17 is copied to the seventh cell of b:

| 2 | | 8 | 9 | 10 | | 17 |

The predecessor of 17 in a is 3 and $c[3] = 2$, so 3 is copied to the second cell of b:

| 2 | 3 | 8 | 9 | 10 | | 17 |

The predecessor of 3 in a is 15 and $c[15] = 6$, so 15 is copied to the sixth cell of b:

| 2 | 3 | 8 | 9 | 10 | 15 | 17 |

The sort is complete when the last for loop copies b to a.

4. After initializing the array c to zero, the next for loop sets $c[k]$ to the number of occurrences of value k in the array input array a:

$$c[2] = c[3] = c[4] = c[5] = 1.$$

The next for loop modifies c so that $c[k]$ is equal to the number of elements in a less than or equal to k:

$$c[2] = 1, \quad c[3] = 2, \quad c[4] = 3, \quad c[5] = 4.$$

The next for loop copies the items from a into the array b, which will be sorted. Copying begins with the last element in a.

The last element in a is 5. Since $c[5] = 4$, 5 is copied to the fourth cell of b:

			5

The predecessor of 5 in a is 4 and $c[4] = 3$, so 4 is copied to the third cell of b:

		4	5

The predecessor of 4 in a is 3 and $c[3] = 2$, so 3 is copied to the second cell of b:

	3	4	5

The predecessor of 3 in a is 2 and $c[2] = 1$, so 2 is copied to the first cell of b:

2	3	4	5

The sort is complete when the last for loop copies b to a.

5. Suppose that $a[s] = a[t]$, $s < t$. When a is copied to b, $a[t]$ is copied *before* $a[s]$. After $a[t]$ is copied to $b[c[a[t]]]$, $c[a[t]]$ is decremented. Therefore, when $a[s]$ is copied to $b[c[a[s]]]$ $(= b[c[a[t]]])$, the index of $a[s]$ in b is less than the index of $a[t]$ in b; that is, $a[s]$ precedes $a[t]$ in b. Therefore, counting sort is stable.

8. *counting_sort*(a, m) {
```
    // set c[k] = the number of occurrences of value k in the array a.
    // begin by initializing c to zero.
    for k = 0 to m
        c[k] = 0
    n = a.last
    for i = 1 to n
        c[a[i]] = c[a[i]] + 1
    // modify c so that c[k] = number of elements ≥ k
    for k = m − 1 downto 0
        c[k] = c[k] + c[k + 1]
```

```
// sort a with the result in b
for i = 1 to n {
    b[n + 1 − c[a[i]]] = a[i]
    c[a[i]] = c[a[i]] − 1
}
// copy b back to a
for i = 1 to n
    a[i] = b[i]
}
```

9. Since the least significant digits are all equal to 4, after using counting sort to sort on the least significant digit, the array is unchanged.

The array becomes

| 4 | 34 | 9134 | 20134 | 29134 | 134 |

after sorting on the 10's digit.

The 100's digits are, in order, $0, 0, 1, 1, 1, 1$. Thus, after using counting sort to sort on the 100's digit, the array is also unchanged.

The array becomes

| 4 | 34 | 20134 | 134 | 9134 | 29134 |

after sorting on the 1000's digit.

The array becomes

| 4 | 34 | 134 | 9134 | 20134 | 29134 |

after sorting on the 10,000's digit and is now sorted.

12. The array becomes

| 10000 | 1000 | 10 | 100 | 1 |

after sorting on the 1's digit.

The array becomes

| 10000 | 1000 | 100 | 1 | 10 |

after sorting on the 10's digit.

The array becomes

| 10000 | 1000 | 1 | 10 | 100 |

after sorting on the 100's digit.

The array becomes

$$\boxed{10000} \; \boxed{1} \; \boxed{10} \; \boxed{100} \; \boxed{1000}$$

after sorting on the 1000's digit.

The array becomes

$$\boxed{1} \; \boxed{10} \; \boxed{100} \; \boxed{1000} \; \boxed{10000}$$

after sorting on the 10000's digit and is now sorted.

13. Radix sort calls counting sort with $m = 10$. Counting sort thus requires an array c of size 10, which is a constant amount of storage. Counting sort also requires an auxiliary array b the same size as a. Thus, the space requirement of counting sort, and by extension radix sort, is $\Theta(n)$.

Section 6.5

1. After partition (Algorithm 6.2.2) is called, we obtain

$$\boxed{3 \; | \; 14 \; | \; 31 \; | \; 28 \; | \; 40 \; | \; 15 \; | \; 17 \; | \; 51} \; .$$

$$\begin{array}{cccc} \uparrow & \uparrow & & \uparrow \\ 1 & 2 & & 8 \end{array}$$

The partition element 14 is placed at index 2.

Since we want the element that would be at index 4 if the array were sorted, and $2 < 4$, we next call partition on the part of the array to the right of 14. The result is

$$\boxed{17 \; | \; 28 \; | \; 15 \; | \; 31 \; | \; 40 \; | \; 51} \; .$$

$$\begin{array}{ccc} \uparrow & \uparrow & \uparrow \\ 3 & 6 & 8 \end{array}$$

The partition element 31 is placed at index 6.

Since $6 > 4$, we next call partition on the part of the array to the left of 31. The result is

$$\boxed{15 \; | \; 17 \; | \; 28} \; .$$

$$\begin{array}{ccc} \uparrow & \uparrow & \uparrow \\ 3 & 4 & 5 \end{array}$$

The partition element 17 is placed at index 4. The algorithm thus terminates having found 17 as the fourth smallest element in the array.

4. After partition (Algorithm 6.2.2) is called, we obtain

$$\boxed{3 \; | \; 14 \; | \; 15 \; | \; 17 \; | \; 28 \; | \; 31 \; | \; 40 \; | \; 51} \; .$$

$$\begin{array}{cc} \uparrow & \uparrow \\ 1 & 8 \end{array}$$

The partition element 3 is placed at index 1.

Since we want the element that would be at index 4 if the array were sorted, and $1 < 4$, we next call partition on the part of the array to the right of 3. The result is

14	15	17	28	31	40	51

$\uparrow$　　　　　　　　　　　　　　　　　$\uparrow$
2　　　　　　　　　　　　　　　　　　8

The partition element 14 is placed at index 2.

Since $2 < 4$, we next call partition on the part of the array to the right of 14. The result is

15	17	28	31	40	51

$\uparrow$　　　　　　　　　　　　　　　$\uparrow$
3　　　　　　　　　　　　　　　　8

The partition element 15 is placed at index 3.

Since $3 < 4$, we next call partition on the part of the array to the right of 15. The result is

17	28	31	40	51

$\uparrow$　　　　　　　　　　　$\uparrow$
4　　　　　　　　　　　　　8

The partition element 17 is placed at index 4. The algorithm thus terminates having found 17 as the fourth smallest element in the array.

6. An array containing n elements sorted in increasing order with $k = n$ requires time $\Theta(n^2)$ (see Exercise 4).

9. If n is odd, $\lfloor n/2 \rfloor = (n-1)/2$. Thus, the last expression in (6.5.1) becomes

$$c_1 n + \frac{8c_1}{n}\left[\left(n - 1 + \left\lfloor \frac{n}{2} \right\rfloor\right)\left(n - \left\lfloor \frac{n}{2} \right\rfloor\right) \cdot \frac{1}{2}\right]$$

$$= c_1 n + \frac{8c_1}{n}\left[\left(n - 1 + \frac{n-1}{2}\right)\left(n - \frac{n-1}{2}\right) \cdot \frac{1}{2}\right]$$

$$= c_1 n + \frac{8c_1}{n}\left[\left(\frac{3n-3}{2}\right)\left(\frac{n+1}{2}\right) \cdot \frac{1}{2}\right]$$

$$= c_1 n + \frac{3c_1}{n}(n-1)(n+1)$$

$$= c_1\left(4n - \frac{3}{n}\right).$$

Chapter 7: Greedy Algorithms

Section 7.1

1. The algorithm first chooses one coin of denomination 25. The new amount is $37 - 25 = 12$. The algorithm next chooses two coins of denomination 5. The new amount is $12 - 10 = 2$. The algorithm concludes by choosing two coins of denomination 1.

4. We use induction on A to prove that to make change for an amount A, Algorithm 7.1.1 and an optimal solution use the same number of coins. The cases $A = 1, \ldots, 13, 25$ are readily verified.

The inductive assumption is that to make change for an amount k, where $k < A$, Algorithm 7.1.1 and an optimal solution use the same number of coins. Suppose first that $13 < A < 25$. Let Opt be an optimal solution. Now Opt must use a coin of denomination 13. (If Opt does not use a coin of denomination 13, it is restricted to coins of denomination 1. Because $A > 13$, Opt must use at least 13 1's. But now Opt is not optimal because it could trade in 13 coins of denomination 1 for one of denomination 13.) Now Opt with one coin of denomination 13 removed is optimal for $A - 13$. (If Opt with one coin of denomination 13 removed is not optimal for $A - 13$, there is another solution for $A - 13$ that uses fewer coins. Adding a coin of denomination 13 to the solution to the $A - 13$ problem produces a solution for A using fewer coins than Opt, which is impossible.) By the inductive assumption, Algorithm 7.1.1 for $A - 13$ and Opt with one coin of denomination 13 removed use the same number of coins. Adding a coin of denomination 13 to the output of Algorithm 7.1.1 for $A - 13$ yields the output of Algorithm 7.1.1 for A. Thus the output of Algorithm 7.1.1 and the optimal solution use the same number of coins for $13 < A < 25$.

Suppose that $A > 25$. Let Opt be an optimal solution. If Opt uses a coin of denomination 25, Opt with one coin of denomination 25 removed is optimal for $A - 25$. (If Opt with one coin of denomination 25 removed is not optimal for $A - 25$, there is another solution for $A - 25$ that uses fewer coins. Adding a coin of denomination 25 to the solution to the $A - 25$ problem produces a solution for A using fewer coins than Opt, which is impossible.) By the inductive assumption, Algorithm 7.1.1 for $A - 25$ and Opt with one coin of denomination 25 removed use the same number of coins. Adding a coin of denomination 25 to the output of Algorithm 7.1.1 for $A - 25$ yields the output of Algorithm 7.1.1 for A. Thus the output of Algorithm 7.1.1 and the optimal solution use the same number of coins for $A > 25$ if the optimal solution uses a coin of denomination 25.

Suppose that the optimal solution does not use a coin of denomination 25. If it uses only one coin of denomination 13, it can make change for at most 25. (It is restricted to using at most 12 coins of denomination 1.) Since $A > 25$, it must use at least two coins of denomination 13. We now replace two coins of denomination 13 with one coin of denomination 1 and one coin of denomination 25. The resulting solution uses the same number of coins as the optimal solution and so is also optimal. We now have an optimal solution that uses a coin of denomination 25.

We may now repeat the argument in the previous paragraph to conclude that the solution produced by Algorithm 7.1.1 is optimal. The inductive step is complete.

7. Algorithm 7.1.1 is optimal for this set of coins. We use induction on A to prove that to make change for an amount A, Algorithm 7.1.1 and an optimal solution use the same number of coins. The cases $A = 1, \ldots, 11$ are readily verified.

   Suppose that $A > 11$. Let *Opt* be an optimal solution. If *Opt* uses a coin of denomination 10, an argument similar to that in the solution to Exercise 4 shows that the output of Algorithm 7.1.1 and the optimal solution use the same number of coins.

   Suppose that the optimal solution does not use a coin of denomination 10. If it uses at most two coins of denomination 4, it can make change for at most 11. (It is restricted to using at most three coins of denomination 1.) Since $A > 11$, it must use at least three coins of denomination 4. We now replace three coins of denomination 4 with one coin of denomination 10 and two coins of denomination 1. The resulting solution uses the same number of coins as the optimal solution and so is also optimal. We now have an optimal solution that uses a coin of denomination 10. We may now again argue as in the solution to Exercise 4 to conclude that the solution produced by Algorithm 7.1.1 is optimal. The inductive step is complete.

10. Algorithm 7.1.1 is not optimal. A counterexample is $A = 15$.

13. Algorithm 7.1.1 is not optimal. A counterexample is $A = 48$.

16. The denominations $1, 5, 11$ show that the condition is not sufficient. The denominations $1, 5, 10, 20, 25, 40$ show that the condition is not necessary.

Section 7.2

1. The edges sorted by weight are

$$(2, 3), (3, 5), (3, 4), (1, 2), (1, 4), (4, 5), (2, 5).$$

   (Ties were broken arbitrarily.)

   Edge $(2, 3)$ is chosen first. Next $(3, 5)$ is chosen. Next $(3, 4)$ is chosen. Next $(1, 2)$ is chosen, and the algorithm terminates.

4. In general, the worst-case time of Kruskal's algorithm is $\Theta(m \lg m)$, where m is the number of edges in the graph. For a complete graph on n vertices,

$$m = \frac{n(n-1)}{2} = \Theta(n^2).$$

   Replacing m by n^2, we obtain

$$m \lg m = n^2 \lg n^2 = 2n^2 \lg n = \Theta(n^2 \lg n),$$

   which is the worst-case time of Kruskal's algorithm when the input is the complete graph on n vertices.

7. e is an edge between components of T'. If there was another edge e' between components of T', whose weight is less than that of e, we could add it to T' to obtain a spanning tree whose weight is less than T's. Since T is a minimal spanning tree, this is impossible. Therefore, e is a minimum weight edge between components of T'.

10. Suppose that e is incident on vertices v and w. Removing e from T produces a disconnected graph with two components. Vertices v and w belong to different components. We suppose that v belongs to component C_1 and w belongs to component C_2. There is a path P from v to w in T'. As we move along P, at some point we encounter an edge $e' = (v', w')$, with v' in C_1 and w' in C_2. Since adding e' to $T - \{e\}$ produces a connected graph, $(T - \{e\}) \cup \{e'\}$ is a spanning tree. Clearly, $(T' - \{e'\}) \cup \{e\}$ is a spanning tree.

11. False. A counterexample is

Edge sets $\{(1, 2), (1, 4), (3, 4)\}$ and $\{(1, 3), (2, 3), (3, 4)\}$ give distinct spanning trees of weight 12.

Section 7.3

1. Since the minimum weight of an edge from either vertex 2 or vertex 4 to the current tree is 3, either edge $(1, 2)$ or $(1, 4)$ may be chosen. We suppose that $(1, 2)$ is chosen.

The minimum weight edge from vertex 3 to the current tree is 1, the minimum weight edge from vertex 4 to the current tree is 3, and the minimum weight edge from vertex 5 to the current tree is 4. Therefore, edge $(2, 3)$ is chosen next.

The minimum weight edge from vertex 4 to the current tree becomes 2, and the minimum weight edge from vertex 5 to the current tree becomes 1. Therefore, edge $(3, 5)$ is chosen next.

The minimum weight edge from vertex 4 to the current tree is 2. Thus, $(3, 4)$ is the last edge chosen.

4. *print_mst*(*parent*) {
    for $i = 1$ to *parent.last*
      if (*parent*[i] != 0)
        println("(" + *parent*[i] + "," + i + ")")
}

7. When h is implemented using an array that is always sorted from largest to smallest weight, the worst-case times for the various operations are:

Operation	*Worst-Case Time*
$init(key, n)$	$\Theta(n \lg n)$
$del()$	$\Theta(1)$
$isin(w)$	$\Theta(1)$
$keyval(w)$	$\Theta(1)$
$decrease(w, ptr.weight)$	$\Theta(n)$

Each for loop takes time $\Theta(n)$. The *init* operation takes time $\Theta(n \lg n)$. The delete operation *del*, which takes time $\Theta(1)$, is in a for loop whose time is $\Theta(n)$; thus, the total worst-case time for the delete operations is $\Theta(n)$. The *total* time for the while loop is $\Theta(m)$ since each iteration of the while loop inspects another node on some adjacency list and there are $2m$ nodes altogether. Each *isin* and *keyval* operation takes constant time to evaluate. The decrease operation *decrease*, which takes time $O(n)$, is in the while loop whose total time is $\Theta(m)$; thus, the total worst-case time for the decrease operations is $O(mn)$. Since $m \geq n - 1$, the dominant term is mn and the worst-case time is $O(mn)$.

10. No, if we assume that the m edges input to Kruskal's algorithm are arranged so that sorting them takes time $\Theta(m \lg m)$. In this case, Kruskal's algorithm requires time $\Theta(m \lg m)$. Since the worst-case time of Prim's algorithm is $O(m \lg n)$ and $m \geq n - 1$, Prim's algorithm will not take longer (asymptotically) than Kruskal's algorithm.

13. The inequality can be verified directly for $n = 4$ and $n = 5$. For $n \geq 6$, we argue as follows. The formula

$$\sum_{i=u}^{v} i = \frac{(v + u)(v - u + 1)}{2},$$

with $u = \lceil (n - 2)/2 \rceil$ and $v = n - 2$, gives

$$\sum_{i=\lceil (n-2)/2 \rceil}^{n-2} i = \frac{(n - 2 + \lceil (n - 2)/2 \rceil)(n - 2 - \lceil (n - 2)/2 \rceil + 1)}{2}.$$

Now

$$n - 2 + \lceil (n - 2)/2 \rceil \geq n - 2 + (n - 2)/2 = \frac{3n - 6}{2}.$$

Since $m - \lceil m/2 \rceil \geq \lfloor m/2 \rfloor \geq (m - 1)/2$ for every positive integer m,

$$n - 2 - \lceil (n - 2)/2 \rceil + 1 \geq \frac{n - 1}{2}.$$

Therefore,

$$\sum_{i=\lceil (n-2)/2 \rceil}^{n-2} i \geq \frac{3n - 6}{2} \cdot \frac{n - 1}{2} \cdot \frac{1}{2}.$$

A little algebra shows that if $n \geq 6$,

$$\frac{3n - 6}{2} \cdot \frac{n - 1}{2} \cdot \frac{1}{2} \geq \frac{n(n - 1)}{4}.$$

Section 7.4

1. The first path is from 1 to 1 of length 0.

Vertices 2 and 4 can extend the shortest path from 1 to 1 as follows

Vertex Added	To Path	Path Length
2	1	3
4	1	3

Since both extensions have length 3, we may add either vertex. We arbitrarily add vertex 2 and edge $(1, 2)$ to the path from 1 to 1 to obtain the path $1, 2$ of length 3. We now have the following shortest paths

Shortest Path	Length
1	0
1, 2	3

Vertices 3, 4, and 5 can extend the shortest paths found as follows

Vertex Added	To Path	Path Length
3	1, 2	4
4	1	3
5	1, 2	7

Since length 3 is the minimum, we add vertex 4 and edge $(1, 4)$ to the path 1 to obtain the path $1, 4$ of length 3. We now have the following shortest paths

Shortest Path	Length
1	0
1, 2	3
1, 4	3

Vertices 3 and 5 can extend the shortest paths found as follows

Vertex Added	To Path	Path Length
3	1, 2	4
5	1, 4	6

Since length 4 is the minimum, we add vertex 3 and edge $(2, 3)$ to the path $1, 2$ to obtain the path $1, 2, 3$ of length 4. We now have the following shortest paths

Shortest Path	Length
1	0
1, 2	3
1, 4	3
1, 2, 3	4

Vertex 5 can extend the shortest paths found in one way

Vertex Added	To Path	Path Length
5	1, 2, 3	5

so we add vertex 5 and edge $(3, 5)$ to the path $1, 2, 3$ to obtain the path $1, 2, 3, 5$ of length 5. We have now found all the shortest paths

Shortest Path	Length
1	0
1, 2	3
1, 4	3
1, 2, 3	4
1, 2, 3, 5	5

4. *print_short_paths*(*predecessor*) {
    for $i = 1$ to *predecessor.last*
      if (*predecessor*[i] != 0) {
        recurs_short_paths(i, *predecessor*)
        println()
      }
  }

  recurs_short_paths(i, *predecessor*) {
    if (i != 0) {
      recurs_short_paths(*predecessor*[i], *predecessor*)
      print(i + " ")
    }
  }

7. When h is implemented using an unsorted array, the worst-case times for the various operations are:

Operation	Worst-Case Time
init(*key*, n)	$\Theta(n)$
del()	$\Theta(n)$
isin(w)	$\Theta(1)$
keyval(w)	$\Theta(1)$
decrease(w, *ptr.weight*)	$\Theta(1)$

Each for loop takes time $\Theta(n)$. The *init* operation takes time $\Theta(n)$. The delete operation *del*, which takes time $O(n)$, is in a for loop whose time is $\Theta(n)$; thus, the total worst-case time for the delete operations is $O(n^2)$. The *total* time for the while loop is $\Theta(m)$ since each iteration of the while loop inspects another node on some adjacency list and there are $2m$ nodes altogether. Each *isin* and *keyval* operation takes constant time to evaluate. The decrease operation *decrease*, which takes time $O(1)$, is in the while loop whose total time is $\Theta(m)$; thus, the total worst-case time for the decrease operations is $O(m)$. Since $m = O(n^2)$, the dominant term is n^2 and the worst-case time is $O(n^2)$.

10. False. A counterexample is

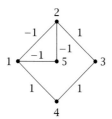

with start vertex 1.

Section 7.5

1. *PEN*

4. *SALAD*

5. 0111100010

8. 0110000100100001111

9.

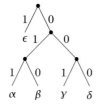

12. 2600

15. The key algorithm is *recurs_print_codes*. The input is a non-null vertex in a Huffman coding tree and a string. The algorithm performs a traversal of the subtree of a Huffman coding tree rooted at the vertex. The string is the bit string traced from the root to the vertex. If the vertex is a terminal vertex, the algorithm prints the character and the bit string, which, in this case, is the code for that character. If the vertex is not a terminal vertex, the algorithm appends 1 to the bit string and calls itself on the left subtree of the vertex. It then appends 0 to the bit string and calls itself on the right subtree of the vertex. We assume that the algorithm $concat(s, t)$ appends the string t to the string s and returns the result. The process is started by calling *recurs_print_codes* with input the root of the Huffman coding tree and the null string.

```
print_codes(root) {
    recurs_print_codes(root, "")
}
```

```
recurs_print_codes(vertex, s) {
    // check for terminal node
    if (vertex.left == null)
        println(vertex.character + " " + s)
    else {
        recurs_print_codes(vertex.left, concat(s, "1"))
        recurs_print_codes(vertex.right, concat(s, "0"))
    }
}
```

Section 7.6

1. Since

$$\frac{p_1}{w_1} = 0.04167, \quad \frac{p_2}{w_2} = 0.03333, \quad \frac{p_3}{w_3} = 0.02,$$

the greedy algorithm takes all of objects 1 and 2, and 30 of object 3, for a profit of

$$5 + 5 + \frac{30}{200} \cdot 4 = 10.6.$$

4. The total amount of objects selected

7. Consider the profits and weights of Example 7.6.1 with capacity 620. The greedy algorithm will take all of objects 1, 2, 4, and 5 for a profit of 21. But taking all of objects 1, 2, 3, and 4 gives a profit of 22.

Chapter 8: Dynamic Programming

Section 8.1

1.

1	1	2	3	5	8

4. The following table shows the values of f, $f\_twoback$, and $f\_oneback$ at the bottom of the for loop:

i	f	$f\_twoback$	$f\_oneback$
3	2	1	2
4	3	2	3

Thus the algorithm returns 3.

7. We use induction. The base cases ($n = 1, 2$) were discussed after Algorithm 8.1.3.

Suppose that when we execute $fibonacci\_recurs(k)$, $0 < k < n$, the number of times that the base cases are computed is f_k. When we execute $fibonacci\_recurs(n)$, we recursively invoke $fibonacci\_recurs(n - 1)$ and $fibonacci\_recurs(n - 2)$. By the inductive assumption, $fibonacci\_recurs(n - 1)$ invokes the bases cases f_{n-1} times, and *fibonacci_recurs*$(n - 2)$ invokes the bases cases f_{n-2} times. Thus the total number of bases cases computed is $f_{n-1} + f_{n-2} = f_n$. The inductive step is complete.

10. Let w_n be the number of ways a robot can walk n meters. By inspection,

$$w_1 = 1, \quad w_2 = 2, \quad w_3 = 4.$$

Suppose that $n > 3$. The robot begins by taking a 1-, 2-, or 3-meter step. If the robot begins with a 1-meter step, it can complete the walk in w_{n-1} ways. If the robot begins with a 2-meter step, it can complete the walk in w_{n-2} ways. If the robot begins with a 3-meter step, it can complete the walk in w_{n-3} ways. Therefore,

$$w_n = w_{n-1} + w_{n-2} + w_{n-3}.$$

We write a dynamic programming algorithm to compute this sequence:

```
robot_walking(n) {
    if (n == 1)
        return 1
    if (n == 2)
        return 2
    if (n == 3)
        return 4
    w_threeback = 1
    w_twoback = 2
    w_oneback = 4
    for i = 4 to n {
        w = w_threeback + w_twoback + w_oneback
        w_threeback = w_twoback
        w_twoback = w_oneback
        w_oneback = w
    }
    return w
}
```

13. $\Theta(n)$

Section 8.2

1.

		j											
		0	1	2	3	4	5	6	7	8	9	10	11	12
	1	0	1	2	3	4	1	2	3	4	5	1	2	3
i	2	0	1	2	3	4	1	2	3	4	5	2	3	4
	3	0	1	2	3	4	5	6	7	8	9	10	11	12

4.

		j											
		0	1	2	3	4	5	6	7	8	9	10	11	12
	1	F	F	F	F	F	F	F	F	F	F	T	T	T
i	2	F	F	F	F	F	T	T	T	T	T	T	T	T
	3	T	T	T	T	T	T	T	T	T	T	T	T	T

7. *coinset*$(i, j, denom, C)$ {
    while $(j > 0)$
        if $(i == denom.last \ || \ C[i][j] < C[i + 1][j])$ {
           println("Use coin " $+ i$)
           $j = j - denom[i]$
        }
        else
           $i = i + 1$
}

The worst-case time is $\Theta(j + n + 1 - i)$.

10. In the graph

$2, 1$ is the shortest path from 2 to 1, and $1, 3$ is the shortest path from 1 to 3, but $2, 1, 3$ is not the shortest path from 2 to 3.

Section 8.3

1.

			j	
		1	2	3
	1	0	60	54
i	2		0	30
	3			0

4.

Dimensions	Optimal Grouping
$5 \times 4, 4 \times 3, 3 \times 2, 2 \times 1$	$(1 * (2 * (3 * 4)))$
$7 \times 2, 2 \times 2, 2 \times 5, 5 \times 7$	$(1 * ((2 * 3) * 4))$
$1 \times 2, 2 \times 1, 1 \times 2, 2 \times 1$	$((1 * 2) * (3 * 4))$
$7 \times 5, 5 \times 2, 2 \times 1, 1 \times 5$	$((1 * (2 * 3)) * 4)$
$1 \times 2, 2 \times 3, 3 \times 4, 4 \times 5$	$(((1 * 2) * 3) * 4)$

6. Change

    if $(q < s[i][j])$
        $s[i][j] = q$

to

    if $(q < s[i][j])$ {
        $s[i][j] = q$
        $index[i][j] = k$
    }

8. $C_1 = 1, C_2 = 2, C_3 = 5, C_4 = 14, C_5 = 42$

11. By Exercise 10, the number of groupings of n matrices is C_{n-1}. By Exercise 9, $C_{n-1} \geq 4^{n-2}/(n-1)^2$.

Section 8.4

1.

			A	L	W	G	Q	V	N	B	B	K
		0	1	2	3	4	5	6	7	8	9	10
	0	0	0	0	0	0	0	0	0	0	0	0
S	1	0	0	0	0	0	0	0	0	0	0	0
L	2	0	0	1	1	1	1	1	1	1	1	1
W	3	0	0	1	2	2	2	2	2	2	2	2
O	4	0	0	1	2	2	2	2	2	2	2	2
V	5	0	0	1	2	2	2	3	3	3	3	3
N	6	0	0	1	2	2	2	3	4	4	4	4
N	7	0	0	1	2	2	2	3	4	4	4	4
D	8	0	0	1	2	2	2	3	4	4	4	4
K	9	0	0	1	2	2	2	3	4	4	4	5

4.

			A	B	A	B	C	P
		0	1	2	3	4	5	6
	0	0	0	0	0	0	0	0
S	1	0	0	0	0	0	0	0
L	2	0	0	0	0	0	0	0
W	3	0	0	0	0	0	0	0
O	4	0	0	0	0	0	0	0
V	5	0	0	0	0	0	0	0
N	6	0	0	0	0	0	0	0
N	7	0	0	0	0	0	0	0
D	8	0	0	0	0	0	0	0
K	9	0	0	0	0	0	0	0

5. Consider the strings *CAECE* and *ACE*, whose c-table is

			A	C	E	
		0	1	2	3	
	0	0	0	0	0	
C	1	0	0	1	1	←
A	2	0	1	1	1	
E	3	0	1	1	2	←
C	4	0	1	2	2	
E	5	0	1	2	3	←

The arrows mark where the entries in the far right column go down by one. Noting the characters corresponding to these rows, we obtain the "longest common subsequence" *CEE*.

8. True. If a longest common subsequence s did not begin with A, we could add an A to the beginning of s to obtain a longer common subsequence.

11. True. In fact, *every* longest common subsequence ends with A. If a longest common subsequence s did not end with A, we could add an A to the end of s to obtain a longer common subsequence.

14. Yes—regardless of whether $a[i] \neq b[j]$.

16. If $i, j > 0$ and $a[i] \neq b[j]$, $c[i, j] = \max\{c[i-1, j], c[i, j-1]\}$. Since $c[i, j-1]$ is in the same row as $c[i, j]$, $c[i, j-1]$ must be computed *before* $c[i, j]$.

Section 8.5

1.

$$A^{(1)} = \begin{pmatrix} 0 & 2 & 3 & 16 \\ 2 & 0 & 5 & 3 \\ 3 & 5 & 0 & 3 \\ 16 & 3 & 3 & 0 \end{pmatrix}, \qquad A^{(2)} = A^{(3)} = A^{(4)} = \begin{pmatrix} 0 & 2 & 3 & 5 \\ 2 & 0 & 5 & 3 \\ 3 & 5 & 0 & 3 \\ 5 & 3 & 3 & 0 \end{pmatrix}.$$

The matrix *next* is

$$\begin{pmatrix} 1 & 2 & 3 & 2 \\ 1 & 2 & 1 & 4 \\ 1 & 1 & 3 & 4 \\ 2 & 2 & 3 & 4 \end{pmatrix},$$

and row i, column j, of the matrix

$$\begin{pmatrix} 1\,1 & 1\,2 & 1\,3 & 1\,2\,4 \\ 2\,1 & 2\,2 & 2\,1\,3 & 2\,4 \\ 3\,1 & 3\,1\,2 & 3\,3 & 3\,4 \\ 4\,2\,1 & 4\,2 & 4\,3 & 4\,4 \end{pmatrix}$$

shows the output of *print_paths*(i, j).

4. Relative to the ordering Atlanta, Denver, Los Angeles, Miami, Philadelphia, Seattle, the matrix is

$$\begin{pmatrix} 0 & 1 & 0 & 0 & 1 & 0 \\ 0 & 0 & 1 & 0 & 0 & 0 \\ 1 & 0 & 0 & 0 & 0 & 0 \\ 0 & 0 & 0 & 0 & 0 & 1 \\ 0 & 0 & 0 & 0 & 0 & 0 \\ 0 & 0 & 0 & 0 & 0 & 0 \end{pmatrix}.$$

7. $\{(i, j) \mid i > j\}$

10. Lines

> for $i = 1$ to n

and

> for $j = 1$ to n

can be interchanged. All other permutations do not give a correct algorithm.

13. In the graph

there is a path from 3 to 5, but there is no shortest path from 3 to 5.

16. A necessary and sufficient condition is that for all i, j, and k,

$$A(i, j) \leq A(i, k) + A(k, j).$$

19. The graph of the relation is

The matrices are

$$A^{(1)} = A^{(2)} = \begin{pmatrix} 1 & 0 & 1 & 1 \\ 0 & 1 & 0 & 0 \\ 1 & 0 & 1 & 1 \\ 0 & 0 & 1 & 1 \end{pmatrix}, \qquad A^{(3)} = A^{(4)} = \begin{pmatrix} 1 & 0 & 1 & 1 \\ 0 & 1 & 0 & 0 \\ 1 & 0 & 1 & 1 \\ 1 & 0 & 1 & 1 \end{pmatrix}.$$

22. $A^{(k)}(i, k) = A^{(k-1)}(i, k)$ and $A^{(k)}(k, j) = A^{(k-1)}(k, j)$.

25. A is the matrix of a relation on $\{1, \ldots, n\}$.

```
reflexive_closure(A) {
    for i = 1 to A.last
        A[i][i] = 1
}
```

The worst-case time of the algorithm is $\Theta(n)$.

Chapter 9: Text Searching

Section 9.1

1. 4

4. Consider the case where the text consists of n copies of the same symbol.

8. The following program will list locations of all matches.

```
simple_text_find(p, t) {
    m = p.length
    n = t.length
    i = 0
    while (i + m ≤ n) {
        j = 0
        while (t[i + j] == p[j]) {
            j = j + 1
            if (j ≥ m)
                println(i)
        }
        i = i + 1
    }
}
```

11. "???-??-????"

Section 9.2

1. The algorithm will make 10 comparisons.

4. Consider a text of all zeros.

Section 9.3

1. The shift table for "barbara" is

−1	0	1	2	3	4	5	6
1	1	2	3	3	3	3	7

4. The shift table for "cancan" is

−1	0	1	2	3	4	5
1	1	2	3	3	3	3

6. The algorithm will make 22 comparisons before finding a match.

9. The algorithm will make 31 comparisons before finding a match.

Section 9.4

1. For example, "moon" in "darkness at noon"

3. We have $shift["n"] = 1$, and $shift["a"] = 2$, and $shift["b"] = 5$. For all other letters, the shift is 6.

6. The pattern "banana" will be shifted three times, two positions in each shift, before the algorithm terminates with a match at position 6. 18 comparisons are necessary.

9. Consider $p = ba^{m-1}$ and $t = a^n$, where a^k denotes k copies of a.

Section 9.5

1. The edit distance of "center" and "centre" is 2 as witnessed by the entry $d_{5,5}$ in the following table:

		−1	0	1	2	3	4	5
			c	e	n	t	r	e
−1		0	1	2	3	4	5	6
0	c	1	0	1	2	3	4	5
1	e	2	1	0	1	2	3	4
2	n	3	2	1	0	1	2	3
3	t	4	3	2	1	0	1	2
4	e	5	4	3	2	1	1	1
5	r	6	5	4	3	2	1	2

4. Running the algorithm gives us the table

		−1	0	1	2	3	4	5	6
			t	o	n	i	g	h	t
−1		0	0	0	0	0	0	0	0
0	n	1	1	1	0	1	1	1	1
1	i	2	2	2	1	0	1	2	2
2	t	3	2	3	2	1	1	2	2
3	e	4	3	3	3	2	2	2	3

showing that "ni", "nig", and "nigh" are the best matches for "nite" in "tonight" (all with an edit distance of 2).

7. Extend the algorithm to store in every cell (i, j) not only the value $ad_{i,j}$ but also a pointer to the cell that realized the minimum value, that is, one of $(i-1, j)$, $(i-1, j-1)$, or $(i, j-1)$ (if there is more than one cell that realizes the minimum, choose one cell arbitrarily). Finally, after computing the full matrix, trace the history of the minimum value in the last row.

9. "??:?? ?m, ??/??/????" (matched, for example, by "07:00 am, 12/03/2001")

12. Yes. For example, there is a match for the pattern "?" in the text "I", but there is no match for the pattern "??".

13. We have $P = \{01, 10\}$ with $\ell_1 = 0$ and $\ell_2 = 3$. After processing the subpattern 01, the array c is equal to $[1, 0, 0, 0, 1, 0, 0, 0, 0, 1, 0, 1, 0, 1, 0, 0]$ (since there are matches for 01 in positions 0, 4, 9, 11, and 13). After processing the second subpattern 10, c becomes $[1, 0, 0, 0, 1, 1, 0, 1, 0, 2, 0, 2, 0, 1, 0, 0]$ (the matches for 10 are in positions 2, 8, 10, 12, 14; therefore c is increased in positions 5, 7, 9, and 11). This means we have matches for the don't care pattern "01?10" at positions 9 and 11 (k being 2).

16. There are two matches.

Section 9.6

1. The set of all binary strings that start with the digit 0

4. The set of all binary strings that do not contain the sequence "11"

5. "$(0|1|2|3|4|5|6|7)*$"

8. "$0 * 1?0 * 1?0*$"

11. "$(0|1)(00|10|01|11)*$"

14. Use the same idea as in Exercise 9.6.4.

17. Most major languages, including Java, C++, Perl, Visual Basic, and Python, support regular expressions.

19. The regular expressions "$(0 * |01*)(1|10*)$" can be represented as

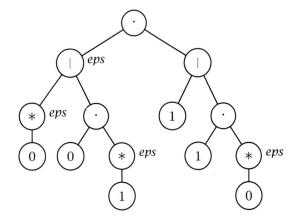

22. The regular expressions "$0 * 1 * 0$" can be represented as

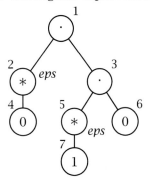

Initially the set of candidates is $\{4, 7, 6\}$. After receiving a 0, the candidate set remains $\{4, 7, 6\}$, as it does after processing the second 0. The following 1 then changes the candidate set to $\{7, 6\}$, and the final 0 results in an empty candidate set. At that point the matched attribute of nodes 6, 3, and 1 is true showing that "0010" matches the pattern "$0 * 1 * 0$".

24. The regular expressions "(01|0)(0|10)" can be represented as

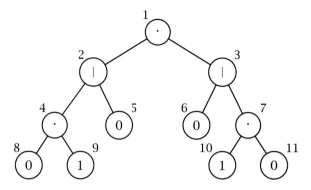

Initially, the set of candidates is $\{8, 5\}$. After receiving a 0, the candidate set is updated to $\{9, 6, 10\}$. The 1 changes the candidate set to $\{6, 10, 11\}$. The final 0 results in an empty candidate set. Both node 6 and node 11 were matched by this final 0, showing that there are in fact two different ways that 010 matches the pattern "(01|0)(0|10)".

Chapter 10: P and NP

Section 10.1

1. Depth-first search on a graph $G = (V, E)$ takes time $O(|V| + |E|)$, which is linear in the size $|V| + |E|$ of the graph.

4. Since $\sqrt{n} = n^{1/2}$ the answer is $k = 1$.

8. $s_f(t) = \lceil \sqrt{t} \rceil$ for $f(n) = n^2$.

11. $s_f(t) = 2^t$ for $f(n) = \log n$.

13. The instances will be larger by a multiplicative factor depending on the degree of the polynomial.

15. $1000n$

18. n^{1000}

21. If $f(n) = O(n^k)$, then, by definition, there are n_1 and a such that $f(n) \leq an^k$ for all $n \geq n_1$ (assume that $n_1 \geq 2$). Let $c = \max\{an^k \mid n < n_1\}$, and choose $k' \geq 2k$ such that $2^{k'/2} \geq a$. Then for $n < n_1$ we have $f(n) \leq an^k \leq c \leq n^{k'} + c$, and, for $n \geq n_1$, $f(n) \leq an^k \leq 2^{k'/2}n^k \leq n^{k'/2}n^k \leq n^{k'/2}n^{k'/2} \leq n^{k'} \leq n^{k'} + c$, so in either case $f(n) \leq n^{k'} + c$.

24. $c = \log_2 3 \approx 1.58$

Section 10.2

1. Color Western Australia and Queensland red, the Northern Territory and New South Wales green, and South Australia, Victoria and Tasmania blue.

4. Western Australia, the Northern Territory, and South Australia form a K_3, which requires at least three different colors.

7. None, since this leaves Chennai isolated

10. A K_4 has exactly three Hamiltonian cycles:

$$(1, 2, 3, 4, 1), \quad (1, 3, 2, 4, 1), \quad \text{and} \quad (1, 2, 4, 3, 1).$$

13. There is a tour of length 4160.

Section 10.3

1. The solution

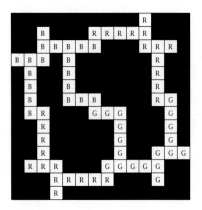

   corresponds to coloring the upper-left vertex blue, the lower-right vertex green, and the remaining two vertices red.

4. If $n \neq m$, player I has the following winning strategy: Always move the rook to the diagonal, that is, to $(\min\{n, m\}, \min\{n, m\})$ (since $n \neq m$, this is a real move). In the next move, player II must move the rook off the diagonal again, so we will again have $n \neq m$, and player I can continue playing the strategy until $n = m = 1$. This shows that all the positions in $\{(n, m) \mid n \neq m\}$ are winning positions for player I. A similar argument shows that all remaining positions are winning positions for player II, concluding the proof.

7. If a clause consists of two literals, $\ell_1 \vee \ell_2$, then replace it by two clauses $\ell_1 \vee \ell_2 \vee y_1$ and $\ell_1 \vee \ell_2 \vee \overline{y}_1$, where y_1 is a new variable.

Section 10.4

1. If C is a set of vertices that form a clique in G, then the same set of vertices form an independent set in $\overline{G}$, hence $\omega(G) \le \alpha(\overline{G})$. Similarly, an independent set I in $\overline{G}$ forms a clique in G, hence $\alpha(\overline{G}) \le \omega(G)$.

4. There are five different maximal independent sets including the vertex $\overline{x}_2$ in C_1. For example, we can pick $\overline{x}_2$ in C_1, x_3 in C_2, $\overline{x}_1$ in C_3, $\overline{x}_4$ in C_4, and $\overline{x}_1$ in C_5. The corresponding truth assignment sets x_1, x_2, and x_4 to false, and x_3 to true.

8. The following picture shows a possible 3-coloring of the graph for

$$\varphi = (x_1 \vee x_2 \vee \overline{x}_3) \wedge (\overline{x}_1 \vee \overline{x}_2 \vee x_3) \wedge (x_1 \vee \overline{x}_2 \vee x_3).$$

The truth assignment corresponding to this coloring sets x_1, x_2, and x_3 to false.

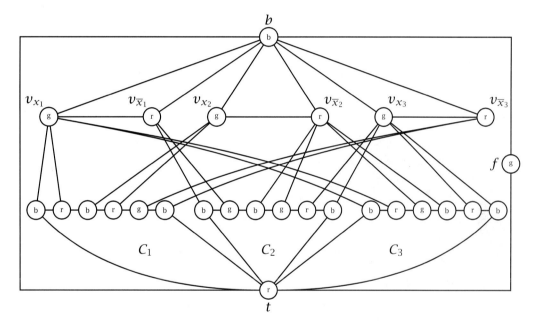

Section 10.5

1. Yes, $21 = 1 + 9 + 11 = 2 + 3 + 4 + 12$.

4. A score of four is possible.

Chapter 11: Coping with NP-Completeness

Section 11.1

1. The independence number is 4.

3. Since φ contains a clause with two literals, namely $(x_2 \vee x_4)$, we first investigate $\varphi[x_2 \to \text{false}][x_4 \to \text{true}]$, which is $x_3 \wedge \overline{x}_3$. Letting x_3 be true (since it is a single literal clause), yields false, hence there is no satisfying assignment under the assumption that x_2 is false and x_4 is true. Hence we next try $\varphi[x_2 \to \text{true}]$, which is $x_1 \wedge (\overline{x}_3 \vee \overline{x}_4)$. Since this formula contains a clause with one literal (x_1), we set x_1 to true. This, in turn, yields $(\overline{x}_3 \vee \overline{x}_4)$. We try letting $\overline{x}_3$ be false and $\overline{x}_4$ be true. This reduces the formula to true; that is, we have found a satisfying assignment, namely, let x_1, x_2, and x_3 be true and x_4 be false.

6. Let A be the adjacency matrix of G. We need to check for all $i, j \in U$ that $A[i, j] = 0$. This is easily done in time $|U|^2$ as the following code illustrates.

```
for each i ∈ U
    for each j ∈ U
        if (A[i, j] == 1)
            return false
return true
```

9. Exhaustively test all possible assignments, of which there are 2^n. Since checking a single assignment takes time $|\varphi|$ the algorithm will run in time $O(|\varphi|2^n)$.

12. We solved this problem in Section 4.5.

Section 11.2

1. If the entry and exit point of the maze are both in the outer wall of the maze, then both left-hand rule and right-hand rule always succeed (why?).

4. Let p_k be the probability that the random walk reaches t *for the first time* in the kth step. Clearly, $p_0 = p_1 = 0$. Since the first time t is reached can only be an even move, we know that $p_k = 0$ for all odd k. Consider an even $k \geq 2$. Since we assume that k is the first time t is reached, the random walk had to be going back and forth between s and v for $k - 1$ steps, which happened with probability $2^{-\lfloor(k-1)/2\rfloor} = 2^{-(k/2-1)}$ (since at the odd steps, there is only a $1/2$ probability of going back to s from v). Finally, in the kth step, it had to decide to move to t rather than s, which happened with probability $1/2$; hence, $p_k = 2^{-(k/2-1)} * 1/2 = 2^{-k/2}$ for even k. Therefore the expected value is

$$\sum_{k \geq 0} k p_k = \sum_{k \text{ is even}} k 2^{-k/2} = 2 \sum_{k \geq 0} k 2^{-k} = 4.$$

To see that $\sum_{k \geq 0} k 2^{-k} = 2$, use Exercise 9(a) in Section 2.2, and let n go to infinity.

Alternately, let X be the random variable that counts the number of steps to get from s to t. Let $Y = X/2 - 1$. Then Y has a geometric distribution with $p = 1/2$, since the probability that Y equals k is the probability that X equals $2k + 2$ [which we know to be $2^{-(k+1)}$]. Hence Y has expected value $p/(1 - p) = 1$, and, because $X = 2Y + 2$, X has expected value 4.

7. Start a depth-first search at s (which takes linear time), and check whether t was visited.

10. The following code implements a Monte Carlo version of *randomized_st_connectivity*, which errs on the negative side with probability at most $1/2$.

```
monte_carlo_randomized_st_connectivity(G, s, t) {
    counter = 2|V|³  // where G = (V, E)
    vertex = s
    while (vertex ! = t and counter > 0) {
        vertex = random vertex from N(vertex)
        counter = counter − 1
    }
    return vertex == t
}
```

13. No, there is not. Why?

Section 11.3

1. I is the set of all instances, that is, the set of all sequences $(s_1, \ldots, s_n)$, where all s_i lie in $(0, 1]$. $C(s_1, \ldots, s_n)$ is the set of all possible packings of $(s_1, \ldots, s_n)$ into bins. For a particular packing $c \in C(s_1, \ldots, s_n)$, $m(c)$ is the number of bins used in that packing.

4. Use the algorithm to compute $\alpha(G)$, and then check whether $\alpha(G)$ is at least k.

5. Since there is a total of 358 minutes of music, we need at least $\lceil 358/78 \rceil = 5$ CDs.

6. The *next_fit* algorithm uses six CDs.

9. The *next_fit* algorithm uses five bins.

12. Take a complete bipartite graph with one vertex in the first partition and $n - 1$ vertices in the other partition.

15. The claim means that $m(greedy\_coloring(x)) \le n/2\chi(G)$; that is, *greedy_coloring* is never worse than $n/2$ times the best possible value $\chi(G)$. If $\chi(G) \ge 2$, then the inequality is always true, since *greedy_coloring* never uses more than n colors. Hence only the case $\chi(G) = 1$ needs to be considered. However, if $\chi(G)$ is 1, then G does not contain any edges, and hence *greedy_coloring* will only use one color, also making the inequality true.

Section 11.4

1. $klam_f(n) = \lceil t/n \rceil$

3. $klam_f(n) = \lceil t^{1/n} \rceil$

6. Consider covering the edges in a simple path.

9. Traversing the adjacency list of a vertex v completely to count its neighbors could take too long. However, this is not necessary: We can begin traversing the list of vertices adjacent to v, and stop and return true when we have found at least k neighbors, and otherwise (less than k neighbors) return false. This will take time $O(k)$.

12. Use three colors to color the board.

13. There are four matchings of size 3.

Section 11.5

1. It will loop forever since it terminates only if a solution with no collisions is found.

4. If we identify boards that can be obtained from each other by rotation or mirroring, then there is only one solution of the 4-queens problem.

Chapter 12: Parallel and Distributed Algorithms

Section 12.2

1. If $i = \lceil \lg n \rceil - 1$, then $j = 2^i - 1 = 2^{\lceil \lg n \rceil - 1} - 1 \geq n/2 - 1$, which is $\Theta(n)$.

4. Using *er_broadcast*, distribute x into a new array b of the same size as a, and then have processor i check whether $a[i]$ equals $b[i]$ (in one parallel step). The running time is $\Theta(n)$, and the work is $\Theta(n \lg n)$.

7. The following table is a trace of the algorithm.

	$a[0]$	$a[1]$	$a[2]$	$a[3]$	$a[4]$	$a[5]$
start	31	24	71	3	12	28
$i = 0$	55	24	74	3	40	28
$i = 1$	129	24	74	3	40	28
$i = 2$	169	24	74	3	40	28

10. No, it might not run correctly since the final blocksize would be $2^{\lfloor \log n \rfloor}$, which could be strictly less than n. For example, run the algorithm with $a = [1, 2, 3]$ and $\otimes = +$.

13. Since $n = 10$, *blocksize* is 4 ($\lg \lg 10$ is roughly 1.7). The following table shows the computation of the first part of the algorithm.

	a[0]	a[1]	a[2]	a[3]	a[4]	a[5]	a[6]	a[7]	a[8]	a[9]
start	2	2	2	2	2	2	2	2	2	2
$j = 1$	4	2	2	2	4	2	2	2	4	2
$j = 2$	8	2	2	2	8	2	2	2	4	2
$j = 3$	16	2	2	2	16	2	2	2	4	2

The next table traces the second part of the algorithm.

	$a[0]$	$a[1]$	$a[2]$	$a[3]$	$a[4]$	$a[5]$	$a[6]$	$a[7]$	$a[8]$	$a[9]$
start	16	2	2	2	16	2	2	2	4	2
$i = 2$	256	2	2	2	16	2	2	2	4	2
$i = 3$	1024	2	2	2	16	2	2	2	4	2

16. Similar to Example 12.2.21. The value of n' is 6, hence in the first loop i will run from 0 to 2, and from 0 to 5 in the second loop.

19. The exercise amounts to computing the values of $i!$ for i ranging from 1 to 10. The following table traces the computation.

	$a[0]$	$a[1]$	$a[2]$	$a[3]$	$a[4]$	$a[5]$	$a[6]$	$a[7]$	$a[8]$	$a[9]$
start	1	2	3	4	5	6	7	8	9	10
$i = 0$	1	2	6	12	20	30	42	56	72	90
$i = 1$	1	2	6	24	120	360	840	1680	3024	5040
$i = 2$	1	2	6	24	120	720	5040	40320	362880	1814400
$i = 3$	1	2	6	24	120	720	5040	40320	362880	3628800

22. The result is

$$a = [r, r^2, hr^2, hr^3, r^3, hr^3, h, hr, r, r^2, hr^2, hr^3, h, hr, r, r^2, hr^2, hr^3].$$

24. The algorithm will have three phases. In the first phase, you need to use the sequential algorithm to compute prefixes of blocks of length $\lg n$. In the second phase, you use *parallel_prefix* to compute the parallel prefixes on the $n/\lg n$ last elements of these blocks. In the third and final phase, you again use a sequential algorithm to compute the prefixes for the remaining elements.

27. The algorithm will take six parallel steps, including the initialization step.

30. The professor is right. Find an example, and show how to improve the algorithm.

Section 12.3

1. We will just show part of the claim, namely, that the uppermost wire will output the smallest value. After the first layer, the first two wires and the last two wires are ordered by themselves. Since in the second layer we compare the first wire to the third wire, the first wire will contain the smallest input.

4. This can be shown by induction.

5.

0	1	2	3	4	5	6	7	8	9	10
10	9	9	7	7	5	5	3	3	1	1
9	10	7	9	5	7	3	5	1	3	2
8	7	10	5	9	3	7	1	5	2	3
7	8	5	10	3	9	1	7	2	5	4
6	5	8	3	10	1	9	2	7	4	5
5	6	3	8	1	10	2	9	4	7	6
4	3	6	1	8	2	10	4	9	6	7
3	4	1	6	2	8	4	10	6	9	8
2	1	4	2	6	4	8	6	10	8	9
1	2	2	4	4	6	6	8	8	10	10

8. The formula does not depend on whether n is even or odd.

11. After running D_8 we obtain $(4, 3, 2, 1, 8, 7, 6, 5)$. Running D_4 on both halves gives us $(2, 1, 4, 3, 6, 5, 8, 7)$. Finally running the four D_2 sorts the sequence, and we get $(1, 2, 3, 4, 5, 6, 7, 8)$.

14. After running D_{16} the sequence is sorted.

17. By definition, a cyclically increasing sequence is a sequence that can be rotated so that it becomes increasing. Therefore, a sequence is cyclically increasing if and only if all of its rotations are cyclically increasing.

20. M_8 occurs as part of the network shown in Example 12.3.17.

23. The drawing of M_8 as part of the network shown in Example 12.3.17 does not have wire crossings.

25. We use S_8 without wire crossings as shown in Example 12.3.17. After the two S_4, the sequence is $(1, 7, 11, 11, 2, 3, 4, 9)$. The next layer (the disentangled D_8) turns this into $(1, 4, 3, 2, 11, 11, 7, 9)$. In the next layer we get $(1, 2, 3, 4, 7, 9, 11, 11)$, which remains unaffected by the final layer.

28. Use induction on k to show that S_{2^k} has depth $k(k + 1)/2$.

31. The first layer of comparators will turn the sequences into

$$(12, 23, 4, 7, 1, 6, 17, 19, 2, 3) \quad \text{and} \quad (1, 1, 0, 0, 0, 0, 1, 1, 0, 0).$$

In the next step we obtain

$$(12, 4, 23, 1, 7, 6, 17, 2, 19, 3) \quad \text{and} \quad (1, 0, 1, 0, 0, 0, 1, 0, 1, 0).$$

The next even layer turns this into

$$(4, 12, 1, 23, 6, 7, 2, 17, 3, 19) \quad \text{and} \quad (0, 1, 0, 1, 0, 0, 0, 1, 0, 1)$$

followed by

$$(4, 1, 12, 6, 23, 2, 7, 3, 17, 19) \quad \text{and} \quad (0, 0, 1, 0, 1, 0, 0, 0, 1, 1).$$

Another even layer results in

$$(1, 4, 6, 12, 2, 23, 3, 7, 17, 19) \quad \text{and} \quad (0, 0, 0, 1, 0, 1, 0, 0, 1, 1)$$

followed by

$$(1, 4, 6, 2, 12, 3, 23, 7, 17, 19) \quad \text{and} \quad (0, 0, 0, 0, 1, 0, 1, 0, 1, 1).$$

This turns into

$$(1, 4, 2, 6, 3, 12, 7, 23, 17, 19) \quad \text{and} \quad (0, 0, 0, 0, 0, 1, 0, 1, 1, 1)$$

and then

$$(1, 2, 4, 3, 6, 7, 12, 17, 23, 19) \quad \text{and} \quad (0, 0, 0, 0, 0, 0, 1, 1, 1, 1).$$

One more step leads to

$$(1, 2, 3, 4, 6, 7, 12, 17, 19, 23) \quad \text{and} \quad (0, 0, 0, 0, 0, 0, 1, 1, 1, 1).$$

The network would continue, but there would not be any more changes. Note that throughout all of the steps, numbers less than 10 have a 0 in the corresponding position of the binary sequence, and numbers larger than 10 have a 1 in the corresponding position.

Section 12.4

1. $n - 1$

4. The solution is a Hamiltonian path in the 3-dimensional hypercube. For example, we can use the path $(000, 010, 011, 001, 101, 111, 110, 100)$.

7. Suppose that two vertices in the hypercube are labeled $u0v$ and $u1v$ (where u and v are binary sequences, possibly empty). That means they belong to the hypercube that is formed by all of the vertices whose labels begin with u. Within that hypercube, they are adjacent since they were created as two copies, $0v$ and $1v$, of the same vertex v in the inductive construction of the hypercube.

10. Example 12.4.2 shows that in a d-dimensional hypercube we can get from any vertex to any other vertex in at most d steps, giving us an upper bound on the diameter. For the lower bound, consider the vertices with labels $(0, 0, \ldots, 0) \in \{0, 1\}^d$, and $(1, 1, \ldots, 1) \in \{0, 1\}^d$. In a hypercube, adjacent vertices differ in exactly one coordinate; therefore, it takes at least d steps to get from $(0, 0, \ldots, 0)$ to $(1, 1, \ldots, 1)$.

13. The array will be sorted after the first phase of the second stage, as shown:

sorting rows (phase 1)   sorting columns (phase 2)

1. Stage

16	3	2	13	→
5	10	11	8	←
9	6	7	12	→
4	15	14	1	←

2	3	13	16
11	10	8	5
6	7	9	12
15	14	4	1

2. Stage

2	3	4	1	→
6	7	8	5	←
11	10	9	12	→
15	14	13	16	←

1	2	3	4
8	7	6	5
9	10	11	12
16	15	14	13

16. The array will be sorted at the end of the first phase of the fourth stage.

19. There are examples of size 3×3.

20. For example, a spiral-shaped path from a corner to the center will have diameter $\Omega(n^2)$.

23. The following diagrams are a trace of the algorithm. In steps (1) through (9), the rules are applied until all pixels are 0 in (10). Steps (11) through (20) play back the history in reverse order, labeling the pixels.

1	1	1	1	1
1	0	0	0	1
1	0	1	0	1
1	0	0	0	1
1	1	1	1	1

(1)

1	1	1	1	1
1	0	0	0	1
1	0	0	0	1
1	0	0	1	1
1	1	1	1	0

(2)

1	1	1	1	1
1	0	0	0	1
1	0	0	1	1
1	0	1	1	0
1	1	1	0	0

(3)

1	1	1	1	1
1	0	0	1	1
1	0	1	1	0
1	1	1	0	0
1	1	0	0	0

(4)

1	1	1	1	1
1	0	1	1	0
1	1	1	0	0
1	1	0	0	0
1	0	0	0	0

(5)

1	1	1	1	0
1	1	1	0	0
1	1	0	0	0
1	0	0	0	0
0	0	0	0	0

(6)

1	1	1	0	0
1	1	0	0	0
1	0	0	0	0
0	0	0	0	0
0	0	0	0	0

(7)

1	1	0	0	0
1	0	0	0	0
0	0	0	0	0
0	0	0	0	0
0	0	0	0	0

(8)

1	0	0	0	0
0	0	0	0	0
0	0	0	0	0
0	0	0	0	0
0	0	0	0	0

(9)

0	0	0	0	0
0	0	0	0	0
0	0	0	0	0
0	0	0	0	0
0	0	0	0	0

(10)

6	0	0	0	0
0	0	0	0	0
0	0	0	0	0
0	0	0	0	0
0	0	0	0	0

(11)

6	6	0	0	0
6	0	0	0	0
0	0	0	0	0
0	0	0	0	0
0	0	0	0	0

(12)

6	6	6	0	0
6	6	0	0	0
6	0	0	0	0
0	0	0	0	0
0	0	0	0	0

(13)

6	6	6	6	0
6	6	6	0	0
6	6	0	0	0
6	0	0	0	0
0	0	0	0	0

(14)

6	6	6	6	6
6	0	6	6	0
6	6	6	0	0
6	6	0	0	0
6	0	0	0	0

(15)

6	6	6	6	6
6	0	0	6	6
6	0	6	6	0
6	6	6	0	0
6	6	0	0	0

(16)

6	6	6	6	6
6	0	0	0	6
6	0	0	6	6
6	0	6	6	0
6	6	6	0	0

(17)

6	6	6	6	6
6	0	0	0	6
6	0	0	0	6
6	0	0	6	6
6	6	6	6	0

(18)

6	6	6	6	6
6	0	0	0	6
6	0	18	0	6
6	0	0	0	6
6	6	6	6	6

(19)

Section 12.5

1. This problem can be solved in time $\Theta(1)$ and message complexity $\Theta(n)$.

4. Adapt the ring-broadcasting algorithm (Algorithm 12.5.2) utilizing the acknowledgment feature to achieve synchronization.

7. The idea for the solution is that once a leader has been elected, that leader can broadcast a message announcing the termination of the election.

Index